THE BIG BOOK OF GARDENING

Where harmony dwells—an old-world cottage and its appropriate garden

THE BIG BOOK OF

GARDENING

A COMPREHENSIVE GUIDE
FOR THE HOME GARDENER, GIVING ALL
NECESSARY ADVICE ON THE CULTURE
OF FLOWERS, VEGETABLES
AND FRUIT

By Charles Boff

ODHAMS PRESS LIMITED
LONG ACRE, LONDON

LIST OF PLATES

(*Between pages 192 and 193*)

Our thanks are due to Carters' Tested Seeds, Ltd., for kind permission to reproduce the picture of Primula malacoides on Plate 3 and double-tuberous Begonia on Plate 27; to Allwood Bros. for Dianthus Allwoodii on Plate 25.

CONTENTS

SECTION I

THE GARDEN SCHEME

IT IS A pleasure to take over a garden site: an unplanted area in which things may be arranged to one's own satisfaction from the very first. There is equal pleasure in achieving one's own order out of another's chaos: in taking over an already made garden all the features of which call for rearrangement. In the gardener's soul the urge to excel is never quenched.

There is nothing secret about the processes needed to change a piece of ground into a lovely, and maybe profitable, garden. But the processes are numerous, entailing real labour as well as giving pleasure. Best results are secured not by haphazard sowing and planting but by a well-considered sequence of operations, all of which this book describes in simple detail.

When to Start. There is neither beginning nor end to the gardener's working calendar. A start may be made in January, or August or any other month: the ground comes into bearing in due season. Weather and time (or lack of time) and the obstinacies of some soils are, of course, circumstances to be reckoned with. Seasons may conspire to interfere with your plans. But these vagaries may be countered, within reasonable limits, when a certain degree of skill has been acquired.

How to Start. There are tidy-minded folk who contrive a flower garden out of a tiny town patch, complete with handkerchief-size lawn, wherein every blade of growth appears to have been washed and combed and smoothed five minutes ago. Others, working to a larger scale, achieve a happy result with a mixture of everything, but the unplanned comming-

Fig. 1.—*The well-planned site. The brightest flowers are prominent, and a stretch of lawn, the fruit and vegetable sections being in the background*

ling of flowers and vegetables and fruit is to be avoided.

No need to be a slave to convention. But one should bow to limitations of space and accept not only the natural needs of plants in general but—this is of very great importance—their requirements beyond the first year or two of their existence. First sketch out your scheme on paper, however roughly, and discuss it at leisure. This is the natural starting point for the construction of a garden "out of nothing" or for the reconstruction of an established one.

Alternative Plans. The ground may be devoted entirely to flowers and lawn, or to vegetables or fruit. But the ideal is to embrace all these, each in a separate department. It is possible, of course, to grow flowers or vegetables among fruit trees and bushes while the latter are still young and small, but the possibility soon passes with the increasing demands for more root-and-branch space inevitably made by the fruit.

The temptation to mix things is great and must be resisted. Far better to be content with a very miniature orchard, away from the flowers; and, if it is a toss-up between flowers and vegetables, to extend one's activities beyond the

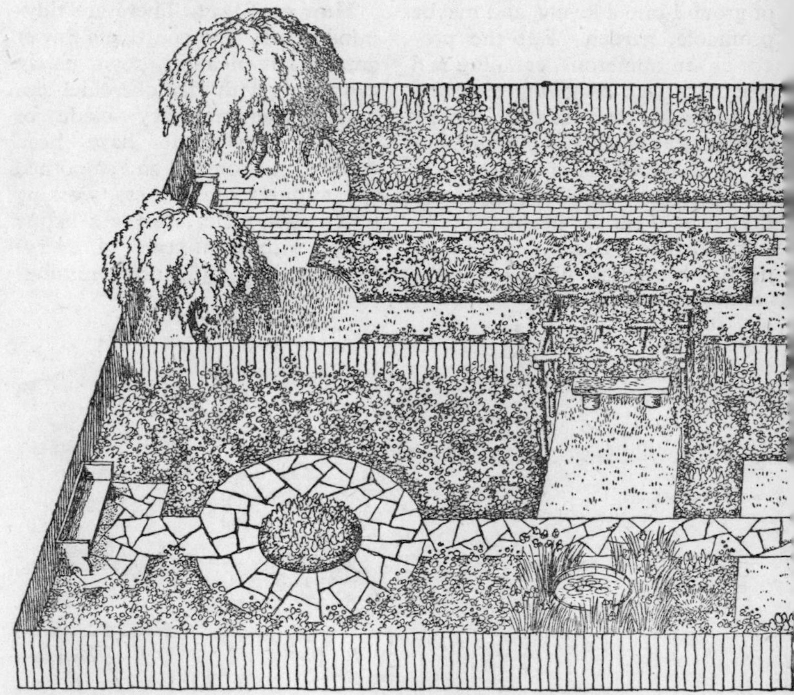

Fig. 2.—*Lay-outs for two adjoining cottage gardens are suggested here. Crazy paving is adopted in one instance for the paths, brick paving in*

home garden and cultivate, in addition, a nearby allotment.

Consider how your garden will look, not only in spring and summer, but through the year. Aim at creating the most pleasing view from the dwelling: there, prominently, should be the brightest flowers and a stretch of verdant lawn, the fruit and vegetable sections in the background (see Fig. 1). Attractive as the fruit and vegetable quarters undoubtedly can be, they hold their beauty for only part of the year. Flowers and the lawn are good to look upon and will give pleasure the year round.

There are flowers specially suited for beds in spring, and summer flowers to take their place as they wane in beauty. Even when the summer flowers have gone the beds need not be bare for there can be plants in flower during autumn and winter. The herbaceous border will take, in addition to its permanent occupants, spring and summer bedding plants, as well as many bulbous subjects. These things, then, should have pride of place from one's windows.

Flower Garden Features. The straightforward flowers and the lawn may be considered the mainstay, with a rock garden (it can be quite small) and a rose garden (or

the other. Shade, essential to the enjoyment of a garden in summer, is provided in the one case by two trees, in the other by a rose-covered arch

Fig. 3.—*This might well be the show-piece of the flower garden where space is ample. In adopting such a design it should be borne in mind that considerable labour is entailed in maintenance: mowing the turf and trimming its edges; weeding the flower beds; tying and pruning the roses trained to the semicircle of poles. But many will think it worth the toil*

a simple rose bed) as very desirable incidentals. There may be what is known as a dry wall constructed for plants which rejoice in wall pockets and crevices, and even a cottage garden may include a small pool for interesting aquatics (see Fig. 2).

An ornamental pool is always a popular feature and lends itself well to attractive formal designs, such as that shown in Fig. 3. This type of lay-out, however, is only suitable for large gardens, where help is available, as keeping it in good order involves a considerable amount of labour.

A cold frame or, more ambitious, a greenhouse adds to the enjoyment and profit. And, of course, you must have a garden seat, preferably with not too dense shade, which suggests a tree. Here it is well to remark that tiny saplings grow sometimes at incredible speed, and this must be considered when choice is made of subjects for planting. The slender and beautiful sapling of today may be your embarrassment of tomorrow, blocking out light and air where these can ill be spared.

The house walls can be clothed with any of a number of attractive subjects: the sunniest aspect will suit a grape-vine which can be coaxed into considerable productivity; or flowering climbers, including clematis, wistaria and rose, may be trained to cover almost any wall-space.

If your flower garden is tiny you may want to augment it with window-boxes. These can be extremely successful if due care and time are combined in their management. But only if attention can be spared from the garden proper at the height of its busy season should summer window-boxes be considered.

Labour Saving. Your garden is a recreation and must never become a burden. To make the lazy spell possible, think in terms of labour saving when possible. A turfed path can be very lovely (see Fig. 4), but it demands frequent mowing and weeding and, generally speaking, the lawn itself will give you enough of that. Before flower beds are cut in the lawn, the pros and cons of their upkeep in that position should be considered. Their edges must be trimmed frequently and if their shapes are fanciful the hand-shears must reinforce the lawn-mower in the tricky angles. Generally speaking such beds should be discreet, for, if overdone, they will destroy a garden's character and charm.

Anything that can reduce labour in the garden is worth consideration. By way of further illustration, the covering of a wall or fence with virginia creeper should not lightly be embarked upon.

That creeper will grow quite swiftly, and its leaves in autumn assume most brilliant hues. But the leaves fall, in vast quantity and over a period of weeks, and sweeping them up can be very toilsome and a waste of valuable time.

A Corner Unplanted. Waste materials become a real embarrassment if their accommodation is omitted from the planning scheme. Annual weeds, leaves and lawn-mowings should go on to the compost heap, in some corner of the garden, there to decay and become most valuable humus for digging in. Similar space should be arranged for the year-round collection of hard rubbish: twigs and broken stakes and the roots of perennial weeds, such as convolvulus and twitch and dock and dandelion, all to be burned as they accumulate and become dry enough.

This strictly utilitarian corner can be screened from sight (see Fig. 5) by rambler roses or, economically enough, in the vegetable garden by runner beans. Or a hedge will conceal it: a line of shrubs needing to be kept within

Fig. 4. *A turfed path, ending in a rest-inviting seat, can be a lovely garden feature, though the turf entails labour in mowing and weeding. The grass edges also require frequent trimming*

Fig. 5.—*A strictly utilitarian corner whose unavoidable untidiness is screened from sight by rambler roses or other climbing plants*

bounds and good to look upon by regular pruning.

A corner of a different kind—this a sunny one, well away from trees—may hold a garden frame, and comprise a small area in which flower and vegetable seeds can be sown in spring and summer for later planting out, and adjacent space for transferring seedlings until these are ready for their final positions. In planning a garden the real need for such "nursery beds" should not be overlooked.

Greenhouse Possibilities. The scope of the gardener is vastly increased when a greenhouse is available. It does not save labour, it increases it, for the attention a greenhouse demands is considerable. But no garden can possibly be thought complete without one. It should be sited away from shade and if it can be heated, however slightly, from late autumn to advancing spring, it can prove a possession beyond price.

Thriving Vegetables. In apportioning part of the garden to vegetables, it should be borne in mind that these are no mere Cinderellas. They render big returns—but not for nothing. Bits of ground where flowers, shrubs or lawn failed because of shut-in conditions, poverty of soil or some other reason, cannot suddenly produce worth-while crops of potatoes or anything else. Crops under big, spreading trees or in ground not properly prepared cannot be other than leggy, caterpillar-plagued and disease-stricken.

Branches overhanging from a neighbouring garden, and their trespassing roots, should be cut hard back after amicable arrangement with their owner (see Fig. 6). If the ground is bordered by a hedge, the roots of this should be similarly dealt with; the hedge itself will not be affected and the ground will be vastly improved. (See Fig. 7).

Naturally, all hedges should be kept well within bounds by regular trimming and the trimmings burned with other hard rubbish to get rid of them and provide useful wood-ash. But the bonfire habit should be avoided as the smoke may cause annoyance to neighbours.

Fruit Quarters. Walls and fences can be put to no more useful purpose than the support of fruit of some kind, ranging from blackberries and loganberries to a grapevine. But one's ambition in the direction of home-grown fruit doubtless will not be satisfied at that. An open space will carry its row or rows of wire-supported raspberry canes, its strawberries, bushes of gooseberry and currant (red, white or black), and so on (see Fig. 8).

In taking over a garden it may be discovered that existing fruit trees and bushes are old and unproductive. They should be cut down, if it seems that long neglect has ruined them, and their roots grubbed out entirely with axe and pickaxe. The ground they occupied should then be dug deeply and enriched with compost (in default of manure) so that their successors shall start with everything in their favour.

Fig. 7.—*Roots of a hedge bordering a plot rob the soil of nourishment needed by crops. A trench dug close alongside will enable masses of roots to be removed, without having an injurious effect on the hedge itself*

Fig. 6.—*Tree branches overhanging from neighbouring ground and casting unwanted shade should be removed, after arrangement with their owner. Also the trespassing roots should be cut back, a trench being opened out for this purpose*

Crowding is not permissible in the fruit quarters. To the lukewarm gardener it may seem that interest here lies only in the period of the fruit harvest, and that to leave precious ground beneath the spread of branches bare is lamentable waste of space. Not so. One *can* plant vegetables and flowers beneath them, and between fruit

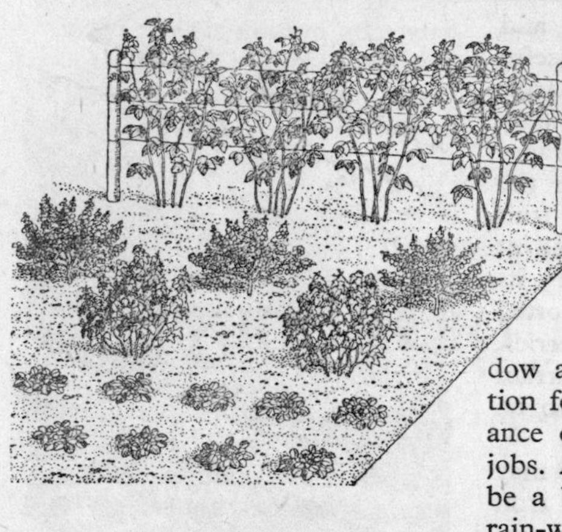

Fig. 8.—*An unshaded space will carry its row of supported raspberry canes, its well-spaced bushes of gooseberry and currant, and two or more rows of strawberry plants*

bushes, but cultivation of the fruit then becomes extremely difficult, and the intruding vegetables or flowers suffer because of shade and over-keen competition with the roots of the trees and bushes.

Indispensable Shed. For storing the lawn-mower and roller, the hose, tools, empty seed boxes and garden paraphernalia in general, a rain-and-weather-proof shed is a necessity. It should have a door that fastens and an ample window that opens; and beneath the window a bench of sturdy construction for the comfortable performance of potting and other inside jobs. At one side, or end, should be a barrel to catch and contain rain-water from the roof via a short length of piping leading from the guttering. That water supply may prove invaluable.

Methodical Clearance. Time and effort can be wasted if a decisive plan is not followed in clearing a piece of ground preparatory to putting it to a new purpose or preparing a weed-infested area for cultivation. The garden scheme will have all the better start for a clean commencement—which can be achieved in the manner shown in Fig. 9.

Fig. 9.—*The piece of ground may be covered with grass and weeds, but if it is tackled methodically and well dug it is soon brought under control*

First remove all rubbish such as bricks, tin cans, etc. Make a bonfire and burn all perennial weeds. Next divide the area into halves by putting a piece of string down the middle. Then proceed with digging as described in the next chapter.

SECTION II

THE ART OF DIGGING

DIGGING is no top-speed, frantic business. For the good of the job and the well-being of the digger it must be done at a leisurely pace. It must not be left to accumulate so that a hot-sweat bout is necessary just as seed sowing or planting becomes imminent. As soon as possible after flowers or vegetables have been cleared the piece of ground should be dealt with.

Soil needs to settle down somewhat before seed is sown or plants set out, and this it cannot do if the necessary attention is delayed until, say, March, when other essential jobs are clamouring to be tackled.

Digging that is rushed is certain to be scamped; the benefits that come of a proper handling of spade or fork are not attained.

Why Dig? Obvious reasons are the burial of weeds and the covering-in of manure. The ultimate reason is the ensuring of really profitable plants. By breaking up the soil to a good depth the downward path of roots is made easy. Essential air is let into the ground. Unused stores of plant food are opened up. The soil becomes fertile to a greater depth. And most plants in deeply dug soil suffer less in dry periods than those in ground inexpertly or lazily turned over.

When to Dig. The time to dig is when the ground is not so wet that it squelches underfoot; when it is not frozen; when it is not snow-covered. Heavy ground—of a clay-like nature—is best dug in early winter, the surface being left lumpy for wind and frost to crumble and sweeten it. If the digging is delayed until, say, early February the surface should be broken down as finely as possible with spade or fork as the work proceeds. Soils of a lighter nature can be dealt with at any time; though if some weeks in advance of sowing the surface should not be fined down unduly, or it will become hard-caked under the action of rain and wind, and so need forking over again.

Spade or fork should always be used to the greatest possible depth except when, say, summer bedding is about to be planted in ground well dealt with for the preceding spring bedding, or, in the kitchen garden, when a follow-on crop is to be sown or planted immediately. In this case it is sufficient if the surface is turned over and weeds removed.

Spade versus Fork. Ground that is clay, or of a clayey nature, is as a rule more easily worked with fork than spade. Stony, gravelly

Fig. 10.—*Turf to be stripped from a piece of ground should be lifted methodically and stacked out of the way of later digging. Note that the spade-blade is nearly horizontal, and that the inside of the right knee is lending power to the push as each section of turf is cut through below*

or sandy soil demands a spade. Whichever tool is used, it should be of medium weight; a quite small one does better work in hands unaccustomed to digging, and without undue strain on the muscles.

Clearing the Ground. The disposal of whatever covers the surface naturally comes first. If it is turf, this could be buried deeply during the digging—turned grass-side down into the bottom of the digging-trench and there chopped up with the spade. It contains valuable plant food which the roots of garden subjects of every kind will appreciate.

Fig. 11.—*Note positions of the digger—shoulders, hands and feet—relative to the spade. This is the attitude, and the manner of holding the spade, before the blade of the nearly upright tool is thrust into the ground*

Fig. 12.—*The spade-blade is pressed into the soil with the ball—not the instep—of the left foot. The hands are in the best positions for easy working*

If the turf contains grubs such as wireworms or leatherjackets (they will be obvious enough if present) scatter lime or fresh soot thickly over it before covering in. Or pare it from the surface (Fig. 10) with a sharp spade used nearly horizontally, before digging begins, and make a heap of it, grass-side down, somewhere on the plot, and leave it for a year to decay. Then open out the heap to enable birds to demolish whatever grubs have survived, and dig it in as though it were manure. Part of this good, fibrous soil should be saved for

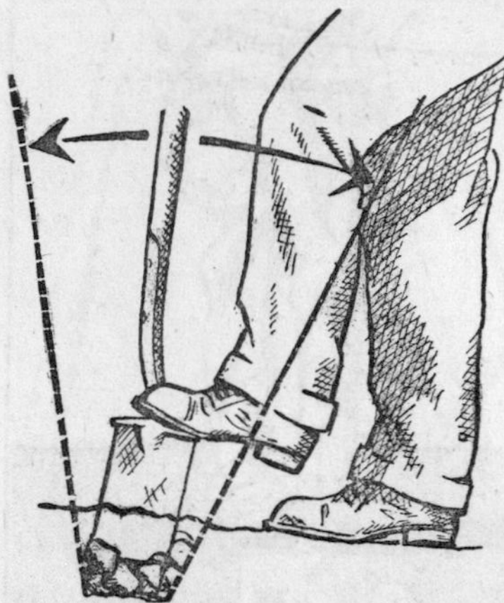

Fig. 13.—*Side view of digger in Fig. 12, showing how the spade-blade is worked backwards and forwards to enable it to penetrate stony soil. Pressure is maintained with left foot*

filling seed boxes and flower pots.

Heaping up pared-off turf and burning it is wasteful—unless it is very weedy with couch grass, dandelion, dock, thistle, nettle or other perennial-rooted persistent weeds; in which case burning is the safe plan. The resultant ashes are rich in potash and should be forked into the surface a week or two before sowing or planting.

Where tall weeds of the foregoing nature occupy the ground the roots should be got out with the fork, and after the soil has been knocked from them the tops and roots should be added to the general woody refuse heap for destruction at the next bonfire.

Handling Spade and Fork. The spade is the "founder of the feast," and on the method of its handling depends the absence or presence of blisters and the condition of the digger's leg and back muscles at the end of thirty minutes of hard toil in the garden.

Stand over the spade (or fork), feet close together, the left foot a little in advance of the right; right hand loosely clasping the D at the top of the handle, back of the hand uppermost; left hand gripping the handle about one-third down, back of the hand towards the left knee (Fig. 11).

Keeping the spade as upright as possible, press the blade (or tines of the fork) full depth into the soil with the ball—not the instep—of the left foot (Fig. 12). Don't jump on it. If necessary, work the blade (or tines) backwards and forwards, maintaining pressure with the left foot, until it has gone down full depth (Fig. 13).

Then slide the left hand down the handle, remove the foot from the tread of the tool, push downward with the right hand and lift with the left and raise the "bite"

Fig. 14.—*Hands and feet are in this position as the bite of soil is raised. The soil will be tipped as is here indicated by the arrow*

of soil (Fig. 14); then with a twist of the right wrist throw the soil forward and completely over so that it falls upside down (Fig. 15). The left-handed digger will naturally reverse those hand and foot positions.

Those motions become automatic after a little practice, and the digger finds it quite easy to keep an open trench at his feet—as described in the next paragraph—until the digging is completed.

Digging One Spit Deep. A spit represents the full depth of spade-blade or fork-tines, the soil being broken up and turned over to that depth.

Begin operations by taking out a trench 1 ft. wide and 1 ft. deep, right across one end of the strip which is to be dug. Wheel the excavated soil to the opposite end and there dump it in barrow loads, in a straight line, for filling in

Fig. 15.—*With a twist of the right wrist the spadeful of soil is tipped forward and right over so that it falls upside down into the digging trench*

Fig. 16.—*Ground being dug one spit deep. Soil from the first trench has been wheeled to the far end, for filling in the final trench. The arrows indicate how the opening of each successive trench fills in the previous one*

the final digging trench (Fig. 16).

Return to the right-hand end of the top trench and stand facing it. Raise the spade (or fork) a foot or so, vertically, then jab it into the soil 4 in. or 5 in. from the inner edge of the trench, the wrist working quite loosely. That represents the first bite of soil. Then manœuvre the tool as already described, finally disposing of this first bite by throwing it upside down into the back of the trench. If it is heavy soil, leave it lumpy for the weather to work upon it; if, however, the digging is being done as late as February, break the lumps down as finely as possible.

Move along to the left, the width of the tool, for the second bite. It makes for cleaner digging if a nick is made with the spade-blade at the inner extremity of each bite (Fig. 17). Make the nick, lever out and dispose of the second bite in the same manner as the first; and

Fig. 17.—*Digging is easier and cleaner if a nick is made with the spade-blade at the inner extremity of each bite before levering it out*

in that way work along to the extreme left of the strip.

A second trench, 1 ft. wide and 1 ft. deep, is now open at the digger's feet. This will be filled in and a third trench opened by working along to the right. So the digging proceeds, right to left, left to right and back again, until the digger finds the heaps of soil (taken from the first trench) at his heels.

This soil thrown into the final trench, the digging is completed.

Division of Strip to be Dug. In dealing with a wide strip of ground it is sometimes more convenient to get rid of the soil taken from the first trench by disposing of it in the following manner.

Divide the wide strip by an imaginary line down the centre, and wheel (or throw) the excavated soil across this line, parallel with the trench. Then proceed with the digging down the full length of the first half of the strip, ending with an open trench. Cross over the imaginary line, take out a trench (at the same end), and use that soil for filling in the trench with which the first strip terminates (Fig. 18).

Working backwards from that end, the digger duly finds the first heaps of soil at his heels, these being used to fill in the final trench.

Level Digging. Much needless raking will be saved if a correct level is secured as each succeeding digging-trench is opened and closed.

Other points to observe: keep the trench straight; drive the spade-blade (or fork-tines) full depth and vertically each time; adjust width

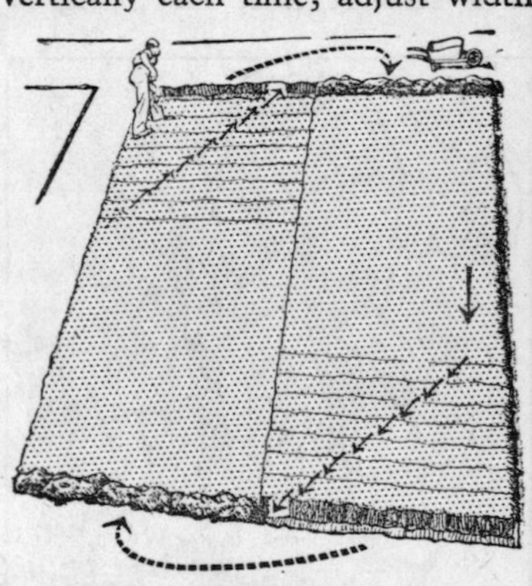

Fig. 18.—*A wide piece of ground to be dug should be divided down the centre with an imaginary line and one long half dug at a time. The soil from the first trench is wheeled across the line. The last trench in the first half is filled in with soil from the first trench in the second long half*

of bite to the nature of the soil—narrow for clay, wider for easily worked ground; pick out all weed roots and grubs revealed.

Keep the Spade Clean. Labour is lightened and the work expedited by keeping the tool clean. As soil accumulates on it, scrape it off with a piece of wood fashioned like a label with sharpened edge (Fig. 19). This scraper can be carried in a pocket where it can be got at for immediate use. It will be needed quite frequently when heavy or moist soil is being dealt with.

Digging-in Manure. The ideal time for manuring heavy soil is early winter; late winter for light ground. Decaying vegetable refuse should be got into the ground during winter if possible.

It should be buried at the bottom of the digging-trench. If a soil

Fig. 19.—*Labour is lightened if the spade-blade is kept clean during the digging. A small wooden scraper should be carried for that purpose*

Fig. 20.—*In bastard trenching the ground is dug two spits deep, the soil 1 ft. down being turned over, broken up, and left where it is. The top soil is kept at the top, and moved on as has been indicated in Fig.* 21

Fig. 21.—*When the foot-down soil has been dealt with, the top soil from the next trench is turned forward on top of it. The digger here is breaking up the soil at the bottom of that next trench*

fumigant (such as naphthalene) is to be applied, fork this into the surface *after* the digging.

The manure or vegetable refuse may be forked into the trench from the wheelbarrow, or be spread over the surface before digging begins and be scraped into each trench as encountered. The latter method means that the digger must tread on the material as he works backwards; he may therefore find the barrow method preferable. Another method is to spread the manure or refuse in heaps over the plot and so be able to deal with it by the forkful.

Bastard Trenching. If ground is never dug deeper than one spit the soil below that depth remains so hard packed that plant roots find it no easy matter to penetrate it.

It is therefore advisable to dig two spits deep every third year, the method being known as bastard trenching. One-third of the vegetable plot should be so treated each year, so that in three years the whole of the ground has been broken up to the depth of approximately 2 ft.; the two-thirds that are not being bastard trenched being dug one spit deep.

The deeper treatment of the soil improves the prospect of crops very considerably, facilitating deep penetration by roots and making more readily available buried stores of food and moisture.

In this case the digging trench is 2 ft. wide and 1 ft. deep. The first trench opened, the digger gets

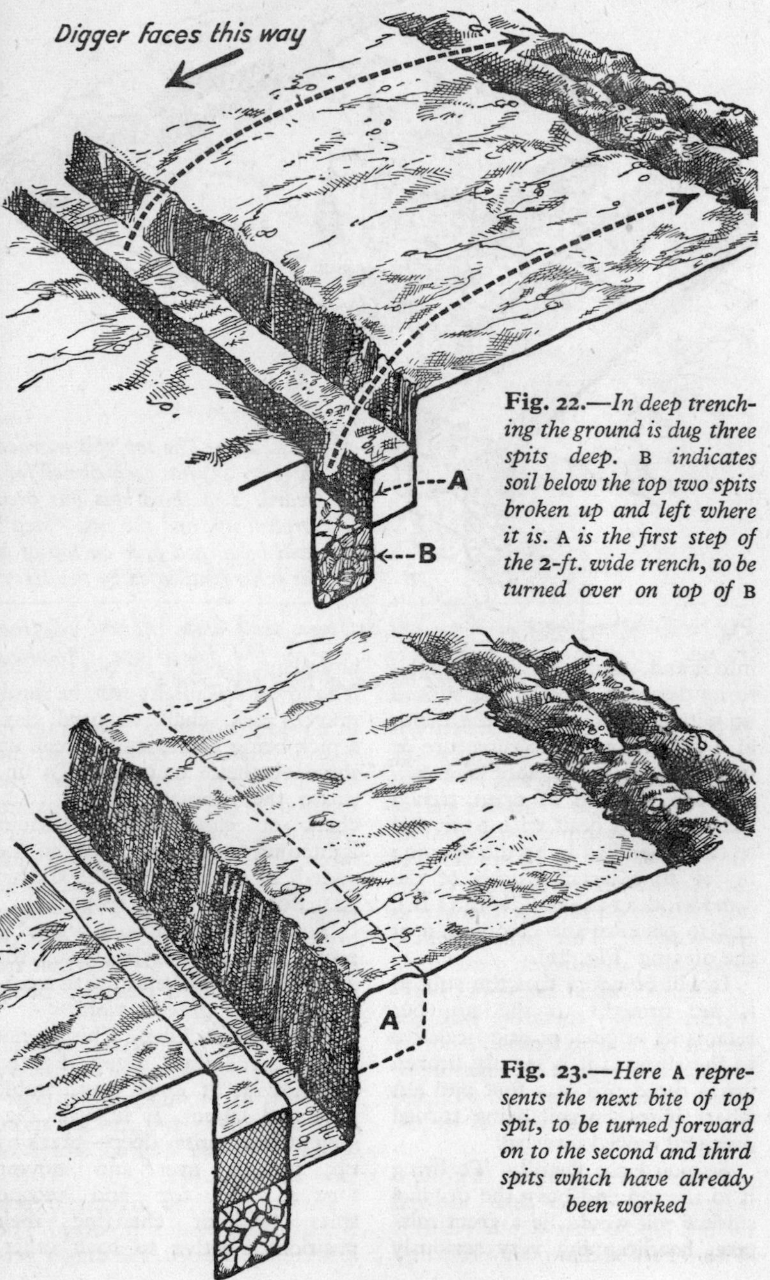

Fig. 22.—*In deep trenching the ground is dug three spits deep.* B *indicates soil below the top two spits broken up and left where it is.* A *is the first step of the 2-ft. wide trench, to be turned over on top of* B

Fig. 23.—*Here* A *represents the next bite of top spit, to be turned forward on to the second and third spits which have already been worked*

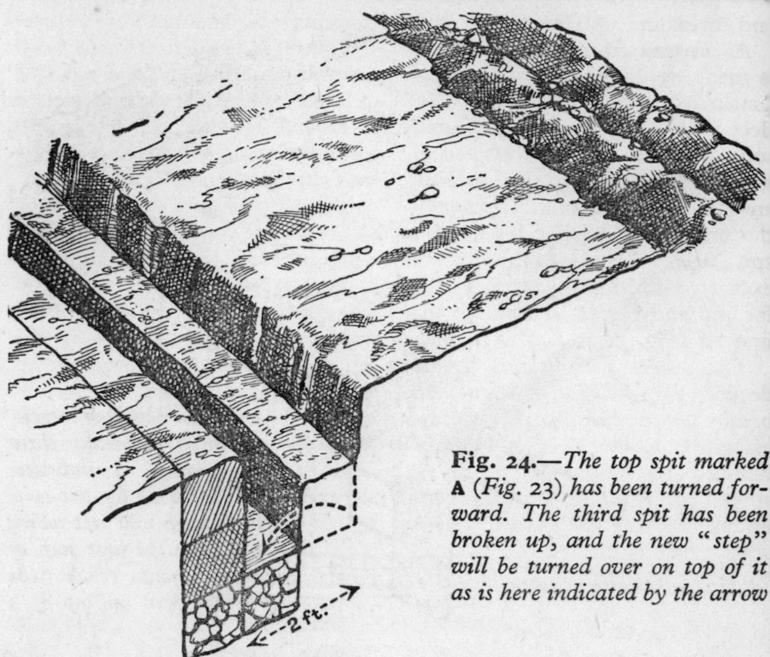

Fig. 24.—*The top spit marked* A (*Fig.* 23) *has been turned forward. The third spit has been broken up, and the new "step" will be turned over on top of it as is here indicated by the arrow*

into it and, standing at right-angles to its direction, breaks the subsoil up with spade or fork to the depth of 1 ft., mixing in any manure or vegetable refuse available (Fig. 20).

When the run of open trench has thus been dealt with from end to end, it is filled in by the opening up of an adjacent trench of the same width (2 ft.) and depth (1 ft.), and so on until the completion of the digging (Fig. 21).

It will be noted that the subsoil is *not* brought to the top but retains its original position relative to the surface; it is simply broken up to the depth of a foot and left where it is, top soil being turned over and moved forward.

Subsoil lacks fertility. To bring it to the top and bury the original surface soil would be a great mistake, handicapping very seriously any plants sown or set out therein. The lower soil might even be sand, gravel, rock, chalk or hard clay, a pick being necessary to break up these obstinate materials. To improve the drainage of the rock, chalk or clay subsoil, various lightening materials need to be added, as explained in the section All Sorts of Soils (page 31).

The more manure or vegetable refuse is mixed with the subsoil, the more fertile it becomes, with a correspondingly greater yield.

Deep Trenching. This is not to be embarked upon lightly, entailing as it does considerable time and labour. It involves digging three spits deep—breaking up, turning over and moving forward the top and second spits (without changing their positions relative to each other) nd breaking up the third spit.

As in bastard trenching a start s made by digging, at one end of strip, a trench 2 ft. wide and 1 ft. leep and removing the excavated soil to the far end. But instead of nerely breaking up the subsoil, another trench is made therein—the width of spade or fork and a spit deep. This second lot of excavated soil is also taken to the far end and placed in front of the first lot (Fig. 22).

The digger then stands in the deeper part of the trench and breaks up the bottom thoroughly, leaving it where it is. A layer of manure or vegetable refuse is spread evenly on top of the broken-up bottom, and the first step of the wide trench is then turned over, in spadefuls or forkfuls, on top of the covering of manure or refuse.

This also is then covered with manure or refuse and the top spit of what will be the second trench is moved forward, in bites, and turned over on top of it. There is now exposed another stretch—1 ft. wide and two spits deep—of subsoil, and there is a new step (Fig. 23).

Break up the new bottom, manure it and turn the new step over on to it, covering this in turn with manure and then with the top spit of the third trench (Fig. 24). Repeat this until the last trench is to be filled with the subsoil that was wheeled away from trench number one, covering this with the top soil from the same.

Labour of this arduous nature is not necessary for the production of normal crops.

SECTION III

SPADE, FORK AND HOE

THE tools really necessary for the home producer of vegetables, flowers and fruit are not numerous. But for the sake of one's pocket and results it is necessary to know how to select those that are essential, how to use them to the best effect and with the least expenditure of labour, and how to prolong their useful existence.

"Must" Number One. A spade is absolutely indispensable. And a spade is *not* a shovel (Fig. 25). The latter has no tread to the top of the blade; it is meant to be used flat, scoop fashion, and it is impossible to dig with it. A spade has a flat tread and is normally used upright. It has a sharp cutting edge for easy penetration of the soil, and a bright blade.

Size and weight are of great importance. The large heavy spade wielded with such apparent ease by the expert tiller of the soil is a painful hindrance in the hands of the inexpert. Quality is governed by price; the digger's comfort by the spade's size and weight.

The manner of using it is explained in the previous section. Like every other tool used on the land it should be put away under cover in a clean condition, blade and handle being scrubbed if necessary. Soil caked on the handle is a fertile source of blisters; on the blade, it hinders every thrust.

The Digging Fork. Size and weight also count for much in the digging fork (Fig. 25, H). The four tines, or prongs, may be flat or rounded, for digging clay or other heavy ground difficult to move with a spade.

It is also used for breaking down surface clods after digging; removing raked-up stones and rubbish; collecting and spreading manure and vegetable refuse; lifting potatoes and root crops generally. A heavy type of fork with broad flat tines is used by professional potato diggers, but in ordinary circumstances the common garden fork will serve all purposes including the forking-in of manures, fertilizers, or soil fumigants needing to be worked into the top 2 in. or 3 in. only.

A fork may fail at the hardest jobs, such as breaking up exceptionally obstinate subsoil. A pick will then be needed; but unless this tool is required extensively its purchase is scarcely worth while, if one can be borrowed for occasional use.

Handle and tines of the fork, and handle and head of the pick, should be cleaned with a scrubbing brush before the tool is put away (Fig. 27).

Small Handfork. This diminutive edition of a digging fork, small but sturdy, is useful for weeding close around plants where the hoe cannot easily or safely reach; for loosening surface soil in the seed bed; and for lifting young plants from soil too clayey for easy work with the trowel. Keep it clean from end to end by scraping or scrubbing (Fig. 25, J).

Multi-purpose Hoes. For annihilating weeds, which rob soil of food and compete with crops for air, light, space; for keeping surface soil loose, thus checking evaporation of moisture and letting in air, warmth, rain; breaking down clods; making drills for seed sowing and planting; earthing up potatoes, and so on—a hoe is invaluable. It should be one of the hardest-worked tools.

The Dutch hoe (Fig. 25, G) has a flat blade for working just below the soil surface; it is used with a jabbing, sliding motion, the operator walking backwards over the ground. It uproots weeds, or severs them at a vital part, a job most effectively performed when sun is shining strongly so that the disturbed weeds are quickly withered; after which they should be raked off and added to the soft refuse heap for later digging in. The flat blade leaves a more or less dusty top to the soil, this serving to bottle up moisture below. Its use is always advisable after the surface has been consolidated by trampling or heavy rain.

The draw hoe (Fig. 25, F) has an upright blade at right angles to the long handle. It is used with a chopping motion so that slices of the surface are detached. The operator walks forward over the hoed ground—not backwards as when the Dutch hoe is being used. This is the tool to use when the Dutch hoe is ineffective, as on clayey soil or where weeds are thicker and of coarse growth; and for drawing soil up to potato tops (earthing up).

The draw hoe is also used in conjunction with the garden line,

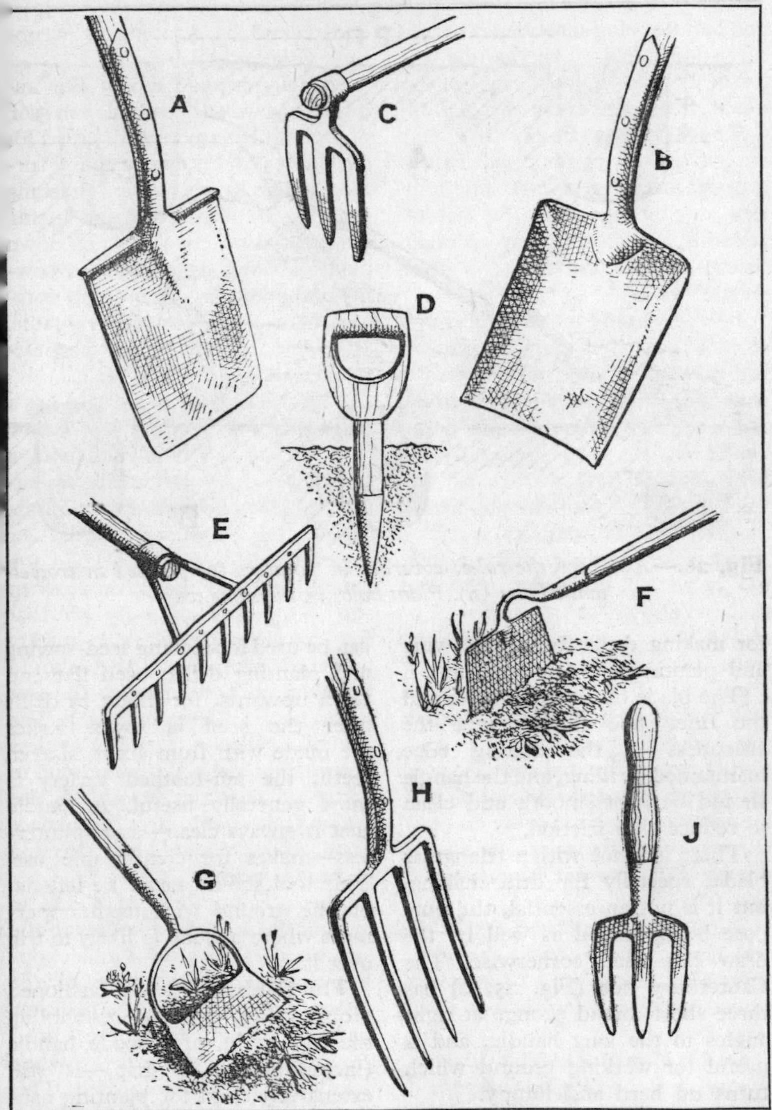

Fig. 25.—*Note how a spade* (A) *differs from a shovel* (B). *The Canterbury hoe* (C) *is useful for breaking hard and lumpy clods. A dibber* (D) *quickly makes small planting holes. A metal-headed rake* (E) *finds ample employment. The upright-bladed draw hoe* (F) *is for heavier work than the flat-bladed Dutch hoe* (G). *Size and weight count for a good deal in the digging fork* (H); *the small handfork* (J) *is useful for general weeding and transplanting*

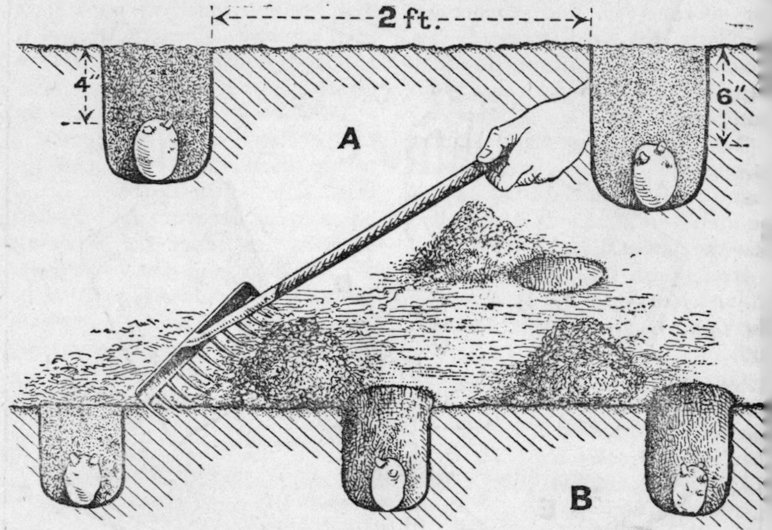

Fig. 26.—*A use for the rake; covering in potatoes* (B) *planted in trowel-made holes* (A). *Plant bulbs in the same way*

for making drills for seed sowing and planting out (*see* page 42).

The blade of the Dutch hoe and the draw hoe should have the sharpness of the cutting edge maintained by filing, and the handle should be kept smooth and clean to reduce skin friction.

There is a hoe with a triangular blade, specially for drill making, but it is not an essential, the purpose being served as well by the draw hoe used cornerwise. The Canterbury hoe (Fig. 25, C) has three short, broad prongs at right angles to the long handle, and is useful for working ground which turns up hard and lumpy.

The Rake. A metal-headed garden rake (Fig. 25, E) finds ample employment on stony ground; is useful for drawing hoed-up weeds into heaps; and for general levelling. If turned teeth upwards and at an angle, a corner of the rake can be used for making seed-sowing and planting drills; used flat and teeth upwards, for filling in drills after the seed is sown. Rakes are made with from six to sixteen teeth; the ten-toothed variety is most generally useful. A handle that is always clean—and splinterless—makes for comfortable use. This tool should never be left flat on the ground with teeth uppermost where anyone is likely to trip over it.

The Dibber. The old-fashioned dibber (Fig. 25, D)—resembling the top 12 in. of a spade handle (including the D grip)—is still extensively used for planting cabbage, potato, etc. But there are drawbacks to it. The pointed end makes a hole that terminates in a point, the result being that the potato or bulb dropped into the hole does not fall to the bottom; the roots it sends out will have to grope r a time to find anchorage. imilarly, the small roots of, say, cabbage seedling dropped in may ang fire for a period for lack of an nmediate grip.

The dibber is perhaps quicker n operation in fairly loose ground han a trowel, but the latter should e used in preference. In stubborn lay the dibber, though tipped with steel point, is not easily forced n, and it leaves a solid-sided hole hrough which roots penetrate with ifficulty.

Garden Trowel. The garden rowel (Fig. 28) is not the flat-bladed kind as used by plasterers, but is scoop-shaped. The method of using it depends on the object in view. If sizable plants are to be set out from pots or boxes, a circular hole should be scooped out with the trowel, larger and somewhat deeper than the mass of soil and roots in the pot. The plant is then placed into position in the hole, and some of the excavated soil is scraped back around it and firmed down with the other end of the trowel or with the fingers.

Small flower, vegetable and other plants without a mass of roots are quickly planted if the trowel is held with the concave surface towards the operator, pushed deeply and vertically into ground and then pulled backward—that is, towards the user (Fig. 28, c). The trowel is held in that position until the roots have been inserted. Then the trowel is removed and the hole filled in firmly.

This works admirably in light soil which would immediately trickle back into a scooped-out small hole before the roots could be inserted; but it might be found necessary to adopt the scooping method in ground that was clayey.

The hole should always be deep enough to take long roots—as sweet-pea and onion seedlings—without being bunched up or folded.

A straight-edge line—a length

Fig. 27.—*After each bout of digging the fork should be water-scrubbed or dry-cleaned—according to its condition—before being put away under cover. Clean tines mean easier digging. A clean and smooth hand-grip on fork, or any garden implement, means fewer blisters*

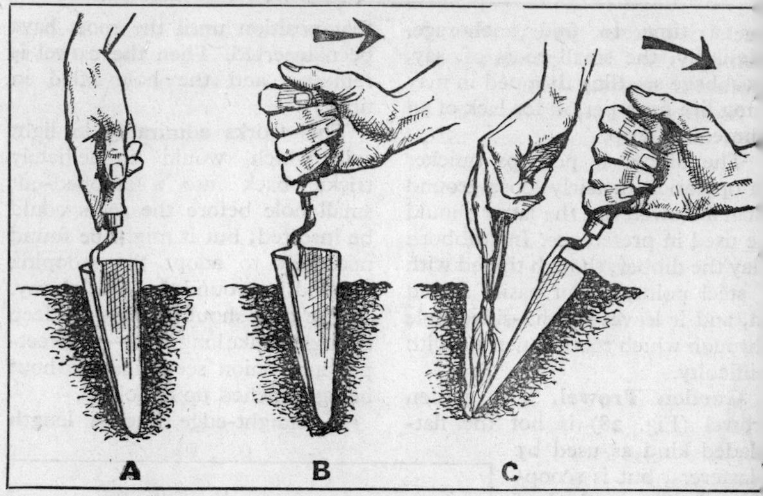

Fig. 28.—*Small plants of all kinds are quickly transplanted with a trowe used as here. Pushed vertically and deeply into the ground* (A), *then drawn towards the user* (B) *the trowel is held in position until the plant roots are inserted* (C) *in the hole thus made. Then the trowel is removed and the hole filled in firmly with the other end or the fingers*

of stout cord—should always be handy for use in securing straight seed drills and planting rows, the cord to be stretched tightly between two sticks, one thrust into the ground at each end of the drill or row, and almost touching the soil. Out of use, keep the cord wound around its two sticks; and put it away clean and dry.

Barrow, Sieve, Watering Can. A wheelbarrow is nearly, if not quite, indispensable; a stout box on two pram wheels and provided with two handles will serve in absence of the real thing.

Soil and leaf-mould, for preparing seed beds and making composts (mixtures of soil and leaf-mould or rotted manure) for filling seed boxes and for potting, should be passed through a sieve (or riddle) with a $\frac{1}{4}$-in. mesh. This item cannot very well be dispensed with.

A stoutly made watering can of ample capacity is necessary not only for giving plants plain water during dry spells but for administering foods and tonics in the form of liquid animal manure or liquid artificial fertilizer. When water is to be given to seedlings in the form of a gentle shower the watering can should be fitted with a removable rose—a perforated cap that fits the end of the spout. If a hose is used for watering it should be of the non-kinkable type.

Powder Blower. A distributor in the form of bellows or blower for scattering insect-killing and disease-controlling powders over stems and foliage is a worth-while investment. A homemade substitute consists of a small muslin bag attached by a piece of string about 6 in. long to the end of a stick; the bag is filled with the powder, the eck tied, then jerked over the lants, the dry powder being jected in small clouds.

Syringe. Sprayers for applying lear water or liquid insecticides take several forms, their simplicity or complexity depending on price. The application of insecticides, etc., is dealt with in the section PESTS AND DISEASES (page 397).

SECTION IV

ALL SORTS OF SOILS

A MASS of chalk, or stones, or sand, gravel or dust, or wet or solid clay is no inspiring ight to the would-be grower who nas one or other as the medium in which to attain worthwhile results. But no kind of ground is hopeless; it can be tamed and made fertile.

The Perfect Soil. The nearest approach to this is a good loam, which is defined as "fertile soil consisting of clay and sand, together with humus"—humus being decayed animal and vegetable matter. If sand predominates it is known as light loam (light, as applied to soils, having nothing to do with the colour); if there is more clay than sand in the mixture it is termed heavy or clay loam; in the intermediate state it is called medium loam.

This type of soil is easily dug and handled, and with the very moderate use of manures or decayed vegetable refuse and artificial fertilizers will produce excellent flowers and crops of all vegetables.

Fertile Clay. Magnificent crops can be produced from clay ground when this has been dug deeply, strawy stable manure or leaf-mould (rotted tree and other leaves), and sand, or sharp grit, fire-ashes from the house, or charred woody bits from the bonfire, being mixed in as freely as possible during the deep digging.

If dug in early winter and left with rough, lumpy surface, frost and wind will pulverize it (Fig. 29). Lime scattered over the surface after digging will sweeten it and help further to break it down. A fortnight or so before sowing or planting, the surface should be forked over and clods shattered, and then ash from the bonfire (or from the burning of wood) be raked or forked in as generously as possible.

If water is disinclined to soak away, this can be corrected by deep trenching (*see* section THE ART OF DIGGING, page 15), or by digging a trench—and leaving it open—across or lengthwise of the plot, this open trench having a slight fall to a ditch (Fig. 30) that can take the drainage water.

Thin layers of clay can be burned if mixed with coal slack and piled in a loose, conical heap over a foundation of glowing wood or coal. A stick or crowbar should be poked into the heap occasionally to create a through draught. The clay crumbles under the influence

Fig. 29.—*Heavy ground dug in early winter should be left with rough, lumpy surface; frost and wind will pulverize it. The surface should not be fined down if the ground is to lie fallow long, or surface-drainage will be impeded and puddles of water may collect here and there on it*

of the heat and forms splendid material for forking or raking into the surface of the clay plot.

Cultivated clay remains rather difficult to dig, but it has the advantage of retaining moisture below the immediate surface during drought, the crops showing no distress when vegetables on lighter soils are almost at the end of their tether because of lack of water.

Even lettuce, spinach, radish, mustard and cress can be grown on cultivated clay, or clay-like ground, if sown in deep drills filled with leaf-mould and finely broken clay or old potting soil.

Long-rooted carrots, beet and parsnips are at a disadvantage in this medium and in shallow soi the stump-rooted varieties of ca rot, and globe beet and turni rooted parsnip, should be sow (Fig. 31), though it is possible produce excellent long carrots, an parsnips, if stations are special prepared for each plant. Holes 1 f or 1½ ft. deep and 4 in. across a made with a crowbar, then fille with old potting soil mixed wit leaf-mould. Three seeds are sow on each prepared surface, and th seedlings reduced to one. Th roots are able to go right dow and plump up unhindered.

With potatoes and most othe crops to be grown in clay the saf rule is to seek the advice of neighbouring growers as to which varieties they have found to d best under local conditions. Thi applies to all other types of soil.

Sandy Troubles. Thirsty an hungry, sandy ground must b given moisture-holding substance such as decaying vegetation, helpe out perhaps with spent hops from a brewery, or hop manure, these being worked in freely throughout as great a depth as the cultivator cares to dig. Chopped-up turf can be added, and seaweed (dug in either wet or dry) if available, and broken clay will help further to give the sandy ground body.

Crushed or powdered chalk, about 1 lb. to the square yard, forked into the surface after moisture-holding materials have been dug in, will provide essential lime (in mild form) and help bind the loose particles together.

Inhospitable Subsoil. A few inches of good top soil may hide a subsoil of chalk, sandstone, gravel, almost pure sand, or clay, with or without any evidence of this

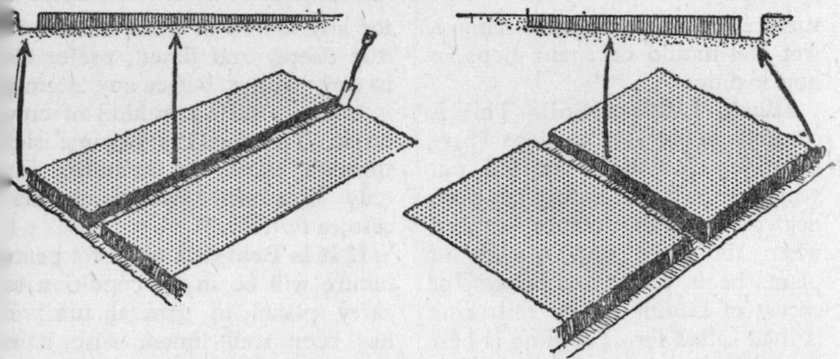

Fig. 30.—*If water is disinclined to soak away it can be encouraged to do so by means of an open trench running the length or breadth of the plot, the trench arranged to have a slight fall to a ditch or other waterway*

appearing on the surface. In such circumstances the term shallow is applied to the top soil, which suffers not only from lack of depth but from easy and excessive dryness in droughty periods and perhaps extreme wetness in rainy spells; all of which conditions have to be combated by the cultivator.

Also there is nothing much for most plants to live on down below the fertile few inches. The sand or gravel subsoil needs to be packed with all the humus-providing material (manure, leaves, lawn mowings, chopped turf, etc.) that can be collected and mixed deeply with it.

Similar materials need to be packed, with the aid of a pick, into chalk, sandstone, clay subsoil, with the important addition of road grit, house-fire ashes, brick dust, mortar rubble, or charred bonfire remains, to assist drainage.

The shallow soils are specially awkward in the case of long-rooted carrot, beet, parsnip, whose ends would buckle up on meeting the hard lower layer; varieties with shorter roots should be sown. Examples are: Scarlet Intermediate carrot, midway in length between Long Red and the stump-rooted Scarlet Model; parsnip, variety Turnip-rooted; beet, Crimson Globe.

Stony Ground. A few stones in soil are all to the good; they assist drainage. In excess they are a nuisance. Frequent raking off will dispose of larger stones; to improve the quality of the soil dig in any animal manures available, spent hops and all forms of vegetable waste—from lawn mowings and seaweed to tree leaves and the muck from a ditch bottom.

Dusty Stuff. This, again, needs to be packed, deeply, with humus-providing materials as mentioned above. It is waste of time to scratch the materials into the surface; they must be worked in to spade-blade depth at least, rougher portions of the material being trodden into the bottom of the digging trench. If chopped turf can be added, or broken clay or heavy loam, the redemption of this very thin type of soil is brought nearer.

Much can be done, in addition, to assist plants in spring and early summer by covering the soil surface around them with manure, wet leaf-mould or spent hops or hop manure.

Black, Lifeless Soil. This is common in old town gardens where manuring has been carried out year after year and liming has been neglected. There comes a time when the yield and quality of plants begin to decline because of excess of humus in the soil; lime is then called for. The lime is best forked into the surface in winter—hydrated (slaked) lime, about 1 lb. per square yard.

Many town garden soils have the same appearance but have not been manured for years. The remedy is to lime in winter and dig in manure or decayed vegetable matter a few weeks later if the soil is thin; if the ground is heavy, dig in manure deeply in winter and lime the surface when digging is completed.

A piece of "sick ground," where, for example, a fowl run has been for any length of time, should b dug deeply and limed, preferabl in early winter, before any attemp is made to raise any kind of cro on it. The soil has become sic through excess of manure, an only lime will sweeten it an restore fertility.

If it is Peaty. A plot of a peat nature will be in no condition t carry plants in general until i has been well limed. Also it i worth every effort to mix with it throughout a good depth, plent of clay or heavy loam if either ca be obtained.

Animal Manure. The idea manure for enriching clay or other heavy soils is stable manure; for light soils, pig or cow manure. Scarcity of these is a big stumbling block, and artificial fertilizers are not a substitute for them. Alternatives and methods of using them are fully dealt with in the section, FERTILIZERS AND MANURES.

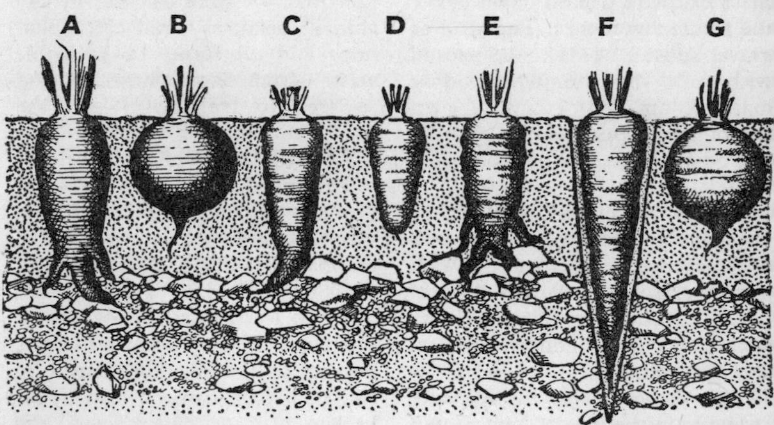

Fig. 31.—*Beet* (A), *carrot* (C) *and parsnip* (E) *of long-rooted types are at a disadvantage in heavy or "shallow" soils. Globe beet* (B), *stump-rooted varieties of carrot* (D) *and turnip-rooted parsnip* (G) *have a much better chance, though excellent long carrots and parsnips can be grown in this obstinate ground if stations are specially prepared for each plant* (F) (*see text*)

SECTION V

FERTILIZERS AND MANURES

It is a common practice to buy fertilizers and then wonder what to do with them; a bad example of putting the cart before the horse. Animal manures, scarce and still more expensive, are not considered; and for lack of knowledge of substitutes the ground is starved of the humus without which artificial fertilizers are of little value.

Replacing Plant Food. The object in manuring ground is to replace the foods which all plants extract from the soil.

Ground is fertile by reason of the humus it contains. Humus is the residue of decayed animal and vegetable matter. The stock of it is added to by digging in natural (organic) manures such as stable, farmyard, sheep, goat, rabbit, fowl and pigeon manure; and such matter as spent brewery hops, hop manure (an excellent substitute for stable manure), seaweed, and rotting or rotted vegetable material as collected in the refuse heap which should find a place somewhere on every cultivated piece of ground.

These are supplemented by wood ash (the result of burning wood, or woody refuse), soot and blood. Chemical fertilizers—artificial manures—supplement these. They are necessary additions. But they do *not* add any humus to the soil.

The First Concern. Prevention of waste should be the first concern in dealing with any animal manure that can be obtained. If for any reason the manure cannot be dug in at once, it should be protected against rain by placing it under an open shed, or covering it with boards, galvanized-iron sheets, sacking, old bits of carpet or lino, or anything similar. This prevents much of the goodness being washed out of it.

The ideal procedure is to dig in animal manure in *early* spring if the soil is light; in autumn or early winter if the soil is heavy.

Stable and Farmyard Manure. Horse manure frequently contains wood shavings, used for bedding in the stable; this should not be used. If it contains straw it is particularly useful for digging into clay and other heavy soils, the straw helping to break up the ground and render it more porous. It should not be used for cabbage or other crops that have to stand through the winter, or they grow lush and in that condition may be injured by frost. And no animal manure should be nearer the surface than spade-blade depth where root crops—carrot, parsnip, beet—are to be grown, or the roots will fork and split.

Cow and pig manure are specially valuable for light soil, helping to retain moisture; they are apt to keep heavy soil wet and cold.

Dug in at the rate of about 28 lb. per sq. rod (30¼ sq. yd.), sheep, rabbit and goat manure are appreciated by all plants.

Fowl and pigeon manure is strong stuff, and can cripple or kill if used to excess. Store under cover with equal parts of dry soil, sandwich fashion. Mix the accumulation and powder it when required for use—any time during the actively growing season, a trowelful per yard run of row hoed or lightly forked in, about once a fortnight. Follow with a good watering if the ground is dry at the time.

In Liquid Form. All animal manures, and those artificial fertilizers that are soluble in water, may be given in liquid form in spring and summer; but not to plants still in the seedling stage.

Put the animal manure in a sack or other bag of coarse texture (Fig. 32) and suspend this in a barrel of water, about 1 peck to 36 gal. of water—½ peck in the case of fowl and pigeon manure. Allow it to soak for a couple of days, poking the bag occasionally with a stick; then use the liquid, diluted with an equal quantity of plain water, to soak the soil occasionally alongside rows of onion cabbage, and other vegetables.

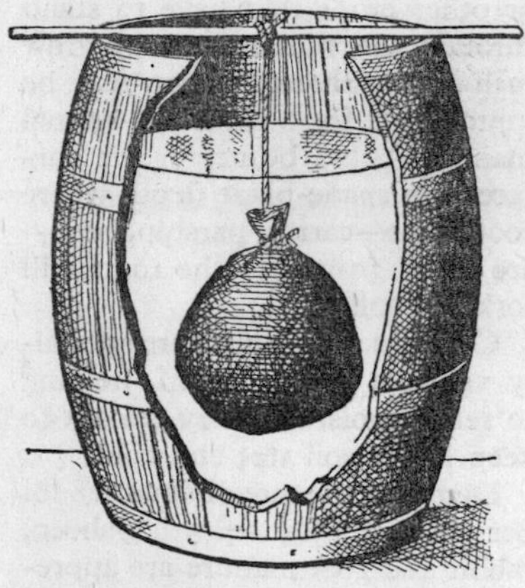

Fig. 32.—*Liquid manure is made by filling a small sack or other coarse bag with manure and suspending it in a barrel of water. The liquid is ready for use after a couple of days*

As liquid is taken out, replace it with water until the richness is exhausted, as shown by the increasing clearness of the barrel's contents. Manure left in the bag should then be emptied out alongside any vigorously growing crop. Smaller quantities can be prepared in a bucket or watering can.

Artificial fertilizers can be mixed with water—in the watering can—at the rate of about 1 oz. per gal. and applied at that strength.

Vegetable Refuse. All disease-free waste greenstuff, potato-tops, weeds (excepting vigorous-rooting dock, thistle, nettle, couch grass or "twitch," and wild convolvulus, all of which should be burned), lawn mowings, grass cut from hedge sides and ditches, bracken, should be collected in a heap or pit to rot down. As layers of material are added they should be sprinkled with finely crushed chalk, or sulphate of ammonia, ½ lb. to the sq. yd., or with soot, to assist the rotting down and increase the value of the mass.

This organic matter is of such value for enriching the soil that the pile or pit of it repays every trouble taken in its collection. The stuff can be dug in whenever a piece of ground is vacant.

Woody Refuse. The bonfire (Fig. 33) is another source of valuable plant food, the ash that results from the burning of cabbage stalks, sticks, old stakes, weed roots, hedge trimmings, diseased potato-tops, pest-infested leaves, bracken, containing potash. This last is required by all crops, especially such as contain starch and sugar, as potato, beet and tomato plants.

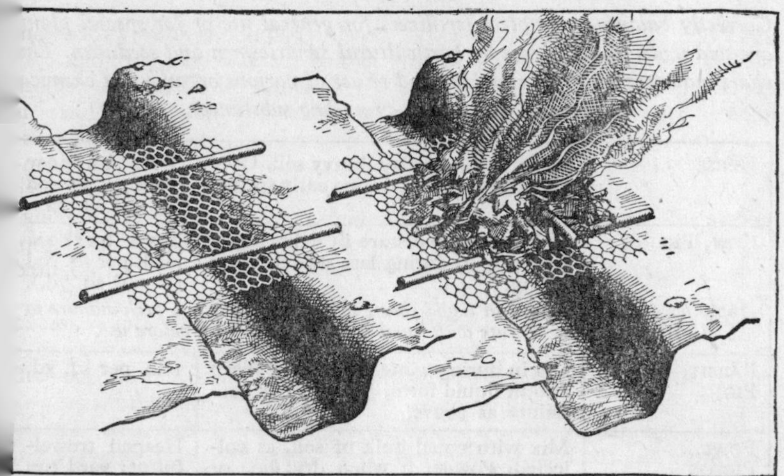

Fig. 33.—*Woody refuse, weed roots, hedge trimmings, cabbage stalks, etc., are a source of valuable potash. Burned on a wire-netting platform over a trench open at both ends (this ensures a good draught), the ash can be scraped from the trench and stored under cover until it is wanted*

This wood ash must be kept under cover and dry until required for use, or much of its value may be washed out by the rains. Scatter it over the soil at the rate of a heaped trowelful per sq. yd. a week or ten days before sowing or planting. Use it also as a top dressing before earthing up potatoes and hoe it in around other actively growing plants. Too much wood ash should not be used on light soils, which it makes still lighter.

Green Manuring. Another method of putting humus into the soil, and improving the moisture-holding quality of light, sandy ground, consists in sowing broadcast a mixture of vetches and rye during September, the top growth being dug in the following spring; or a mixture of mustard and rape in summer, digging in the top growth in autumn—4 oz. of mustard seed and 1 oz. of rape per rod.

Artificial fertilizers are required in order to supplement manure or vegetable refuse already dug in. Special mixtures for the various plants and crops can be bought ready for use, with directions. These are correctly balanced, the fertilizers being mixed in suitable proportions. Quick-acting stimulants should be applied separately, according to each plant's requirements.

The Chief Needs. Foremost among the chemicals required by all plants are:—

(*a*) Nitrogen, to assist the production of leaf and stem and fast growth. It is required specially by the cabbage tribe and flowering plants generally.

It can be supplied in the form of sulphate of ammonia, 1 oz. per sq. yd., hoed in at intervals of about a fortnight during spring and summer; nitrate of soda, a mere pinch

SOIL ENRICHERS AND TONICS

Correctly balanced, complete fertilizers for general use or for special plant are sold under trade names by horticultural sundriesmen and seedsmen. Thi chart indicates the nature and method of use of various organic and chemica manures and humus-providing substances.

<table>
<tr><td>HORSE</td><td>Helps break up clay, heavy soil. Used in light soil, dig in during early spring.</td><td>Two barrow loads per sq. rod (= $30\frac{1}{4}$ sq. yd.).</td></tr>
<tr><td>COW, PIG</td><td>Helps retain moisture in light, sandy soil; dug in during late winter, early spring.</td><td>Two barrow loads per sq. rod (= $30\frac{1}{4}$ sq. yd.).</td></tr>
<tr><td colspan="3">Apply horse, cow, pig also in liquid form, to growing plants, ½ peck manure to 18 gal. water. Dilute with equal volume clear water before use.</td></tr>
<tr><td>RABBIT, GOAT, PIG</td><td>Dig in during winter. Goat and sheep also in liquid form, ¼ peck to 18 gal. Dilute as above.</td><td>1 lb. per sq. yd.</td></tr>
<tr><td>FOWL, PIGEON</td><td>Mix with equal bulk of soil, as collected. Powder it when dry; hoe or fork in around growing plants, spring and summer.</td><td>Heaped trowelful per yard run of row.</td></tr>
<tr><td colspan="3">Use also in liquid form, spring and summer, ¼ peck to 18 gal. water. Dilute with equal volume clear water before use.</td></tr>
<tr><td>DECAYED VEGETABLE MATTER</td><td>Leaves, weeds, grass, disease-free greenstuff generally, collected in heap to rot down. Supplies humus; helps to retain moisture.</td><td>Bury not less than 9 in. deep.</td></tr>
<tr><td>HOP MANURE</td><td>Substitute for stable manure, for all soils and plants.</td><td>Dig in two handfuls per sq. yd., any time.</td></tr>
<tr><td colspan="3">Use also as surface dressing—put down wet—in late spring, summer.</td></tr>
<tr><td>SPENT HOPS</td><td>Obtained from breweries. Provides humus, helps retain moisture in light soil.</td><td>Dig in liberally, any time of year.</td></tr>
<tr><td>SEAWEED</td><td>Provides humus, potash. All crops. May be dug in either wet or dry, in winter.</td><td>Dig in generously and deeply.</td></tr>
<tr><td rowspan="2">GREEN MANURE</td><td rowspan="2">Adds humus; helps retain moisture in light, sandy soil. Sow mixture of vetches and rye, thickly, September. Or sow mustard and rape mixture in summer.</td><td>Dig in top growth the following spring.</td></tr>
<tr><td>Dig in top growth late autumn.</td></tr>
<tr><td>DRIED BLOOD</td><td rowspan="3">These provide nitrogen for encouragement of leaf, stem, fast growth. Required specially by cabbage tribe, lettuce, all flowering plants. Use at intervals, spring and summer; hoe in.</td><td>A sprinkling.</td></tr>
<tr><td>SULPHATE OF AMMONIA</td><td>1 oz. per sq. yd.</td></tr>
<tr><td>NITRATE OF SODA</td><td>Small pinch per plant.</td></tr>
<tr><td colspan="3">Also in liquid form: sulphate of ammonia 1 oz. per gal.; nitrate of soda ½ oz. per gal. of clear water.</td></tr>
</table>

KAINIT	These five provide potash, one of chief requirements of potato, tomato, beet, root crops generally; all flowering plants.	3 oz. per sq. yd., autumn, or winter only.
NITRATE OF POTASH (Saltpetre)		1 oz. per sq. yd., summer.
SULPHATE OF POTASH		1 oz. per sq. yd., spring.
SEAWEED ASH	Into surface before sowing or planting.	Trowelful per sq. yd.
WOOD ASH	Into surface before sowing or planting.	Trowelful per sq. yd.
Also in liquid form: nitrate of potash and sulphate of potash 1 *oz. per gal. of water, applied to growing crops.*		
BASIC SLAG	Phosphates, specially required by peas, beans, turnip.	4 oz. per sq. yd., heavy and peaty soils, autumn or winter.
BONEMEAL	Roses, herbaceous plants.	4 oz. per sq. yd., autumn.
SUPERPHOSPHATE	Sweet peas, chrysanthemums.	2 oz. per sq. yd., spring and summer.
Also in liquid form: superphosphate 1 *oz. per gal. of water.*		
SALT (Agricultural)	Useful to cabbage tribe, beet, asparagus.	2 oz. per sq. yd., autumn or spring.
SOOT (Liquid form)	All plants, spring and summer. ¼ peck in 10 gal. of water.	4 oz. per sq. yd.
QUICKLIME (Calcium oxide)	Clay, heavy soils. Slake on ground, fork into surface.	½ lb. per sq. yd.
GROUND LIME	This is powdered quicklime. Use similarly.	½ lb. per sq. yd.
HYDRATED LIME (Calcium hydroxide)	This is water-slaked quicklime, in powder form and non-caustic. Sold in small bags with directions for use. Suitable for heavy and medium soils.	
GROUND LIMESTONE (Carbonate of lime)	Powdered chalk. For light or sandy soil.	1 lb. per sq. yd.

per plant, also at intervals; soot, ½ lb. per sq. yd. during summer, of greatest use on light soil; dried blood, sold by horticultural suppliers, with directions, hoed or forked in during spring and summer. Liquid blood obtained from a slaughter house can be prepared for use by mixing it with a heap of sifted soil; when this has dried, scatter it where required.

(*b*) Potash, to help produce starch and sugar. It is one of the chief requirements of potato, tomato, beet, and can be supplied as kainit, 3 oz. per sq. yd., dug in during autumn or winter only; sulphate of potash, in spring, 1 oz. per sq. yd.; nitrate of potash (saltpetre), 1 oz. per sq. yd., during summer. Wood ash, from the bonfire, is a free source of supply, as also is the ash of burnt seaweed.

(*c*) Phosphates, which help to maintain health generally and encourage root development. Plants in general benefit by an extra allowance in the form of superphosphate of lime, 2 oz. per sq. yd. during spring and summer; or bonemeal, which is slow in action and should be forked into the surface in autumn or winter, about 4 oz. per sq. yd., or basic slag, for heavy and peaty soils, 4 oz. per sq. yd., autumn or winter.

(*d*) Lime, which is not a manure but, like humus, must be present in soil in sufficient quantity to ensure fertility. Soil overloaded with humus becomes acid or sour, and plants fail. The forking in of lime will correct this. But liming must not be overdone, or the humus will be destroyed. Both lime and humus must be present—in the right proportions.

Mossy growth on soil surface indicates either lack of lime or poverty of soil; in the latter case the trouble is corrected by manuring or by the use of fertilizers. The lime content can be determined as described in the next paragraph.

Testing for Lime. Pour a little spirits of salts (hydrochloric acid) over a saucerful of soil. If nothing happens, apart from the soil soaking up the acid, lime will certainly have to be added to the plot where the sample came from.

If it bubbles and froths, sufficient lime is present. If bubbling and frothing is feeble, a moderate dressing of lime is called for.

How to Use Lime. Once the plot has been put right as to lime it should be kept so, but all-over annual dressings are not likely to be necessary. It is generally sufficient if one-third of the plot is limed in a year, other portions taking their turn in following years. More frequent dressings, however, may be given to the soil containing the destructive club root or finger-and-toe disease which attacks roots of cabbage and turnip; lime checks this. An additional use is as a soil pest (slug, etc.) destroyer.

As a general rule lime should be forked into the surface during winter. It gets to work more quickly if applied in powder form. In that condition it should be broadcast on a windless day, the trowel or spade, or tin with perforated lid, with which it is distributed, held close to the ground.

What Lime to Use. Quicklime will destroy whatever humus there may be in light or sandy soil; in this case apply a dressing of calcium carbonate (carbonate of lime), commonly known as chalk, ground chalk or ground limestone, 1 lb. per sq. yd.

Quicklime, calcium oxide, also known as burnt lime, lump lime, shell lime, or caustic lime, is burned chalk. It should not be allowed to make contact with stems or leaves or any vegetable. Note should be made of the fact that it burns—hands, face, clothing.

It is useful for sweetening and pulverizing clay and other heavy soils, and is generally needed by newly broken grassland. It should be forked into the dug surface, ½ lb. per sq. yd.

Before spreading, quicklime should be slaked. A convenient method is to distribute it in small heaps, cover these with soil, and later scatter the heaps evenly.

In powdered form quicklime is known as ground lime. The finer the powder the quicker it gets to work. Lumps of lime left on the surface remain idle; ½ lb. per sq. yd. is the quantity to apply, the rate being doubled where club root is troublesome. Note that ground lime is *not* the same as ground (powdered) limestone or chalk.

For general purposes the most convenient form of lime is that sold in small bags, under various trade names, as hydrated (water-slaked) lime. Its chemical name is calcium hydroxide. It is non-caustic, and should be used as directed by the suppliers.

General-purposes Mixture. Lime is best applied separately, as already indicated. It should never be mixed with animal or hop manure. Superphosphate must not be mixed with lime or nitrate of soda; or sulphate of ammonia with lime or basic slag.

The three chief chemical requirements, apart from lime, may be mixed together and given as a general dressing a week or so before the spring sowings in the following form: superphosphate three parts, sulphate of potash one part, and sulphate of ammonia one part, these representing respectively the essential phosphates, potash and nitrogen.

Special individual requirements are mentioned under the names of plants in the alphabetical sections. The trouble of selection and mixing is saved if special proprietary mixtures are purchased.

SECTION VI

SEED SOWING, OUTDOORS AND IN

ONLY seed supplied by a firm with a good reputation is worth sowing; the rest may be rubbish. But even the world's most expensive seed cannot produce good results unless (*a*) the soil is prepared beforehand, and (*b*) the seed is then sown properly.

For some plants it is desirable to provide a special seed bed, the seedlings to be transplanted later to the places where they will ultimately produce their flowers or crops. Of vegetables, cabbage, broccoli, brussels sprouts, etc., come into this category (Fig. 34).

Other kinds may be sown in boxes or pots in frame or greenhouse, for later transference to open ground; such as half-hardy and tender flowering plants, and onion, leek, celery and tomato.

Others will be sown in the places where the plants are to mature, as carrot, turnip, beet, parsnip, radish; because of the

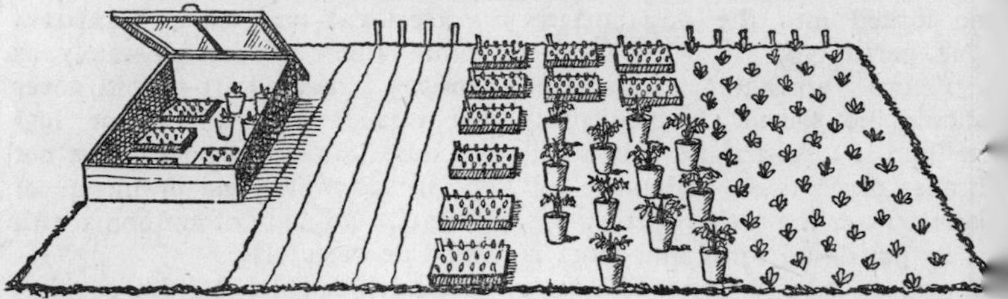

Fig. 34.—*A seed bed and nursery ground such as this is very desirable for bringing on seedlings for later planting out in prepared rows where they will produce their crops. The area also provides room for a frame*

nature of their roots they will not bear the upheaval of transplanting. Beans, peas may be sown in their rows, and all hardy annuals.

Remain where Sown. For these the ground should be dug (and if necessary or desirable, manured) well in advance. If this can be done only a short time before sowing the ground may be spongy, and will then need firming, by treading or rolling.

The time to sow is governed to some extent by the state of the soil and by the weather; and sowing in a cold locality, or in a heavy or wet soil, cannot take place until later than is practicable in a warmer district or in a light, dry soil.

Preparing the Surface. It is necessary that the top inch or so of soil shall be crumbly—that is, have a good tilth. This is an aid to germination (sprouting). Seed may remain dormant a considerable time if buried among clods or put into ground that has become pasty on top with heavy rain or made hard by too much trampling.

The hard or pasty surface should be loosened with a digging fork and left for a day (longer if necessary) for the wind to dry it out. A vigorous raking should follow.

If a surface is covered with lumps and clods these should be broken with fork or hoe or rake. Wood ash forked or raked in will help to get the surface friable.

It is then possible to make drills—shallow trenches—for the reception of the seed (Fig. 35). For all small seeds these may be V-shaped; for larger seeds—pea, bean—the drill should be as wide at the bottom as the top.

Making a Drill. Sowing rows should be spaced according to the needs of the plant concerned.

Use a garden line as a straight-edge, stretched tightly between two end sticks and almost touching the ground. To open up the drill use a draw hoe, with a chopping motion, the edge or one side of the blade being guided by the taut line. If the drill is to be flat-bottomed, the blade should be used parallel with the ground; if V-shaped, the blade should be at an angle so that only one corner is used.

A corner of the rake, held teeth upwards, will do the job—in the case of a V-shaped drill—as well as the hoe (Fig. 36).

The operator walks backwards, facing the opening drill, and so that the garden line shall not shift he presses it down with one foot, shuffled backwards along it.

Making a Drill

Fig. 35.—*Wide, flat-bottomed drills for the larger seeds can be made with draw hoe and garden line* (A). *Dry ground should be watered before sowing* (B). *When the water has drained away the seeds are spaced out* (C), *and the row labelled. In heavy ground the drill should be shallower (upper arrow) than in light ground (lower arrow). Ground too heavy for drill-making with the hoe can be dealt with as at* (D); *edges of the drill first being spade-nicked* (E).

Fig. 36.—V-*shaped shallow drills can be made with a corner of the draw hoe* (*top sketch*) *or of the rake held teeth upwards* (*centre*); *a semicircular drill* (*bottom*), *by pressing the rake handle into the ground with one foot*

Depth of Drill. If only shallow drills are required, as for very small seed, these are made with least trouble by placing the handle of hoe or rake flat on the ground and parallel with the garden line and pressing it down with both feet.

Depth depends on the amount of soil-covering the seed requires. But in dealing with ground that dries out quickly in spring and summer it is advisable to make drills 2 in. or so deeper than is really necessary; the seeds are given their normal covering, the space that then remains above them forming a convenient channel for receiving water when this has to be given later on to the plants.

Seed put into dry ground will wait for moister conditions before it starts to germinate. If drills really are dry, fill them with water overnight, or two or three hours before sowing—a much better plan than watering the ground immediately afterwards (Fig. 35B).

Water given after sowing and before seedlings show above ground may cause the surface to cake, with the result that they have difficulty in breaking through the stiff crust.

Several Drills at a Time. Open out the number of drills required for the day's sowing operations, so that when sowing starts it can be completed without interruption. Space them with care, shifting the line to left or right as necessary. Avoid overmuch trampling of the ground; if operations are followed by heavy rain, puddles may form. If a plank is available for standing on, use it.

Fig. 37.—*Economy in both seed and labour is effected by sowing small seed in groups of three. The seed is trickled from a torn-off corner of the packet held low*

Sowing the Seed. Make a little seed go a very long way. It results in a saving of money and labour. Final distances at which plants sown in the open are to stand are indicated in the alphabetical sections. Seed should be sown with those distances in mind.

If a continuous stream of seed is sown along a drill most of the seedlings will have to be pulled up and thrown away. Larger seeds can be spaced out one by one. Small ones can be trickled out of the seed packet, one corner being torn off for that purpose, in groups of about three at intervals (Fig. 37); or a little can be held in the closed right hand and trickled out carefully between thumb and first finger.

Fig. 38.—*Sown seed can be covered by shufflng the feet carefully along both sides of the drill, or drawing soil back into it with the inverted rake*

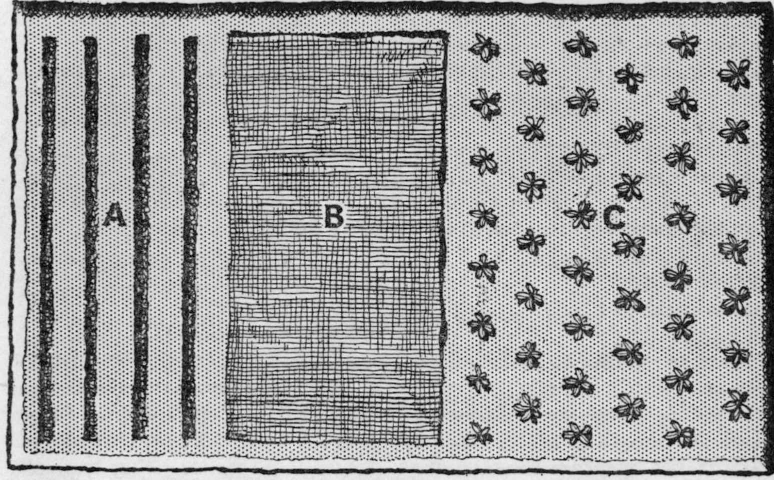

Fig. 39.—*Seedlings to be transplanted a few inches apart* (C) *before they go into their permanent rows can be raised in shallow drills about 4 in. apart* (A). *If the soil is light and there is no rain the seed bed can be prevented from drying out by covering the sown rows with wet sacking or other material* (B) *until the seedlings are up*

Seed can be made to go three times as far with careful sowing.

Label as You Go. As a row is sown and before the drill is filled in it should be labelled (Fig. 35C). The average memory is short and faulty. Little wood slivers as used for labelling pot plants are too fiddling for outdoors; also they are easily displaced. A common practice is to push a stick into the end of a row and fit the emptied seed packet into a notch in the stick's top. It answers—unless wind blows the packet away or rain pulps it.

Serviceable labels can be sliced from box-wood, or from old stakes. Or a stake can have one side cut flat for pencilling on. A handy length is 1 ft., one end pointed for pushing into the ground. The name of the vegetable or flower and its variety should be printed as close as may be to the top end. And the names will remain legible longer if the pencil is pressed hard into the wood.

Covering the Seed. Sown seed can be covered, to the required depth, by shuffling the feet along both sides of the drill. If this is to be completely filled in, the quickest way is to work the displaced soil into the drill with the back of the rake (Fig. 38), patting it down gently afterwards, if fairly dry, to ensure firmness over the seeds.

A fall of rain may have made the soil so wet since the drills were opened that it cannot be returned above the seed except in lumpy condition; which is not favourable to speedy growth. It is as well to be prepared for this by placing beforehand a quantity of dry soil under cover specially for filling drills. Old potting soil serves excellently. The scheme should be adopted specially where soil is naturally heavy and disinclined to crumble.

Finish off by passing the rake down between the covered-in rows.

Protection for Seed. Old dry soot (not straight from the chimney—it is likely to burn tender seedlings) sprinkled along the rows will keep birds, slugs, mice and cats at a distance. Even the most persistent cat will acknowledge defeat if confronted by pepper-dusted rows.

To discourage birds from indulging in dust baths above the seed, place twigs of evergreen (laurel, etc.) flat along the rows; this also provides shade in hot, sunny weather and cuts out any need for watering.

Position for Seed Bed. Seedlings to be transplanted should be raised in a special bed, or in boxes or pots. Later shifting to permanent quarters will not upset them. In the case of wallflowers, cabbage and other greens, the shift actually benefits them; the disturbance induces the young plants to form a network of roots instead of sending down one long tap-root.

It should be away from shade and overhanging tree branches. The site should be dug 1 ft. deep, and if the soil is heavy, sand, grit or wood ash mixed in freely will put things right. The seedlings will not need a rich root run to start with, so no manure should be added.

In the home garden the best place for a seed bed is a border backed by fence or wall facing the south or south-west. For spring sowings especially, seedlings get just the encouragement they need in a warm border of this description. If the border is narrow the drills should run parallel with the path; otherwise at right angles.

Seed Bed Drills. As the seedlings are due for early transplanting the drills need not be more than 4 in. apart, and quite shallow, made as already explained. To prevent light soil drying, during a rainless spell, cover the sown rows with wet sacking or something similar until the seedlings show above surface (Fig. 39).

There may be a temptation to broadcast seed over the bed instead of sowing in neat drills. But this wastes seed, causes overcrowding

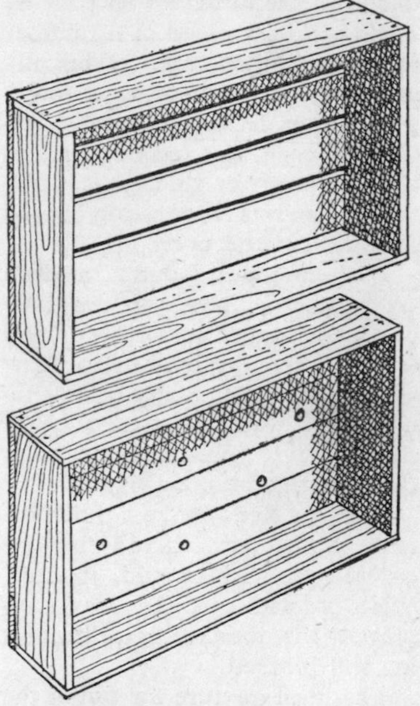

Fig. 40.—*Seed boxes must be efficiently drained, by spaces between the bottom slats (upper sketch), or by ¼-in.-diameter holes bored in the bottom. To prevent the spaces or holes becoming clogged with soil they should be covered with leaf-mould, or leaves should be placed over them*

Fig. 41.—*Seeds germinate more quickly if the soil is warmed before it goes into the box. This can be done by heaping it over a heated brick*

and weak growth, adds to the labour of thinning out and makes weeding difficult.

Sowing in Boxes. It is possible to steal a useful march on time by sowing in boxes seed of a number of plants that are commonly raised by outdoor sowings. Sweet peas, onion, leek, beans, peas, lettuce, cabbage, etc., can be reared in a sunny frame or greenhouse until the time arrives for planting out the seedlings in the open.

Wooden boxes about 2 in. deep are handiest. These can generally be obtained from seedsmen. There are cracks in the bottom to allow of free drainage. Boxes which do not allow water to escape easily should have $\frac{1}{4}$-in.-diameter holes bored in the bottom (Fig. 40).

Soil for Seed Boxes. The bottom of the box should first be covered with leaf-mould, if available; or with enough leaves to prevent the drainage holes becoming soil blocked.

The ideal mixture for filling the box consists of two parts good soil and one part of leaf-mould, both being rubbed through a $\frac{1}{4}$-in.-mesh riddle; enough fine sand or sharp grit being added to make the mixture feel gritty when passed through the fingers. Good garden soil, sifted, without leaf-mould, will do at a pinch; but it *must* be porous with sand or grit.

Seeds get a flying start if the prepared soil is warmed before being filled into the box—by full exposure to sun in a frame; or by being spread out on the bench in a heated greenhouse; or being heaped over a brick heated in a kitchen oven (Fig. 41).

Filling Seed Boxes. Prepared soil should be neither wet nor dry when it goes into the box. It must be made firm by pressing down with the fingers along the two sides and two ends (Fig. 42); then press the surface all over with the clean bottom of a small flowerpot, or a broad piece of flat, smooth wood.

The firmed surface should be $\frac{1}{2}$ in. from the top of the box. Rub the surface lightly with the finger-tips, to crumble it; sowing can then proceed (Fig. 43).

For quick germination sow the seed as thinly as patience will

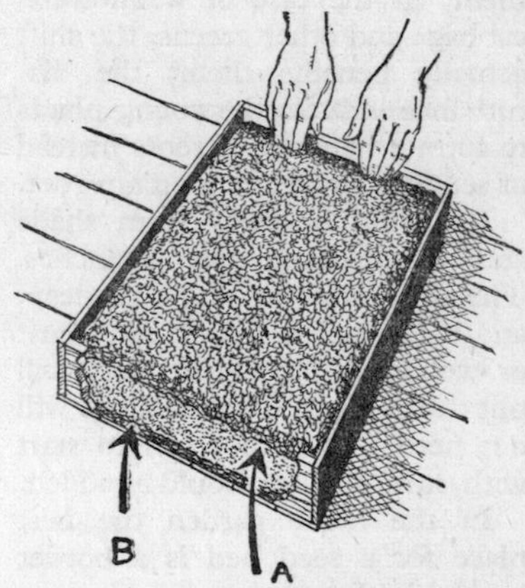

Fig. 42.—*Soil* (A) *should be made firm in the seed box by pressing it down the sides with the finger-tips. The bottom lining of leaf-mould or leaves is indicated by the arrow* (B)

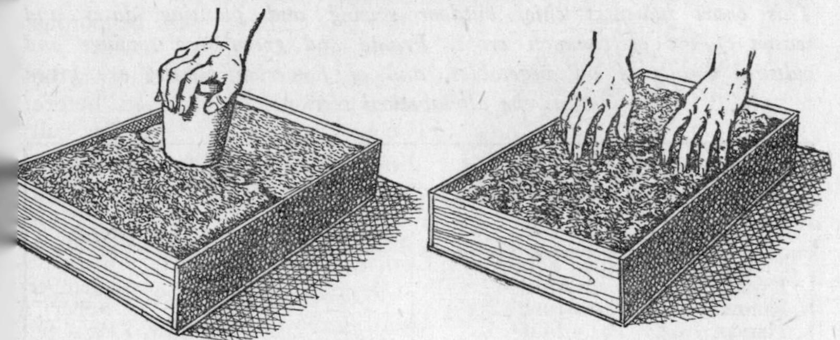

Fig. 43.—*The soil firmed down the sides of the box, the surface is then compressed with the clean bottom of a small flowerpot (left). The surface is then crumbled lightly and evenly all over with the finger-tips (right)*

allow, cover with a sprinkling of sifted soil and press this down lightly with the flowerpot bottom or piece of flat, smooth wood. With quite small seeds deeper soil delays germination. But seeds of pea and bean may be dropped, singly, into holes 1 in. deep, the holes then being filled up with soil.

Moisten the soil with water applied from a can fitted with a fine rose, carefully, to avoid disturbance of the shallowly covered seed. Then place the box in a sunny frame, kept closed until the seedlings appear, or in the greenhouse.

It helps germination and saves later watering if the boxes are covered with paper, to shade the soil surface; better still if a sheet of glass can be placed between paper and box. This covering is to be removed when the first seedlings show (Fig. 44).

When large enough to handle, the seedlings will be planted out in the open ground in the case of quite hardy plants; tender ones will be transferred to other boxes and grown on for a time in frame or greenhouse for later planting out in their prepared places. Each box should be labelled as soon as the seed is sown.

Sowing in Pots. Flowerpots of about 3 in. diameter are quite large enough, scrubbed, inside and out, and thoroughly dried. Clean crocks placed in the bottom will keep the drainage hole clear. Fill up with

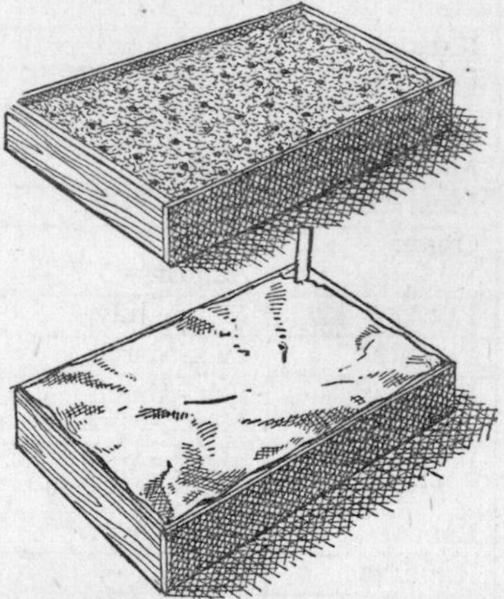

Fig. 44.—*Seed should be sown in the prepared box as thinly as possible; larger seeds should be spaced out (top). Germination is assisted and watering saved if the surface is then covered with paper—preferably with a sheet of glass beneath the paper*

CHIEF VEGETABLE AND SALAD CROPS

This chart indicates chief outdoor sowing and planting dates and season of use of common crops. Frame and greenhouse sowings and cultural details of all vegetables, and of flowering plants, are given in the alphabetical sections

Crop	*Sow in open*	*Plant out*	*When ready*	*Available until*
ARTICHOKE (Jerusalem)	—	Feb.-March	November	March
BEAN, Broad Dwarf French Runner Haricot	Nov., Feb.-May Late April May, June Early May	— — — —	June July July November	August September October Late winter
BEET	April-late June	—	July	March
BROCCOLI	March-May	May-July	October	May
BRUSSELS SPROUTS	March-April	May-June	November	March
CABBAGE Spring Autumn	 July-August April	 October June	 February October	 May January
CARROT	March-April	—	July	April
CAULIFLOWER	Early April	May-June	July	October
CELERY	April	June-July	Oct.-Nov.	March
CRESS	March-Sept.	Ready for use about sixteen days after sowing		
KALE	Early April	June-July	December	April
LEEK	March	July	October	April
LETTUCE	March-August	Ready about ten weeks after sowing		
MARROW	May	May-June	August	November
MUSTARD	March-Sept.	Ready about 12 days after sowing		
ONION	March August	May-June —	September March	May June
PARSLEY	March-July	—	June-Oct.	All the year
PARSNIP	Feb.-March	—	November	March
PEA, Early Maincrop	Feb.-March March-April	— —	June July	July August
POTATO, Early Maincrop	March-April April-mid-May	— —	July Late Sept.	September May
RADISH	March-Sept.	Ready five to six weeks after sowing		
RHUBARB	—	March	April	July
SAVOY	March-April-May	May-July	August	March
SHALLOT	—	Jan.-Feb.	July	March
SPINACH (Summer)	Feb.-August	—	May	September
SWEDE	May-July	—	October	March
TOMATO	In heat	Late May	July	October
TURNIP	August	—	October	December

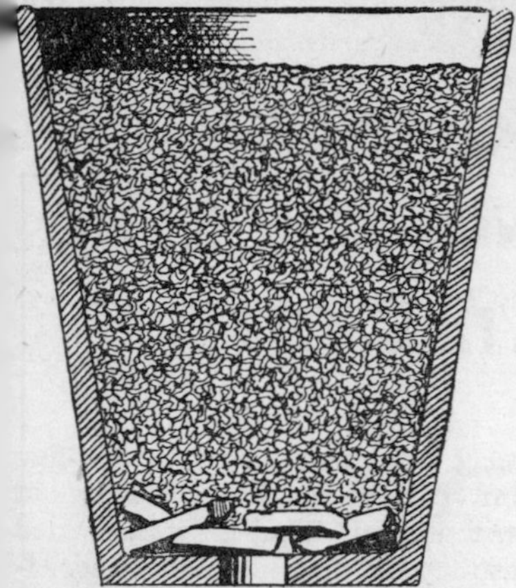

Fig. 45.—*Before seed is sown the pot should be scrubbed inside and out and dried. Broken pieces of pot are then placed over the drainage hole, and prepared soil firmed in to within half an inch of the top*

Fig. 46.—*To moisten the soil in a pot in which seed has been sown the pot should be immersed almost rim deep in a bucket of water, with the chill taken off, until water soaks up through the hole to the soil surface*

good, porous soil (mixture similar to that for seed boxes); press this down with the thumbs and level off the surface $\frac{1}{2}$ in. from the pot top (Fig. 45).

Sow very thinly, cover with a soil sprinkling, gently firm this, and place the pots in frame or greenhouse. Glass and paper over each (until the seedlings appear) will retain moisture in the soil and assist germination.

How to Water Seed Pots. When watering becomes really necessary, immerse the pot almost to its rim in a bucket of water with the chill taken off (Fig. 46). Hold the pot there until water soaks up to the soil surface; withdraw it, allow surplus to drain out, and give no more water until the soil obviously needs it. Pots of seedlings should be watered in the same way; not with the watering can.

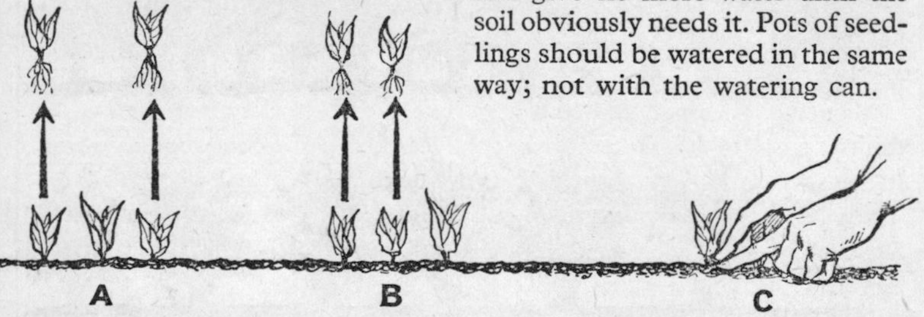

Fig. 47.—*In thinning out, seedlings should be removed complete with their roots. Seedlings that are to stay and have been loosened should be firmed again with the fingers* (C). *Here the seeds have been sown in groups of three, each group being reduced to a single seedling—the strongest—*(A) *and* (B)

SECTION VII

THINNING OUT, TRANSPLANTING, PRICKING OFF, PLANTING OUT

THE man who makes two blades of grass grow where only one grew before does a good job of work. But the man who tries to crowd vegetables or flowers makes a mistake. The more space plants have, within reason, the more profitable the yield. This need for ample space begins with the seed, and the need becomes greater through subsequent stages of growth. The operations of thinning out, transplanting, pricking off, potting on and planting out will not wait. They must be tackled as they fall due, in manner according to each plant's requirements.

Seedlings in Open Rows. Only mustard and cress crops are required to grow densely, to produce thick top growth that can be cut with scissors when required for making salads or sandwiches. The seed, to make gathering easier, is

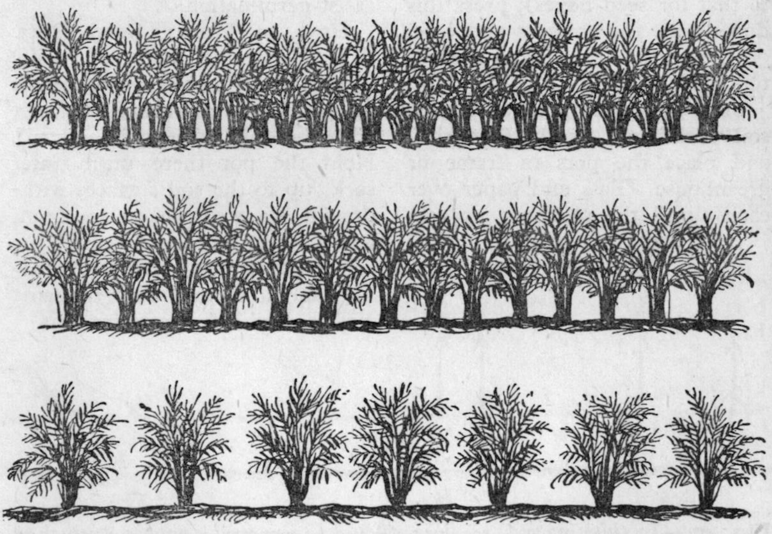

Fig. 48.—*The top sketch shows an unthinned row of carrots. These have been thinned out to 3 in. to 4 in. apart in the centre sketch. The final thinning out of the plants has been carried out in the bottom sketch*

Fig. 49.—*Thinning out in progress in a row of beet. Alternate plants will later be pulled for the table, leaving the remainder to reach full size*

sown closely in beds (or boxes) and not rows.

Other plants are required to grow on as spaced-out individuals in separated rows, and the spacing out in each row needs to be done as soon as they are large enough to handle—not with a hoe but with the fingers.

Surplus seedlings should be pulled up complete with roots and without unnecessary disturbance of those that are to remain. It is most easily done when the soil is moist, and any loosened seedlings that are to stay should be made firm again in the ground with the fingers (Fig. 47).

The thinnings (pulled-out seedlings) need not all be thrown away. In dealing with carrot, beet, onion, these should not be thinned out to their final distances in one operation. Thin out to 3 in. or 4 in. apart at first; later, the between ones can be pulled up and put to good use in the kitchen (Figs. 48, 49, 50).

Those which transplant readily —onion, pea, bean (not carrot, beet, parsnip, turnip), and some hardy annual flowers—can be used to fill in any blanks there may be, provided they are lifted with trowel or handfork complete with roots (Fig. 51) and at once watered into their new places if the soil is dry.

Transplanting from Seed Bed. According to their own requirements seedlings will be moved either to the nursery part of the bed, at about 4 in. apart (cabbage, broccoli, wallflower, etc.), there to grow on for final planting out; or direct to their final places.

Meanwhile they should be kept free of weeds, and some thinning out may be desirable. Before any thinning out or transplanting is done the soil should be watered if at all dry; not merely moistened on the surface, but soaked for 2 in. or 3 in. down. That enables the small plants to come away with soil attached to the roots, and growth will not be checked when they are re-planted.

If sun shines hotly they will move all the better if their disturbance is left until the cool of evening. If their planting-out places are dry, make the soil wet an hour

Fig. 50.—*At the first thinning, the seedlings shown between brackets will be pulled up. At the next thinning those marked with a × will go, leaving the remainder at their final distances as is shown in the lower sketch*

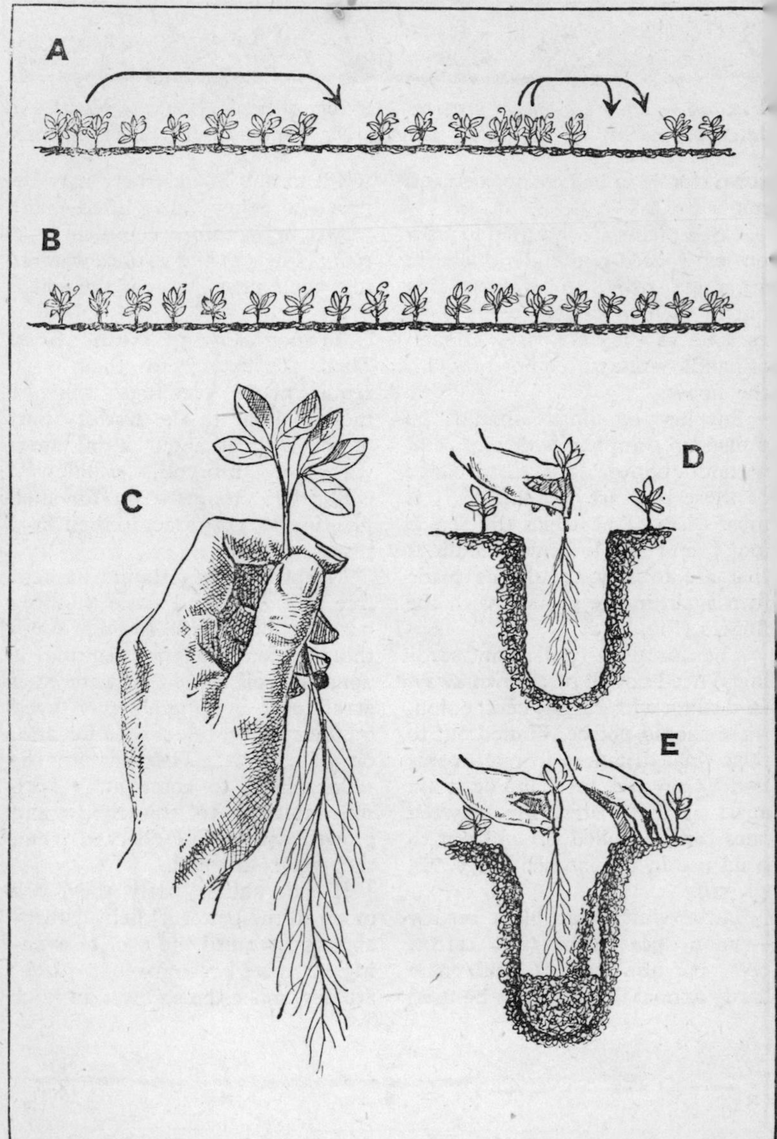

Fig. 51.—*Seedlings which transplant readily should be thinned in the seed row, crowded ones being replanted to fill blank spaces* (A). *The result is seen at* (B). *They should be lifted with roots* (C), *planted in sufficiently deep holes where blanks occur* (D), *and the holes filled with crumbled soil* (E)

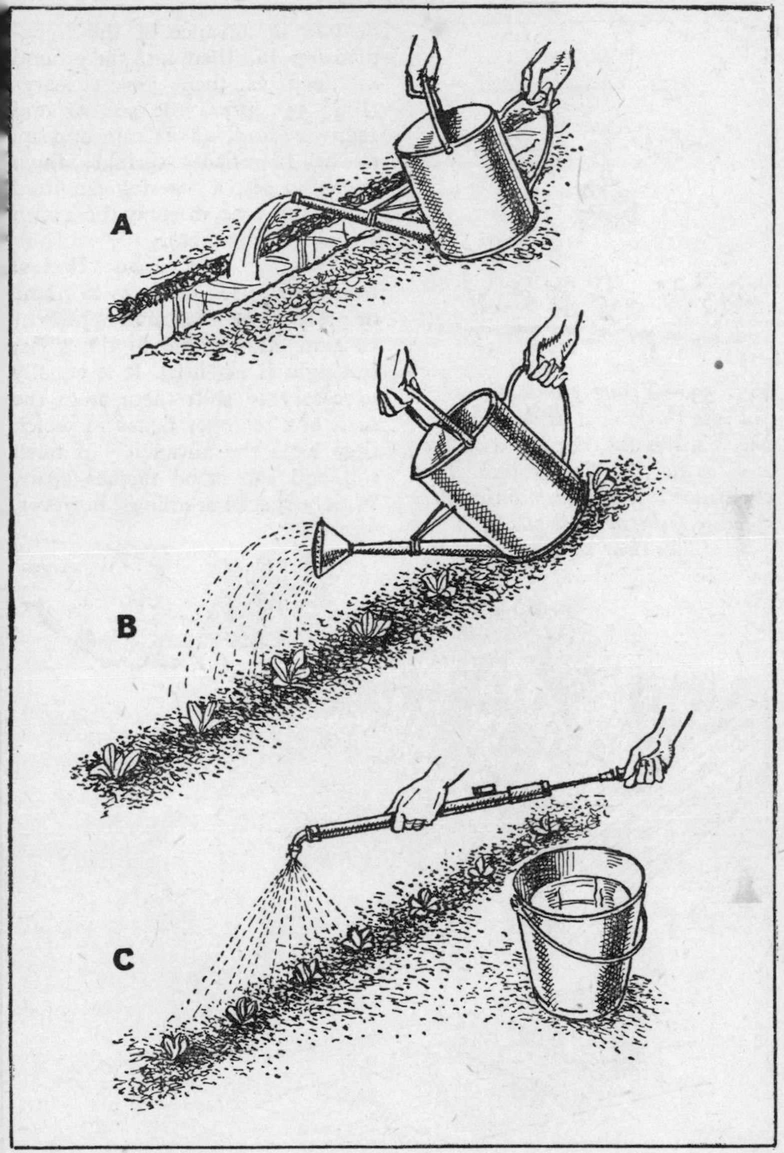

Fig. 52.—*A quick getaway is assured for newly-set-out young plants if a drill is prepared for their reception and (if the ground is dry) filled with water an hour or two before planting. They also benefit greatly from an overhead sprinkling from a watering can* (B) *or spraying with a syringe* (C)

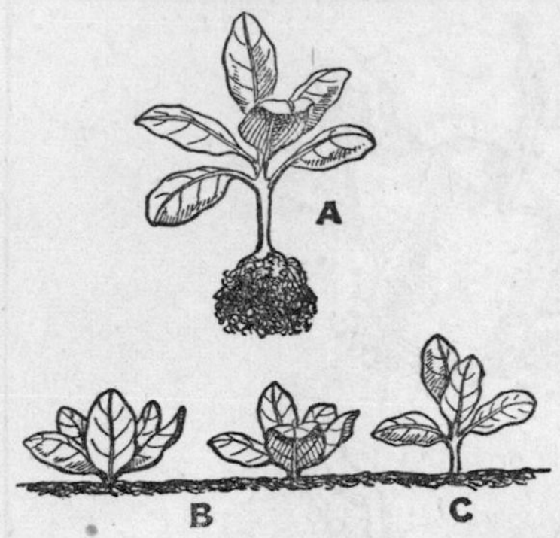

Fig. 53.—*Young plants should be put into the ground as deep as their lowest leaves* (B), *not left with bare stem as at* (C). *They recover from the disturbance of transplanting more speedily if lifted with plenty of soil at their roots* (A)

or two in advance of the transplanting. Put them into the ground as deep as their lowest leaves (Fig. 53), press the soil around each one and, unless rain appears to be imminent, sprinkle them overhead with a watering can fitted with a fine rose, or spray them with a syringe (Fig. 52C).

Pricking Off Into Boxes. Seedlings raised in boxes in frame or greenhouse must always be kept as close as possible to the glass; full light is essential. It is equally necessary to shift them from the seed box to other boxes in which they have the advantage of fresh soil and can stand farther apart. Widely spaced seedlings, however,

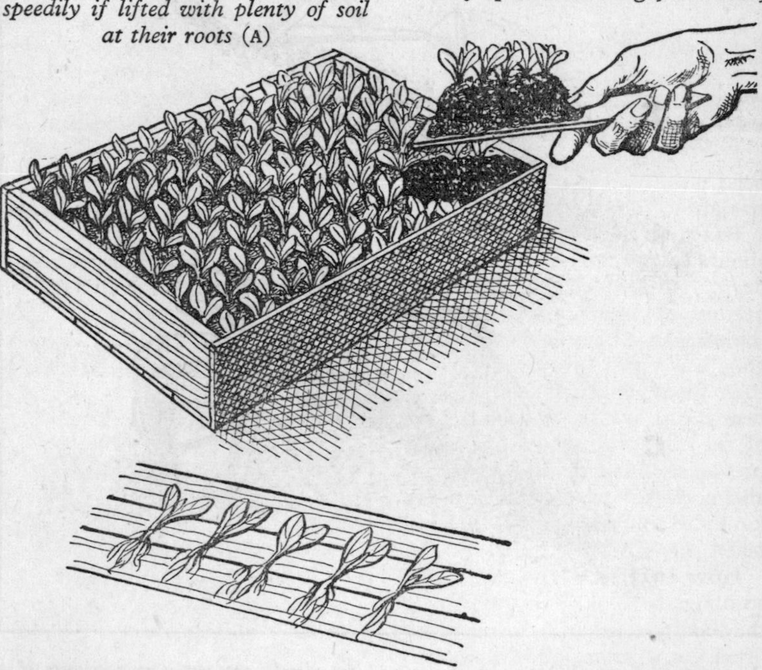

Fig. 54.—*Seedlings to be pricked off from a box are lifted out a few at a time, with a label, and the few carefully separated and laid out ready for transference to another box in which they are placed farther apart*

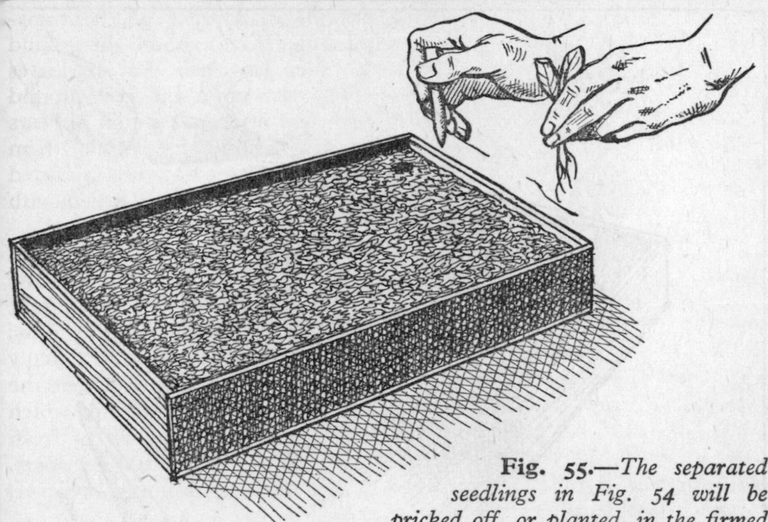

Fig. 55.—*The separated seedlings in Fig. 54 will be pricked off, or planted, in the firmed soil of the prepared box, in holes made with a piece of pencil or wooden skewer. A start should be made at one corner of the side farthest from the operator—who is here making the mistake of working from the near end and so will have to reach over rows of seedlings as these are pricked off*

need no intermediate shift but go straight to their prepared rows.

Boxes to receive the seedlings should be not less than about 2 in. deep. If the drainage holes in the bottom are covered with leaf-mould the pricked-off seedlings will make good use of this rich material when their roots get down to it. Fill up firmly and evenly, to within ¼ in. of the top, with the soil mixture previously advised for seed boxes; and note that seedlings take more kindly to soil that has had the chill taken off it.

How to Prick Off. First the seedlings have to be removed from the seed box, a small cluster being lifted out with the aid of a wooden label thrust in beside them to the full depth of the box. The label is then used lever fashion; the hoisted-up little group is placed on the bench, the roots are carefully separated and the few seedlings laid out side by side (Fig. 54).

One by one they are taken and placed in their respective holes in the soil of the prepared box. The holes are made, about 2 in. apart each way, in straight lines, with a

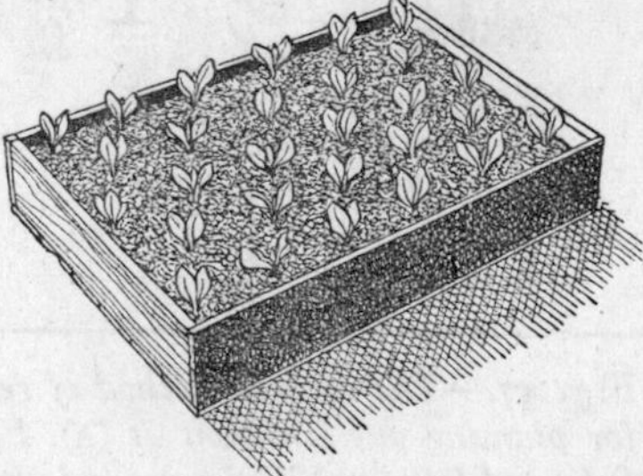

Fig. 56.—*A box of pricked-off seedlings. Note how the rows run diagonally, seedlings in one row being placed to fall opposite gaps in the next*

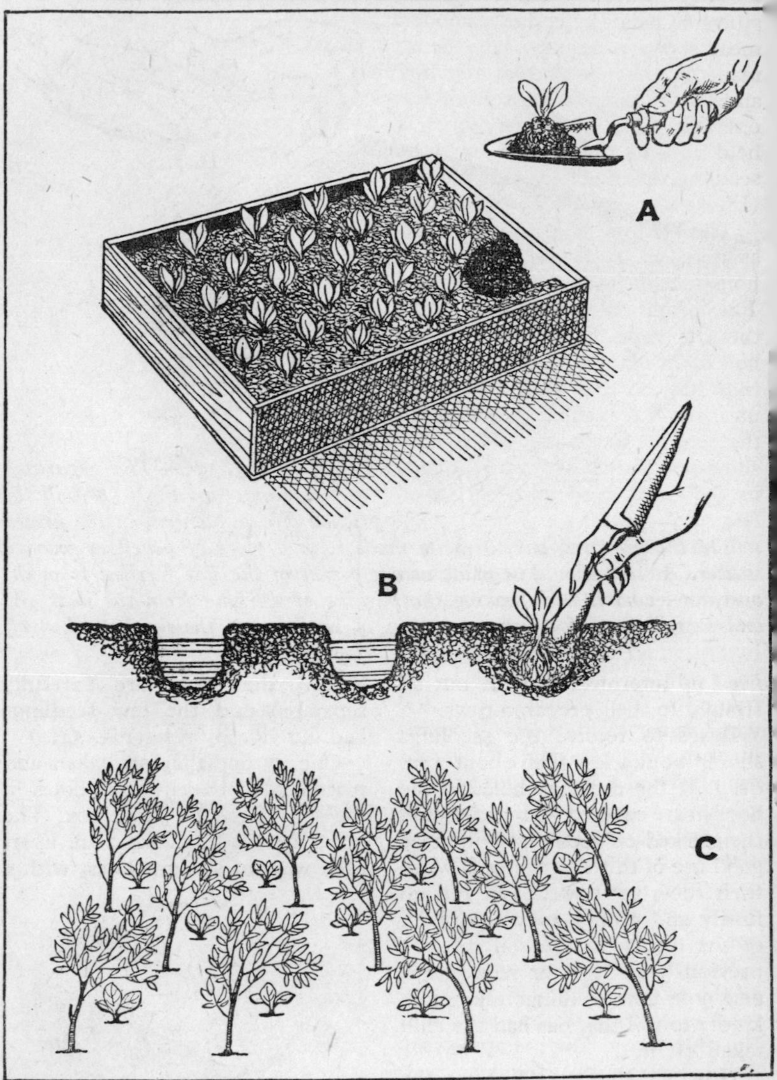

Fig. 57.—*The correct method of removing pricked-off seedlings from a box for planting out is shown at* (A). *Each should be planted in a trowel-made hole and left firm in the ground; holes should be filled with water an hour or two beforehand if the soil is dry* (B). *In very bright weather the young plants should be shaded at first, as indicated at* (C), *with leafy twigs or small pieces of evergreen thrust slantwise into the rows*

stump of pencil or end of a wooden meat skewer; the first hole being made at the left end of the box and at the side farthest from the operator. The miniature dibber is held in the right hand and the seedling manipulated with the left (Fig. 55).

The seedling goes into the hole as deep as its lowest leaves; the hole is then closed with the dibber. The second seedling is taken up in the left hand, transferred to the hole then made for it 2 in. to the right of the first one, and so on until the box is filled. Seedlings in the second, fourth and sixth rows should be planted opposite the gaps in the first, third and fifth rows (Fig. 56).

The Filled Boxes. As each box is filled, smooth the surface around and between the seedlings with the finger-tips. Fill up gently with lukewarm water, and when the box has ceased to drip replace it in the frame or greenhouse and shade with paper from direct sunshine for two or three days; otherwise the plants may droop, which delays growth.

Thereafter watering is a matter of importance. Soil must never be so sodden that it approaches muddiness; nor should it ever be dried out.

Planting from Boxes. When all the soil in a box is occupied by roots is the ideal time to plant out. But the outdoor temperature may be too low, or the ground too wet. Then the young plants must be fed with weak liquid manure or artificial fertilizer to keep them going. Lack of sufficient food, and too dry soil, will cause a halt in growth which may later lead—especially with celery—to the plants

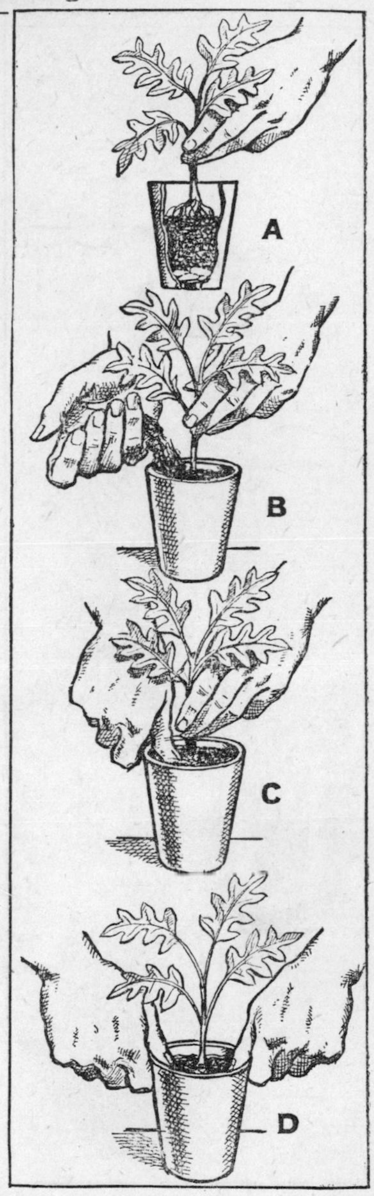

Fig. 58.—*How to pot seedlings. The process and references are explained in the text on pages* 60 *and* 61

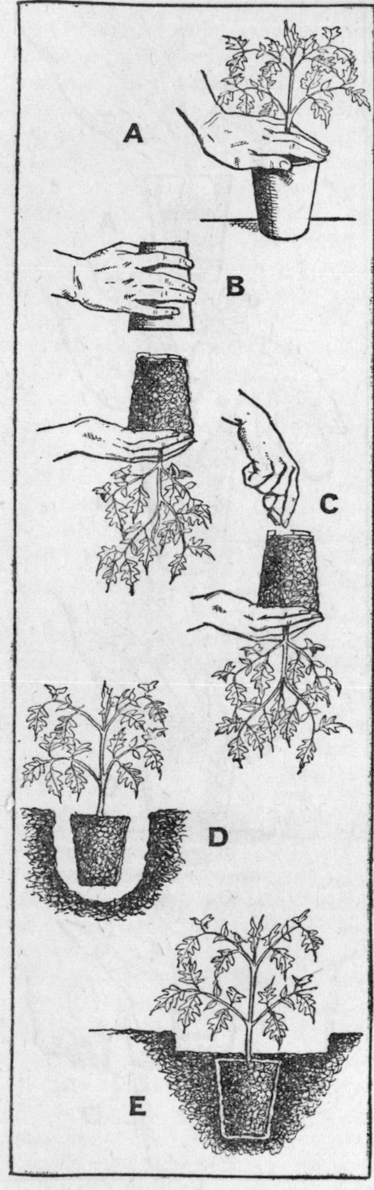

Fig. 59.—*How to remove a plant from a pot. For references and explanation* *see text on page* 61

bolting: that is, flowering and forming seed and becoming useless as a crop.

Hardening off is a necessary preliminary before planting out frame- or greenhouse-raised seedlings. They need to be accustomed, by increased ventilation, and gradually, to outdoor conditions.

The day previous to planting out, the soil in the box should be moistened right through if it is not damp enough; and the drills, or other planting stations, should be treated similarly.

Starting at one end of the box, get the plants out singly, with a trowel, scooping this beneath the roots; and plant each in a capacious, trowel-made hole, the lowest leaves to be flush with the soil, and the latter made firm above the roots. They will appreciate shade for a couple of days in sunny, hot weather; leafy twigs, or bits of evergreen stuck slantwise into the rows, will serve the purpose (Fig. 57).

Transferring to Pots. Absolutely clean pots are necessary for potting on. If pots are dirty inside the plants will not turn out cleanly when it comes to planting out (or shifting to still larger pots). Cover the drainage hole of each pot with two or three pieces of crock, and firm-in a little soil mixture as already described.

Lift the seedlings, with soil attached to their roots, with a label, from the seed pot, separate carefully, and transfer one by one to the partly filled pots. These are quite large enough for a first shift if they measure about 3 in. across the top.

Support the plant with the left hand (Fig. 58A), place it in position in the pot, fill in with soil (Fig. 58B) and press it down lightly with the thumb (Fig. 58C). Then, with both hands (both thumbs on top of the soil), lift the pot and tap it down a couple of times on the bench, to settle soil well down among the roots. Press again, with both thumbs (Fig. 58D), leaving the surface rather less than ½ in. below the top of the pot.

Fill up with lukewarm water, and return the potted seedlings to the frame or greenhouse.

Planting from Pots. When planting-out time arrives the young pot plants will probably have filled the pots with roots. They will have been hardened off—accustomed to hardier conditions by increased exposure to the open air.

To remove plant from pot, place the fingers of the left hand across the pot's top, the stem of the plant passing between the second and third fingers (Fig. 59A). Then invert plant and pot and, holding this with the right hand, tap the rim smartly on the edge of the wheelbarrow or on the spade handle. The ball of soil should then come out, unbroken (Fig. 59B). If it is reluctant to do so, poke a piece of stick through the drainage hole and push against the piece of crock covering it.

The plant is now supported upside down between the fingers of the left hand. Remove the crocks from the bottom of the ball of soil (Fig. 59C), then turn the plant right way up into the planting hole that has been made for it with the trowel (Fig. 59D). Scoop soil back into the hole, around and over the ball, and firm it with the end of the trowel handle. In dry soil leave a depression for watering (Fig. 59E).

If tall-growing plants are being dealt with, stake them at once.

SECTION VIII

FRAME AND GREENHOUSE

WITH odd sheets of glass to trap and retain sun-heat, exclude rain and cold weather, it is possible to extend the season of various plants quite considerably. Wooden boxes with bottoms removed and provided with movable glass tops serve as miniature frames. With a 6-ft. frame, constructed of a few lengths of timber, or built up with turves, and topped with an old window frame (glazed), still more can be done. A homemade greenhouse extends the possibilities still further.

Warming the Soil. Patches of seed bed covered with pieces of glass propped up with sticks to form inverted-V shelters (Fig. 60) in the early days of the year will warm up and become dry enough after a week or so to make extra-early seed sowing less risky than it would otherwise be.

If odd pieces of glass are not available, cloches with wire frame-work can be purchased. The soil having been made reasonably dry with their aid seed sowing can go ahead—lettuce and radish as early

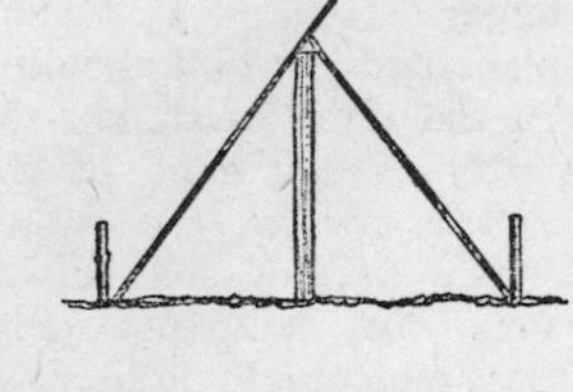

Fig. 60.—*End view (top) and side view of seed-bed warming device. Note how the glass is made secure*

as January, the thinned-out crop being allowed to finish under the glass. Provided there is sufficient length of glass covering, the usual February and March vegetable and flower sowings can all be advanced in spite of inclement weather.

If the covering is deep enough (from apex to ground) it can be used to shelter boxes of February-sown onion and leek; and tomato, celery and the less-hardy flowering plants can all be raised.

Ventilation and Watering. Protection must be continued after the seedlings are up until the weather is warm enough for safe removal of the glass, which will need to be covered with sacking, strips of old carpet or something of similar nature when frost threatens.

It is important that the ends of the inverted-V shelters be closed with glass, otherwise wind whistles through and the value of the protection is seriously lessened. But plants must have air, at all stages of growth, and this should be admitted whenever possible by displacing slightly the glass at that

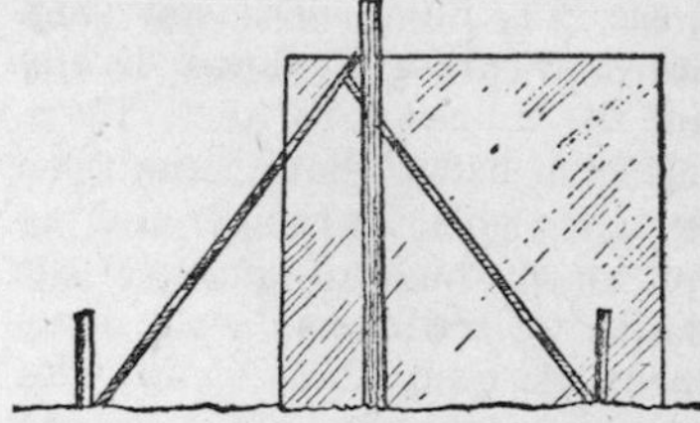

Fig. 61.—*Ends of the glass shelter should be closed. Air is admitted by moving the end-glass to one side*

end which does not face the wind (Fig. 61). The shelter should be closed up again before evening.

The shelters are, naturally, best able to make use of whatever sun there may be if placed beyond the reach of shade from trees, walls, fences; though it helps considerably if the position is sheltered from north and east winds. If the sun refuses to shine the glass will at least be a barrier to chill air and rain.

When watering becomes necessary the water should be given not under the glass (that would chill the air inside and give rise to damp conditions) but outside, a drill being drawn with the hoe down each side of the shelter, or inward-sloping holes about 4 in. deep made with a crowbar, and filled with

Fig. 62.—*This side view of Fig. 61 shows the complete arrangement of glass and supporting sticks, and the outer watering drill on the right*

water. The moisture will soak inwards, below the surface, to the roots.

Seedlings will need all the light they can get, so the glass must be kept clean, inside and out; soil splashed up by rain should be wiped off. Slugs and snails will appreciate the milder conditions—and whatever young plants there are—inside the shelter, and they must be watched for. If high winds are prevalent, the supporting sticks may need special attention.

The Box Frame. This may be a cut-down packing case, with no cracks for wind to penetrate, with pieces of glass over the top, the latter to be cut at an angle so that it slopes to the sun—facing the south (Fig. 63). As with an ordinary garden frame, boxes or pots of seedlings should be raised to within a few inches of the glass.

A crack of air should be given when the weather allows, and when water is given it should have the chill taken off and not be splashed about. The atmosphere needs to be kept reasonably dry. Sacking or other material used to give additional night protection must be put

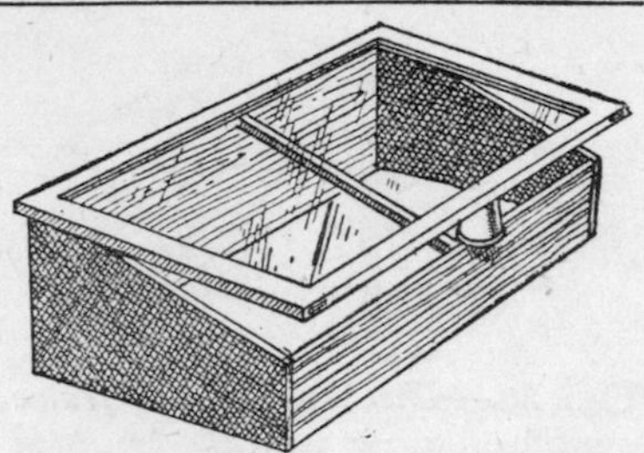

Fig. 64.—*A frame should be ventilated on the side from which the wind is not blowing. Here the wind is coming from the back*

on dry. And if frost comes the material must be left in position until weather is again normal.

A Garden Frame. The dimensions of the garden frame are not important. If it is homemade the length and breadth will probably be governed by the quantity of wood and glass available for constructing the light—which is the term applied to the glass and its framework. The area might well be adapted to an old window frame, or a couple of these (Figs. 64 and 65).

The body of the frame could be built of grass turves, each about 1 ft. long and 9 in. wide, and as thick as possible, these to be laid like the

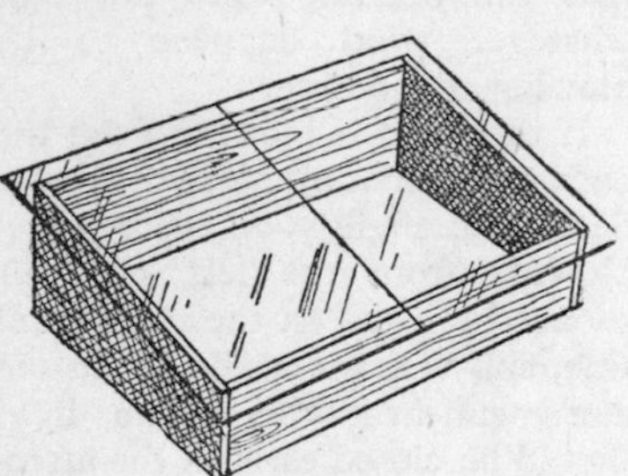

Fig. 63.—*A frame can be made from a cut-down packing case with glass to cover the top. It should be deeper at the back, and slope south, to catch all the sun possible*

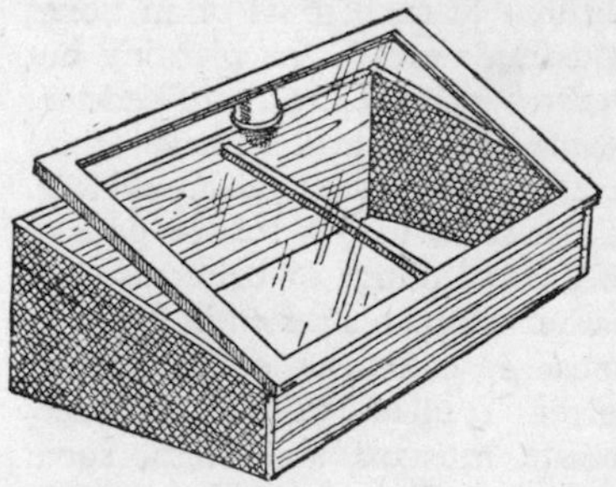

Fig. 65.—*Wind is blowing against the front of the frame here, so ventilation is given at the back; if the wind were blowing from the left, the right side would be propped up*

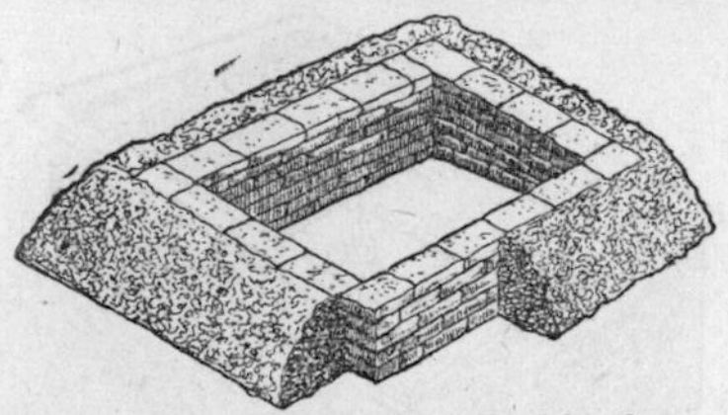

Fig. 66.—*The body of this frame consists of turves laid like bricks in a wall, with sifted ashes heaped around the outside and made firm*

bricks in a wall so that they interlock (flat, and grass side down). To make such a frame still more weatherproof sifted house-fire ashes could be heaped up around outside the walls (Fig. 66).

Possibilities of a Frame. Broad beans and peas can be sown in boxes in November and wintered in the frame for planting out at the end of March for cropping in June; dwarf and runner beans in April for planting out in late May or early June for cropping in mid-July; and so on. Cauliflowers sown outdoors in September could be wintered in the frame for planting out in April; they would be ready for use in early June. The finest sweet peas are those sown in autumn in small pots or in boxes and frame-grown for planting out in early spring. Cuttings of bedding plants and of shrubs thrive there.

The frame need never be idle. If not filled with boxes or pots of seed or seedlings or being used to harden off plants raised in a greenhouse it could be cropped with carrot (pulled young), lettuce, radish, mustard and cress, sown in the bed. This should be of really good soil, its surface should slope at the same angle as the glass and it should be not more than about eight inches from the glass.

Pots and boxes should also be quite close to the light, raised up on empty boxes or inverted flower pots (Fig. 67).

Position of Frame. The frame should face south, and should be exposed to full light. Though the presence of a fence or wall to shield it from north or east winds is desirable this should not be allowed to darken it unduly. The frame should not be too close to any such shelter. Also it should stand where water is not likely to collect around it.

Frame Management. Unnecessary watering must be avoided, a too moist atmosphere not being conducive to rapid and healthy growth. Ventilation needs care. In winter the merest crack of air during the brightest periods may be sufficient. In high summer the frame light may be removed completely during the day and replaced at night, well propped up at the front or either end.

In the spring particular care is called for in this matter, air then being given by propping up the frame light with a small pot or wedge of wood in such a manner that the opening does not face whatever wind happens to be blowing at the time.

If the wind is blowing from the back of the frame, the front should be opened slightly, and vice versa; blowing from the left side, air should be given on the right-hand side, and vice versa. To retain the day's sun-heat the frame light should be closed early in the afternoon or evening.

The glass needs always to be clean, inside and out; if there are holes or cracks to let rain through, stop them with a bit of putty.

The soil, if this is occupied by plants, should be kept loose on the surface by stirring it occasionally with a pointed stick.

Dry sacking or other material should be placed over the frame light at the first suspicion of frost and be kept in position with heavy pieces of wood or bricks, the covering to remain on until frost has departed (Fig. 68).

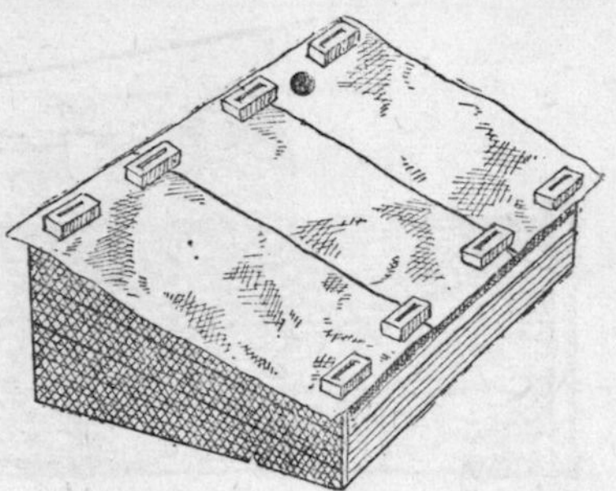

Fig. 68.—*To keep out frost the frame light should be covered with dry sacking or other material*

A Warm Frame. A cold (unheated) frame can be converted to a warm (heated) one by placing it on a hotbed made of stable manure and tree leaves mixed in equal parts, the warmth given out by this converting the frame into a miniature heated greenhouse (Fig. 69).

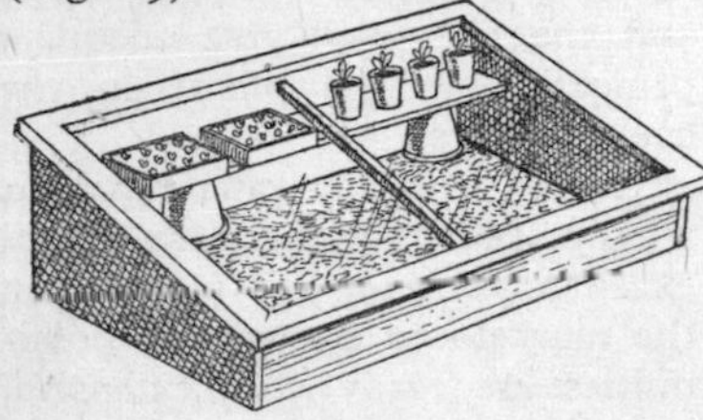

Fig. 67.—*Whatever occupies the frame should be as close up to the glass and full light as possible*

The object of mixing leaves with the manure is to secure moderate, steady, long-lasting heat. Manure alone would give greater heat but of shorter duration. The stable manure should be less than a month old and should not contain wood shavings (as frequently used for bedding horses). The heap should be forked over three or four times in the course of a fortnight and the leaves mixed thoroughly with it.

It is then fit for making up into a bed on which the frame will stand, the bed being built up in layers, each layer firmed down by beating it with the fork. When it is finished it should exceed the area of the frame by about 18 in. in each direction, and be about 18 in. in depth. Stakes driven in at each corner, and along back and sides, form a useful guide in building it.

Heat for Three Months. The bed made reasonably firm all over, the frame is placed upon it but without the frame light—to allow the steam to escape. At the end of five or six days a layer of soil about 9 in. deep at the front (the surface to slope at same angle as the frame light) is placed inside the frame and the frame light put on. It will take about twenty-four hours for the soil to warm through, and seed may then be sown.

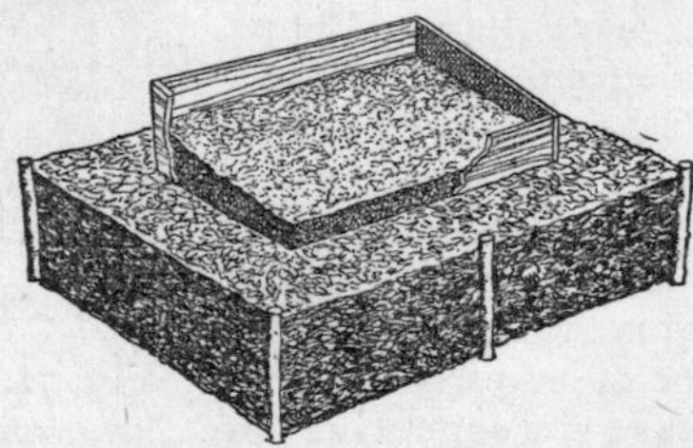

Fig. 69.—*An ordinary garden frame placed on a hotbed of manure becomes a miniature heated greenhouse*

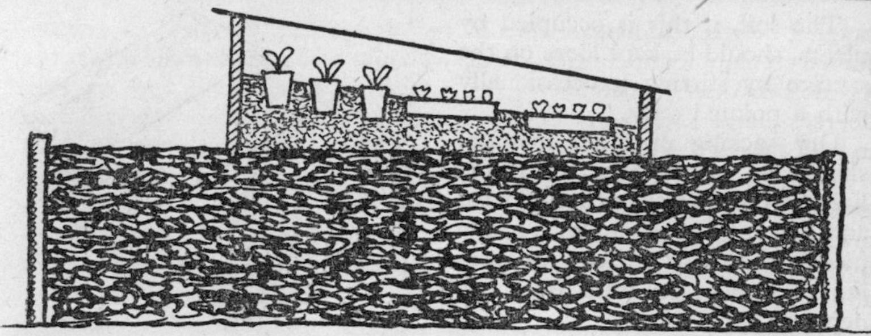

Fig. 70.—*Seed boxes and pots should be sunk to the top edge or rim in the soil which partly fills the hotbed frame. A thermometer should be kept in the frame to check the temperature which should be maintained at a maximum of 70 degrees, ventilation being attended to as necessary*

If the seed is to be sown in boxes or pots these should be sunk to the rim or top edge in the soil (Fig. 70). A thermometer should be kept in the hotbed frame and ventilation attended to so that the temperature does not rise above about 70 degrees.

Useful heat will be maintained for about three months. When the bed has served its turn (there would be very little difficulty in getting a good crop of cucumbers or melons from the frame in summer) the material will not be wasted. It will be as valuable as it was in the beginning for digging into the ground.

Greenhouse Crops. A greenhouse is a glorified frame in which sun heat is trapped, and in which leek and onion and other seedlings for growing on outdoors can be raised early and with ease irrespective of weather conditions, with tomatoes to fill it all summer and well into autumn. Its general management follows the lines laid down for the unheated frame. Sheets of old newspaper placed between plants and the glass will give adequate protection to the plants in the event of frost.

Heated with hot-water pipes, or a lamp (Fig. 71)—there are several excellent ones for this purpose on the market—or electrically, possibilities are really very extensive,

Fig. 71.—*A greenhouse can be efficiently heated by means of a stove specially made for this purpose, placed centrally, on the ground. Plants can be further protected in frosty weather by pinning sheets of newspaper between them and the glass*

ranging between tomatoes sown in January (night temperature about 55 degrees) and cucumbers (55 degrees), and early new potatoes in pots (55 degrees) for April eating.

Greenhouse Flowers. The extension of activities and interests made possible to the flower grower by a greenhouse is very considerable. The raising of seedlings of a big range of half-hardy annuals is simplified. The seed can be sown quite early in the year, and the seedlings hardened-off in the garden frame.

The wintering of rooted cuttings of bedding plants is shorn of its problems, and the wintering of plants lifted from the summer flower beds, too. Even if no heat is available, cuttings can be taken (and rooted) from indoor-wintered bedding plants in early spring, to supplement the stock secured by late summer cuttings.

Furthermore, the greenhouse can be gay with flowering plants in pots for most, if not all, of the year. Bulbs can be brought into flower in pots of soil or bowls of fibre, long before the blooms could make an outdoor appearance.

Chrysanthemums, both the late-flowering, big-bloom, indoor kinds and the border varieties, can be flowered to perfection under glass without undue skill or trouble. Carnations, geraniums and pelargoniums, roses, azaleas and hydrangeas, all come within the category.

Bedding Plants. Lifted from the summer flower beds when frost is approaching and transferred to pots, most of the "popular" plants will continue to flower on for weeks. These include geraniums, fuchsias, lobelias, petunias, heliotrope, begonias and many others.

These—or the best of them—should be lifted from the flower bed with fork or trowel with as little disturbance to the root-mass as possible.

If the soil in which the plants are growing is dry, it should be watered freely the day before the plants are dealt with. If the watering is delayed until just before potting, there will be a sodden root-mass to deal with.

The plants lifted, yellowing leaves should be picked off and the potting proceeded with, added soil being made reasonably firm—especially down the pot-sides. A piece of stick, shaped like a ruler, is useful for firming around the plant's own ball of soil.

The potted plants should then be watered, and for a day or two placed in a shady position in the greenhouse if the sun is shining. After that they should be exposed to full light, and turned occasionally so that all sides are given a share.

Early Spring Flowers. A similar procedure can be followed with primroses and polyanthuses, and a whole range of rock plants, lifted from one's own garden or bought for this special purpose. After flowering, the plants are not discarded but planted outdoors for further periods of usefulness.

Greenhouse Arrangements. A hanging shelf near to the glass enables fullest use to be made of all available space. It is an excellent position for pot plants of all kinds. In this respect it differs from the shelf, or shelves, along the back wall of a lean-to greenhouse.

A shelf in the latter position is likely to receive little sunlight over much of the day, but that is no drawback where ferns are concerned. Ferns in pots can be very decorative subjects indeed.

If the staging consists of open slats, it is an advantage to close in the top with slates or galvanized iron sheeting and to cover this with an inch or two of washed gravel. This material can be kept moist (a desirability in hot weather), and can be cleaned by washing when it begins to lose its fresh appearance.

Below the Staging. Quite unintentionally on the owner's part the space beneath the greenhouse staging may develop into a store of empty flowerpots, old seed-boxes and other items whose proper place is the garden shed. This accumulation in the comparative gloom affords a wonderful abiding and breeding place for pests. Scrupulous cleanliness here is absolutely essential.

If the floor beneath the staging is soil, this is likely to become sour unless forked over regularly. If any suspicion of odour arises from it, a generous sprinkling of lime mixed into the well-broken surface will put things right.

A concrete central path is desirable. Without it, the ground tends to become puddled when much watering, syringeing and damping-down are done in summer. In default of concrete, a wooden duckboard prevents messiness.

Propagating Case. Whilst the general run of seed sowing and

Fig. 72.—*It is possible to maintain a moister atmosphere in hot weather if the greenhouse staging is covered with washed gravel, as above; it looks neater, too. A wooden duckboard to walk on prevents messiness underfoot*

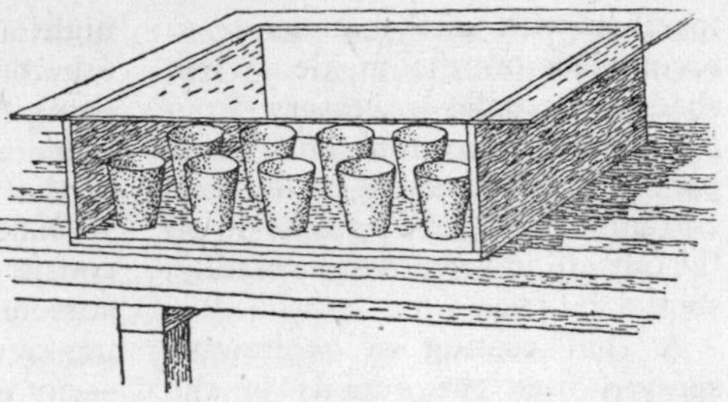

Fig. 73.—*An ordinary flat-topped wooden box, with a sheet of glass to cover it, makes an admirable propagating case in the greenhouse*

the striking of cuttings can be done on the staging or the light shelf, occasion may arise when closer conditions than the greenhouse ordinarily affords would be desirable. This additional degree of "closeness" may be contrived with the aid of a wooden box and sheet of glass standing on the staging. This propagating case, or small frame, will receive the pots of sown seed or of cuttings, and the glass top will be kept closed down (and if necessary shaded from direct sunlight) until the seedlings are up or the cuttings have taken root.

The underside of the glass should be wiped free of moisture every morning. The temperature within the box will be noticeably higher than that of the greenhouse itself, making it necessary that the interior of the propagating case should be moderately moist. But that moisture must be controlled (hence the daily wiping of the glass), otherwise damping-off may occur.

General Attentions. Pot plants, whether these be cuttings or plants intended to flower in the pots, need frequent inspection. The removal of yellowing leaves and the loosening of the surface soil are two foremost considerations. The loosening is most easily and safely done with a piece of pointed stick, and leaf removal should be done with finger and thumb or knife or scissors, since a hasty tug may prove disastrous. The frequent handling ensures the early detection of pests, which may otherwise escape notice until they are causing serious trouble. Also it enables one to detect the plant which is receiving too much, or not getting sufficient, water. The pot which is very light or unduly heavy contains a plant which is thirsting for water or is too sodden.

Both conditions may be brought about by incautious syringeing. Whilst it is very desirable that the atmosphere of the greenhouse and the surface of the staging or shelf should be well charged with moisture in sunny, warm, "growing" weather, heavy syringeings may overload pots with water or perhaps keep the surface soil moist whilst the mass of the soil goes dry.

The spray from the syringe should be kept to the surroundings, and if necessary to the foliage, and be kept from the soil. The central pathway, and beneath the staging, should be sprayed. Routine watering (twice daily in hot weather) should be attended to before syringeing.

Greenhouse Management. There cannot be too much light in the greenhouse, especially in winter. In the neighbourhood of towns the amount of dust that settles on the outside of the glass can be truly astonishing. This must be removed, together with dirt that tends to accumulate on the inside. When shading becomes necessary from full sunlight, any thin and transparent material, such as old lace curtains, that can be hooked up on the outside and removed as readily, should be used.

A thin coating of whitewash sprayed over the outside of the glass is excellent in a really sunny and protracted summer. But as it is unusual for summers in Britain to be of that nature, the whitewash spray may prove a drawback rather than a help.

The growing of a climbing rose, or a grape vine, in the general-purposes greenhouse is not advisable, because of the shade likely to be cast—a shade that would be appreciated by ferns, for instance, but certainly not by the ordinary run of plants.

Control of Temperature. As with the management of a garden frame, extremes of temperature are to be avoided, which means that ventilation by night demands as much thought as by day. The avoidance of a draught is one of the main cares. The interior should never be allowed to become so stuffy that the ventilators and door have suddenly to be opened wide. If a hot, dry blast strikes one on entering the greenhouse, something is wrong; it should be a mellow warmth, whether conjured up by the sun or by artificial heating.

It should be remembered that a brisk night wind, even in summer, can "whip" the warmth from a greenhouse in the same way that sudden exterior cold can reduce the inside temperature.

The temperature of an unheated greenhouse can be maintained at night at a higher level than would otherwise be the case by timely damping down on a warm afternoon and simultaneous reduction of the ventilation.

Damping down the greenhouse consists in moistening the interior surroundings with a fine rose watering-can or, preferably, a syringe—not using cold water but tepid. If the ventilators are almost closed at the same time the temperature will soar (without doing any harm) and be maintained with but a gradual drop throughout the night.

To be really effective, the damping down, and closing of the ventilators, should be done just before the sunshine goes off the greenhouse in the late afternoon, a little ventilation being given before it becomes dark.

On an overcast day, with a gradual fall in outside temperature likely, the damping down should be omitted. A little experience enables the greenhouse owner to distinguish at once between an atmosphere which is warm and moist and buoyant and that which is dank and stuffy.

Water Supply. A tub of water kept in the greenhouse will ensure a supply, of the same temperature as the atmosphere, always being available to meet plants' requirements, both for application to the soil and for syringeing—to promote rapid growth—in fine weather.

As regards watering, pots containing seeds or seedlings should be immersed not quite rim-deep until moisture rises up through the soil to the surface. Boxes of seedlings should be given water gently from the spout of a watering-can (not through a rose). Seedlings will not then be flattened.

SECTION IX

THE FIGHT AGAINST WEEDS

THE fight against weeds is never-ending and must be persisted with however much you dislike it. Weeds are not only untidy, they take up space and nourishment required for your chosen plants.

Winter Weeding. There are circumstances in which it is not possible to use hoe or fork and hand-weeding is non-effective. These conditions become apparent in the flower garden especially in winter, when the hardy herbaceous border is being cut over—that is, the old stems are being shortened more or less to ground level.

Then, amidst a big clump of pæony or spreading patch of iris, hitherto hidden and unsuspected trespassers are likely to be revealed. These trespassers may be young plants of perennial sunflower which have strayed underground, possibly several feet from their parent plant, or offspring of a strong-growing Michaelmas daisy.

Treasured as perennial sunflower and Michaelmas daisy may be in their allotted places, they are none the less weeds when they become misplaced. When their offspring appear in the centre of, say, pæony or iris clumps, it is quite ineffectual to pull off their tops. It may be possible to extract their roots with the aid of a deeply inthrust table-knife or screwdriver. The probability is it will prove necessary to dig up the clumps entire and free them of the weed-roots when one has them right out of the ground, the cleaned clumps then being carefully replanted.

In the Rockery. Here it may be brought home forcibly to the grower that weeding can be not only a challenge which must be taken seriously but also accomplished laboriously. It may be necessary to remove some of the rocks or large stones completely in order to free plants of the competition of their stronger neighbours, replacing the rocks after the cleaning up has been done. This is the only satisfactory method when certain obstinately persistent weeds, such as couch grass or twitch, become introduced to the rockery.

It is because of the numerous "safe" root-runs afforded by the rocks and stones that normal methods of weeding fail here.

Occasional re-making of the rockery, or a portion thereof each year, affords the best opportunity of maintaining this feature of the garden in a weed-free and cleanly condition.

Seed Rows and Boxes. Slow and cautious weeding is necessary among seedlings—with the fingers, when the soil is moist but not wet. If the soil is dry the weed-tops may break off; if wet, weeds and seedlings may come up in a mass together.

The fingers of one hand should be used to steady the soil-surface close up to or around a seedling or small group of seedlings, whilst the other hand extracts the weeds. However carefully it is done there will be some undesirable disturbance of the seedlings, and to remedy this the soil should be pressed gently down as the weeds are pulled out.

Before the seed rows or boxes are thus dealt with, it must be determined which really are weeds and which the rightful seedlings. It may seem an elementary point, but confusion as to which is which may well lead to the elimination of the desired seedlings and the retention of the weeds.

In the Lawn. The use of lawn sand (which can be purchased, with directions) aids the maintenance of a clean sward of turf. And a very great deal can be done with a stiff-bladed table knife or screwdriver to reduce the plantains, daisies and other obstinate weeds. The tool is pressed into the turf close to the weed and worked completely around it so that its grip is loosened and it can be pulled up entire.

With a little practice a good space can be covered in this way, particularly after the lawn has been mown. The slight disturbance caused to the turf here and there can be obliterated with a tread of the foot. But in dealing with dense patches of weed it may be necessary to cut the bad portions right out, using new turf as replacement or filling the depression with good soil and sowing seed there.

Hard sweeping with a stiff broom will help get rid of moss, the sweepings being gathered up and burned. The alternative is to "claw" it out of the turf with a sharp-toothed rake. Fuller details appear in the chapter AN ATTRACTIVE LAWN.

Weeds and Fruit. Reliance should be placed mainly on hand-weeding around fruit bushes and trees and canes. Here the roots lie a very short distance below the surface, and fork or spade used to dislodge weeds may do considerable harm. Even the hoe, if used too vigorously, may interfere with those precious, fibrous surface-roots of the fruit.

Because of this, weeding in the fruit section is apt to be neglected, with corresponding harm to the fruit. Even large apple or pear trees are the better for having a cleared and weed-free circle about their bases.

The removal of weed masses from around raspberry canes, strawberry plants and so on is likely to remove also soil from above the plants' shallow roots. Whatever soil can be shaken back from the weed roots will help as replacement, but it may be necessary to add fresh soil from elsewhere in the garden.

Weed-free Paths. Grass and other undesired plants always seem to grow more luxuriantly on a garden path than elsewhere. Even on asphalt, moss will secure a hold and defy a hard yard broom applied in an effort to effect its removal. A proprietary weed-killer will clear it away, as it will clean a brick or any other type of path.

Moss on gravel can be dealt with in the same way. Or the gravel may be turned over as deeply as possible, so that the moss is no longer at the surface, and then rolled. Larger weeds, of perennial nature, may need to be uprooted with a knife.

The ash path may be hoed, to remove moss and so on, the debris being swept up and a roller used to consolidate the disturbed ash. Or the proprietary weed-killer can be

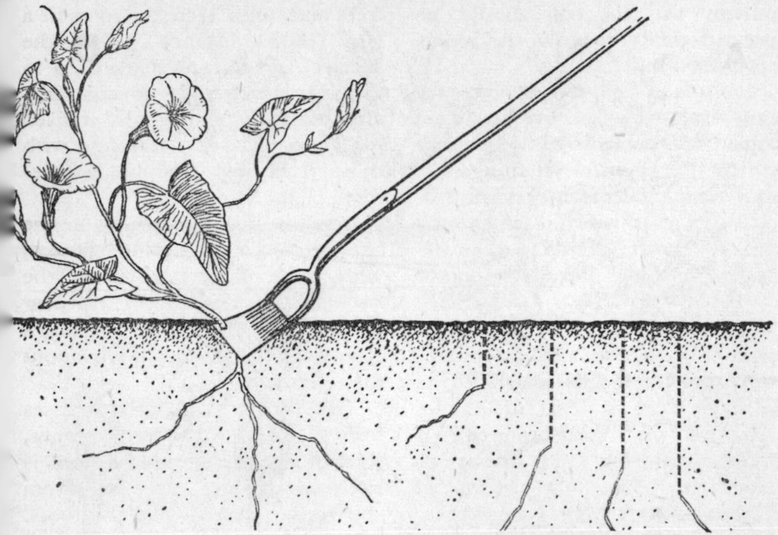

Fig. 74.—*Pieces of bindweed (wild convolvulus), dandelion, twitch, thistle, nettle, plantain, and dock left in the ground by the hoe (left) or during digging (right), will give rise to more plants as if the hoe had never been used*

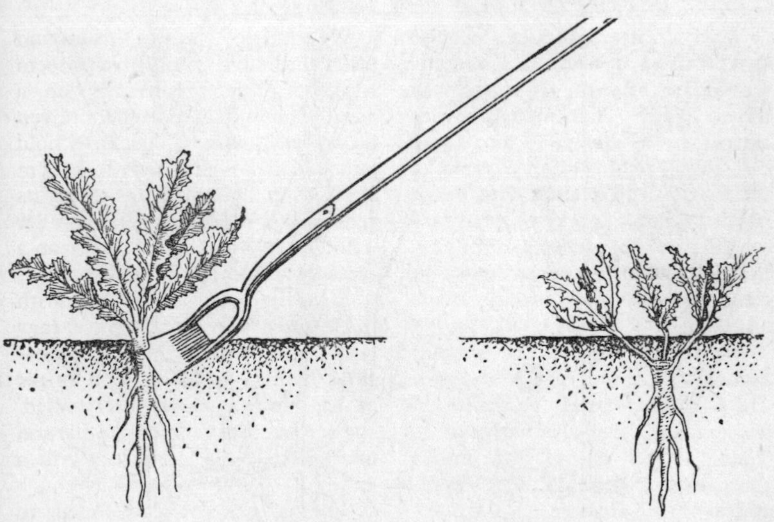

Figs. 75 and 76.—*A thistle which has been decapitated with the hoe (left) will quickly start to grow again. The soil should be loosened deeply with fork or spade, soon after rain or watering, and the whole weed, roots and all, removed by a twist and pull, to be subsequently burnt*

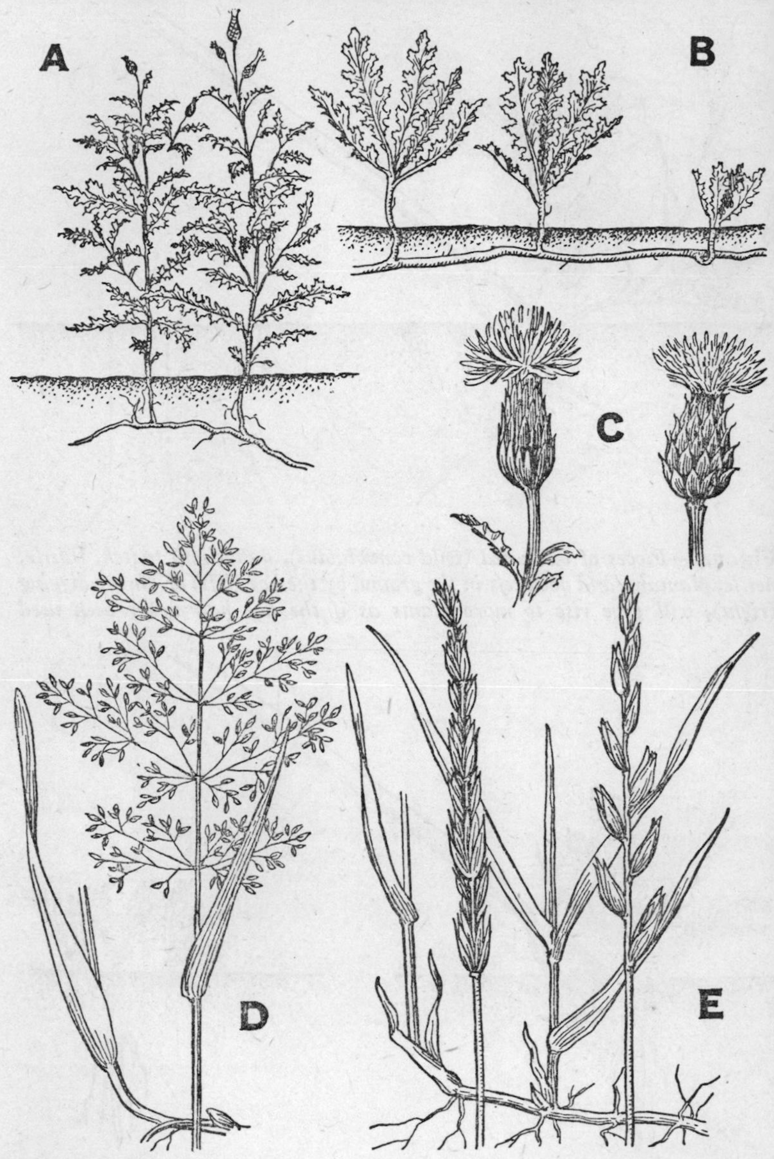

Fig. 77.—*Perennial weeds which should always be grubbed out complete with all roots. The creeping thistle* (A) *travels underground by creeping roots* (B)*; its flower-heads are shown at* (C). *Common bent grass or black twitch* (D) *and couch grass or twitch* (E) *also have creeping roots.*

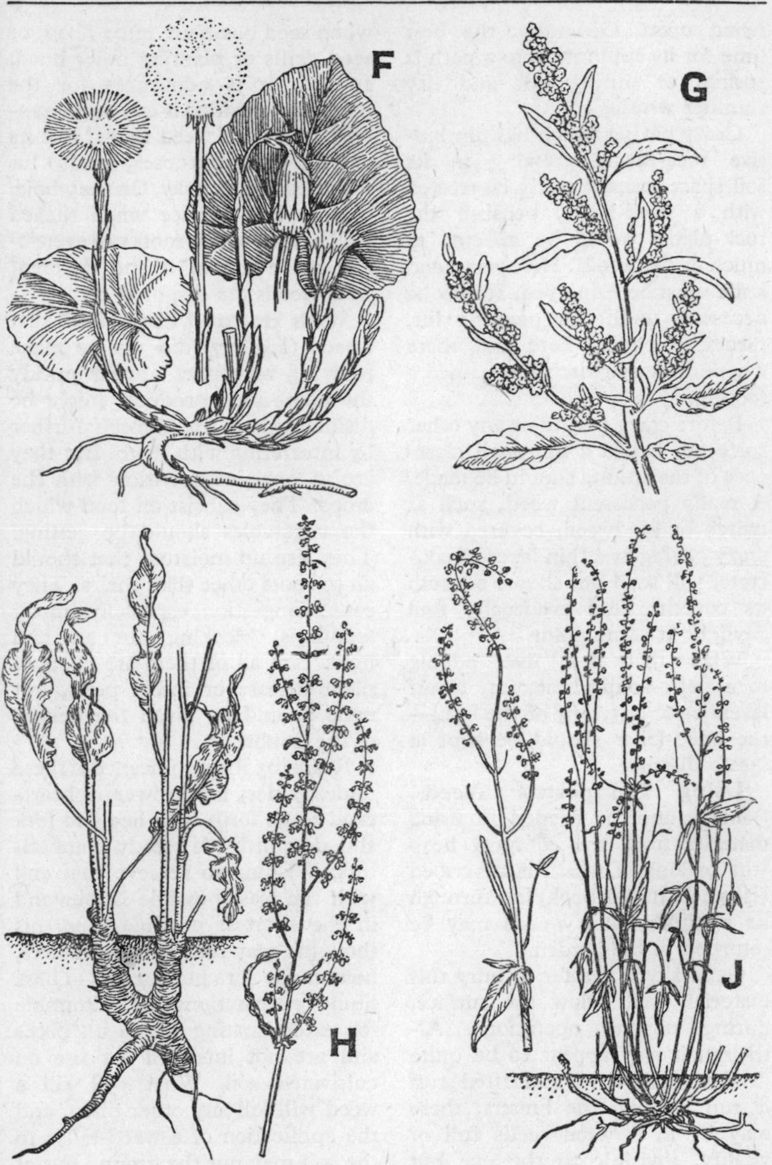

Coltsfoot (F) *should be grubbed out entirely, and the same should be done with curled dock* (H) *and sheep's sorrel* (J)*; they are all perennials. Goosefoot* (G) *is an annual and cutting through the stalks with the hoe will kill it; it should be destroyed in good time before it flowers and seeds*

relied upon. Generally, the best time for its application to a path is spring, or during hot and dry summer weather.

Crazy paving which has diminutive rock-plants growing in its soil spaces cannot easily be treated with a weed-killer, because the rock-plants would be affected as much as the weeds. Here hand and knife must be employed. It may be necessary to lift, or partially lift, pieces of paving here and there where dock or twitch has gained a footing.

Before crazy paving or any other surfacing is laid a thorough clearance of the ground should be made. A really persistent weed, such as twitch or bindweed, covered with crazy paving or a thin layer of concrete, will send out shoots beneath its covering and eventually find daylight at some point.

Where there is a "live" edging to a path—pinks, catmint, dwarf lavender or anything of the kind—the weed-killer should be kept at a safe distance.

Using Composted Weeds. Some caution is needed in using material from the compost heap (the making of which is described elsewhere in this book) lest through its medium many weeds may be returned to the garden.

Generally it is safer to bury this material, well below the surface, during digging operations. Although it may appear to be quite dead when the dried and sifted stuff is run through the fingers, there may be in it weed seeds full of vitality, invisible to the eye but waiting the opportunity to set up in competition with other plants.

This thoroughly decomposed material presents a temptation when seed boxes are to be filled, or seed drills or planting holes lined. Indeed, it is admirable for the purpose, provided it can be guaranteed free from weed seeds. But its use for those purposes, as also for top-dressing, is risky. On the whole, it does best service when tucked well below, where roots can eventually make use of it and dormant weed-seeds are disposed of.

With Hoe and Fork. If all that weeds (Fig. 77) did was to make rows of vegetables appear untidy the home food producer might be disinclined to tire himself further by interfering with them. But they are in open competition with the crops. They subsist on food which the vegetables should be getting. They use up moisture that should go to roots other than theirs. They cause congestion, especially among seedlings, blocking out air and light. Not all of them are hosts of plant disease or insect pests, but none should be given the benefit of the doubt.

Realizing the significance of these undesirables, the grower is heartened to go forth with hoe and fork and demolish his weedy competitors. Wishing to achieve that end with the least possible labour and in the shortest possible time, his thoughts may turn to weed-killers, homemade or purchased. These liquid preparations are admirable for exterminating weeds on paths and are not intended for use on cultivated soil. What will kill a weed will kill any other plant, and the application of a weed-killer to the soil may put the ground out of action for weeks—perhaps months.

A Clean Sweep. Only where a start is being made with badly weed-choked ground and it seems

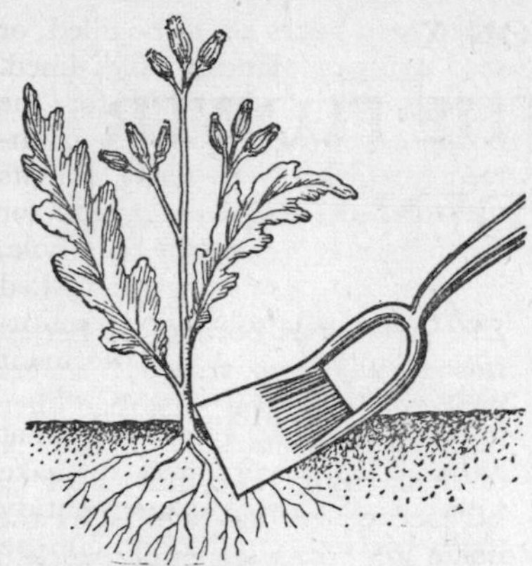

Fig. 78. — *Groundsel and other annual weeds cut short with the hoe will perish for a certainty. They must not be allowed to run to seed*

impossible to clear it by any other method—and, moreover, the site can be left idle all winter—is the use of a weed-killer there to be entertained. The weeds—thistles, nettles, dock, etc.—would first be cut down, with a grass hook or similar tool, as close to the ground as possible. Then the tops would be raked into heaps for burning. When these are disposed of, and the ash from the burning saved dry for returning to the dug ground, the weed-killer could be used to soak the stumps, roots and ground.

A very effective solution for this clean-sweep purpose is made by mixing 1 lb. of commercial sodium chlorate with every 3 gal. of water.

Three or four weeks later the ground should be dug, all scraps of weed root picked out and placed in basket or barrow for burning. Then, at the turn of the year, cultivation could begin in earnest.

Among the Crops. It is the perennial (come up every year) weeds that are the greatest nuisance. One can dispose of all visible top growth, but the roots—unless pulled out complete—are not discouraged. Portions of root of bindweed, twitch, plantain, dandelion, dock, thistle, nettle, will send up fresh growth as though the hoe had never been that way (Fig. 74).

The only certain method of dealing with them is to loosen the soil as deeply as possible with the fork or spade, then grasp the top of the weed and twist and pull at the same time. The anchorage of these strong rooters is less secure in wet soil, so the easiest time to weed is after rain or watering.

Perennial weed roots encountered during digging should be pounced on and put aside for burning. It simply does not do to bury them. They have incredible powers of self-resurrection and will get to daylight again.

Weeds as Manure. Annual weeds (one year of life) come up more easily than the others, and even if the ground is too hard and dry to get out groundsel, chickweed, shepherd's purse, complete with their shallow roots, decapitation with the hoe is effective discouragement (Fig. 78). These annuals should be added to the soft refuse heap or pit, to rot down for digging-in in due course in the manner of manure.

But all weeds carrying seed heads should be burned without delay.

When to Weed. Before the weeds have a chance to flower is the time to tackle them; never should a weed be allowed to distribute its seed. For hand weeding, the soil should be moist. Hoeing is most effective in hot, dry weather, when the hoed-up or decapitated weeds will soon wilt.

SECTION X

PLANNING THE FLOWER GARDEN

THE BEST time to plan a new flower garden is high summer; for then one can see where most shade falls—from walls, fences or trees. In winter one can be grievously misled, for bare branches seem not to overshadow the ground to any degree that matters, and walls and fences look to be but warmth-engendering backgrounds for one's flowers. So if you have to plan in winter, you must try to imagine the circumstances and conditions of summer.

The occupants of flower beds and herbaceous borders do better, in so far as the majority of them are concerned, in sunshine than they do in shade. Hence the importance of their siting. The making of an herbaceous border (which, as the name implies, is generally stocked with hardy plants which live on from year to year) is an arduous task and, once it is done, the removal of the border is no easy matter, any more than is the removal of a flower bed, which generally holds plants of a fleeting nature. Before their sites are decided upon, all possible later drawbacks should be considered.

Fig. 79.—*A formal layout for the small front garden is generally advisable. The unpleasing effect of bits and pieces can be avoided by adopting one of these designs. Different plants can be used each year to provide variety*

Wild versus Formal. Growing flowers implies some degree of formal arrangement, for they occupy space and, in relation to one another, can produce all manner of pleasing and unpleasing effects. The unplanned garden is not merely informal, it is a wilderness entirely lacking in character. This should not be confused with a wild garden where a piece of sparse woodland, copse or moorland is allowed to retain its character with the introduction of appropriate plants placed for natural effect.

On the other hand, the geometrically shaped beds of an older generation, crammed with "carpet bedding" planted thickly in stiff patterns, were works of art, costly to fill and demanding an enormous amount of labour to maintain. This severely formal style is still encountered in a set-apart space in public parks and large private gardens, but it is now exceptional. On quite a small scale, however, it might well be adopted in the small front garden (see Fig. 79), which too often presents an unlovely spectacle of bits and pieces.

Fig. 80.—*A crazy-paving path, featuring a sundial, might be edged broadly with thrift or pinks or catmint; with low-growing rock plants (as dwarf saxifrage, sedum and so on) where spaces between the slabs of paving allow*

The conventional square front plot gives excellent results when formality is adhered to: the simplest scheme perhaps being to have a bird-bath or sundial set centrally on a small circle of crazy paving surrounded by lawn, the latter bordered by narrow strips of soil planted with wallflowers or polyanthuses for spring display, very dwarf dahlias or antirrhinums, or other low-growing plants for summer (see Fig. 80).

Beds versus Borders. Generally the greater garden space is at the rear of the house, and its layout is largely dependent on its shape. It may be long and narrow, or broad and short, or square. In the long and narrow flower garden one would have mixed borders rather than beds. When the latter are cramped circles of a mere 3 ft. across, the ultimate effect, however skilled the treatment, is

Fig. 81.—*Charming effects of forethought are shown here. The garden boundary (left) is of strained wires, with poles spaced at intervals and clothed with roses or other flowering climbers*

bound to be somewhat insignificant.

When space is available for a mixed border with turf in front of it, and more turf, or possibly a well-groomed yew or holly hedge, as background, there is tremendous scope for floral effect. As opposed to such a border, with a minimum width perhaps of 6 ft., one may have to be content with a mixed border 3 ft. or so wide and tight up against a fence (see Fig. 81), and it can be a thing of beauty the whole year round.

The border should have a straight front edge, whether that edge be lawn or path; and it should not slope from back to front, but should be level, to make watering in spring and summer less of a nuisance. Plants should be graded according to height, tallest at the back, shortest at the front. And it need not necessarily be filled with herbaceous plants; spaces should always be left for annuals and for bulbous plants.

A Brilliant Bed. Caution has already been offered concerning the small, niggardly bed. Infinitely better than a dozen meagre ones is a bold oblong, 8 ft. by 6 ft. or thereabouts, or a circular one 8 ft. across—and in as open a position as the garden will afford. Either can be filled brilliantly with dwarf polyantha roses, or dwarf bedding dahlias, or scarlet salvias, or violas, or hardy carnations, or geraniums. The ultimate choice will depend on whether the plants are to be more or less permanent (as are the roses or carnations) or whether they are to be removed at summer's

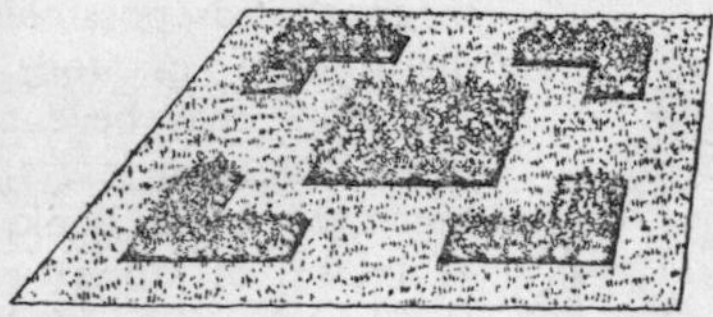

Fig. 82.—*Alternative layouts for the conventional garden, comprising small, shaped beds of dwarf flowering plants separated by turf*

end and their places taken by bulbs for spring flowering, or those mightily reliable stand-bys the polyanthuses and wallflowers.

In siting a bed on a lawn, it is as well to choose a position that is not central. Not only does a centre bed detract from the apparent size of a lawn, but it is definitely in the way if any activities are to be pursued on the turf. Site it near one end, or towards a corner, whatever lawn there is behind it being not less than 3 ft. wide—for convenience of mowing and of walking (see Fig. 83).

Mainly for Cutting. A family grievance commonly arising out of the garden is that the flowers must not be cut for fear of spoiling Father's display. The answer to that is a border set apart specially for the production of cut-flowers, preferably in a place where you are not for ever staring at it and being offended by the spectacle of blanks where the cutting-scissors have been busy.

This extremely useful cutting-border can be filled with a great diversity of plants, annuals specially suitable including aster, clarkia, cornflower, godetia, larkspur, mallow, marigold, sunflower and, of course, sweet pea. Perennials will include carnation, coreopsis,

Fig. 83.—*If a flower bed is to be a feature of a small lawn it should be positioned near one end, with walking space behind it. The bed will not then interfere with general activities on the turf, as it would if centrally placed. It is also more convenient for mowing*

Fig. 84.—*An unlevel plot may be terraced neatly and attractively as here. Small rocks, or irregular slabs of stone, are used to form a rockery against the face of the bank between the higher and lower portions of the garden*

delphinium, erigeron, gaillardia, rudbeckia and, for autumn especially, chrysanthemums.

Because this border is mainly intended for cutting, the plants should not be crowded. They need as much room for full development as do those in other beds and borders and as much preparation and attention.

Awkward Plots. If the garden is not as level as one would wish, there is the possibility of terracing and so making a virtue of having different soil levels (always with the minimum of labour, which means the least possible disturbance of soil). The slope may be cut in two or more parts, separated by a bank, or banks, of stone or small rocks embedded in the soil "face." Behind this the necessary levelling may proceed. Steps cut in the bank and reinforced with stone slabs or concrete or thick timber can be made very attractive, and the bank itself can be planted as a rock garden (see Fig. 84).

The ordinary run of plants cannot be induced to grow with any degree of success where a slope is considerable. Lack of sufficient water in dry weather would wither them. Even on a gentle slope the hose needs to be kept almost constantly employed in spring and summer when rain holds off.

There may be an abrupt slope up to, or down to, a boundary. The simplest treatment consists in planting it with rambler roses, the roots to be at the base of the slope, the shoots as they extend being pegged to the soil of the slope. Or it may be covered with the swiftly spreading and always attractive *Cerastium tomentosum* (snow-in-summer), roots being planted in autumn or early spring.

A magnificent summer display may be arranged by sowing the abrupt slope, in March, with nasturtiums a foot or so apart; but nasturtiums should be considered only if the soil is good and can be kept reasonably moist. If the slope is a mass of stones, use the cerastium, which is long-suffering and difficult to kill. Another alternative is to bed the stony slope with small rocks and treat it as a rock garden, with good soil provided in "pockets" for each plant. Naturally, to begin with, it must be cleared of weeds and other rubbish.

Wind and Boundary. In working out a plan for flowers remember that the first considerations are plenty of air and sunlight. In confined quarters it may be desirable to have the flowers as far removed as may be from wall or fence or hedge, to secure maximum sunlight. On the other hand, in a very open and exposed garden it would be wise to give the flowers whatever shelter from strong winds the natural features of the ground afford.

A wind-break of some kind is desirable, and circumstances will dictate its nature if one has to be provided. It may be a fence or wall or hedge, to break the blast and, perhaps, afford privacy. But nothing that shuts out good air and strengthening sunlight should be tolerated: a warning appertaining also to the use of trellis in the garden.

Wooden trellis erected as a screen may not cast much shade when bare, but when carrying a load of foliage its shade may be altogether too dense for the liking of flowering plants growing nearby.

SECTION XI

MANAGEMENT OF FLOWER BEDS AND BORDERS

A ROUGH-AND-READY distinction between flower beds and borders is that beds have temporary occupants, whereas the borders are mostly filled with hardy and permanent plants. The aim is to keep the beds and borders always attractive: in the case of flower beds by emptying them when their beauty has passed and refilling them with plants that will restore their attraction: in borders by planting bulbs and annuals between the permanent tenants.

Through the Four Seasons. Follow-on plants for replacing in the beds those which have bloomed and had their day are, in a well-managed garden, on hand when required—being drawn from a reserve: bulbs which were stored from the previous year, or plants brought along in the "nursery" patch or frame from the seedling or cutting stage. Unless this system of home-raising and storing is followed, the restocking of even two or three small beds may prove startlingly expensive, though it occurs only once a year.

There is no need to stray beyond the limits of simplicity to get good

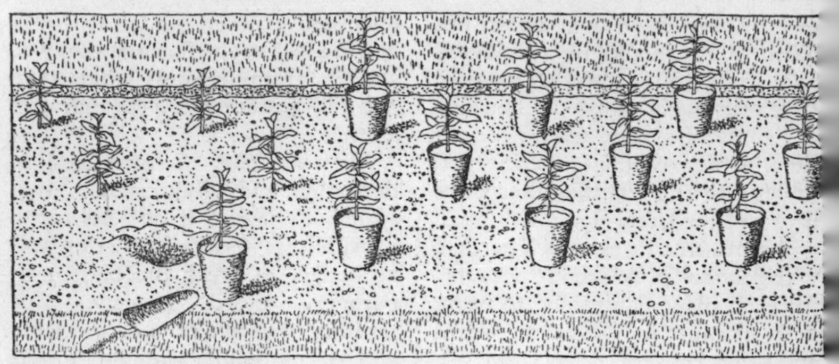

Fig. 85.—*Before setting out the plants in a flower bed it is advisable to stand the pots containing them (or the knocked-out plants themselves) as markers in the positions which they will ultimately occupy*

effect. Garishness is a thing to avoid, so colour combinations call for thought. There was a time, not so long ago, when the well-tried favourite arrangement of a summer flower bed (and even window-box) involved red geraniums surrounded or bordered by white marguerites or white alyssum and finished off with an outer ring or edging of blue lobelia.

Much more simple and restful effects can be secured: in spring with polyanthuses in mixed colours, or forget-me-nots and white narcissi interplanted, or white arabis and scarlet tulips, or wallflowers alone or with daffodils, or red and white double daisies, or violas. The summer beds may be filled with scarlet salvia, or with antirrhinums, or scarlet geraniums, or dwarf dahlias, or a mixture of yellow calceolarias and blue violas. Pleasing combinations or single plantings are numerous enough, worked out with the aid of this book and a plant catalogue or two.

In autumn and winter the beds are not left bare; they will be carpeted with the foliage of the follow-on plants of the season that is to come.

Planting the Beds. The mechanics of spacing and planting are simple enough. The habit of growth of any plant dictates the amount of elbow-room it requires; it may be denied its natural right to space, of course, but it will not do itself justice. The amount of vacant ground between plants at the time of their setting out may seem a woeful waste, but at the height of their season of flowering it may be impossible to see a square inch of soil between them.

Planting distances decided on, a good working plan is to mark each site with a short stick or stake thrust into the ground, each being withdrawn in turn as a hole is made with the trowel. If planting from pots, the latter can be used as markers (see Fig. 85). Thus perfectly even spacing is easily achieved. Alternatively, the plants themselves may be laid out as markers, but too much preliminary handling is likely to shake soil from the roots. The more soil clinging to the roots at planting time the better. No such objection applies, however, to dormant bulbs.

An elementary, though frequently overlooked, precaution is to plant bulbs—when these are to be mingled with wallflowers or other plants—*after* the ordinary plants are in place in the bed.

Nearly always it is most convenient to start planting in the centre of the bed, the outer plants, or edging, going in last. Too much trampling of the soil can be avoided by standing on a piece of board, if all parts of the bed cannot be reached from the surround. However small the area, the outer plants should stand well back from the edges, so that no complications arise when the turf needs to be mown there or the path swept.

Planting the Borders. Here the object is not to get the greatest possible number of different plants into one border but to get the most attractive and long-lasting display. All those plants known as hardy herbaceous perennials (they defy the weather and live on from year to year; delphinium and Michaelmas daisy are examples) show to greatest effect when planted in clumps of three or more of the same kind; though in a very narrow border one would not attempt to follow that practice with such strong growers as pæonies.

Annuals, both hardy and half-hardy, should be present in the border; and bulbs provide most welcome colour there, though their foliage proves unsightly when approaching the yellowing stage. If bulbs are to be used they should be planted well to the back of the border; where later foliage will hide their tops after flowering. Or they should be lifted when flowering is over and temporarily replanted elsewhere for their own foliage to ripen out of sight.

Happy-go-lucky arrangement of plants in the mixed border can

Fig. 86.—*The planting of a mixed border should be preceded by the adoption of a plan. Here flowering shrubs, hardy herbaceous perennials, and at the front annuals, are employed to the best advantage. Reference numbers:* 1, *hollyhock;* 2, *delphinium;* 3, *anchusa;* 4, *rudbeckia;* 5, *helenium;* 6, *Michaelmas daisy, pink, and* 7, *mauve;* 8, *shasta daisy;* 9, *phlox, red, and* 10, *pink;* 11, *erigeron;* 12, *China aster;* 13, *godetia;* 14, *clarkia;* 15, *African marigold;* 16, *English marigold;* 17, *sweet alyssum;* 18, *lobelia. Forsythia blooms in spring, buddleia in summer*

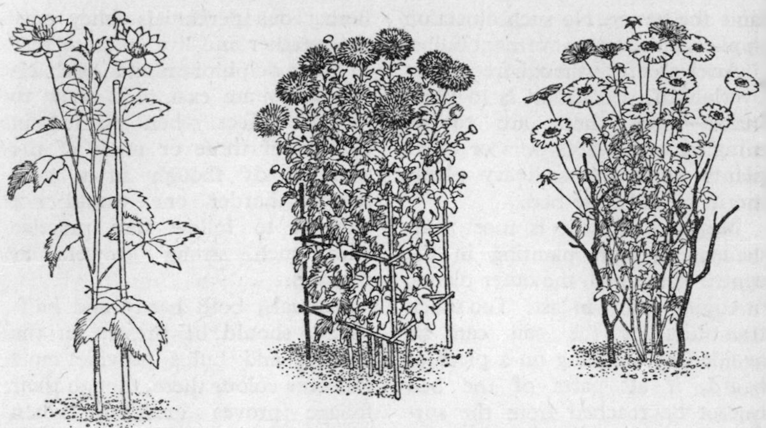

Fig. 87.—*Staking should be done early and neatly, the type of support being suited to each plant's habit. A tall, single stake may suffice for a dahlia (left). Strong bushy growth, as chrysanthemum (centre), may need a triangle of stakes connected by raffia or string. Annuals of light growth (right) will be sufficiently supported by twiggy sticks*

have really pleasing results, but the safer plan is to *have* a plan, a prearranged scheme which, for the sake of variety, can be varied in a subsequent year if so desired (see Fig. 86). A plan is desirable if for no other reason than that it enables one to avoid the error of placing short plants too far back and having the giants too far forward. It is not necessary to have plants graded too exactly, as to maximum height, from back to front, but generally the tallest should be at the back and the shortest at the front.

Tidiness First. One should not have to do much tidying up after planting. Soiled or broken leaves should be cut or pinched away *before* the plants go in—and the rubbish placed in trug or barrow straight away. No soil will be carried to the turf or path adjacent if sacks, or sheets of newspaper, are laid down to catch whatever may fall during operations. This applies equally to beds and borders, and the precaution is specially necessary where adjacent turf is concerned: small stones left on the grass may cause damage to the blades of the lawn-mower.

After planting. In dry weather the plants may need watering in at once, each being given sufficient water to settle the soil thoroughly around the roots. If there is much sunshine, sheets of newspaper laid lightly upon the plants will prevent their wilting in the first few hours.

Frequent watering may be necessary in very dry weather and when growth is really active. Mere sprinklings are waste of time. The soil should be soaked, and the following day the surface should be loosened with hand fork or hoe. In the absence of rain, a good watering should precede feeding with artificial fertilizers or liquid manure—

and dry fertilizers should be lightly hoed or hand-forked in or washed in with careful watering.

Weeding will mostly be done by hand, it being the habit of weeds to snuggle close up to the plants, where an incautious stroke with the hoe might prove disastrous.

Early Support. Stakes should be given to all plants likely to need them *before* there is sign of the necessity. If staking is left to the last minute it becomes difficult; stems may become deformed, or sudden heavy rain may level plants to the ground.

A single stake may suffice for a dahlia plant, the growths being looped singly to it as they extend upwards, whereas a chrysanthemum, or Michaelmas daisy clump, may need a triangle of three stakes (see Fig. 87). A clump of annuals may get sufficient support from three or four twiggy sticks disposed around and between them without ties.

A most important point is that the support shall be strong enough for its task and tall enough for the maximum growth. When the latter stage is reached, the support may be shortened so that its tip is not visible. In every case, early placing of stakes ensures that later foliage will conceal them.

Ties may be of string or raffia or patent garden twine. The quickest and safest way of tying is to twist the material first around the stake, then loop the two ends around the stem (or stems) and knot them (see Fig. 88). Bunching or strangling must be avoided; room for later growth or expansion must be left. It is sometimes desirable to attend to this tying three or four times through the season, higher ties being called for as plants push upward.

Removing Seed Heads. The surest method of prolonging the floral display in beds and borders is to remove every flower as it fades. A faded flower is prelude to a seed head, and the production of seeds speedily wears a plant out. In the case of the lovely Canterbury bell this picking off of faded flowers can be very wearisome, a daily task, unfortunately not to be avoided. Left to go to seed, their season of beauty is regrettably short. Dahlia and marigold also are prodigious seed-producers, and every day during summer they need going over with fingers or scissors.

The nipping or scissoring calls for some care, because another flower bud waiting to burst is generally but a short way to the rear. Some seed-pods are attached

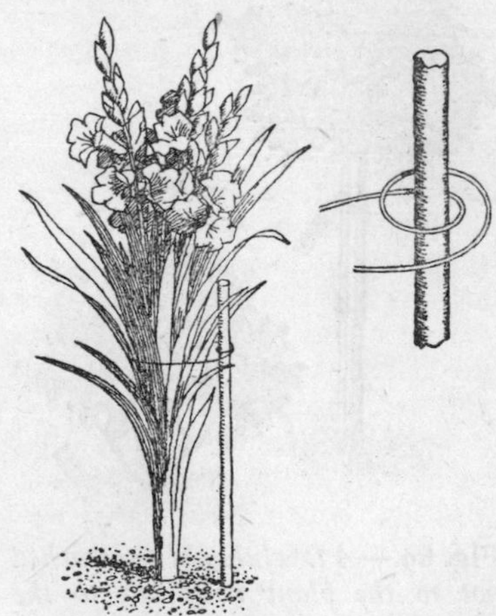

Fig. 88.—*Method of securing the tying material to the stake is shown on the right. On the left, a gladiolus plant encircled by the same tie*

so stubbornly to their stem that their removal is almost impossible with the fingers alone. Hollyhock is a case in point.

Towards the close of summer a seed-pod here and there may be left to ripen its contents, if seed is to be saved for sowing. Or seed may be allowed to fall naturally, to secure self-sown seedlings for next year's display. Annuals, such as clarkia and nasturtium, are specially prodigal with their seedlings.

Replanting the Border. There comes a time in autumn or early winter when the herbaceous border takes on a bedraggled air. It must then be cleaned up. The old ripened stems of phlox and hollyhock, golden rod and others should be cut down to within a couple of inches of the ground and conveyed to the rubbish-fire for burning—along with the withered annuals. Fallen leaves and bits of stick should be cleared away, so that no hiding place remains for slugs and snails, woodlice and other destructive pests.

Fig. 89.—*A label should be attached not to the plant itself but to the plant's stake, and high up (left). Where the plant requires no stake it should be given a substantial wooden label large enough not to be overlooked and trodden in or kicked aside*

The soil surface can then be loosened with hoe or fork, a watchful glance being kept for seedlings worth preserving. In the case of an old-established border, however, harder work is indicated, extending perhaps to complete replanting, carried out in the following manner.

A patch of spare ground is prepared for the temporary reception of plant clumps as these are lifted with the fork, no more being transferred than is necessary to clear a length of border for dealing with comfortably in an afternoon, or whatever continuous time is at one's disposal.

Dig the cleared piece of ground, to its full width, at least a spade-blade deep (or equivalent depth with the fork) and mix in rotted material from the compost heap, or old manure, placing on one side any bulbs that may be turned up. Leave the surface level, and replant.

To prepare the lifted clumps for replanting, remove soiled or broken leaves, shake off some (not all) of the soil and, if the clump is large, divide it—pulling it apart with the hands, or using a knife, or wrenching it asunder with the aid of two forks thrust into it back to back and then pushed apart. Clumps may be left undisturbed for several years, but they begin to deteriorate after about the third year; and such as retain their foliage in winter (as erigeron) provide a grand home for large numbers of pests.

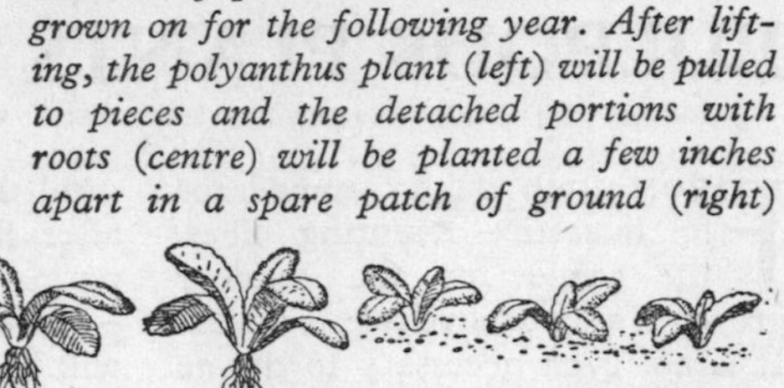

Fig. 90.—*After the spring flower display such hardy perennials as polyanthus will be grown on for the following year. After lifting, the polyanthus plant (left) will be pulled to pieces and the detached portions with roots (centre) will be planted a few inches apart in a spare patch of ground (right)*

The old and woody centre of a clump is almost certain to be worn out, so that portion may well be discarded after the division. The latter results, of course, in a larger number of plants than the border will hold. The temptation to crowd them all in is to be resisted.

Unreliable Memory. Labels may become destroyed or lost or displaced if they are not firmly wired to a permanent stake, or if not of metal or stout wood and thrust securely into the ground where they are sufficiently obvious for manœuvring feet to avoid them (see Fig. 89).

The average memory in a garden is as fickle as the weather, and name and variety of some choice plant, so well known at planting time, is bound to fade unless committed to a label—which should be safeguarded as suggested already. Their handling demands extra care when a border is being replanted.

Emptying the Beds. Flower beds occupied by roses or other shrubs (which see) are, naturally, exempt from the seasonal flurry of work associated with beds devoted to plants of a transitory nature—the spring and summer bedding. With the latter, as soon as the seasonal display is over the object is to get the soil cleared and dug and filled with the next occupants as quickly and efficiently as circumstances allow.

Methodically, sacking or old newspaper is laid down on path or grass adjoining and the wheelbarrow brought close alongside. Then, with digging-fork or hand fork, the flowered-out plants are lifted, working from the outer edge inwards. The natural habits of the plants, and one's conveniences will dictate their disposal.

For example, when the spring show is ended, polyanthus will be divided and planted in the nursery quarters for use next autumn (see Fig. 90); bulbs will be replanted close together elsewhere to finish their growth; wallflowers will be discarded, new stock to be raised from seed; forget-me-nots will be thrown on the soft rubbish-heap, with the exception of three or four which will be cast into some odd corner to drop seed and in due course produce seedlings.

Digging and manuring will follow, affording an opportunity of exposing underground pests, which should be destroyed on the spot. If there has been disease among the plants, any tops showing the taint at this time should be burned and not added to the compost heap.

SECTION XII

BULBOUS PLANTS OUTDOORS

FROM frail, dainty snowdrops to majestic, flaunting lilies, the scope for the outdoor grower is as extensive as it is varied. It is not even necessary to devote a flower bed to the bulbs of one's choice. Small patches in the mixed border can give infinite pleasure. There are kinds specially adapted to the rockery. Others give a charming display in a natural setting of rough grass. Some may be grown in formal rows, where space can be spared, specially for cutting.

Bulbs for Bedding. For bedding purposes, to give a spring display, a short selection would include hyacinths, daffodils, tulips and crocuses. The effect is heightened if the bulbs are provided with a carpet of plants which will flower along with them, the bulbs being interplanted with wallflowers, forget-me-nots or polyanthuses. This scheme not only makes the bulbs go further but it ensures that the bed looks attractive in winter-time.

Choice of Varieties. If a mixed bed of hyacinths or tulips is required, consideration should be given to the blending of colours. Moreover, the hyacinths or tulips should flower simultaneously and be of the same height.

The tabulated list on the opposite page should help you in selecting and planting your bulbs.

Bulbs in Grass. Daffodils, narcissi and crocuses planted in grass among fruit trees, or in a corner of the lawn which for their special benefit can be left unmown until the tops have withered away after flowering, are more or less permanent occupants of the ground —unlike the bedding bulbs, which will be lifted to make way for the summer bedding.

In the Rockery. Small varieties of narcissi, the lovely little grape hyacinth (Muscari), and snowdrops will enliven the rockery in what otherwise is a dull season. Their placing should be considered in relation to sunlight, and the pockets of soil which receive them should be of good depth and quality.

Planted in groups of not less than six or so, their gradual increase and spread should be envisioned. Snowdrops especially will occupy more and more space as season follows season, and this inclination ought not to be thwarted by planting the bulbs where closely adjacent rocks will hem them too closely in.

Bulbs in the Border. When planning to plant bulbs in the mixed herbaceous border, it should be borne in mind that such items as tulips and hyacinths will need to be lifted after flowering, as explained on page 85.

Daffodils and narcissi may be regarded as more or less permanent occupants so long as they are planted well to the back of the border, where they can be left undisturbed after flowering and the unsightliness of their withering foliage will be hidden by summer-flowering plants in front of them.

A border edging of crocuses is very attractive, but the bulbs

OUTDOOR-FLOWERING BULBOUS PLANTS
Including Tubers and Corms

Name	*Time to Plant*	*Flowering Season*	*Height in Inches*	*Apart in Inches*	*Depth to Top of Bulb Inches*	*Remarks*
Anemone	March	Spring	12	6	3	Mixed border. Good for cutting.
Begonia	Late May–early June	Summer	18	12	Tuber-tops to be exposed	Summer bedding; and in pots.
Chionodoxa	September	March	6	1	2	Sunny position in rockery.
Crocus	October–December	Spring	4	3	2½	Spring bedding; edging to beds; borders.
Daffodil and Narcissus	October onwards	Spring	12	4–6	4	Spring bedding; clumps in mixed border. Good for cutting.
Gladiolus	March	Summer	Up to 36	6	3	Clumps in mixed border. Good for cutting.
Hyacinth	November	Spring	12	8	3–4	Spring bedding; window-boxes; mixed border.
Iris	August–October	October–June	18	6	3	Clumps in border. Good for cutting.
Lily	September	Summer	Up to 72	At least 6	Up to 6	Plants in clumps of 3 or more; leave undisturbed.
Montbretia	October–March	August	Up to 36	2	3	Massed in mixed border. Good for cutting.
Ranunculus	February	Spring, early summer	Up to 18	4	Claws downwards, 2	Clumps in mixed border. Good for cutting.
Snowdrop	Sept.–December	January–March	6	1	2	Clumps in mixed border. Good for cutting.
Snowflake (Leucojum)	September onwards	March and May	12	3	4	Clumps in border and in rockery.
Tulip	October–December	March–June	Up to 18	6	4	Beds; borders; window-boxes.
Winter Aconite	October–December	January–March	4	2	2	Among ferns; in the rockery.

should be removed and stored in due season, to allow of the planting of a summer-flowering edging.

Bulbs for Cutting. Daffodils, narcissi and gladioli are such splendid flowers for indoor decoration

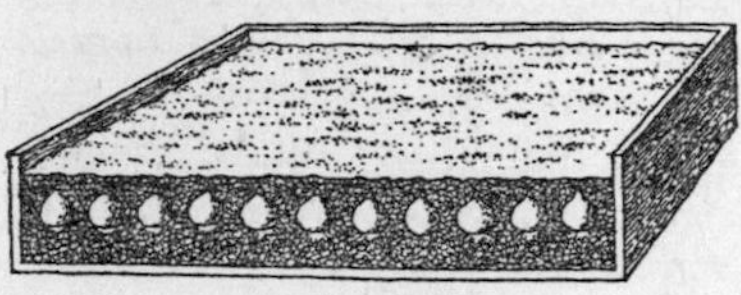

Fig. 91.—*Preparatory to outdoor planting, bulbs may be started into growth in a shallow box of good soil placed outdoors or in a frame*

that they are deserving of a special planting where their cutting will not spoil the outdoor scene. That is, a certain number of them should be reserved from the mixed border and the bulbs placed where no unsightly gaps will be left when the blooms are taken, even if this means encroaching on the vegetable garden to provide them with a straight and strictly utilitarian row.

When to Plant. As early in late summer or in autumn as the bulbs are available is the best time to plant. It is a mistake to wait until winter. This early planting may sometimes give rise to some difficulty when there is delay in removing the summer plants from a bed which the bulbs are intended to occupy. But this can be got over by planting the bulbs closely together in boxes of good soil where they will commence growth and remain until the bed is ready for their occupation (Fig. 91.)

How to Plant. If a bed is to be filled, the bulbs and the spring-flowering plants to accompany them should be laid out on the prepared surface. This ensures even spacing. The spacing and the actual planting should be done without treading on the soil, for though bulbous plants require a moderately firm root run they are not happy in ground that has been consolidated overmuch.

It is a mistake to use a dibber for planting bulbs. When the latter are dropped into dibber-made holes they are apt to be "hung up," whereas the base of the bulb should rest on the earth, from which it obtains the nourishment necessary to development. This is certain if a trowel is used. In any case a trowel is required for the planting of the accompanying "carpeting" flowers, and there would be no point in using both tools. (Fig. 92.)

A spade may allow of quicker work than a trowel when bulbs are to be grouped in the mixed border. Sufficient soil is taken out to allow of correct depth planting in each group position, the bulbs are then half-covered with the finest of the soil removed (to prevent them being moved on to their sides, or

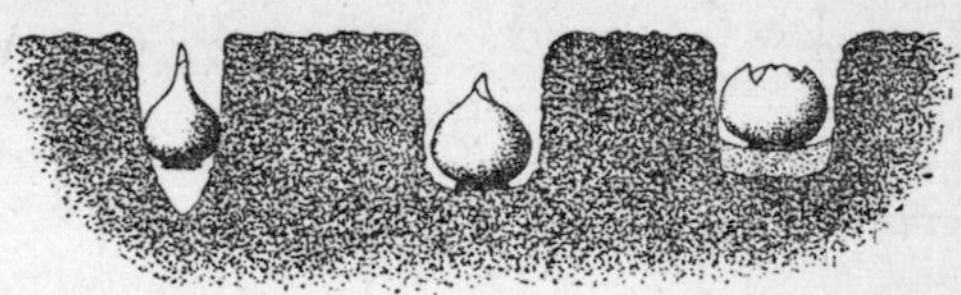

Fig. 92.—*A dibber should not be used for bulb planting; the bulb is likely to be "hung up," as at the left. In a trowel-made hole the bulb sits comfortably* (*centre*). *Lily bulbs appreciate being bedded on a little silver sand or sharp grit at the bottom of the hole* (*right*)

otherwise displaced), and the remainder of the soil replaced.

When planting is to be done in grass, a small and close area is most conveniently dealt with by rolling back a strip or two of the turf. The soil below is then dug and, if necessary, enriched, the bulbs laid in position, and the turf replaced above them. (Fig. 93.) The loosening of the soil will necessitate the removal of a little of it to allow of the turf being replaced level with the surrounding surface. The turf should not be refirmed by heavy rolling, nor by being beaten with a spade, but pressed lightly down with the foot.

Fig. 93.—*Bulbs planted in grass give better results if the turf is first cut and rolled back. The soil can then be dug and enriched if necessary before replacing the turf*

The planted area of turf should then be avoided by traffic. Especially when growth is commencing, the tender shoots are likely to be injured by trampling feet. And it should be further stressed that mowing or other cutting of the grass must be avoided until the tops of the plants have withered.

Soil Preparation. The temptation to hurry bulbs into unprepared ground must be resisted. Moderately rich soil, well dug, is necessary to enable the bulbs to flower well and also, which is equally important, to build up for the following year's flowering.

When the flower bed has been cleared of its summer occupants, or the intended patches in the mixed border marked out, digging to the depth of a spade-blade should proceed, stones, weeds and other rubbish being removed at the same time. Rotted manure, leaf-mould, or old compost material, should be worked in evenly and not deposited in a layer at spade-blade depth. Bone-meal dug well in is also very effective for spring bulbs. They do not like to be in contact with fresh stable manure. Dealing with heavy soil, it is advisable to work in sharp grit to improve drainage. Lilies in particular are in danger of rotting in winter-wet ground, and with these the safest plan is to drop sharp grit, or silver sand, into the planting holes so that the bulbs are kept from direct contact with the soil. Builder's sand should not be used for this purpose; it is apt to cake hard and solid after becoming wet, thus defeating the grower's purpose.

Staking. Bedding hyacinths need support for their top-heavy spikes of bloom. Each should be given an unobtrusive stake and a raffia tie to keep it vertical, otherwise the blooms will flop over and become soil-stained, or the flower stems may even snap off. The stakes should be at some distance from the stems to avoid possible piercing of the bulbs.

Tall and strong stakes will be needed for lilies of various kinds, either a stake to each stem or three disposed around a clump, the three being looped around with string or strong raffia.

Gladioli need individual stakes,

except when grown in a row for, say, cutting. In the latter case one strong stake at each end of the row can be inserted, and string or thin wire run from one to the other, the growths being looped back to this horizontal support.

Overcrowded Bulbs. Daffodils and narcissi which have been left long in one position—in the mixed border or in grass—are bound in due course to show signs of deterioration, flowers not being produced in satisfying abundance. The bulbs should be forked out of the ground and pulled apart with the fingers, the best of the divisions being replanted in rich soil in a position where they can remain, out of the general way, until they attain flowering size, when they can again take their place in the border or elsewhere.

This building-up will not take place unless they are in rich soil, in a position exposed to the sun, and where they can be reached with the watering-can if that becomes necessary.

Harvesting Bulbs. The ideal time to lift bulbs for storing is when the tops have withered. More often, it becomes desirable to get them out of the ground (to make way for other plants) whilst the foliage is still green. The fork should be used to loosen the soil so that the bulbs come up, without tugging, complete with their top growth. The latter still has work to do, and so the lifted bulbs should be replanted temporarily, quite close together, in a piece of good soil, until the tops die down.

Then they can be lifted finally, the soil shaken from them, and laid out to dry, on a hard path, or under an open shed. Not until they are reasonably dry should the bulbs be stored away, in shallow boxes or in paper bags, complete with labels. If rats or mice are likely to find access thereto some traps should be set in the store, for bulbs present a great attraction to hungry rodents. Individual cultural requirements of bulbous plants are given in the chapter FLOWERS IN DETAIL.

SECTION XIII

ROCK GARDEN, DRY WALL AND POOL

SEPARATELY OR combined, even on quite a small scale, these can be intriguing features of the garden (see Fig. 94). The purpose of a rockery (or rock garden) is to provide a home for plants that flourish naturally where rocks appear through the soil surface and those that show to best advantage amidst miniature "alpine" scenery.

A dry wall, up to about 3 ft. in height as a rule, is built of blocks of rugged stone with soil between them instead of the mortar of an ordinary brick wall. It may be backed substantially by soil, for support, and rock plants will thrive

Fig. 94.—*Rockery, dry wall and small formal pool can be charmingly combined. The dry wall, carrying rock plants on both sides or faces, here serves as a novel division between two parts of the garden*

between the facing-blocks where their roots may reach the soil behind.

The pool may be nothing more than a sunken tub filled with water and stocked with dwarf aquatic plants. It may be a concrete-lined excavation housing flowering water-lilies and goldfish. It may be sited in the lawn or combined with the rockery.

Siting the Rockery. A fair share of sunlight is its due. Beneath trees, where shade is too prolonged and the drip of rain from branches is inevitable, is no place for it. Moderately good soil, with small rocks or sizable stones embedded therein, can be the foundation of much floral loveliness. A heap of rubbish flung up in haste, with bits of stone stuck in upright—resembling a disturbed graveyard in miniature—will never make an attractive rockery.

A position may be in readiness for it: a mound or steep bank of soil which can be so worked upon as to appear, even in its first season, as though the rocks and plants had always been there. Through it a path or paths will be driven, and crazy-paved. A greater likelihood is that it will have to be built up from ground level, the necessary soil coming, perhaps, from the pool site—a happy coincidence of jobs. Or it may be below soil level, with a step or two leading down to it, the excavated material being placed around the sides to extend it upwards.

A sunken rock garden is specially fascinating (see Fig. 95). But it should be considered only where natural drainage is very free. Where the soil is of heavy nature and moisture-holding, it is not practicable: in a wet winter it may become a pool.

Building Material. This may present difficulties. Plain bricks, concrete slabs and anything else that looks conspicuously artificial must be counted out. There may be suitable rock or stone in the neighbourhood to be had for the taking, or at small cost. To buy it from a distance is costly. An alternative is large stuff from demolitions, picked up perhaps in a builder's yard.

In the absence of flat, thick stone for the crazy paving, concrete blocks of irregular outline may be made in moulds and laid. Or the path may be concreted over to the depth of a couple of inches, with lines scored across with a trowel to simulate the real thing. These, at best, are only inferior imitations.

Banking-up. Building will normally proceed from the front, soil being added as each layer is completed and packed down firmly. Every stone or rock has to be very firmly embedded, so that shifting is out of the question. A flat-surfaced rock of good area may lie almost level here and there, in contrast with bolder upright mass (see Fig. 96).

There must be adequate pocke of soil in which to plant, of cours and, provided the soil is not t heavy in nature, most rock plan will get along nicely witho special preparation. Later, whe the rockery is a going concern, may be found desirable to repla soil for special subjects with pe or leaf-mould.

Planting. If constructional wo is carried out in winter, it reasonable to suppose a timely fa of rain will settle soil and rock sufficiently for planting. Otherwis it may be necessary to apply wate generously, to bed the whole dow planting the following day.

Plants of too vigorous natu should be excluded from the sma rockery or they may quickly tak possession of the whole. There an extensive range of moderatel vigorous and dainty subjects fro which choice may be made. Ther are even small shrubs that can b included—dwarf varieties of ber beris and cotoneaster and specia conifers.

And, of course, there are man bulbous plants, including earl

Fig. 95.—*A partly sunken rockery has fascinating possibilities. It shoul be placed where water is not likely to collect in wet weather. The pathway through it need not be more than eighteen inches wide*

Fig. 96.—*In rockery construction every piece of material used should be firmly embedded, so that accidental shifting is out of the question, as shown here in section*

flowering irises, grape hyacinths, scillas, snowdrops and winter aconites, crocuses, and miniature narcissi such as *Cyclamineus*, and bulbous anemones.

Spring-flowering saxifrages, in variety, are always successful. A tuft or two of golden alyssum is invaluable as background for the lowlier but charming *Viola gracilis* and *Gentiana acaulis*. There are erinus varieties, and omphalodes, and dwarf phlox and that great stand-by aubrietia.

With early summer come the flowers of androsace, armeria, dianthus and echeveria, thyme and the stonecrops (sedum) and sempervivum and many another.

For crevices in the rock-garden path are the acænas, *Arenaria balearica*, *Dianthus deltoides*, sedums and mossy saxifrages, thyme and others.

Maintenance and Renovation. Watering is as necessary as elsewhere in the garden, more especially in a dry spring and early summer. Many rock plants, whose roots have travelled to the moister conditions beneath the larger stones, will get along fairly well without the watering-can or hose; but the general run of plants profit from this attention. With watering goes weeding, and sometimes it may be necessary to remove a rock or stone completely to enable a persistent weed's roots to be withdrawn.

There will be a battle for space when plants are thriving. Those with obvious desire to swamp a neighbour must be curbed, by cutting back the trespasser carefully in summer or by division of it when flowering is over.

Autumn is probably the best time for a general overhaul of the rockery—removal of withered leaves and other rubbish being important as lessening chances of survival of lurking slugs and woodlice and other pests. A dry and sunny day lessens the discomfort and expedites the labour.

Then, too, a wastage of soil due to rain and watering and weeding may need to be made good, fresh soil being packed close around stems and any loosened plants firmed in with the fingers. Any winter losses should be made good

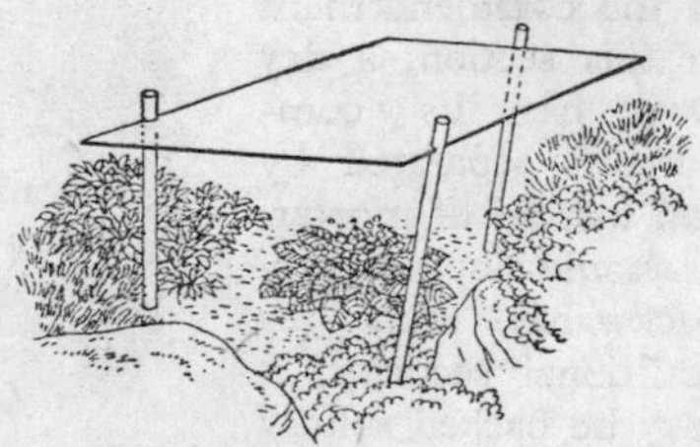

Fig. 97.—*A piece of window-glass supported by notched sticks will give winter protection to rock plants that are known to suffer from cold and (or) heavy rains*

Fig. 98.—*A piece of rock or stone may be sloped (firmly embedded) above a treasured rock plant at the coming of winter to shield it*

in early spring, when a further picking over will do good.

Some rock plants are apt to suffer in winter unless protection is given against heavy rain. The orthodox method is to support a piece of window-glass, roof-fashion, above the doubtful ones—generally those with woolly leaves—by means of notched sticks (see Fig. 97). Or a piece of rock or stone of suitable shape may be sloped above a treasured plant as a canopy (see Fig. 98). Propagation is dealt with in the section HOW TO INCREASE FLOWERING PLANTS.

Dry-wall Gardening. As mentioned at the commencement of this section, a dry wall has its components separated by soil instead of mortar. It should slope slightly backwards and, for additional security, it may be backed solidly by a mound as high as itself (see Fig. 99). Rock plants of a trailing nature are specially suitable, planted in the spaces between: aubrietia, golden alyssum, white arabis, stonecrop and so on. Small, hardy ferns, such as are found growing wild in woodlands and some hedgebanks, can be introduced, and the top of the low wall can be crowned with catmint (nepeta) and dwarf lavender. As a quick filler, of temporary nature, dwarf nasturtium can be relied on.

Unless the dry wall is already in existence, planting is most easily carried out as the wall is built up stone by stone. Seed-sowing, however, is best left until the erection of the wall is complete.

If a wall of this kind is to divide one part of the garden from another it may be built double-faced, an ample body of soil dividing the two sides. For stability, it should be broader at the base, and the top should be not less than about 18 in. across. Naturally, the soil-filling will be made firm at all stages of construction, and if there is any doubt at all about the foundation this should be rammed very solid

Fig. 99.—*The dry wall should slope slightly backwards and, for additional security (unless it be double-faced), should be backed solidly by earth as high as itself*

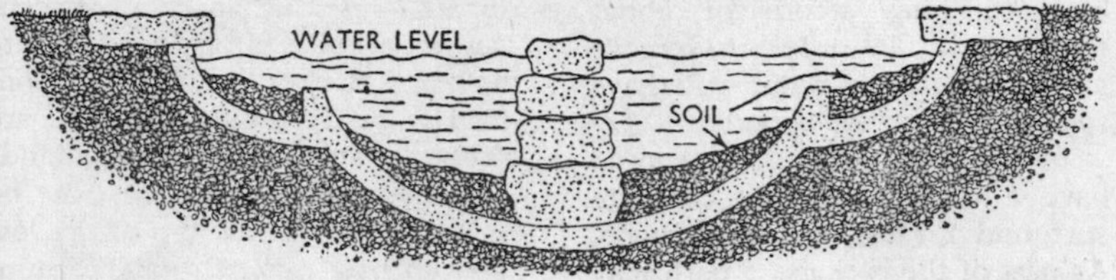

Fig. 100.—*Cross-section of a still-water garden pool, showing how a ledge is contrived to hold soil at a higher level than that which covers the bottom —for plants whose roots need to be only an inch or two below water*

before ever the first stone is laid.

In spite of the misleading word "dry," quite a lot of water will be needed by this wall, at least until the occupants have been long enough in position to have driven their roots well inwards.

A Pleasant Pool. A formal design—circle or oblong—fits in best where the pool or pond is to be a feature of the lawn (see page 10). Where it is to be combined with a rock garden, formality should be forgotten and the pool's outline made irregular. There is no need to have the finished depth greater than a foot or eighteen inches.

To facilitate the annual clean-out (necessary to ensure the water does not become unpleasant) the bottom should be level. This is desirable in the absence of a controlled outlet, the provision of which takes the garden pond into the "professional" and costly class.

The first constructional step consists in marking out the site; the second, removing the soil and disposing of it, without trampling the turf too much if the lawn is the site. The sides of the excavation should slope outwards, and these should be made absolutely firm, and the bottom rammed. A mixture of cement one part, sand three parts, made into a stiff paste with water, will then be plastered over the bottom and sides to the depth of about three inches.

The bottom is treated first. The sides are built up on succeeding ledges (see Fig. 100). This mixture must be given several days to harden, and then should have its first water-filling emptied out

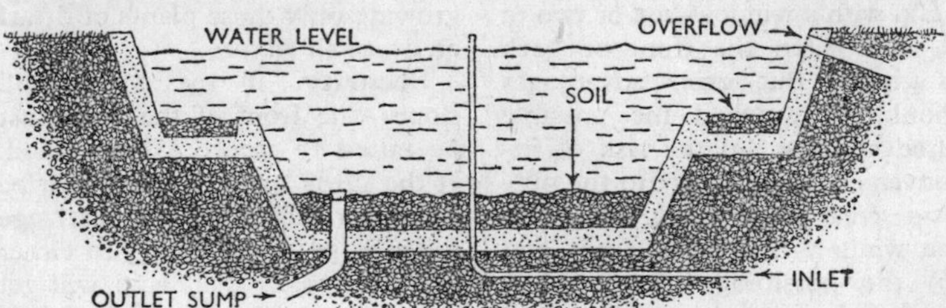

Fig. 101.—*Inlet and overflow pipes make this pool a really ambitious effort. Depth of soil at the low level should be so adjusted as not to clog the outlet pipe when the latter is opened at the top*

after this has stood for about three weeks, in order to remove any chemical the water will have soaked up from the concrete.

In the lawn, the pond should have a crazy-paving or concrete surround not less than a foot wide. As part of the rockery, a path may terminate at the water or extend part of the way around the rim.

Stocking the Pool. The small pond, such as is dealt with here, should not have the bottom covered with soil for the rooting of plants. The cleanest plan is to place a water-lily root in an old rush-basket filled with good soil, the top being loosely tied, sinking the whole slowly in the water where it is to stay (see Fig. 102). It may be necessary to weight it with a brick or rock, but this will not be seen when the foliage spreads on the surface.

Aquatic plants needing less soil than the vigorous water-lily can be accommodated in flower-pots (6 in. or more across the top) sunk in position. Goldfish (or others) can be added, but not before the plants are all there and growing well. If the water-level sinks with evaporation, this loss can be made good with bucket or hose.

Fig. 102.—*Planting a water-lily in a soilless pool is best achieved by enclosing the roots in an old rush-basket or piece of sacking filled with rich soil, tying the mouth somewhat loosely, and sinking it into position*

SECTION XIV

WINDOW-BOX GARDENING

A GREAT DEAL can be done with a window-box or two to brighten the front or back of a house. But against advantages should be weighed the possible disadvantages: (*a*) the risk of inconvenience or damage to the outdoor scene below when the soil in the window-box is watered; and (*b*) the possibility of excluding much light from the room behind the box.

Special circumstances may rule out the first consideration (*a*), and the second (*b*) can be met by growing only those plants of dwarf or dwarfish stature.

Security. If the window-sill slopes, the front of the box must be raised to secure a level stand. If the sill is level, the box must be raised an inch to enable drainage water to get away easily. In either event it means that wind will get under the box and a gale might dislodge it. To circumvent that, the box should be secured at either end to the brickwork (see Fig. 103), or fastened in some other way. The weight of the box will be considerable when it is filled with soil, and reliance should not be placed on a perhaps rickety window-frame gripping a screw or two tenaciously enough to prevent accident.

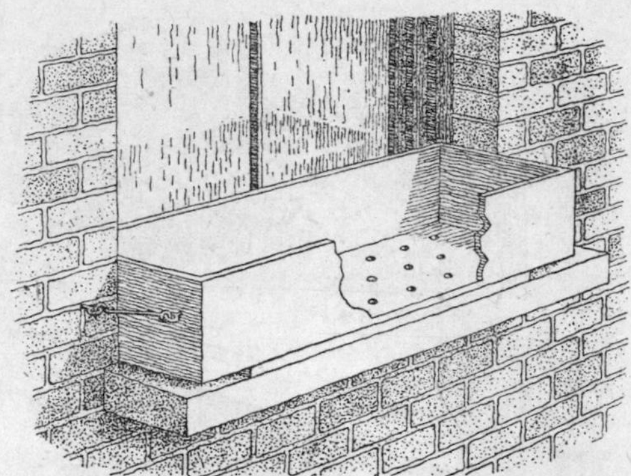

Fig. 103.—*Well-prepared window-box, drainage holes bored in the bottom, front edge raised to secure a level stand, and secured at both ends to the brickwork*

Construction. Wood ¾ in. thick should form the box: front, back, two ends and bottom. Length of the box should be such that a comfortable fit is made between the sides of the window-opening. From back to front it can extend not more than a couple of inches beyond the edge of the sill. Depth can be about 7 in. For drainage purposes, ½-in. holes should be bored in the bottom at intervals of about 9 in. The whole of the outside should be painted, preferably green.

Filling with Soil. To prevent soil being washed out through the drainage holes, these have to be covered with leaf-mould or hop manure or rough stuff from the compost heap, spread an inch thick over the bottom.

Soil as good as can be obtained should be used for filling, to within an inch of the top when made reasonably firm. If soil is scarce, a small outlay at the nurseryman's for a good mixture is justified.

Planting. In autumn, a variety of bulbs can be planted. If the position is windswept, taller subjects such as daffodils, narcissi and tulips and hyacinths should be ruled out, and the shorter things, such as Muscari (grape hyacinth), snowdrops, crocus, chionodoxa and scilla be concentrated on. To hide the bare soil at once, forget-me-nots can be planted as a carpet through which the bulbs will push.

Or the box may be planted with polyanthuses in mixed colours, or double daisies in white, pink or red, or mixed. If the box is not unduly exposed to harsh winds, wallflowers are not ruled out.

For the summer, geraniums or petunias or dwarf antirrhinums will do excellently. If something quite short is required one may choose between viola, white (sweet) alyssum, ageratum and heliotrope (cherry pie), planted in late May. (See Fig. 104.)

Attentions. Watering every day may be needed in late spring and throughout summer, enough being given at a time for some to trickle from the bottom. The soil may dry so that it leaves the sides of the box, a gap presenting itself all around the surface and the water running away as fast as it is given

Fig. 104.—*The window-box (as prepared at Fig. 103) neatly planted and in full summer beauty*

over as often as necessary for faded blooms and withered leaves. And it should not be expected that the common ills to which the garden in general is heir will give the window-box a miss. Green- and black-fly may appear, and slugs and snails and woodlice. These should be dealt with in accordance with instructions in the section PESTS AND DISEASES OF FLOWERS AND VEGETABLES.

Plants that show inclination to topple beneath wind-buffeting may be made firm by pressing around the "collar" with the finger-tips, or unobtrusive but firm stakes may be the solution, with ties as necessary.

The remedy for this shrinkage is to rub a finger-tip or piece of stick around the sides so that the small gap is filled again; then give the water.

The plants should be picked

SECTION XV

HOW TO INCREASE FLOWERING PLANTS

CONSIDERABLE COSTS can be saved in the garden by the simple propagation of plants of all kinds. Methods are as interesting as they are varied, and can be carried out successfully by whoever takes the trouble to avoid the penalty which follows non-observance or defiance of a few simple gardening laws. The legendary "green fingers" are the reward of care and knowledge.

Sowing. The obvious way of increasing plants, and the one most frequently adopted, is to sow seed. The mechanics of the various operations involved, from the preparation of sowing-soil onwards, are explained in Sections VI, VII and VIII, and individual requirements are given in Sections XVI and XXII.

Root Division. This method consists in taking a plant clump to pieces, each piece complete with root or roots, and planting the divisions. This applies to plants of a perennial nature. It is the simplest way of working up, and rejuvenating, stock in the herbaceous border.

A clump of common flag (iris)

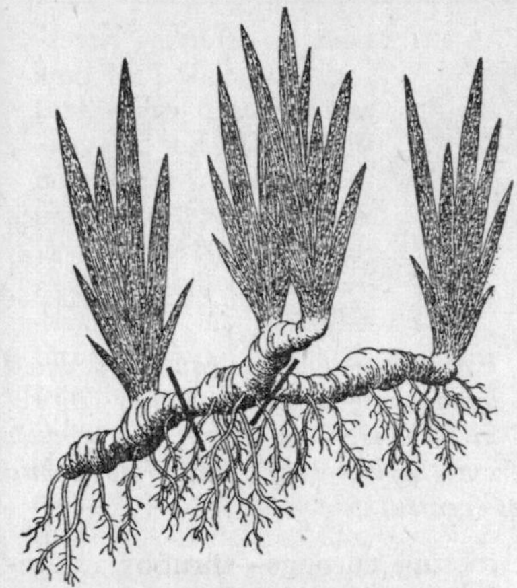

Fig. 105.—*How a clump of flag iris can be divided into portions ready for replanting*

has simply to be levered out of the ground, with the fork, and the brittle root-stocks cut through where division is to be made. Phlox (for example) when it has become an oldish clump is a tougher proposition, the root-mass needing to be levered apart with fork or trowel (Figs. 105 and 106).

Commonly, the centre portion of a clump should be discarded as worn out and the young, outer pieces replanted in good soil, constituting a fresh start. Thus is rejuvenation as well as increase achieved. Most favourable times for root division of this kind are autumn and early spring.

The dahlia lends itself to division, but the operation is of a gentler nature. Dahlia tubers are taken in spring from the indoor winter store and, still in clumps, are packed closely together in light soil, or broken leaf-mould, in boxes, so that they are just covered. Placed in the cold frame or the greenhouse, several shoots will be produced from each clump, and each single tuber carrying an active growth can be separated (carefully) from its old central stem and potted or boxed in fairly rich soil to grow on. Sometimes a half-dozen or more new dahlia plants can be secured from an old clump (see Fig. 107).

Root Cuttings. Anchusa, Oriental poppy, verbascum, phlox, echinacea and other hardy plants with lengthy roots like bits of string or thin rope can be increased by root cuttings. Soil is trowelled

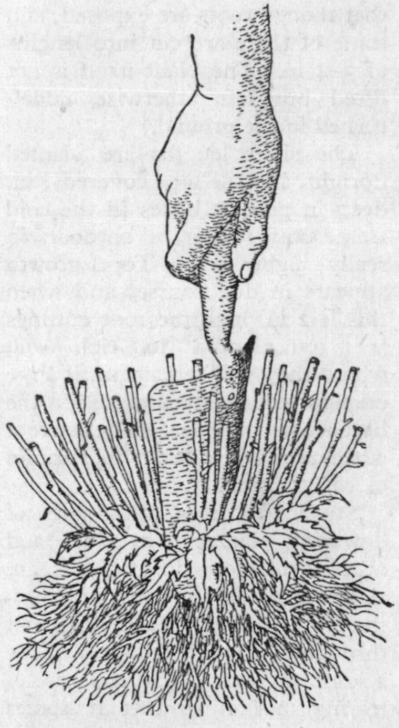

Fig. 106.—*Herbaceous plants which make thick root-masses can be divided into portions with the aid of a trowel thrust forcibly through from above after the mass has been lifted*

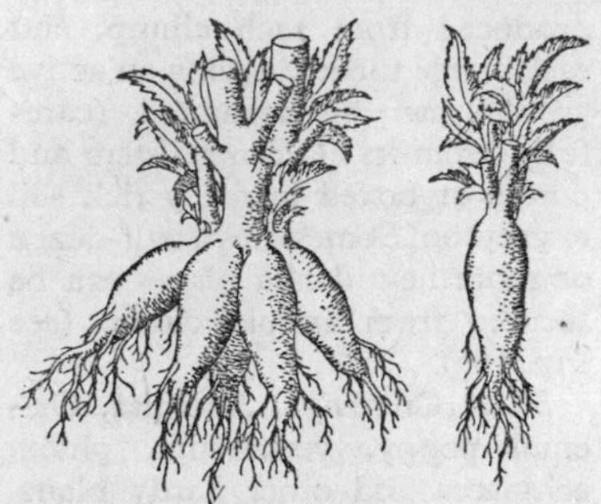

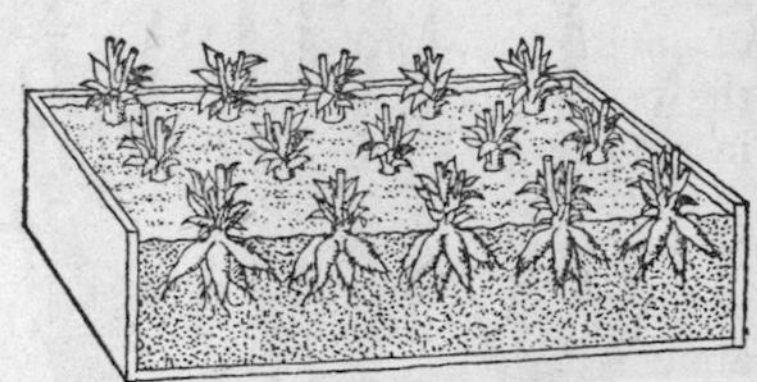

Fig. 107.—*Dahlias can be increased by packing wintered clumps (entire) in a box of soil (right) to produce new shoots. They are then removed from the box (left) and divided into single tubers (centre)*

away from one side of the plant so that thongy roots are exposed, and some of these are cut into lengths of 3–4 in. (The plant itself is not lifted but left otherwise undisturbed in the ground.)

The short lengths are planted upright, and the tops covered ¼ in. deep in pots or boxes in the cold frame until spring, or outdoors in really light soil. Top growth appears in due course, and when this is 2 in. high the root cuttings are transplanted to rich soil, where they will remain until large enough to take their places in the herbaceous border. These root cuttings may be taken in autumn or early spring.

Stem Cuttings. All sorts of flowering plants, from roses and other shrubs to bedding plants, are easily increased by stem cuttings, the piece of stem selected being cut through cleanly immediately below a joint, or removed with a careful tearing motion so that it comes away with a piece ("heel") of the parent plant attached (see Fig. 108).

Dealing with summer bedding plants, September and October are the most favourable months for rooting cuttings—shrubby calceolarias and violas and pansies in the garden frame; geraniums, fuchsias, marguerites and others of that type in the greenhouse. Frame cuttings should be about 3 in. long and

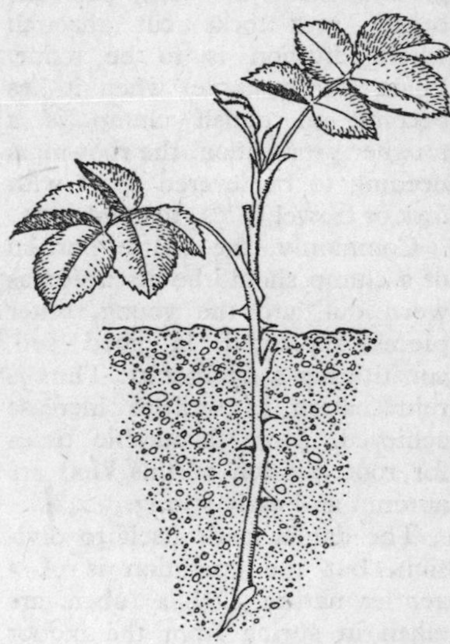

Fig. 108.—*A typical stem cutting (in this instance a rose). The oblique end falls just below a joint, and the stem may be cut through there, or it may end in a "heel" as shown in this illustration*

should be planted 3 in. apart and to the depth of about ¾ in., direct in the bed of the frame or in pots or boxes.

Fig. 109.—*Typical geranium cuttings inserted equidistant in small pot, each touching the side*

Cuttings for striking in the greenhouse (and wintering there) may be about 4 in. long, inserted an inch deep in shallow boxes or small pots, four in a pot 3½ in. across the top, close around the sides (see Fig. 109). The rooting medium should be a good compost containing silver sand and sifted leaf-mould, or as near to that as circumstances allow.

It is a considerable help to successful "strikes" if, before inserting the cuttings, the soil surface is covered with ¼ in. of silver sand: some of this will trickle to the bottom of the planting-hole as the latter is made and the base of the cutting will rest upon it. Flower pots should be properly crocked for drainage, and boxes should have ample holes in the bottom.

After the cuttings are inserted they should be settled in with a moderate watering (using a rosed can) and no more water should be given until the soil shows plainly that it is needed. The garden frame should be kept closed, and shaded against direct sunshine, for two or three weeks; cuttings on greenhouse shelf or bench should likewise be shielded for a time from sunshine.

Preparing Stem Cuttings. Ends of shoots cut off for rooting must not have any ragged portions at the cut, which is to be directly below a joint, and the lowest pair of leaves should be snipped off. They should not be flabby, though with pansies and violas the cuttings are naturally somewhat soft. Geranium cuttings should be really hard and firm, and sun-tinted red or brown; and there will be fewer casualties among them if they are laid out on the greenhouse shelf for a few hours for the cut ends to dry, before inserting. This drying must not be overdone.

Cuttings taken with a "heel" should have the latter trimmed neatly, because ragged tissue is likely to decay and to ruin the prospect of rooting.

The Rooting Period. During winter, cuttings demand all the light possible, whatever air can be given them without risk (stagnant conditions are deadly), and they are happy with the minimum of water. When this *has* to be given it must be kept from the foliage. Yellowing leaves should be picked off (remembering how slight as yet is the cuttings' hold of the soil), and pests watched for.

Little, if any, new top growth will be apparent before spring, and not until ample roots have been produced should boxed or potted cuttings be moved on to ampler quarters, repotted singly in small pots or at least 4 in. apart in boxes.

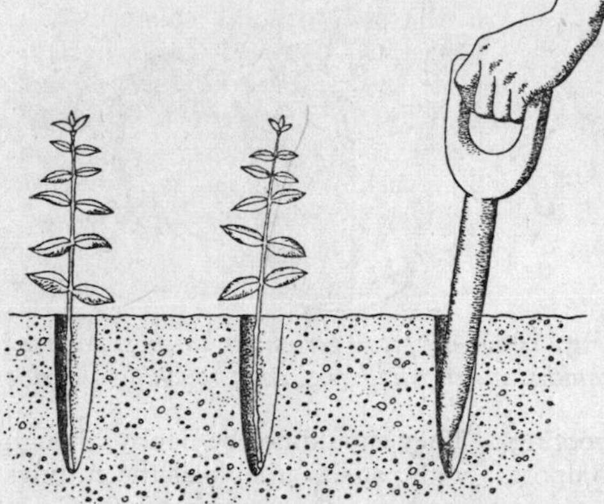

Fig. 110.—*Shrub cuttings inserted about half their depth, in dibber-made holes each with sand or grit at the bottom*

Those in the frame bed may remain there (with increasing quantities of air) until the season is ripe for planting out.

Rose and Shrub Cuttings. These may be a foot or so long, prepared as in a previous paragraph, and should be planted about half their depth in light soil in the open, each in a dibber-made hole with sand or grit at the bottom, the soil around them then being trodden quite firmly (see Fig. 110). They should be given a full year in which to root. Where roses are concerned, this method of propagation applies only to the bush and rambler types; standards are made by budding (which see).

Pipings. These are a form of cutting, in which the shoot is not squared up with a knife below a joint nor has it a "heel" of the parent plant. It is a method specially successful in the case of pinks and carnations.

Selected shoots (they should *not* have flowered) from strong and healthy plants are pulled from their sockets—one hand holding the parent stem, for safety—and then, with no further attention beyond the snipping off of the lowest leaves, are planted about an inch deep in sandy or gritty soil (see Fig. 111).

Only the straightest and healthiest unflowered shoots are worth troubling with. Weakly ones, even if they root, will result in weakly plants. Diseased shoots are certain to spread trouble.

These pipings should be about 3 or 4 in. long, and the time to root them is June–July. They may be inserted 2 in. apart around the rim of small pots in the frame or go direct into the bed of the frame. After they have been watered in, the frame should be closed for three or four weeks and lightly shaded (with newspaper,

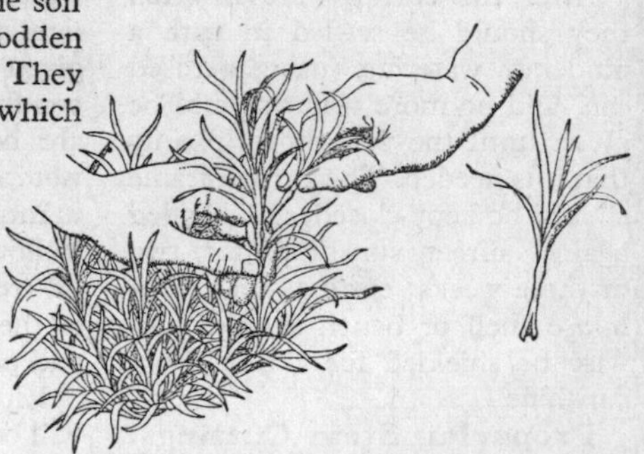

Fig. 111.—*Pinks are easily increased by "pipings"—young, unflowered shoots pulled carefully from their socket (right). One hand should hold the parent stem whilst the piping is pulled upwards*

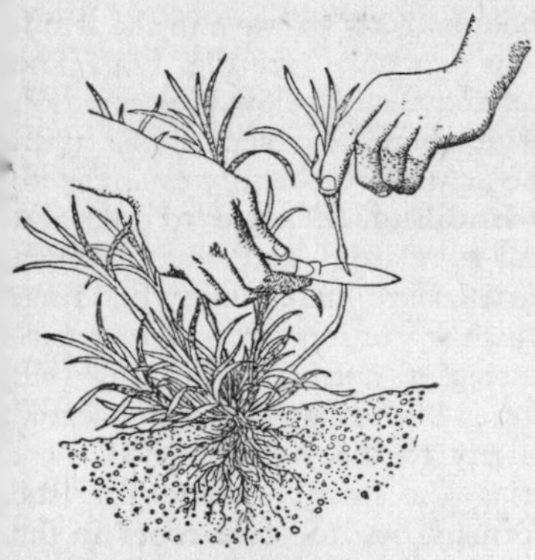

Fig. 112.—*Carnation layering. A nick is made in a chosen, unflowered shoot, about a quarter-inch below a convenient joint, the knife-blade then passing upwards through the joint and a quarter-inch or so beyond*

not heavily with sacks) against continual sunshine. They may then be gradually accustomed to full air, for planting in their flowering quarters in autumn.

Layering. To induce a shoot to send out roots by the layering method it is necessary to make a knife-cut through the shoot, as near to its base as possible, or at a point where the shoot can be persuaded to make easy contact with the soil, then to cover the cut portion with 2 in. of good soil. The shoot must be safeguarded against any movement, and be kept well watered, until rooting has taken place. It is then severed from the parent plant, lifted with its roots—which were produced where the knife-cut was made—and transferred to its own flowering place.

Carnations, bush and rambler roses and a large variety of shrubs can be increased quite easily in this way. Dealing with a carnation plant in the open ground, shoots which have *not* flowered are selected. Near to the base of each a nick is made in the stem $\frac{1}{4}$ in. or so below a convenient joint, the knife-blade then passing upwards through the joint and $\frac{1}{4}$ in. beyond it (see Fig. 112).

The shoot is then pressed gently to the ground so that the cut opens and remains open, 2 in. of good soil being firmed over it at that point. If the shoot shows inclination to rise up, it should be kept in close contact with the ground by means of a wire "pin" (see Fig. 113). If a number of shoots of one plant are to be dealt with, they should all be prepared and then soiled over together. Time to do this is early summer. By the end of autumn abundant roots should be sent out, and the shoots should be in condition for severing from the clump and transplanting; or transplanting may be deferred until the spring. If the plant is in a pot, the

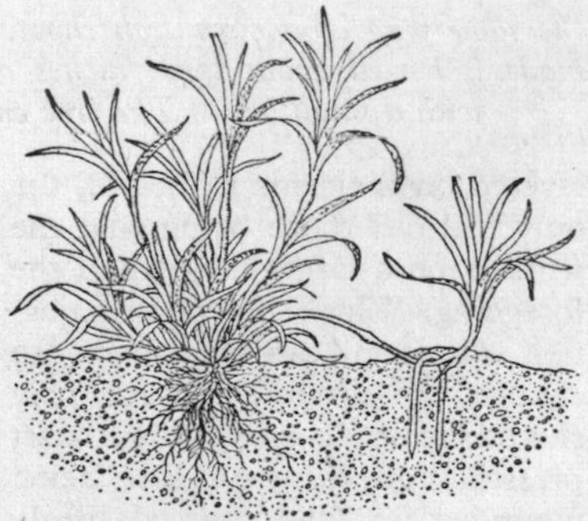

Fig. 113.—*The shoot prepared as in* Fig. 112 *is then gently pressed to the ground, with the cut open as shown, and kept down with a wire pin. Then soil is pressed carefully down over it*

latter may be sunk in the open ground, thus enabling the details to be carried out quite easily without the roots being disturbed. Carnations are very impatient of dry soil, so it is advisable to water the ground around the plant before commencing operations and to keep the soil above the layered portions reasonably moist.

Shoots of bush and rambler roses and shrubs in general are layered on the same principle, the only real difference being that the work is on a larger scale than the foregoing. Where the nicked portion of stem can be made to contact the ground a 3-in. hole should be made and the cut part pressed into it, good soil being mounded up (and pressed firmly down) on it. To prevent the shoot springing out, a weighty stone may be placed above the buried part or a substantial "pin" be used *behind* the cut—that is, towards the parent plant. If the free end of the shoot is likely to wave in the wind, tie it to a stake (see Fig. 114). The soil above and below the operation point should be kept moist until the new plant is firmly established.

Fig. 114.—*A bush or rambler rose or other shrub shoot can be layered in the same way as a carnation shoot. The portion of stem where the cut is made is buried about three inches deep, covered over and weighted down with a small brick. The free end is staked to prevent movement*

Budding. All standard roses and half-standards and many bush varieties are increased by budding, which operation consists in transferring a dormant leaf-bud (*not* flower-bud) taken from any selected variety to the stem or shoot of a briar (the stock) and inducing the dormant bud to "take root" in the briar's own tissue.

The transference takes place in July–August. None of the briar's own leaf growth is allowed below the point of budding, nor beyond it when the bud has definitely "taken." And so the briar is caused to assume henceforth the character and flowers of the rose variety from which that leaf-bud was taken.

The requirements are: (*a*) a briar, or briars, with a good length of perfectly straight stem, for standards, planted the previous autumn for budding in July–

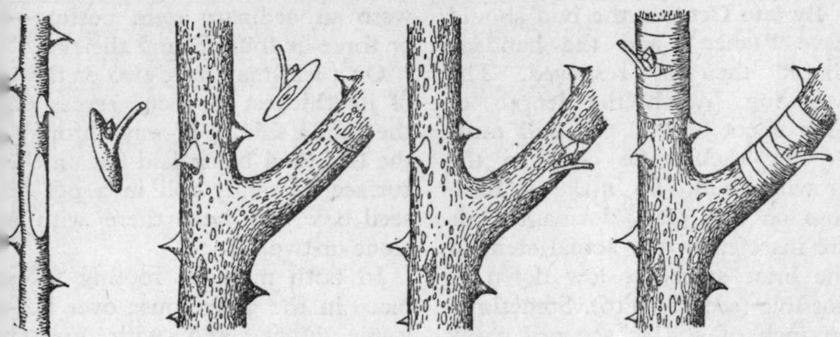

Fig. 115.—*Budding a standard rose. Four stages—left to right:* (1) *bud removed from flowering stem, about half-way down;* (2) *prepared bud in position, seen from underside;* (3) *bud inserted in T-cut;* (4) *two buds inserted and bound with raffia*

August, and (*b*) freshly cut dormant leaf-buds from the variety of rose to be propagated.

To make a standard, three well-spaced shoots or branches at the top of the briar's straight stem are shortened back (if necessary) to a foot in length, and any other shoots there may be are removed. As near as possible to the base of each of the three shoots a slit is made in the soft outer skin, about an inch long, and then a crosswise cut at the slit's outer end.

All the cut edges are then very gently prised up, to allow of a small portion of the tissue taken with each dormant bud to be slipped in. The bud is cut from the parent with about an inch of the parent skin (or outer bark) attached: $\frac{1}{4}$ in. above the bud, $\frac{3}{4}$ in. below it.

The leaf at whose base the dormant bud nestles is cut off, leaving its stem as a most convenient handle. The soft wood backing the bud and strip of skin is very carefully removed, and the bud with its strip is inserted in the T-cut and pressed close to the parent tissue. The edges of the cut are then smoothed down to overlap the bud portion and a bandage of moistened raffia is applied to hold it down, but leaving the actual bud uncovered (see Fig. 115). Contact between the cut surfaces must be near-perfect; and the bandage must not be so tight as to cut the tissue.

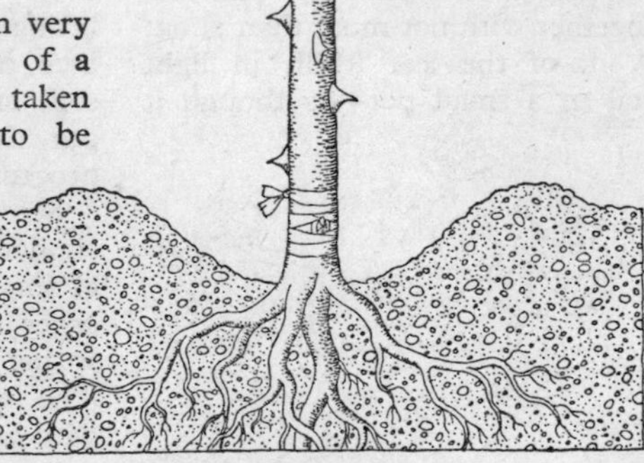

Fig. 116.—*Making a bush rose. The prepared dormant buds are inserted in the actual briar stem, as low down as possible—a little soil being first scooped away to give easier access*

By late October the bud should have "taken" and the bandage should then be removed. The following March the length of briar shoot beyond the bud must be cut back quite close to the growing bud. To make a bush rose on this plan, dormant buds are inserted in the actual stem of the briar stock, as low down as possible (see Fig. 116). Sometimes an inch of soil is scooped away from the briar's base and the buds inserted in that exposed area.

The success of rose budding depends largely on a free flow of sap at the time of operating. To ensure that, in dry weather the ground around the briar should be soaked with water, and kept moist, well in advance; and after the buds are inserted they should be syringed every dry evening.

Leaf Cuttings. Plants which have fleshy, thick-ribbed leaves, such as gloxinias and tuberous begonias, can be increased by inducing a single leaf to take root. A full-grown healthy leaf is cut from the plant with about ½ in. of stalk, and this is inserted, together with not more than about ¼ in. of the leaf itself, in light soil in a small pot—as though it were an ordinary stem cutting—or three or four around the rim.

Fig. 117.—*Offsets of sempervivum will take root if planted up to the neck in gritty soil*

Or a leaf may have two or three of its thickest ribs cut across on the underside, half-way through, the leaf then being laid flat on the surface of sandy soil in a pot or seed box and held there with a stone or two.

In both methods rooting takes place in the greenhouse over hot-water pipes, and with greater certainty if the pot or box is kept very close for a few weeks—as in a larger box with the top completely covered with a sheet of glass, and shaded from direct sunlight.

No more water may be given than is necessary to keep the leaf alive until the stem-tip or the rib-nicks have rooted, which should be in something under two months. The pot or box is then transferred to the more open conditions of the greenhouse shelf, bits of leaf as this withers being picked away. The tiny plants are then grown on as individuals.

Offsets. Bulbous plants make tiny bulbs at their base, commonly overlooked or thrown away at lifting time. If they are planted an inch or so deep, in well-drained soil, and kept watered when top growth appears, they make steady progress to flowering size.

Sempervivums and plants of similar nature are usually prodigal of small offsets which are only too eager to take root any time from spring to autumn (see Fig. 117). The offsets should be removed with whatever length of stem (and root, if any) they possess and inserted as deep as their base in gritty soil in a pot or box, and given the shelter of a frame until growing well.

SECTION XVI

FLOWERS IN DETAIL

ACHILLEA

A GENERAL-PURPOSE flower for the herbaceous border, and especially good for cutting for indoor decoration, achillea blooms throughout the summer. *A. ptarmica* reaches about 2 ft. in height and bears sprays of pure white double flowers. *A. eupatorium* is yellow flowered and reaches 4 ft.

Achillea needs no special attention during summer, and in late autumn the plants are tidied up by having old flower-stems and withered tops removed.

Propagation. A hardy perennial, increase is rapid. Clumps may be lifted and divided and the pieces replanted, in October or March. Seedlings may be raised by sowing outdoors in early summer, shifting the small plants in autumn to a spare patch for spring planting; or the young plants may be set out in autumn where they are to bloom the following year.

AGERATUM

One of the most useful and showy of the smaller plants, dwarf ageratum is invaluable for filling small beds or edging larger ones. It is effective also as a continuous front line to the mixed border. Flowering continues throughout summer.

There are blue and white varieties up to about 9 in. in height, and, good for cutting, a taller blue, reaching about 18 in.

Propagation. A half-hardy annual, ageratum will not serve for a second year. Plants should be discarded after flowering and fresh stock raised by sowing seed in a frame or greenhouse in March, transferring the seedlings, 2 in. apart, into shallow boxes of good soil, and hardening off for planting out in late May where they are to flower, 8 in. apart.

Achillea

AGROSTEMMA

A distinctive plant, with silvery-white foliage and crimson flowers, the perennial species *Coronaria* is known as rose campion. It grows 2 ft. high and flowers during July–August.

The annual species include *Cœli-rosa* (Rose of Heaven), with rose-coloured flowers on 18-in. stems.

Propagation. The perennials

are planted in autumn or early spring, and are easily raised by sowing outdoors in early summer for flowering the following year.

The annuals are raised by sowing in March, outdoors or in boxes in a frame, transplanting to their summer flowering quarters as soon as large enough.

ALSTRŒMERIA

Sometimes known as the Peruvian lily, this hardy perennial flourishes in any sheltered, sunny position. *A. aurantiaca* has spotted, yellow or orange flowers, carried on stems 2–3 ft. high, and blooms in July and August. *A. Ligtu* is very fine with large heads of salmon, rose, terracotta and almost red, on 3-ft. stems, in July and August. It is not quite so hardy as *A. aurantiaca*, but will grow well in a sheltered and sunny position. *A. Ligtu* resents disturbance when once established and should be planted for permanence.

Propagation. The fleshy, tuberous roots of *A. aurantiaca* may be planted, 4 in. deep and about 4 in. apart, in October and April. During these months an established clump may be lifted and the roots divided and replanted. *A. Ligtu* is usually raised from seed sown thinly in a box in frame or greenhouse in March, and the seedlings pricked off into boxes ready for planting out in May or early June.

Withered stems should be removed in late autumn.

ALYSSUM

Sweet alyssum is a familiar hardy annual used for filling small beds and edging larger ones.

It does not exceed about 9 in. in height, and the fragrant small flowers commonly smother the plants. Its dwarf form, Lilac Queen, has pale lilac-coloured flowers. The white variety, Little Dorrit, grows only 3–4 in. high.

Propagation. The hardy annuals are increased by sowing seed in a small box in frame or unheated greenhouse in March, transferring 2 in. apart to other boxes, and planting out when large enough.

Alyssum saxatile compactum is

Anchusa

the hardy perennial golden-flowered kind, very useful indeed for the rock garden. It reaches a height of about 6 in. and spreads in compact masses, flowering in early spring and onwards. Flowering at an end, the plants should be cut over to keep them dwarf for the following year. No winter protection is needed for the old plants.

Propagation. Golden alyssum is increased by sowing seed outdoors in early summer, for the next spring's flowering. Cuttings of young shoots of this perennial may be rooted in a cold frame in April. Time to plant is October or April as most convenient.

ANCHUSA

Sometimes known as bugloss, anchusa provides a colour not too plentiful in the garden—true blue. *A. italica*, 3–4 ft., produces masses of long sprays and it should be given ample space in the herbaceous border and staked as necessary. *A. cæspitosa* is a new and attractive dwarf species that blooms from May until September. Both are hardy perennials.

A hardy annual form reaches about 18 in.

Annual anchusas are persistent seed producers, and it is necessary to pick off sprays of bloom as they fade—to prolong the flowering season, which except in the case of *A. cæspitosa*, takes place in June.

Propagation. The hardy annual may be sown in March, where it is to flower the same year.

The perennials may be divided in October, after the old flowered stems have been cut back to the basal growth. Seed may be sown outdoors, or in a frame, in early summer, for next year's flowering.

ANEMONE

The hardy herbaceous perennials here are represented by the white-flowered Japanese anemone and its varieties (see Plate No. 2). Height is 4 ft., the flowering season August–September. The mixed border is the place for this excellent cut-flower, which will grow well in moderate shade.

Propagation. Roots may be divided in October or March, and seed sown outdoors in early summer for flowering the following year.

Quite different from the foregoing in appearance are the tuberous-rooted perennial anemones, represented by the Poppy and the St. Brigid forms. A variety of colours is available. Height is about 12 in. and flowering occurs in spring, at which season they are very welcome for cutting for indoor decoration. They make effective patches at the front of the mixed border, planted 3 in. deep and 6 in. apart.

Winter Treatment. Although the tuberous kinds are reasonably hardy it is advisable to lift them when the foliage, after flowering, withers and store the tubers indoors away from the damp and frost, for replanting the following March.

Propagation. Seed of the tuberous anemones may be sown thinly outdoors in May, where the plants are to bloom the following year, the seedlings being thinned out to 6 in. apart.

ANTIRRHINUM

The snapdragons give a brilliant and prolonged display throughout the summer and, excepting the dwarf varieties, are excellent for cutting. The tall varieties reach about 3 ft. and should be given plenty of space in the border.

The intermediate varieties are more adapted to the summer flower beds, height being from 15 to 18 in. For quite small beds and for edging large ones the dwarf varieties are admirable.

The plants must be prevented

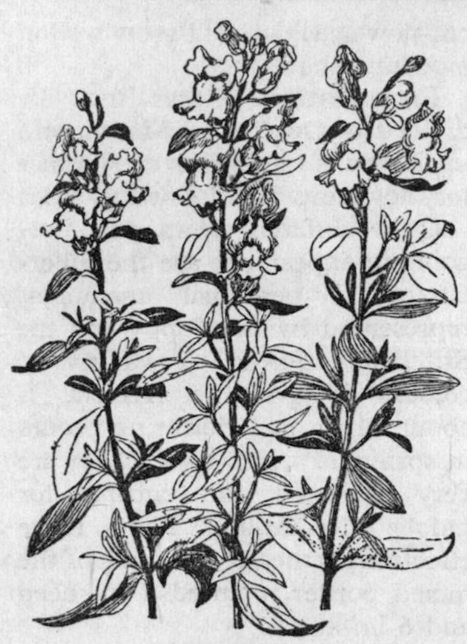

Antirrhinum

from seeding by the regular removal of flowered-out stems, otherwise the season may be shortened.

Propagation. Although antirrhinums are classed as perennials, they are seldom satisfactory after the first year. Plants may be raised by sowing seed in a heated greenhouse from January to March, shifting the small seedlings to boxes and gradually hardening off for planting out after the wallflowers and other spring-flowering plants have had their day.

Seed may also be sown in early summer in boxes in a frame for flowering the following year. Before the frosts or heavy winter rains arrive, the boxes with the seedlings pricked off 3 in. apart should be placed back in the frame.

AQUILEGIA

One of the comparatively few plants that will flower really well in semi-shade (where sun reaches for only part of the day) is the columbine. Red, yellow, white, blue-and-white and other colours are available. Flowering season ranges from May to August and height varies from 1 to 3 ft.

A hardy perennial for the mixed border, it provides many graceful blooms for cutting.

Propagation. Clumps may be divided in October or March, the normal months for planting.

Seed may be sown in the open in June to give strong plants for flowering the following year.

ARABIS

The white, double-flowered variety of arabis or rock cress is a general-utility plant of great value. It can be used as a "carpet" for spring bulbs, for edging, as clumps at the front of the border and for the rock garden, where its trailing habit shows to great advantage.

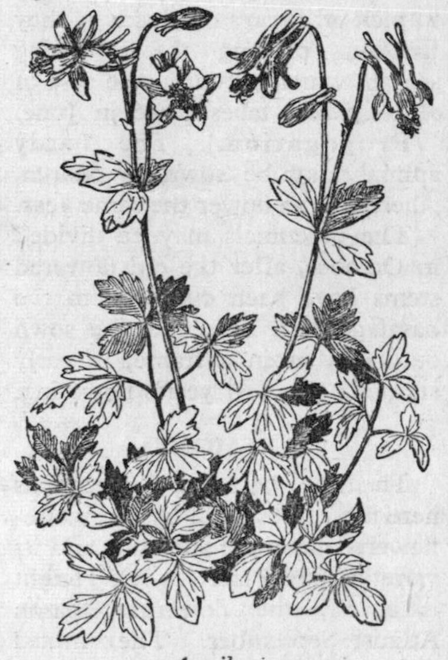

Aquilegia

A hardy perennial, it will stand considerable cutting back when it encroaches on other plants. It grows 4 to 6 in. high.

Propagation. Clumps may be divided during October–November, which is the normal planting time.

Cuttings taken in August root readily in a lightly shaded spot outdoors or in a frame.

Arabis seed in variety may be sown in June in the open ground, the seedlings to be transplanted, when large enough to handle, to where they are to bloom in spring.

ARMERIA

The long-stemmed, rosy-pink flower heads of thrift are effective in a number of ways: for cutting, for providing splashes of colour in the mixed border, as edging for the border or the garden path and for a sunny position in the rockery.

A hardy perennial, its height is about 18 in. and it may be planted in October or March.

Propagation. Clumps may be lifted and divided in autumn or spring, a speedy way of raising a large stock from small beginnings.

Seed may be sown in April, in a frame, the seedlings being shifted early to 2–3 in. apart, and planted out in autumn where they are intended to flower.

ASTER

Popularity came deservedly to the China aster, a half-hardy annual noted for its extensive range of colours. A remarkable diversity of flower forms is shown in the various types, which include Ostrich Plume, Comet, Ray, Victoria and Single (see Plate No. 26). Flowering season is from August to October, and height ranges from 15 in. to 2 ft.

It is in the front rank for cutting purposes, and in August plants may be lifted (after a good watering) and potted for flowering in greenhouse or conservatory.

First-class Blooms. Though one may not require them for show purposes, asters respond so generously to good treatment that it is worth providing them with rich soil: well-dug ground containing rotted material from the compost heap, or old manure.

Habit is naturally bushy, and to enable the plants to branch freely they should be set out at least 18 in. apart. There is a considerable quantity of flower to be borne, and the season can be extended to the utmost by applying liquid manure, or a general-purpose artificial fertilizer, occasionally.

Normally, the plants do not require staking, but if support seems necessary (as it may be in wet weather), this can be given by inserting twiggy pieces of stick unobtrusively among the foliage.

Syringeing with clear water is appreciated, especially in the early stages. At the first sign of wrinkling of the leaves (due to aphis or other pests) an insecticide should be applied—preferably by means of a syringe, the liquid being driven forcibly into the heart of the plants and also against the underside of the leaves.

Propagation. Seed should be sown very thinly and shallowly, during March, in boxes in frame or greenhouse, the seedlings being shifted early, 2 in. apart each way, into other boxes, and hardened off for planting out when about 3 in. high. For somewhat later blooms, sowing may be done outdoors in April. If entire beds cannot be given up to these plants they may be set out, in clumps, in the mixed border.

For perennial asters see Michaelmas daisy.

AUBRIETIA

This hardy perennial evergreen, seldom exceeding 4 in. in height, is admirably adapted to carpeting spring beds, edging beds, borders or paths, and for planting in the rockery. It is available in rose, mauve, lavender, violet and purple, and blooms through spring into early summer, providing lovely banks of colour.

Planting and Treatment. Plants may be set out in October or March. Aubrietia is naturally straggling in nature, but does not resent fairly hard cutting back if that becomes necessary to keep it in place. This should be carried out immediately after flowering.

Propagation. Soft tips of growth taken in June root freely in a shaded frame.

Seed may be sown in May–June, in the open or in a box in the frame, for planting out in autumn where the plants are to flower the following spring. Seedlings vary considerably in colour.

Aubrietia

BALSAM

Equally at home as a pot plant in the greenhouse, as filling for a summer bed, or for planting in the mixed border wherever there may be spaces, the half-hardy annual balsam grows to about 18 in. Colours include white, pink and scarlet. Given good soil and plentiful watering in dry weather, the display is excellent.

Propagation. Seed may be sown outdoors in May, where the plants are to flower, the seedlings being thinned out to allow of ample space. Earlier flowering is secured by sowing in a frame in March–April and planting out in May.

BEGONIA

Some of the most striking examples of summer bedding consist of begonias. Other kinds of begonia provide winter blooms in the warm greenhouse; and the Rex varieties (also for the greenhouse) are notable for their large, handsome foliage (see Plate No. 27). They well repay initial expense.

Tuberous-rooted half-hardy perennial begonias are superb for summer bedding and for growing in pots. There are double and single kinds in various colours, and blooms are sometimes 5 or 6 in. across. Height is about 18 in.

Planting time is late May or early June. Distance, 12 in. apart. Rich soil is desirable, but plants need not necessarily be in full sunshine.

Summer Treatment. Syringeing with an insecticide, before the plants commence to flower, may be necessary if greenfly appear. Otherwise, apart from watering in dry weather, little attention is needed.

Balsam

Winter Treatment. Plants will go on flowering until the first frost. Before the latter can harm them they should be lifted and placed under cover until the withered stems can be removed. All soil should then be shaken from the tubers and these be packed in dry soil, in boxes, for wintering wherever they will be safe from frost and damp.

Starting Stored Tubers. The warmth of a heated greenhouse is desirable for starting the stored tubers into growth, early in March. These should then be removed from the dry soil and placed almost touching in rich, light soil in boxes, the tops of the tubers to be just above the soil surface.

Very careful watering is called for until the new growth is really active. They should be hardened off gradually for planting out in May–June.

Those that flowered in pots in the greenhouse and were duly dried off after flowering should be repotted in fresh, rich soil in March, carefully watered, and grown on for flowering again.

Propagation. New plants may be raised by striking cuttings of the young shoots taken from restarted tubers in the greenhouse.

Seed may be sown in carefully prepared compost in February–March, in the warm greenhouse, the seedlings being transplanted 2 in. apart into shallow boxes and later shifted singly into 4-in. pots. After hardening off they may be set out in their flowering places in late May–June.

Fibrous-rooted, half-hardy perennial begonias (*Semperflorens* type) grow not more than 1 ft. in height and may be used for filling or edging summer beds, also for flowering in pots, in the greenhouse, conservatory or window-box. They must not be allowed to suffer through lack of water.

The small blooms are produced in clusters. A variety of colours is available. They should be planted 6–9 in. apart, soil and summer treatment being similar to that advised for the tuberous-rooted kind.

Winter Treatment. Before damaged by frost the plants may be lifted and boxed in good, well-drained soil for growing on in the warm greenhouse.

Propagation. A few plants only need be saved if it is intended to raise stock from cuttings in spring.

It is less troublesome to sow seed in February–March, as advised for the tuberous-rooted kind, if the necessary facilities are available.

Winter-flowering fibrous-rooted begonias, typified by Gloire de Lorraine, are warm greenhouse plants with large numbers of small pink flowers. Flowering of some of the batch of plants can be deferred until early spring by picking off all flower buds up to about a fortnight from the date when flowers are required.

Staking. To increase their bushiness, young plants of this winter-flowering type should have the tips of shoots pinched off; this induces the production of more shoots. The stems require support, and as many ties as necessary should be given to a central stake (height up to 18 in.) or to three or four stakes around the circumference of the pot.

After Flowering. When the last flowers have faded, much less water should be given, just sufficient to keep the plants alive, until March. Then the soil should be moistened through, and when growth becomes apparent the plants should be removed from their pots, a little of the old surface soil and the crocks removed, and repotted (using pots a size larger) to flower once more.

Propagation. Cuttings of winter-flowering, fibrous-rooted begonias are taken when growth recommences in spring. As the rooted cuttings increase in size they should be transferred to larger pots, until—through a succession of shifts—they are in 6-in. pots, in which the plants will flower.

Foliage Variety Rex is a fibrous-rooted begonia for greenhouse culture from first to last. The large, handsome leaves are in various rich colours.

Liquid manure should be given occasionally during summer, and in winter the plants should be kept growing slowly.

Propagation. Increase of the Rex begonia is by leaf-cuttings (see the section HOW TO INCREASE FLOWERING PLANTS), also by seed sown in spring in the warm greenhouse, the seedlings being shifted through successive sizes of pots until they stand singly in the flowering size (6-in.) pot.

BOCCONIA

The stately plumed poppy, *Bocconia cordata*, is a hardy herbaceous perennial demanding ample space to display its finely cut, greyish foliage. It is a distinctively ornamental subject for a lone position—in a small bed of its own—in a lawn, and it makes an outstanding picture in a wide herbaceous border.

The buff-coloured feathery flowers are produced in July, and the height is 5–6 ft. The flower stems should be cut down after blossoming.

Propagation. Suckers taken from ground level, and planted in pots or a box in the frame in July, should make sturdy young plants for setting out the following April.

Seed may be sown in June, outdoors or in a frame, for planting out the following April.

BRACHYCOME

Swan River daisy is a hardy annual in the cut-flower class. It will flower throughout summer in a sunny border. Colours are blue, mauve and white. Height is about 1 ft.

Propagation. Seed sown in March–April in a frame, for planting out when large enough in

Brachycome

May, will result in early flowers. Or seed may be sown outdoors, in the flowering position, in April, the seedlings to be thinned out well.

CALCEOLARIA

The half-hardy perennial class of calceolaria is an old favourite for summer bedding. Of shrubby habit, height is about 1 ft., and flowers are obtainable in a variety of colours.

Plants should be massed, at about 9 in. apart, for best effect.

Winter Treatment. After flowering, if just a few plants are concerned they may be lifted, cut back half-way, and wintered in a frame for replanting outdoors the following year. It is less bother to take cuttings and discard the old plants.

Propagation. Short shoots, not more than 4 in. long, may be taken as cuttings in September–October and planted 3 in. apart in shallow boxes, for growing on in a frame. The latter should be covered with matting or sacking when frost threatens and the interior of the frame be kept dry. In spring, when growth is active, the rooted cuttings should be given fresh soil in other boxes, at 4 in. apart, and gradually hardened off for planting out towards the end of May.

Greenhouse Calceolarias are larger flowered than the foregoing, up to 2 ft. in height and available in a range of colours. They are treated as biennials: sown for flowering (under glass) the following year (See Plate No. 13.)

General Treatment. A winter temperature of 45 deg. is desirable. When growth is really active the plants should be lightly syringed (with clear water of the same temperature as the greenhouse) occasionally and the immediate surroundings moistened; dry atmosphere must be avoided. Light shading from direct sunshine is also necessary. When the flowering-size pots are filling with roots, weak liquid manure should be given twice a week—up to the appearance of colour in the buds.

Propagation. From a sowing in May–July (in the greenhouse) plants will be had in flower during May–August the following year. The extremely small seed is covered with the merest sprinkling of very fine soil, and the seedlings shifted singly to quite small pots ("thumb" size), thence to pots 3½- to 4-in. top diameter. In these they pass the winter, a shift to the flowering-size pot (6–7 in. diameter) taking place in March.

CAMPANULA

Hardy perennials for the mixed border, these campanulas flower on long stems most useful for cutting. Varieties are to be had in white and in various shades of blue, up to

4 ft. in height, the main species being *Persicifolia*, *Lactiflora* and *Glomerata*.

General Treatment. Graceful in habit, flowering stems may need to be given inconspicuous stakes. Flowers as they fade must be picked off—precautionary note being made of the fact that follow-on flower buds are produced just behind each original flower. Scissors or fingers should do the severing—without tugging. When the season definitely is over the old flowered stems should be cut down.

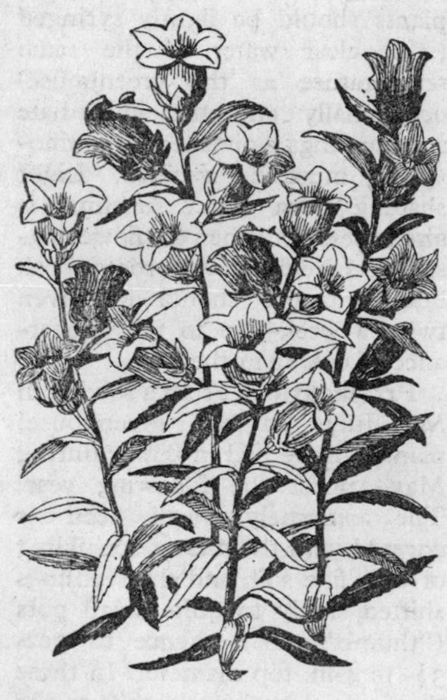

Canterbury Bell

Propagation. Root-clumps may be divided in autumn and spring. Seed may be sown in June, in a prepared patch outdoors or in a box in the frame, for transplanting in autumn to next year's flowering positions.

CANARY CREEPER

This member of the nasturtium (Tropæolum) family is distinctive by reason of its bright yellow flowers and its useful habit of quickly covering whatever it is set to clamber over—trellis, archway and so on.

A half-hardy climbing annual, it will reach a height of about 10 ft., flowering from early summer well into autumn.

Propagation. Seed should be sown outdoors in April where the plants are to flower, in poor soil, the seedlings being thinned out to at least a foot apart.

CANDYTUFT

The hardy annual candytuft (see Plate No. 18) is an admirable gap-filler along the front of the herbaceous border. Its flowers, 6–12 in. high, in rich colours, are produced throughout the summer. It is known botanically as *Iberis*.

Propagation. Seed of annual candytuft should be sown in March–April, where the plants are to flower, and thinned out to about 6 in. apart.

Evergreen Perennial Candytuft, in various colours, 6–9 in. in height, provides valuable early blossom in spring in patches in the rockery or at the front of the mixed border.

Propagation. Seed of the perennial candytuft may be sown in a box in the frame in April and planted out when large enough, to flower the following spring.

The roots may also be divided, in autumn or early spring.

CANTERBURY BELL

The best known of the campanulas (see also under that name), the hardy biennial Canterbury bell provides a wonderful display in the mixed border through the early summer months. It is to be had in a variety of lovely colours, in single, double, and cup-and-saucer varieties, up to 3 ft. in height.

General Treatment. Plants should be set out at not less than 18 in. apart. It is necessary to nip off all blooms as they fade (a daily task) or the plants soon become exhausted.

Propagation. Seed may be sown in the open in late spring or early summer, the seedlings, before they crowd, being shifted to 6 in. apart to make big plants for setting out in autumn or the following early spring in their selected flowering places.

CARNATION

Hardy perennial border carnations, in the mixed border or in a bed to themselves, will flower in summer and provide a quantity of long-stemmed blooms for cutting. There is a considerable range of colour, and height is about 2 ft. (see Plates No. 24 and 25).

How and When to Plant. September–October is the most favourable season for planting, or early spring—not later than April. The soil needs to be well dug and drained, and lime should be added if not already present in any quantity.

Plants should be set out about 18 in. apart, in a sunny position, and the soil made quite firm around them. Border carnations are thoroughly hardy and may remain undisturbed for 3–4 years.

Summer Treatment. Drought is not conducive to flowering; frequent hoeing, and watering as necessary, and prompt removal of weeds, are essentials. Liquid manure or general fertilizer may be given at 10-day intervals when the flower-stems begin to "push."

Stakes will be needed before the weighty growths begin to topple.

To produce large, well-formed blooms in the show class, each flowering stem should be allowed to carry only one flower, all buds below the topmost being removed—very cautiously, with finger-nails or the tip of a penknife.

Carnation Troubles. Greenfly and other pests of carnation foliage can be abolished by syringeing with a nicotine spray; they must not be allowed to become numerous.

Stem eelworm may cause sudden collapse of a plant here and there; the plant should be removed, complete with roots and attached soil, and burned, this being a most infectious ailment.

Wireworms sometimes eat through roots and stems; the underground pests should be destroyed by dressing the soil with Bamfirite or naphthalene at the rate of 3 oz. per sq. yd.

Badly spotted and blotched leaves should be cut off and burned, the attacked plants then being dusted with sulphur.

Propagation. Border carnations may be increased by layering and by seed.

Only strong, young (unflowered) shoots on the best plants are worth layering, in July–August, after flowering, the rooted layers to be lifted and transferred in autumn to the flowering site or potted or boxed and wintered in a frame. Autumn planting is preferable. (For method see page 107.)

Seed sown in February–March, in greenhouse or frame, the seedlings grown on in boxes or singly in small pots, hardened off, and planted out in October, secures specially good results. Or seed may be sown in June, in a frame, and the seedlings grown on as hardily as possible for spring planting.

Annual Varieties of carnation, in various colours and about 18 in. high, are sown in February, in a frame or unheated greenhouse, for flowering outdoors in August of the same year. Before frost comes, the strongest of these annual varieties may be lifted and potted to continue flowering for a time indoors.

Cerastium

Perpetual-flowering carnations constitute a class specially useful for winter and spring flowering in the greenhouse where the heat in winter can be kept up to an even temperature of 45 deg. There is the further advantage that plants after flowering under glass may be planted out in the open in May to continue flowering until early September, when they should be repotted and returned to the greenhouse.

Propagation. Cuttings of perpetual-flowering carnations taken in spring provide plants for flowering (under glass) the following spring. They generally root quite easily.

Seed may be sown in January to secure plants to bloom in the following winter. To cause the young plants to become bushy, the top of the seedling is removed when the plant is about 6 in. high. When the additional shoots which arise from that "stopping" have themselves made 6 in. of growth their tops are pinched off, this second operation being timed to take place not later than the end of June.

CELOSIA

The half-hardy annual *Celosia plumosa*, given rich soil and a sunny spot, makes a decidedly gay summer bed. Up to 2 ft. in height, the large feathered plumes are in yellow, scarlet, crimson and other colours.

Celosia cristata, the cockscomb (so called from the resemblance of its huge flower-heads to a cock's comb), in various colours, is equally effective.

Propagation. Seed may be sown early in the year in a heated greenhouse, or in April in a frame, for planting out of doors in late May or early June.

CERASTIUM

Known familiarly as snow-in-summer, from the dense covering of small, starry, white flowers above the 6-in. carpet of ornamental foliage, *Cerastium tomentosum* is a hardy perennial of astonishingly rampant growth.

It may be used for edging, for planting in ample space in the rockery, and for speedily covering any waste area. It flourishes in the poorest, dry and stony ground.

It needs to be kept within limits, ·t only by cutting hard back after ·wering but by uprooting the ·er-spreading outlying portions of ·ch clump.

Propagation. Seed may be ·wn in the open, in June, for ·ansplanting, and clumps may be ·vided in March, even the smallest ·visions generally possessing roots.

CHERRY PIE

The delightfully scented helio- ·ope or cherry pie is a half-hardy ·erennial requiring a sunny posi- ·on and good soil. In an outdoor ·ed it will reach 2 ft. in height before ·e end of summer. It is to be had ·ı lilac and purple.

Planting-out time is late May, ·r June, when there is no risk of ·rost, and the plants should be ·taked when the need becomes ·vident.

It is adapted also to pot culture. ·s a permanent occupant of the ·eated greenhouse it may be trained up pillars and over rafters.

After Flowering. Heliotrope plants will not survive the first frost outdoors. They may be lifted and repotted in September, removed to the greenhouse, kept rather dry throughout winter, and side shoots and withered tips pruned back during February.

Propagation. Seed may be sown in early spring in the heated greenhouse, for planting out in late May.

Cuttings of shoots about 3 in. long may be taken in March or in August in the greenhouse.

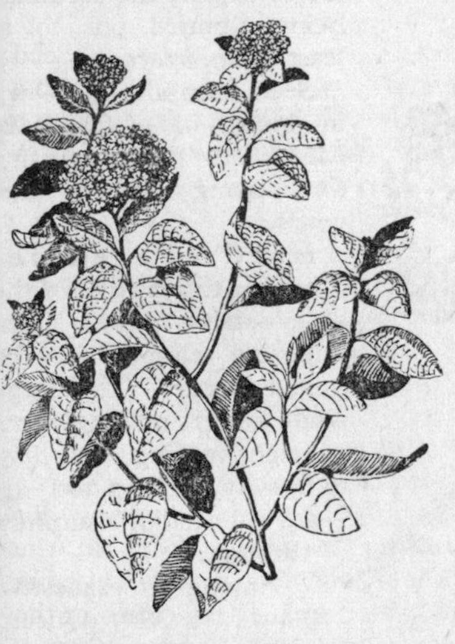

Cherry Pie

CHIONODOXA

The beautiful little March-flowering chionodoxa has earned for itself the title Glory of the Snow. A hardy bulbous plant, it is typified by the form *Luciliæ*, 6 in. high, carrying dainty, star-shaped, blue-and-white blossoms.

It does well in a sunny position in the rockery and the bulbs should be planted in September, 2 in. deep and about an inch apart, remaining undisturbed for 3–4 years; after which they should be lifted and replanted in fresh soil.

In pots, for indoors, chionodoxa does equally well. Several may be grown in a well-drained pot, covered an inch deep and spaced an inch apart, in September. The pot or pots should be stood outdoors, with sifted household ashes piled around and above to the depth of about 2 in. Little top growth but plenty of root formation will occur from then until January or March, when the pots should be taken into the greenhouse, or inside a sunny window, for flowering.

Propagation. Offsets are produced around the bulbs, and these may be removed (after lifting) in September and planted as already described in detail.

CHRISTMAS ROSE

A winter-flowering hardy perennial for the open border, *Helleborus niger*, 1 ft. high, produces white flowers when bloom is specially precious, from December to March. *Helleborus orientalis*, in pink, bronze or purple, reaches about 15 in.

Planting. Roots may be set out about a foot apart, in rich soil but not too sunny a position, in October or March.

It is an advantage if some rough protection can be given overhead—as with odd pieces of glass—in the event of snow or heavy rains when flowering time approaches.

To prevent the flowers being soil-splashed in rainy weather (when overhead shelter cannot be arranged) a surface layer of dried bracken or something similar may be put down around the roots.

Chionodoxa

Propagation. Clumps may lifted and divided in July. Seed m be sown, in a frame, in winter. rich, moist soil is needed.

CHRYSANTHEMUM

Remarkably diverse types ma this big family one of the mc useful, as it is also one of the mc abundant-flowering, of all cult vated plants. For general decorati purposes, in the open garden, greenhouse and conservatory, ar for cutting, chrysanthemums a not excelled (see Plates No. 30–31

Hardy Annual Chrysanthe mums are suitable for the mixe border, for beds and for windov boxes.

They are obtainable in variou colours, height ranging from 1½ t 3 ft.

Propagation. Annual chrysan themums are increased by sowin seed outdoors from March to Ma (this extended period securing succession of plants) where the are to flower, the seedling being thinned out to a least 12 in. apart.

Seed may also be sown in boxes in a frame in March, to provide plant for setting out in du course.

Hardy Perennia Chrysanthemums, of th ox-eye-daisy type, form imposing clumps in the mixed border. The large white flowers on long stems —height varying, according to variety, from 2 to 3 ft. —are to be had the summer through.

Among the earliest to flower is May Queen. In June, Shasta Daisy ens its big buds, and the new irral Pride unfolds in July.

Requirements. This hardy per- nial type may be planted in :tober or March, in good soil. irge clumps will have formed by : third or fourth year. They ould then be lifted, divided, and planted; the soil first being riched, if they are again to occupy e same position.

Propagation. Simple root- vision in autumn or spring pidly increases the stock.

Seed may be sown in early ımmer (April–July) in the open ound or in a box, for trans- anting, when large enough to ındle, to a prepared position here they will grow on for planting ı autumn or spring in their owering places.

Border Chrysanthemums of ıe familiar "bush" kind are btainable in a great range of amed varieties and colours, in eight up to 3 ft. or more, for owering outdoors from August nwards. The Korean group has ıostly single flowers and is valu- ble for border effect.

When ample growth has been ıade they may also be lifted and otted for flowering in the unheated reenhouse or conservatory.

Young Plants. Purchased border hrysanthemums are generally in he form of quite small rooted uttings, for planting in the open order from mid-April onwards.

They should be set out not less han 18 in. apart, in ground that ıas been deeply dug and is not poor. To make these small plants bushy ınd therefore productive of a greater quantity of bloom, each hould have its tip nipped off at ıbout the end of May. This results

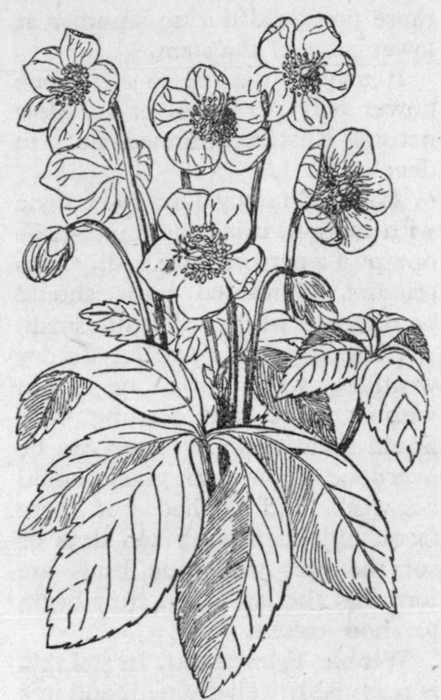

Christmas Rose

in more shoots per plant, and these in turn should have their tips removed towards late June.

So accommodating are these border chrysanthemums that they may be transplanted from a nursery up to the time of commencing to flower, providing they are shaded for a few days after transplanting, syringed daily, and kept well watered.

Staking. Support in the form of pea sticks should be given early, or the first downpour of rain will almost certainly bring the stems down to ground level.

Thinning-out Buds. Some sacrifice in the number of flowers per plant is called for if individual blooms or clusters are to be up to standard. This involves the removal of some buds where they are crowded in big clusters, and of all those produced during summer at lower parts of the stem.

It may be desired to allow one flower only per stem, or to allow natural clusters (thinned out) to develop.

This bud removal has to be done with caution, using the finger-nails or tip of a penknife or small, sharp scissors. Unwanted buds should be removed whilst still quite small.

Watering and Feeding. In dry weather, water may be given without stint; but feeding with liquid manure or fertilizer can be overdone. Whatever is given should be weak, and applied not more frequently than every ten days or so: the first when the buds are forming, the last when they begin to show colour.

Winter Treatment. In soil that is reasonably well drained, and in a not too severe winter, border chrysanthemums may be left undisturbed after flowering—apart from cutting down the old tops, and the division of clumps when these are becoming large.

Choice kinds, however, will be safer if lifted and the clumps packed closely together in lig soil in a frame or substantial wood box with a glass cover. Protecti from undue moisture and ha frost is all that is required.

Propagation. Seed may sown in a heated greenhouse February, for flowering outdoo the same year. The easiest meth (and one to be adopted with choi named varieties) consists in divi ing the clumps, in April, into many single shoots as can be tease away with a few roots.

Greenhouse Chrysanthe mums. Japanese and decorativ chrysanthemums, of which ther are many named varieties, f winter flowering under glass a grown throughout in pots.

They may be purchased a rooted cuttings in (or out of) ver small pots, and though at first the require some artificial heat (if the are to be in the show class) the are later grown on as hardily a possible.

Unfortunately, transferring the from the small pots straightway t the ultimate flowering pots—10 in or more top diameter—is no

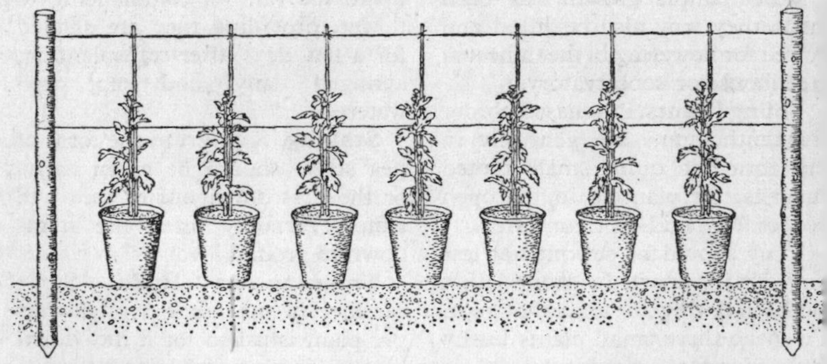

Fig. 118.—*When pot chrysanthemums are placed out of doors, about the end of April, thin stakes may be tied to wires strained between end-posts to prevent the wind blowing them over*

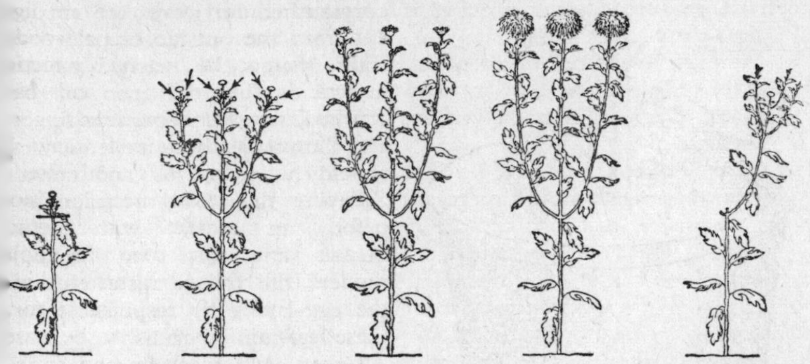

Fig. 119.—*Stages in disbudding chrysanthemums. Only three blooms should remain on each stem. The plant on right is the result of not removing surrounding shoots when small. The bud will not develop*

possible. There must be a succession of moves, through various sizes, as the pots become filled with roots.

At about the end of April the plants are given tall stakes and the pots are placed in full sunshine outdoors, there to remain until taken into the greenhouse for flowering. (See Fig. 118.)

Three Stems Only. Generally, the big-bloom greenhouse chrysanthemums are restricted to three stems only per plant, each of the three terminating in a single flower. No other bud or side growth is allowed to develop.

The plant starts, of course, with a single stem, and this is caused to produce the desired three stems by cutting off the top of the young plant in, say, mid-April (though in some varieties the young plant "breaks" naturally into the desired side growth). The date of this and subsequent operations depends on the variety, guidance being given in the specialists' lists.

Removal of the tip (or the natural "break" itself) may cause more than three shoots to develop. If so, the strongest three only are allowed to remain. Some weeks later a flower bud will develop at the top of each, together with tiny shoots. Those shoots are to be rubbed away, or removed with a penknife tip, the bud remaining. That is known as "securing or taking the bud." (See Fig. 119.)

Those "first crown" buds (three in number) will become the big blooms. If the variety is to be flowered as "second crown" buds, the first bud appearing on each of the three shoots must be nipped out, and all but one of the little shoots clustering around it removed. This still leaves three shoots only, and in due course these will produce buds at their tips—three "second crown" buds, which will be allowed to develop without competition from any other buds or shoots.

If "terminal" buds are desired, the "second crown" buds and all but one of the surrounding shoots must be removed: again leaving the plant with only three shoots, which

Fig. 120.—*Cuttings of pot-flowered chrysanthemums should be made from small shoots arising direct from the soil*

will in due course be surmounted by clusters of "terminal" buds, each cluster to be reduced to one flower bud only.

Propagation. Big-bloom indoor chrysanthemums after flowering should have the stems cut down almost to soil level, the soil in the pots being kept just short of really dry. Shoots produced direct from the soil (not from the stem bases) are removed as cuttings in January and onwards and struck in light soil in small pots placed in a glass-topped box in the greenhouse. Rooting takes, as a rule, about three weeks, after which the potting-on processes commence. (See Fig. 120.)

Chrysanthemum Troubles. The leaf-mining maggot, whose activities within the tissues of chrysanthemum leaves are apparent from the outside as pale thin trails, cannot be reached by an insecticide; but the grub can be crushed, in position, between finger and thumb. Badly tunnelled leaves should be picked off and burnt. Spraying the leaves occasionally, before an attack, with weak quassia and soft soap (mixed) renders the foliage distasteful to the egg-laying fly responsible for these leaf-mining grubs.

Green- and black-fly and thrip do great damage to growing points. They should be destroyed by spraying with a good insecticide or dusting with an insecticide powder.

Earwigs should be trapped in inverted empty pots stuffed lightly with dry crumpled newspaper or moss or hay, supported on sticks among the plants. They go to the

Cineraria

pots for shelter, and should be turned out and destroyed.

In the greenhouse, pest destruction and prevention is achieved by fumigation with one of the numerous proprietary articles marketed for this purpose.

CINERARIA

Favourite greenhouse pot-plants, cinerarias offer an extensive colour-range in the *Stellata* class (up to 2 ft. high, and branched) and in the large-flowered varieties (shorter, and generally unbranched).

General Treatment. Overwatering has to be sedulously avoided; result of carelessness in this direction is limp leaves, a sudden partial collapse of foliage. There is no remedy.

Plants may be considerably weakened by the leaf-miner. For treatment see preceding paragraph, Chrysanthemum Troubles.

Light shade from direct sunshine should be provided at all stages.

Propagation. A greenhouse biennial, seed may be sown in the greenhouse (slightly heated) in April for winter flowering, or in June for flowering the following spring. The seed should be sown very thinly and shallowly and the young plants potted on, in stages, before roots occupy all the soil.

CLARKIA

In pink, white, mauve and other colours, the hardy annual clarkia (see Plate No. 18) is an outstanding decoration for any mixed border throughout the summer, and the cut-flowers are long-lasting in water.

Tall varieties grow up to 2½ ft., others up to 1½ ft.

Convolvulus

Ordinarily good soil suffices, away from shade. Clarkias may also be grown in pots.

Propagation. Seed may be sown, thinly, where the plants are to remain and flower, in March, the young plants being early thinned out to 6 or 9 in. apart.

Where slugs and woodlice are specially troublesome to seedlings, sowing may be done in a box in a frame, the seedlings being planted out when they have made about 2 in. of growth and then surrounded with soot.

CONVOLVULUS

For quickly covering trellis, archways and similar objects, the hardy annual climbing convolvulus is most useful. A range of colours is available, and height is up to about 8 ft. Varieties in the minor class are non-climbers, height being about 12 in.; these are useful for bedding.

Propagation. Seed should be sown in March where the plants are to flower and the seedlings thinned out to about 1 ft. apart.

Those known also as ipomæa are not quite hardy and should not be sown outdoors before early May. These are excellent also for clothing greenhouse pillars.

COREOPSIS

Long-stemmed flowers for cutting, and ability to thrive in unpromising town gardens, are the hall-marks of coreopsis. Its place is the mixed border.

In various colours, the hardy annual varieties range in height between 18 in. and 3 ft.

Coreopsis

Propagation. The annual varieties may be sown outdoors in March, where they are to flower, and thinned out.

Perennial varieties of coreopsis, such as the yellow-flowered *grandiflora*, reach about 2½ ft. in height.

Propagation. Seed of perennial varieties may be sown in June, in the open ground or in a box in the frame, for planting out in autumn to flower the following year.

Increase of the perennial kinds is also by division of clumps in autumn or spring.

CORNFLOWER

There are annual and perennial forms of cornflower and neither demands much skill in cultivation. Both are splendid in the mixed border or for cutting in early summer. *Centaurea cyanus*, the annual cornflower mostly grown (see Plate No. 19) is available with blue, purple, pink and white flowers on stems up to 3 ft.

Good soil, a sunny position, early thinning out and ample watering are necessary aids to strong and prolonged flowering.

Propagation. Seed may be sown in March, where intended to flower, and the seedlings thinned to 6 in. or more apart. For early spring flowering a sowing made outdoor in early autumn should succeed if the soil is well drained, the winter not too severe and soil pests not troublesome.

Of the perennial cornflowers, *C. montana* and *macrocephala* are two of the best. The former blooms in May and early June, has blue and white flowers, and is of a rather sprawling habit, whilst the latter blooms in July with yellow flower heads, in form rather like a thistle. Both are quite hardy and may be increased by division of the roots as soon as growth appears in spring.

Reasonably good soil is wanted. If rich, the plants are likely to continue leaf production at the expense of flowers.

COSMEA

The large, long-stemmed flowers of cosmea—in white and various shades of rose and crimson—are set off to advantage by light, feathery foliage, and both flowers and foliage are long-lasting when cut for house decoration.

A half-hardy annual for the mixed border, cosmea needs plenty of space in which to develop, tall varieties making imposing bushes up to 4 ft. in height; dwarf varieties are limited to about 2 ft.

Early Flowering. Cosmea varieties listed as "early" are preferable. Late ones are often caught by frost before they have attained anything like full beauty. Normally, flowering persists through summer until frosts put an end to all the half-hardy annuals.

Reasonably good soil is wanted. If too rich, the plants are likely to continue leaf-production at the expense of flowers. If the trend seems to be in that direction, overgrowth can be checked by gently levering the plant up with spade or fork so that some roots are broken.

Propagation. Seed sown very thinly in pots or boxes in a frame or greenhouse during February–March should give sturdy plants for setting out, 2 ft. or so apart, towards the end of May (after hardening off).

The seedlings should be shifted early, singly into small pots or 2 in. apart into boxes, for growing on.

CROCUS

A hall-mark of spring in the garden is the crocus, that hardy little bulbous plant which makes such a lovely edging to the mixed border, lights up odd pockets in the rockery, and is so much at home in grass which need not be mown short until the crocus tops have had their day and ripened and withered (see Plate No. 6).

Planting the Bulbs. Holes about 3 in. deep and 3 in. apart should be made with a trowel and the small corms dropped singly to the bottom, right side up.

Time for this is October–December. The earlier-planted corms give better results the following spring.

After Flowering. Crocus corms may be left undisturbed for four to five years at a time, when they should be lifted and the clusters divided for replanting.

Lifting time is June–July. Anywhere under cover and dry (and safe from mice) suffices as a storage place until replanting time. It weakens plants for the following year if the old foliage is removed before it has quite withered.

Propagation. When old flowered corms are lifted, young cormlets will be found attached. These may be detached, and planted in autumn.

New plants can be raised from seed sown in a box in a frame in autumn; but three or four years must pass before the flowering size is attained.

Autumn-flowering Crocus. The less familiar autumn-flowering kinds are happiest in a mixed border or in grass where they can remain undisturbed. Planting time is August–September.

CYCLAMEN

The exotic-looking greenhouse cyclamen differs considerably in its requirements from the lesser-known hardy outdoor cyclamen. The former is exclusively for pot culture under glass. (See Plate No. 13.) The outdoor varieties give no trouble at all.

Hardy Cyclamens. These are perennials, reaching to about 6 in. in height. There are spring-flowering and autumn-flowering species, in shades of red and pink or white.

Planting the Corms. Time to plant is August–September, about 2 in. deep and 2–3 in. apart, in peaty soil, or loam containing plenty of leaf-mould.

They show to advantage in the rockery; better still, massed at the foot of a tree where the ground is otherwise bare (with peat or leaf-mould dug in).

After Flowering. The small foliage, ivy-leaf shape, and attractively mottled, should be allowed to wither away, the corms remaining undisturbed. Subsequent flowering is further encouraged if some of the old surface soil is scraped away and replaced with fresh good soil.

Propagation. The hardy outdoor cyclamen can be increased by sowing seed (a packet of mixed colours giving excellent results) in a box in a cold frame in summer, the small seedlings being planted out the following spring and allowed time in which to establish themselves for flowering.

Indoor Cyclamen. These lovely plants are most simply grown from corms, purchased from a nurseryman and already in some condition of active growth or in a dormant condition. The alternative is seed sowing. Normal flowering period is November to late April.

Winter Treatment. In the heated greenhouse, watering must not be neglected. The soil in the pots should be kept evenly moist (not sodden), and water should not be poured on to the corm—the top of which must be above the level of the soil.

Flowers and leaves that wither should be removed at the base: that is, where they rise from the corm.

The supply of water should be lessened when the flowers have faded.

Summer Treatment. When there is no longer danger from frost, the pots of flowered-out cyclamen should be placed out in the open, in light shade. Little water will be needed until about late August, when the corms should be removed from the old soil and repotted in fresh compost, ready for removal to the heated greenhouse (for flowering again) in late September.

Propagation. Greenhouse cyclamen may be raised from seed (obtainable in a variety of colours) sown in August–September in light and rich soil, in a temperature of about 55 deg. The seedlings should be removed singly to 3-in. pots the following March–April, by which time the corms should be more or less the size of peas.

The next shift, about June, will be into the flowering-size pots: 5 or 6 in. top diameter. From then, until removed to the greenhouse, the pots may stand in a frame, with light shade from direct sunshine.

At all times the top of the corm should rest just above the soil surface to prevent moisture from settling in the hollow crown and causing decay.

DAFFODIL

The hardy bulbous daffodil (botanically a section of narcissus) is obtainable in a large variety of flower forms and colours (see Plate No. 4). The chief use is for growing in beds, for spring flowering. It is also very effective when planted in grass, the one drawback to this position being that the grass should not be cut whilst any of the foliage is green. Small clumps may also be employed to enliven the rockery, and window-boxes may be made gay with daffodils. The mixed border may be included as a planting site.

There is no difficulty in growing them in pots for out-of-season flowering in the greenhouse (cold or heated) or the home.

For Outdoor Flowering. Bulbs should be planted if possible in October whilst the soil is still warm, though later planting is not necessarily unsuccessful.

Planting holes should be made with a trowel, the top of the bulb resting about 4 in. below the soil. They may be spaced 4–6 in. apart.

After Flowering. Foliage should be allowed to remain on until it is quite withered and comes away at a slight tug.

Daffodils which have to be removed from the flower beds to make room for summer occupants should be temporarily replanted in an odd spot for growth to be completed, after which the bulbs should be lifted, all soil removed, and then stored under cover until planting time comes again.

Clumps in the border may be left undisturbed for three years or so, when it becomes advisable to lift, divide and replant in fresh soil. Those permanently planted in turf may remain in position until there is evidence of a falling short in flowering capabilities.

Daffodils in Pots. If daffodils are to be forced into flower, a greenhouse temperature of about 55 deg. is needed. Procedure is the same whether the plants are to be thus forced or brought along more gently in ordinary living-room conditions.

Pots of 5-in. top diameter are usually preferred, bulbs being so placed therein as to be almost touching, the tips of the bulbs, when the potting is completed, to be just visible above the soil surface.

The object then is to encourage root formation before top growth. This is achieved by standing the pots out in the open under a layer of sifted ashes so that they are covered to the depth of about 2 in.

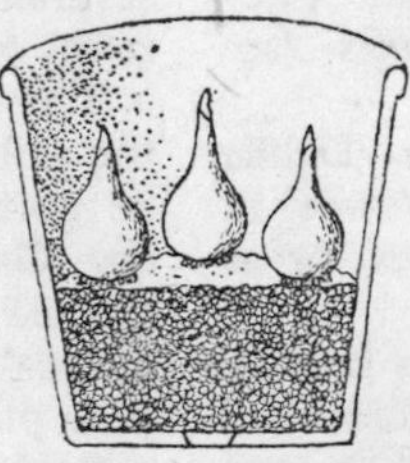

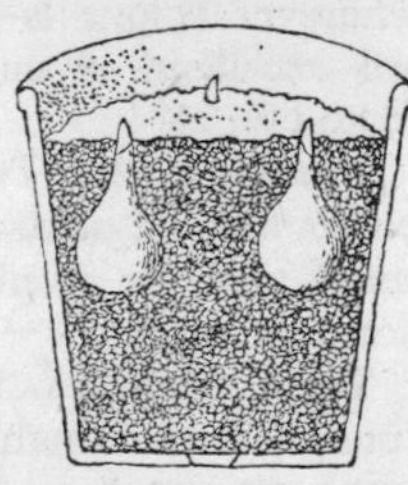

Fig. 121.—*Tips of daffodil bulbs when potting is completed should be visible above the soil (right). At the left, the same bulbs are shown in position for the final filling-in*

When not less than ½ in. of top growth has been made (progress being observed by temporary removal of ash), pots may be taken into the greenhouse or living room—after they have been scrubbed externally and all evidence of ash removed.

Exposure to full light should be deferred for a few days, after which they may have it in abundance. Over-watering and too dry conditions are to be guarded against.

After flowering, the plants should be removed from the pots and planted permanently outdoors for future flowering.

Propagation. Daffodils may be increased by removal of the small side-bulbs or offsets revealed after lifting. Planted as though they were full-size bulbs, these offsets will attain flowering size in due course if placed in good soil.

DAHLIA

There is a type of dahlia for almost every garden purpose, from the huge double flowers of the 5 ft. high decorative class to the dwarfs of 12 in. or so. They may be massed in beds, displayed in small clumps, or dotted about wherever colour is wanted. They are excellent as cut-flowers (see Plate No. 28).

Planting the Tubers. Dahlia plants may be obtained growing in small pots, or from boxes, or as dormant tubers.

Time to plant outdoors is early June, plants bought before then being sheltered in frame or cold greenhouse to protect from frost. Rich soil is needed—really deeply dug and well manured if exhibition blooms are hoped for.

Tall varieties should be planted 3–4 ft. apart, this being varied down to 18 in. for the dwarfs.

Dormant Tubers. It is desirable to start dormant (leafless) dahlia tubers into growth before planting out in early June. However, clusters of tubers may be planted direct from the winter store during April. It should be noted that undivided clumps do not give such a good display as single tubers.

The time to start old clumps into growth is February–March in a heated greenhouse, April in a frame (the latter being covered with sacks or mats on cold nights, for this perennial plant is not hardy).

The clumps, undivided, should be placed side by side in good soil in boxes deep enough to accommodate the longest tubers, only the tips of these to be visible above the soil. They need then only little moisture until growth is really active.

When between one and two inches of top growth has resulted the clumps may be divided, each division (single tubers or otherwise) to have one good growth. A knife will be needed to effect severance from the old central stem, or careful tearing may do it.

The divisions then go back into the soil in the boxes, or they may be potted separately, for growing on. Gradual hardening off (increased exposure to open-air conditions) must precede the early June planting.

Stakes and Ties. Even the dwarf types of dahlia may need staking if the position is a wind-buffeted one. The tall kinds demand really strong support. Stakes should be inserted 6 in. from the plant (in order not to damage the roots) and should be as high out of the ground as the nurseryman's catalogued height for the variety concerned.

Generally, one strong stake per plant suffices, growths being looped in as necessary. Breakage, due to wind or rain, of the succulent stems is frequent in the absence of sufficient ties.

Summer Treatment. In a treacherous early summer it may be advisable to protect the young plants at night for a period after setting out by covering them with inverted boxes or large pots, or even newspapers. This, however, is rarely necessary in the case of June-planted dahlias which have been properly hardened off.

A thorough watering as often as the soil becomes dry is desirable. And when the first petals are expanding a fortnightly feeding with liquid manure (animal or artificial) may commence.

Up to the time of flowering, syringeing in the evening of each hot day with sun-warmed water (not cold, straight from the tap) is a great help.

To prolong flowering, every faded bloom and its length of stem should be removed before seed-pods have a chance to form.

Show-class Bloom. Though dahlias require rich soil the excessive use of artificial or natural manures or fertilizers must be avoided, otherwise rank growth and deformed flowers are inevitable. Preliminary digging to the depth of 2 ft. is more important than summer feeding.

Big-bloom types cannot perfect an unlimited number of flowers. Therefore, flower buds of these varieties should be reduced to one per cluster. Also, the number of side shoots should be restricted.

Smaller varieties and single-flowered types do not, as a rule, call for this restriction of flowers and growth.

Dahlia Troubles. Greenfly can be a nuisance in the early stages. The remedy is to syringe the small plants (on a dull day) with an insecticide or dust them thoroughly with one of the proprietary powders.

Slugs may be troublesome. Covering the soil around each plant with soot or lime keeps them at bay. Hoeing occasionally, and hand-picking revealed pests, helps considerably.

Earwigs are the traditional foes of dahlias, flower buds especially suffering. Here inverted flower-pots stuffed loosely with dry crumpled newspaper, or hay or moss, and supported on stakes among the plants, are effective. The material is taken out each day and shaken and the ejected earwigs which have sought sanctuary there are destroyed—swiftly, for their movements are rapid.

Winter Treatment. Autumn usually is well advanced before the dahlias show signs of wear and tear. The first touch of frost will blacken the growth, and then the tuber clumps should be dug up and freed of their stems, 4-in. stumps of the latter only remaining.

The lifted tubers are then to be hand-cleaned of soil and placed for a few days under cover where drying will proceed without danger of frosting. They may then be piled into any convenient box or other receptacle, without soil, and in that manner stored indoors for the winter, with neither moisture nor heat.

The lifting should be done with a fork, thrust vertically into the ground several inches from the base of the plant. Any tubers which may be split, broken or otherwise injured in the process should be removed straightway. Their inclusion in store would induce decay in others.

Double Daisy

Propagation. Division of tuber-clusters is dealt with in a previous paragraph under the heading Dormant Tubers.

Increase may also be effected by cuttings of the young shoots taken when these are about 2 in. in length, in the heated greenhouse.

Seed may be sown in February–March in the heated greenhouse, April–May in cold greenhouse or sunny frame, thinly in fine soil. The resultant seedlings are moved on, at about 3 in. apart, into shallow boxes, or they may be placed singly in 4-in. pots.

Full exposure to light will keep the young plants strong and sturdy, and progressive hardening off will prepare them for planting in June.

DAISY, DOUBLE

A bed massed with double daisies (*Bellis perennis*) in full flower in spring is a magnificent sight. A line of these hardy perennials edging the mixed border is scarcely less attractive.

Height when in flower is about 6 in., and the fine blooms can be had in white, pink, crimson or mixed.

Planting. Position is not important, double daisies appearing to do equally well in sun and in light shade, but the soil must be good.

The plants should be set out at about 9 in. apart, the large leaves and spreading habit demanding all that space. Planting time is October, after the summer bedding has been cleared away.

Propagation. Double daisies may be increased by division of old plants, after lifting in June (when flowering is at an end or approaching it). Side growths come easily away, each with a few roots, and these should be set out, 6 in. apart, in a lightly shaded spot, to grow on for the autumn planting.

Normal method of increase is by seed, sown in June–July, in shallow boxes in a frame or in the open, the seedlings being set out later, 6 in. apart, for planting in autumn in their flowering places.

DELPHINIUM

One of the tallest, most stately and lovely of hardy perennials for the mixed border, the delphinium produces from early summer onwards long spikes studded with large flowers in shades of blue, purple and intermediate shades as well as white, very desirable for cutting (see Plate No. 9).

Planting. In a garden where the soil is light in nature and normally well drained, autumn planting is always advisable. But it should be deferred to late March or early April where the soil is heavy and inclined to lie wet and cold in winter.

Something of the maximum effect is lost when delphiniums are planted singly. Preferably they should be in groups of three or four, towards the back of the border. The roots should be 18 in. apart. Height ranges up to 6 ft.

Summer Treatment. Early staking and tying will prevent snapped stems. If flower-spikes of show class are required, the number of stems should be limited to not more than three (in the case of well-established plants).

The habit is naturally branching, and as the central flower-spikes approach the fading stage they should be cut away to their base, allowing more space for the development of flowering side shoots.

Delphinium Troubles. Slugs and snails are the great affliction here. These climbers have a habit of eating through flower-spikes and causing them to topple. Some may be hand-picked from the stems.

The use of a good soil fumigant will go far to lessen the danger from these pests.

Winter Treatment. Top growth should be cut down to within about 6 in. of the ground in late autumn or early winter, and hard and gritty ashes (sifted from the house fires) heaped over each clump and left there until new growths push through in spring.

Propagation. Clumps of delphinium may be left undisturbed for three years or so, when they will benefit from division and replanting in autumn or in March when growth first appears.

Named varieties are increased by division or cuttings, hybrids by seed. This may be sown as soon as ripe, outdoors or in a frame. The seedlings should be transferred about 4 in. apart into boxes for wintering in the frame if the garden soil is heavy and winter-wet. If the soil is light and well drained, the seedlings may be set outdoors in temporary quarters in autumn for final planting in spring, or they may be planted direct in their flowering places.

ERIGERON

One of the cheeriest and most persistent flowers in the summer garden, *Erigeron speciosus* (sometimes called the Midsummer daisy) carries numbers of large, daisy-like blooms of pale mauve with yellow centres; height is 1½ ft. And there are hybrids of *Erigeron aurantiacus* in various colours, height about 12 in. It is a most useful cut-flower.

Planting. A hardy perennial, erigeron will be a more or less permanent occupant of the mixed border, and at least 18 in. should be allowed between these plants when setting out in autumn or early spring. They soon develop into quite large clumps.

Summer Treatment. It is

Erigeron

advisable to stake each clump early, or flower stems are likely to become distorted. Three sticks inserted triangle-fashion outside the clump and linked with raffia or other tying material will give adequate support. Faded flowers should be snipped off, to prolong the season of beauty.

Winter Treatment. Old flower stems and long shoots should be cut back in late autumn to young basal growth.

Propagation. Erigeron is easily increased by division of clumps in autumn or early spring.

Seed may be sown in June outdoors or in a frame, for planting out in autumn to flower the following year.

ESCHSCHOLTZIA

This hardy annual is also known as Californian poppy (see Plate No. 18). It calls for massing in the mixed border, or in a small bed, and in pockets in the rockery.

Height is about 12 in. It is obtainable in shades of yellow, rose and white, and there are double and semi-double varieties. It is not particular as to soil, but the position should be sunny.

For indoor decoration the flowers should be cut in the bud stage, with full length of stem.

No staking or tying is required; the plants look after themselves throughout summer.

Propagation. Seed may be sown in March, outdoors where the plants are to flower the same summer, and the seedlings thinned out, before they crowd, to about 3 in. apart.

EVENING PRIMROSE

The hardy evening primrose (Oenothera) varies in height from 12 in. to 4 ft., according to variety. It is extremely free flowering, in delightful shades of yellow, in the mixed border. It should be planted

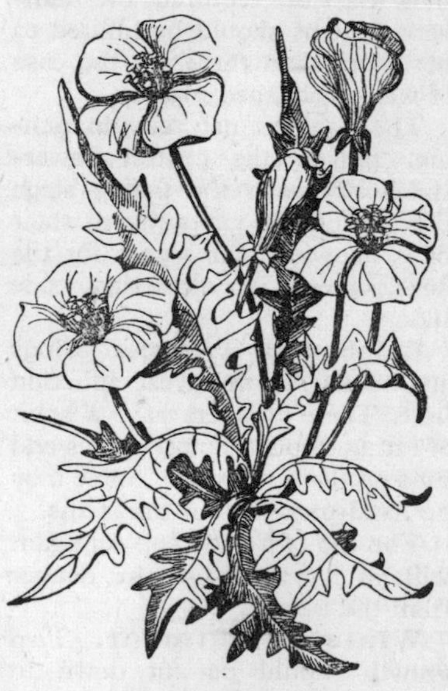

Evening Primrose

in October or March, and as a rule no staking is required.

Propagation. Plants usually scatter plenty of seed, and attention in autumn or spring to these "chance" seedlings quickly increases the stock. Both biennial and perennial varieties may be increased by seed sown outdoors in June, for planting out in autumn or spring.

Winter Treatment. The biennial varieties die, of course, after flowering. The perennial kinds are cut back in autumn, and are best lifted and divided and replanted after three years.

EVERLASTING FLOWERS

A number of easily grown annuals are called everlasting on account of their ability to remain fresh (as to the flowers) for an indefinite period.

Cut with full length of stem just before the flowers are fully open they will furnish dry vases for any length of time, and can be made up into charming bowls and baskets filled with dry moss.

These everlastings include acroclinium (12 in.), ammobium (2½ ft.), helichrysum (3 ft.), rhodanthe (12 in.), annual statice or sea lavender (18 in.), and xeranthemum (2 ft.), in various colours (see Plate No. 22). These are unrelated plants, and florists use them extensively in winter for the purposes just named.

Planting. Good soil is desirable, and a sunny position. Planting time is spring or early summer and the taller ones should be about 9 in. apart. Staking is not necessary, and even in an outstandingly dry summer the everlastings appear to escape distress.

Drying the Flowers. Blooms are produced throughout summer, and they should be cut, with a good length of stem, before the crisp-petalled flowers are fully open, and when there is no dew or rain upon them.

The harvested stems should then be tied in small bundles (single handfuls) and hung head downwards in an open shed, or other airy place, to dry thoroughly.

At the approach of frost they should be taken indoors and withered foliage stripped off.

Propagation. Seed may be sown thinly in boxes in March, the seedlings pricked off 4 in. apart into other boxes, and the plants hardened off for their flowering quarters as soon as large enough to go out.

Seed may also be sown outdoors, but an early start in the frame is desirable.

FLAX

Garden varieties of flax or Linum include a scarlet and a

Flax

white, annuals 12 in. high; a pale blue annual about 15 in.; a perennial blue and perennial white both 2½ ft.; and an 18 in. high form of the perennial blue. The latter are forms of *Linum perenne.*

Flowering period is June to September, and to enable plants to remain in bloom throughout that time dead flowers should be promptly removed.

Forget-me-not

They are valuable subjects in the herbaceous border, the perennial varieties preferring light soil.

Propagation. Annual flax may be sown in March, in clumps in the open border where they are to remain and flower, the seedlings being thinned out to about 3 in. apart.

The perennial varieties should be sown in pots or a box in the frame, in June, the seedlings being shifted into other boxes when an inch or so high, sheltered in the frame throughout winter. They can be planted out of doors, about 12 in. apart, in March–April. The perennials may also be increased by root-division in spring.

FORGET-ME-NOT

Rich blue flowers of the hardy biennial myosotis, massed or in bold lines, or interplanted with other spring-flowering plants, such as polyanthus primroses, are almost in a class apart.

A tall variety, 12 in. high, is useful for cutting; there is a dwarf blue, 6 in., for where space must be considered.

Forget-me-nots are very obliging as to soil, but they demand plenty of water in dry weather.

Propagation. Seed may be sown thinly in June, outdoors, and the seedlings transplanted in autumn to where they are to flower the following spring.

Seed is produced very freely, and if one or two of the finest plants are transferred (when flowering is finished) to an odd corner—or even thrown down there—plenty of self-sown seedlings will arise.

FOXGLOVE

The delightfully graceful Digitalis is a hardy biennial with big claims for inclusion in every mixed border and wherever a tallish plant is required. It flourishes in a lightly shaded position as well as in full sun, and if the spot is damp so much the better. The Shirley strain contains the finest types.

Summer Treatment. Stems on which the blooms have faded should be cut away to allow of development of later side shoots with their flowers.

Propagation. A myriad seedlings will spring up around an old plant if it is allowed to develop seed. These may be transplanted, when each has made four leaves, to where they are to flower the following year. Or seed may be sown outdoors in June-July and the seedlings given the same treatment as those naturally sown.

FREESIA

Delicious perfume distinguishes the flowers of this half-hardy greenhouse bulbous perennial. Obtainable in a number of colours and shades, they are excellent for cutting. Height is about 12 in.

Potting the Bulbs. For winter and spring flowering in the heated greenhouse, freesia bulbs may be potted during August and onwards, 1 in. deep and 2 in. apart, in good soil in pots with a top diameter of 4½ in. or thereabouts.

Until growth is apparent little water will be required. When flower buds appear, a weekly dose of weak liquid manure is helpful.

Staking. The top growth of freesias is grass-like and needs the support of five very thin sticks thrust down the pot sides at equal distances and linked with raffia.

After Flowering. The bulbs will function equally well in subsequent years if, after flowering, the soil in the pots is gradually allowed to become quite dry. The pots, with their bulbs in the dry soil, should remain in the greenhouse, in full light, until the following August. Then the bulbs should be removed from the soil and potted in new compost.

Propagation. Increase is by

Foxglove

Freesia

potting offsets produced by flowered bulbs, and also by seed sowing.

Seed may be sown from January to March for flowering the following summer, very thinly in pots of the $4\frac{1}{2}$-in. size, in the heated greenhouse.

The seedlings should be thinned out to the best five and encouraged to flower by the application of liquid fertilizer once a week from the time the pots show plenty of roots. Treatment is then as given for freesia bulbs.

FUCHSIA

A charm all its own is possessed by this half-hardy shrubby perennial which for long has been a favourite for summer bedding and for growing in pots and tubs and window-boxes.

There are forms with single and double flowers, in varying shades.

Planting Outdoors. End of May or early June is the outdoor planting season. A sunny position is required, and good soil, and the plants should be set out at least 12 in. apart.

Summer Treatment. Bud dropping may be troublesome if the plants are allowed to become dry. The soil must be kept reasonably moist.

Each plant should be neatly staked and tied.

Winter Treatment. In late September or October the outdoor plants should be lifted, with all their roots, and planted in good soil in pots or boxes and wintered anywhere under cover where frost is excluded. It is an advantage during this winter period if the fuchsias can be exposed to full light.

Very little water will be needed, just sufficient to keep the soil from being dry, until the following March, when the plants should be repotted or boxed in fresh soil and started into growth in full light and whatever warmth can be given, such as that of a sunny greenhouse or window, with continuing protection against frost.

Spring Treatment. Old fuchsia plants restarted into growth generally require some pruning when the new growth is becoming active. It may be sufficient to cut back dead ends of shoots to sound tissue. Harder pruning may be called for if it is desired to reduce the size of a plant.

Propagation. Seed sown in the early weeks of the year, in a heated greenhouse, and the seedlings potted on as necessary, will provide plants to flower the same year.

Increase by cuttings is the normal procedure. These are formed of young new shoots taken in the spring. They may be up to about 3 in. long and should terminate, as to the lower end, in a joint.

Inserted an inch or so apart around the side of a small pot filled with good compost and placed in a heated greenhouse or inside a sunny window, rooting soon takes place—the more quickly if the cutting-pots are stood in a shallow box having a glass top.

When it is obvious, from inspection of the potful of soil, that the cuttings have rooted, these should be transferred singly to small pots. When the new plants are about 6 in. high the tips may be nipped off to induce bushiness.

To create standard fuchsias—plants with a bare length of single stem and a bushy head—the young plants are allowed to run up to the required height before the tips are removed. The top shoots that will then be produced should be nipped back occasionally until a good thick "head" has been secured. All growths below the "head" must be removed on appearance.

Hardy Fuchsias. These are shrubs, in several species, height up to 6 ft., for moderately warm positions outdoors. They are sometimes cut down by frost, but new growth arises from the base. The form *Riccartoni* in particular makes a serviceable hedge in suitable weather conditions. The flowering season is July to September.

GAILLARDIA

One of the most dependable hardy perennials for the mixed border, brilliant in flower, with long stems for cutting, the gaillardia will thrive in practically any kind of garden soil, provided it is well drained.

There are also annual varieties, in height ranging from 1 ft. to 3 ft., and colours represented are crimson and gold, yellow and scarlet, red and yellow. Flowering continues throughout summer.

The perennials especially make imposing clumps in the mixed border. They like a warm, sunny position and they are not affected by drought.

Propagation. The annual varieties of gaillardia may be sown in March, outdoors where they are to flower, the seedlings being thinned out to about 12 in. apart.

The perennials are quickly increased by division of root clumps in March and October or by root cuttings taken in October. Also

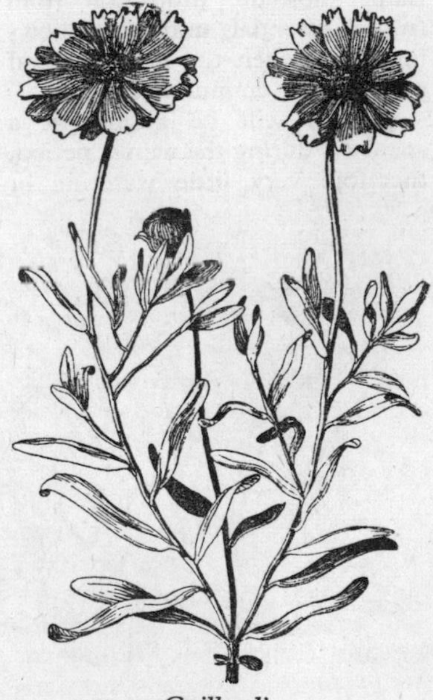

Gaillardia

by sowing seed outdoors in June for flowering the following year. The seedlings should be shifted to a spare patch, 4–6 in. apart, and planted out in March where they are to flower.

GAZANIA

A free-flowering half-hardy perennial, no more than 12 in. high, for edging summer beds or the mixed border, and for planting in the rockery, gazania is specially brilliant in a hot and dry summer. Colours range from cream to red.

Planting. Late May or early June is soon enough for the plants to go out, after being hardened off. Distance, about 9 in. apart.

Winter Treatment. The plants should be lifted in October and potted separately or placed fairly close together in boxes of soil, and sheltered in greenhouse or sunny frame (absolute protection from frost is essential) until the following May, when the hardening-off process may commence.

Growth will be almost at a standstill during the winter period, therefore very little watering or other attention will be required.

Propagation. Small side shoots from the base of the plant may be inserted in the frame in July or August, and wintered therein, the frame being matted over against frost.

Seed may be sown in the heated greenhouse in March, or later in a sunny frame, and the seedlings placed separately in pots, or 4 in. apart in boxes, for planting out in late May or early June.

GENTIAN

Trumpet-shaped flowers of perennial gentian, in shades of blue, are an immense acquisition to the rockery or mixed border. Flowering season ranges from May to August, according to the variety, and height varies from the 4 in. of the intense-blue variety *acaulis* to the 2 ft. of *Hascombensis*.

Planting. March and October are the best planting months. The position should be in full sun, and the soil should be made quite firm around the roots.

During spring and summer they should be kept moist, in the absence of rain, but good drainage is essential at all times.

Propagation. Division of roots in March is the easiest method of increase.

Seed may be sown during March in the frame, in soil very finely sifted. The seed should be lightly pressed into the surface only—not covered—and the seedlings be transferred early to light soil and fully exposed to sunshine. Seed of gentian is generally slow to germinate, a period up to two

Gentian

years sometimes elapsing before seedlings show.

GERANIUM

The always popular bedding and greenhouse geraniums are, botanically speaking, all pelargoniums. These are classified, in respect chiefly to the leaf-markings, as zonal, bicolour, tricolour, bronze and so on; there is also the scented-leaved type, and the trailing or climbing ivy-leaved geranium. They are half-hardy perennials.

Massed in beds or window-boxes, grown in pots in greenhouse or conservatory or in living-room windows, they give a display of flower and foliage that is satisfying in the extreme (see Plate No. 12).

Planting. End of May or early June (according to temperature and soil condition) is the outdoor planting season. The plants should not be closer than 9 in. apart, and the soil should not be too rich or leaf growth will outpace the flowers.

They should, of course, be properly hardened off before being set out; and the more soil they have attached to their roots at the moment of planting the more speedily they settle down.

Watering in after planting is advisable, unless a downpour follows. If hot sunshine or drying winds occur during the first days, the trouble of lightly shading the plants with newspaper or something similar is amply repaid.

Summer Treatment. Once established in the bed, geraniums do not seem to mind drought. In a window-box they must be well supplied with water.

Removing faded blooms and yellowed lower leaves is essential.

Staking is seldom necessary, except with ivy-leaved geraniums; the alternative with these is to allow them to assume the trailing position and peg them neatly over the soil.

Winter Treatment. When the summer bedding is over—in October, as a rule—outdoor geraniums should be lifted, for wintering under cover where frost and damp are excluded but full light has free play. In a mild winter and early spring they may scrape through in an ordinary frame, if this is matted over on cold nights. A spare room indoors would serve in the absence of a frame or a greenhouse, the latter being the ideal.

The lifted plants should be transferred to pots or boxes containing light soil, unduly long roots being cut back first and the longest top growth being shortened by about one-third.

The soil should be kept just moist enough to prevent the stems shrivelling. Dying leaves must be removed, and the tops kept free of moisture.

It is not necessary to save all one's stock of bedding geraniums for the following season. The rooting of cuttings from the best plants, in late August or early September, renders that unnecessary.

Propagation. Short, hard-feeling side shoots, tinged with red (an indication of "ripeness"), taken from the bedding geraniums in August make the best cuttings. Their removal, if done with reasonable care, will not be noticed and the plants in the bed will continue in flower for weeks.

They may be rooted in pots or shallow boxes, should be wintered in the greenhouse (or in circumstances as similar as may be

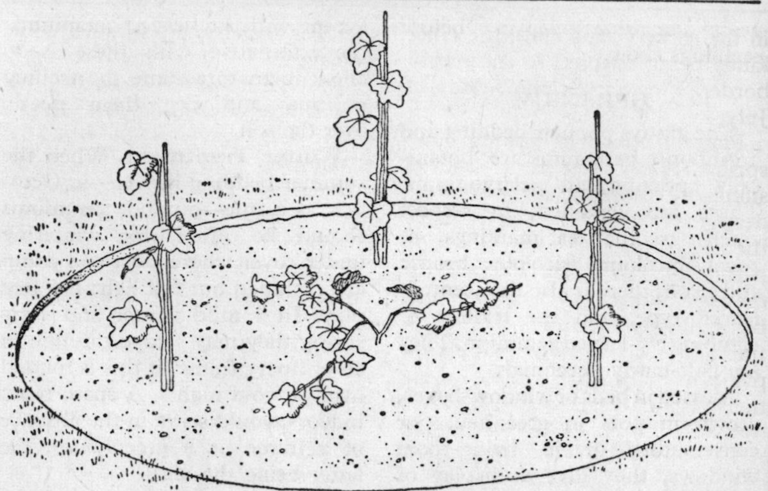

Fig. 122.—*Ivy-leaved geraniums are used outdoors most effectively when a number are trained prostrate, the shoots being pegged down. A few may be left as "dot" plants—that is, trained upright to individual stakes*

contrived), and be potted on or given more space in other boxes in the spring. The general procedure for the treatment of such stem-cuttings is explained in the section "How to Increase Flowering Plants."

To make the cuttings bushy, in or about March the tips should be removed. Side shoots may be "stopped" similarly when they have extended to 2–3 in.

Greenhouse Geraniums. The so-called show and fancy pelargoniums are grand plants for greenhouse decoration. Short cuttings are rooted in July–August in frame or greenhouse, shifted singly to 4-in. pots when rooted and given full light in a temperature of about 45 deg. At the turn of the year they will be due for the shift to 5-in. pots in which the plants (made bushy by "stopping" the cuttings as explained in the previous paragraph) will flower.

When flowering is over, these greenhouse pelargoniums should be placed (still in their pots) temporarily outdoors, in the sun. In July or August the shoots may be shortened to within an inch or so of their base, after which the appearance of new young shoots announces that it is time to shift the plants (after shaking away loose soil from the roots) into pots a size or two larger, using rich soil. They will be rehoused in the greenhouse in September or early October.

Herbaceous Geraniums. These are sometimes known as crane's bill, from the elongated shape of the seed pods. They are hardy herbaceous perennials, with flowers ranging from pale pink to deep purple according to variety, and varying in height from 4 in. to 2 ft.

The shorter varieties look well

in the rockery (full sun), the taller kinds being adapted to the mixed border. Flowering time is May to July.

Planting time is autumn and spring. They need no special summer treatment. In winter the dead tops should be cut back to the live crowns.

Propagation is by division of the roots in autumn or spring; and by seed sown outdoors or in a frame in early summer to provide plants for flowering out of doors the following year.

GERBERA

Known also as the Barberton or Transvaal daisy, this half-hardy perennial has marguerite-like flowers in scarlet and other colours, throughout summer. Height is about 18 in.

They make excellent pot plants for the greenhouse, and for the mixed border in warm and sheltered positions.

Planting time is late March–April, soil and weather conditions being guiding factors.

Winter Treatment. Before winter frosts arrive, a safety precaution is to cover the old clumps with dry straw, or bracken or cloches until spring. Alternatively, the plants should be wintered in a frame.

Propagation. Root division in spring is the simplest method of increase. Seed may be sown in greenhouse or frame in spring, to provide next year's flowering plants.

GEUM

Once seen in flower, this hardy herbaceous perennial is always remembered. Height is up to 2 ft., the flowers persist from June to October and they are favourites for cutting.

Two foremost varieties are the double scarlet-crimson Mrs. Bradshaw and golden-yellow Lady Stratheden.

Removal of old flower stems in autumn leaves the plants tidy for winter.

Propagation. Increase is by division of clumps in autumn and

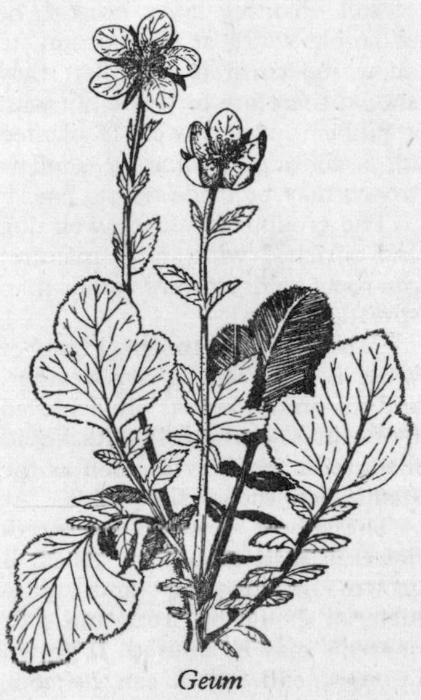

Geum

spring (the normal planting seasons). Seed may be sown in June, outdoors or in a frame, for planting in flowering positions the following autumn or spring.

GLADIOLUS

In full bloom these bulbous perennials are majestic plants. They may be grown in clumps in the mixed border, or in lines, or in a patch of their own for cutting —they are extremely decorative.

Height is up to 3 ft. or more. There are several types or sections of gladiolus, the most important being the early flowering *Colvillei* sorts and the later flowering large-flowered and *primulinus* types; colours cover an extremely wide range.

Planting. The corms should be planted in March, spaced 6 in. apart and covered with about 3 in. of soil. Planting holes need to be of ample width at the bottom, to allow the corm to rest flat; they should therefore be made not with a dibber but a trowel. If planted in a continuous line, a shallow trench may be made with a hoe.

The ground should be well dug and enriched with stable manure; the roots go downward rather than spread outward.

Summer Treatment. Plenty of water is necessary in dry weather, and maximum results are achieved by feeding occasionally with liquid manure or fertilizer as soon as the stems show the swelling buds.

The flower-spikes of the large-flowered sorts should be staked, if grown in clusters, and tying material should be broad and soft, or stems may be injured. If grown in lines, end stakes can be connected with strands of wire or thick string and the stems looped thereto. The *Colvillei* and *primulinus* varieties are self-supporting if planted deep enough.

Winter Treatment. When top growth becomes yellow the plants should be forked up, soil shaken from the corms, and the tops bunched and tied; or the stems may be cut off 4 in. above the corms. The latter should pass the winter under cover, safe from frost and damp and mice.

Where the ground in winter is dry rather than wet and cold, corms may be left undisturbed a couple of years in mild climates.

Propagation. Small corms—offsets—at the base of those which have flowered, may be planted about 2 in. deep in March, grown on for a season and lifted and stored. After the next planting they should flower.

Seed may be sown in a warm greenhouse in February, for growing on outdoors. Seedlings generally need to pass their third season before flowering.

GLOBE THISTLE

This quick space-filler has the vigorous habit of a thistle, with great round flower-heads in deep blue, or white. Height is 3 to 5 ft., and its place is at the back of the mixed border. It is listed in nursery

Globe Thistle

catalogues as *Echinops ritro.*

Echinops, of which there are several forms, is a hardy perennial, for planting in autumn or spring where space is not too precious. Once established it will look after itself, producing plenty of flower-crowned stems strong enough to require no staking.

It should be tidied up for the winter by having the top cut back to near ground level.

Propagation. There is no difficulty here about root division, in autumn or spring. The smallest slips of thongy root will form independent plants. Indeed, difficulty is sometimes found in keeping echinops within bounds.

Seed may be sown outdoors in June, for planting out in autumn in the following year's flowering position.

GODETIA

One of the most satisfying of the hardy annuals for the mixed border, godetia flowers all through summer, in most attractive colours. It is excellent for cutting (see Plate No. 18).

Tall varieties reach to about 2½ ft. Others vary between 8 and 18 in., and there are doubles and singles.

It is not particular as to soil, and staking is not necessary.

Propagation. Seed may be sown in March–April, outdoors where the plants are to flower a few weeks later. Seedlings should be thinned out to 3–6 in. apart. Godetias also make very attractive pot plants.

Gypsophila

GYPSOPHILA

A search for "something" to mix with cut-flowers occurs in most gardens in summer. Gypsophila, in one or other of its varieties, is the ideal "something" — particularly with sweet pea blooms.

The dried flowering stems are invaluable for winter indoor decoration, mixed with everlasting flowers (which see).

There are hardy annual and perennial varieties; colours include white and pink, and heights range up to 4 ft.

A dryish position is appreciated in the mixed border. Heavy soil may be made suitable by lightening it with old mortar broken up, or crushed natural chalk.

Planting time for the perennial varieties is autumn and spring.

Propagation. Seed of the annual gypsophilas may be sown, very shallowly, in March–April, in the open where the plants are to flower during the summer. The seedlings should be thinned out 4–6 in. apart.

The perennials may be increased by cuttings in spring, and by seed sown in June, in the open or in a frame, the young plants being set out in autumn where they are to flower the following year.

HEUCHERA

In clumps in the mixed border, and dotted about in the rockery, heuchera gives plenty of blossom in coral red, pink, creamy white and other colours according to variety. Height varies from 18 in. to 2 ft.

It likes a sunny position with plenty of air and light. The soil should not be too heavy. It fails to establish itself in clayey ground.

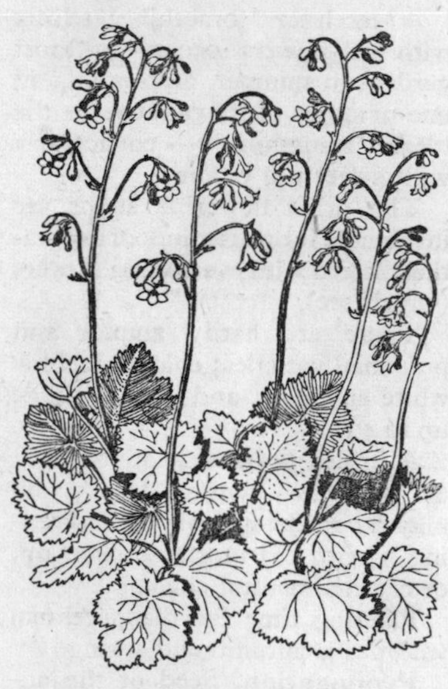

Heuchera

Planting time for this hardy perennial is spring.

Propagation. Increase is by division of clumps in spring; and seed may be sown in fine soil in the frame in March, for planting in the chosen flowering positions the following spring.

HOLLYHOCK

There is nothing bashful about a well-grown hollyhock; a height of 10 ft. is not unusual. There are double and single varieties, in various colours. Hollyhock, although a hardy perennial, can also be treated as a biennial. It should be represented in every mixed border.

Planting. Good soil deeply dug is required to produce first-class blooms. Planting time is April, and plants should be not less than 18 in. apart. They should be at the back of the mixed border, with plenty of head room and sunshine.

Summer Treatment. Staking is a prime requirement, and it should be done before wind damage occurs.

Seed production should be discouraged, to prolong flowering. To this end, the round seed-pods as they form should be cut off. Their short stems are tough and they cannot be tugged off without risk of damage to the stem. It is a task demanding some patience.

Fungus Trouble. Rust spots on hollyhock foliage are troublesome. Attacked leaves should be cut off and burned. The disease is almost certain to be repeated the following year. To safeguard young plants these should be sprayed during March–April with Bordeaux mixture, a second spraying following when the flower-spikes begin to extend.

Winter Treatment. The old plants should be cut right down, in autumn, leaving only the basal growths.

Propagation. Seed is the best means of increase and may be sown in June, in the open or in a box in the cold frame. It is safer to winter the young plants in the frame, in pots or boxes, setting them out the following spring in their flowering quarters.

HONESTY

Quaintly named, this plant is botanically called *Lunaria biennis*. A hardy biennial, height about 2 ft., it produces purple or white flowers in early summer. Its chief attraction, however, is in the flat, oval seed-pods. When the outer covering of these pods is rubbed off, between the fingers, thin silvery tissue is revealed.

For winter decoration, stems should be cut full length and dried in an open shed or airy room.

Propagation. Honesty scatters its seed freely, and as a rule there is no lack of seedlings in summer and autumn for the production of the next year's flowers.

Seed may be sown in June, in the open or in a box in the frame, the seedlings to be set out, about 6 in. apart, in a spare patch until they may be conveniently planted in the border in autumn.

HYACINTH

A bulbous plant of all-round usefulness is the ever-popular hyacinth. If expense or other consideration excludes its massing in beds in the garden, a bulb or two here and there in the mixed

Hollyhock

Honesty (see page 151)

border will exude fragrance from flower-spikes of surpassing beauty.

The common kinds, too, may be grown in window-boxes, and in flowerpots and water-glasses for indoor flowering. The choice, small-flowered Roman hyacinths are for pot-culture in a heated greenhouse or warm room.

Planting. For spring flowering in beds or window-boxes the bulbs should be planted in November, 3–4 in. deep and 8 in. apart. Good soil and a sunny position are required.

Each flower-spike should be given a stake before it commences to topple. Without support, heavy rain—or a snowfall—may snap stems.

After Flowering. Bulbs may be left, without risk of injury, in the mixed border, unless the position is wanted for other plants. They should be lifted from beds (and elsewhere) in June, or somewhat earlier if summer bedding is waiting to be planted.

After lifting, the bulbs should be laid out in an open shed for a few days to dry, then be stored in bags (or otherwise) until wanted again for planting in the autumn.

Hyacinths in Pots. Ordinary bedding hyacinths will flower early in pots in an ordinary living-room, earlier still in a heated greenhouse.

One bulb in the centre of a 5-in. or 6-in. pot will do well, given good compost. It should rest half-in and half-out of the soil, and to encourage maximum root production the pot or pots should be buried under sifted fire-ashes outdoors, the ashes covering the top of the pot to the depth of about 2 in.

Some time in late January, or February, the pots should be removed from the ashes, scrubbed clean, and placed in the greenhouse or living-room. The top growth will be quite short, and almost white. Green colour will appear under the influence of light, and when growth is really noticeable water may be given to the soil.

The flower-spike should be neatly staked and tied, the stake being pushed into the soil far enough to keep it rigid.

Indoor culture should not be attempted a second year with the same bulb. Flowering over, it should be planted outdoors.

Hyacinths in Glasses. Special glasses with a constricted neck are used for flowering these bulbs, without soil, indoors. The bulb should be placed in the glass vessel during November–December, and the vessel filled with water sufficient to reach the base of the bulb. The water should be maintained at that level—just touching the bulb.

The glass can then go into a cupboard or other dark position until roots are working well down into the water, which is the time for its removal to full light. After flowering the bulb may be planted outdoors.

Roman Hyacinths. These should be potted during August–October. A 5-in. pot will accommodate three bulbs, these to be covered an inch deep. The pots should be placed under ashes outdoors until top growth appears, the plants then being given greenhouse or window treatment as already described. A temperature of about 55 deg. is most suitable. The bulbs are not worth saving after they have flowered in any degree of warmth.

Propagation. Small bulbs (offsets) produced at the base of flowered bulbs may be removed at lifting-time and planted out in the ordinary way, though not more than 6 in. apart and in a spare patch where they can grow on to full flowering size.

IRIS

There is an almost bewildering range of forms and colours in the irises, which are most commonly represented by the "bearded" section—familiarly known as "flag" iris. There is also a "beardless" section, and bulbous representatives include the Dutch, Spanish and English Iris.

Planting Flag Iris. A well-drained position in full sun suits these best. They appreciate lime in the soil, and if the latter is heavy it should be lightened with sharp grit, mortar rubble or crushed chalk.

There are April, May and June flowering varieties in this section, of diverse and beautiful colours, and the most suitable planting time is as soon as possible after flowering—this ensuring a fair show of blossom the following year.

If such early planting is not practicable, the next best period is September–October or March.

The root-stocks (rhizomes) should not be completely buried but be left half-exposed, that being the natural habit. Planting is most effective in clumps, these to be undisturbed for three or four years, when they should be lifted, divided and the best portions replanted.

Propagation. Division of clumps is simple, preferably shortly after flowering.

Winter Treatment. The stiff blades of foliage wither in autumn and winter, and these should be cut right back—without damage to young new growths which may be "shooting." Early removal of the old tops is desirable, otherwise the withered blades droop to soil level and give snails and slugs a winter hiding-place.

Beardless and Japanese. Many of the beardless section of iris prefer a damp position, as by the side of water, and all the Japanese section do best where there is ample moisture. A sunny spot in the mixed border will serve, if plenty of water can be given during the growing season.

Flowering period is, generally, June to August. Other details as given under flag iris apply.

Bulbous Irises. Height of these ranges, according to class and variety, between a few inches and

2 ft., and flowering time varies between October and June.

Planting time is August to October, the bulbs being placed 3 in. deep and up to 6 in. apart. They may remain undisturbed for about three years, when they should be lifted and replanted.

Propagation of bulbous irises is by offsets (small bulbs at the base of old ones) planted in autumn.

JACOB'S LADDER

Among the oldest garden favourites, varieties of Polemonium range from 6 in. to 2½ ft. in height. They have ornamental leaves, and the sprays of flowers in blue—not forgetting a white variety—are admirable for cutting.

A hardy perennial, planting should take place in autumn or spring. Full exposure to sun is needed, in the mixed border for taller varieties, in the rockery for the dwarfer ones.

Taller varieties need staking in exposed positions. Old stems should be cut down in autumn, after flowering.

Propagation. Root division in autumn or spring is a ready method of increase.

Seed may be sown in June, outdoors or a box in the frame, to produce plants for flowering the following year.

LARKSPUR

For general garden decoration and for cutting, the hardy annual *Delphinium ajacis*, or larkspur (see Plate No. 19), is indispensable. Fine spikes in blue, white, rose, scarlet and other colours are very freely produced with both single and double flowers.

Heights range from 12 in. to 3 ft., and they make a grand display in clumps or groups in the mixed border.

They flower throughout the summer and do not require staking unless the position is very windy. As stems go out of flower they should be cut off, to prolong flowering.

Propagation. Self-sown seedlings spring up plentifully in autumn, and if these survive the winter they flower well in advance of those raised from a spring sowing.

Seed may be sown in March–April, preferably where the plants will remain to bloom. Seedlings should be thinned out early to about 9 in. apart.

LILY

Strikingly beautiful, up to 6 ft. or more in height, lilies are offered by the specialist firms in numerous species. Bulbous perennials, they are suitable for the mixed border —all hardy varieties from the old Turk's Cap lily to the majestic Golden-rayed Lily of Japan.

Planting. October is the most suitable month for planting the bulbs, and for best effect they should be in clumps of three or more, spaced at least 6 in. apart and up to 6 in. deep.

Summer Treatment. Staking needs attention before the tops begin to sway, and the bulbs should be left undisturbed in the ground for as many years as possible.

When, by natural increase, the plants have obviously become overcrowded the bulbs should be lifted (when the tops have withered in autumn) and replanted, in soil enriched with old manure or leafmould.

Lilies vary considerably in their requirements. Some are stem-rooting, i.e. produce a set of surface roots from where the stem rises from the ground. Such types of lily require to be grown among low shrubs or plants in order to provide the necessary protection from the sun's rays which tend to scorch them.

Water must be given, with no niggard hand, in dry weather. Lilies respond to liquid manure or artificial fertilizer given sparingly from the time the buds begin to form until the petals begin to show.

The tops should be allowed to ripen naturally when flowering is over.

Failure to Flower. This may be due to too dry conditions or poor soil, apart from the fact that lilies need a year or so to become established after planting.

If general condition is poor, the bulbs should be transplanted, in autumn, to another spot where the soil has been enriched with leaf-mould, thoroughly decayed material from the compost heap, or really old manure.

If the soil is heavy and inclined to lie wet in winter there is a risk of lily bulbs decaying unless there is placed at the bottom of each planting hole a handful of sharp grit or sand for the bulb to rest upon. Similar material, if sufficient is available, should surround the bulbs also, before soil is returned above them.

Propagation. Offsets, or baby bulbs, removed from old bulbs when these are lifted in autumn, may be planted 1 in. deep and 2 in. apart in light soil outdoors or in a box in the frame, for planting out the following autumn where they can grow on to the flowering stage —which may occupy three or more years.

Seed may be sown in light soil in March, in a box in frame or greenhouse, about $\frac{1}{8}$ in. deep and 1 in. apart. Seedlings should grow on undisturbed until the following year. Then, when the foliage withers in autumn, the small bulbs (which should then be about the size of hedge-nuts) should be taken from the soil in the box and planted outdoors to assume flowering size—which may take five or six years.

LILY OF THE VALLEY

Deliciously scented, prized for cutting, this hardy herbaceous perennial is one of the prime beauties of spring. It is sometimes reluctant to "get going," but once

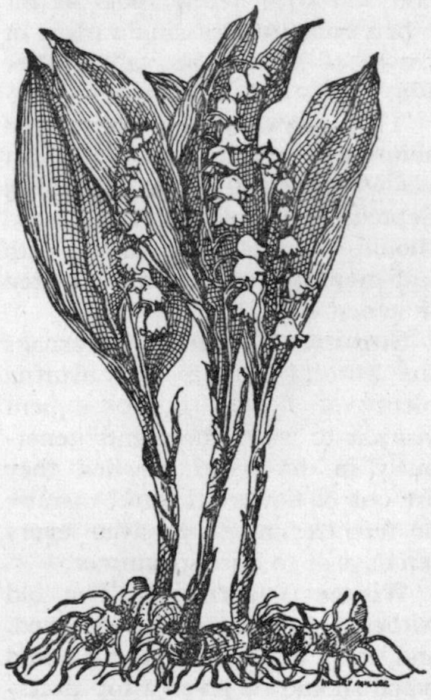

Lily of the Valley

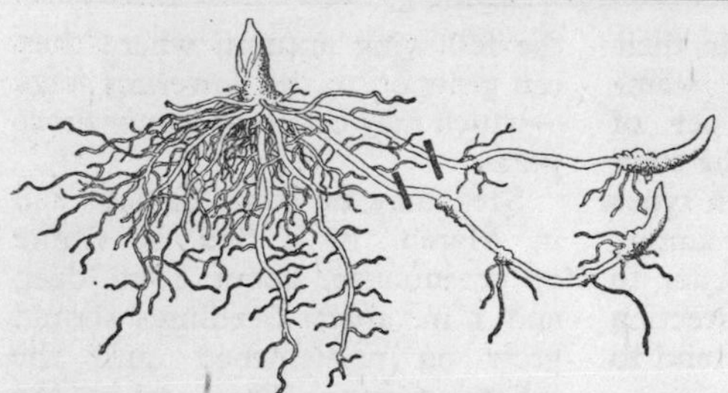

Fig. 123.—*A root-mass of lily of the valley has here produced two young "crowns." These should be cut off obliquely, as shown, and replanted to form two new plants*

established it does magnificently.

It may be grown in a shady border (not gloomy or heavily overhung by trees), or in a semi-shaded patch facing south for extra early flowering.

Planting the Crowns. An inch or so of root-stem as thick as an ordinary pencil, pointed at the top end and with a few roots at the other, constitutes a single plant or crown of lily of the valley. (See Fig. 123.)

These crowns may be planted about 3 in. apart, the top end just below the soil surface, during September–October. The ground should be well dug first, with leaf-mould or old manure mixed in generously.

Summer Treatment. Perhaps the surest method of ensuring plenty of flowers in subsequent years is to water the plants generously in dry weather when they are out of flowers. Liquid manure or fertilizer may be given every ten days or so during summer.

Winter Treatment. The old withered tops should be removed, and early in the year the planted patch should be given a top dressing, an inch thick, of sifted leaf-mould or rotted manure.

The bed may have become so crowded in the fourth year that replanting is necessary. The plants should be forked out and the crowns separated, the largest of these being planted together, the smaller ones elsewhere —for these smaller ones may need a year or so in which to plump up.

Propagation. The quickest method of increase is by division of old clumps, as explained in the preceding paragraph.

Seed may be sown in June, outdoors, in a lightly shaded position, to supply plants for permanent planting in due course.

LINARIA

The annual toadflax (see Plate No. 18) produces throughout summer dainty flowers resembling miniature antirrhinums (snapdragon). Varieties are obtainable in white, golden-yellow, mauve and other colours, height ranges from 9 to 12 in., and clumps in the mixed border are very effective.

Perennial varieties include the dwarf (4–6 in.) *Linaria alpina* and Mauve Gem, suitable for the rockery. Also the fascinating little *Linaria cymbalaria*, familiarly known as Kenilworth ivy, creeping freely over the rockery stones, at home on old walls (its roots lodged in small crevices), and a useful subject for a hanging basket.

Propagation. Annual varieties may be sown in the open, where they are to flower, during March, thinned out to 2 in. apart.

Perennial varieties are increased by division in March and October; and by seed sown outdoors or in a frame in June, to provide plants for flowering the following year.

LOBELIA

The compact little bedding lobelia, up to 6 in. high, conceals itself entirely beneath blossom in the summer flower beds. In blue, mauve and white it is also much used for edging beds and mixed borders (see Plate No. 6).

The spreading varieties, in blue, mauve, white, serve similar purposes and can be used to edge window-boxes and furnish hanging baskets.

The tall varieties, up to 12 in. high, in blue, white, rose, are used for summer beds, borders and for growing in pots.

The foregoing are half-hardy perennials, and may be treated also as half-hardy annuals where there is no warm greenhouse in which to winter old plants lifted from the summer beds.

They are planted out towards the end of May, after hardening off, and spaced 6–9 in. apart.

Propagation. The foregoing lobelias may be raised by sowing seed, very shallowly in a box of light soil, in February–March in the warm greenhouse or during April in a sunny frame.

The small seedlings should be moved on, 2 in. apart, into shallow boxes and gradually hardened off for late May or early June planting for summer flowering.

Plants may also be raised, in March, from cuttings from old plants lifted from outdoors in late September and wintered in the greenhouse; or the old plants may be divided in March. The cuttings—a temperature of about 55 deg. is needed—should be rooted, 2 in. apart, in light soil in shallow boxes.

Hardy perennial Lobelias. About 2 ft. high, these look well in clumps in the mixed border. Colours are scarlet, and various shades in the hybrids of *Lobelia cardinalis*.

Planting. These should be set out in spring, in a sunny position, and well supplied with water in dry periods whilst growth is active. If the soil is heavy and lies wet in winter, the hardy perennial lobelias should be transferred to pots in autumn and wintered in a warm greenhouse or frame.

Propagation. Increase is by root-division in March, and by seed sown during June in the frame, to provide flowering plants for the following year.

LOVE-IN-A-MIST

Botanically, this plant is Nigella, a most attractive and free-flowering hardy annual (see Plate No. 19) which holds its charm to the very end of summer. There are blue, white and purple varieties, height is about 18 in., and both foliage (which is finely cut and graceful) and flowers are admirable for cutting.

Propagation. Seed may be sown in March, where the plants are to flower a few weeks later, and the seedlings thinned out to 6 in. apart.

A sowing outdoors in September is worth risking, for plants that pull through the winter are unusually strong and early to flower.

To prolong flowering, withered

blooms should be picked off before seed forms.

LOVE-LIES-BLEEDING

Amaranthus caudatus is the botanical name of this hardy annual which is notable in the mixed border for its long, drooping,

Love-lies-bleeding

crimson flowers or tassels. Height is 2–3 ft.

Seed may be sown, where the plants are to flower in summer, during March–April, and the seedlings thinned out to a few inches apart. A sunny position is needed.

LUPIN

Lupins are among the foremost selections for the mixed border in summer, and for cutting where bold spikes of bloom are appreciated. There are hardy annual and hardy perennial varieties, and so-called tree lupins (see Plate No. 9). Many colours and shades are represented and height ranges from the average 2 ft. of the annuals to the 5 ft. of the tree lupins.

Annual Lupins. These are raised by sowing seed, very thinly, during March–April, where the plants are to flower in the summer of the same year. The seedlings should be thinned out to 18 in. apart, for they are strong growers. Sowing direct in the flowering position is advisable because these lupins do not readily transplant.

Perennial Lupins. These hardy herbaceous lupins are planted in spring or autumn, preferably in groups of three or four and separated by about 18 in. They should be given stakes before wind damage occurs. Slugs and snails have a habit of climbing the flower-spikes and eating through the soft stems so that the spikes topple before the presence of the pests is suspected. They should be watched for on the plants and destroyed. Stems should be cut down in October.

Clumps should remain undisturbed for three years, then be lifted and rooted side growths taken and replanted in enriched soil.

Propagation is as described, in spring, and by seed sown in June, in the open or in a frame, for plants to flower the following year.

Tree Lupins. Of bushy habit, these have bright yellow or white or mauve flowers, according to variety. Hybrids in a number of shades also are obtainable.

Propagation is by seed sown in June, outdoors or in a frame, for flowering the following year.

Frost may cut back the tops completely in winter, but new

growth should arise from the base. Top growth that survives winter should be trimmed back in spring to secure shapeliness.

MALLOW

Hardy annual Lavatera (see Plate No. 18) makes astonishing growth in the one season of its life. Of bushy, spreading habit it reaches a height of 3 ft. and flowers prodigiously throughout summer. The flowers, large and showy, in shades of pink and in white, are carried on long stems—making this very useful for cutting.

Propagation. Seed may be sown, very thinly, from March to May, in the flowering position and the seedlings thinned out to 18 in. apart. Or plants may be raised in a box in the frame, or unheated greenhouse, and transplanted.

As flowers fade they should be nipped off. Big flat seed-pods left to ripen seed soon put an end to flowering.

Musk Mallow. The hardy perennial mallow (Malva) may be planted, in the mixed border, in October or March. Height is about 2–3 ft. Propagation is by seed sown in June, outdoors or in a frame, to provide plants for flowering the following year.

MARIGOLD

The old English marigold (Calendula) and the French and African marigolds (Tagetes) between them fit in with practically every garden requirement, the English type being especially valuable for cutting (see Plate No. 23).

They flower from June until well into late autumn; indeed, they are generally the last of all the annuals to be lifted and cast aside.

There is extensive choice of variety in the three types, height ranging from 6 in. to 3 ft., colours varying between clear orange and warm lemon and crimson to brown and striped or blotched, and there are doubles and singles.

Taller varieties look well massed in the mixed border. Shorter ones are more useful for filling summer flower beds, and for edging and window-boxes.

English Marigold. This hardy annual is indispensable for cutting. Height is ordinarily about 1 ft., but giant types are 2½ ft. Colour is mostly in shades of orange or lemon.

Summer Treatment. Marigolds can survive without water in rainless periods, but they are infinitely better with it. No staking is required. Seed formation should be prevented by the prompt removal of faded flowers. These items also apply to the French and African marigolds.

Propagation. The old English marigold may be increased by seed sown direct in the open, from early March to May, where the plants are to flower in a few weeks' time. Drastic thinning out of seedlings to at least a foot apart is necessary.

Generally it is more convenient to sow English marigold seed about 1 in. apart in a box in March–April in the frame or unheated greenhouse, the seedlings before they become crowded being transplanted to the flowering quarters.

French and African. These marigolds generally are planted out in late May, the taller ones about 16 in. apart. The miniature *Tagetes signata pumila*, height 6 in. to 1 ft., is specially useful for edging small beds. They should be set out 6 in. apart.

Propagation. French and African marigolds may be treated as hardy annuals by sowing outdoors in late April or early May. But earlier flowering and stronger plants are assured by sowing in a warm greenhouse in March, or in a sunny frame in April, boxing the seedlings at 3 in. apart, hardening off, and planting out in late May.

MICHAELMAS DAISY

This can be one of the chief and brightest attractions in the garden in late summer and autumn (see Plate No. 29). Perennial asters (as they are less commonly known) are admirable for cutting, colours ranging from white to blue, deep mauve and pink, heights from 9 in. to 4 ft. and more.

Planting. Autumn and spring are the seasons for planting, in sun or light shade, in moderately good soil. Plants of the taller varieties, set out at about 18 in. apart, make magnificent clumps.

Staking and tying need early attention.

Winter Treatment. The tops should be cut down to nearly soil level in early winter and burned on the hard rubbish heap. Individual root-masses should be lifted and divided every third year, in autumn or spring.

Propagation. Division of roots, in autumn or spring, is the simplest method of increase, and essential in the case of choice named kinds.

Seed may be sown in the warm greenhouse during February to produce plants for flowering in the autumn of the same year. Or, for flowering in the following year, in the sunny frame in June, the seedlings being transplanted to a spare patch outdoors for the winter or wintered in boxes or small pots for the following spring planting.

MIGNONETTE

The charm of mignonette (see Plate No. 19) lies in its wonderful perfume, and on that account as much as for the attractiveness of the flowers—there are white, red and yellow varieties—it is valued for cutting. Height of well-grown plants is 12–18 in.

Summer Treatment. It appreciates generous watering in dry weather, and if seed-pods are removed promptly the bushy plants continue long in flower.

Propagation. Seed may be sown, in the spot where the plants are to remain and flower, from early March to May—the later sowings prolonging the flowering season.

Monarda

The soil should contain lime in some form, such as slaked lime or crushed mortar or broken chalk, and the seed bed should be made really firm before sowing. As soon as the seedlings can be handled they should be thinned out to at least 3 in. apart.

MONARDA

The big, bold flower-heads of sweet bergamot or bee balm (Monarda) are produced freely in almost any kind of soil. In the well-cultivated ground of the mixed border this hardy perennial is a real acquisition. There are white, pink and scarlet varieties, and the foliage is strongly and pleasantly scented.

Flowering time is June–September, and height is from 2 ft. to 3 ft.

Planting. Roots may be planted in autumn or spring, preferably to form clumps, in sun or light shade. The plants will not stand drought, so water must be given in rainless weather.

Winter Treatment. Old flower stems should be cut hard back in early winter, and as the plant spreads at an astonishing rate it may be necessary to limit the area of occupation, by lifting, dividing and replanting during October–November.

Propagation. Increase is by root division, during October–November or in March.

MONTBRETIA

Graceful, showy spikes of bloom are produced in August by this hardy tuberous-rooted perennial. In golden yellow, scarlet, orange and other colours, they are valued for cutting. Height is up to 3 ft.

Planting. The effect is most pleasing when the plants are massed in the mixed border. The small tubers (or bulbs) should be planted 3 in. deep and 2 in. apart in early March.

Montbretia

Winter Treatment. It is advisable to lift and replant every year. If they must be left in position for two or three years they should be top-dressed in March with old manure.

The old, withered tops should be cut to ground level in early winter.

Propagation. Increase is by means of offsets produced by the old tubers, planted separately in good soil at lifting time.

NARCISSUS

The value of narcissi, in many varieties, in the garden in spring, and in pots for extra early flowering indoors, need not be stressed. The culture of this hardy bulbous perennial is identical with that of daffodil, which see.

NASTURTIUM

A patch of waste ground or other piece of the garden which threatens to present a problem as to its occupants—because of the poor nature of the soil or lateness in preparing it for planting—can be beautified in very short time by sowing seed of nasturtium (see Plate No. 19).

Choice lies between the sweetly scented Gleam varieties (tall, semi-tall, and dwarf), the dwarf Tom Thumb class, and the giant climbing varieties which clamber up rough sticks or trellis to the height of 10 ft. The flowers of them all are excellent for cutting, and there is great diversity of colour.

The dwarfer kinds may be massed in beds or used to edge the mixed border.

Summer Treatment. Poor rather than rich soil is required. In rich soil the foliage is likely to hide the flowers.

Abundance of water should be given in rainless weather or the plants may collapse and perish.

Green- or black-fly sometimes fastens on the plants so that the latter are completely ruined. At first sign of this pest the plants should be syringed forcibly, above and below, with an insecticide, this to be followed, on the next day, by a clear-water syringeing.

Seed-pods should be picked off daily. They are produced in such profusion that flowering quickly ceases under the burden, unless the pods are removed without delay.

Propagation. Seed may be sown outdoors during April–May, where the plants are to remain and flower. The seed should be put in singly and about an inch deep, seedlings being thinned out to not less than 9 in. apart.

Seed may also be sown earlier—in March—in frame or greenhouse, singly in small pots or well spaced in boxes, the plants to be slowly hardened off for planting out in favourable weather in May.

NEMESIA

For the filling of a summer flower bed—after the wallflowers and polyanthuses have been lifted—or a length of narrow border in a sunny position, the half-hardy annual nemesia (see Plate No. 19) is excellent.

Colours include yellow, pink, white and blue, and height of most varieties is about 12 in. There are dwarfs that reach only 6–8 in.

Propagation. For summer bed-

Nemesia

ding, seed may be sown towards late March or in early April in greenhouse or sunny frame, the seedlings being shifted early, about 2 in. apart, into boxes and, after hardening off, planted in the flowering positions in late May.

Seed may also be sown in position outdoors in May and the seedlings thinned out to 3 in. apart.

NEMOPHILA

The cultivation of this old favourite summer-flowering hardy annual is of the simplest. It will thrive in almost any soil, but for first-class results well-prepared ground is required.

Height is from 4 to 12 in., according to variety, and flowers are in blue, white and various shades.

Propagation. Seed may be sown in March, where the plants are to remain—as edging to a bed of taller plants or to a mixed border, or massed at the front of a wide border. Seedlings should be thinned out early to about 2 in. apart. They spread rapidly.

NEPETA

Hardy perennial catmint makes a glorious show of mauve or blue flower-spikes, which are well adapted to cutting and mixing with other cut-flowers. From early summer to late autumn the beauty persists.

Height varies from 1 ft. to 2½ ft., according to the species, and catmint is perhaps seen at its best in the form of continuous edging. It does well also as clumps in the border, and in the rockery where there is room for its bushy, spreading growth.

Planting. Autumn or spring planting is the rule, and they should be spaced about 9 in. apart.

Winter Treatment. Where frosts are generally keen it is advisable not to cut back the old tops until spring, the old growth affording some protection to the new shoots—the latter commencing to appear in early winter. The old growth may be cut back with shears, or a sharp knife.

When the plant has filled its allotted space it should be lifted and divided with a sharp knife.

Propagation. Stock can be speedily worked up by simple root division in spring. Seed may be sown in the open in June, for planting out in autumn or spring.

NICOTIANA

The flowering tobacco plant, Nicotiana, sweetly scented and free-flowering, sends its perfume far and wide in the dusk of a

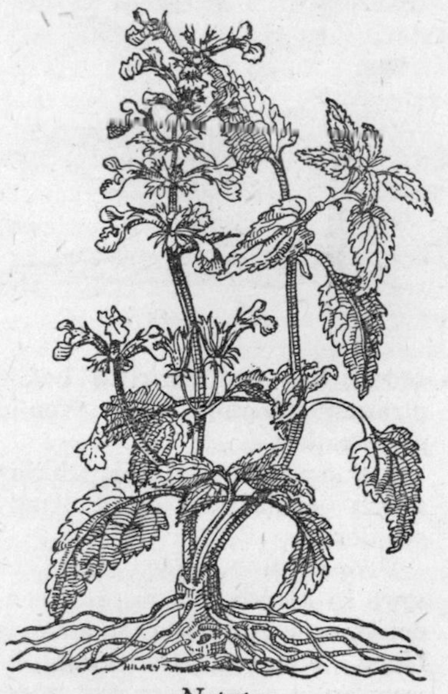

Nepeta

summer's evening. Colour of blossom ranges through white, crimson, scarlet, and lovely shades of the hybrids. Height varies from 15 in. to 6 ft., according to variety.

Planting. A half-hardy annual, this plant is normally set out—in beds, or clustered in the mixed border—in late May or early June, not less than 12 in. apart.

Flowering tobacco is both hungry and thirsty, so the soil should be

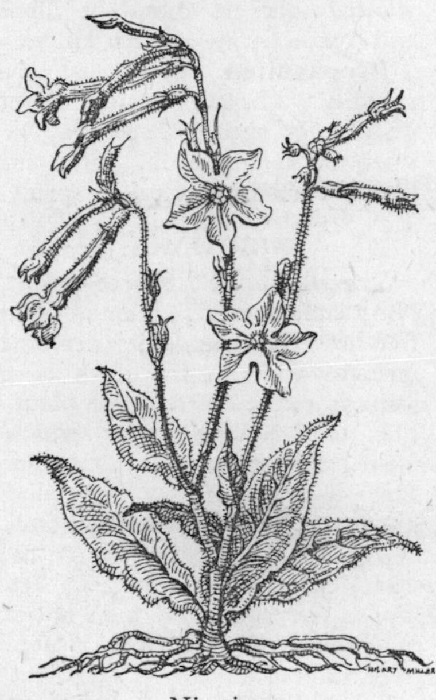

Nicotiana

deeply dug and enriched before planting and ample water given in dry weather.

Staking may be necessary during a wet summer or in a windy position.

Propagation. Seed may be sown in March in a warm greenhouse, or in April–May in a sunny frame. The seedlings should be transferred 3 in. apart into boxes filled with good soil, and hardened off before planting out.

PÆONY

The enormous flowers of pæony, produced in May–June, delicately perfumed, make a wonderful display in the mixed border (see Plate No. 11). Height of this hardy herbaceous perennial is up to about 4 ft. Colour ranges from snowy white to deep crimson, and there are single and double varieties.

Planting. Time for planting is October or March. Rich soil dug 2 ft. deep is needed, for the roots like to be undisturbed for years. The habit is bushy, and plants should be 4 ft. apart, with the tops of the roots about 2 in. below the soil.

Summer Treatment. Dry spells call for watering-can or hose. Staking should be given early attention, for the blooms are heavy and a downpour of rain can do considerable damage.

Winter Treatment. The tops should be cut down to soil level when the border is being tidied up in early winter.

Propagation. Pæonies need to become well established before much bloom can be expected. But where a plant has assumed somewhat formidable dimensions it may be lifted and divided into rooted pieces for transplanting, during September or October.

Root cuttings may also be taken, and without undue disturbance of the plant. For method, see the chapter HOW TO INCREASE FLOWERING PLANTS.

Seed may be sown in a sunny frame during summer, the resulting plants being set out in rich soil for growing on to flowering size. It usually takes about eight years for seedlings to develop to flowering plants.

PANSY

In rich soil pansies produce abundance of big blooms of wonderful colour and texture. There are a number of varieties, and if a bed cannot be devoted to them they may be planted in the forefront of the mixed border.

Planting. A position which receives a certain amount of shade during the hot days is preferable. Plants may be set out, 9 in. apart, in October or March.

Summer Treatment. Ample water is required in dry spells, and liquid manure or artificial fertilizer is appreciated. Blooms should be picked off as they fade.

If extra-large blooms are required, one flower only should be allowed to each stem.

If cuckoo-spit or greenfly appears, an insecticide should be forcibly applied. Either pest is capable of much damage, and the plants should be cleaned before flowers begin to open. Insecticide cannot be applied later without ruining the blooms by "spotting."

Winter Treatment. Pansies become very untidy by the time the cessation of flowering draws near, on account of the long, prostrate growths. The latter should be cut hard back to young shoots if the attempt is to be made to carry the plants over winter. Although pansy is classed as a hardy perennial, it is in all ways more satisfactory to raise new plants yearly.

Propagation. Cuttings may be taken in July–August. Choose young shoots, up to 3 in. in length, rising from the centre of the plant. The old, hollow stems which carried flowers are not suitable. The young shoots, trimmed squarely below the bottom joint, should be inserted about 3 in. apart, in shallow boxes in the frame. They should be wintered in the frame, but otherwise treated as hardily as possible. The rooted cuttings will be due for planting out the following March.

Pentstemon

Seed may be sown in June, outdoors in a shaded spot or in the frame, the seedlings to be planted out in October or March.

PENTSTEMON

For filling a summer flower bed or grouping in the mixed border, the hardy perennial pentstemon is a good choice. Height is up to about 3 ft., and the colour range is from white to crimson according to variety. It is good for cutting.

Planting. Good rich soil in a sunny spot is required, and the plants are set out during March–April, about 9 in. apart. When flowering ceases in autumn, the old tops should be cut back.

Propagation. Seed may be sown in June, in a cold frame or outdoors, the young plants being wintered in the frame or in a sheltered and warm spot outdoors, for spring planting.

Root division may be carried out in April.

Stem cuttings, about 3 in. long, may be taken in August and rooted in shallow boxes in the frame or cold greenhouse, for planting the following spring.

PETUNIA

Large, showy flowers of petunia are decidedly decorative in a summer bed or when the plants are grouped in the mixed border.

Petunia

Bedding varieties range up to about 12 in. high, those more suited for growing in pots in the greenhouse up to 18 in. There is a fine range of colours, with single or double flowers.

Outdoor Petunias. The planting month is June, in rich soil in a sunny position. Plants should be about 9 in. apart.

Plants which it is desired to keep over winter, to provide cuttings in spring, should be lifted in autumn, potted and placed in the greenhouse with protection from frost.

Propagation. Seed may be sown in April, in sunny frame or greenhouse, or earlier if the greenhouse is heated. Treating petunia in this way, as a half-hardy annual, is less troublesome than treating it as a half-hardy perennial. The young plants should be hardened off before placing out in their flowering positions in early June. Young shoots up to 3 in. long will root in light soil in spring in a temperature of about 55 deg.

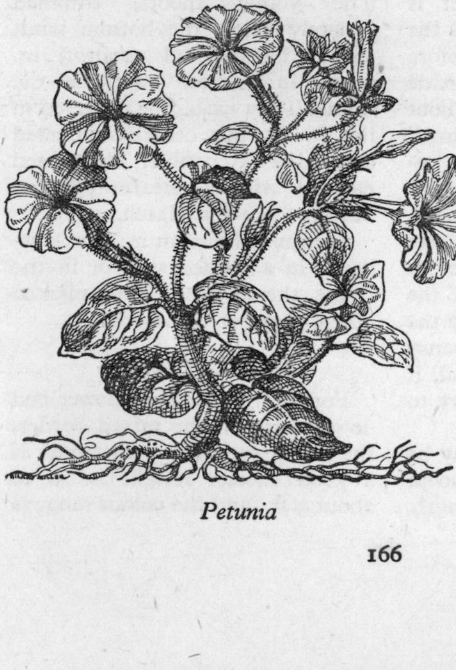

Indoor Petunias. When the time comes to clear the summer flower beds, the best of the petunias may be lifted and transferred to rich soil in 5-in. pots to continue to flower for weeks in the greenhouse or inside a sunny window.

The larger-flowered petunias specially suitable for the greenhouse should be potted, as early in the year as possible, singly in 5-in. pots, using rich compost. To secure these early plants seed should be sown during February or March in a temperature of about 65 deg. and the plants grown on in a temperature of not less than 55 deg. From October to March the temperature should not fall below 40 deg.

PHLOX

Large heads of close-massed flowers in striking colours, according to variety, distinguish the phlox. There are two kinds—half-hardy annuals and hardy herbaceous perennials, including a number of attractive alpine forms.

Annual Phlox. These range in height from 6 to 12 in. and flower from early summer to the end of September. They may be grown in groups towards the front of the mixed border, used for summer bedding (after the spring-flowering bedding plants have been removed) and the dwarfer ones for edging.

Propagation. Seed of annual phlox may be sown direct in the flowering positions, during April–May, and the seedlings thinned out to about 9 in. apart.

Generally it is more convenient —as when a bed is to be filled with annual phlox—to sow in March in the sunny frame or greenhouse. The seedlings should be shifted at 2 in. apart to shallow boxes, grown on in the frame or greenhouse and hardened off for planting in late May.

Perennial Phlox. These should be in every mixed border. They are invaluable, flowering from July to late September, and ranging in height from 18 in. to 4 ft.

Roots should be planted at 18 in. apart, in autumn or spring, in well dug and enriched soil.

Phlox

Summer Treatment. Perennial phlox should be staked early and kept well watered. Established plants will produce quite a lot of stems, and if the very best results are wanted these should be reduced to not more than six per plant—the remainder being cut back.

Winter Treatment. The old stems should be cut down almost to ground level in early winter. After about three years in one position clumps tend to become worn out. Before that happens the clumps should be lifted and divided and replanted in fresh soil. If they must go back into the same places, the soil should either be changed or dug deeply and enriched.

Propagation. Perennial phlox is quickly increased by root division in autumn or spring. The root-masses are tough, and if divisions cannot be teased apart with the fingers they should be separated by means of a sharp knife.

When dividing, the young side growths only should be replanted, the old and woody central portions being useless.

Seed may be sown as soon as ripe, but germination is apt to be slow, seedlings often failing to appear until the following spring.

PHYSALIS

Physalis comprises both hardy and tender perennials, the most familiar of the hardy forms being *P. Franchetti*, called the Chinese lantern plant on account of the

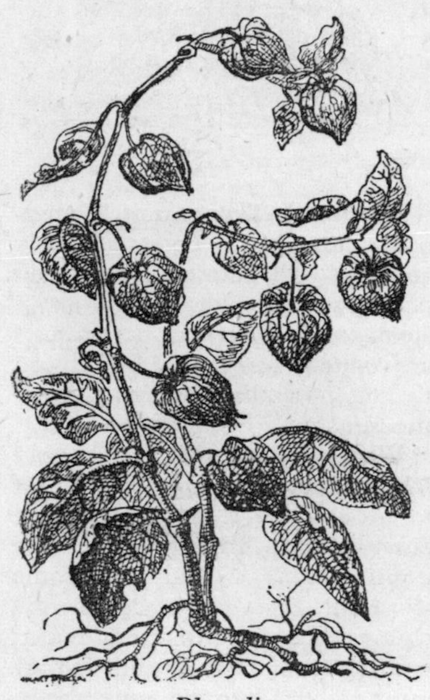

Physalis

yellow seeds being enclosed in a large lantern-shaped bladder that turns red in the autumn and may be dried for use in winter decorations. This is one of the easiest hardy perennials to grow and, when established, will quickly spread. It is propagated by division of roots in October or March.

Winter Cherry. The foregoing plant is sometimes known as winter cherry, but this name belongs properly to the small, shrubby, scarlet-berried *Solanum capsicastrum*. Seed is sown in a warm greenhouse in February or March, or cuttings of the young shoots from plants that have been cut back may be taken during the same period. A temperature of 65 deg. is required. Plants raised the previous year and well established in pots may be cut back in February to 1 in. New growth will soon appear and when about ½ in. in length the plant may be repotted in a good compost.

From June to September the plants are best stood outdoors on a well-drained position in full sun. Alternatively, to save watering, they may be turned out of their pots and planted in the border. In the latter case they may be repotted in September, for removal to the greenhouse, where the berries that will have followed the small flowers will gradually colour.

PINK

Pinks are included in the great family of Dianthus, which includes the carnation, sweet william and a number of other forms. They are hardy perennials, flower with the greatest freedom—in a big range of colours—and are sweet scented and most useful for cutting. Average height of border varieties is about 12 in. (see Plate No. 24).

Planting. Autumn and spring are suitable seasons for planting, about 9 in. apart in a sunny position. The soil should be good, and not lacking in lime. If there is doubt as to the latter, one of the prepared garden limes, or broken natural chalk, should be worked in before planting.

Rockery Pinks. These are suitable for the front of the border, but specially valuable for the rockery on account of their dwarf habit—about 2 in. upwards. Some flower as early as April–May, others June–September. Growers' lists contain quite a number of delightful varieties.

Summer Treatment. Prompt removal of faded flowers is necessary with all pinks and carnations. Too dry soil may result in the withering of buds before these have a chance to open. A reasonable degree of moisture at the root must therefore be aimed at. Weak liquid manure or fertilizer given from May onwards is a great help.

The withering of buds is sometimes due to lack of vitality in the plants. These are apt to become woody and leggy with age and such plants are not worth keeping. The stock must be kept young and vigorous by timely propagation.

Winter Treatment. The plants are tidied up when flowering is at an end for the year by cutting back all old flower stems. In the case of vigorously spreading varieties this may be done with shears.

Accumulation of fallen leaves and general debris over and around the plants is harmful. When clearing away such rubbish, opportunity should be seized to remove weeds which have a habit of pushing up beneath the mat of foliage of the pinks.

Propagation. All kinds of pinks are readily increased by cuttings or pipings, taken in June; and some, which produce sufficiently long growths, by simple layering. These operations are explained in the chapter HOW TO INCREASE FLOWERING PLANTS.

Seed may be sown, in spring, in a frame or cold greenhouse, the small seedlings being transplanted to a spare patch outdoors for autumn planting in their ultimate flowering places.

POLYANTHUS

Fine heads of blossom, excellent for cutting, ranging in colour from white to crimson, place the polyanthus (which family includes the common primrose) among the high-ranking plants for a spring display. They will fill a bed of any size to perfection, and may be sited in any odd patch of good soil that receives the early spring sun.

Planting. They should be spaced about 9 in. apart, in rich soil made firm about the roots. Autumn planting is desirable—after the summer bedding has been lifted. The plants will survive the hardest winter, when other spring bedding subjects, such as wallflowers, are crippled. They are also useful plants for a shaded border.

Propagation. After flowering, the plants should be lifted (making way for the summer bedding), and if they are to be retained for flowering again in subsequent years they should be divided into separate "crowns" and planted in good soil in a reserve spot until the following autumn.

Even if the site in which the polyanthuses have flowered is not wanted for other purposes during summer the plants should be lifted and dealt with as in the preceding paragraph. If left too long undisturbed, polyanthuses be-

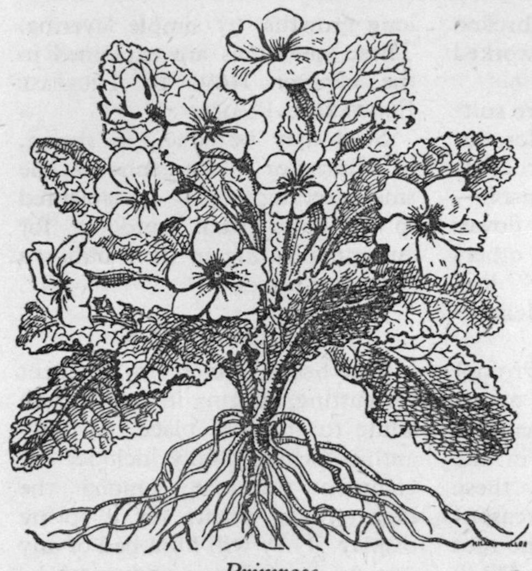
Primrose

come very "woody" with consequent deterioration in number and length of flower stems.

Seed may be sown outdoors in June, or in a frame, the small seedlings being shifted to good soil at about 6 in. apart, for planting out in autumn or early spring.

POPPY

Both the annual and the perennial varieties of poppy are valuable for the masses of colour they display in the mixed border, varying greatly in form and colour and ranging up to 3 ft. in height (see Plate No. 10). They require good soil in full sun.

Annual Poppies. Single and double-flowered varieties may be had in bloom throughout the summer if seed is sown in small successive batches from March to May.

The seed should be sown very thinly and shallowly, in groups, and the seedlings thinned out early to about 9 in. apart for the finest results.

Perennial Poppies. These include the oriental poppy, and help to fill that pause which always comes between the end of spring bedding and the first burst of flowers from the summer bedding.

Roots may be planted in October or March, in good soil and about 18 in. apart, preferably towards the back of the mixed border—in which position the flowered-out plants will be more or less concealed by the later subjects. The foliage usually looks somewhat forlorn when the flowers have departed, hence this "screening."

Staking is generally necessary. In late autumn the old stems should be cut back to the young basal growth.

Propagation. Seed may be sown at any time from May to August, outdoors, to secure plants for setting out in autumn or spring in their flowering positions.

Root division is another method of increase. But perennial poppies are prone to resent too frequent disturbance. Root cuttings may also be taken, as explained in an earlier chapter, How to Increase Flowering Plants.

PRIMULA

Members of this family differ considerably in form and colouring, but whether they be the hardy perennial varieties or the greenhouse kinds their decorative value is great (see Plate No. 3). The indoor primulas are specially valued for the production of winter blooms, whilst the hardy, outdoor varieties range over almost the whole year in their time of flowering.

Outdoor Primulas. Some of these are giants of their kind, reaching 2 ft. in height. Suitable for the mixed border, they thrive also in shady and damp spots. Moisture at all times of growth is essential.

Dwarfer varieties, ranging from 4 to 12 in., are delightful subjects for the rockery.

Planting time is autumn or spring, in rich soil, and the plants may remain in position, undisturbed, for two or three years, when they should be divided and replanted.

Propagation. Increase of hardy perennial primulas is by root division in autumn and spring, and by seed.

Seed may be sown in June or July, in a box in frame or greenhouse, very thinly, and the seedlings set out in the open after hardening off. In this nursery patch they should be well watered, then transferred to their flowering positions in autumn or the following spring.

As with all primulas, germination of the seed may be irregular. Seedlings should be shifted on as they become large enough to handle, with the least possible disturbance of the soil in which later seedlings are slowly developing.

Indoor Primulas. These fine plants include the *sinensis, obconica* and *malacoides* sections. Though heat is necessary to raise seedlings, the plants should be treated as nearly hardy when that stage has been passed. Given protection from frost, plants in 5-in. pots will flower well in the cold greenhouse or a living-room.

The *sinensis* primulas reach about 15 in. in height and are treated as annuals or biennials. The dainty *malacoides* varieties, about the same height, are treated similarly. *Obconica* varieties, 1 ft. in height, are treated as greenhouse perennials.

Propagation. Increase of the indoor primulas is by seed, sown in May–June, very thinly, in a temperature which should not fall lower than 50 deg. The tiny seedlings should be removed, as ready, to small pots—placed around the edges at about 2 in. apart.

By successive stages they finally stand singly in 5-in. pots. Two points call for special attention: the plants must "sit" flush with the soil, and water must be given with great care or they may damp (or rot) off.

As soon as the seedlings recover from their first shift the pots should be placed in a lower temperature.

Obconica varieties may be grown on from year to year, old plants being repotted in spring, at which time also they may be divided. The other indoor kinds are raised from seed each year.

PYRETHRUM

There are lovely colours and shades among the hardy perennial pyrethrums, and as the flowers are borne on long stems they are specially useful for cutting, during early summer. There are double- and single-flowered varieties, and height is 2 ft. or more.

Pyrethrum

Planting. Roots may be planted in spring or in August. The latter period may appear somewhat unusual, but if that time is chosen rather than autumn the plants are enabled to become well established before winter, and flowering the following year is assured. Rich soil is desirable.

Planting in clumps is most effective, spaced about 18 in. apart. Neat staking may be necessary when plants are approaching the flowering stage. The old growth should be cut back in autumn.

About every third year the clumps should be lifted and divided.

Propagation. Root division in spring or August is a quick and certain means of increasing the stock. Established plants make great masses of root, and division, from the top downwards, should be made with a sharp knife.

Seed may be sown in June, in a box in the frame, to provide plants for flowering the following year.

Foliage Pyrethrum. The ornamental-leaved pyrethrum, familiarly known as Golden Feather, is a hardy perennial in demand for bedding along with other summer subjects and also for edging. Height is about 6 in.

Propagation. Increase of foliage pyrethrum is by seed and by division. Seedlings are the more satisfactory, seed being sown early in the year in a warm greenhouse.

For division, a few plants should be lifted in autumn, shortened back, and wintered in the frame or cold greenhouse. As early in the following year as practicable they should be pulled to pieces and the small divisions, each with a few roots, inserted 3 in. apart in good soil in shallow boxes and grown on in the frame for bedding out later in the season.

RANUNCULUS

These tuberous-rooted relatives of the buttercup are extremely showy in spring and early summer. Height is from 6 to 18 in., there is great diversity of colours and they are good cut-flowers.

Planting. Clumps in the border are effective, a moist position being greatly appreciated. In default, plenty of water should be given when rain holds off.

Planting time is February, the tubers being placed claws downwards 2 in. deep and 4 in. apart.

Winter Treatment. After flowering, and when the foliage has yellowed, the tubers should be lifted, dried in the sun or in an open shed, then stored away from frost and damp until replanting time.

Propagation. Seed may be sown in spring in greenhouse or sunny frame, the seedlings being hardened off in due course and kept watered until the tops wither. The small tubers should then be removed from the soil and stored for planting out in the following February in the flowering position.

RED-HOT POKER

See TRITOMA.

ROSE

The great diversity of types, and of form of flower, is apt to be bewildering to the gardener making the acquaintance of roses in a practical manner for the first time. A visit to a rose specialist's nursery is the finest form of quick initiation.

Types of Roses. There are hybrid tea roses, simple tea roses (for planting where spring frosts are only very mild), hybrid perpetuals, Austrian roses and their hybrids, single roses, dwarf polyantha roses, China and moss roses, Japanese and damask roses, Provence or cabbage roses, Bourbon roses and briars, Scotch and musk roses, climbers and ramblers, and others generally described in the catalogues (see Plates Nos. 15–17). Each has its special points, and of all it can be said they are beautiful—some species, notably *moyesii* and *hugonis*, continuing the beauty of blossom into large and handsome "hips" to cheer the days of winter.

Habit of Growth. By exercising the art of "budding," nurserymen produce certain roses in standard form. That is, these have straight single stems 3–4 ft. in height, devoid of shoots throughout that length and with a "head" of branches which bear the blossoms. Shape is maintained through the years by wise pruning.

Climbing and rambling roses are formed into standards with heads of drooping branches, the latter being maintained in the drooping form by tying the individual growths to wire shapes provided for that special purpose. These are known as weeping standards. (See Fig. Nos. 124 and 125.)

Also there are half-standards, with "clean" straight stems 2–3 ft. high.

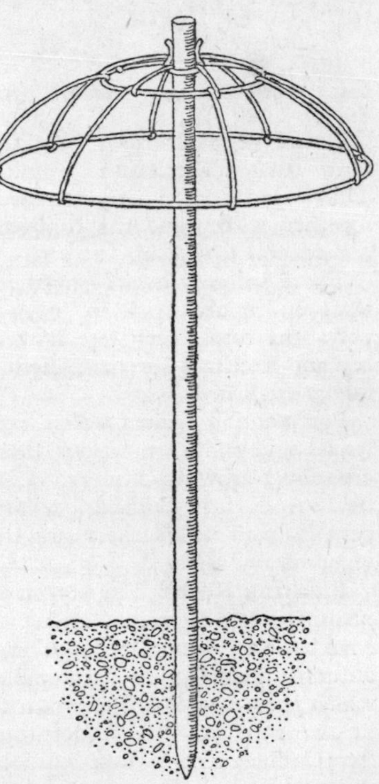

Fig. 124.—*A metal-headed trainer, such as this, provides support for the long, downward-drooping growths of a weeping standard rose*

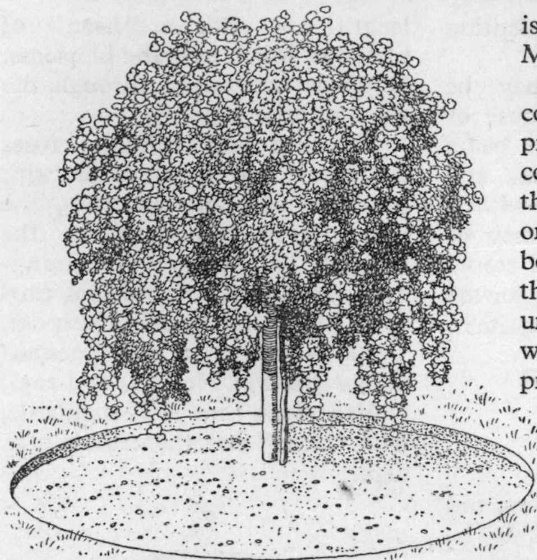

Fig. 125.—*Weeping standard rose in bloom*

is more safely carried out in March.

Unfortunately, the weather conditions are not always propitious when the plants come to hand. If the ground then happens to be frozen, or very wet, the roses should be kept under cover with the roots covered with earth until the ground becomes workable, when planting may proceed.

If the plants arrive before the ground has been prepared, they may be laid in a shallow trench and the soil heaped back over the roots and as much of the stem as can be covered, until the preparation is completed.

Dwarf or bush roses take the form that description implies. They are used mostly in beds together with standards to break the general low level.

There are very dwarf—no more than up to about 18 in. high—polyantha roses, very free flowering and excellent for permanently filling small beds.

For planting against walls, high fences and similar positions there are robust-growing climbing varieties. And for clothing pillars, pergolas and trellis there are the vigorous ramblers.

Planting Roses. The season of planting extends from October to March, but, generally speaking, autumn planting is preferable, whilst there is still a little warmth in the soil, and the roots thus have inducement to take hold of the new earth before winter shuts down on all growth.

Where the ground lies wet and heavy and cold in winter, planting

Soil Preparation. The site should be dug 2 ft. deep and enriched with old (not fresh) manure, or quite rotted material from the compost heap. The hole to receive the plant should be sufficiently ample in area to allow of the roots being spread out as horizontally as possible. And it should be of such depth that, when the final filling-in of the hole is completed, the new soil level will fall where examination of the stem reveals a soil mark, the latter having been acquired at the nursery. (See Fig. 126.)

In the case of dwarf (bush) roses, however, planting may be deeper, with advantage—the point of union of stem and branches being covered about 2 in. deep. That will induce the branches which have been "worked" on to a stumpy briar stem to take root on their own and assist the briar's roots in the business of providing

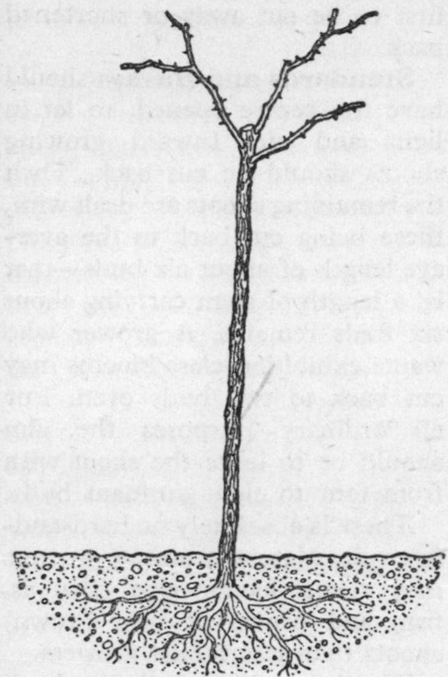

Fig. 126.—*Planting a standard rose. The few roots should be spread out as flat as possible*

nourishment for growth. (See Fig. 127.)

Early Support. If the plant obviously needs support, as does a standard or half-standard, it should be given a stake before the soil is filled in above the roots, it being possible then to see where to drive in the stake without damaging roots. As a rule, a rose has remarkably few roots to begin with and these should be regarded as precious. Any of the thicker ones which have been broken or badly bruised in transit should be cut back to sound tissue.

Ramblers and climbers, newly planted, should be loosely tied to the trellis or pillar or other support, to begin with. The soil will sink a little, and some "play" in connexion with the tie will enable the roots to sink at the same time.

Firm Root-run. A point not to be overlooked is the condition of the prepared ground both before and after planting. The loose soil at the bottom of the hole should be trodden so that it is reasonably compact before the roots are placed thereon.

When the hole has been filled to within about an inch of the top, careful pressure of the foot will firm it down. More soil is added, and firmed, the surface being made crumbly afterwards with fork or rake. Complications arise when, because the ground is very dry at planting time, the hole is filled with water before the roots go in. It is not then possible to firm the soil properly. A couple of days should pass after watering before planting takes place.

A better plan than filling the hole with water is to soak the roots for twenty-four hours in water, and then to plant. Then, after the soil has been made firm, water can be given from above.

Pruning Roses. Standard and bush roses and dwarf and climbing roses are pruned during the latter part of March or early April in

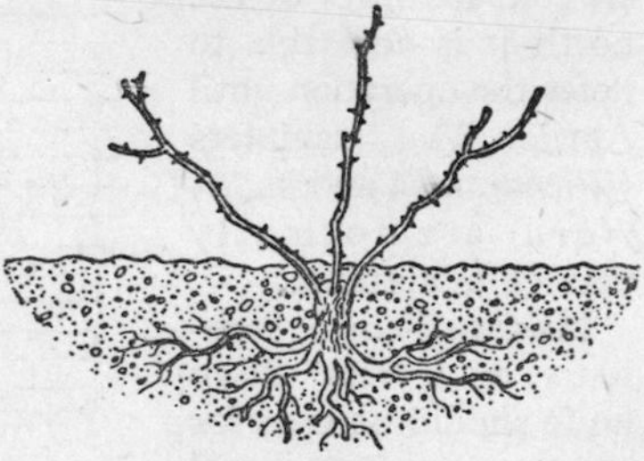

Fig. 127.—*Planting a dwarf bush rose. Point of union of stem and branches may be covered about* **2** *in. deep, as shown here*

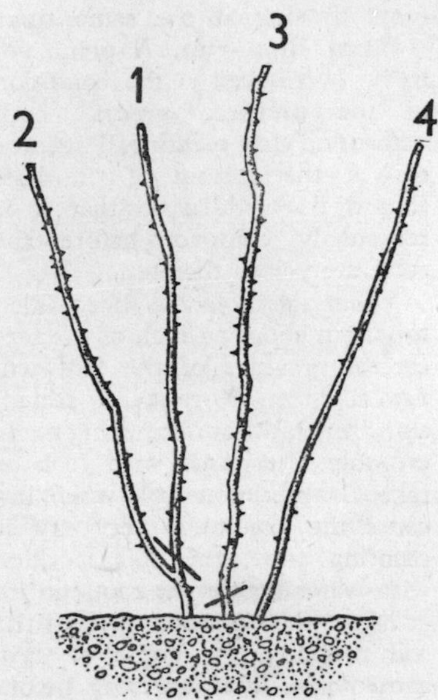

Fig. 128.—*In pruning a rambler rose the aim is to secure new and unflowered growths of greatest possible length. Old growth* (1) *would be cut back to where new growth* (2) *arises very low down. Really old growth* (3) *without new growth should be cut right away. New growth* (4) *from ground is left untouched*

reasonably mild districts. In cold localities of the north it is advisable to defer the operation until April. The ramblers (*Wichuraiana* and *multiflora*) are normally pruned in autumn.

How to Prune. Secateurs or a very sharp knife should be used for pruning, the former tool being preferable. Very thin, very soft or dead growth is always the first to be cut away or shortened back.

Standards and Bushes should have the centre opened, to let in light and air. Inward growing shoots should be cut back. Then the remaining shoots are dealt with, these being cut back to the average length of about six buds—that is, a length of stem carrying about six buds remains. A grower who wants exhibition-class blooms may cut back to two buds even. For all ordinary purposes the aim should be to leave the shoot with from four to eight dormant buds.

There is absolutely no hard-and-fast rule. Naturally strong growers may retain longer ripe (that is, firm and brown or near brown) shoots than less robust growers.

The shape of the standard or bush should be considered. It would be unwise to prune so as to upset the balance of the plant.

Weeping Standards need to have their heads maintained in good shape, which is done mostly by careful tying-in to the circular support. The vigorous, long shoots may be left almost full length, to droop right down, only the oldest

Fig. 129.—*How the growths of a climbing variety* (not *rambler*) *should be spaced out against a fence or wall*

shoots, obviously becoming worn out, being cut back.

In all cases, a shoot should be pruned back to a bud which points outwards; growth produced by that bud will follow the outer slope.

Dwarf Polyantha should have the old flower stems cut back, some of the oldest wood removed, and the remainder of the shoots cut back to within 6 or 9 in. of their base.

Climbing roses need no general shortening back. Dead wood must go, then if there is any crowding of the growths thinning out is done by cutting away some of the oldest (three years or so) shoots. The object is to retain and maintain a vigorous and fairly young framework of "foundation" branches.

Rambler types are thinned out in the autumn. They call for much more severe pruning than the climbers (that is, the climbing teas and hybrid teas, perpetuals and Pernetianas). The ramblers (Dorothy Perkins and similar type) should have as much as possible of the old flowered wood cut away each autumn, the object being to retain the best of the long, strong and unflowered growths—these being produced during the summer whilst the previous summer's shoots are flowering.

Aim should be to secure new, strong shoots or canes arising from or near to the base of old wood—as close down to the ground as possible. (See Fig. 128.)

The first step in dealing with rambler roses is to remove all ties so that the growths are free of restraint. Only then is it possible to cut away or shorten unwanted shoots without risk of considerable damage to the remainder.

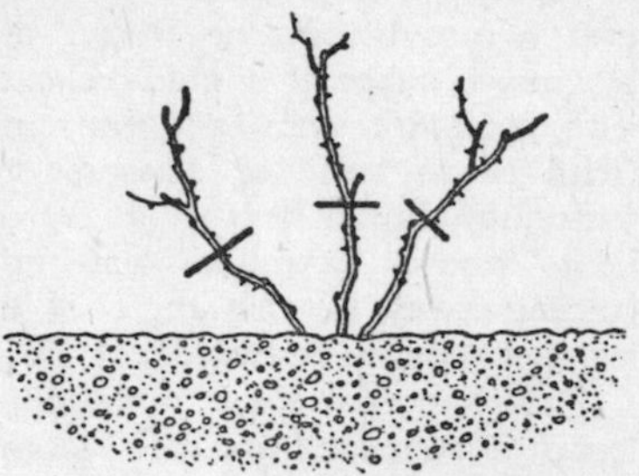

Fig. 130.—*A newly planted bush rose should be pruned back so that each growth is left with not more than three or four dormant leaf buds*

When thinning out is completed, the remaining growths are tied into place.

Newly planted roses should not be allowed to carry too much flowering growth the first year. Bush roses in particular should be hard pruned after planting, all shoots being cut back to within three or four buds of their base. It is necessary to harden one's heart to do this, but the plant must be allowed to become established in one full season before the strain of blossoming is felt. (Fig. 130.)

Summer Treatment. Watering of first-year roses in particular should be attended to. Not driblets but a thorough soaking each time whilst growth is active.

Ties and stakes should be examined occasionally, this applying equally to all seasons of the year. Ties must not cut the stems, and stakes must not chafe. A "cushion" of sacking or other material between the stem and the top of the stake (or whatever it threatens to rub) should be provided, and a strip of thick material interposed between the stem and the tie itself.

Cutting Rose Blooms. Whenever a rose bloom, or cluster of blooms, is taken it should be cut with plenty of stem, and the cut (with sharp knife or scissors or secateurs) should be just above a joint whose dormant leaf-bud (tucked away in the angle of a leaf-stem) points outwards.

The chances are the remaining length of stem will produce bloom again later on in summer or in early autumn.

Flowered stems from which petals have fallen should be shortened in the same way.

As with all cut flowers, roses should be gathered when the sun is not full upon them. The ideal time is reasonably early in the morning, and again in the cool of evening. In water, they last days longer than blooms cut when the sun is full out and they are dry.

Rose Troubles. Greenfly (aphis) is a recognized foe. Syringeing with an insecticide (when the sun has gone down in the evening, or during a really dull day), followed twelve hours or so later by a clear-water syringeing (both need to be very forceful), will effect a clearance. The operations should be repeated two days later, to make certain.

But this is no guarantee that this trouble is over for the season. A fresh attack should be watched for, and promptly dealt with.

Where greenfly cluster thickly on shoot-ends they may be disposed of between finger and thumb. Those who object to this method may dip the shoot-end into a vessel containing insecticide solution and switch the shoot-end about so that all parts of the greenfly become moistened. This latter method is only possible, of course, when the shoot is long enough to be bent over into the solution.

Buds which appear to have been nibbled probably contain a small caterpillar. Bud and caterpillar should be sacrificed together.

Leaf-markings may give rise to considerable disquiet in the rose-grower's mind. The commonest of these diseases are known as black spot and rust. The latter may be halted by dusting the leaves (healthy and otherwise) when they are damp with dew, or after a light syringeing, with powdered sulphur. Black spot is more obstinate and is only really effectively dealt with in early spring. For this disease, and for rust, a spraying then with any of the well-known fungicides prepared for this purpose is strongly advised.

These diseases are likely to spread from the fallen leaves, so where they can be gathered up they should be burned.

A soft, felty growth on shoots, especially in late summer, is indicative of mildew. Dusting with green sulphur, when the shoots are damp, is a good remedy.

Feeding Roses. There are special artificial compounds obtainable for applying to the soil around roses in spring and summer, and if these can be obtained excellent results follow.

The ideal is to spread a layer of rotted stable or farmyard manure on the soil above the area of the roots in early spring, covering it from sight under a sprinkling of soil.

Routine Tasks. Weeding, by hand and by hoe, cannot be neglected. The surface soil should be kept in a crumbly condition (though that is difficult with ground approaching clay) with hoe or fork, at all times. Caution has to be exercised when the hoe is used close up to stems.

Propagation. Increase of rose plants is commonly by means of cuttings and by budding, both operations being detailed in the chapter entitled HOW TO INCREASE FLOWERING PLANTS.

RUDBECKIA

A list of the dozen best easy-to-grow flowers for general garden decoration and for cutting would surely include rudbeckia, sometimes known as cone flower. There are hardy annual and also hardy perennial varieties, and colours include rich golden yellow with chestnut markings. Their place is a sunny spot in the mixed border.

Annual Rudbeckia. Height of these is about 18 in. They are raised by sowing seed in March, where they are to flower in the summer of the same year, and thinning out the seedlings to about 9 in. apart.

Or seed may be sown, very thinly, in a box in the frame, for transplanting to the flowering positions.

Perennial Rudbeckia. These flower well into autumn, and height ranges from 2 ft. to 8 ft. according to variety. Roots may be planted in autumn or in early spring, not less than 2 ft. apart, the taller varieties going to the back of the border.

Small plants rapidly develop into large clumps, and these should be lifted, divided and the best portions replanted, every second or third year.

Rudbeckia purpurea is now known as *Echinacea purpurea* and comprises a number of fine varieties with bright purple flowers having dark brown cones at the centre.

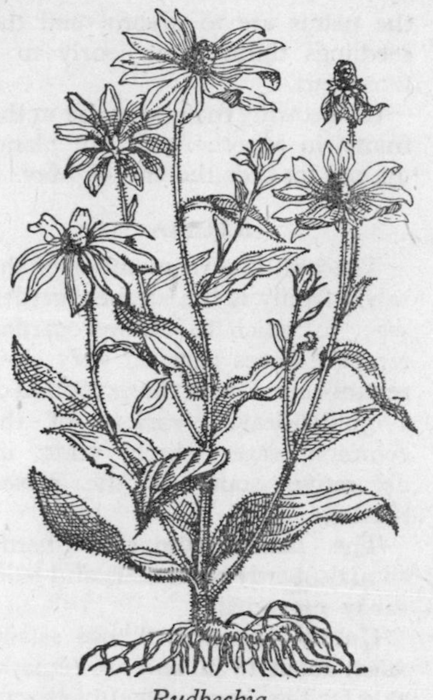

Rudbeckia

Propagation of perennial rudbeckia is by root division in March–April and in October. Also by sowing seed in June, outdoors or in the frame, for planting out in autumn.

SALPIGLOSSIS

The funnel-shaped flowers of salpiglossis, delicately veined and marked, can be had in white, blue-and-gold, crimson and other rich colours. It is a half-hardy annual valuable for cutting. It may be grouped in the mixed border, or it may fill a small bed, forming a great attraction from July onwards.

Height is up to about 3 ft.; there are varieties not exceeding 15 in.

Propagation. Seed may be sown in mid-April outdoors where the plants are to bloom, and the seedlings thinned out early to a foot apart.

Or a sowing may be made in the frame, in March–April, for planting out towards the end of May.

SALVIA

The best-known member of the salvia family is the kitchen garden sage, to which the flower garden representatives bear no very close resemblance—with the exception of a golden-leaved variety of the common sage which adds its decorative quota to the mixed border.

The family comprises hardy annuals, hardy perennials and half-hardy perennials.

Hardy Annuals. These salvias reach about 18 in. and are remarkable for the showy spikes of bracts, coloured purple or soft pink. A clump in the border is very attractive.

Salpiglossis

Seed may be sown in March where the plants are to remain for the summer, or they may be sown in a box in the frame and transplanted.

Hardy Perennials. As border plants these salvias are very handsome, with flowers of blue, pink and white or purple, according to variety, and ranging up to 3 ft. in height.

Roots may be planted in autumn or spring. Increase is fairly rapid, so clumps should not be left too long undisturbed. About every third year they should be dug up, divided, and the youngest and strongest pieces replanted. The old tops should be cut down in late autumn.

Half-hardy. The half-hardy perennial salvias are choice plants for summer beds, or summer clumps in the mixed border. Representatives are the scarlet-flowered *Salvia splendens* and the blue *Salvia patens*.

Planting time is late May or early June, at least 9 in. apart. They may be raised by sowing in a temperature of not less than 45 deg. in February–March, for flowering the same year. Cuttings of young shoots (taken from the old plants wintered in the heated greenhouse) may be rooted at the same time.

These half-hardy perennial salvias should be lifted before the frost spoils them—in October—and preserved for the following year: *splendens* in pots or boxes in the greenhouse; the tuberous roots of *patens* to be stored in sand or dry, sifted soil away from frost and damp. Both kinds need to be started into new growth in March.

SAPONARIA

Very free-blooming, annual varieties of saponaria are always worth a place in the mixed border. The variety *vaccaria*, in pink or white, and about 2 ft. in height, is specially useful for cutting. There are also compact annual varieties not more than 6 in. high.

These may be sown in March, where they are to flower a few weeks hence, and thinned out before they become crowded. To prolong the season, two or three more sowings may be made at intervals of two or three weeks.

Hardy perennial varieties, about 6 in. high, look well at the front of the border and in the rockery. Roots may be planted in October or March. Increase is by root division in autumn or spring, and by seed sown in June for planting out next autumn or spring.

SAXIFRAGE

Perhaps the best known of all the saxifrages is the easily grown London Pride, with its dainty sprays of pinky flowers in spring. It has many entirely dissimilar relatives, including the encrusted section, the mossy section and the megasea section, all beautiful in their own distinctive way.

Encrusted. These saxifrages are so called because of the encrusted appearance of their silvery leaves, growing in neat rosettes. They thrive in full sun in the rockery, and may be planted in spring.

Propagation of the encrusted kinds is by seed sown in March in the frame, using gritty soil. The seedlings should be shifted singly to small pots, for planting out of doors the following spring.

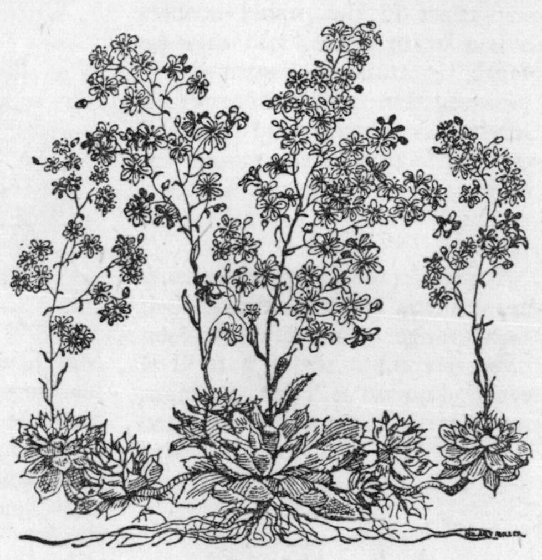

Saxifrage

Small pieces detached when flowering is over, and inserted as cuttings in sandy soil in the frame, soon take root.

Mossy. Refreshingly green and charmingly moss-like, these saxifrages do well in light shade in the rockery. They are also used for planting in the cracks between crazy paving. They should be planted in autumn or in spring.

Propagation is by seed sown in the frame in March, for planting out in autumn or the following spring. The old plants may also be increased by division in spring, worn-out bits being rejected. Small pieces taken as cuttings during summer will root in the shaded frame.

Megasea. This is the giant-leaved section and in general appearance most unsaxifrage-like. The large and shiny leaves are evergreen, and the pink flowers are borne in bold spikes. It shows to best effect in the mixed border, in sun or in shade, and may be planted in autumn or spring.

Propagation is by division in October or March, and by seed sown in March in the frame, for planting out in autumn.

SCABIOUS

A great favourite for cutting, the scabious bears its flowers—in a fine range of colours—on long stems. Height is about 3 ft. The section known as sweet scabious (see Plate No. 19) may be treated as an annual, seed being sown in March in a heated greenhouse for planting out in May. Or the seed may be sown outdoors in the flowering position, in early April, and thinned out—or carefully transplanted — to about 8 in. apart.

Sempervivum

If, owing to lateness of season or other cause, it fails to flower, it is worth while wintering the plants in the frame for setting out the following spring.

The Caucasian scabious is a hardy perennial, about 2 ft. high, with mauve or heliotrope flowers admirably adapted to cutting. There are also a number of Caucasian hybrids. Roots may be planted in March, in the mixed border, and should be well dressed with lime. Clumps should be lifted, divided and replanted about every three years in the spring when growth appears.

Propagation of the Caucasian scabious is by division in October or March. Also by seed sown in June, in the frame or outdoors,

Sedum

to provide plants that will flower the following year.

SCHIZANTHUS

The dainty blossoms produced in great profusion by Schizanthus have given this plant the alternative name of butterfly flower. It is a half-hardy annual.

For flowering in pots under glass, or for planting out in the open in late May, seed may be sown in a heated greenhouse in March–April. Or an outdoor sowing, where the plants are to flower, may be made in late April. Seedlings should be thinned out at about 9 in. apart.

SEDUM

Familiarly known as stonecrop, from its habit of spreading over stones and old wall-tops, the hardy perennial kinds of Sedum are invaluable in the rock garden.

All are quite dwarf, and flower colours include yellow, white and violet. Planting time is from autumn to spring.

Propagation. The plants spread rapidly, especially when grown—as they should be—in full sun, and it is an easy matter to increase them by division. This may be done in autumn or early spring.

Seed may be sown in a frame, or outdoors, in June, to provide plants for setting out in the following autumn or spring. The soil for sowing should be gritty, and the seed simply be pressed down to the surface and not covered over completely even with fine soil.

SEMPERVIVUM

Hardy perennial varieties of Sempervivum, or houseleek, will grow when rooted in the merest cracks in the rockery, on the tops of old walls, and even on roofs if given a fair start in a mixture of clay and soil pressed securely to the surface.

Dryness is essential, or there may be few flowers.

Flower spikes (chiefly in red, yellow and purple) rise in June-July, and height varies from 3 in. to 12 in.

Planting time is March, and propagation is by division and by seed as advised under Sedum.

SILENE

Early summer flowers of the hardy annual varieties of silene are most welcome, in shades of pink and rose, in the mixed border. Height is from 12 in. to 18 in.

Silene

Other varieties, of dwarf habit—up to 4 in.—make attractive edging.

Annual varieties may be sown in March–April, and thinned out to about 6 in. apart.

Hardy perennial varieties of silene, from 2 in. to 6 in. high, are suitable for the rockery and the front of the mixed border. Propagation of these is by division in March–April, and by seed in June to flower the following year.

Snowflake

SNOWDROP

From January to March is the flowering season of the snowdrop. Planting time is from September to the end of the year, and the small bulbs should be placed 2 in. deep and spaced 1 in. apart.

Anywhere in the mixed border, in sun or slight shade, snowdrops will thrive; and the wonderful whiteness of the drooping blooms will enliven the rockery if bulbs are planted in "pockets" of rich soil.

Snowdrop

Propagation. Increase is by small bulbs produced as offsets by the older ones. These may be detached in autumn and planted as ordinary snowdrop bulbs. But disturbance of snowdrop groups is inadvisable. Only if the flowers come in fewer numbers—indicating general weakening—should the bulbs be lifted, as the foliage ripens, sorted and replanted elsewhere, or in enriched soil if they are to occupy the same place.

Seed may be sown in June, in a box outdoors or in the frame. But great patience is called for; seedlings take about three years to attain flowering size.

SNOWFLAKE

White-and-green flowers of the snowflake appear later in the year than their rivals the snowdrops. The spring snowflake (*Leucojum vernum*) blooms in March; the summer snowflake (*Æstivum*) in May. Height is about 12 in.

This hardy bulbous plant is at home in the rockery, massed in the grass under a tree, and in the mixed border. It is important that the bulbs should not be disturbed for some years after planting: a point to bear in mind in connexion with the border. The plants require a year at least in which to become properly established, and after that they should be allowed to remain in the one position until deterioration is becoming apparent.

Planting Snowflake. September onwards is the period for planting the bulbs, 3 in. apart and 4 in. deep. If to be "naturalized" under a tree, some thought needs to be given to the soil. Snowflake will not succeed amidst a mass of tree roots. The soil should be forked over and made reasonably rich before the bulbs go in.

Propagation. Small bulbs produced as offsets may be removed, when an old clump is lifted for division in September, and planted separately in good soil.

SOLIDAGO

Its familiar name of golden rod serves to describe the flowering aspect of this hardy herbaceous perennial. The long golden plumes of blossom are borne in great profusion from August onwards, and where large vases or jars are to be filled with cut flowers it is always dependable. Height is up to 6 ft.

Planting. Roots of Solidago may be planted at any time from October to spring, in sun or shade, at the back of the mixed border. It thrives, too, in any moist position.

Staking in the early stages of growth is necessary. In early winter the tops should be cut down almost level with the ground.

Propagation. Solidago is a rampant grower and one small piece will form an extensive clump in about three years. The clump should then be lifted and divided, the best of the divisions (the young, outer portions) being replanted. Increase by this method is wonderfully rapid.

SOLOMON'S SEAL

The graceful, arched growths of this hardy herbaceous perennial (*Polygonatum multiflorum*) would be attractive even without the plentifully produced drooping white flowers. It commences to flower in May, and height is about 2 ft.

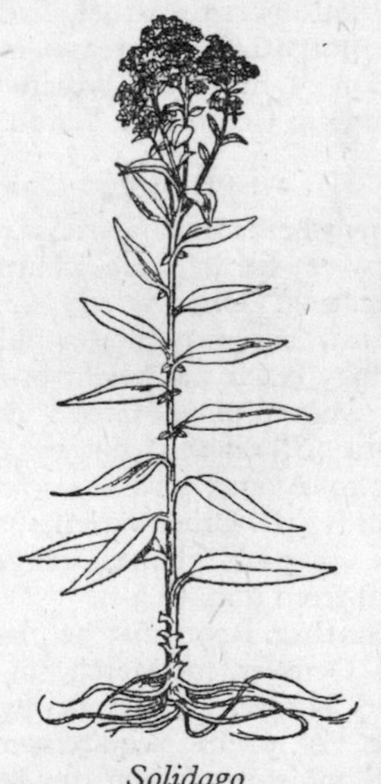

Solidago
(*Golden Rod*)

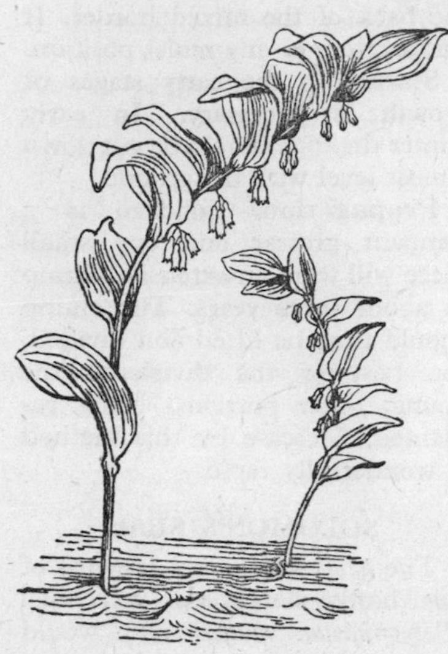

Solomon's Seal

Planting. Roots may be planted in autumn or spring. The plant does not object to partial shade.

Propagation. Increase is by division of the roots, which may be done in October or March.

SPIRÆA

Hardy herbaceous Spiræas (meadowsweet family) are charming for cutting. One variety, *Spiræa gigantea*, has rosy flower-plumes and may reach the height of 8 ft. The white-plumed Goat's Beard Spiræa (*S. aruncus*) flowers from June to August and the average height is 5 ft. Other varieties, with white or pink plumes, range in height from 6 in. to 3 ft.

Planting. Roots may be planted from October to March, in the mixed border, in sun or partial shade. A prime requirement is ample moisture. When the height of the variety demands staking this should be seen to early. Old growths should be cut down in early winter.

Propagation. Increase is by division of the roots, in October or March. Normally, clumps should be lifted, divided and replanted about every third year.

STATICE

This, in any one of its several forms, is admirable for cutting and drying for winter indoor decoration (see Plate No. 22). Even if not wanted for that purpose, the long flower-spikes are very attractive in summer and autumn in the mixed border. There are annual as well as perennial varieties of this sea lavender.

Annual Statice. Varieties *spicata* (puce), *suworowii* (bright rose) and *sinuata* (blue or white or rose) are from 12 to 18 in. high. Propagation of these is by seed sown in March–April, where the plants are to flower, the seedlings being thinned out to about 9 in. apart. Or seedlings may be raised in a box in the frame for transplanting.

Perennial Statice. Hardy herbaceous perennial varieties include *latifolia*, mauve, 2 ft.; *incana*, or silver cloud, with masses of small white blossom, 18 in.; and one specially delightful in the rockery, of lavender shade and 8 in. high.

Planting time for the perennial varieties is March. Increase is by root division in March, and by seed sown in June (outdoors or in a frame) to provide plants that will flower the following year.

STOCK

For filling beds or massing in the mixed border, stocks are available in a number of classes and colours (see Plate No. 18). All are beautiful, and all deliciously scented. Height ranges from 10 to 18 in. They are treated as half-hardy annuals or biennials, and plants should stand (according to height of variety) from 9 in. to 15 in. apart. To keep the plants flowering, seed pods should be removed as they form and not left to ripen seed.

Ten-week Stocks. These flower throughout summer if seed is sown in a heated greenhouse during March, the young plants being set out in late May, or if sown in the frame in April and set out in early June. Or seed may be sown outdoors in late April where the plants are to flower, and the seedlings thinned out.

The wallflower-leaved stocks are treated similarly. The night-scented stock may be sown outdoors in April where the plants are to remain and flower.

Intermediate Stocks. Treated as annuals, these may be sown during February–March in a heated greenhouse, and planted out in early June for flowering July onwards.

As biennials, seed is sown in August–September in the frame and the plants wintered therein—in pots or boxes—for the following year's summer bedding.

Brompton Stocks. For flowering indoors during winter, these are sown in the greenhouse during June–August. For planting out the following year, seed may be sown as advised above under Ten-week Stocks.

Spring Flowering. This class of stock is treated as a biennial, plants for flowering outdoors in spring and early summer being raised the previous June–July by seed sown then in a frame or outdoors.

Where the soil is light and dry in winter and conditions generally mild, these will prove hardy out in the open. But where the reverse conditions obtain it is safer to winter the plants in the frame, setting them out in early spring as soon as it appears safe to do so.

SUNFLOWER

Everyone's fancy does not run to those varieties of sunflower which produce blooms as large as a soup-plate. Fortunately, there is a wide choice among the annuals and the perennial forms of Helianthus.

Ordinarily good soil suffices, and a sunny position. Plenty of water will need to be given in dry spring and summer spells, and stakes should be provided early.

Sunflower

Annuals. In this class of sunflower height ranges from about 12 in. to 10 ft. or more. There are large-flowered and small-flowered varieties. Colours are mostly red, yellow and bronze.

The small-flowered annuals are specially useful for cutting, and as the height ranges up to not more than 4 ft. they are adapted to small spaces.

Propagation of annual sunflowers is by seed sown in April–May, outdoors where the plants are to flower the same summer; or seedlings may be raised, for transplanting, in pots or boxes in frame or greenhouse. The seeds, which are large, should be spaced singly and well apart.

Perennials. As with the annuals, there are several choice varieties of perennial sunflower. Roots may be planted in October or March, where there is likely to be plenty of space for development.

Increase is rapid, new thick roots travelling underground several feet and then producing their stems above ground. Old stems should be cut down in early winter, and the opportunity taken of discarding such plants as have journeyed beyond their appointed area.

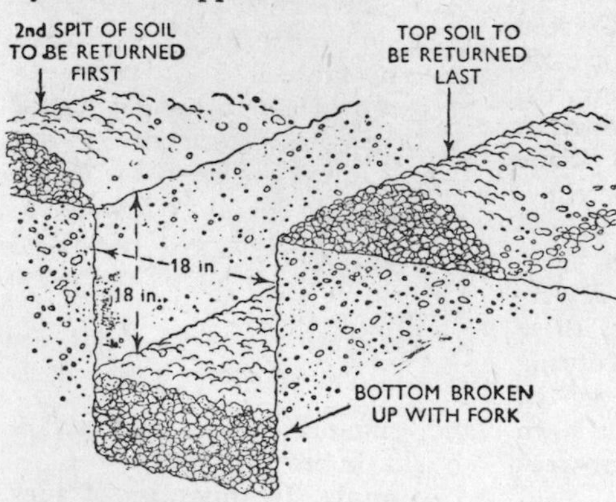

Fig. 131.—*Preparing a sweet-pea trench. First remove soil to width of at least* 18 *in., placing the two layers as shown and returning them in reverse order after bottom soil has been broken up*

Propagation of perennial sunflowers is by division of root-clusters in October and March, and by seed sown outdoors or in frame or greenhouse during spring.

SWEET PEA

Though fragrance seems to have departed very largely from modern varieties of sweet pea, considerably larger flowers and longer stems than of old compensate for that loss. There are long lists of named varieties from which to choose (see Plate No. 14). For those without special fancies or requirements there are sweet-pea seed mixtures.

Where to Grow Sweet Peas. The ideal is a fully open position, away from trees and the shade of walls and fences. They can be grown in clumps of a half-dozen plants in the mixed border, but they are more effective and more easily attended to when grown in a row or rows.

In order that both sides of a row shall benefit from all the sunlight possible, the rows should run north-south and should be at least 5 ft. apart.

The Root-run. A deep and rich root-run cannot be dispensed with. There is all the difference in the world between sweet peas just rubbing along in shallow poor soil and those flourishing in ground that has been dug deeply and enriched.

The site of a row should be prepared in autumn, if possible; failing that, as early in the year as may be. A strip at least 18 in. wide should be opened, the good top-soil being placed all on one side. Lower soil should be removed in part (and disposed of elsewhere) to the depth of 6 in. if that is the depth of rotted manure or old material from the compost heap that will be added.

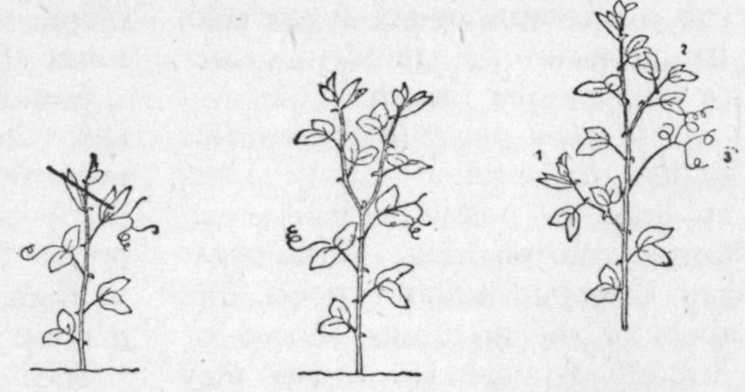

Fig. 132.—*When a sweet-pea seedling has made four pairs of leaves the top should be removed. This will cause production of shoots*

The remaining lower soil should be broken up with the fork and the manure or compost worked into it. The good top soil is then returned above it, and this may be enriched —a week or so before sowing or planting—with one of the special artificial fertilizers, plus plenty of dry wood-ash. The latter alone is helpful, if the artificial cannot be obtained.

Where the garden soil dries out very quickly in rainless weather it is an advantage to leave the surface of the prepared run 3 in. or so lower than the general level; this makes for ease in watering.

Obtaining the Plants. If the facilities (frame, labour and time) are available for an autumn sowing, that is perhaps the best plan of all.

An outdoor autumn sowing may be made during September–October where the soil is well drained and the position a warm one. A spring sowing in the open may be made during February–April. Or seedlings, ready for planting in position, may be purchased in early spring.

How to Sow. For autumn in a frame, pots or boxes filled with good soil are needed. In this soil the seed may be sown about ½ in. deep and at least 1 in. apart. The frame should be kept closed until the seedlings show through, then plenty of ventilation is called for. Only in very frosty weather need the frame light be closed.

If watering is carefully done there will be no losses from damping off.

When the seedlings have each made four pairs of leaves, the tip of the plant should be pinched off; and when new growth begins to form, the seedlings will be the better for potting singly into 3-in. pots, in which they will remain until planted out in spring.

The object in removing the tip of the plant is to cause the production of a number of shoots. If the very best results are wanted, only two—or even one—of those shoots should be allowed to grow per plant.

For outdoor sowing the seed should go in about ¾ in. deep. They should not be scattered freely, for the plants should eventually stand at about 9 in. apart, preferably in a single row.

How to Plant. Seedling sweet peas raised in pots or boxes may be transplanted to their flowering places in early March, if weather and soil conditions are favourable. In the north of England it is safer to wait another month.

With most plants it is desirable to disturb the soil around the roots as little as possible before and during transplanting. With sweet peas the opposite holds good. The roots of the seedlings should be carefully disentangled, so that they hang down straight and are practically bare of the old soil. For each plant a trowel-hole should be made of such depth that the disentangled roots go straight down. Fine soil is then shuffled with the foot or coaxed with the hands into the hole, and the planting completed by pressing soil firmly round the plants.

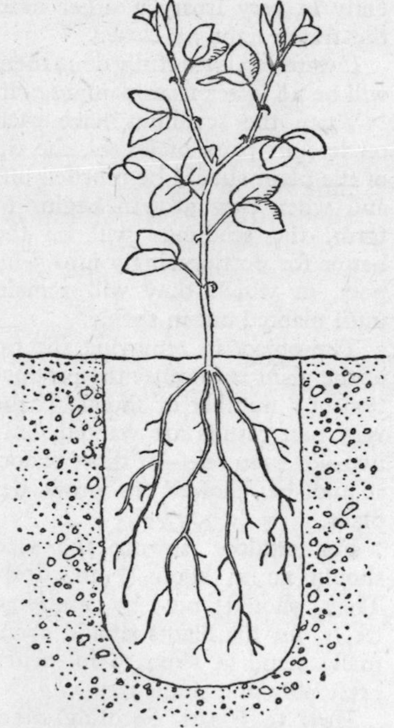

Fig. 133.—*How to plant a sweet-pea seedling. The roots, freed of soil, should hang straight down in the hole*

Staking Sweet Peas. Immediately they are planted out—or, if outdoor sown, when about 3 in. high—each plant should be supported by a twiggy stick a foot or so high. The permanent supports may be positioned later.

Well-grown sweet-pea plants will need stakes standing 8 or 10 ft. out of the ground. When it is possible to secure canes, these are best of all. In default of canes, unbranched beech or other sticks should be thrust in upright.

To these the plants will be tied, at as frequent intervals as growth requires. One plant per stake is the rule.

Summer Treatment. The really long and straight stems bearing big flowers are secured by removing all side-growths and tendrils as these appear. The side-growths are not wanted; the stems which were retained after the tops of the seedlings were nipped off should remain unbranched. If tendrils are allowed to remain these represent loss of growth, and by wrapping themselves around flower stems they lead to distortion.

These attentions take up considerable time and must be continued to the end of the season if "show" results are wanted.

Weeding and watering demand frequent attention also. And flowers as they fade must be removed, to prevent the formation of seed pods —for if pods begin to plump up with seed the strain upon the plants will be such that flowering will be speedily curtailed.

Sweet-pea Troubles. A few losses among the seedlings must be

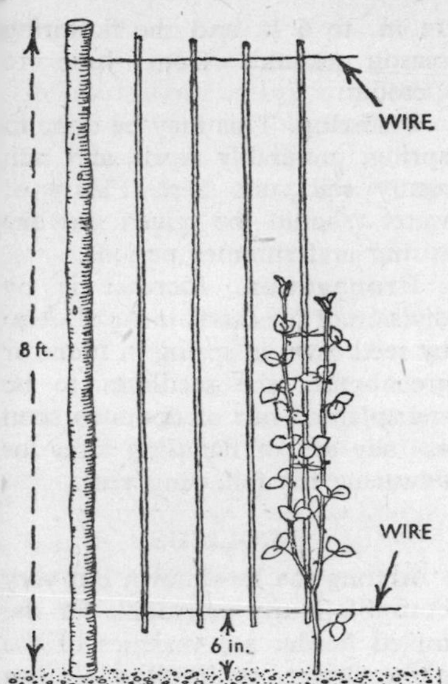

Fig. 134.—*Thin, strong canes tied vertically 9 in. apart to two wires strained between end-posts make ideal sweet-pea supports.*

expected, especially when seed is sown outdoors. Any seedling which suddenly takes on a sickly look should be uprooted and burned. The trouble may be disease or an underground pest. If disease, the removal and burning will prevent its spread. If underground pest, a little work with the trowel where the sickly seedling stood may reveal the creature for destruction.

Slugs may be very troublesome, especially to plants in the early stages. The soil and the young plants should be dusted freely with old (not fresh) soot, or with dry wood ash, to render them distasteful. Anything that can be done in the way of trapping or hand-picking should be pursued diligently.

Greenfly and blackfly may be ruinous in some seasons. They must be fought with insecticide, liquid or powder, from the first appearance.

Sparrows and other birds are sometimes a menace, pecking at young shoots and even destroying flower buds. Bits of bright tin or other metal suspended at intervals among the plants, so that these oddments sparkle and tinkle, often prove effective bird-scares.

SWEET WILLIAM

One of the old-fashioned favourites which have been mightily improved by the plant-breeders, sweet william is a gay and sturdy plant in the mixed border and a wonderful subject for bedding, and charming for cutting.

Colours include pink in various shades, scarlet, crimson, white—the choice of variety is ample—and height is about 18 in. Flowering time is early summer.

Propagation. Sweet william is a hardy biennial, and seed may be sown outdoors during May–July. As soon as the seedlings can be handled they should be transplanted about 6 in. apart, and shifted again in autumn to their flowering places for the following year. They should be spaced about 12 in. apart, in good soil.

THALICTRUM

This hardy perennial provides finely cut foliage, somewhat resembling maidenhair fern, very useful for mixing with cut flowers. Indeed, the species *adiantifolium* is sometimes called the hardy maidenhair; it grows about 18 in. high and has miniature white flowers in June–July.

Other varieties range from 3 ft.

Sweet William

to 6 ft. and bear flowers of various colours. The variety *dipterocarpum*, tallest of all when well grown, does best in poor soil in full sunshine.

Planting time is October to March.

Propagation. Increase is by root division in spring. Also by seed sown in frame or greenhouse in summer, for planting out in autumn where the plants are to remain. They do not like disturbance, so frequent transplanting of established plants should be avoided.

TRITOMA

Sometimes known officially as Kniphofia, familiarly as red-hot poker, this hardy perennial does well in a sunny position in the mixed border. The tall spikes of flowers may be had in various shades of red and of yellow. Height ranges, according to variety, from 12 in. to 6 ft. and the flowering season extends from June to October.

Planting. This may be done in spring, preferably April, and rich sandy soil suits best. Plenty of water should be given in dry spring and summer periods.

Propagation. Increase is by division of the roots, in April. Also by seed sown in spring in frame or greenhouse, the seedlings to be transplanted out of doors as soon as they are of handling size, for flowering the following year.

TROLLIUS

Among the less-known but very desirable hardy perennials for the mixed border are varieties of the globe flower, or Trollius. It has attractive foliage and showy blooms in shades of lemon, orange and white. Flowering time is May–July, and heights range from 18 in. to 2½ ft.

It is a most accommodating plant, flourishing in full sun, or in half shade, and in damp positions.

Planting. At any time from October to early April, when the weather is reasonably mild and the soil workable, roots may be planted. The plants should be allowed to stay in position for three or four years, when it will become necessary to lift and divide and replant.

Propagation. Trollius is increased by root division in autumn or spring. And seed may be sown in June, in the open, for transplanting in autumn to the next year's flowering places.

TULIP

The outdoor flowering period of these hardy bulbous plants may be extended from March to June,

PLATE I

PAGEANT OF THE FLOWERS

In most of the pages in this section are presented groups of typically lovely varieties of the main kinds of garden flowers.

The flowers are arranged roughly in the sequence in which they bloom throughout the year, although of course the periods of their blooming may overlap by weeks or even months.

Anemone *Japonica*

ANEMONE

Garden anemones show great diversity in form, colour and height, and it may not always be easy to appreciate the relationship between the different types. The tuberous-rooted kinds, that flower outdoors in spring, can have their season extended considerably by arranging for small batches to be planted at intervals. The tall perennial Japanese anemones, in white or delicate shades of pink, are useful in a mixed flower border, as they bloom in late autumn when other flowers are scarce. All types of anemone are excellent for cutting; they are long-lasting in water

Anemone de Caen

Anemone Hepatica

St. Brigid Anemones

Anemone Blanda

Anemone Fulgens

PLATE 3.—*Primula malacoides, with its pale mauve blossoms, is a decorative pot-plant in greenhouse or living-room, in autumn and winter*

Trumpet Daffodils

DAFFODIL AND NARCISSUS

Spring outdoors in Britain without these hardy bulbous-rooted plants is unthinkable. Daffodils tall and stately, with massive trumpets, golden yellow or creamy white or a mixture of the two; narcissi, no less lovely but usually with smaller cups, some bunch-flowered, and in contrasting colours—you cannot have too many of them! Sited in masses in the borders, or less formally in grass (under and around the fruit trees), they are a feast of beauty. They do well in window-boxes. Dainty miniature types are specially suited to the rockery

Poeticus Cassandra

Barri Conspicuus

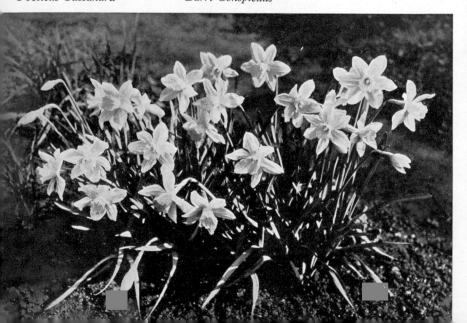

Narcissi (left) and (below). Poeticus, or the Poet's Narcissus, always a prime favourite, is white or pale yellow with a red eye. Barri varieties usually have bright-coloured shallow cups with perianths of bright yellow or white. A thick clump of narcissi in a wild part of the garden is wonderfully effective

TULIP

There is much difference in the heights, shapes and colours of tulips, and the numerous varieties offer a wide choice, ranging between the Darwins, Parrots and others to the Cottage types that are last of all to flower. Some kinds bloom early and others bloom late. Thus the flowering period can be extended from March to June. Tulips lend themselves particularly well to formal planting massed in beds, but the long-stemmed varieties are improved by a carpeting of low-growing spring-flowering plants such as yellow alyssum or forget-me-nots

Murillo Tulips (double)

One of the most popular varieties of Darwin tulips is Clara Butt (below)—a soft shade of salmon-pink. Massed together as shown in the picture they make a wonderful splash of colour. Cutting a few, here and there, for indoor decoration will not spoil the effect

Rembrandt Tulips

Parrot Tulips

PLATE 6.—*Crocus (above) and lobelia (below) are typical examples of spring- and summer-bedding respectively. In short grass below the fruit trees or as border-edging, the golden yellow or white, mauve or purple of the crocuses is delightful. Dwarf, neat and compact, in blue, mauve or white, types of lobelia persist in bloom from early summer until late autumn. It is a favourite window-box plant*

PLATE 7.—*In May patches of brilliant colour fill the eye in the well-ordered garden. The flowering shrubs burst into bloom. Tulip beds and bold irregular border plants are vivid against the fresh green of the turf*

PLATE 8.—*Flag irises add charm to the summer border, especially when flanking a grassy path. Irises show great diversity in type, form and colour*

PLATE 9

DELPHINIUM AND LUPIN

In early summer, delphiniums, six feet or more in height, bear spires of elegant blossom in varying shades of blue. Lupins rival them closely, though of lesser height, in many striking colours. The bushy tree-lupin, in yellow, white or mauve, is useful in the mixed border

Tree Lupin

Delphiniums (above), and (below) a fine show of lupins in full blossom

Shirley Poppies

POPPY

Scarlet is the traditional poppy colour, but garden poppies can now be obtained in a great variety of shades. Iceland poppies range between orange, yellow and white, while some varieties of meconopsis, the Himalayan poppy, have blue or purple flowers. Meconopsis Baileyi *is a glorious Cambridge blue. There are annual and perennial types, single- or double-flowered, ranging up to three feet high. The poppy is not an exacting grower. It will flourish in any reasonably good soil, but likes plenty of sun, and space in which to develop fully*

Cardinal Poppy

Iceland Poppies

Fairy (*semi-double*)

Meconopsis Baileyi

Oriental Poppies

Double Iceland

PLATE 11

PÆONY

This is a plant that demands space in which to produce its large, showy blossoms in May and June. The garden pæony that we know today in so many beautiful varieties has been produced by intercrossing a few natural species, chiefly the herbaceous P. officinale *and shrubby* P. moutan (*native of China*) *with their hybrids. Some of the newer hybrid pæonies are so unbelievably lovely that they defy description. Flowers are single or double, or semi-double, white to deep crimson, some delicately perfumed. The so-called tree pæonies, reaching about four feet in height, will flourish in sheltered, sunny shrubberies*

Duchess of Albany

A group of double pink pæonies (below) at the height of their flowering season in June makes a fine show in the herbaceous border. The blooms are not unlike old-fashioned full-blown roses and they have a faint, delicately elusive perfume. They have a rather short flowering season, but their foliage is always ornamental, especially the early purplish-red shoots

Moacan

Fashion

GERANIUM

The summer bedding and greenhouse plants popularly known as geraniums are correctly known as "Zonal Pelargoniums." The true geraniums are hardy herbaceous plants suitable for border or rock garden. They vary in height from 4 in. to 2 ft.

Geranium Harmony

Pelargonium A. E. Blake Amos

Ivy-leaved Geranium

Scented-leaved P.

Regal Pelargonium

Geranium grandiflorum

PLATE 13

GREENHOUSE PLANTS

One of the advantages of a greenhouse is that one can be sure of flowers for indoor decoration the year round. An even greater advantage, where the greenhouse can be adequately heated, is that one can grow in pots some of the rarer, more exotic plants

Group of Cacti

Cyclamen

Gloxinias

Streptocarpus

Calceolaria

Coleus (flame nettle)

Rochea Coccinea

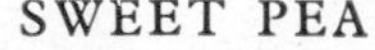

SWEET PEA

One of the most popular of summer flowers, for indoor decoration the sweet pea has few equals. To prolong the season of flowering, cut blooms as they appear. Not least of this flower's attractions is its delicate, subtle perfume

Basket of mixed Sweet Peas

Morning Mist

Ambition

Amethyst

PLATE 15.—*June in the flower garden. A large bed of bush roses*

ROSE

A universal favourite, the rose is cultivated in almost every country of the world. Colours vary between reds, yellows, white and intermediate shades. In form and habit the plants are grouped broadly as bushes, standards, ramblers or climbers. Many are in flower before May is out, and many still bloom in October and beyond

Étoile d'Hollande

Hector Deane

The Doctor

Basket of Roses

Madam Butterfly

Lemon Pillar

Moss Rose

Mermaid

Flamingo

Dorothy McGredy

PLATE 17

Rambler roses are good for covering arches (below) as they are rapid growers. Where space allows, a plot should be set aside as a rose garden. Bush roses do not like to be crowded by other flowers and lend themselves so perfectly to formal designs that it pays to grow them in their own beds in an open position

Polyantha Golden Salmon

Ten-week Stocks

POPULAR ANNUALS

The great stand-by in the garden—thus can be described that very large and popular collection of plants known as annuals. Annuals are plants of one season, but most of them fortunately are easily renewed from seed. Many are hardy and can be grown out of doors. Others, half-hardy, should be started under glass and planted out as seedlings. According to their kind they can be used to fill beds or to edge them, to occupy odd gaps in the border and to be grown in groups apart for cutting

Godetia

Candytuft

Eschscholtzia

Linaria

Lavatera

Clarkia

Because annuals in general bloom so readily, the soil and treatment they really require are often denied them. To correct treatment, as outlined in this book under their individual names in the FLOWERS IN DETAIL *section, they respond readily. By contriving earlier and later sowings the flowering season may be extended, and it helps tremendously if withering flowers are picked off so that no strain is placed upon the plant by seed production. Generally speaking, annuals, like most other plants, require adequate space in which to develop properly. Most annuals will flourish in reasonably good garden soil*

Larkspur

Cornflowers

Sweet Scabious

Nigella (Love-in-a-mist)

Mignonette

Nasturtiums

Nemesia

PLATE 20.—*Lilies in a cottage garden. How much careful planning has gone to make that air of informality and peaceful permanence! Below we see an interesting contrast between the brightness of the flowering border and the dark-green formal shrubs. Background is always of importance, even to the widest and most thickly planted border*

LILY

An almost tropical look is given to the flower garden by any group of lilies, but with few exceptions most lilies are perfectly hardy in the British Isles. The choice is wide, in colours ranging from golden or scarlet, orange-red or purple, to lustrous white. Some are delightfully fragrant. Some lilies multiply quite readily when not interfered with in a programme of general replanting in the mixed border. Others take a year or two to establish themselves. During vigorous growth lilies like plenty of water, but the soil should be well drained

Lilium Harrisi

Lilium Tigrinum

Lilium Beerensii

Lilium Auratum

Lilium T. A. Havemeyer

Lilium Croceum

Lilium Rubellum

EVERLASTING FLOWERS

So far as outdoor duration is concerned the general title "everlasting" is a misnomer for these free-flowering annuals; but the spikes of summer-cut flowers, if hung head downwards first to dry, will retain their fresh appearance the winter through

Helichrysums

Xeranthemum

Acroclinium

Pink Statice

Statice sinuata

MARIGOLD

There is little superficial resemblance between the varied types of flowers, any more than there is between the heights. There are 6-in. dwarfs for edging summer beds or lining the front of a border, as well as 3-ft. bushes for the centres of large beds or for filling spaces in the border. Flowers may be single or double and in varying shades of yellow, orange and brown. All are annuals, hardy or half-hardy, and among the simplest to grow. The flowering season extends from early June throughout the summer

Prince of Orange

French Marigolds

Legion of Honour

Dixie Sunshine

African Marigolds

Semi-double Hybrids

French Marigolds

PLATE 24

CARNATION AND PINK

Carnations are often avoided as a "specialist" flower, yet the border types and the annual varieties will flourish out of doors if planting and general treatment conform with simple requirements. The perfume of a carnation is in a class apart, and even when the blooms are absent the foliage is ornamental. As for pinks, there are 12-in.-high types for the border and dwarfs for edging and for planting in cracks in split stone in the rockery

Malmaison Carnation

Dianthus Neglectus

Dianthus Loveliness

Carnation Dianthus

Double White Pinks

Dianthus Winteri Winifred

PLATE 25.—*Typical Dianthus Allwoodii*

CHINA ASTER

This half-hardy annual (invaluable for cutting) may be raised outdoors as a hardy annual by sowing when the weather is kind in April. The large blooms of some of the modern types are so heavy that staking is necessary, though the plants themselves may not exceed two feet in height

Single Asters

Giant Comet

Victoria Aster Aurora

Ostrich Plume Aster

Sunshine semi-double

PLATE 27

BEGONIA

Fibrous-rooted dainty-flowered edging plants for summer beds, and big-blossomed tuberous-rooted types for bed display and pots: each kind in its way is very desirable. Other types are suitable for the greenhouse alone. The hardier ones are summer visitors only to the garden

Single tuberous Begonia

Double tuberous Begonias

Exquisite (fibrous)

Double tuberous Ruth Wald

Mixed tuberous

Coltness Gem (dwarf)

DAHLIA

Since the dahlia was first introduced into Europe in the eighteenth century it has been a favourite object of experiment with horticulturists, and changes and improvements brought about have been almost innumerable. There are doubles and singles in a wide variety of colours

Pompon F. K. Hirsch

Cactus Picotee

Collarette Dahlias

Bishop of Llandaff

Orchid Dahlias

Large decorative Dahlias

PLATE 29

MICHAELMAS DAISY

In late summer and autumn these perennial asters bring colour to the mixed border. The long-stemmed flower-branches are invaluable for picking when other flowers for cutting are sometimes scarce. Heights range up to about 4 ft., and colours from pale mauve to pink

Beechwood Challenger

Barr's Pink

Desire

Luteus

King George

CHRYSANTHEMUM

Another flower which has received special attention from the horticulturists is the chrysanthemum. What we know today as the florist's chrysanthemum has been evolved by a long process of selection and cultivation

Chrysanthemums Golden Beauty

Japanese Edith Cavell

Early H. Larwood

Fred Baker

Large decorative

PLATE 31

The Japanese chrysanthemum is a type well known today and it has reached a very high state of perfection. Sizes in general range from enormous "mop-heads" to the small tight "pompons" of the Korean chrysanthemum. Forms of flowerhead show a fascinating variety. Colours, too, are rich and varied

Newcastle

Healsville Sunset

Basket of chrysanthemums (below), all Crensa varieties, in autumn colourings ranging from yellow to golden bronze. With its firm stems and graceful foliage the chrysanthemum perhaps more than any other flower lends itself to indoor decoration, either in pots (brought in from the greenhouse) or in vases of every shape and size

Anemone-flowered

Korean Venus

PLATE 32.—*Colour in the rock garden provides one of the greatest pleasures of spring, but judicious choice of plants will result in flowers all the year round*

by planting according to section or class as listed in the bulb catalogues.

There are large numbers of varieties and differing colours in each section (see Plate No. 5). The outdoor position should be sunny, and a rich, well-drained soil is appreciated.

Planting. From October to December is the planting season, the bulbs which go in earliest holding greater promise of blossom. Planting depth is 4 in. and the bulbs should be spaced about 6 in. apart.

After Flowering. As soon as flowering is at an end the bulbs may be forked up, to make room for whatever is to follow them in bed or border. To enable them to complete their season's growth the lifted bulbs should be replanted at once in a reserve piece of ground, and watered as necessary. When the tops begin to yellow the bulbs may be lifted again, dried off, and stored under cover (where they will be safe from mice) until required for re-planting the following October.

Alternatively, the bulbs may be left in position until July August when they may be lifted and stored straightway after drying.

They may be left in the ground a season or two, if the soil is well drained in winter, then lifted and divided. But it is preferable to replant them yearly, in well-dug and enriched soil.

Tulips Indoors. For flowering indoors or in the greenhouse, the bulbs should be potted from September to November, three to a 5-in. pot, in good compost, the tips of the bulbs to fall just below the surface of the soil.

The filled pots should then be placed outdoors or in the frame and covered with sifted ashes to the depth of about 2 in. When inspection reveals that about ½ in. of top growth has been made, the pots should be removed from the bed of ashes to where the plants are to flower.

Those which have been flowered in an ordinary living-room, or in an unheated greenhouse, may be planted outdoors for future flowering. If forced—as out-of-season tulips generally are, in a temperature of 55–65 deg.—the bulbs are not worth keeping for a second year.

Propagation. Increase of tulips is by the small bulbs, or offsets, produced at the base of mature bulbs. Planted in good soil, tulip offsets will flower at the end of three or four years. Seedlings demand still greater patience, any-

Tritoma
(Red-hot Poker)

thing up to six years elapsing between the sowing of the seed and the appearance of bloom.

Verbascum
(more popularly known as Mullein)

VERBASCUM

Fine upstanding hardy perennials or biennials, in height from 2–6 ft., the verbascum or mulleins flourish in ordinary soil in a sunny border, and the flowers—ranging through white, pink, mauve, purple and yellow—are borne on slender stems or strong spikes, according to variety.

The perennials may be planted in autumn or spring, and are increased at those seasons by division of the crowns, also by seed sown outdoors in April to provide plants for flowering the following year.

The biennial verbascums are raised from seed sown outdoors in April, the seedlings being moved (when they have produced four leaves apiece) to a spare patch, at about 6 in. apart. There they remain until the following April, when they should be set out in the flowering quarters.

VERBENA

Apart from the beauty of the flower-heads—in white, pink, blue and other colours—verbena is noteworthy for the fact that it suffers not in the least from drought. A dry and sunny summer seems to add to its brilliance.

The half-hardy perennial varieties for summer bedding are planted out in late May. The hardy perennials, including scarlet and violet colours, may be planted in autumn or spring.

Propagation. The half-hardy varieties may be raised from seed sown in a frame in March–April,

Verbena

or earlier if a heated greenhouse is available. The young plants should be moved early to shallow boxes or singly into small pots, and to induce bushiness the tips should be nipped off some time before planting out in late May.

Increase is also by cuttings taken in August and rooted in the frame, the young plants being wintered in a frost-proof greenhouse.

Hardy perennial varieties are increased by root division in spring; by cuttings inserted in a frame in August; and by seed sown in a frame in June to give flowering plants for bedding out the following year.

VERONICA

The hardy herbaceous perennial veronicas are specially adapted to the small mixed border. They are neat in growth, and the dwarf varieties are admirable in the rockery. The taller ones produce many dainty spikes of flowers for cutting. Colours are shades of blue, and white, with attractive, evergreen foliage. Height ranges from 2 in. to 3 ft. or more.

Planting Veronica. Either autumn or spring is a suitable period for planting roots. They are not particular as to soil, but they appreciate watering in dry growing weather.

Tops of the taller varieties should be cut down in early winter. After three years in one position, clumps should be lifted, divided and replanted.

Propagation. Root division, in October or March, is an easy method of increase. Seed may be sown in June, outdoors or in the frame, to provide plants for flowering the following year.

VINCA

Where there is space for it to spread, Vinca or periwinkle is a useful rock-garden plant, and in shady places generally it makes rampant growth. Hardy and evergreen, the plants produce charming blue or purple or white flowers from June to September. One variety has silver variegated foliage.

Planting. Of a naturally trailing disposition, periwinkle seldom reaches more than a foot in height. Wherever a shoot-end makes contact with the ground, there it will take root, so there is no difficulty here about propagation.

Roots may be planted at any time from autumn to spring.

VIOLA

Some of the most cheerful spring bedding is provided by hardy

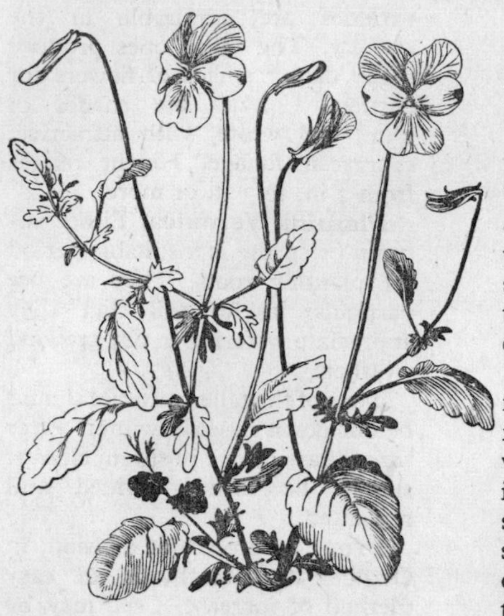

Viola

Propagation. Three simple methods may be followed: division of roots, cuttings and seed.

Division is carried out in September – October, plants being forked up and pulled carefully to pieces. Each plant will yield a number of divisions, each with roots, and these should be replanted at once.

Stem cuttings may be taken in early September and rooted in a box in the frame. These will provide plants for flowering the following year. The shoots to select are quite small ones, at or near the centre of the plant, and if these are eased away carefully some of them may be secured with a few roots.

perennial violas, always popular favourites. For edging purposes and for the rockery there are specially compact varieties. All are lovely, and if all faded flowers are nipped off, regularly, the plants persist in flowering well into late autumn. Colours include mauve, white, yellow and bronze.

Planting. For spring bedding viola plants are usually set out in April, at 9 in. apart. They may also be planted in October, for the following year's display.

Summer Treatment. Weeding, by hand or with the hoe, and watering in dry weather, are routine tasks. The prompt removal of fading blooms has already been mentioned.

Straggling growths which have flowered themselves to a standstill may be trimmed back in August. Their removal aids the plants in continued flowering.

Length of cuttings should not exceed 3 in. At the lower end those which have not a root or two already attached should be cut through immediately below a joint and the lowest leaves snipped off. The cuttings are then inserted firmly in sandy soil, about 2 in. apart, and the frame kept closed (and lightly shaded from direct sunshine) for about three weeks.

After that period, plenty of ventilation is necessary, but the rooted cuttings should remain in the frame until the following spring.

Whilst the young plants are in the frame they will need constant watching. Watering must be done with great care and only when absolutely necessary. Decaying leaves should be cut off directly they are observed and not left to spread trouble. The surface soil between the plants should be broken gently occasionally with a piece of pointed stick or hand fork.

Slugs and snails (*and* garden tortoises) are specially fond of viola plants at all stages of growth, and these creatures must be kept from cuttings and seedlings by hand-picking or dusting with old soot.

Seed may be sown in June, for flowering the following year, outdoors or in the frame, and the seedlings transplanted to a nursery patch—for planting out in October; or they may remain there, with proper attention, for early spring planting.

VIOLET

One of the most deliciously scented of all hardy perennials, the violet is quick to respond to careful treatment—and to show its resentment of neglect. There are a number of varieties, with blooms single or double, in blue, purple, white and other shades.

Planting. During April–May plants may be set out for flowering the following spring. They should be not less than 9 in. apart, and rows at least 12 in. apart.

The position should be where they are naturally shaded from direct summer sunshine during the hottest midday hours, as on the north-facing side of a fence, or wall or hedge. It is possible to grow them very successfully in a fully exposed position, but this entails considerable attention to watering and syringeing and it lays them open to attack by the devastating red spider—against which a nicotine solution or other insecticide has to be used.

The soil should be deeply dug, and rich with old manure or quite rotted material from the compost heap. Firmly planted, these conditions will result in abundant flowers. The same conditions are inducive to the growth of weeds, and these will have to be hand-picked constantly.

Summer Treatment. Coolness and moisture being two prime requirements, the violet bed will have to be kept watered when it is out of bloom in summer, as well as when the flowers are being enjoyed in springtime. An artificial fertilizer watered in occasionally will strengthen the plants, and the latter should be forcefully syringed with clear water at intervals during hot, dry weather, to discourage red spider.

In good soil, violet plants are very productive of runners—straying shoots which seek to develop rooted plants at their tips. Except for a few which may be needed for propagation (see later paragraph)

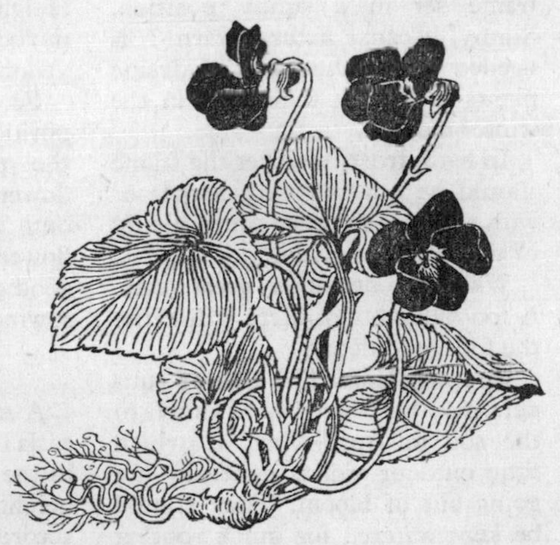

Violet

Virginian Stock

these runners should be cut off before they attain any size, for they weaken the plants.

Winter Blooms. To have violets in bloom in winter, outdoor plants should be lifted, complete with roots and soil, in September, and planted 8 in. apart in rich soil in a frame set in a sunny position. Sunny, because natural warmth is needed to encourage the frame plants to give of their best in the winter months.

In hard, frosty weather the frame should be covered with a mat or with sacking; at other times plenty of air should be given.

Watering demands great care. A too moist atmosphere will cause the foliage to decay.

Propagation. The tips of runners may be pegged hard down to the soil in April–May, at which time outdoor violets generally are going out of bloom. They should be kept watered for quick rooting to be encouraged. The rooted plants are severed (with scissors or sharp knife) from the parent plants in autumn or the following spring and planted elsewhere.

Another method of increase is by division of clumps, as soon as possible after flowering.

Seed may be sown outdoors or in a frame in June, the seedlings being shifted to a nursery patch when large enough, for planting out the following spring.

When an established bed shows signs of deterioration—smaller flowers on shorter stems—it should be scrapped and another formed, in really rich soil.

VIRGINIAN STOCK

Malcomia, or Virginian stock, is an early-flowering hardy annual for massing in a mixed border, or for dwarf edging, and for dotting about in clumps in the rockery. Height is 6–9 in., and colours include crimson, red, white and yellow.

Seed may be sown in a sunny position outdoors, in March, where the plants are to remain and flower, the seedlings being thinned out. To keep up a supply of the flowers throughout summer, it is a good plan to make small successive sowings from March to May.

VISCARIA

A no-trouble hardy annual, viscaria is very effective when grouped in the border, at the front, for the height is not more than 6–12 in., according to variety. Colours include pink, blue and white.

Seed may be sown outdoors from March–May, where the plants are to flower, and the seedlings thinned out.

WAHLENBERGIA

Belonging to the same order as the campanulas, and quite hardy, species of Wahlenbergia adorn the sunny rockery in summer with bell-shaped flowers on short and slender stems, height ranging from 2 to 6 in. These include *W. serpyllifolia*, with violet-blue blossoms produced one to a stem, and *W. tenuifolia*, similar in colour but with six or more blooms per stem.

Planting. From October to April the plants may be set out, in ordinary soil, where the low-growing foliage is not likely to be overrun by taller-growing neighbours.

Propagation. Cuttings may be taken in summer, and tufts may be divided during March-April.

WALLFLOWER

Often disappointment is expressed regarding this sweetly-scented, spring-flowering plant. If that is so, it is due to planting in the spring instead of in autumn, and in ground ill prepared.

There are single and double varieties, and there is an extensive range of colours.

Planting. Strong, bushy plants should be set out in autumn or early winter, in their final positions, about 12 in. apart. The position should be sunny, and the soil should have added to it some old crushed mortar or lime. If the ground is clay-like it should be deeply dug and lightened by working into it—in addition to the old mortar or lime—plenty of grit.

Also, the soil must be really firm before planting; it must be well firmed around each plant as it goes in. After a frost, which is apt to lift the plants, the soil should be trodden around them again—when this can be done without the soil clinging to the boots.

Treated thus, wallflowers commence to bloom early in the year and continue to do so until the summer bedding is due for planting out—provided all seed-pods are picked off regularly.

Wallflower

The Siberian wallflower (*Cheiranthus Allionii*) is an orange-flowered biennial, from 9 to 12 in. high, and flowering to the end of summer if flower pods are regularly removed. Its treatment is the same as for other wallflowers.

Propagation. Wallflowers will bloom a second year, but they are not worth keeping after the first season. Old plants become leggy and are inferior in every way.

Seed may be sown outdoors, or in a box in the frame, in June. When the seedlings have each made a third or fourth leaf they should be moved to a spare patch—in the sun—at about 6 in. apart; the patch having been prepared with old mortar or lime worked in.

Weeding and watering will be necessary until the autumn or early winter, when the plants should be lifted with all the soil possible attached to the roots and set out in their flowering places.

WATER-LILY

The charm of a garden pool is completed by the lovely blossoms of hardy water-lilies (Nymphæa). There are a number of varieties, colours including white, crimson, yellow and other shades.

Planting. Roots of hardy water-lilies are most conveniently planted in rich soil contained in an old basket or piece of sacking tied firmly, the whole then being sunk in the water (see page 100). Time to plant is April to June.

The position should be in full sun, and when it becomes necessary to restore the level of the water (reduced by evaporation) that which is added must be sun-warmed first. The water must be of the same temperature (or higher) as that already in the pool; otherwise the shock is almost certain to interfere with flowering.

Large water-lilies should be planted at least 6 ft. apart, but for the smaller varieties a space of 2–3 ft. will suffice.

Water-lilies

Propagation. Water-lilies may be increased by division, during the period April–June.

WINTER ACONITE

Eranthis, or winter aconite, is a low-growing tuberous-rooted perennial with yellow flowers each set in a whorl of green leaflets. Height is not more than about 4 in. Flowering from January to March, it is of tremendous value in that season of little garden cheer.

Planting. The small tubers may be planted from October to December, 2 in. deep and about the same apart, where they can remain undisturbed for years, among garden ferns, in the rockery, and in good soil under a tree.

Propagation. Winter aconite is increased by division of tubers during October–November. But as this plant, once established, is apt to resent disturbance, clumps should not be interfered with to a greater extent than is necessary for purposes of propagation.

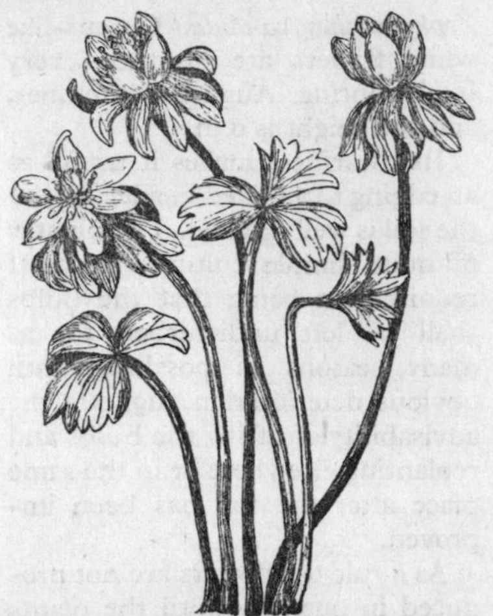

Winter Aconite

WINTER HELIOTROPE

No relationship exists between this plant and the heliotrope (or "cherry pie") of the summer flower beds and the greenhouse; but they have one point in common—delightful fragrance. One does not have to search out the perfume of the winter heliotrope (*Petasites fragrans*). It is all-pervading, and a bunch of the pale lilac flowers, clustered thickly on sturdy spikes, up to 12 in. high, will shed sweetness throughout a room for several days.

Planting. The fleshy rhizomes (rootstocks) may be planted in autumn, to produce a massed effect. An inch covering of soil is sufficient. The position should be a sunny one, to induce early winter flowering; the period ranges from January to March. The plant may be massed at the front of a shrub border, or in a rough piece of ground. If it is introduced to the mixed border it will need to be kept severely in check, owing to the rapidity with which it travels by root extension.

Its strong growth has enabled *Petasites fragrans* to become naturalized on some railway embankments and similar sites in southern England. The woolly leaves are reminiscent of coltsfoot.

Propagation. Increase, as has been noted, is naturally rapid. The garden method—as with most other hardy perennials—is by simple division of root-clumps, preferably in the autumn.

ZEPHYRANTHES

Flower of the West Wind is the English name for this hardy bulbous plant whose botanical title is

Zephyranthes candida. Crocus-like white flowers are produced very freely during August–September, and the height is 6 in.

Its dwarfness makes it useful as an edging to a mixed border, where the soil is well drained. The plant is of quite simple culture, its chief requirement being that the bulbs shall be left undisturbed for as many seasons as possible—until obvious deterioration suggests the advisability of lifting the bulbs and replanting elsewhere or in the same place after the soil has been improved.

As a rule the flowers are not produced in quantity until the plants have been in position a year.

Planting. The small bulbs may be set out 3–4 in. apart and 4 in. deep, during the period August–November.

Propagation. Increase is by removal of offsets ("baby" bulbs) when replanting takes place, the offsets being treated then in the same way as ordinary bulbs.

ZINNIA

One of the most striking of all the half-hardy annuals, the zinnia makes a magnificent show in a summer flower bed or massed in the mixed border. There are single and double varieties, and the flower-heads of some are really massive.

Colours include white, yellow and scarlet, and heights range up to 2½ ft. Long-stemmed zinnias are useful for cutting.

Planting. Being a half-hardy annual, it is usually not safe to plant out the zinnia until the end of May or early in June. The plants should stand not less than 8 in. apart; if sown in the flowering position they should be thinned out to that distance.

Zinnia

Soil should be deeply dug, and rich with old manure or compost-heap material, and the position should be in full sun.

Summer Treatment. Plenty of water needs to be given in dry weather, and as the stems are rather brittle each plant should be neatly staked early in its career.

Propagation. Seed may be sown in the open, where the plants are to remain and flower, in May, the seedlings to be thinned out to at least 8 in. apart.

Earlier flowering is ensured by sowing in a frame or greenhouse in April. The seed should be sown very thinly, and the seedlings moved to a box of rich soil at not less than 2 in. apart. They should be kept growing steadily, then gradually hardened off for planting out in late May or early June.

SECTION XVII

FLOWERING SHRUBS AND TREES

WHERE and why are two points to be settled before shrubs or trees are purchased. They should not be planted where in a year or two's time they will be in fierce competition with other garden occupants, or where they will appear incongruous. The "why" concerns the ultimate usefulness of the tree or shrub: is it wanted primarily for shade and quick growth, or for its flowers, or its berries, or the autumn tinting of its leaves?

Those points decided, it is easier to make a sensible selection. One might well start by ruling out all trees in the forest class—chestnut, lime, sycamore and others with similar large proportions—as they take up far too much space for ordinary purposes. Fortunately, their exclusion still leaves an abundance to choose from.

For Shade and Quick Growth. One of the loveliest of the quick growers is the mountain ash. The dainty silver birch is another, and so is laburnum. Growth of these is not so dense as that of the forest trees, and neither height nor branch-span will be troublesome if secateurs and saw are used occasionally.

For Flowers. Laburnum is mentioned in the previous paragraph, and to it must be added (for selection) lilac in variety, the guelder rose (*Viburnum opulus*), bird cherry, "may" (Cratægus), buddleia, mock orange, crab apple, and that king of shrubs the rhododendron. These are but typical of the nurseryman's stock.

For Berries. Mountain ash, among those already mentioned, is famous for its autumn berry show. For "berries" of a larger nature the crab apple is perhaps unexcelled. Varieties of cratægus, of which the "may" or hawthorn is an example, are magnificently conspicuous at summer's end with never-failing masses of coloured berries. The red and yellow of the holly fruits, and the varied colours of cotoneaster varieties, make early winter memorable.

Tinted Leaves. In autumn, gay colour comes in plenty to the foliage of berberis and cotoneaster, sumach, and varieties of cratægus and guelder rose, among others.

The list on page 204 will enable you to make a quick comparison of the qualities and characteristics of the main kinds.

When to Plant. Those trees and shrubs which naturally drop all their leaves towards the end of the year (they are classified as deciduous) are best planted in late October or in November, the next chance being February–March.

Rhododendron and holly and bay and all those outdoor subjects which are evergreen (that is, are never completely bare of leaves) transplant most successfully in August or September.

ORNAMENTAL SHRUBS AND TREES

Name	*Flower and Season*	*Other Attractions*	*Type*	*Suitable for*
Almond	Rose-coloured March–April	Nuts in late summer	Up to 30 ft.	Specimen tree
Bay	Flowers white, inconspicuous	Fragrant leaves (used in flavouring)	Evergreen up to 40 ft.	Shrub or tree
Berberis Darwinii	Orange-coloured, April–May	Purple berries	Evergreen up to 10 ft.	Any position
Bird Cherry	White, May	Coloured foliage	Up to 20 ft.	Full sun
Buddleia variabilis	Deep lilac, August	Decorative for indoors	Up to 9 ft.	Specimen shrub
Cratægus varieties	White, pink, red, May–June	Berries in autumn	Up to 20 ft.	Any position
Cotoneaster varieties	White, etc., in May	Berries in autumn	Up to 30 ft.	Against walls and fences
Flowering Currant	Deep rose, fragrant, May	Decorative for indoors	Up to 8 ft.	Sunny position
Forsythia	Yellow sprays, March–April	Decorative for indoors	Up to 12 ft.	Wall, pillar or arch
Guelder Rose (Viburnum)	Heads of white flowers, June	Coloured foliage in autumn	Up to 15 ft.	Specimen shrub
Hydrangea paniculata	Heads of white flowers, Aug.-Sept.	Decorative for indoors	Up to 6 ft.	Sheltered spot
Laburnum	Yellow, April–May	Will grow almost anywhere	Up to 25 ft.	Shrubbery or specimen tree
Lilac varieties	Lilac, crimson, white	Decorative for indoors	Up to 20 ft.	Sunny position
Mock Orange	White, scented, June	Strong and rapid grower	Up to 12 ft.	Sunny position
Mountain Ash	Flat heads creamy-white, in May	Scarlet berries, summer, autumn	Up to 30 ft.	Giving light shade
Rhododendron	Many varieties and colours, April onwards	Decorative for indoors	Evergreen up to 15 ft.	Soil free of lime
Silver Birch		Graceful appearance	Up to 50 ft.	Giving light shade
Weigela (or Diervilla)	Rose, red, yellow and white, in May	Decorative for indoors	Up to 8 ft.	Specimen shrub

Whichever class is being dealt with, planting should be done when the soil is neither so dry as to be rock-like nor so wet as to be unmanageable in its messiness. Between those extremes there are abundant opportunities. Much damage is often done by unnecessary exposure of the roots to the air. The ideal is for the plant to arrive for planting with its soil-encased roots wrapped about with sacking. All too frequently the roots are quite soilless and quite dry, in which case they should be soaked in water for a few hours.

How to Plant. For each tree or shrub there should be prepared a hole several inches deeper than the soil-mark on its stem, sufficient of the dug-out soil being returned to raise the level of the hole so that when the subject is planted its soil-mark shall be just below the surface.

The hole should be large enough in area to take the ball of roots and soil with about four inches to spare all round. The sacking is removed after the tree or shrub has been placed in the hole, then filling in proceeds, each layer of surrounding soil being stamped down.

If the roots have no soil about them, the tree or shrub should be bumped gently up and down after the adding of each of the first two or three layers of filling-in soil. This causes the soil to trickle down between all the roots—which should be spread out horizontally, with the fingers, before they are covered.

The soil above the roots has to be very firm, but the surface should be left loose for the top inch or so. It may be advisable to give two or three cans of water immediately after planting, and if dry warm weather follows the evergreen will benefit from a daily overhead spraying.

If a stake is considered necessary, this should be given *before* the hole is filled in, so that injury to roots may be avoided.

How and What to Prune. The first pruning attention may need to be directed at the roots, broken ends being cut back, with an outward sloping cut—before the tree or shrub is lowered into the hole, of course. Once done, that will not need doing again. Top pruning, on the other hand, may be a yearly task, as it is with roses (see under Roses in the section FLOWERS IN DETAIL).

A rough-and-ready general rule as to the time of year for pruning flowering trees and shrubs is to deal with the spring-flowering ones immediately after flowering before new growth begins, and to defer until early spring the pruning of those whose flowering occurs in summer or autumn.

Lilac and laburnum may go for years with no particular attention other than keeping them within bounds—restricting their growth to the height and area desired—by cutting back branches when the leaves have fallen, and in the case of lilac removing all sucker growths that may rise from the ground around the main stem or stems. The suckers should be cut off from the point where they leave the tree's roots, these points being got at by scraping away the soil at the base of the suckers. It makes for tidiness, too, if old flower-spikes of lilac are removed after the flowers wither.

When to Prune. The golden-flowered *Forsythia suspensa*, flower-

Fig. 135.—*To prune forsythia shorten flowered shoots right back to a strong bud at the base (shown by oblique lines) immediately after flowering in early spring*

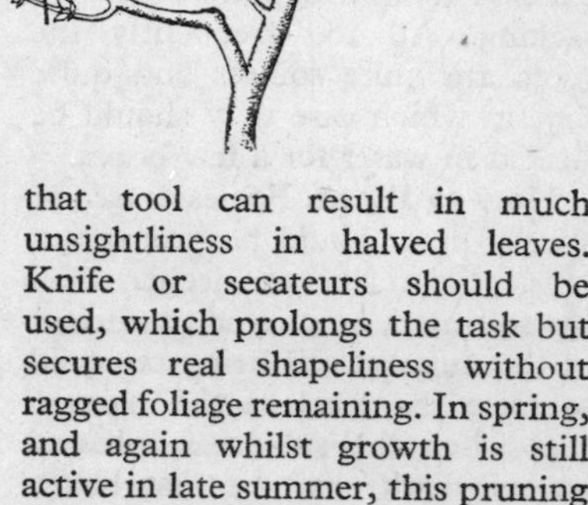

ing very early in spring, becomes a tangle of long whippy shoots if not cut back hard before the new spring growth extends. Pruning consists in shortening all the flowered shoots right back to a strong bud at the base, leaving perhaps no more than an inch of the flowered shoot (see Fig. 135). That basal bud will produce in the course of the summer a shoot up to about five feet in length, and this will be smothered in blossom the next early spring.

This annual removal of old wood after flowering in spring or early summer is practised also with the flowering currant, mock orange (Philadelphus), Deutzia and others. The framework must be retained, of course, but all the flowered wood that can be spared should go, to make room for the developing new wood which needs all the air and sunlight available to strengthen it for flowering in due course.

Buddleia variabilis, whose deep lilac flower-spikes are a magnificent attraction of midsummer, hardy hydrangeas, tamarisk and others, profit by the removal of the flowered wood before growth recommences early in the year; the new growth that follows the cutting back will flower later in the same year.

In pruning evergreens, such as bay and laurel and holly, the temptation is to use the shears, but that tool can result in much unsightliness in halved leaves. Knife or secateurs should be used, which prolongs the task but secures real shapeliness without ragged foliage remaining. In spring, and again whilst growth is still active in late summer, this pruning or shaping of evergreens is most safely carried out.

It should be remembered that if berries are wanted, the flowered shoots of holly, evergreen berberis and the deciduous thorns (cratægus) should not be removed. Berried shoots may be cut for indoor decoration, of course, and new flowering wood will be produced. But if the flowers themselves are cut away there can be no berries.

Tree Lopping. When the top of a tree has to be cut out or large branches shortened or removed, the length of each piece that will fall should be adjusted to the safe space below. That is, if the entire length of branch is likely to smash a fence or the garden frame when it falls it should be sawn off in portions that may be kept more or less under control: an assistant with a stout rope perched higher up the tree can be of great assistance.

If the situation of the branch makes it possible, the first cutting should be done on the underside, so that when the cutting through with the saw from the top side of the branch is completed the branch will fall away cleanly—without tearing the bark of the portion that remains. If the branch breaks away prematurely (a perhaps dangerous possibility which must always be borne in mind) the jagged snag that is left should be sawn or pared back closely and neatly, to guard against decay.

SECTION XVIII

CLIMBING PLANTS AND HEDGES

INVALUABLE as a shed can be in the garden, no one wants to gaze upon it in its natural state. It can be transformed into a thing of beauty, clothed with the foliage and flowers of a climber. Indispensable as is the small area which must be "wasted" as the site of the compost heap and the occasional and unavoidable bonfire, no one wants to look upon that either. Again climbers come to mind to hide the not-too-presentable corner—with the aid of trellis, or strained wires, as the climber's support.

The dreary-looking fence, the bare wall, call for the cheerful climber, and if further sites are wanted for this class of plant they can be provided in the shape of stout timber pillars or home-made archways.

Security for Climbers. Ivy will climb and cling with little or no assistance from the gardener, and the self-clinging Virginian creeper will find its own way to the summit of any support. But others need tying to their archway, or pillar or trellis, or nailing to shed or fence or wall; unless the wall is furnished with wires or simple wooden trellis fixed to stand out an inch from the brickwork to take easy ties (see Fig. 136).

Before erecting an archway, or pathside pillars or trellis, thought should be given to the width of the passageway and how this will be reduced by the bulk of the climbers when these are in the heyday of their beauty. To counter this, the supports should be set back at least a foot from the path edges. They should be sturdy rather than dainty; trellis especially should be well anchored below and secure above. For weight of climbers, especially large-leaved varieties, when wet with rain, can be considerable.

A climber planted against a fence or low wall, lacking upward space, should have the growths spread out as nearly horizontally as possible.

Hardy Climbers. There is no scarcity of plants from which to choose. Climbing roses (not to be confused with rambler roses) include the lovely Gloire de Dijon,

William Allen Richardson, and others of the type (see the section on FLOWERS IN DETAIL for culture.)

Clematis in several varieties is free-flowering and rapid-growing. Time to plant is October–November or in spring. Those that flower in summer and autumn (*Jackmanni* is typical) bear their blooms on shoots produced the same year—that is, from spring onwards. Pruning consists in cutting back these varieties, in November, to within a foot or so of the ground. This apparently severe treatment, carried out each year, results in abundant new growth and blossom. Other clematis varieties flower from the old wood; pruning consists in cutting away, in February or March, straggling and weak growths and preventing overcrowding. The best of the young and ripened wood (which will flower the following year) should be tied in to replace any that is becoming unwieldy.

Ivy is an obvious choice where fairly quick covering is required. There are a number of ornamental-leaved varieties, and pruning is of the simplest, consisting in the use of the shears in spring.

Jasmine, in winter-flowering yellow (*nudiflorum*) and summer-flowering white (*officinale*), grows rapidly over trellis or archway, needing occasional thinning out to keep it within bounds.

Honeysuckle is suitable for most positions, but is happiest where it can ramble unchecked, as over a summer-house. Occasional thinning out is all that is required.

Wistaria for a house-wall can be magnificent with masses of blossom. The first flowering does not come hurriedly, for the blossom is produced on spurs (similarly to the apple) arising on old wood, but it is worth waiting for. The first growths (after planting) need to be tied back to the wall or other support as foundation branches, spaced a foot or so apart. Side growths that come from these should be shortened back, in winter, to within a couple of buds (or about an inch) of their base. That makes the start of the flowering spurs, which are allowed to

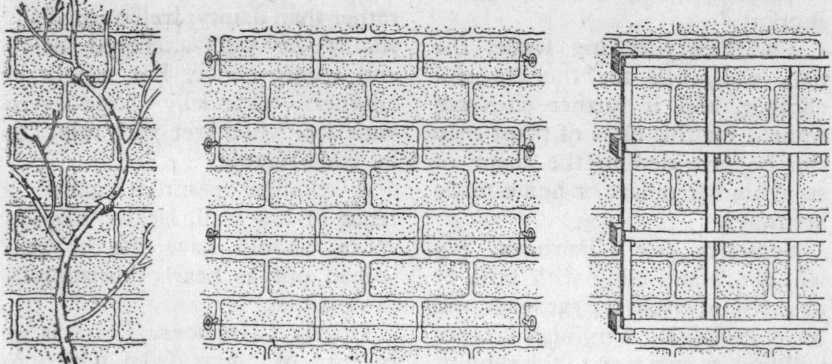

Fig. 136.—*Types of security for climbers. Shoots nailed to wall (left), using special nails with bent-over heads or pieces of material to protect the stem. Wire (centre) or wooden trellis (right) may be fixed to stand out* 1 *in.*

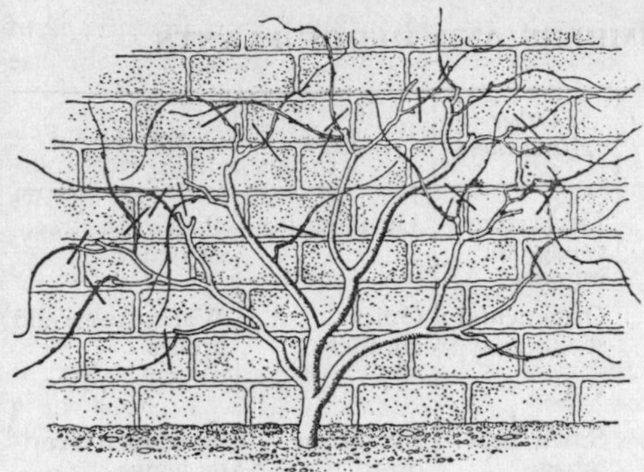

Fig. 137.—*Inducing wistaria to flower. Growths should be tied back to the wall as foundation branches, spaced about 1 ft. apart. Side growths should be cut back in winter as indicated*

make no more than an inch or so of extension each year by shortening back the new growth each winter (see Fig. 137).

Ampelopsis Veitchii, the familiar self-clinging Virginian creeper, needs no attention whatever beyond keeping it within reasonable bounds, and its autumn colouring is superb. But its falling leaves cause tremendous sweeping-up labour in autumn.

Polygonum baldschuanicum is the fastest grower of them all, with cascades of creamy flowers produced as abundantly as its ever-extending growths. It will cover a ruin or a forest tree in incredibly short time. It is perhaps too vigorous for any but a large garden, though a brake of sorts may be put upon it by severe cutting back in winter or spring.

The list on page 210 will enable a quick comparison of some of the main types to be made.

Planting Climbers. One is not over-generous in digging a hole 3 ft. square and 18 in. deep and filling it with really good soil in preparation for a climber. Especially is this necessary when the planting is to be done in a gravel or other pathway at the foot of a wall, a position generally consisting of builder's rubble.

In that position the prepared bed should be bordered with brick or stout timber projecting upwards a few inches—to discourage awkward feet which might collide with and injure the base of the plant (see Fig. 138). Also it is a neat finish.

The soil-mark on the climber's stem is a guide to depth of planting; it should fall just below the new level. The base of the stem should be not less than 6 in. out from the wall. Normally the position is a dry one, and apart from the fact that the gap between stem and wall gives the stem space in which to expand, the roots in the early stages are likely to encounter more

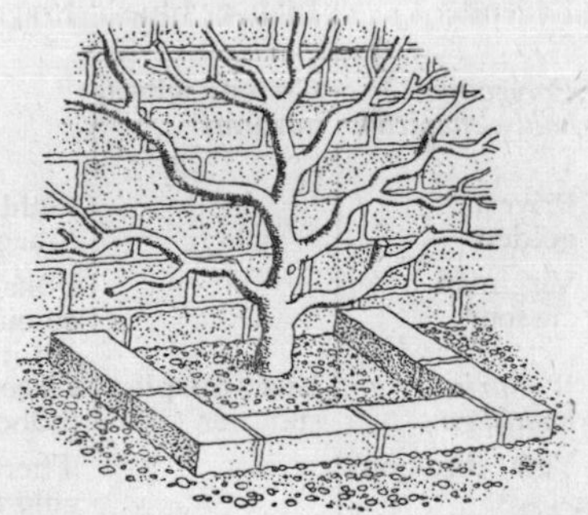

Fig. 138.—*The bed of a wall climber should be bordered with brick or timber to protect the stem from clumsy feet*

POPULAR CLIMBERS AND HEDGE PLANTS

Name	*Flower and Season*	*Other Attractions*	*Type*	*Suitable for*
Beech		Decorative foliage for indoors	Up to 80 ft.	Specimen tree, or hedge
Clematis, many varieties	Various colours, spring or summer	Ornamental seedheads	Quick climber	Walls, trellis and arches
Cupressus Lawsoniana		Small, neat foliage	Evergreen up to 100 ft.	Specimen tree or hedge
Holly	Green, gold or silver, May–June	Red berries, autumn and winter	Evergreen up to 30 ft.	Tree, or impenetrable hedge
Honeysuckle: *Lonicera periclymenum*	Red and yellow, June–September	Fragrant	Twiner up to 10 ft.	Trellis, wall or fence
Lonicera nitida	Creamy white, summer	Fragrant	Evergreen up to 5 ft.	Dwarf hedge
Ivy	Green, in autumn	Berries	Evergreen climber	Walls, fences
Jasminum nudiflorum	Yellow, winter	Decorative for indoors	Climber	Walls, pillars
Jasminum officinale	White, summer	Decorative indoors	Climber	Walls, pillars
Laurel, common or cherry	White, spring		Evergreen up to 20 ft.	Hedge
Lavender	Lilac or blue	Fragrant	Evergreen 3 ft.	Dwarf hedge
Polygonum baldschuanicum	Creamy white, autumn		Rapid climber, up to 20 ft.	Covering large area
Privet, golden		Golden foliage	Evergreen up to 8 ft.	Hedge
Virginian creeper		Foliage colours in autumn	Strong climber	Walls, trellis, fences
Wistaria multijuga	Lilac-purple, summer	Decorative indoors	Climber	Sunny walls, arches
Yew, common		There are gold and silver striped and other varieties	Evergreen up to 50 ft.	Slow-growing hedge

moisture than if crowded to the wall.

The top growth should be tied loosely to the support at first, to enable the plant to sink comfortably along with the soil as this settles down after planting. A tight tie will allow no downward movement.

Hedge Plants. Golden privet (more cheery than the green type) for a position in full sun is generally a fast grower and clips well, and *Cupressus Lawsoniana* can be relied on. The common laurel is a third useful evergreen, and yew and holly can be considered where expense and slow growth are no great drawbacks. In the leaf-losing class is the common beech, splendid on chalky soil and easy to maintain straight-faced; it is happiest when allowed to run up to 6 ft. or more.

Hedge Foundations. Extent of root is vastly more important than quantity of top growth in young plants being purchased for hedge-making, and preparation of planting site calls for great thoroughness. No later generous treatment can make amends for too hurried planting.

When the planting site has been marked out it should be dug at least 2 ft. wide and 18 in. deep, and decayed material from the compost heap should be mixed in throughout that depth. Removal of large stones is advisable. If the dug soil cannot be given a couple of weeks in which to settle down, it should be trodden firmly, planting holes being made at 9-in. intervals. It is not advisable to allow greater space than that between the plants, or the hedge will be slow in "filling up." Use of the garden line will assist straight planting.

It is very tempting to allow a quick grower, such as privet, to run up unchecked until the desired height of hedge has been reached. But that has to be resisted, or the hedge will be lanky and thin, a travesty of what it should be. Cut back to within about 9 in. of the ground after planting, a number of extra stems will be produced per plant. These can be allowed to extend 9 in. or so, anything beyond that being cut off in September.

That gives a thick foundation, and in subsequent years a routine trimming in May and in September (with light clippings, if necessary, in between) will allow gradual extension until the limit of desired height is reached, after which the shears may have to be used frequently and severely.

How to Clip. Until the hedge is reasonably thick and strong it may be necessary to use the garden line as a guide for the shears, both as to face and top line. To ease the labour of clipping, a box or low step ladder may be desirable, to allow of the shears being plied without too great effort when the top of the

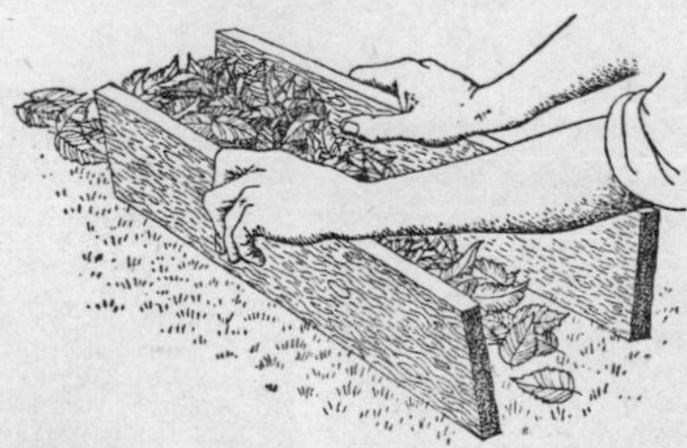

Fig. 139.—*To collect hedge trimmings, leaves, etc., two lengths of board used as a scoop form a handy tool*

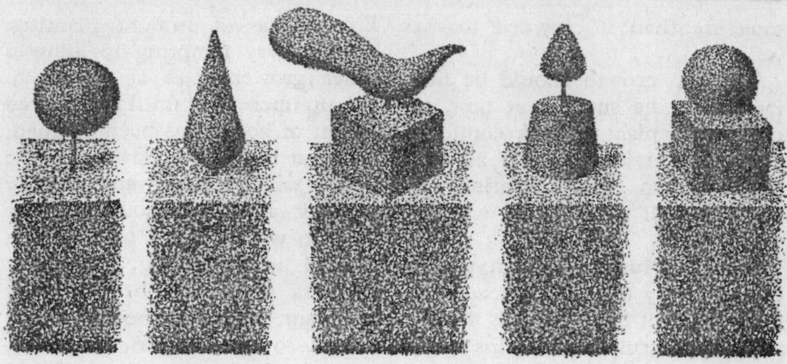

Fig. 140.—*Clipped box or yew may be trained in a variety of shapes to give character to a formal garden. The shape is generally obtained by training the growths in the early stages to a wire framework. Older shrubs may sometimes be cut to the desired shape by skilful clipping and tying*

hedge is not within quite easy reach.

The blades of the shears should be kept flat against the growth, and the length of the hedge should be worked along methodically. That is, a start should be made at one end and the cutting continued until the other end is reached, the wielder of the shears standing back now and again to view his work.

Clearing Up. If sacking or other material is spread out close to the hedge to catch the clippings, clearing up is simplified and speeded. The alternative is to sweep up afterwards, which is not always easy on a gravel path or close-cropped piece of turf. To collect swept-up clippings, two lengths of board form the handiest tool (see Fig. 139).

Fancy Shapes. The art of topiary—the training of growths to the form of a peacock or large ball or other ornamental object—is not to be decried in even the smallest garden where a hedge (or even a single shrub) permits of it. The definite shape is secured generally by training the growths, at an

Fig. 141.—*The top of an established hedge may be cut in various ways to lift it out of the ordinary. Here are three fairly simple suggestions*

early stage, to a framework of wire; but an older shrub may sometimes be cut quite satisfactorily to the form required with secateurs or shears or both, supplemented by a little careful tying. The entire top run of an established hedge may be lifted out of the commonplace in this way (see Fig. 140). A less ambitious plan is to trim the top to rounded or angular form or give it a castellated shape (see Fig. 141).

Renovating a Hedge. A gap occurring here and there can be rectified by planting a young shrub in the space, after digging out the old roots and replacing the worn-out soil in that spot with good soil taken from elsewhere in the garden. Whilst the new shrub is extending upwards, it may be possible to lessen the gap at the top by pulling adjoining growths across it and tying them in position.

A hedge that has become too wide can be split (on one side, preferably that which shows less) in spring or early autumn, with the secateurs and, if necessary, a saw. Daily syringeing, if the weather is dry following this operation, will hasten new growth on the "raw" face.

Where dogs have developed a habit of dashing through a hedge, the best form of discouragement is to strain wire netting tightly across one side.

SECTION XIX

AN ATTRACTIVE LAWN

THE making of a good lawn, unless indeed it be but a few square feet in area, is a task of some magnitude. Points that help to decide the placing of this feature include drainage and general level of the garden, and the amount of shade likely to be cast in summer. The site should not be overhung to any extent by tree branches. It should get as much sun as surroundings allow. Water must run away freely at all times of the year. Therefore, if the garden slopes, the lawn should not be sited at the bottom of the slope where drainage water may be expected to accumulate.

Preparing the Site. Ordinary "lazy" digging—to not more than about 6 in. deep—suffices to prepare the ground for seed-sowing or turf-laying, in favourable cases. If levelling has to be done, guesswork must be counted out. Wooden pegs driven into the ground at frequent intervals whereon to rest the plank (on its edge) that will serve as a ruler, and a spirit-level for testing, are essentials (see Fig. 142). Depressions will be made good by filling in with prepared soil, and bumps will be removed with the spade.

A month or so should elapse before anything further is done. In that time the dug soil will settle, probably necessitating final levelling here and there. The pegs are then withdrawn, the whole surface worked with the rake so that the top inch is left really fine, and stones removed. It should not be necessary to use the roller after that, but if hard clods will not respond to the rake or the fork and the surface seems to give unduly underfoot, a light roller may be moved once across it; then will come another raking to break the surface down again.

When and How to Sow. The weeks of spring (about mid-March to early May) and from mid-August to mid-September are favourable times for sowing. The most expensive seed is cheapest in the long run, and it should be used at the rate of 2 oz. to each square yard, broadcast sown, the hand with the seed being held as close to the ground as possible.

It helps even distribution if the garden line is used to mark off yard-wide strips, one strip being sown at a time—and when there is no appreciable wind. Then comes the covering of the seed, which is done by scattering sifted soil over it or by raking it carefully into the surface; the merest covering only is required.

A light roller should then be used, once lengthwise, once crosswise. If birds threaten to take dust-baths there or devour the seed, they must be kept from the surface by netting strained a few inches above, or by covering the entire area with sheets of newspaper (weighted at the corners with stones) or with sacking or other material, this being left in position until the seed has germinated.

Besides being a deterrent to birds, the covering assists germination by preventing the surface becoming too dry. Drought is hateful to young grass, and if dry conditions prevail the area must be sprinkled frequently.

The First Cutting. This comes when the young grass is up about four inches; it should not be left to become longer. Alternatives for the first cutting are a light mower used cautiously and set not to cut close, or sharp hand-shears. An expert with a keen scythe would make a perfect job of it, of course.

Apart from that essential shortening, and the removal of young weeds, feet should be kept from the young grass for three months or longer. If spraying in dry weather can be done without treading on the turf, so much the better; otherwise tennis shoes should be worn. Heel-marks are easily made in turf at this stage.

How to Lay Turves. Putting down good turf on a site prepared as for seed sowing is the quickest way of getting a lawn. If they have been cut expertly turves should all be of even thickness, and about three feet long by a foot wide. But no turves should be used which

Fig. 142.—*Wooden pegs driven in at intervals with their tops protruding about 2 in., a straight piece of timber on edge, and a spirit-level, are aids in securing a perfectly level site*

show many weeds, or which contain pests such as wireworms or leather-jackets, or which are thin in texture. It is these latter drawbacks, plus cost, which generally decide that seed shall be sown.

If good turves are available, they should be laid without stretching and so that they "lock" in the manner of bricks in a wall (see Fig. 143). Any slight adjustment of surface level that individual turves may require must be attended to at once, for no amount of subsequent rolling will secure a good level after the turves are down.

Fig. 143.—*For turfing a lawn, each rolled length of turf is carried to its position and there unrolled. They are laid in final position one by one so that they interlock*

A light roller should be used, twice lengthwise and twice crosswise of the area, when all the turves are in place. A spade should not be used in its stead, for that tool is apt to beat the life from the turf. A last look after the rolling may reveal gaps, and unfilled corners where bits of turf broke away; these should be filled with soil and a pinch of seed sown. Turf laying may be done at any time of the year excepting in frost, snow or very wet weather.

How to Patch a Lawn. Bare or thin patches should be forked over to the depth of about 3 in. and the top inch made quite fine before seed is sown in these gaps. If patching is to be done with pieces of turf, the latter should be cut to fit after the space has been prepared.

This must not be done hastily, or the general level may be ruined. Pieces of wire netting laid down over the patches will safeguard against accidents, and a moist root-run (ensured by use of the watering-can) will encourage speedy and strong growth. Such areas should later be given gentle treatment, at mowing time especially.

Repairing Broken Edges. The need to repair may be avoided by using a wooden run-up at any spot where the wheelbarrow is to leave the path for the lawn (see Fig. 144). Where a break in the lawn-edge does occur, the plan is to cut away the area, about 2 in. beyond the extremities, and turn it around so that a sound edge is once again presented (see Fig. 145). Grass seed sown in the reversed broken part, after filling with sifted soil, will soon obliterate any sign of the patch.

When turf has to be cut and lifted in this way and the regulation tools (edging iron with half-moon cutting-edge, and flat-bladed turfing-iron for lifting) are not available, a sharp spade can be used. The precaution of holding the spade at the correct angle must not be overlooked, either in the vertical or the horizontal cutting.

Routine edge trimming is done with hand clippers, or hedge-trimming shears, or with the long-handled shears made specially for this purpose. Only where the turf edge is ragged all along or a new alignment is wanted should the half-moon edging iron be used for this trimming; otherwise turf will be wasted.

Mowing and Weeding. Any plant other than grass in the lawn need not necessarily be regarded as a weed for prompt extraction. Clover and yarrow are invaluable; in the driest summer, when the grass itself is yellowing, these two remain green, and there is nothing better for "thickening" the turf where this has to stand up to much wear and tear.

Dandelion, daisy and other obvious intruders can be looked for during the mowing, any that occur in the immediate path of the machine receiving attention at once. An old screwdriver pushed in and worked around the root will enable the latter to be pulled out complete and the blank that is left will be scarcely noticed.

If the lawn is very weedy, however, the task should be done apart from the mowing. A yard-wide strip worked methodically from end to end effects a thorough clearance so far as the weeds large enough to handle are concerned. Others, such as moss, should be raked out and swept up and cleared away, or one of the advertised lawn sands may be used to destroy them on the spot.

Fig. 144.—*A wooden "run-up" for the wheelbarrow (or roller) prevents broken turf-edges*

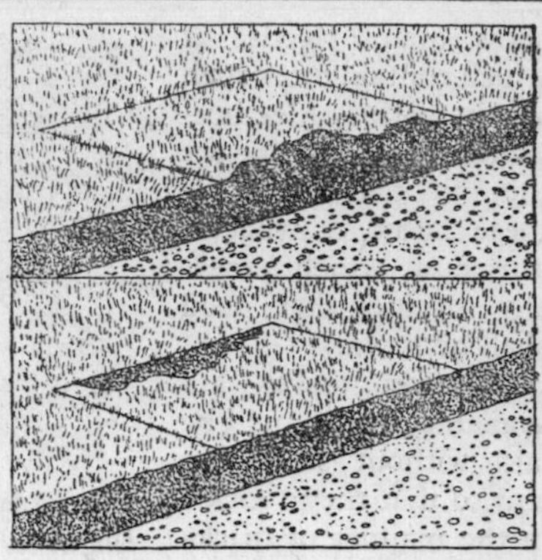

Fig. 145.—*A worn lawn-edge can be repaired by cutting out the piece of broken turf and replacing it carefully reversed*

Regular mowing, carried out when the grass is not too wet and before it begins to look overgrown or ragged, does as much as anything to keep a stretch of turf in first-class condition. Mowing should be done, on alternate occasions, lengthwise of the lawn, then crosswise; this ensures that all the grass —including that in slight dips— will encounter the knives.

The machine should be cleaned on every occasion after mowing, and be oiled, at all points, before mowing. And, on every occasion before the machine goes into action, the lawn should be swept or hand-picked for stones. The mower should not be set so low that it taxes the strength to push it. An indication that the bottom blade is too low is provided by the occasional upflinging of soil; the knives are slicing off small bumps, and the machine should be adjusted accordingly.

If stiff pieces of grass-stem ("bents") spring up after the mower passes over them they should be pulled out by the roots; otherwise this wiry weed quickly spreads and the turf becomes very coarse.

The lawn mower should not be put away with the hose at the end of summer. It should be kept in action, except during frost or snow or heavy rain, as long as the grass continues to grow.

Other Routine Maintenance. Water needs to be given generously in dry, growing weather—before there is any indication of yellowing or of small cracks in the turf. And one good "feed" a year will help it along tremendously; artificial fertilizers for this special purpose are obtainable.

The fertilizer should be broadcast on a windless day, hand held well down, and be watered in if rain does not fall soon after. Or the fertilizer may be dissolved in water and applied with a rosed can. The best time to apply it is immediately after mowing.

Sweeping occasionally with a stiffish besom, held nearly horizontally, the sweeper's back well bent, is included in the programme. Broad, sweeping strokes quickly cover the ground (see Fig. 146). This is altogether apart from any necessity to clear up fallen leaves. It keeps the soil surface "fresh," and distributes worm-casts. Lacking a besom, a stiff yard-broom does the same work, though it entails more muscle-ache.

The presence of worm-casts indicates, of course, activity of worms beneath the surface. This is all to the good so long as the casts are not an insufferable nuisance. The tunnels the worms make assist surface drainage, and the casts which the broom distributes are a form of good top-dressing for the turf. If it is essential that the worms be killed, a watering solution for the purpose is obtainable from horticultural stores.

Bare patches in the grass may be due to the root-eating activities of a leaden-hued, unpleasant-looking grub known as the leather-jacket, the infant of the daddy-long-legs (crane-fly). An effective way of dealing with this is to flood the area with water, then lay down sacks or something similar. Removal of the sacks an hour or two later generally reveals the sluggish

Fig. 146.—*A besom for sweeping the lawn should be held horizontally, and broad, sweeping strokes made as far to left and right as the sweeper's arms and back will allow*

grubs lying on the surface of the ground; it is then a matter of moments to pick them up and feed them to the fowls or dispose of them in equally effective manner.

Mention of the garden roller is left to the last because the ordinary lawn is better without it. Its frequent use results in extremely hard-packed soil in which the grass-roots cannot properly survive. Only where the turf is badly kicked up and must be firmed down again should the roller be passed over it, sparingly, and the roller should be a light one. Generally speaking, the roller should be kept to the paths. The turf receives far more benefit from the garden fork being thrust upright into the ground, every yard or two, and then gently levered over so that the turf is eased up slightly. Especially is this useful when surface drainage is not too efficient.

SECTION XX

PATHS AND EDGINGS

A SURFACE level, dry and clean, comfortable to walk on and goodly to look upon, sums up the ideal garden path. It is seldom all these. But a near approach thereto is worth the striving. Basic facts are: (*a*) importance of foundation, and therefore drainage; (*b*) nature of the surfacing and how this is maintained. Surfacing materials range from sifted ash (from household fires) to asphalt, other possibilities being gravel, bricks, crazy paving and an imitation of the latter contrived with cement.

Ash Paths. Fine siftings from coal or coke fires spread evenly and to the depth of about an inch, moistened and then well rolled, consolidate very thoroughly. The surface can be maintained in that condition by rolling after a shower. If the rolling is done frequently enough, the ash will not kick up or blow up dustily even in the driest weather.

But the foundation must be there. If it is not, the line of the path (no footpath should be less than 3 ft. wide) should be marked out and dug out to the depth of about 9 in., the excavated material being disposed of elsewhere. The trench should then be filled in, to within about 2 in. of the top, with clinkers, coarse siftings from the fires, or stones. This material, spread out evenly, is then made wet, and either rammed as hard as possible or rolled several times with a heavy roller.

The filling of sifted ash may then go on, and its surface raked so that it rises slightly from both sides towards the centre (see Fig. 147). Hard rolling follows. If possible, the path should slope evenly to one end. After the first heavy rainfall it should be inspected for slight depressions, and should any suspicion of a puddle be detected the level there should be made good with more ash (and the roller).

If one of the other surfacing materials previously mentioned is available, but not in sufficient quantity to do the whole of the paths, preference may perhaps be given to the crazy paving, brick, or whatever it may be, for paths close up to or within view of the house, the ash being reserved for the far end of the garden.

Clean Gravel. If this can be obtained at moderate cost it is worth consideration. Given a good foundation, maintenance consists in an occasional raking over (followed by rolling) to keep the top fresh-looking and free of depressions, and maybe weeding now and again.

Weed-killers for use on garden paths are obtainable. But neither gravel nor ash paths in an average garden should be allowed to become so weedy as to demand the employment of a weed-killer. Hand-weeding once a week will save the cost of that.

It should be noted that rolling is more effective when the gravel (or ash) is moist after rain or hosing.

Crazy Paving. The thicker the stone slabs for use as crazy paving the better. They should be bedded on 2 in. of sifted fire-ash, or sand, into the surface of which the underside of each slab can be "wriggled" to secure an even lay.

Imitation crazy paving is made with a cement mixture, one part cement, three parts sand, and just enough water to make the whole a kind of stiff paste. This is put down to a depth of not less than 1½ in., in one solid layer. The crazy effect is secured by scoring the surface across (not right through) at intervals, with the trowel, when the mixture has almost set.

Before the mixture is spread, the ash or sand bed should be made quite moist; and to prevent the mixture drying too quickly the finished surface should be covered with old sacks for a day or so. The finished surface should be left rather rough — not polished smoothly with the trowel; a non-slippery surface is secured by levelling off with a piece of board on edge.

Brick Paths. A path made of bricks can be very attractive (see

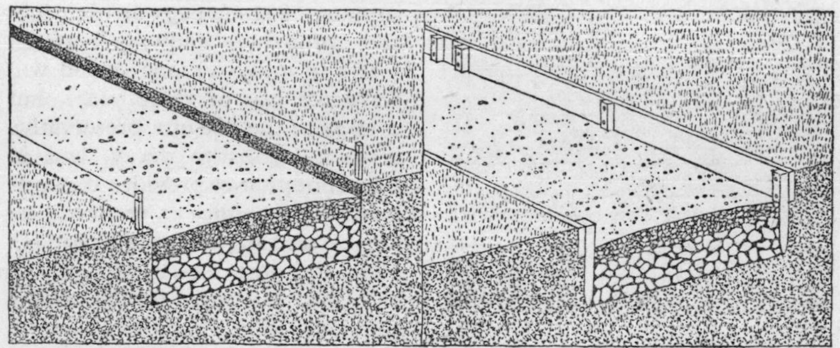

Figs. 147 and 148.—*Two garden lines should be used to mark the site of the new path. The excavation is then partly filled with rammed or rolled clinkers, then given a rounded surface of ashes or gravel. A wooden edging needs the support of stout pegs*

Fig. 149). Old bricks bought cheaply are an economical proposition and practically everlasting in a well-made path, that is, one with a proper foundation and absolutely level.

The ash or sand bed above the foundation should be moistened after rolling, then coated with an inch or so of the cement mixture and the bricks bedded on that, as close together as possible. A little of the mixture should be plastered on to the adjoining brick sides so that these make secure joins. A plank on edge used along with a spirit-level will help to secure a uniform level of the brick path surface.

Fig. 149.—*Brick paths can be made most attractive by arranging the bricks in a formal design. Any one of the above designs would look well*

Asphalt. This material, laid by an expert, gives a trouble-free path, dry, even-surfaced, neat-looking and very hard-wearing. It is almost completely resistant to weeds and is easily swept. But cost may rule it out of count.

Edgings. Generally, the choice of a path-edging lies between timber and bricks. If both are available at reasonable cost, the bricks will win. They should be bedded deeply enough to hold themselves secure, preferably before the path is given its surfacing.

If wood is used it should be not less than an inch thick, and its life is lengthened if it is first painted generously with creosote or other wood preservative. It will need the support of stout pegs at each join and probably midway between (see Fig. 148). Thinner wood will serve for two or three years, but even with the use of a preservative it soon begins to decay, and in that condition it provides concealment for woodlice (a terrible pest among seedling plants of all kinds), slugs and other undesirables.

"Live" edgings, for decorative purpose only, include catmint (Nepeta), pinks and dwarf box shrubs, the latter extensively adopted in the vegetable garden by our forebears but because of trouble and expense now seldom seen.

SECTION XXI

PLANNING THE VEGETABLE GARDEN

WHATEVER the period of year there is always something to be done among the vegetables, whether it be the pleasurable task of pulling, cutting or picking a crop of one's own production, or the less agreeable task of digging in preparation for crops yet to be. In any case, there can be enjoyment in the anticipation as in the actual realization.

Quickest, biggest and best possible results are natural objectives. They are secured not by haphazard sowing and planting, but by a well-thought-out sequence of operations.

Where to Start. This consideration may be of even greater importance than the "when." The site may be a portion of the home garden formerly occupied by flowers and henceforth to be devoted to vegetables. It may be an allotment left derelict by a previous tenant, say a 10-rod plot—roughly 30 ft. by 90 ft.—which is as much as the average man can handle in his spare time. It may be quite a small patch, from which the grower will be happy to collect quite moderate dividends.

Home or Away. It is worth considering whether to break away from the home garden in so far as vegetables are concerned and acquire an allotment, to be worked in addition. One consideration revolves around the question of distance. It should not be too far away. For when days are short and darkness comes early and there is digging to be done, the short period of after-work daylight is too scanty for much of it to be wasted in travelling to an allotment.

Economy. If there is an allotment society in the neighbourhood, considerable benefits may accrue from becoming a member of it. If no such local society exists, one could be formed. The value of this co-operation lies in the saving effected in bulk purchases of seed, manures, insecticides, tools and requisites generally. Apart from these commercial considerations there is the mutual good fellowship which may not, perhaps, be experienced by one playing a lone hand.

How to Start. Whatever the area and its immediate condition it should be considered, by way of a start, in terms of a period of several months. The grower has to take a long view, planning not for the immediate present but for the quite near future. Once that future has been caught up with, in a manner of speaking, one remains level with immediate requirements—so long as the ahead planning continues uninterrupted.

All over the plot there will be changes of occupant, a succession of crops. There will be periods when, a crop having been removed, part of the ground lies bare, pre-

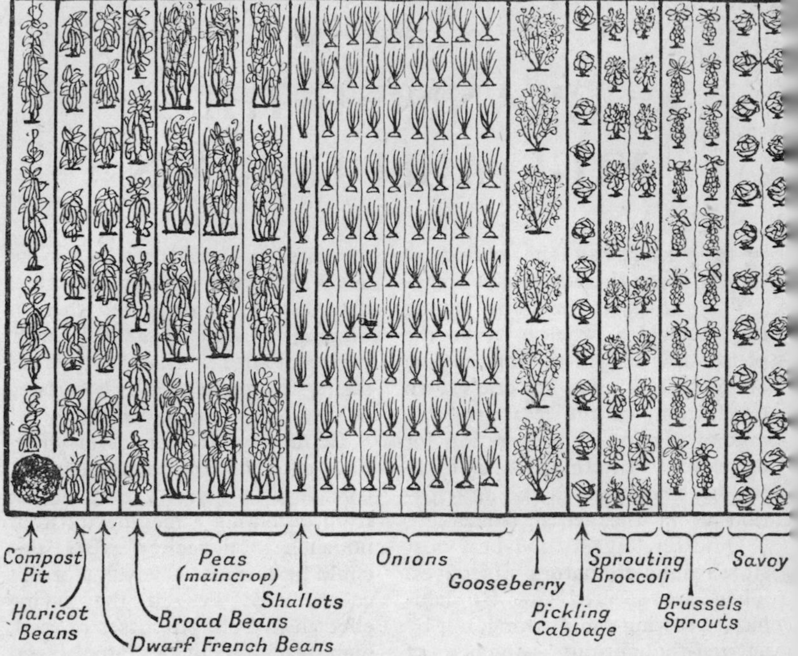

Fig. 150.—*Layout for a 10-rod plot, adaptable to suit any special circumstances. For arrangement see text. Note the 6-ft. strip at the east end for items often*

senting the opportunity for digging and manuring to prepare for the crop to follow.

Before any seeds or young plants are bought, note should be made of what vegetables are to be grown, and in what relative quantities. This is necessary to avoid a shortage of any particular crop or a glut at any time. It then becomes possible to make a rough plan, on paper, for a full year's guidance.

A Working Plan. The fact that seeds or seedlings or roots of those vegetables which one specially desires cannot all be got in at once makes planning easier and labour lighter. Not only do exact planting and sowing dates depend on weather and locality, the particular variety of a vegetable may have something to do with it. And dates may be varied with a view to securing a succession—that is, a steady supply over a period—of a particular crop (Fig. 154, page 227).

The 10-rod cropping plan (Fig. 150) contains suggestions which the individual grower will adapt to his own special needs and circumstances. The vacant piece of ground will not be dug from end to end before any sowing or planting is done. The aim is to get it producing something as soon as possible. Therefore, as one section of ground is prepared it will be got into production, and so on until the whole plan is at last in operation.

Ten-rod Cropping Plan

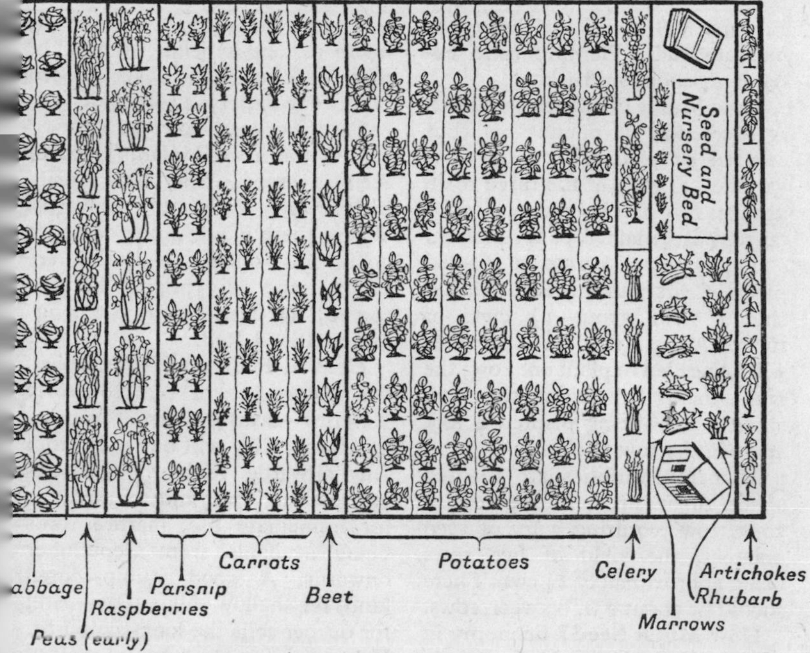

forgotten in the hurry to get a new piece of ground cropped. Runner beans fill the row on extreme left; tomatoes occupy half the celery row on right

The Potato Section. Eight rows of potatoes, the rows spaced 2 ft. apart, should yield about 4 cwt. If that is not considered sufficient for the needs of the family, more space will have to be planted with potatoes, and other vegetables reduced as to number of rows or omitted altogether.

Local inquiry of enthusiastic and successful food producers will secure information as to which are the most suitable varieties to plant; most suitable, that is, for the district and soil. Potatoes have their likes and dislikes in regard to both.

The class (or type or group) of potato is also of importance. Varieties classed as first earlies are ready for use about mid-July and onwards; second earlies are ready in August; maincrops are ready for lifting in late September or early October for storing for winter use.

First earlies are planted in late February in very favourable (warm and sheltered) districts, mid-March being a safer date. In cold midland districts the end of March is early enough, whilst mid-April is more appropriate farther north and in Scotland. Good first early varieties are Arran Pilot and Epicure, good croppers on most kinds of soil.

Second earlies include Great Scot and Ben Lomond, both suitable for ordinary or heavy soil. April is early enough for these.

Maincrops include Arran Banner for all types of soil, and King

Edward VII for fairly heavy or medium soils. Planting time extends to about mid-May.

How Many Potatoes to Plant. A succession of potatoes is thus secured by planting a variety, or varieties, of each of the three main groups: first and second earlies for current use, maincrops for storing.

Three rows (across a 10-rod plot) of first and second earlies should yield about 1½ cwt. of tubers. About 4 lb. of seed potatoes will be needed to plant one row; the seed—that is, tubers each weighing about 2 oz.—being planted a foot apart in the row.

Maincrop varieties are planted about 16 in. apart in the row, a 30-ft. row requiring 3 lb. of seed potatoes, the yield of five rows being approximately 2½ cwt. There should be about 2 ft. between rows.

How Much Seed? Economy in small seed sowing means not only money saved but time saved in thinning out—that is, removing crowded seedlings; and time saving is a big consideration, whether a 10-rod plot or a small piece of the home garden is being worked. In many cases a small packet of seed of any one variety is sufficient.

Beet. For one row, as allowed for on the 10-rod plan, ⅓ oz. of seed is ample. Sow late April–early May; ready July onwards. Where there is not much depth of good soil suitable varieties are Globe and Egyptian Turnip-rooted; for deeper soils the long-rooted Blood Red.

Carrots. Four rows, 1 ft. apart, will require ⅔ oz. of seed. Sow early varieties—Scarlet Horn, Nantes—in March; they will be ready from July onwards. Maincrop varieties are sown in April and thinned out for immediate use, mature roots being available from September onwards. A good stump-rooted kind, for shallow soil, is Favourite; for deeper soils the long-rooted St. Valery.

Parsnips. Two rows of parsnips 18 in. apart take ½ oz. of seed.

Sow February to March; they will be ready from November

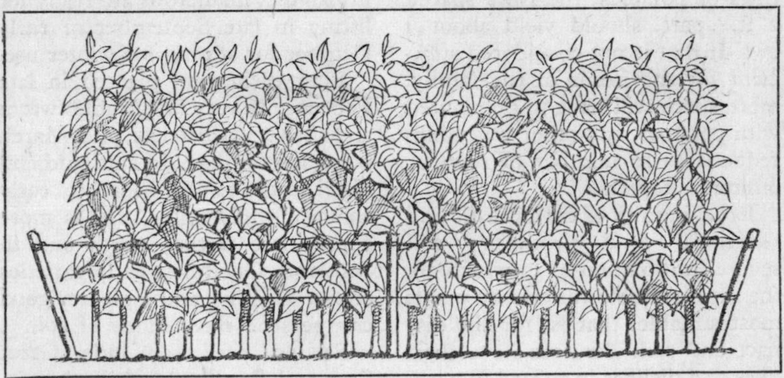

Fig. 151.—*A windbreak is very desirable when a plot is exposed to rough winds from some particular quarter. A row of Jerusalem artichokes provides the necessary protection here. String stretched between end-stakes may be needed to prevent the very tall artichoke tops from being blown over*

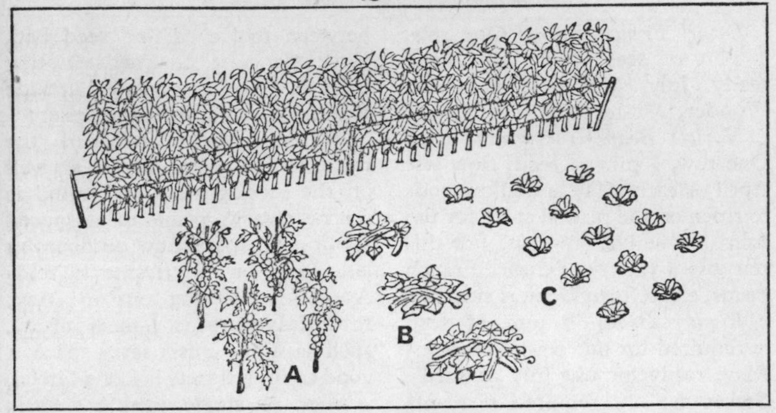

Fig. 152.—*Tomatoes* (A), *ridge cucumbers* (B) *and lettuce* (C) *will specially appreciate a windbreak of Jerusalem artichokes*

onwards. For deep soils, use the long-rooted variety, Hollow Crown; for shallow soil, Turnip-rooted.

Early Peas. Allowed one row in the plan, sown February to March, ready in June, require ¼ pint of seed. Varieties include Pioneer and Little Marvel, both about 2 ft. in height. For three rows of main-crop, 2½ ft. apart, sow ¾ pint of seed; they will be ready July to August. Varieties include Fillbasket and Senator, both about 3 ft. in height.

For two rows of each of the "greens" on the 10-rod plan allow $\frac{1}{16}$ oz. of seed; this should be sown in the seed bed for transplanting.

Cabbage. Sow April, plant out July, rows 2 ft. apart, ready October onwards. Varieties: Winningstadt, Nonpareil.

Savoy. Sow May, plant out July to August, rows 2 ft. apart, ready January to March. Varieties: Ormskirk, Dwarf Green Curled.

Brussels Sprouts. Sow late April, plant out May to June, rows 2 ft. apart, ready November to January. Varieties: Dwarf Gem, Matchless.

Broccoli. There are two types of broccoli—sprouting and autumn. For sprouting sow late April, plant out July, rows 2 ft. apart, ready April to May. Varieties: Purple Sprouting, White Sprouting. For autumn, sow late March or early April, plant out late May to early June, ready September to October. Varieties: Michaelmas White, Self-protecting Autumn.

Pickling Cabbage. Sow March to April, plant out July to August, ready November onwards. Variety: Large Blood Red (also for cooking).

Onions. Sow in boxes, under glass, in the early weeks of the year, ¼ oz. of seed which will give plants for eight rows. Ready for lifting in September. Variety: Bedfordshire Champion does well on all soils, and is an excellent keeper.

Shallots. One row will take forty bulbs at 9 in. apart. Plant January to February; ready in July for harvesting and storing.

Broad Beans. Allowed one row, require ½ pint of seed. Sow February to March, ready July onwards. Varieties: Mammoth Windsor and Green Longpod.

Dwarf French Beans. One row, ¼ pint of seed. Sow late April, ready July. Varieties: Canadian Wonder, Masterpiece.

Haricot Beans (for winter use). One row, ¼ pint of seed. Sow late April or early May and allow pods to ripen on the plants; store for use from November onwards. For this purpose a variety of dwarf French beans, e.g., Green Gem, is suitable.

Runner Beans. ¼ pint of seed is required for one row. Sow mid-May, ready for use July onwards. Stakes are not required if plants are kept low and bushy by removal of the growing tips at intervals after they have reached a height of about 2 ft. Varieties include: Scarlet Emperor, Painted Lady.

Fig. 153.—*What is meant by a succession of crops. Cabbages in foreground, planted first, come in earlier*

Tomatoes. A line of tomato plants, 18 in. apart, might occupy the position shown on the plan. Set out in late May, tomatoes would be ready for picking late July and onwards. Varieties include: Princess of Wales, Sunrise, Golden Queen (yellow).

Celery could occupy a trench to the right of the tomatoes, twenty plants set out 8 in. apart in June; ready October onwards. White varieties: Solid White, Giant White; red: Major Clarke's Red, Standard Bearer.

Rhubarb, for pulling in April and onwards, could be accommodated between tool shed and seed bed, three plants, 3 ft. apart. Planting time is March; varieties include Reading Ruby and Champagne.

Marrow plants, between the rhubarb and celery, would do well on the level ground (a mound is not necessary), plants to be spaced about 2 ft. apart. Sow outdoors in late May, or in a frame in mid-April for planting out in May; ready July onwards. A bush variety, such as White Bush, saves space; a good trailing variety is Long Green.

Sage (a single bush), *parsley, mint* and other herbs would run parallel with the tomato row.

Break the Cold Winds. A row of Jerusalem artichokes makes an admirable windbreak (Figs. 151, 152). In the plan they are positioned at the east end of the plot. Plant the tubers 1 ft. apart, in February to March; ready November onwards.

Intercropping. Lettuce, radish, spinach, mustard and cress and similar quick-growing small plants are most conveniently grown between rows of other vegetables which grow comparatively slowly and are longer in occupation of the ground, such as the cabbages and other greens whilst these are still small, and between pea rows. These catch crops will be cleared away before the rightful occupants of the ground are in need of the full space allotted to them. The sides of the celery trench can be utilized in the same way. Radish and spinach can also be sown between onion rows.

But there must be no attempt to crowd anything unduly, and as only small quantities of radish, lettuce, mustard and cress are wanted at a time, sowings should be small and made at intervals of several days.

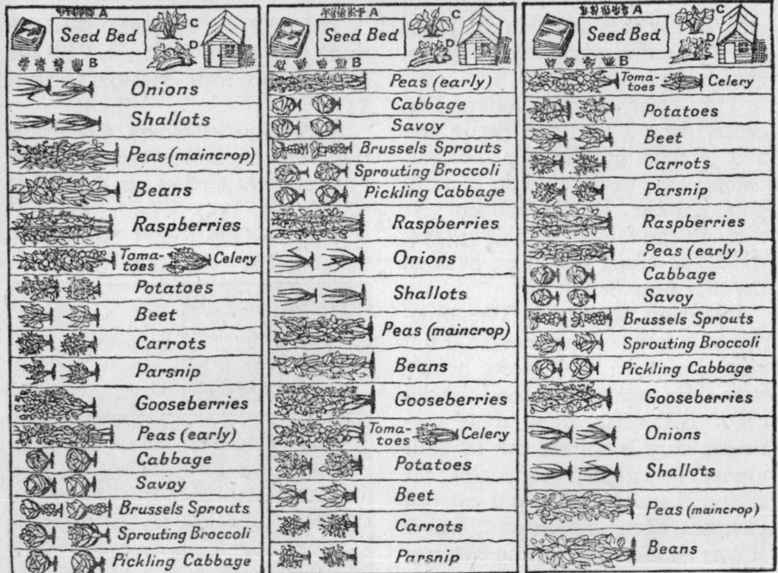

Fig. 154.—*(Left) How the crops shown in Fig. 150 would best be arranged the second year. (Centre) Third-year changes. (Right) In the fourth year the crops are back in the positions they occupied the first year. Near the seed bed are planted* (A) *artichokes,* (B) *herbs,* (C) *rhubarb,* (D) *marrows*

Follow-on Crops. When the early potato rows have been cleared turnip seed can be sown there as a follow-on crop to provide tops the following spring; a suitable variety is Green-top White. Alternatively, while the early potatoes are still in occupation young plants of broccoli or Brussels sprouts could be set out between the rows.

When the onions have been lifted, spring cabbage (for use in spring) could go in—sown in August, planted out in October; suitable variety, Flower of Spring.

Shallots might be followed by colewort, a very hardy little cabbage, sown in June, set out in August, ready October onwards.

Early peas have a good follow-on in spinach beet. Leeks may be planted after the maincrop peas, and swedes sown after broad beans.

Rotation of Crops. Change of position for vegetable crops from year to year is attended by such good results that it should be practised wherever possible. Permanent crops, such as rhubarb, seakale, asparagus, are best left undisturbed for a number of years; others are better for a change of site.

The 10-rod cropping plan provides for an effective change-over annually. The second year the crops would be disposed as in Fig. 154. Tomato, celery, potato, beet, carrot and parsnip would be grown on the section previously occupied by the early peas and the greens. The latter would be on the section previously occupied by the onions, etc., whilst this crop would be in the top section which the potatoes, etc., had occupied.

Third-year changes (Fig. 154, centre) would find the early peas and greens in the top section; onions, etc., in the middle section; potatoes, etc., in the bottom section. In the fourth year (Fig. 154, right) the crops would be back in the first year positions.

Rotation Reasons. The practice of rotation is not essential but very desirable. Soil pests which have their own special food fancies cease to flourish when their particular crop is shifted out of their immediate circuit; wireworms, for example, and potatoes and carrots. Diseases, such as club root, which afflicts all members of the cabbage tribe (including turnips), are encouraged to die out in the soil when the vegetables which they concern are moved to another section of the ground.

As soil pests and diseases have their own special needs, so different kinds of vegetables have their own special food requirements which the grower can meet, to some extent, by providing an annual change of site. The cabbage tribe use up a considerable amount of lime but not much potash, which is the reverse of the requirements of potatoes and beet. So when the two latter are moved on into the greens section their needs are partly provided for.

Furthermore, members of the cabbage tribe do not send their roots far down into the soil, which means that plant food some inches down remains untouched, and is available for deeper-rooting vegetables such as beet, carrot and parsnip which may follow on.

The subject of plant foods is more fully dealt with in the section, FERTILIZERS AND MANURES (page 35).

Direction of Rows. Co-operation with the sun is secured when rows are arranged to run north and south (Fig. 155). The sun in its daily round shines first on the east side of each row, then down the rows, via the south, and finally cast its rays from the west. Thus both sides of each row are exposed to maximum sunlight.

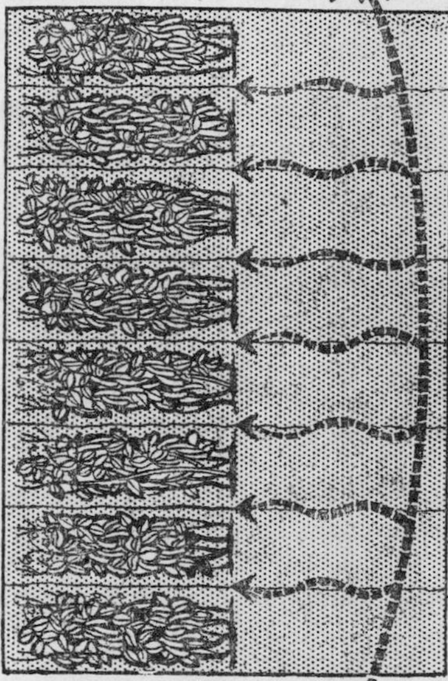

Fig. 155.—*If possible arrange rows to run N. and S. This exposes both sides of each row to maximum sunlight, and results in increased yield of crop. How the sun gets at both sides is shown by the arrows*

Such is not the case when rows run east-west (Fig. 156). North-facing sides of rows are cheated of their right. They get little if any sun. This is not such an important point in the case of onions and similar low-growing vegetables, but sunless sides of rows of taller plants such as peas and beans show plainly by smaller yield how very dependent such crops are on exposure to sunlight.

Layout Ideas. In the 10-rod plot layout (Fig. 150) it will be seen

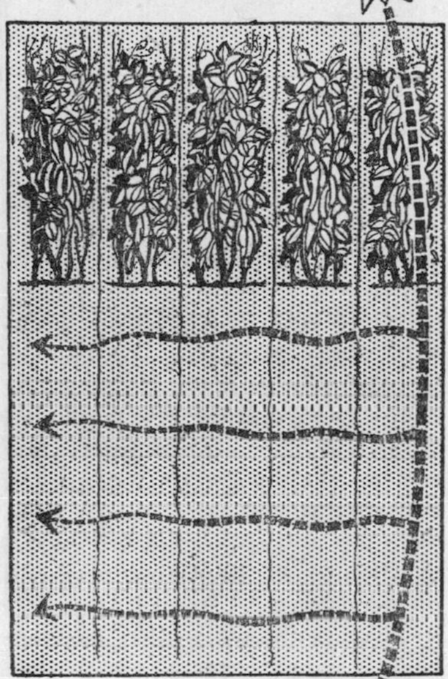

Fig. 156.—*When rows run E. and W., the north-facing sides of tall plants get little if any sun, as is here indicated by the arrows*

that a strip, about 6 ft. wide and the width of the plot, is occupied by various items the necessity for which is apt to be overlooked in the hurry to get a new piece of ground under a full load of crops.

Tool shed and frame may be left to the last. The combined seed and nursery bed must certainly come first. This essential bed is for the raising of seedling cabbage and other plants, which will be transplanted to the nursery part of the bed to grow on for a space in readiness for setting out in the rows where they are to remain. Other seedlings—lettuce, for example—will be transferred direct to the open ground.

It is a convenient space, also, for seed boxes containing young celery, leek and onion plants awaiting planting out. Vacancies not otherwise occupied from time to time could be cropped with radish, and mustard and cress.

Space for Fruit. On the 10-rod plot plan space is indicated for a row each of raspberry plants and gooseberry bushes; black, red or white currants could be planted as alternatives. These divide the plot (exclusive of the 6-ft. wide top strip) into three equal parts. To utilize space to the full, blackberries or loganberries could be planted against the shed sides. Cultural details will be found in the FRUIT section, pages 473–550.

A Bit of Glass. A frame of some kind (Fig. 157), sheltered from the north if possible, and with the glass sloping to the south, is invaluable for raising early seedlings and for wintering others. A frame can be made of oddments, and may be of any size according to the glass available. An old glazed window frame makes an excellent "light" (or top). Other devices to trap heat in spring and keep out frost in winter can be contrived with boxes and odd pieces of glass.

The grower will not be too ambitious if he visualizes a small greenhouse for securing extra-early crops. The management of frame,

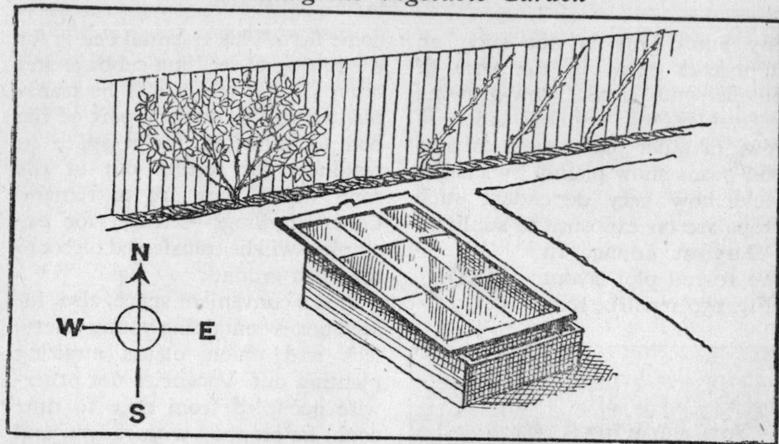

Fig. 157.—*A frame is most useful when sheltered from the north, and with its glass sloping to the south. This enables maximum sun heat to be trapped*

greenhouse and home-made handlights is dealt with in the section, FRAME AND GREENHOUSE (page 61).

Space Saving. An allotment plot will be surrounded with paths, of a sort, and to bisect it with another would be waste of valuable space. Where paths have to be made into orderly condition around a piece of ground they can be surfaced with stones raked off the plot, or with fire ashes or not too coarse clinkers, rolled or rammed for ease of walking. A narrow grass strip as edging looks attractive, but it is a nuisance inasmuch as it needs clipping to secure and maintain neatness, and it provides a harbourage for slugs and snails. A neat enough job results by throwing soil back with the spade from each of the four boundaries so that a slight dip is left along the sides.

Rough Bit of Ground. A rough and weedy bit of soil, or the odd strip that cannot be properly dug and prepared because of lack of time, should be brought under control by forking up or hoeing off the weeds, raking away the general rubbish, and then planting potatoes or Jerusalem artichokes. Though the resultant yield may be below average, those hastily planted crops will help to break up the soil and by their vigorous top growth will discourage the weeds that were left and those that are bound to spring up after this scamped preparation.

This is a makeshift measure which should be adopted only under pressure of time or in other special circumstances. It is, at any rate, preferable to leaving a portion of the ground uncared-for and an eyesore.

Too Late to Sow. It is definitely cheaper and vastly more satisfying to raise one's own plants from seed than to depend on someone for the necessary seedlings. But when it is not possible or convenient to sow, young plants of the cabbage tribe, seedling onions, leeks, celery and other items can be purchased. Nurserymen have these available at the appropriate seasons. It is as well to be sure of the source—of the standing of the grower. Diseased seedlings may introduce into the soil trouble that will take long to eradicate.

One needs to inspect the roots as well as the tops of young plants. Seedlings of the cabbage tribe, for instance, may reveal the presence of club-root disease, or the little root swellings caused by gall weevil grubs. In no circumstances can it be worth while to turn one's back on such risks.

Sunny and Shady Borders. In the home garden, fences or walls that back a sunny border in the vegetable quarters—a border facing the south or south-west—can be made profitable with tomato plants, runner beans trained up strings or wires, or blackberries and loganberries tied or nailed closely back.

The sunny border of light (fairly crumbly), well-drained soil is capable of producing potatoes, dwarf French beans, turnips, lettuce, spinach and carrots, well in advance of any in more exposed ground. And the earliest outdoor grown peas and broad beans may be secured by sowing in such a position in November. The border may be so narrow that it is not possible to grow these crops in the orthodox rows; but provided the plants are given the requisite elbow room it comes to much the same thing.

A small area of such a border may be reserved (if provision has not been made elsewhere) as a seed bed and "nursery ground" for the production of seedling plants needed for filling the main, exposed beds.

During hot summer days the border which gets full sun, though ideal for tomatoes, is no longer suitable for lettuce, radish and similar salad plants which thrived there earlier on. In summer these require a certain amount of shade, and altogether moister conditions than are afforded in light soil in hot sunshine. They will be happier between rows of peas or beans, where they will receive some shade from the tall growth, or in a border of good soil which faces north, as in the suggested layout for the small home vegetable garden shown on page 232 (Fig. 158).

Shady Allotment. The more sunlight that reaches *all* parts of an allotment, all the year round, the better. There one wants no shady border. It is an unfortunate fact that allotments here and there are too near big trees, and if such a site is viewed in winter, when the trees are bare, it may not appear to be such a bad outlook. But when those trees carry their loads of leaves and the roots are busy sucking nutriment far and wide out of the soil, the outlook is definitely bad.

If there is no alternative to an allotment of that description and it is possible to deal with the trees and their roots as explained and illustrated in Section I, there are possibilities but they entail much labour. If there is a small and heavily shaded corner only, it could be made use of as the site for the indispensable compost heap.

Mid-town Possibilities. The grower whose plot is situated in a smoky town is somewhat handicapped by these shut-in conditions, more particularly when the effort is made to produce potatoes and cabbages in a narrow area between fences. But certain crops, unless

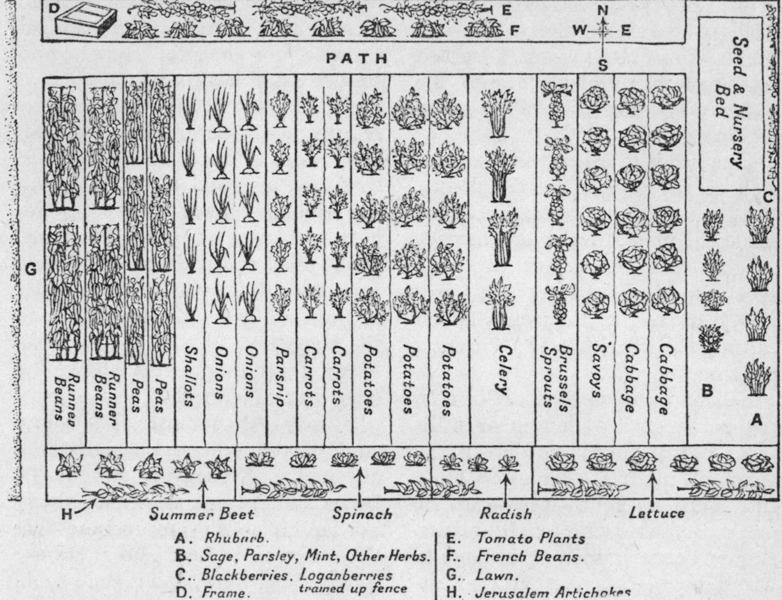

Fig. 158.—*Suggested layout for a vegetable plot in the home garden. The narrow borders can be put to special uses, as shown and explained above*

luck is exceptionally bad, may do well provided the ground has been deeply worked and well manured for their reception. These include rhubarb, dwarf French beans, runner beans, vegetable marrows and tomatoes.

The two latter must definitely be where the maximum sunshine falls, a sunny spot against a warmth-reflecting wall or fence being essential for the tomatoes. Even in a country or suburban area where there is no smoke, the tomato crop may fail to ripen in a coldish summer without the backing of a warm (south-facing) wall or fence.

Radish, lettuce and spinach sometimes do surprisingly well in a smoky area—given rich soil and moisture to induce really rapid growth—though lettuce and spinach are apt to be discouraged by the burden of dirt deposited upon them out of the sooty atmosphere. The deposition of smuts can be defeated by the use of cloches, frame-lights, or odd pieces of glass supported above the plants: this protection to be washed frequently so that the passage of light remains unhindered.

SECTION XXII

VEGETABLES IN DETAIL

ARTICHOKE, CHINESE

APART from the fact that man cannot live on potatoes and cabbage alone, an unusual vegetable makes a very welcome change. The Chinese artichoke (Fig. 159) brings a new flavour to the table. It is a vegetable which is very easily grown, and occupies but little ground.

The plant, which bears no resemblance whatever to either the globe artichoke or the Jerusalem artichoke, grows about a foot high, and underground tubers form the crop. The tubers vary in length from 1 in. to 3 in., are spirally twisted, and about 1 in. thick at the widest part—the centre.

A sunny position is needed; the ground should be dug not less than a foot deep, and it must be well drained. Yield will be greater if the position was manured for a previous crop.

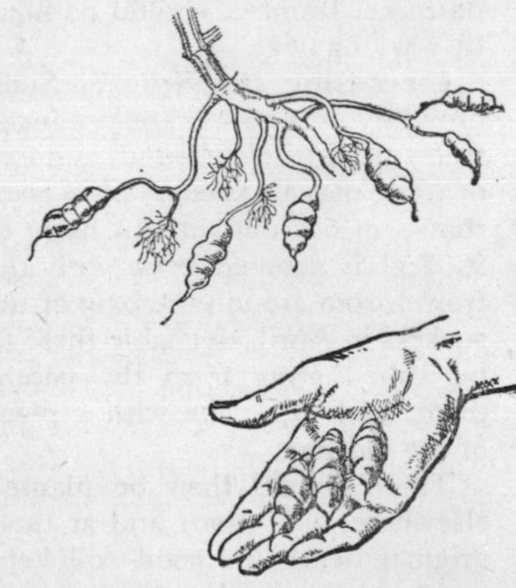

Fig. 159.—*Chinese artichoke tubers are dug in October and can be stored until about February*

There is only one variety: the Chinese Artichoke, *Stachys tuberifera.* Five pounds of tubers will plant a 30-ft. row.

Ready for Use. Tubers are ready for digging in October, and available until February.

When and How to Plant. In March or April, tubers (obtainable from seedsmen) should be planted 3 in. deep and 9 in. apart, in a drill made with the draw hoe. If more than one row is to be planted, it is advisable to space the drills 12 in. apart.

Watering, Hoeing. Plenty of water is required, in July and August especially. Weeds should be hoed up as they appear.

Lifting, Storing. If the ground is light in nature the tubers will pass the winter quite safely where they are for lifting as required; dry bracken or straw placed on the surface above them will prevent it becoming too hard in severe frosty weather for the fork to penetrate. Or the crop may be dug up in November and stored under a layer of sifted ashes under cover.

Preparing for Table. Wash and peel the tubers before cooking. Food value is good. Flavour is somewhat similar to that of the Jerusalem artichoke.

ARTICHOKE, GLOBE

The globe artichoke (Fig. 160) is a luxury plant for the home garden where space is not otherwise in demand; in a small area it is out of place and not profitable. Globe artichoke is a perennial (comes up every year), makes a bushy clump 5 ft. high, has coarse silvery leaves 3 ft. long when fully grown and looks rather like a vigorous thistle —for to that tribe it belongs.

Parts that are cooked and eaten are the globe-shaped, half-grown flower heads and their fleshy bases; these are 4 in. to 5 in. in diameter, bluish-green in colour. Also the young growths, when blanched as explained in the next column.

Full exposure to sun, and deeply dug and manured ground, are two essentials. If there is no manure for digging in, bury plenty of rotted leaves and similar vegetable refuse a foot or more deep.

Variety Green Globe is excellent for ordinary purposes.

Ready for Use. The unopened flower heads, or globes, are ready for cutting in June. Production continues until October.

When and How to Plant. The purchase of young plants is preferable to sowing seed; it saves time and only a few are likely to be required. Plant in late March or early April, 3 ft. apart; if more than one row, space these 4 ft. apart. In dry weather plenty of water will need to be given.

Cutting for Use. Remove the flower heads, each with a portion of stem, before they begin to open. They would expand fully during August, if allowed to, and would be useless. Continue to take the globes as these attain sufficient size.

Preparing for Table. Cut off a small portion of the top of each, cut away the piece of stalk, remove soiled or broken outer parts, and wash in cold water, before cooking. Globe artichokes come well up the food scale and are particularly easy to digest.

Production of Chards. Plants remain profitable for not more than four years. But before they are discarded they can be put to one further use—the production of chards, or blanched young growths, which are welcome in the kitchen department. Procedure is as follows:

When the plant has surrendered its last good globe, some time during summer, remove the flower stems completely and cut back the leaves to within a few inches of the ground. New growth will quickly appear, and when this has reached the height of about 2 ft. wrap it round with clean, dry hay or straw, or thick paper, so that all light is excluded. Tie this material securely, and mound up sifted ashes or dry soil round it. The new shoots will be sufficiently blanched in the course of about six weeks; ashes and wrapping are then removed and the whitened chards are cut.

The worn-out plant can then do no more. Its place should be filled by a young one.

Increasing the Stock. Side-growths, or suckers, are produced freely from below ground, and two or three may be taken from a plant that is in bearing without harm to it. Soil is scraped back with the trowel from around the base of the suckers in April, to enable these to be knifed away from the parent plant, each complete with a piece of the old root.

These should then be planted elsewhere, 3 ft. apart and at their original depth, in good soil kept moist as required; the strongest might produce a few small globes the first year. Small suckers taken later than April would be better planted singly in 5-in. pots and wintered in a cold frame, for planting out the following spring.

Winter Protection. Plants should be cut down in November, and banked round with sifted ashes. If hard frost threatens, dry bracken or leaves should be spread over the tops, this to be removed during fine weather. In March the ashes, having served their protective purpose, should be taken away, and the soil around hoed or forked.

ARTICHOKE, JERUSALEM

The most important of the three kinds of artichoke, the Jerusalem artichoke (Fig. 161) is worthy of a place on every allotment and in every garden. If the potato vanished from the earth, the Jerusalem artichoke would take its place.

The plant grows as high as 10 ft. in three or four months and resembles a tall sunflower plant; as it should, for it belongs to that tribe. Its worth, however, is in the underground tubers, which are produced most generously—up to a bushel per plant in really good soil. These have the appearance of much-bumped and dented potatoes.

It is a general utility plant. It will grow in the open or in shade; in the heaviest soil (so long as this does not lie wet) and in the lightest and driest. A hungry, undug stretch of the vegetable plot will satisfy it. It will hold its own in the weediest patch. But to give biggest and most tubers it needs the encouragement of well-dug soil; rough leaf-mould mixed in helps good results.

Varieties: Purple, or Red-skinned, and White, or Silver-skinned. The white is superior in flavour to the older purple variety.

Fig. 160.—*Where space is not too precious the globe artichoke should certainly be grown. The globe-shaped, half-grown flower heads—one is shown here—are tasty eating*

Four pounds of tubers will plant a 30-ft. row.

Ready for Use. Tubers are fit to dig in October or early November, and are available up to March.

When and How to Plant. February and March are the planting months. Small tubers, or large ones cut into three (each division to have an eye), are planted, without the necessity of previous sprouting. They need to be a foot apart; rows to be 3 ft. apart. Put down the garden line as a guide for draw hoe or spade in making a planting drill, this to be deep enough to allow the tubers placed therein to be covered with 4 in. of soil.

If the ground is heavy, make separate planting holes with the spade (instead of a continuous drill) and place the tubers just under the surface, stalk end uppermost. Unlike potatoes, the plants do not need earthing up.

As a Windbreak. The thick, strong stems and dense growth of the Jerusalem artichoke form an efficient barrier against cutting winds, and a line of tubers may be planted for this purpose. But if the tall tops are exposed to gales they will need some support; thick string, or wire, stretched between end stakes will take the strain.

A line of these plants will also provide welcome shade in summer for lettuce, radish and other salad plants.

Lifting, Storing. The best plan is to leave the tubers in the ground, after cutting down the stems in November, and dig them up as wanted. Dry straw or bracken spread on top will ensure easy digging when a few tubers are to be forked up in frosty weather. The alternative is to lift the entire crop, in November, and store in a dry shed or cellar. Sifted ashes or loose soil thrown over the heap will keep them safe.

Clear the Ground. The last of the tubers left to winter in the ground should be got out in February and placed in store. If Jerusalem artichokes are again to occupy the same line the cleared ground will need deep digging and whatever vegetable refuse can be tucked into it. Leaving old tubers year after year in the same bit of undug ground results in a jungle of tops and a mass of undersized tubers for the crop.

A sufficient number of the best should be set aside each year for the February to March planting.

Preparing for Table. Wash, or scrub, and peel tubers before cooking. Food value is considerable.

ASHES

Coal and coke ashes contain no plant food; in no way may either be regarded as a manure or fertilizer. But they have much value where clay or other heavy soil is to be dealt with, sifted ashes dug in generously and deeply helping to break the ground up and keep it broken up so that it is more inclined to crumble. The drainage of ground thus dealt with is greatly improved.

The ashes do not need weathering. They may be dug in (after sifting) straight from the house fires or stokehold. They cannot serve the foregoing purposes if left scattered on the surface; they must be mixed in with the soil to the depth of 1 ft. at least. They should not be used where potatoes are to be planted, or the skins of these may be scratched and scabbed by the sharp particles. Neither should they be added to light soil, or this will be made still lighter.

Sifted dry ashes will keep slugs and snails away from lettuce and other plants; ashes lose their value in this respect whilst wet, regaining it when the particles again become dry and sharp.

They can be used for mounding up around plants which require such protection in winter; for mounding up around the outside of a garden frame to make this more weatherproof; and for surfacing paths, a roller being used to compress them after rain.

Wood Ash. Ash that results from the burning of wood and woody refuse of all kinds—tree and hedge prunings, old pea and bean sticks, cabbage stalks, dead stems of Jerusalem artichokes, dock and other coarse weeds, diseased potato tops—is in a quite different category. It is rich in potash; potato, onion, beet and tomato especially derive benefit from this. The wood ash should be kept dry

Fig. 161.—*Jerusalem artichoke tubers are planted whole* (B) *or, if large, cut into portions* (A) *and spaced out* (C); *section of hoe-made drill* (D). *Or planting holes may be made with the spade* (E). *In a windy district support may be needed by the top growth* (F). *A bunch of tubers ready for lifting* (G)

and under cover (or rain will wash most of the potash out of it) for forking, hoeing or raking into dug ground a week or ten days before sowing or planting onions or beet. For potatoes it should be sprinkled freely in the planting drills and also mixed with the soil at the first earthing up. For tomatoes it should be mixed with the top soil before the plants are set out, and later given as a surface dressing and watered in.

Used in sufficient quantity it makes the surface of heavy ground lighter. It should not be used too freely on light soil.

ASPARAGUS

A luxury vegetable, with only a short annual season of usefulness —not more than about eight weeks —asparagus is not a profitable crop for a small plot; moreover, plants must be in their third or fourth year before shoots can be cut without the plants being weakened. Against all this can be placed the fact that a bed, or row, of asparagus will continue to yield well for twenty years or more. It is therefore an undoubted asset in the home garden not cramped for space.

Parts that are eaten are the plump shoots, not less than the thickness of one's little finger, which rise direct from the roots in May and June.

A sunny, sheltered position is required. If the ground is clay-like it must be broken up 2 ft. deep (but the lower soil is not to be brought to the top) and made more porous by the digging in of ashes, grit or sand. Light soil should be given body by the digging in of manure, or seaweed (asparagus appreciates seaweed, being a seaside native) or leaf-mould in quantity. In any case asparagus demands rich living.

Varieties include: Giant French, Connover's Colossal, Perfection, Argenteuil (purple).

About 250 seeds go to the ounce. Germination period, five weeks.

Ready for Use. Outdoor cutting starts in May and ends in June. Winter and early spring supplies are obtained by forcing strong roots, not less than three years old, in a temperature of 60 to 75 degrees.

Obtaining Plants. As plants need to be three years old before it is permissible to start cutting, the quickest plan is to purchase roots either one or two years old, for planting. They will transplant readily.

If time is no consideration, sow seed outdoors, in April, in a 1-in. deep drill. Cover with that depth of soil, and thin out the seedlings to 6 in. apart; the following spring thin out again, to 1 ft. apart. Those removed, if taken up complete with roots, can be planted to extend the line. When these are three years old move them to the permanent bed or row.

Preparations. The plants may form a single row, or be planted in a specially prepared bed to accommodate two rows. The bed should be about 4½ ft. wide, 18 in. separating the two rows. Plants should be 16 in. apart in the row (Fig. 162). Digging and manuring must be thorough and carried out on the lines already explained. This needs to be done well in advance of planting time, to allow the soil to settle again.

When and How to Plant. Roots should be put in during late March or in April, each row being

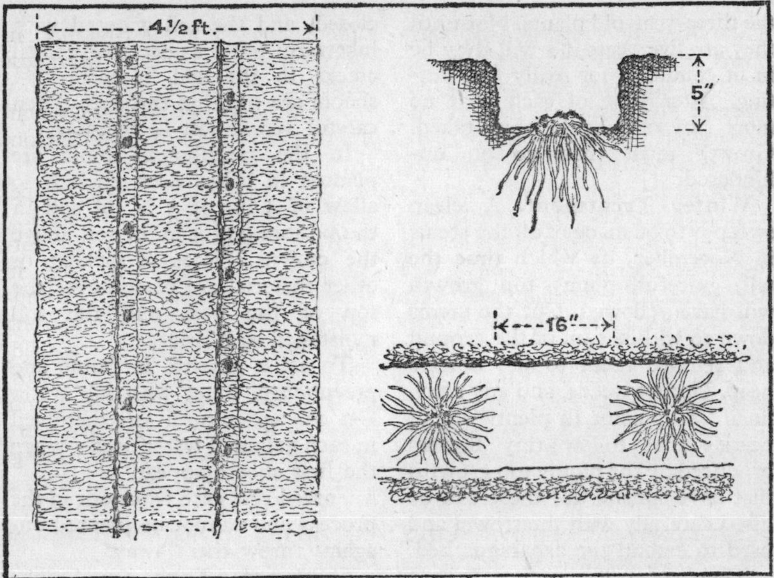

Fig. 162.—*Asparagus roots planted in trench* (*right*), *two rows occupying a 4½-ft. bed* (left). *A well-made bed should continue to yield for twenty years*

marked with the garden line to enable a straight trench to be taken out with the spade. The trench is to be wide enough to take the out-spread roots and deep enough to allow of a covering of 5 in. of soil above the crowns (growing points) at the top of each root mass.

The fleshy, strip-like roots which form a clump are easily broken, so they should be covered in carefully; they should be spread out in all directions before the soil goes back over them.

Watering, Feeding. Soak the bed or row well with water immediately after planting, if the ground is dry, and give plenty throughout spring and summer when rain holds off.

At monthly intervals from May to September sprinkle agricultural salt over the soil surface, 1 oz. per square yard; water it in unless the soil is moist. A handful of wood ash to the square yard, at intervals, will be appreciated.

Gathering the Shoots. The fat shoots for gathering may be cut or broken away below soil level. There is a special knife, with a saw tip, for cutting them; if this is used it must not be pushed so deeply into the ground that there is a chance of roots being injured or other shoots not yet through the surface being accidentally sliced.

The best and quickest plan is to scrape away some of the soil from the base of a shoot and then break this off as low as possible. The gathered shoots may be anything from 5 in. to 8 in. long, including the white, underground part (Fig. 163).

Only a few should be taken from

the three-year-old plants. Not until they are five years old will they be in fit condition for really free cutting. After June of each year no more sticks should be taken. Growth must then go on unhindered.

Winter Treatment. A clean sweep is to be made of all the stems in November, by which time the tall, graceful, plumy top growth will have yellowed. Cut the stems down to within 1 in. of the ground and remove them to the bonfire heap. Uproot weeds, and any seedlings (seeds come in plenty out of berries that follow tiny flowers produced by the plumy top growth) that have sprung up; these can be lifted carefully with the trowel and used to extend the asparagus bed.

Then cover the surface with a thin layer of manure or seaweed, and cover this in turn with a sprinkling of soil.

How to Force Asparagus. The two months' outdoor season can be extended by digging up really strong root clumps, preferably four years old, in February and planting them in a hotbed frame with a temperature of 60 to 75 degrees; or planting them in November, and onwards through winter, in boxes in a greenhouse with a night temperature of about 65 degrees. Either method of forcing will give sticks fit for cutting in about six weeks.

The method of preparing a hotbed frame is described in the section FRAME AND GREENHOUSE (page 61). The asparagus roots for forcing are placed on about 3 in. of soil covering the surface of the hotbed, and good soil is added until the crowns of the roots are covered 5 in. deep. The frame is kept closed, and the soil watered with lukewarm water as necessary, until cracks in the soil indicate that shoots are pushing through. Then careful ventilation is necessary.

In the greenhouse, roots are planted in boxes deep enough to allow of 4 in. or 5 in. of soil in the bottom and 5 in. of soil above the crowns. Pieces of sacking or other material are placed over the top of the box, and the soil moistened as it dries.

To assist growth, in frame and greenhouse, water with salt water —2 oz. agricultural salt dissolved in each gallon of water used—when the first shoots appear.

Forced roots are worn out in the process and cannot be planted out again; throw them away.

Grub-eaten Tops. Small grubs of the asparagus beetle feed on the foliage and may occur in such numbers that stems are almost stripped. Quassia and soft soap solution used as a spray, or derris dusted over the tops, will effect a clearance.

Preparing for Table. Scrape the lower (white) part of the cut shoots with a knife, working the blade downwards from the top, and wash them in cold water, before cooking. Food value lies mostly in the potassium salts contained. Asparagus is very easily digested.

AUBERGINE (EGG PLANT)

A relative of, but bearing no resemblance to, the potato, the aubergine gets its name, egg plant, from the resemblance of its edible fruits to a chicken's egg; though in some varieties the egg is considerably elongated. It is a delicious vegetable when cooked, and can also be eaten raw like a tomato.

Also like the tomato it can be planted outdoors in a warm position against a south-facing fence or wall, or fruited in a sunny greenhouse in pots.

It grows about 2 ft. to 3 ft. in height and is bushy in nature. Varieties include White (nearest in shape and colour to an egg), Long Purple (fruits sometimes 9 in. long), New York Purple. Mixed seed also is sold.

Ready for Use. During summer and autumn. Outdoor season lasts until September.

How and When to Sow. Plants need to be raised in hotbed frame or warm greenhouse; seed to be sown February to March, thinly, in light soil in a small flowerpot or shallow seed box; temperature 65 to 75 degrees. Cover pot or box with a sheet of glass, and paper, until the first seedlings appear.

Potting On. Transfer the seedlings when 2 in. high singly to small pots. When these have become almost filled with roots, shift on into 6-in.-diameter pots. If they are to be grown on in the sunny greenhouse, shift again to a larger size. Potting soil to consist of 2 parts good soil, 1 part sifted leaf-mould or quite old manure, and a sprinkling of silver sand.

Staking, Syringeing. Nip off the top of each plant when about 6 in. high; this will encourage side shoots and bushy growth. Give each a 3-ft. stake, and tie with raffia, but not tightly, as growth extends upwards. Syringe with clear water of the same temperature as the greenhouse, morning and afternoon; this encourages growth and discourages attack by red spider.

Planting Outdoors. In a warm summer the egg plant will do well outdoors, in rich soil, at the foot of a south-facing fence or wall, planted out in June.

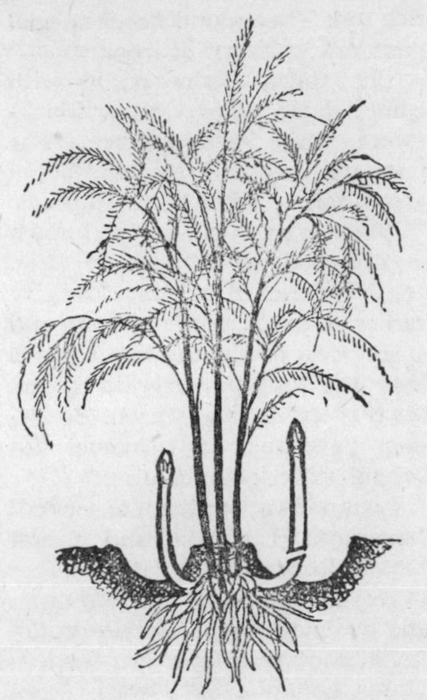

Fig. 163.—*Asparagus shoots are gathered by scraping soil from the base of the plant and cutting or breaking the fat young shoots as low down as possible. The soil is then returned around the plant*

Gathering the "Eggs." These are ready for gathering when fully coloured, tomato-fashion.

Preparing for Table. Wipe the "eggs" with a damp cloth before eating raw or cooking. They are a luxury, not a high-value food.

BEAN, BROAD

Hardy and sturdy, with thick stems and glossy leaves, growing about 3 ft. high, the broad bean gives a heavy crop—though not of long duration—in deeply dug and rich soil. The ground needs special preparation if dry or poor.

The thick, fleshy pods, with white, fluffy lining, follow black-spotted white fragrant flowers. The pods are not edible, the crop being grown for the white or green seeds.

The two main classes are known as Longpods and Windsors (Fig. 164). Varieties in the first class give earlier crops. Windsors (broad and short pods, containing fewer beans than the long-podded kinds) are sown to extend the season. Seedsmen have their own names for several varieties, including:

Longpod varieties, white seeded: Mammoth Longpod and Giant Seville Longpod, for late October to November sowing for early crop, and Prolific Longpod for February (maincrop) sowing; green seeded: Green Longpod and Dwarf Green Gem, the latter about 12 in. high, both for maincrop.

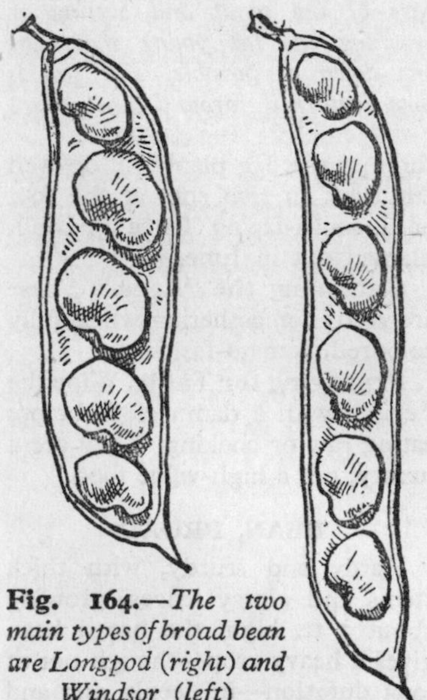

Fig. 164.—*The two main types of broad bean are Longpod (right) and Windsor (left)*

Windsor varieties, white seeded: Mammoth Windsor, Broad Windsor; green seeded: Green Windsor.

About 200 seeds go to the pint, and they germinate in about fourteen days.

Ready for Use. Sown February to March, ready for gathering in July. Autumn-sown early Longpod varieties are ready about ten days earlier than spring-sown.

Soil Preparation. An open position, and rather heavy soil deeply dug and enriched with manure or rotted greenstuff, is ideal for the main crop. A shut-in position, as between close fences, is not favourable; it results in weakly growth, and the crop is generally ruined by the devastating black-fly. Deep and generous soil preparation is essential if the ground is dry or poor.

For an autumn-sown crop the soil must be light and well-drained, sheltered from cold winds and (preferably) sloping to the south; heavy, wet soil is quite unsuitable.

When and How to Sow. Late October or early November for the autumn sowing, but only when the ground is reasonably dry. With the spade take out drills 9 in. wide and 2 in. deep and 2 ft. apart, running north and south if possible. Space out the seed 4 in. apart, in two lines, along the drill bottom; the two lines to be separated by the width of the drill; the seeds in one line to be placed opposite the 4-in. spaces of the twin line. The result is double rows, 2 ft. apart.

This sowing should give pods for picking ten days or so in advance of the February to March sown broad beans. An even more important advantage is that the October to November sown plants

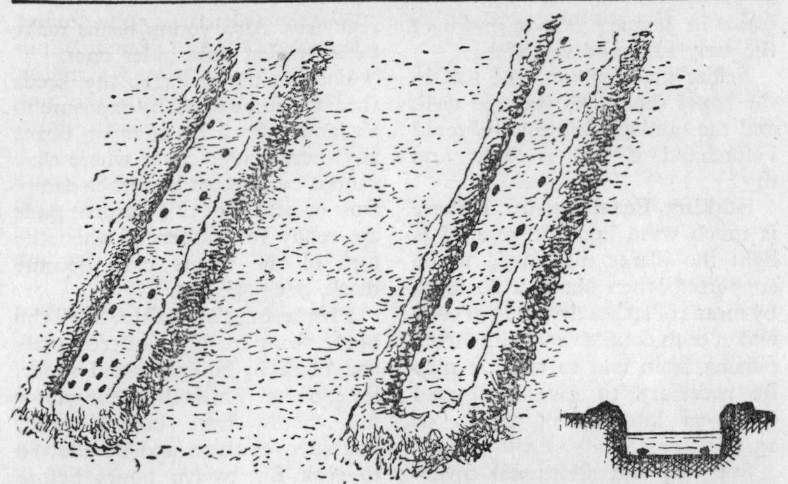

Fig. 165.—*Maincrop sowing of broad beans, in double rows 2½ ft. apart. In light soil the 9-in.-wide drill should be deep enough to leave a 3-in. channel above the covered-in seed (right) for later watering. A few extra seeds should be sown (extreme left) for filling blanks which may occur in the rows*

usually escape the attentions of black-fly because the growth, being more advanced, is more resistant to attack. In the event of hard winter weather, dry bracken, or straw, placed loosely over the young plants whilst the danger period lasts, will prevent disaster.

The Main Crop. For the main crop a fully exposed piece of ground is chosen. Sow in February or March (or in both months, to get a succession of crops) in 9-in.-wide drills 3 in. deep, in double lines as advised for autumn sowing, but spacing the seed 6 in. apart and allowing about 2½ ft. between the double rows (Fig. 165).

If the ground for this spring sowing is light in nature, make the drills 6 in. deep but cover the seeds only 3 in. deep; that leaves a 3-in. channel above for receiving water when the plants need it. Also, water the drills before sowing if the soil happens to be dry then. It will assist the seedlings to make an earlier appearance if the seeds are soaked in cold water for a few hours before being sown. Note that this applies only to light soil in dry weather.

In all cases it is advisable to sow a few extra seeds a couple of inches apart in an odd group for transplanting into any blank spaces that may occur in the rows.

Sowing in Boxes. Wet ground or very cold weather may delay outdoor sowing; in which case time is saved by sowing in shallow boxes filled with good soil and sheltering the boxes in a cold frame or greenhouse. Space the seed 2 in. apart and 1 in. deep. As soon as it becomes possible to plant out, remove the young plants with a trowel and transfer to the prepared rows.

Time is also gained by sowing in

boxes in January one or more of the early Longpod varieties.

Before planting out, the soil in the boxes should be watered well, and the outdoor positions watered beforehand if soil is light and dry.

Staking, Earthing-up. If there is much wind and the ground is light the plants may need to be supported when about 2 ft. high, by means of stakes driven in at each end of each double row, with string passing from end to end. It may be necessary to give additional stakes at intervals of 12 ft. or 15 ft.

Support, and additional covering for the roots, can be given in heavy soil by earthing-up when the plants are about 9 in. high—soil being drawn up to the stems, with the hoe, to the height of 2 in. or 3 in.

Beware of one great Enemy. Black-fly can completely ruin a crop, infesting the pods as soon as these form and sucking all life out of them. The pest appears first on the tips of plants, forming packed black masses. The removal of the tips when plenty of bloom has formed, either before or after black-fly has appeared, helps to beat the pest. Picked-off tips should be burned and the plants sprayed with a handful of soft soap dissolved in 2 gal. of hot water, plus a wine-glassful of paraffin; or with quassia and soft-soap solution.

When seedling leaves are nibbled, this is the work of weevils. The remedy is derris powder, or old (not fresh) soot scattered over the foliage. See page 406.

Picking the Pods. The crop will be greater and more prolonged if pods are picked young, and regularly. Also young beans make better eating than older ones.

For winter storage, the seeds (beans) can be dried by exposure to air and stored in bags or boxes anywhere under cover where they cannot be affected by either damp, frost or heat. For this purpose pods are ready for gathering when the tops of the plants have become black. See page 415.

Preparing for Table. Shell the beans from freshly gathered pods and place in boiling salted water, for cooking. Those dried for winter use should have boiling water poured over them and be allowed to soak for twelve hours before cooking.

Renowned for their food value, broad beans are more easily digested if the individual skins are removed before the beans are eaten.

BEAN, CLIMBING FRENCH

Less vigorous in growth than the runner bean, the climbing French bean is considered the runner's superior in flavour. It grows between 5 ft. and 6 ft. high, and the pods, gathered young and small, can be cooked whole; they differ from the dwarf French bean only in that the plant is a climber.

The roots need plenty to live on, and a sunny and warm aspect gives best results. Crops can be secured all the year round by sowing (and growing on) under glass from July to April. But as that is not possible save in exceptional circumstances only outdoor culture need be considered.

Variety to come into bearing first outdoors is Earliest of All; but Tender and True, and Princess of Wales, are not far behind.

About 180 seeds go to the pint.

Seedlings appear in about seventeen days.

Ready for Use. July sees the first pickings, and the season continues to September or October.

Soil Preparation, Sowing. Deep digging, and the working in of manure or rotted leaves, etc., sowing and other attentions, proceed as described for runner beans. Stakes can be shorter than for runners; it is sufficient if they stand about 5 ft. out of the ground.

Storing, Preparing for Table. The fresh pods are cooked whole, or sliced, and the dried seeds can be used as haricots, as advised under dwarf French beans. Food value is the same.

BEAN, DWARF FRENCH

Dwarf French beans, known also as kidney beans (the seeds are kidney shaped), make sturdy, large-leaved bushy plants up to about 2 ft. in height; stakes are not required. They come into bearing before the runner bean and continue producing pods in quantity throughout summer.

Pods and seeds are eaten together, cooked whole or sliced, and the dried seeds make an excellent winter reserve of food. Soil needs to be as rich as possible and the position open and sunny.

Varieties for earliest outdoor sowing include Superlative and Earliest of All. For the main crop: The Prince, Masterpiece and Canadian Wonder. For a later crop: Green Gem (dried seeds specially useful as haricots).

About 600 seeds go to the pint, and they germinate in about fifteen days.

Ready for Use. Outdoor cropping starts in late June or early July and continues to September. Winter crops are secured under glass by sowing and growing on in a temperature of about 60 degrees.

Soil Preparation. Roots go down deeply, so deep digging is desirable. Vegetable refuse or manure should be worked in below the top 9 in. as far in advance of sowing or planting out as possible. Trouble taken here will be rewarded with long-period cropping.

When and How to Sow. Time to sow outdoors is governed by weather, soil and district. The shelter of a south-facing fence or wall allows of a mid-April sowing if the ground does not lie wet or heavy. These early plants will need protection from frost, provided by an overhead scattering of dry bracken or straw so long as the frost continues.

The last week in April is the earliest for maincrop sowing, successive sowings up to mid-June prolonging the cropping season; mid-May is the earliest date in a cold locality.

Make drills the width of the draw-hoe blade and 2 in. deep. Space the seed 6 in. apart down the centre line of the drill and return the 2 in. of soil above them. Fill drills with water a few hours previous to sowing if the ground is dry. If the soil dries out speedily in summer—as it will do if light in nature—drills should be made about 5 in. deep, leaving a 3-in.-deep channel above the covered-in seed for subsequent waterings. Drills should be 18 in. apart.

Thinning Out. The plants are to stand a foot apart eventually, so thinning out is necessary. Those removed—carefully, with a trowel—can be planted to form another row, or rows. It is not always possible to depend on 100 per cent germination of this seed, hence rather thick sowing is advisable.

The alternative is to sow the seed a foot apart in the drills and sow a clump elsewhere, drawing on the latter to make good any blanks later on in the drills.

Sowing in Boxes. If circumstances make reasonably early sowing outdoors impossible, time is gained by sowing in shallow wooden boxes in frame or greenhouse. Fill the boxes with good soil (a layer of leaf-mould in the bottom if possible, for the roots to grip) and space the seed 2 in. apart and ¾ in. deep.

Keep the seedlings close to the glass, expose to air as much as possible to keep them short and strong, and plant out in drills in May.

Watering, Feeding. The advantage of deep drills is obvious in time of drought; these can be filled and not a drop runs to waste. Liquid manure or fertilizer given when the first pods are forming is a great help. A good artificial mixture for making up at home consists of superphosphate three parts, one part each sulphate of ammonia and sulphate of potash; give 2 oz. of the mixture per 5 yd. of row and water it in. If drills are not deep but level with the surface, hoe the mixture in before watering.

Use the Dutch hoe between rows to annihilate weeds and keep the surface powdery.

Growing in Pots. Dwarf French beans can be forced if the night temperature of the greenhouse can be kept at a minimum of 55 degrees. Pots about 8 in. across the top are half-filled with a mixture of good soil and leaf-mould or stable manure, seeds inserted ½ in. deep and 3 in. apart; the pots filled to within 1 in. of the top with a similar soil mixture when the plants are 6 in. high. Short, twiggy sticks will be required as supports, and full light is essential; also a moist atmosphere, secured by syringeing with lukewarm water on bright mornings.

Pests and Diseases. Slugs will be attracted by the juicy seedlings. Fresh soot scattered on the soil, and old soot dusted over the leaves, will keep them at bay. Red spider will endeavour to ruin greenhouse crops; a moist atmosphere and frequent light syringeings serve as a preventive. See also page 406.

Picking the Pods. These become tough and stringy if not gathered before seed starts to bulge the pods. Careful searching is required to ensure that no pods are overlooked and allowed to become old; these hinder further production.

Storing for Winter. Seed for winter use as haricots is valuable; pods can also be dried or salted; full directions are given on page 415.

Preparing for Table. Freshly gathered pods may be cooked whole, if small, otherwise sliced. They should be topped and tailed and the string down the side removed. Food value is high, proteins, carbohydrates, salts and water being present.

BEAN, HARICOT

All bean seeds serve as haricots. The pods should be left on the plants until the seed is ripe; or taken under cover, where air circulates freely and sun can reach, until the pods have yellowed. The seed is then shelled out, exposed to air to complete drying and then stored in bags or boxes. See under Haricot Beans in the section, Easy Home Preservation of Vegetables (page 412).

BEAN, RUNNER

Rate of growth of scarlet runners is amazing, and the smother of flowers (white, and pink and white, as well as the old-fashioned scarlet) presages generous pickings of long pods. The plants need tall stakes to twine around and climb; though 2-ft. stakes can be used and the plants kept dwarf and bushy, as described in a later paragraph.

Soil light rather than heavy, but rich, is productive of the greatest and most prolonged yield. Full sun is ideal, but some shade during part of the day does not affect cropping.

Varieties include Scarlet Emperor, Improved Painted Lady and Mammoth White Czar (white seeded).

About 180 seeds go to the pint, and average period of germination is about seventeen days.

Ready for Use. First pickings are ready in late July, after dwarf French beans have already been enjoyed. Season extends to October.

Soil Preparation. As with all other tall crops, rows should run north and south; sun then reaches both sides. It is worth while preparing special trenches, 5 ft. or 6 ft. apart for plants to be staked, 3 ft. apart for those to be kept dwarf and bushy, each trench to be 18 in. wide, soil taken out to the depth of 9 in. and placed on one side. The bottom soil is then broken up and decayed vegetable refuse, or hop or animal manure, forked into it.

Part of the excavated soil only is returned, after being enriched with material similar to that forked into the bottom. After the contents of the trench have been firmed by treading, its surface should be about 4 in. below the general level—to facilitate watering later on.

When and How to Sow. The runner bean cannot stand frost at either end of the year. Mid-May is outdoor sowing time, other sowings being made, if necessary, up to mid-June. In northern and other cold districts outdoor sowing is not advisable; plants should be raised in a cold frame for setting out in June.

Sow 2 in. deep in single rows, these to be separated by 5 ft.; or in double rows 9 in. apart, the double rows to be separated by 6 ft., the seed in one row to be spaced opposite the gaps of the twin row (Fig. 166); or in rows 3 ft. apart if plants are to be dwarfed. The plants should stand 1 ft. apart; seed may be sown at 6-in. intervals and the seedlings thinned out; a clump or two should be sown as a reserve for filling in spaces where seed has failed to come up in the rows.

Sowing in Boxes. Cold-district sowings to be made in seed boxes filled with good leafy soil during early May, the boxes to be placed in frame, greenhouse, or light and sunny room indoors. Put the seeds in singly, $\frac{3}{4}$ in. deep and 2 in. apart. Plant out in June.

In warmer districts a similar sowing may be made with safety in April, the plants to be set out in May when the weather is warm and settled.

Plants should be taken from the boxes (the soil previously moistened) with all the soil possible clinging to the roots and planted in ample, trowel-made holes, and at once watered in if the ground is dry.

Supports for the Runners. Thick sticks (no need to have them branched, as for peas) to go firmly into the ground, one to each plant, are used for supports when they are obtainable. They should be pushed into the ground about 3 in. from the plants and, in the case of double rows (9 in. apart), sloped inwards. To make them secure against wind, long sticks should be placed crosswise about 1 ft. down from the top, the upright sticks being tied to the horizontal one crossing them. They need to stand at least 7 ft. out of the ground (Fig. 166).

A light wooden framework—top, bottom, two ends—secured firmly in the ground by end supports, with strings fastened to top and bottom at 12-in. intervals, will take the place of the conventional stakes when these are scarce.

Anything climbable and of sufficient height, such as a trellis, may have runner beans as occupiers of whatever space is available.

Young plants may need coaxing, at first, to climb, by tying loosely to the foot of the stake; or short bits of stick can be pushed into the ground so that the plants are pressed lightly to the stakes they are to climb.

Without Tall Stakes. Plants are kept down to about 2 ft., and the need of tall stakes avoided, by pinching off the tips when they have reached that height. Side shoots will develop, and these will need tipping when 6 in. long; subsequent growths being dealt with similarly. Pod production is not lessened to any appreciable extent.

Watering, Feeding. Soaking the rows with clear water at frequent intervals is a great crop encouragement. Production begins to fall off when the plants suffer from drought. Liquid manure given every ten days or so—after an ordinary watering, or after rain—has excellent results. An artificial fertilizer mixture may be used instead; or nitrate of soda solution—$\frac{1}{4}$ oz. dissolved in each gallon of water. This feeding should start, if possible, when the first pods appear.

Why Flowers Drop Off. When flowers fall off instead of setting—a common trouble in dry weather—this can be put right by syringeing or spraying the flowering parts with clear water every rainless evening. Rainwater is best for this purpose, exposed to the sun so that it is warmed; the chill of hard water straight from the tap is not appreciated.

The flower-dropping complaint is less likely to be experienced if the soil is kept moist as far down as the roots.

Other-trouble Remedies. The first trouble likely to assail the plants—apart from frost, which is avoided by delaying sowing until mild weather, or by raising plants under glass—is slugs; black-fly and red spider are next on the list; and halo blight and anthracnose may be in evidence. These are all dealt with as explained in the chart on page 406.

Saving Space. The gaps of 5 ft. or 6 ft. between rows are necessary for the health of the plants. They

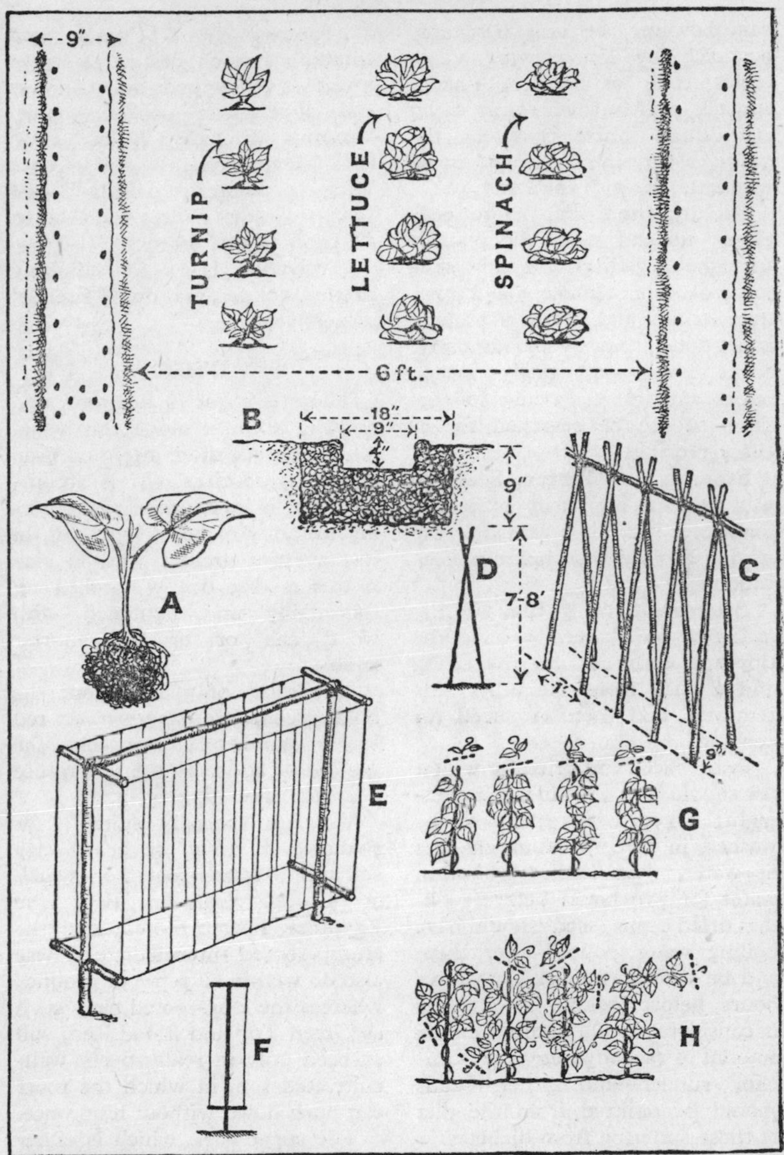

Fig. 166.—*The best type of young runner-bean plant* (A). *Method of preparing trench* (B). *Tall stakes are provided* (C), *end view* (D). *Strings on a support* (E), *end view* (F), *can take the place of tall stakes. Plants can be kept quite dwarf by nipping off the tops* (G) *and ends of side shoots* (H)

can, however, be very profitably occupied by low-growing vegetables such as lettuce, turnip, spinach, radish, sown thinly down the centre. These profit by the shade cast by the beans and in no way interfere with the latter.

Picking the Pods. Before seeds plump up and bulge the pods is the time to gather. The most skilful cook cannot make them other than stringy and coarse if picking is not done promptly and regularly. Some pods may easily escape notice amongst the dense foliage; these should be searched for at every picking.

Storing for Winter. Seeds as well as pods are easily preserved for winter use, as explained in the section dealing with home preservation (page 415).

Preparing for Table. Freshly gathered pods need to have the tips and ends cut off, the string and a strip from the other side removed, and then be sliced for cooking.

Beans sliced and dried for winter use should be soaked in water overnight; salted beans need to be washed in three or four changes of water, then soaked in warm water for two hours before cooking; dried beans (seed) should have boiling water poured over them and be allowed to soak for twelve hours, before cooking. Food value is considerable. On account of the amount of carbohydrates they contain, runner—and other—beans should be omitted from the diet of those suffering from diabetes.

BEAN, WAXPOD (BUTTER)

These are not the flat butter beans sold by grocers and imported from warm climates, but varieties of runner, dwarf French and climbing French beans. The pale lemon or yellow pods are stringless and should be cooked whole. Varieties include Mont d'Or (Climbing French) and Giant Waxpod (runner); Melting Dwarf Wax or Golden Butter and Golden Waxpod (dwarf French).

Cultivation is as for climbing French, runner, and dwarf French respectively.

BEET

There is sugar in beetroot, and on that account alone this vegetable deserves more attention than it usually receives. It is accommodating in its requirements, thriving in sandy or other light soil, in just average ground, and in clay if this is dug deeply, broken up thoroughly and lightened with wood ash or crushed mortar rubble.

The roots only are eaten; the bold green, bronze-green or red leaves should be dug into the ground or added to the soft refuse heap for later digging in.

Varieties specially suitable for shallow, or stony, or heavy clay soil are the round-rooted ones such as Globe, Crimson Ball, the Egyptian Turnip-rooted, and the stump-rooted Intermediate. These also do well in all types of ground; whereas the long-rooted beet, such as Green Top and Blood Red, will succeed only in really deep, well-cultivated soil, in which the roots can push down without hindrance.

The sugar beet, which is either yellow or white skinned, is mostly grown as a field crop for the sake of the sugar which can be extracted from the roots. The method of home extraction consists of boiling the cut-up roots for three to four hours, and again boiling the strained-off liquid until reduced to a syrup, which is bottled for sweetening purposes.

An ounce of seed is sufficient to sow 120 ft. of row. Average time taken for seedlings to appear is about four weeks.

The roots of the beet are ready for lifting in July. Available in store until the following March or April. Round-rooted varieties sown early can be used throughout summer for salad purposes; grown quickly and lifted whilst small they are delicious.

Soil Preparation. Neither heavy nor light soil should be manured for this crop, unless it be old material from a worn-out hotbed, mushroom bed or marrow heap; this may be dug into light, poor soil with considerable advantage. Heavy soil needs to be dug deeply and lightened throughout the full dug depth with crushed mortar rubble, or wood ash (from a bonfire). The latter should be applied generously; the potash it contains is needed by beet. The ideal arrangement is to let beet follow a crop for which special preparations had been made in the way of deep digging and manuring, such as celery, leek, onion, pea, bean.

When and How to Sow. For summer salad purposes a sowing may be made as early as March in a warm, sheltered spot. Otherwise mid-April is safer, with small successive sowings up to the end of June or early July. For this purpose use one of the round-rooted varieties such as Globe or Crimson Ball, and lift them young. They can stand about 6 in. apart.

Drills should be 12 in. apart and about 1 in. deep. Seed for small summer roots should be sown three together at 6-in. intervals; for long roots for winter use and storing, three seeds together at 9-in. intervals. Long-rooted varieties to be sown not earlier than the end of April or the beginning of May.

Thinning Out. If all three seeds at each station germinate, reduce to one. The operation is easier if the soil is moist at the time—after rain or a good watering.

Watering, Feeding. Quick growth is encouraged by plentiful applications of water, and further assisted by surface dressings of agricultural salt in June and July, and wood ash or soot, a trowelful to the yard run of row; these should be hoed in, and then watered in unless the ground is moist.

Forked, Coarse Roots. Long roots develop misshapenly in shallow, stony, or hard clay soil; round varieties have the best chance in these circumstances. Roots will be forked or fanged in recently manured ground. Over-large and coarse-eating roots are the result of sowing long-rooted varieties too early. Eating qualities are also adversely affected by drought, especially from July to August.

Flying and Tunnelling Pests. Sparrows and other birds may give trouble in the early stages; protect the seedlings by dusting with old soot when the leaves are wet with dew or after rain. Repeat the dressing if rain washes it off. Black-fly and leaf-mining grubs to be dealt with as explained on page 406.

Lifting the Roots. To lift the roots push the spade or fork, held upright, into the ground about 6 in.

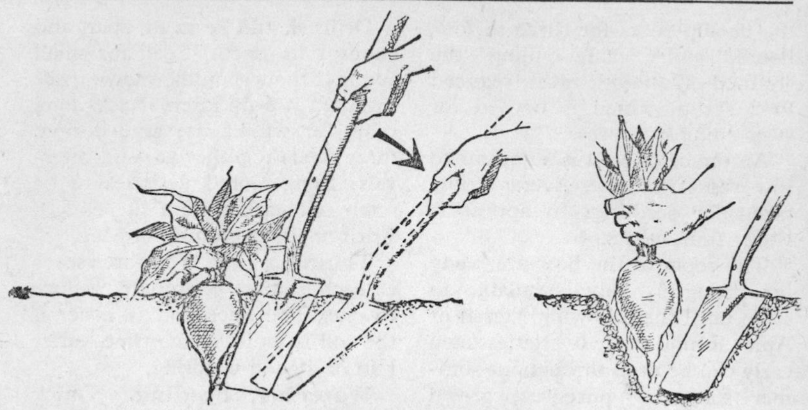

Fig. 167.—*Beet should be lifted with the spade and one hand. Careful manipulation of the spade avoids breaking or bruising the fleshy roots*

from one side of the row. Drive it in deeply, then push the handle down and away from the row. Having thus loosened a root, draw it out of the ground with the left hand, gripping the plant by the leaves low down. The operation needs care; broken or bruised roots bleed and may lose some of their colour (Fig. 167).

Roots for storing should be lifted before they can be damaged by frost; in early October in cold localities. In any case they should be out of the ground by late November.

Storing for Winter. Neither scratched, bruised nor broken roots should go into store. They would decay, and decay quickly spreads. When the roots are lifted, remove the leaves by screwing them off about 2 in. above the top of the root (Fig. 168).

Store them then in single layers in sifted fire ashes or sifted soil, in a frost- and damp-proof shed or cellar. If they must be stored in the open, clamp them where water will not lie (Fig. 169). This operation consists in putting down a 1-in. thick foundation of sifted ashes to form a circular bed. On this the roots are placed one by one, the crowns (root tops) outwards. When all the circular area has been covered with roots one layer deep, cover with sifted ashes. Put down more roots in the same manner, cover with ashes, then more roots, and so on, decreasing the circumference of the pile with each layer so that it finishes as a conical heap.

Give a final covering of ashes, about 3 in. deep, and finish off with a 3-in.-thick layer of dry bracken or straw. Ventilation of the interior is necessary; this is arranged by inserting into the top a twisted bundle (about 2 in. thick and 1 ft. long) of bracken or straw, this to go to the bottom of the final ash covering. In the event of water collecting at the base, dig a trench, right around the clamp, to lead it away.

Replace that part of the covering which is removed each time roots are taken from this winter store for use in the kitchen.

To prepare for table, wash the roots, but do not remove the skin (or peel) until cooked. Beet may be pickled for winter use according to directions in the section, EASY HOME PRESERVATION OF VEGETABLES (page 412). The sugar content represents the chief food value; on this account it should be avoided by diabetics.

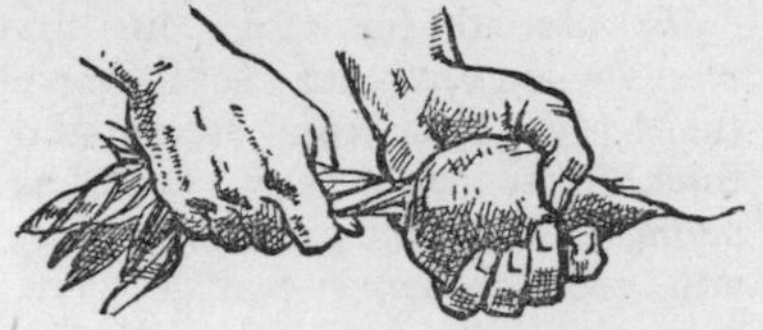

Fig. 168.—*Tops should be screwed from the roots before beet is stored*

BEET, SILVER (SEAKALE BEET)

Silver beet (Fig. 170) is grown not for the roots but for the stems and leaves. The celery-like stalks and the very broad midribs, silvery white in colour, are cooked as seakale. The rest of the leaf is used as spinach.

As a two-uses crop it deserves any space given to it.

Ready for Use. During May and June, and in late summer, according to when sown.

Soil Preparation. Unlike ordinary beet, this plant needs really rich soil, and recent manuring will not harm it. Dig in hop manure, or other animal-manure substitute, or decayed leaves and similar soft refuse. It reaches 2 ft. in height, and needs something rich down below to do itself justice.

How and When to Sow. Sow very thinly in a 1-in.-deep drill, and transplant the seedlings, when large enough to handle, to the prepared row or rows, not less than 12 in. apart in the row; rows also to be 12 in. apart.

Sow at the end of April for late summer use; in August to secure a crop the following May to June.

Fig. 169.—*Store beet in the open, on a foundation of ashes. Alternate layers of roots and ashes are built up* (*left*) *to form a conical heap* (*right*)

To prepare for table, lift the plants when ready for use. Remove the leafy parts from stems and thick ribs, wash and cook as spinach. Wash the stems and ribs, and cook these as seakale. The roots are discarded. Food value is increased by the silver beet plant's twofold use.

BEET, SPINACH (PERPETUAL SPINACH)

Like the foregoing (silver, or seakale, beet) this type of beet has roots which are not to be admitted to the kitchen. Perpetual or spinach beet gives abundant leaf pickings when the ordinary spinach is not available; which labels it at once as an extremely useful vegetable.

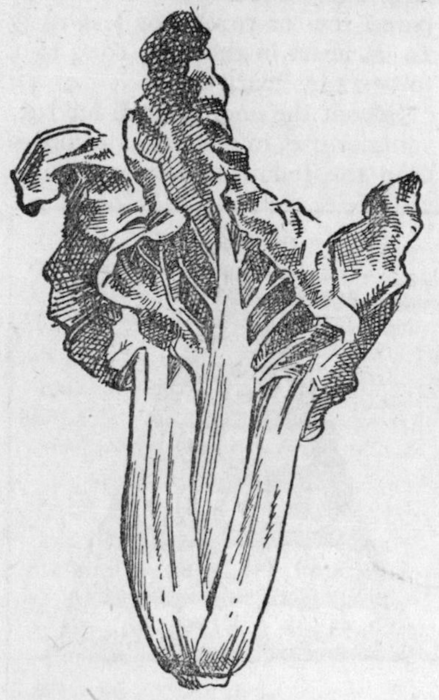

Fig. 170.—*Silver, or seakale, beet is a two-uses crop. Stalks and thick ribs are cooked in the same way as seakale, leaves as spinach*

Ready for Use. During autumn, winter and spring.

Soil Preparation. This is the same as for silver beet. The richer the soil the larger and more frequent the pickings.

When and How to Sow. The first sowing should be at the end of March, and small sowings may be made at intervals—to prolong the crop—up to the end of July. Space the seed very thinly, in 1-in.-deep drills, and transplant the seedlings to the prepared ground, 1 ft. apart each way.

Water as frequently as the ground becomes dry, and keep the surface loose with the hoe. Dry conditions cause this plant to run to seed very speedily, thus ruining the crop.

Gathering the Leaves. As leaves become large enough they may be removed from the plant, only a few from any one plant at a time; or the strongest plants may have all the leaves taken at once, in which case the stripped ones will be out of commission for six or eight weeks, more leaves then being produced. Gathering should cease temporarily during frost.

Preparing for Table. Wash the leaves thoroughly, and cook them entire, as spinach. A tasty and easily digested food. The roots are discarded.

BORECOLE (KALE)

This valuable late winter and early spring green vegetable is dealt with under its more familiar name of kale (page 297).

BROCCOLI

Big white curds, or heads, of broccoli cannot be distinguished by the ordinary eye from those of cauliflower; but the small and plentifully produced heads of sprouting broccoli are distinctive enough. Parts eaten are the large heads of the former, and the small leaf-and-flower heads of the sprouting kind.

An open position is required, and good—but not newly dug and manured—soil is necessary. A really firm root-run is essential to sturdy growth and productiveness. Varieties are numerous. Those which come into use from September to the year end include Sandringham Winter White, Walcheren, Veitch's Self-protecting; from Christmas to April, Mammoth Spring White, Leamington, Snow's Winter White, Adam's Early White, Improved Early Purple Sprouting and Improved White Sprouting; from April to June, Champion, Universal Protecting, Late Queen, Model and Purple Sprouting.

About 1,000 seeds go to the ounce, and seedlings appear in about ten days.

Ready for Use. Autumn, winter, spring and early summer, according to variety (as above). Much depends upon weather as to the date when cutting of heads may begin.

Soil Preparation. Broccoli is well catered for if it can follow a crop that had its site deeply dug and manured (or enriched with decayed vegetable matter); in which case the ground should not be dug again but have the surface forked over. If broccoli must be planted out in newly dug ground this must be made firm and solid, by treading or rolling.

A dusting of hydrated lime may be forked into the surface a week or so before planting; if the soil is light or sandy, however, ground limestone should be used, about 1 lb. to the square yard.

When and How to Sow. Seed to be sown during late March and early April, in ½-in.-deep drills in a prepared seed bed, the seedlings to be kept well watered so that they experience no check in growth. Sow as thinly as possible; crowded seedlings start under a handicap. Should they come up thickly, remove as many as necessary to leave the seedlings not less than 1 in. apart.

Transplanting from Seed Bed. Shift the seedlings early (with a trowel) from the seed bed to a nursery bed, 3 in. or 4 in. apart each way. Leave them firm and low in the soil. Continue watering as necessary. Before they become crowded shift them again, this time into the prepared rows.

Planting Out. The rows where the plants are to remain should be 2 ft. apart, the plants 20 in. apart in the rows, the soil being trodden or rolled if not thoroughly firm. If the ground is light and thirsty, plant in 4-in.-deep drills, to facilitate watering; or leave a depression around each plant to receive water. The trowel-made holes should be large enough to take the roots comfortably, and deep enough to allow the stems to be covered level with the lowest leaves.

Caterpillar Plague. Hand-picking caterpillars from the leaves is a tiresome but effective method of dealing with this pest; or plants may be syringed with salt water, or dusted with derris powder.

Gall weevil and club root may also be troublesome. Remedies and preventives are detailed under cabbage tribe in the chart which appears on pages 406 and 407.

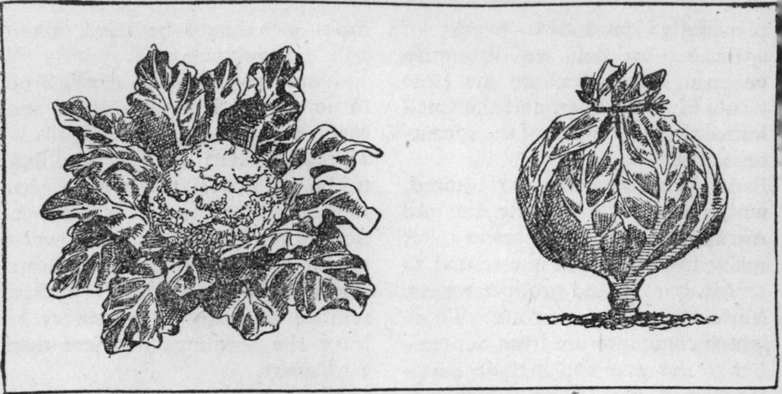

Fig. 171.—*Broccoli not wanted for immediate cutting can be held back by drawing the longest leaves together (right) so as to shield the head*

Cutting the Heads. Large, single heads should be cut before the curds begin to open; small heads of the sprouting varieties to be gathered as they become available, or they will run up to seed.

Large-headed plants ready for cutting but not wanted immediately can be held back by shielding the head against sunshine with the plant's own topmost leaves, these being drawn together over the head and tied (Fig. 171). Or the plants may be dug up complete with roots and replanted deeply and close together where sun cannot reach, the soil then being made wet—a bucket of water allotted to each plant.

Winter Protection. Big-headed broccoli that are to stand through the winter for later use may need protection in the event of hard frost. This is given by laying the plants over so that the heads are directed to the north or west before hard weather comes. Soil is taken with the spade from the north or west side of the row and heaped against the stems on the opposite side and pushed with the foot so that each plant stem becomes nearly parallel with the ground (Fig. 172). Root action is thus checked, and the flow of sap hindered; in which condition the plants are more resistant to frost. More or less advanced heads should be protected, when frost comes, with a layer of dry bracken or other clean litter.

Preparing for Table. Remove soiled outer leaves, cut back leaf-ribs level with the head, pare the stalk closely, wash in salt water (about a teaspoonful to the gallon), and soak head-down in salt water for twenty minutes, before cooking. Wash and soak small heads of sprouting broccoli in like fashion.

The Italian green sprouting broccoli (Calabrese), available during August to September if sown in March, produces one big head and, after this is cut, a number of sprouts. Heads and sprouts are cut with about 6 in. of stem; the stems are peeled and cooked with the rest of the vegetable. Peeled stems may also be used as asparagus.

As a food, broccoli is nutritious and very digestible.

BRUSSELS SPROUTS

Brussels sprouts are a winter vegetable of great worth, each stem a column of close-packed and firm buttons with a small loose cabbage or bunch of greens at the top. Brussels sprouts demand time in which to grow to near perfection. An open position and good, firm soil are prime requirements.

Varieties include Dwarf Gem (the earliest), Aigburth, and Matchless and Rearguard as late varieties.

An ounce of seed represents about 1,000 plants, and period of germination is about ten days.

Ready for Use. November and continuing to March.

Soil Preparation. Heavy or medium soil, dug and manured for a previous crop, is the ideal. Light soils are made suitable by digging deeply and packing with rotted vegetable matter (leaves, weeds, lawn mowings, etc.) as long as possible before planting. If ground is newly dug it must be consolidated by rolling or treading (when it is not wet). A site vacated by another crop needs only to be forked over about 2 in. deep and weeds cleared away.

When and How to Sow. Usual date for outdoor sowings is March, and again in April for a later batch. Sow on a seed bed with well-raked and crumbled surface, very thinly in ½-in.-deep drills a few inches apart. Well water a few hours before sowing if the soil is dry, and keep seedlings moist at the roots.

Transplanting, Planting Out. The seedlings as soon as large enough to handle should first be transplanted, about 4 in. apart, into moist soil, then in May and June (latest ones in July) be planted where they are to remain, 2 ft. apart, in rows 2 ft. apart. Use a trowel, and leave each plant deep and very firm in the ground; soak with water if dry.

Sowing in Boxes. Earliest sowing may be made on a sheltered

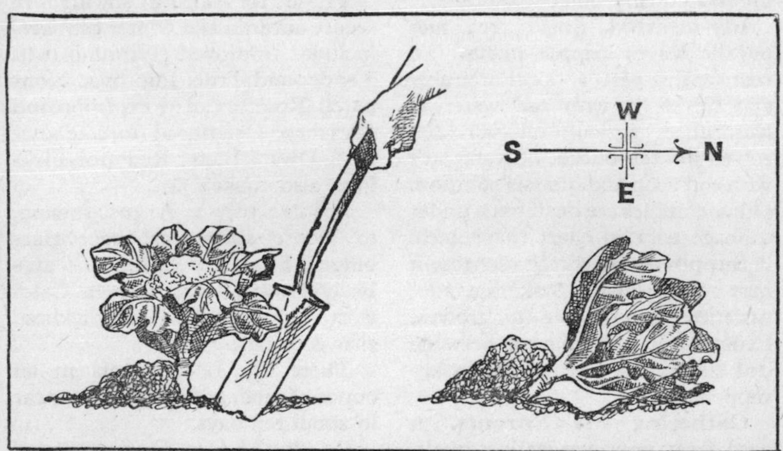

Fig. 172.—*Broccoli to stand through the winter are protected against hard frost by heading over to the north. A spadeful of soil taken from the north side is placed on the south side, pressing the plant right over*

but sunny piece of ground during February. Where conditions are not right for that, sow in seed boxes in a frame or greenhouse, or in a good bed of soil in the frame, which should face south and not be shaded. Sow thinly, keep the frame closed until seedlings appear, then ventilate when weather is mild. Close the frame at night and cover the glass with dry sacking, removing this in the morning.

Transplant the seedlings 4 in. apart each way, in the open, then 2 ft. apart each way in the prepared site.

Leggy Plants, Small and Loose Sprouts. Unless allowed a long growing season, results may be poor—hence early sowing. And ground must be very firm, or growth will be over-tall and sappy, and the buttons anything but firm.

Running to Seed. Plants rush into flower (to produce seed) if there is not sufficient for them to live on down below. They find dry ground equally objectionable.

Fly-infested. Small grey flies on the leaves cripple plants. To remove this pest, spray thoroughly and forcefully with salt water (a handful of agricultural salt dissolved in each bucket of water), or with soft soap and quassia solution. Other troubles are dealt with under cabbage tribe in chart (page 406).

Supports. In windy districts it may be necessary to stake the taller varieties when nearing full growth. Lengths of stout string run between end stakes will give the necessary support.

Gathering the Sprouts. A hard frost improves eating qualities. Remove sprouts by cutting them from the stems with a knife; breaking them off may injure the stems. Take the lowest first from all plants in bearing and work up the stems for subsequent pickings; do not strip a few stems completely. Sprouts evenly matched as to size cook better than a mixed batch. Use the top cabbage finally, when the last sprouts have been taken from the plant (Fig. 173).

Preparing for Table. Remove outside leaves and discoloured ones, trim stalk ends close, wash the sprouts thoroughly, place in salt water for a few minutes, and finally wash in clear water before cooking. They contain salts and antiscorbutic vitamin, though actual food value is not high.

CABBAGE

Cabbage is never so acceptable as when difficult to get. Fortunately it is possible to have fine hearts for cutting during autumn, winter and spring with little trouble and provided that suitable varieties have been selected.

Those for spring sowing, to secure autumn and winter cabbage, include Improved Winningstadt, Tender and True, Improved Nonpareil, Rosette Colewort, Improved Christmas Drumhead (for late sowing), Dwarf Blood Red (for pickling, also cooking).

For late July or August sowing, to secure spring cabbage, Harbinger, Flower of Spring, Ellam's Early Dwarf, Hardy Green Colewort, Large Blood Red (pickling, also cooking).

There are 1,000 plants in an ounce of seed, and seedlings appear in about ten days.

Ready for Use. During spring, from July to August sowings; during autumn and winter, from spring (March or April) sowings.

Fig. 173.—*Brussels sprouts should be picked from the bottom upwards, the top "cabbage" being left to the last*

Soil Preparation. Firm soil that was deeply dug and enriched for a preceding crop suits excellently; it need only be forked 2 in. deep and cleared of weeds. Cabbages are lime lovers, so, unless the ground already contains enough, a scattering of lime should be given (and forked, raked or hoed in) in advance of planting; hydrated lime for medium and heavy soil, ground limestone (1 lb. per square yard) for light ground.

When and How to Sow. First sowing of the year, of one of the earliest varieties (such as Tender and True), may be made in a frame or greenhouse. Outdoor sowings start in March and continue to May—small quantities of seed sown at intervals resulting in plants for setting out in succession. From the earliest of these it should be possible to start cutting in September.

Seed got into the ground in July and August will provide the spring cabbage.

Sow very thinly on a well-raked, sunny seed bed, in drills ½ in. deep, watered beforehand if dry. Keep the seedlings growing by watering as frequently as necessary.

Transplanting, Planting Out. When they are about 3 in. high transplant about 4 in. apart each way into moist soil (Fig. 174). Before they touch, remove them to the rows where they are to finish; rows to be 2 ft. apart, autumn-sown plants to be about 15 in. apart in the rows and spring-sown ones 2 ft.

Four-inch-deep drills taken out

Fig. 174.—*Transplanting members of the cabbage tribe from seed bed to nursery bed before finally planting out encourages a root mass (right) as distinct from the few roots of the untransplanted seedling on the left*

with the draw hoe are advisable if the ground is light and the drainage over-free; planted deeply in these drills, every drop of water given later goes to the roots.

A good start being essential, planting holes (made with the trowel) should be filled with water before the plants go in, unless the ground is already moist enough.

After planting, there should be no bare stem visible; lowest leaves must be level with the surface.

Sowing in Boxes. A February sowing is carried out as described under Brussels sprouts (page 257).

Purchased Plants. If for any reason cabbage plants cannot be home raised, and have to be bought, they should be purchased from a nurseryman who has a reputation to maintain. They should be short jointed, with no suspicion of legginess or yellowness, the roots should not be dry (though soaking in water for three or four hours will remedy this), and above all there should be no swellings at the base of the stems or distortion of roots. The last two symptoms betoken trouble and such plants should be refused (Fig. 175).

Watering, Feeding. That the cabbage responds to frequent drinks in dry weather cannot be doubted; growth is assisted considerably. Feeding also has profitable results—but not until early spring for plants from the July to August sowings. It is desired that these young autumn plants shall be hard of growth, to resist the worst weather that winter can produce, and surface feeding at the wrong time would make them sappy.

One of the special proprietary fertilizer mixtures applied to the soil at intervals, when quick growth and rapid hearting-up are wanted, will have the desired effect. Poultry manure is splendid for all members of the cabbage tribe—a trowelful per plant, hoed or forked in and followed with plenty of water unless the ground is moist enough.

Why Cabbages Bolt. The plants sometimes have a disconcerting habit of throwing up flower stems—bolting, as it is termed—instead of forming the expected compact hearts. This may be due to any one of a variety of causes; such as a check to growth in the seedling stage, due to

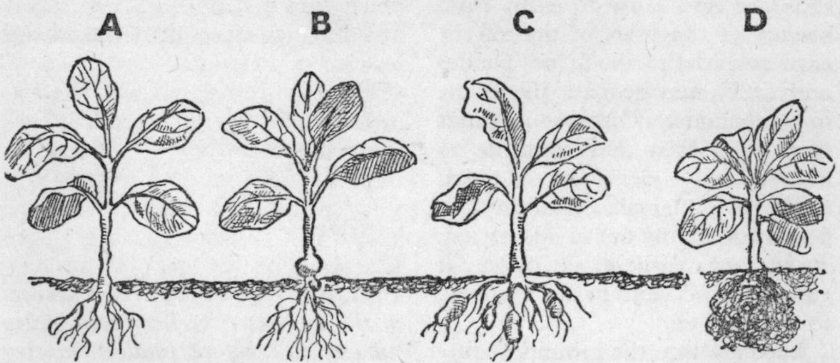

Fig. 175.—*Long-jointed weakly young cabbage plants* (A), *those with stem-swellings, denoting gall weevil* (B), *and those with root-swellings, denoting club root* (C), *should be rejected. The short-jointed, sturdy plant* (D) *is the best*

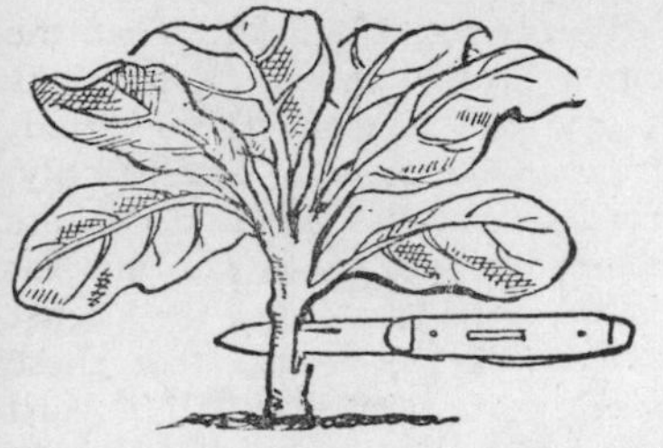

Fig. 176.—*A loose cabbage can be encouraged to heart-up by making a vertical cut in the stem and wedging this open with a piece of stick*

over-crowding or drought; the sowing of poor-quality seed, or sowing a particular variety at an unsuitable time; or the plants decide to throw up the struggle with impoverished or shallow ground and endeavour to produce seed before they perish.

It may be that none of those conditions applies, yet the July to August raised plants bolt. In this case the spring cabbage sowing should be made not in July or early August, but near the end of the latter month, later plants being generally disinclined to bolt.

A cabbage that looks, in autumn or winter, as though it has no intention of forming a heart but prefers to grow loose, can sometimes be saved from waste by a simple surgical operation—a knife blade, held horizontally, cutting edge down, is pushed through the centre of the stem just above the soil; the blade is withdrawn, and a small stone or a sliver of wood is inserted in the cut to keep it open (Fig. 176). This check to the sap-flow is usually effective; if the plant does not heart up, after all, at least a useful picking of greens may be secured.

Loose Hearts. A row of cabbage plants may produce a fine array of hearts, yet all of them deceptive; the hearts are flabby, there is no substance in them. This usually results from planting in newly dug ground. The root run must be firm—rolled firm if need be.

Enemies to Combat. Caterpillars on the leaves, greenfly and flea-beetle, grubs that attack the roots and cause the plants to wilt, other grubs that live in swellings at the stem base, and the club-root disease, are visitations from which no cabbage grower is immune. How to deal with these troubles is indicated in the chart Remedies Against Enemies of Vegetable Crops (pages 406–407).

Cutting the Heads. Time to cut the heads is when they feel firm and solid under the pressure of the fingers. Use a sharp knife, and do not slice off the entire head; let four or five outer leaves remain attached to the stalk that is in the ground (Fig. 177). Then with the knife make two cuts (crossing at right angles) in the top of the stalk or stump, an inch or so deep. This will encourage the later formation of sprouts, or tufts of greens, at the top of the stump that otherwise would have been pulled up and consigned to the bonfire.

Old, yellowed leaves should be removed from plants and added

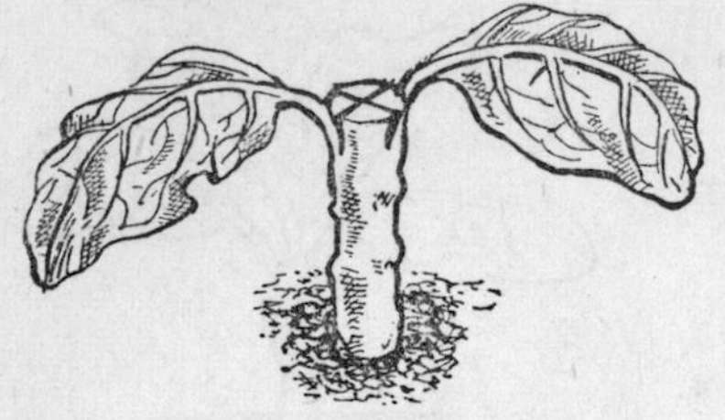

Fig. 177.—*Two cuts made across the top of a cabbage stump, after the head has been taken, result in the formation of useful tufts of greens*

to the general soft-refuse heap (or pit) to decay for later digging in.

Preparing for Table. Remove soiled outer leaves, cut the stalk back close, and cut the cabbage in two—from top to bottom through the centre. If large it could be quartered. Wash thoroughly in cold water, and allow to drain before cooking. Cabbage contains mineral salts and vitamins, but its actual nutritive value is not high.

CAPSICUM and CHILLI

Capsicums for pickling, chillies for vinegar, cayenne and chilli pepper; these are the uses and products of the pods and seeds of *Capsicum annuum* (grows about 1 ft. high) and *Capsicum baccatum* (2½ ft.). Both produce white flowers in summer, followed by the pods or fruits.

Varieties include Mammoth Red, Ruby King, Golden Queen, Long Red (all of which can be obtained in a mixed packet) and Small Red chilli.

Rich soil is required, and the warmth of a greenhouse, or a sunny, sheltered position outdoors.

Ready for Use. Pods ready for gathering in September outdoors; earlier grown under glass.

Soil Preparation. Dig the ground not less than 1 ft. deep and enrich it to that depth with leaf-mould, hop manure, or old hotbed material. For greenhouse plants the potting mixture should also be rich—two parts good loamy soil, one part old manure and a little silver sand or sharp road grit.

When and How to Sow. During February or March in a heated greenhouse; in a hotbed frame or a frame facing south in late March. Sow three or four seeds wide apart in each 3-in. pot and transfer singly to 4-in. pots when the seedlings are about 1½ in. high. Keep well watered and close to the glass.

Those to be grown on in the greenhouse will need shifting into 6-in. pots in due course, with a stake for each plant.

Those to be planted outdoors should be gradually hardened off (exposed by degrees to open-air conditions) when in the 4-in. pots.

Planting Out. Not before the beginning of June, those to be fruited in the open should be planted in the sunniest and warmest position available, as at the foot of a south-facing fence or wall, each to be staked. Space them 1 ft. apart.

Watering, Feeding. Soil backed by a south wall or fence dries out more speedily than open ground; frequent waterings will therefore

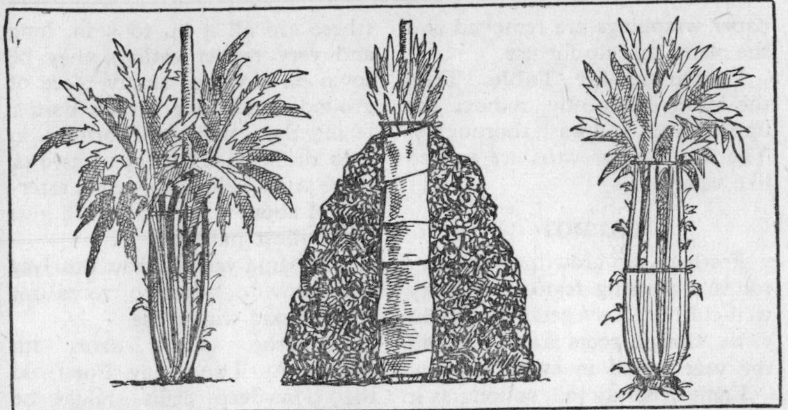

Fig. 178.—*The stalks and thick leaf ribs of cardoons have to be blanched (centre) to prepare them for cooking. A blanched cardoon is shown on the right*

be necessary. Enough water must be given at a time to soak down several inches. Cover the soil surface around the plants with hop manure (put down wet); or feed them occasionally with general-purpose artificial fertilizer mixture.

Picking the Pods. Capsicums for pickling should be gathered before they begin to colour; chillies for vinegar when fully coloured. Ripened pods can be dried and then ground to make pepper.

CARDOON

A large-garden vegetable in the luxury class, and not for small-space growing, the cardoon is as thistly in aspect as the globe artichoke. Parts eaten are the blanched (whitened) stalks and the thick leaf ribs; cut for use, the appearance is that of celery.

Soil must be rich and moist. General requirements are those of celery. They are ready for use in October and onwards.

Soil Preparation. Ground that does not dry out easily is ideal. It should be dug deeply, and whatever manure (or hop manure) is available should be worked in; well-rotted leaf-mould may serve as a substitute provided it is used generously.

When and How to Sow. Late April or early May is the time to sow outdoors, on the prepared site. Sow three or four seeds together, 1 in. deep, at 18-in. intervals. Thin out each group to a single plant when about 2 in. high.

Staking, Watering, Blanching. Two-foot stakes should be put to the plants when about 1 ft. high (Fig. 178), and ample water supplies are essential. In August, or early September, the plants will be ready for blanching. Procedure is as follows: gather the leaves of each plant together at the top, tie them with raffia or string; then wind strips of brown paper around from soil level to the tips; then pack soil completely around the plant to prevent all light from reaching it.

Blanching will be completed in about eight weeks, when soil and paper wrappings are removed and the plants dug up for use.

Preparing for Table. Trim the lower end neatly, remove the upper leaves, and wash thoroughly. The whitened growths are cooked like celery.

CARROT

Feathery top growth of the carrot is a pleasing feature of every well-cultivated vegetable patch; clean, straight roots are in demand the year round in every kitchen.

Light or sandy soil, so long as it is rich enough, produces better crops than heavy, clay-like ground.

For deep soils varieties such as St. Valery and Long Red should be chosen; for shallow ground stump-rooted varieties are most suitable, including Favourite and Early Market Red-cored. Roots of moderate length include Scarlet Intermediate and Matchless.

An ounce of seed will sow about 180 ft. of row. Germination takes about fifteen days.

Ready for Use. July, and on to March (in store).

Soil Preparation. A patch of ground where pea, bean or celery was the previous crop will give good results (provided they were prepared for by deep digging, and manure or rotted vegetable matter was worked in). Clay or other heavy ground needs to be broken up deeply and made lighter by the mixing in of plenty of wood ash and leaf-mould. Soil that is poor and thin is made suitable by digging in leaf-mould; and a heavy dressing of wood ash and soot is very desirable.

When and How to Sow. Early varieties, such as Champion Scarlet Horn, Early Horn, Early Gem (these are all 4 in. to 5 in. long and very tender eating), may be sown on a warm, sunny piece of ground (such as a garden border facing the south) in February, in ½-in. drills made 6 in. apart, two or three seeds being dropped at intervals of about 5 in. These will give the earliest pullings.

The same varieties sown in July will provide welcome roots for autumn and winter use.

Maincrop sowing dates are March, April and May. For these the ½-in.-deep drills should be about 1 ft. apart, the seed groups being 8 in. apart.

Sowing in a Frame. An unoccupied frame can be put to good use by sowing therein one of the early varieties named, in February; this will give roots for pulling in April. The soil bed should be about 8 in. deep and broken finely. Scatter the seed broadcast, very thinly, on the moist surface and cover with sifted soil to the depth of ¼ in. Close down the glass top (the frame light) and give no air until the seedlings show. Then prop up the light 1 in. whenever the weather is mild, closing it down at night and covering with sacking (in case of frost). All light possible is necessary by day, and watering will need care. Ventilation should be increased as the weather becomes more spring-like.

Thin these frame carrots early to 2 in. apart, then to 4 in.

Handling the Seed. Easiest way to sow group fashion in outdoor rows is to empty some seed from the packet into the palm of the left hand and take small pinches between forefinger and thumb of the right hand, dropping two or three seeds at each station. Cover

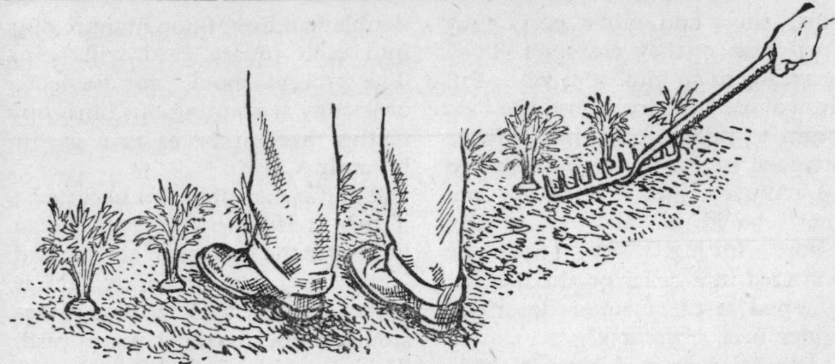

Fig. 179.—*When carrots are thinned out, soil should be pressed back around the remaining plants by treading (left) or with the back of the rake (right). This is to discourage the destructive carrot fly which seeks to lay eggs in loose soil*

with very fine soil, sifted if necessary.

Thinning Out. Each group is to be reduced to one plant when seedlings are about 1 in. high. Alternatively, seed may be sown continuously but thinly along the drill; first thinnings will be too small to use, but later ones will cook deliciously—maincrop carrots standing finally about 8 in. apart, early varieties about 5 in.

It is very necessary that the soil should be pressed back (with rake or foot) around the young plants at each thinning, as a discouragement to the carrot fly which seeks to lay its eggs in loose soil around the top of the root (Fig. 179).

Deformed, Grub-eaten Roots. Carrot roots will inevitably fork and split if they come in contact with either fresh or old animal manure. Obstacles such as stones in the soil will cause roots to grow out of shape; therefore stones should be removed during digging. Long-rooted varieties cannot drive down to the depth they want to go in ground that is only shallowly dug, or chalky or clayey a few inches down; stump-rooted varieties only should be sown in these conditions.

Carrot fly attacks roots from above; its grubs descend and gnaw the roots below. Wireworms tunnel into the roots. Methods of discouraging the former (additional to firming the soil after thinning, as previously mentioned) and trapping the latter are explained in the chart Remedies Against Enemies of Vegetable Crops (page 407).

How to Encourage Growth. Carrots in poor soil are encouraged to get a move on by applications of wood ash, a trowelful to the yard run, sprinkled around the plants and watered in; an occasional sprinkling of dried blood also helps, put down when the soil is moist, or watered in. Soil should be kept loose on the surface between rows by regular use of the hoe.

Lifting the Roots. Use the fork to get the roots up, driving it in a few inches to one side of the row and using it as a lever to loosen the roots' grip; withdraw the roots with the free hand.

Storing for Winter. Roots are hardy, but if maincrop carrots are left in heavy or wet ground too long, slugs and other pests may spoil them; or they may crack. They are ready to go into store when full growth has been made and the tops begin to yellow. Soil that may be attached to the lifted roots should be removed, and if they are wet they should be allowed to dry before storing. They may be wintered in a cellar or shed, or be clamped in the manner described under beet (page 252).

Exception as to lifting is made in the case of early varieties sown in July. These may remain in the ground, for forking up as required.

Preparing for Table. Scrub and scrape young roots, and cook whole. Scrub and peel older ones; remove a slice from the top, also the hard central core there; cut in sections or slices, as required for cooking. Carrots have a high sugar and vitamin A content.

CAULIFLOWER

Compact, close heads of cauliflower make a grand show when plants are well grown. Given a position well in the open, with correct sowing and planting, excellent results should be assured.

Varieties for early summer cutting include Early London White, All the Year Round, Universal; for late summer and autumn, Dwarf Monarch, Autumn Giant, Eclipse.

There are approximately 1,000 plants in an ounce of seed, and average time for germination is about ten days.

Ready for Use. Early summer, late summer and autumn.

Soil Preparation. Heavy soil is best, but light ground is made suitable by stiffening it with material from the decaying weed and leaves heap. In all cases a double handful of hop manure dug into each square yard will help. The ground should not be loose or spongy at planting-out time, but neither need it be as firm as for broccoli.

A sufficiency of lime is necessary; if this is lacking scatter hydrated lime over the surface, if the ground is heavy. Light or sandy soil is better treated with ground limestone, 1 lb. to the square yard. This should be forked into the top 2 in. a few days before the plants are set out.

When and How to Sow. To secure heads for cutting in early summer, sow the early varieties named during August to September, ½ in. deep in a seed bed. To avoid waste of seed and labour of thinning out sow as thinly as possible. When the seedlings are about 2 in. high they should be lifted, with the trowel, and planted in a cold frame, 3 in. apart each way, in good soil.

Water the young plants in, close the frame for two or three days, then get them accustomed again to open-air conditions—by raising the glass a little higher each day for about a week. After that the frame light should be opened wide, or removed, by day, and replaced at night. The protection required is against frost, snow, excessive rain; otherwise, unlimited air is necessary. The plants will remain in the frame until late February or March, or a bit later if bad weather prevails.

To secure heads for cutting in late summer and autumn, sow the varieties already named, in April or early May, in ½-in.-deep drills in a finely surfaced seed bed. From there shift when about 2 in. high to the nursery part of the bed, 4 in.

apart. They will need to be kept steadily growing with plenty of water when rain holds off. Before they touch in the rows, plant out where they are to remain.

Planting Out. This is to be done with the trowel, both from frame and nursery bed—*from* moist soil *to* moist soil. Plant in 4-in.-deep drills, or leave a depression around each plant, as advised for broccoli.

Pest Troubles. See under cabbage tribe in the chart Remedies Against Enemies of Vegetable Crops (pages 406–7).

Watering, Feeding. Spells of dry weather will necessitate free use of the watering-can. Soakings with liquid manure, or surface dressings of poultry manure, help considerably. Also in hot and dry weather it is a help to heads that are forming if top leaves are tied loosely together over them, to shield them from the sun; heavy rains can be kept from the heads in the same way.

Short-period Storing. If heads become ready for cutting more speedily than they can be used, plants may be dug up and replanted close together in a shady spot, the roots to be kept moist; or they can be hung upside down in an airy shed.

Cutting the Heads. These are ready for cutting when full grown. If left too long they will open out into flower, in which condition they are useless.

Preparing for Table. Remove outer leaves, cut back inner leaves level with the head, cut stalk close to base, wash in salt water—one teaspoonful of salt to the gallon of water—soak in another dish of salt water, head down, for twenty minutes, before cooking. Like broccoli, cauliflower is very easily digested—more so than any other green vegetable.

CELERIAC (TURNIP-ROOTED CELERY)

It is a pity so many view with suspicion any vegetable that is not a familiar object in all greengrocers' shops. They miss so much. Change is the spice of life, and celeriac is a vegetable to help break the monotony. Also it is worth acquaintance if only for the sake of growing something fresh. Celeriac's other name — turnip-rooted celery —

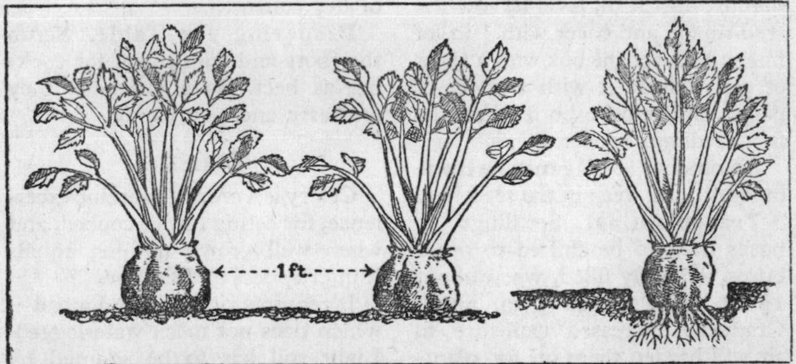

Fig. 180.—*Celeriac is grown for the swollen lower end. Seedlings should be transplanted shallowly—in drills (right) if the soil is light and thirsty*

describes it exactly (Fig. 180). But the stalks are not eaten; it is grown for the sake of the swollen lower end, which somewhat resembles a turnip about as large as a fist. This enlarged root is delicious when cooked like beet.

Rich soil is needed, but less labour is involved than in growing celery; deep trenches and earthing up are not required.

There are about 8,000 seeds to the ounce. Average time for seedlings to appear is about three weeks.

Ready for Use. October and onwards.

Soil Preparation. The site should be prepared by deep digging, and vegetable refuse or manure needs to be worked in; plentifully if the ground is light. Plenty of moisture is needed, and the position should be a sunny one.

When and How to Sow. Earliest plants are obtained by sowing in a greenhouse, with a temperature of about 60 deg., or in a hotbed frame, during March. Fill a seed box (or boxes) with soil and sifted leaf-mould in equal parts, with sifted sand or sharp grit to keep the mixture porous; firm it in, level it, sow the seed thinly, and cover with ¼ in. of fine soil. Cover the box with a sheet of glass, shade it with a sheet of paper, and remove both when the first seedlings appear.

An outdoor sowing may be made in April, ¼ in. deep in the seed bed.

Transplanting. Seedlings in boxes need to be shifted to other boxes, similarly filled, when about 1½ in. high, spaced 3 in. apart. Gradually increased exposure to air will harden them off for planting out in May.

Outdoor-raised seedlings should be transplanted in the same way, 3 in. apart, into good soil kept moist, for final planting out in June.

Planting Out. Set the plants 1 ft. apart; rows (if more than one) to be 1½ ft. apart. Although they need to be in the ground only just deep enough to hold them upright it makes for easier watering if they are planted in hoe-made drills, especially in light and thirsty soil.

Watering, Feeding. The watering-can will have to be used frequently in dry weather or the roots will be slow in plumping up. If weak liquid manure can be given every ten days or so the crop will be all the larger. Soot water (a heaped trowelful of soot stirred into a bucket of water) will help.

Lifting, Storing. The crop is ready for use when the "turnip" ceases to increase in size. The plants may be left in the ground and drawn on as wanted during winter; but if the soil is of a heavy nature and inclined to lie wet the roots are safer in store after November. Twist off the tops and store the roots in sifted fire ashes or sifted dry soil, beyond the reach of frost and damp—as in a shed or dry cellar.

Preparing for Table. Scrub the roots and trim them, for cooking as beet. As a vegetable they are tasty and nourishing.

CELERY

Celery is a crop of supreme excellence, for eating raw or cooked, and when well grown nothing equals it in crispness and flavour.

It requires rich soil, and moist—which does not mean waterlogged. Light soil has to be adapted by generous treatment with manure or rotted leaves and similar material.

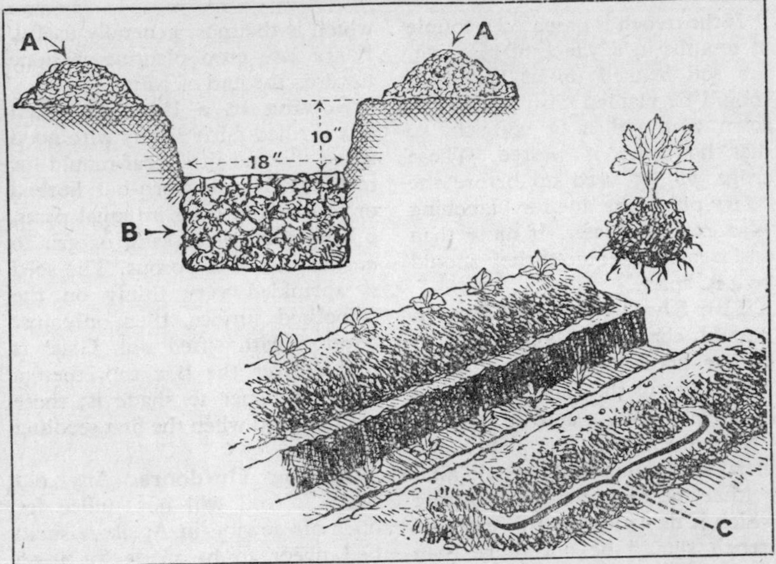

Fig. 181.—*Soil taken from the celery trench is heaped on both sides* (A A) *and the trench bottom broken up* (B). *Celery plants are set out down the centre. The sides can be cropped with lettuce* (*left*), *or spinach or radish* (C)

Excellent varieties include Solid White, Giant White, Major Clarke's Red, Standard Bearer (red).

At least 1,000 plants can be raised from an ounce of seed; germination takes about three weeks, more or less, according to temperature.

Ready for Use. Earliest in October; later sowings and plantings may not be ready until late November or December. Season continues to February.

Soil Preparation. Rich living and continual thirst-quenchings are first considerations. The most satisfactory plan is to dig out a long trench, running north and south, about 10 in. deep, 18 in. wide at the bottom, the sides sloping slightly outwards. The soil taken out is placed on both sides of the trench, an equal quantity on each side, and patted down with the back of the spade to give it a firm slope and prevent any soil falling back into the trench (Fig. 181).

The bottom of the trench is then broken up deeply with fork or spade and packed with rotted vegetable matter, or manure, or a manure substitute (such as hop manure). To make up for lack of these, bonemeal may be forked into the top 2 in. of the trench bottom after this has been broken up. Or a mixture of superphosphate of lime two parts, sulphate of ammonia one part, may be forked in similarly, but not until a week or so before planting. The bonemeal should be used as far as possible in advance of planting. The quantity to use, in both cases, is about 3 oz. to every 6 ft. of trench.

If the trench is prepared a couple of months in advance of planting, the soil banked up at the sides should be planted with lettuce, or sown with radish or spinach, so that no space is wasted. These crops will be used up before the celery plants are due for blanching—as explained later. If more than one trench is required they should be 4 ft. apart.

The Shallow-soil Trench. Should chalk, stubborn clay, or similar hard subsoil lie within a few inches of the surface it would be useless making a 10-in. trench. Celery planted at that depth and in such circumstances would find neither the food nor the moisture which it demands. In this case the trench should be not more than about 4 in. deep, but the ground below should be broken up 1 ft. deep and, as far as is possible, enriched as though it were a really deep trench.

Plants accommodated in this manner cannot be earthed up so thoroughly as is desirable; and lacking the protection against frost given by the more ample soil covering which a deep trench makes possible they are less safe in winter. But the best must be made of circumstances.

Obtaining the Plants. Celery for an early crop needs to be raised in a temperature of about 60 deg., in March, for planting out in May. The main crop is sown in April in a hotbed frame, or in an ordinary frame fully exposed to the sun, or in a sheltered but sunny spot outdoors.

Or young plants may be purchased for planting in the trench during the last two weeks of June—the usual time for the main crop, which is the most generally useful. For a late crop planting is done towards the end of July.

Sowing in a Box. The seed box is filled fairly firmly with good sifted soil and sifted leaf-mould (or material from a worn-out hotbed or mushroom bed) in equal parts, mixed, plus silver sand or grit to ensure that it is porous. The seed is sprinkled very thinly on the smoothed surface, then only just covered with sifted soil. Glass is placed over the box top, then a sheet of paper to shade it; these are removed when the first seedling is visible.

Sowing Outdoors. Any old patch of soil will not suffice for open-air sowing in April. A small bed needs to be made for it—a 3-in. depth of mixture as advised for filling the seed box. Sow as directed in the preceding paragraph, and if a shallow, bottomless wooden box can be placed over the seed patch and the top covered with glass, germination will be speeded up.

Transplanting Seedlings. The very small, indoor-raised plants require to be shifted when 2 in. high to other boxes, filled as before; in these they should stand 3 in. apart. They will remain in these boxes until planted out in the trench. The soil must never be allowed to dry out, and if there is any sign of yellowing of the foliage the plants will have to be fed with weak doses of one of the artificial fertilizer mixtures to keep them growing.

A temporary hold-up in growth may lead to the plants running up to flower later on.

Outdoor-raised seedlings may remain in the seed bed if thinned out to about 3 in. apart, or be transplanted to another bed of rich and moist soil, until large enough for planting out.

Planting Out. The plants are put out—with a trowel—in the trench when they are 6 in. high, lifted from the outdoor bed or removed from the boxes with all the soil that will cling to the roots. An overnight soaking with water makes this final removal easier. Indoor- or hotbed-raised plants must be hardened off first, spending about a fortnight in the cold frame with plenty of ventilation, the boxes then being stood outdoors for a few days without any protection at all.

The sturdy young plants are set out 8 in. apart down the centre of the trench in a single line (Fig. 181); or if space is precious they may form two lines down the trench, separated by the width of the latter, the plants in one row alternating with those in the other. Leave them very firm in the soil and give a good soaking with clear water.

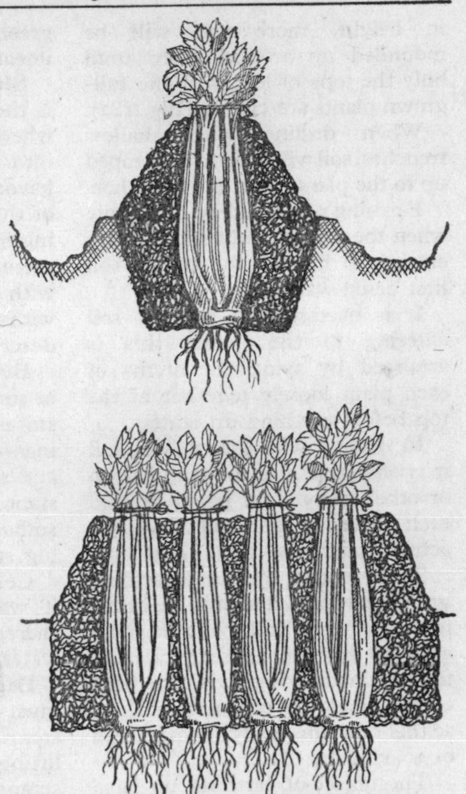

Fig. 182.—*As the celery plants increase in height more soil is mounded up around them*

Watering, Feeding. The soil of the trench needs to be kept moist, not with surface dribblings but with buckets of water so that this gets down below the roots. Feed occasionally with an artificial fertilizer, or with weak manure water if available, or with soot water (a heaped trowelful stirred up in each bucket of water used). Keep the water out of the plant centres or it may cause decay.

Removing Side Growths. Side or sucker growths will arise from the roots. These must be watched for and broken away, or much of the strength of the plant will be wasted.

Earthing Up. When the plants are about 9 in. high, soil from the trench-side mounds should be hoed or spaded into the trench so that about 4 in. of stem is covered, the soil to be worked close up to and completely around each plant, with the hands, the new surface being left level. As the plants increase in height, more soil will be mounded up around them until only the tops of leaves of the full-grown plants are visible (Fig. 182).

When dealing with shallow trenches, soil will need to be scraped up to the plants with the draw hoe.

Earthing up should be done only when the soil from the sides is dry enough to handle, the trench soil first being watered.

It is necessary to prevent soil entering to the heart; this is arranged by tying the stems of each plant loosely together at the top before earthing up starts.

In dealing with heavy, wet soil it is advisable also to wrap brown or other fairly stout paper around each plant so that soil shall not actually touch the stems (Fig. 183).

To complete the final earthing up (after which, it should be borne in mind, plants will make no more growth) pat the sloping sides of the continuous ridge with the back of the spade to consolidate them so that rain runs easily down instead of soaking in.

The object of earthing up is to cause the stems to become white, by excluding light; in the natural green state they are bitter and uneatable.

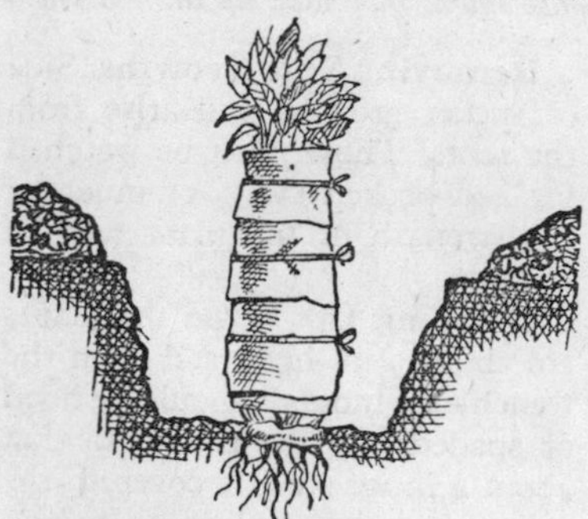

Fig. 183.—*In heavy, wet soil celery plants should be bound around loosely with stout paper before earthing up*

Slugs and Other Enemies. It is the ambition of every slug anywhere near a row of celery to get into one of the hearts and play havoc there. They can be cheated of their prey by occasionally dusting the soil thickly with soot. Other methods of dealing with this pest, with the leaf-tunnelling grub, and with leaf spot disease or rust, are described in the chart on page 407.

Bolting and Rotting. Drought or starvation (or both) during early stages of growth will induce bolting—that is, running up to flower and seed; hence the need for constant attention to watering and sufficient food right from the sowing stage.

Celery will decay at the centre if water is allowed to penetrate there; hence the need for care with watering-can or bucket.

Digging the Sticks. The spade must be handled cautiously or stems may be severed during the lifting of plants. The soil should be scraped down and away from one side of one plant at a time; when it is fully exposed, drive the spade blade slantwise beneath the root and lever the whole plant up and out (Fig. 184).

Celery is ready for use about six weeks after the final earthing up.

Winter Protection. Only in circumstances of extreme wet or cold need all the plants be lifted at once (that is, when sufficiently blanched); they may then be dug up with all the soil possible clinging to the roots and packed in a sheltered spot against a fence or wall or in a shed, with plenty of soil mounded up against their exposed sides as protection.

Fig. 184.—*In digging celery, soil should be scraped from one side, and the spade then thrust down carefully*

Otherwise the plants are best left in the ground for lifting as wanted. In the event of hard weather they should be safeguarded by dry bracken or straw placed over the tops as a temporary covering. When hard frost threatens, a few plants should be lifted and taken indoors; it is not easy digging celery from frozen mounds.

Preparing for Table. Wash the stems thoroughly; cut back green tips as far as the white; cut off roots, and trim the hard base neatly. Food value is not great. Raw or cooked, celery is popular, and holds a high place in invalid diets.

CHARDS

This is the name given to blanched young growths of globe artichoke. *See* under Artichoke, Globe (page 233).

CHICORY

Familiar in association with coffee, chicory (Fig. 185) is not so well known in Britain as a salad or vegetable; but those who are familiar with it hold in esteem the blanched produce from roots lifted from the open and induced to grow in complete darkness in winter.

The common or small-rooted French variety (Barbe de Capucin) is specially useful for filling the salad gap of the year when lettuce and endive (the latter is a close relative) are not available.

The variety Witloof (Brussels chicory), when the roots are winter-grown indoors, produces 9-in.-long, tight-packed heads of thick stems and leaves, which can be used like seakale.

An eighth of an ounce of seed will sow a 30-ft. row. Average time to germinate is about ten days.

Chicory is ready for use autumn to spring, according to treatment.

Soil Preparation. Any well-cultivated soil suffices, but the deeper it is the better; light ground is preferable to heavy.

When and How to Sow. Space out the seed thinly in a drill ½ in. deep, drills to be 1 ft. apart if more than one is required, in May. Water the ground first, if dry.

Thinning Out, Transplanting. Seedlings when 2 in. high to be thinned out about 6 in. apart in

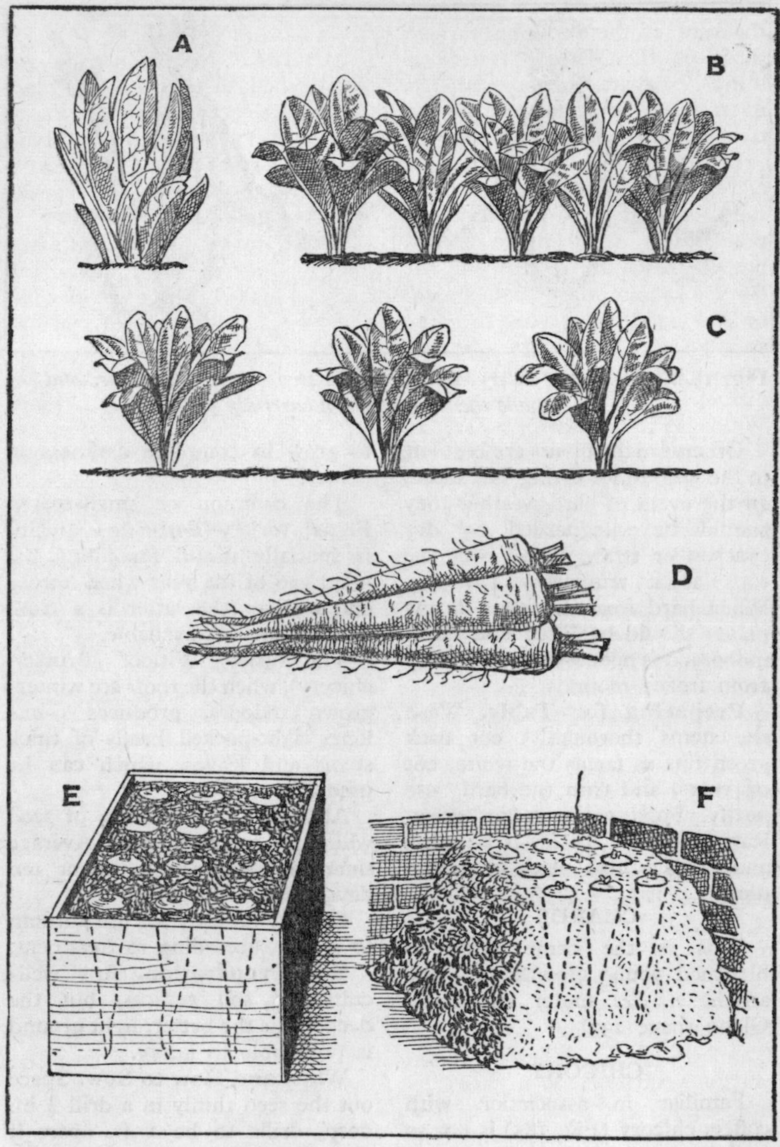

Fig. 185.—*Witloof chicory after forcing* (A). *Plants being grown outdoors* (B) *to provide roots for forcing, and thinned out to 9 in. apart* (C). *Roots* (D) *ready for placing in a box of soil* (E) *or heap of soil in a cellar* (F) *for blanching. Tops of the roots must be level with the surface, as here shown*

the case of the common variety; those of the Witloof variety to stand 9 in. apart. Surplus seedlings, if trowelled up carefully, can be transplanted to extend the row.

Blanching for Winter. Leaves of the common or French variety can be picked green for salad purposes as they become large enough; but the chief use of this and the Witloof is in winter. Roots should be lifted in autumn, a few at a time as required; those of the common variety will be about 1 in. in diameter, whilst the best of the Witloof will be twice as thick. These are planted (top growth cut off to within 1 in. of the root's crown) 2 in. or so apart in light soil in a deep box, the top of each root level with the soil surface.

The box is to be placed in a completely dark cellar or shed, or under the greenhouse bench; in the latter position all light must be excluded, by sacking hung up around the box. Lacking a deep box, the roots will do just as well planted in a heap of light soil—which must be kept moist (but not muddy); darkness is essential.

Crisp, well-flavoured, white leaves are quickly produced; leaf growth is brisker if a temperature of about 55 deg. can be commanded.

Leaves of the common or French variety may be gathered when between 3 in. and 6 in. long. Blanched tops of the Witloof are not cut until about 9 in. high. If heat is used in this winter production the roots will not be worth planting outdoors again.

Preparing for Table. Wash leaves and stems in cold water before using as raw salad or for cooking as a kitchen vegetable.

CHIVE

Member of the onion tribe, the plant called chive is worth a place wherever vegetables are grown. It takes up very little space, and both top and bottom of it can be used—the leaves in salads and soups, the bulbs as mild-flavoured onions.

In the matter of soil it is easily suited, and its position might well be as a decorative edging—decorative, because its small, mauve flowers are produced freely.

Each bulb in time becomes a cluster, necessitating lifting, dividing and replanting every three years; unless the bulbs, harvested in autumn, are stored indoors.

Securing the Plants. Bulbs or young plants may be purchased in March or October for planting during those months, 6 in. apart.

Seed is sown in April, outdoors, in a ¼-in.-deep drill, and the seedlings thinned out to 6 in. apart. Thinnings lifted from moist soil transplant readily.

Gathering. Leaves are taken as wanted, from the outside of each cluster; or one or two plants may be cut right down. In either case fresh leaves soon appear. Young leaves are the best.

Propagation. Unless the small bulbs are harvested each autumn the plants do quite well undisturbed in the ground until clusters become overcrowded. They should then be lifted, in March or October, the clusters divided, and the separated pieces replanted.

CLAMP

A heap of root crops protected against the weather and intended to be a winter store is known as a clamp. Full details as to the making of a clamp appear under beet (page 252) and potato (page 355). General conditions to secure are exclusion of damp, frost, artificial heat, decay.

COLEWORT

This is not a distinct vegetable but a small, compact variety of cabbage, specially useful in winter. Varieties include London, Rosette, Selected Hardy, Hardy Green. It is dealt with under cabbage (page 258).

COMPOST HEAP OR PIT

Decayed or decaying refuse is so valuable for digging into ground where vegetables are to be grown that a heap or pit of this material should always be considered an essential part of every vegetable patch. Everything of a leafy nature (not showing evidence of disease) should be collected in every week of the year.

The longer the stuff is allowed to accumulate, the greater its value. It is more useful in a completely rotted than a half-rotted state, and more useful half-rotted than fresh. Any odour that might come from the accumulation can be checked with a lime dusting.

Leaves and other light material thrown on the heap can be kept in place with a spadeful or two of soil; otherwise in gusty weather they are likely to blow about and cause annoyance. All things considered, a pit is preferable; soil taken out is banked up around the edge of the hole, a scattering being returned over each layer of refuse as this is added.

For full details see under vegetable refuse in the section FERTILIZERS AND MANURES (page 35).

COUVE TRONCHUDA (PORTUGAL CABBAGE)

A substitute is not necessarily an inferior. This certainly holds good in the case of couve tronchuda, or Portugal cabbage; the big white, fleshy ribs of the outer leaves are delicious when cooked as seakale. When the outer leaves have been used there remains the heart, for cooking cabbage fashion; it is tastier for having been touched by frost.

Ready for Use. November and onwards.

Sowing, Planting Out. Small sowings can be made at intervals, on a seed bed, from March to May; the plants are set out 2 ft. apart each way. General culture is as for cabbage; see page 258.

CORN SALAD (LAMB'S LETTUCE)

At any time of the year corn salad is assured of a welcome. The leaves can constitute a salad on their own, or take the place of lettuce when this is not available, and, if the soil is rich enough, the plants assume dimensions which allow of their being cut and used in the place of spinach.

¼ oz. of seed is sufficient for a row of about 30 ft. Seedlings appear in about nine days.

Ready for Use. Small sowings over a long period provide continuous pickings from June to the following spring.

Soil, Position. Ground that has been broken up well and enriched with fertilizer or manure suits corn salad admirably. The position should be sunny, though some shade in summer is required if the soil is light and thirsty by reason of its nature.

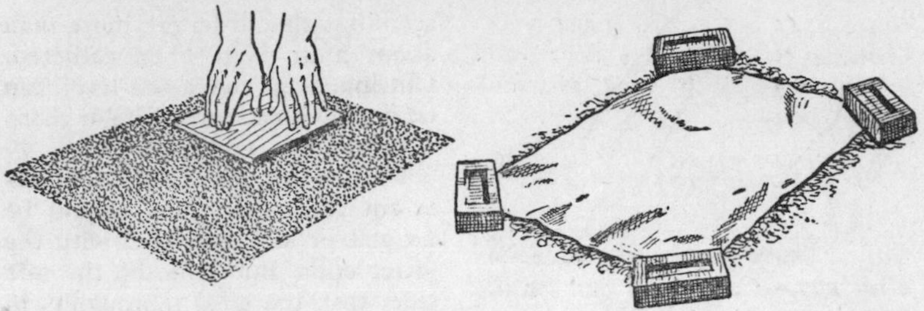

Fig. 186.—*Cress seed being firmed down into moist soil surface (left), then covered with an old mat or other material (right) to assist germination*

When and How to Sow. From February to September small sowings may be made at intervals to produce an uninterrupted supply. The earliest sowing, in February, needs to be in a sheltered, warm spot. The latest sowings, in August and September, will give pickings in winter when the weather is mild, and in the spring.

Seed is sown thinly in ½-in.-deep drills where the soil is other than light; in ground that demands frequent use of the watering-can the drills should be 2 in. deep, the seed being covered ½ in. deep. Drills to be 6 in. apart.

Thinning Out, Transplanting. Plants are to stand 6 in. apart in the row. If thinnings are taken up with the trowel, when the soil is moist, they can be transplanted elsewhere and watered in.

Gathering the Leaves. Young leaves are tender, old ones tough. Plants should therefore be gone over systematically and outer leaves cut before they become old. When a number of pickings have been taken plants may be cut right down, which finishes them off.

Preparing for Table. Use the leaves fresh, as soon after gathering as possible, and wash them to remove any dust or grit.

CRESS

Gathered in the seedling stage and used for making sandwiches, or as a salad component, cress has a flavour all its own. Light soil, moisture and warmth are the three requirements.

Varieties: Curled and Plain.

An ounce of seed will sow two square yards.

Ready for Use. Cress is ready for cutting about sixteen days after sowing. It can be had the year round if sowings are made indoors from October to March. If it is required to go with mustard it should be sown about four days earlier than the latter.

Soil Preparation. As a crop, cress can be snatched from between rows of other plants not yet occupying their full allotted space. The soil surface should be raked very finely and then be watered in readiness for sowing.

When and How to Sow. Small sowings, at intervals, can be made in the open from late March to September. Sow the seed thickly broadcast, on the surface of the moistened ground, press it down with a piece of flat, smooth wood (Fig. 186), then place over it a sheet of paper, or an old mat, until seedlings appear; the darkness will

Fig. 187.—*Cress being cut for use with sharp scissors*

assist germination and hungry birds will be baffled.

Sowing in Boxes. It is not necessary to sow in the open ground during spring and summer; boxes may be used. They are prepared in the same way as for winter indoor sowings—filled fairly firmly with light, gritty soil, with a level surface; the soil is made wet (chill first taken off the water); seed is sown, touching, all over the surface and lightly pressed down. The box is covered with glass and paper until germination has taken place, when exposure to full light becomes necessary.

Winter Crops. A temperature of about 55 deg. is needed for the production of cress when outdoor sowings are not possible—that is from October to March. Inside the sunny window of a living-room at that temperature will do as well as in a heated greenhouse.

Change of Soil. It is not wise to attempt to take more than two crops of cress from the same box of soil or from the same small patch outdoors; give the third in succession a change of site or a freshly filled box.

Before sowing a box or outdoor patch a second time, scrape off top ½ in. of soil and replace with fresh.

How to Gather Cress. The seedlings should be not more than about 2 in. high when gathered. Cutting, ¼ in. above soil level, can be done with a sharp knife or sharp scissors (Fig. 187).

Preparing for Table. If cress is cut cautiously there should be no grit or soil entangled with the lower ends. But to be on the safe side wash the cress thoroughly, in cold water, before use.

CUCUMBER

Given a warm summer, an outdoor crop of cucumbers is not difficult to procure. The requirements, in addition to sun heat, are rich soil and a warm root run (which means fresh manure down below), moist conditions above and below, and a suitable variety of cucumber for cultivation in the open.

These items cannot be called exacting; and when the prize is freely produced fruit (for fruit it is, though accepted as a vegetable) only a trifle short of hothouse standard, every exertion on the grower's part is most adequately rewarded.

Varieties for outdoor growing include King of the Ridge (a beautifully straight cucumber, sometimes

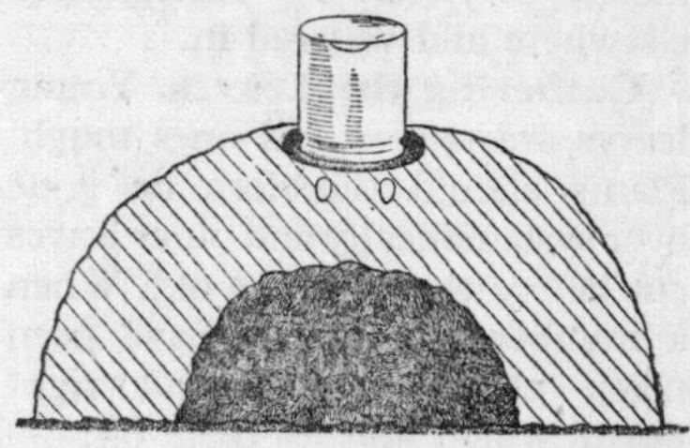

Fig. 188.—*Seeds of outdoor cucumber sown under an inverted glass jar on a mound of soil above a bucketful or more of fresh stable manure*

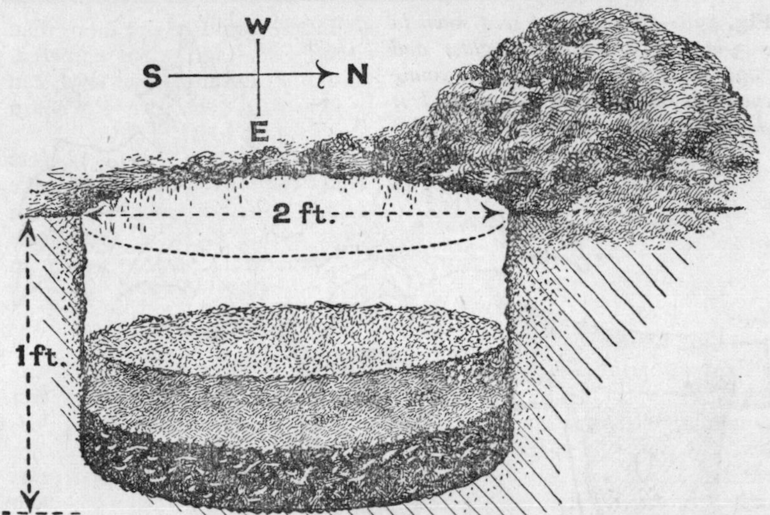

Fig. 189.—*In light soil cucumbers do better planted in holes. Soil from the hole is heaped up on the north side—to break the cold winds*

reaching 16 in. in length), Long Green, Prolific, Stockwood, Bedfordshire Prize, Long Prickly and Short Prickly or Gherkin, which is just right for pickling. These are true ridge cucumbers and should not be confounded with varieties for greenhouse and hotbed frame cultivation. They are called ridge because it is customary to grow these outdoor varieties on ridges or mounds of soil above a few inches of manure.

There are approximately 500 plants in an ounce of cucumber seed. Germination takes about ten days—more or less, in accordance with temperature.

Ready for Use. Early August and September, outdoors. Earlier crops are available from a hotbed frame, still earlier from a heated greenhouse, as explained later.

Soil Preparation. The ideal procedure is as follows: a bucketful of fresh manure is dumped in a heap where each plant is to be grown (in full sun) and on top of that two buckets of good soil are placed (Fig. 188). Light, sandy soil is unsuitable; it should be of heavy and moisture-holding nature. The soil is firmed down, and is then ready—in late May or June—to receive indoor-raised plants; or two seeds may be sown on each heap in late May.

Alternatively, dig a hole for each plant 2 ft. in diameter and 1 ft. deep, placing the excavated soil on the north side (to break the wind) and emptying a bucket of manure into the hole. Tread the manure down and cover with about 4 in. of soil, in readiness for planting or sowing (Fig. 189). This is the better plan when the ground is light and parts easily with its moisture.

It is desirable that the manure shall be fresh, to supply the necessary bottom heat. Enough can

Fig. 190.—*A cucumber seed sown in a 3-in. pot covered with glass and paper (left). Depth at which the young cucumber plant is to be planted is shown by the dotted line (right)*

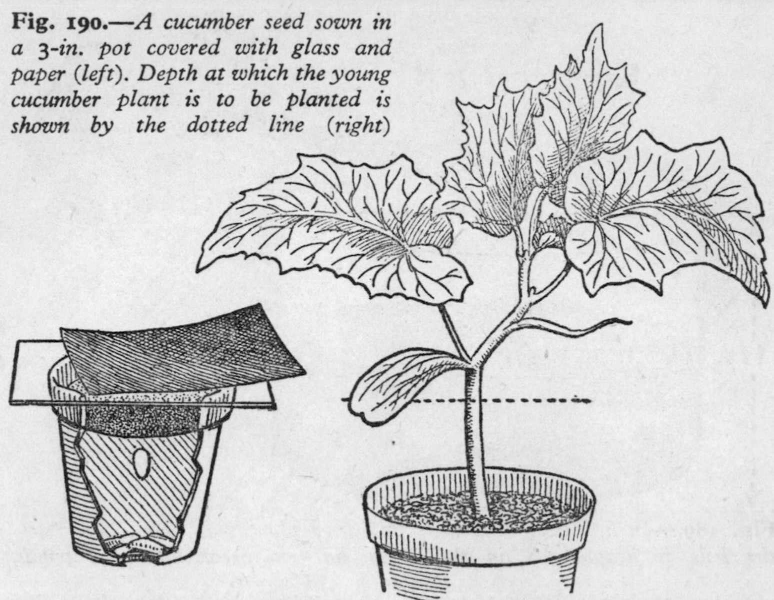

sometimes be secured from road scrapings, and the manure can be made to go farther by mixing with it an equal bulk of tree leaves—last year's, collected from below woodland trees.

When and How to Sow. Naturally, plants for setting out are obtained earlier from an indoor than an outdoor sowing. If a temperature of about 55 deg. is available, as in a heated greenhouse or hotbed frame, ridge cucumbers can be raised from seed sown in late April or early May, for planting out in late May or June. Three-inch pots are filled with good, sifted soil, and in the centre of each a single seed is sown, on edge and about 1 in. deep. Cover the sown pots with paper and glass, remove this covering when the seedlings are breaking through the soil and stand them in full light close to the glass (Fig. 190).

Seed raised in a hotbed frame will germinate more quickly if the pots are sunk to their rims in the hotbed material or in the soil covering it.

Seed may rot before it can germinate if the soil is kept too wet, and young plants may rot at the collar (surface level) unless watering is deferred until need for it is apparent.

Planting Out Ridge Cucumbers. By the time weather is safe for planting out (late May or early June) the plants will be about 6 in. high and the pots filled with roots. Plants that have made rather more progress should not be left to starve in the 3-in. pots until planted out; they should be moved into 5-in. pots filled with really rich soil (old, rotted manure, or sifted leaf-mould, mixed with good garden soil).

A few days spent in a cold frame,

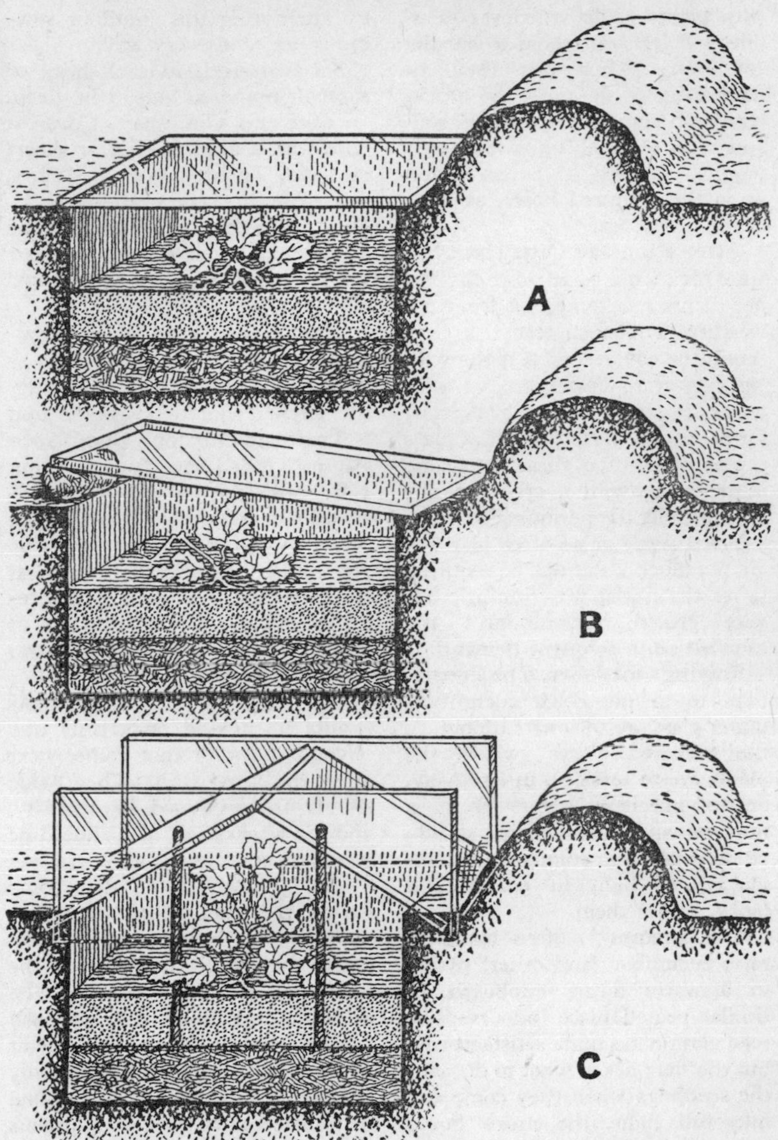

Fig. 191.—*Protection is given to the young cucumber plant by covering the hole with glass* (A). *Ventilation is given by propping up the glass on one side* (B). *Four pieces of glass are used to give later protection* (C). *The glass should be used at night and during chilly periods in the daytime*

with plenty of air whenever possible, will accustom them to hardier conditions. They can then be turned out of the pots, the crocks removed from the unbroken soil-and-roots mass, and planted singly on the prepared heaps or ridges, or in the manured holes, as deep as the lowest leaf.

After Planting Out. Until late June the planted-out ridge cucumber plants run some risk from the weather. To lessen this risk they should be covered each night with large inverted flowerpots, or with boxes. Progress will be brisker if, for the pots or boxes, sheets of glass can be substituted, these remaining in position (with a crack of air) during chilly day periods (Fig. 191).

For a week or so after planting out not much water will be required (after the initial watering-in), but once growth recommences the can will be in frequent demand.

Sowing Outdoors. The alternatives to raising ridge cucumbers under glass are to sow outdoors, in the prepared places (where the plants are to remain), in late May, or to purchase plants from a nurseryman. Bought plants should be deep green in colour and short-jointed; if light in colour and lanky, refuse them.

The attempt is often made to raise cucumber (and other) plants in a warm airing cupboard or similar heated place indoors. The seed germinates quite satisfactorily, but the snag lies in what to do with the seedlings when they come out into full light, the move being accompanied by a noticeable drop in the temperature of their surroundings. The consequent check to growth sets them back to a marked extent. Nothing is gained by attempting this; outdoor sowing is better in every way.

Set two seeds in each heap or ridge or prepared hole, 1 in. deep, on edge and 3 in. apart. Cover at once with a glass jam-jar or sheets of glass, or a glass-topped box, shaded with paper until the seedlings are visible. Then remove the shading and give air by degrees, until the protection can be removed altogether.

Only the stronger of each pair of plants is to remain. As soon as it can be seen which is the better, the weaker should be pulled out.

Training Outdoor Cucumber Plants. When the plant is about 1 ft. long (the habit is trailing—stakes not required) the growing point should be nipped off (Fig. 192). This operation is known as stopping, and the result is the production of side shoots (known as laterals) on which flowers and then the cucumbers will form.

The tips of the side shoots should be nipped off a little way beyond the joint that comes next after the tiny fruit. These side shoots are produced in quantity, and the weakest of them should be removed completely.

The yellow flowers that come before the cucumbers are either male (pollen-bearing) or female. Only the latter bear fruit—the immature cucumber can be seen as a distinct bulge behind each female flower—and the fruit develops without fertilization. Only if seed is required should pollen be transferred to the central organs of the female flowers.

Watering and Feeding. Drought is fatal to these plants. A bucket of water should be given to each plant as often as watering

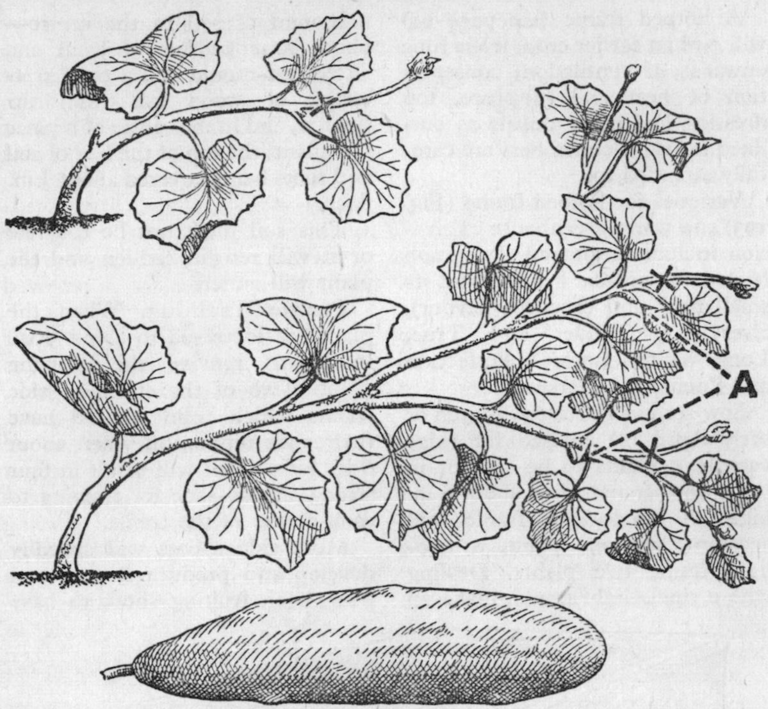

Fig. 192.—*The growing point of the outdoor cucumber plant is nipped off (above, at* X*). The result is the production of side shoots, whose ends are nipped off (below, at* X*) one leaf beyond the young fruit* (A)

is necessary, and they should be syringed, or dewed overhead from a watering-can fitted with a fine rose, every warm and dry morning and evening. Sun-warmed rain-water is best; cold water straight from a tap is apt to check growth.

If roots (like whitish cords or threads) appear at the surface, a top dressing of rich soil, put down about 2 in. thick and compressed with the fingers, will help fruiting tremendously.

When a heavy crop of fruit is formed, give a dose, once a week, of dried blood, a teaspoonful in each 2 gal. of water, or the same amount of superphosphate of lime.

Leaves showing signs of decay should be cut or nipped off and removed to the soft rubbish heap or the bonfire.

Protection for the Cucumbers. The undersides of the fruits, where they lie flat on the soil, may become discoloured unless a piece of board or slate is placed beneath.

Cucumbers in a Frame. Ridge varieties can also be grown in a cold frame, where the plants are under better control (as regards sun heat and moist atmosphere) than outdoors. Sowing and planting details are the same, but the plants are trained as explained here for hotbed crops.

A hotbed frame (see page 61) will give an earlier crop, from June onwards, if ventilation, conservation of heat and moisture, top dressing and other details as outlined for ridge cucumbers are carefully attended to.

Varieties for hotbed frame (Fig. 193) and warm greenhouse cultivation include Improved Telegraph (noted for prolific bearing and its small neck and excellent flavour), Every-day, Tender and True, Long White, Lockie's Perfection and Rochford's Market.

Sow seed in February, March or early April (as advised for ridge varieties); plants to be set out in the hotbed frame when about 6 in. high. A single-light frame will accommodate one plant, a two-light frame two plants. Dealing with a single-light frame, make up a mound of soil in the centre—about four pailfuls of loam and sifted leaf-mould and a good scattering of wood ash from the bonfire, and in the centre of it place one plant, the top of the ball of soil and roots being covered about ½ in. deep.

This soil must not be too fine or it will remain sodden and the plant will suffer.

Frame Training. When the plant has increased to about 9 in. in length remove the growing point. Two of the strongest side shoots which result should have their ends nipped off when about 6 in. long. That will result in four strong shoots—one for training to each corner of the frame.

More side shoots will speedily develop and produce flowers and fruit, each fruiting shoot to have

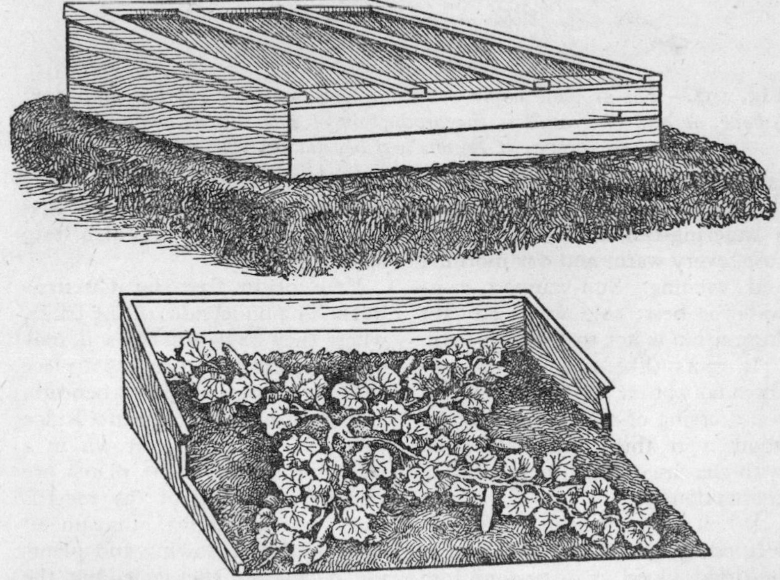

Fig. 193.—*A hotbed frame produces excellent cucumbers. A single plant, in the centre, has its side shoots trained out to reach the four corners*

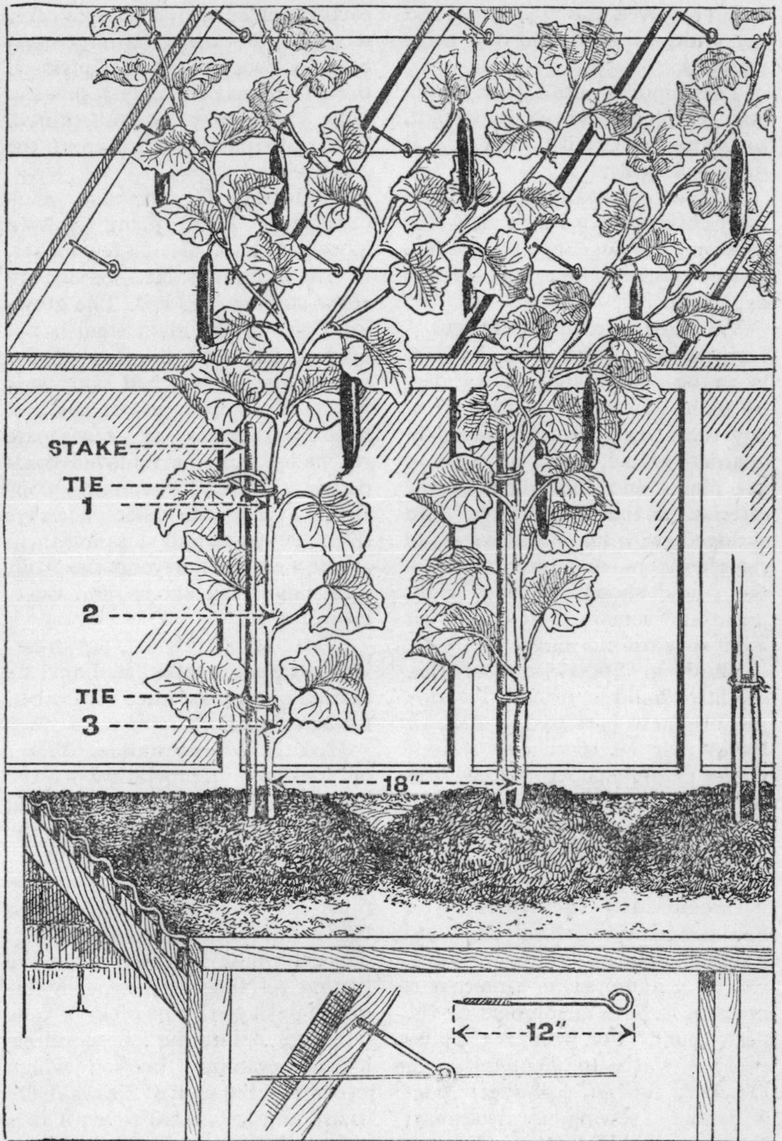

Fig. 194.—*Greenhouse cucumbers, planted in mounds of soil on the bench and trained up stakes and then to horizontal wires. Method of fixing the latter is detailed at foot of sketch. Side shoots are allowed only when the roof glass is reached. Earlier ones (1, 2, 3) are removed as soon as they form*

its tip removed at one joint beyond the fruit, as explained for ridge varieties.

The thinning out of weak shoots and crowded leaves is important, to ensure free circulation of air and plenty of light.

As roots show through the surface, cover with 2 in. of rich soil. Watering, syringeing and feeding to be carried out as already explained.

Ventilation and Moisture. A temperature of 80 deg. by day is to be aimed at, and 55 deg. by night. Give only a little air at any time (cold draughts must be guarded against), and as soon as the plants and the whole of the interior of the frame have been syringed (with lukewarm water) in the afternoon—about five o'clock—the frame should be shut right down and remain closed until air is given next morning.

Shading. Some form of thin shading should be provided during the brightest part of the day, or leaves may be scorched. Single sheets of newspaper placed over the glass (held down by pieces of board or brick) will serve, the shading to be removed as danger of scorching passes.

Greenhouse Cucumbers. If a day temperature of 80 deg. and a night temperature of 55 deg. can be maintained in winter, it is possible to have cucumbers all the year round. For winter supplies seed is sown in September or October; for an early-year start a January sowing is necessary; February or March for a summer crop.

Young plants are set out in mounds of soil about 18 in. apart on the greenhouse bench (Fig. 194), each provided with a stake to carry it up to the wires running horizontally beneath the roof glass. If these training wires are not present, long canes may be substituted, fixed horizontally 9 in. from the glass.

Training Greenhouse Cucumbers. Each plant is tied loosely, at intervals of a few inches, to its upright stake—loosely, to allow stems to expand. The growing point of the main stem is not nipped off until the top of the greenhouse is reached, but side shoots that appear before the first horizontal wires or canes are reached should be removed completely. Thereafter training consists in tying side shoots sideways to the supports and stopping them at the first joint beyond the fruit, removing weak shoots and overcrowding leaves.

Watering, syringeing, top dressing, shading, ventilation should be carried out as explained for hotbed frame cucumbers.

Health Maintenance. Water of the same temperature as the house is to be used for watering and syringeing. An effect of the latter may be to give an always-damp appearance to the soil; this must not be taken as evidence of the condition of the soil below. To determine whether roots are getting all the moisture they require, push a stick or piece of cane 6 in. or 8 in. into the soil, withdraw it and examine the soil which adheres to the end. If this is really moist, conditions are right; if it is not moist, give water at once.

Soil used for covering surface roots (top-dressing) should be warmed to the temperature of the house before being put down.

If leaves are deep green in colour, all is well; a yellowish tint is a sign that too much water is being given, or the temperature is too low, or insufficient light is reaching them.

These conditions apply also to hotbed frame cucumbers.

Troubles and Remedies. Almost invisible mites known as red spider flourish on plants in a too dry atmosphere. The pests congregate on the underside of leaves and suck out the sap so that the foliage has a sickly appearance. Hence the necessity for repeated syringeings, below the leaves and overhead and sideways, all the interior woodwork and brickwork of greenhouse or frame also being kept moist.

Greenfly may put in an appearance. It should be checked by spraying with one of the proprietary insecticides; or greenhouse or frame may be fumigated (see page 411).

Woodlice, if troublesome, can be trapped by placing pieces of decaying board here and there on the soil; the woodlice will seek these hiding places and can be collected and destroyed.

Eelworm is an underground worker, attacking the roots and forming knobs or swellings thereon. An affected cucumber plant, which ceases to grow, and wilts, should be uprooted and burnt, and the soil taken out and buried.

Mildew on the leaves is checked by dusting, after a light syringeing, with flowers of sulphur; the treatment to be repeated on second and third days.

Leaf-spot disease is evident as yellow or brown spots spreading into extensive blotches; any cucumber plant so attacked should be removed and burnt.

Canker eats into the base of the main stem and the plant is destroyed unless the disease is dealt with promptly. The cankered part should be bared—by scraping away as much of the soil as necessary—then dressed with slaked lime or flowers of sulphur, the powder to be well rubbed in.

Gathering the Cucumbers. These should be cut whilst the withered flower is still attached to the far end and before there is any indication of the fruit yellowing at the stem end.

Preparing for Table. Pare off the green skin, and if the cucumber is to be sliced start cutting from the lower end; the stalk end is always bitter. As a food, cucumbers are low down in the scale, and are not too digestible; but those facts are outweighed by their tastiness and their value in every salad bowl.

ENDIVE

Top of the list of autumn and winter salad plants, endive takes the place of lettuce when that is unobtainable. In summer the leaves can be cooked and eaten like spinach; for this purpose the plants need not be blanched, that operation (described later) being necessary to make the leaves white and crisp for raw salad use.

Light and well-drained soil is most suited to its needs, dug at least a spade blade deep and either manured or enriched with an artificial fertilizer.

Varieties include Mossy Curled and Digswell Prize, for spring sowing; White Curled and Green Curled, for early summer sowing; Winter Curled, Oval-leaved,

Winter Lettuce-leaved and Improved Round-leaved (Batavian varieties) for August sowing.

About 2,000 plants are represented in an ounce of seed, and germination takes place in about nine days.

Ready for Use. The year round, according to variety and date of sowing.

Soil Preparation. Roots of endive need to go down deeply. In shallow or undug soil the crop is likely to fail. The spade should therefore be used to a good depth. If manure is unobtainable for mixing with the dug soil, sulphate of potash, raked into the dug surface at the rate of 1½ oz. per sq. yd., is a great help.

When and How to Sow. As only a few plants are required at a time, quite small sowings should be made at intervals of a few days. Sow in April and May, in a sunny position, for early summer supplies; crop will be ready in about ten weeks. Sow in June and July for the main crop; in August for a late crop to stand through the winter, these plants being available for use in about fifteen weeks and onwards.

Seed may be sown in ¼-in.-deep drills for later planting out or where they are to remain, this being the better plan in soil that is quick to dry out. In the latter circumstances the drills may be about 2 in. deep (though the seed is to be covered only about ¼ in. deep), these to be filled with water in rainless periods. They should be 1 ft. apart.

Planting Out, Thinning Out. Seedlings in temporary drills are to be planted in their final places when about 2 in. high, crowded plants to be thinned out meanwhile. Those in permanent drills to be thinned out, as soon as they can be handled, to 1 ft. apart.

The ground should be soaked with water before planting out, unless enough rain has fallen.

Watering, Feeding. Dry soil encourages seeding—plants quickly run up to flower and are wasted. It is essential that roots be kept moist. An occasional pinch (per plant) of nitrate of soda greatly assists leaf production.

How Blanching is Done. When plants have thickened up at the centre they should be blanched—a few at a time—by excluding all light (Fig. 195); this removes some of the natural slight bitterness and prepares them for salad purposes. Average time for blanching to be completed is about three weeks.

To secure the absolute darkness necessary, boards or tiles may be placed on edge along both sides of a row, upper edges meeting above the plants to be blanched. The leaves should be dry when this is done, and slugs and snails (extremely partial to endive) should be looked for around the plants and also on the tiles or boards.

Another method consists in covering each plant with an inverted flowerpot, the interior first being searched for pests, the drainage hole being covered with a flat stone to block out light. It may be necessary to bunch the leaves together to get them into the inverted pot. Plants of more vigorous growth—too large for flowerpot treatment—should have the leaves drawn together at the top and banded there with raffia; dry hay or leaves heaped over them will complete the blanching process (Fig. 196).

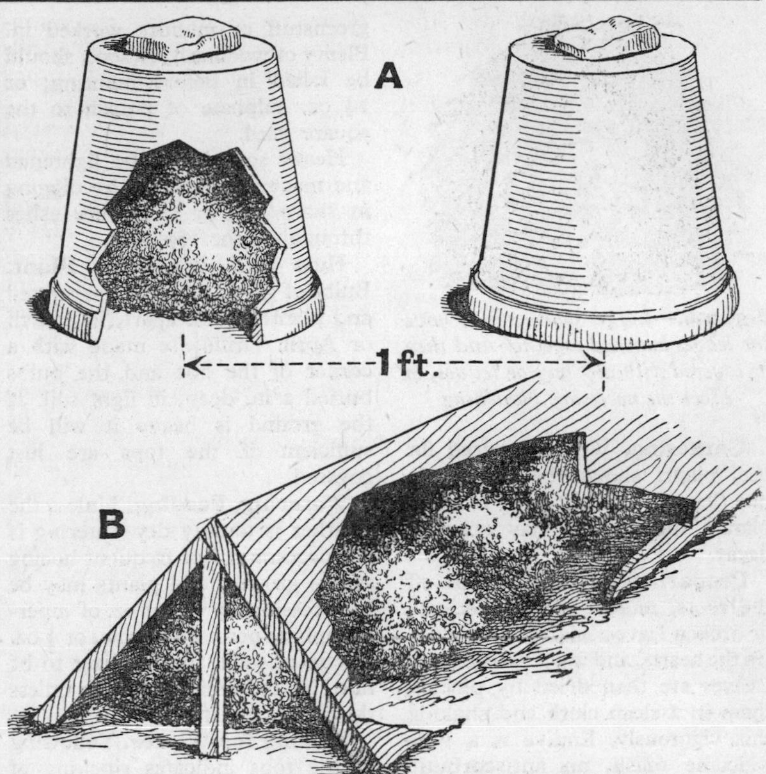

Fig. 195.—*Endive may be blanched by covering each plant with an inverted flower pot* (A) *or by means of planks* (B) *placed over a row to exclude light*

Winter Treatment. Plants that are to stand through the winter (for winter and early spring use) where soil normally lies cold and wet will be much safer in a frame after the end of October; each to be taken up with a trowel, with all the soil that will cling to the roots, and replanted at once, 6 in. apart, in good soil in the frame.

Water them in, but keep moisture from the leaves. The interior of the frame is to be kept as dry as possible and the frame light shut down in foggy or misty weather and during frost. The air must be kept moving in the frame, so some ventilation is necessary when outside conditions allow. Further to avoid decay, broken leaves should be picked off when the plants are transferred to the frame.

At the first hint of frost, dry sacking or mats should be placed over the frame light and there remain until the frost has gone. Covering the glass, or part of it, will also effect blanching.

In the absence of a frame, plants may be replanted at the foot of a fence or wall facing south or west and there covered up.

Fig. 196.—*Larger endives may have the leaves bunched together and then be covered with dry hay or leaves, to effect the necessary blanching*

Gathering. When required for use, plants should be pulled up like lettuce. If left too long to blanch the centres may start to decay.

Preparing for Table. Cut off the roots, remove soiled, decayed or broken leaves, examine for slugs (in the hearts) and wash thoroughly. Leaves are then dried by placing them in a clean cloth and shaking this vigorously. Endive is a very welcome relish, an antiscorbutic and a mild laxative.

GARLIC

Garlic, a small but powerful member of the onion tribe, resembles the shallot in growth, but the bulbs, or cloves, are white or silvery. It is for its bulbs that the plant is grown. It gives no trouble in light or sandy soil but is not so happy in ground of a heavy nature. It is propagated by means of bulbs, and 1¼ lb. will plant a 30-ft. row.

Ready for Use. Bulbs are ready for lifting in July or August and can be stored under cover for use until spring.

Soil Preparation. A deep root run is appreciated, with rotted greenstuff or manure worked in. Plenty of wood ash, or soot, should be raked in before planting; or 1½ oz. sulphate of potash to the square yard.

Heavy soil should be lightened and made more porous by digging in sharp grit or sifted fire ashes throughout the top foot.

How and When to Plant. Bulbs of garlic should be separated and planted 9 in. apart, in March or April. Drills are made with a corner of the hoe and the bulbs buried 2 in. deep, in light soil. If the ground is heavy it will be sufficient if the tops are just covered.

Watering, Feeding. Unless the weather is unduly dry watering is not necessary. But frequent hoeing assists growth, and plants may be fed occasionally with 1 oz. of superphosphate per yard of row, or ½ oz. nitrate of soda, the fertilizer to be hoed in, and then watered in unless the soil is moist.

Storing for Winter. Yellowing of the tops indicates ripening of the bulbs. The clusters should then be forked up and laid out on dry ground in the sun for a few days; or the tops bunched together and hung in a shed. Shelter from frost and damp is required for winter storage.

Preparing for Table. Remove tops, roots, and outer skin. Taste and aroma are both powerful. Garlic should therefore be used with caution. To impart the flavour to food a cut bulb is rubbed on the warm dish in which the food is to be served up.

GOURD (AND PUMPKIN)

For soup, jam and pie making, gourds and pumpkins give a huge

Fig. 197.—*Gourds and pumpkins planted in good soil* (A) *above leaf-mould or old manure* (B) *make rapid growth, which is further assisted by pegging down the shoots at intervals and covering with soil* (C, *and lower right*). *A piece of board* (D) *keeps the pumpkin from contact with wet ground*

return for trouble expended. They are grown in the manner of their close relative the vegetable marrow; requirements are rich soil (old manure or decaying green refuse), plenty of sun, and water in dry weather.

Varieties include Mammoth (mixed colours), Veitch's Giant (up to 100 lb. in weight), Large Yellow; the smaller, ornamental gourds are not for eating.

A small packet of seed will provide more plants than are likely to be required. Germination takes from three to twelve days, according to temperature.

Ready for Use. July and onwards. Can be stored for winter.

Soil Preparation. A heap of decaying garden refuse covered with 1 ft. of soil, in full sun, with plenty of space for the growths to ramble, will produce a big crop of fruit. Where soil is sandy, or quick-drying, better results come from planting in holes, 3 ft. apart, containing a few inches of old manure or leaf-mould covered with about 4 in. of good soil, with a 4-in. depression, 1 ft. in diameter, for watering (Fig. 197). If no animal manure is used, mix superphosphate of lime with the surface soil, 2 oz. to the square yard.

When and How to Sow. Plants for setting out in late May or early June are secured by sowing seed singly, 1 in. deep and on edge, in 3-in. or 4-in. pots filled with soil and sifted leaf-mould in equal parts, in April, in a temperature of 55 deg. (greenhouse or hotbed frame). Kept close up to the glass, seedlings of pumpkin or gourd make strong, rapid growth.

Or seed may be sown outdoors, where the plants are to remain in prepared places, in late May; two seeds 1 in. apart, the weaker seedling to be removed. Cover with sheets of glass, giving little ventilation for about a fortnight.

Planting Out. Indoor-raised plants should be slowly accustomed to outdoor conditions by hardening off in a cold frame for a few days. Or they may be stood out under a sunny fence or wall for a week, covered with a box or other protection at night, previous to planting out in late May or early June. Day protection also may be necessary if weather is not warm. Plant as deep as the lowest leaves, 3 ft. apart, and water in at once.

Watering, Feeding. It is almost impossible to give these plants too much water in dry weather. Growth is assisted by syringeing on warm evenings, or spraying the leaves from a watering-can fitted with a fine rose; sun-warmed rain-water is preferable to that straight from a tap.

When fruit is showing they will respond to weekly doses of dried blood, a teaspoonful stirred into each 2 gal. of water.

Training. If shoots are pegged down to the ground here and there, well spaced out, with bent wire, and covered at the joints with 2 in. of good soil patted down, extra roots will be produced (from the covered joints) and the plants will be so much the stronger. Decaying leaves should be cut away.

In a rainy season the underside of fruits will be safeguarded against decay or other injury if pieces of board are interposed between them and the ground (Fig. 197).

For winter storage purposes fruit should be cut when they cease to swell and be hung up by the stalk-end anywhere under cover where neither frost nor damp can affect them. Gathered dry and unbruised, they should remain in good condition for months.

Preparing for Table. Pare off the skin, cut open, remove pips, and proceed according to recipe requirements. Pumpkins and gourds are palatable and filling.

HERBS

Seen in old gardens, and offered as seeds or plants in nurserymen's catalogues, are quite a number of herbs whose names are unfamiliar to most home food producers; the most useful are dealt with here. The familiar indispensables, such as mint, parsley, sage, thyme, are dealt with under their names on other pages. See also Herbs Dried for Winter, page 416.

Angelica. Grown for its leaf-stalks, which are cut when young for candying. It is a perennial (comes up every year) requiring a shady position and plenty of moisture. Seed is sown during April, or in August, in a ½-in.-deep drill, very thinly, the young plants as soon as they can be handled being set out 2 ft. apart each way. Flower stems should be removed as soon as they appear. Height, 4 ft.

Basil. Tips of the plants, and leaves, add a distinctive flavour to salads and soups. For winter use gather when the flowers appear. Dry the tips and leaves, powder them, and store in a tightly corked bottle or stoppered jar. Sweet basil (1 ft. high) and bush basil (6 in.) are both annuals (of one year's duration only). Plants (Fig. 198) are raised from seed sown in light

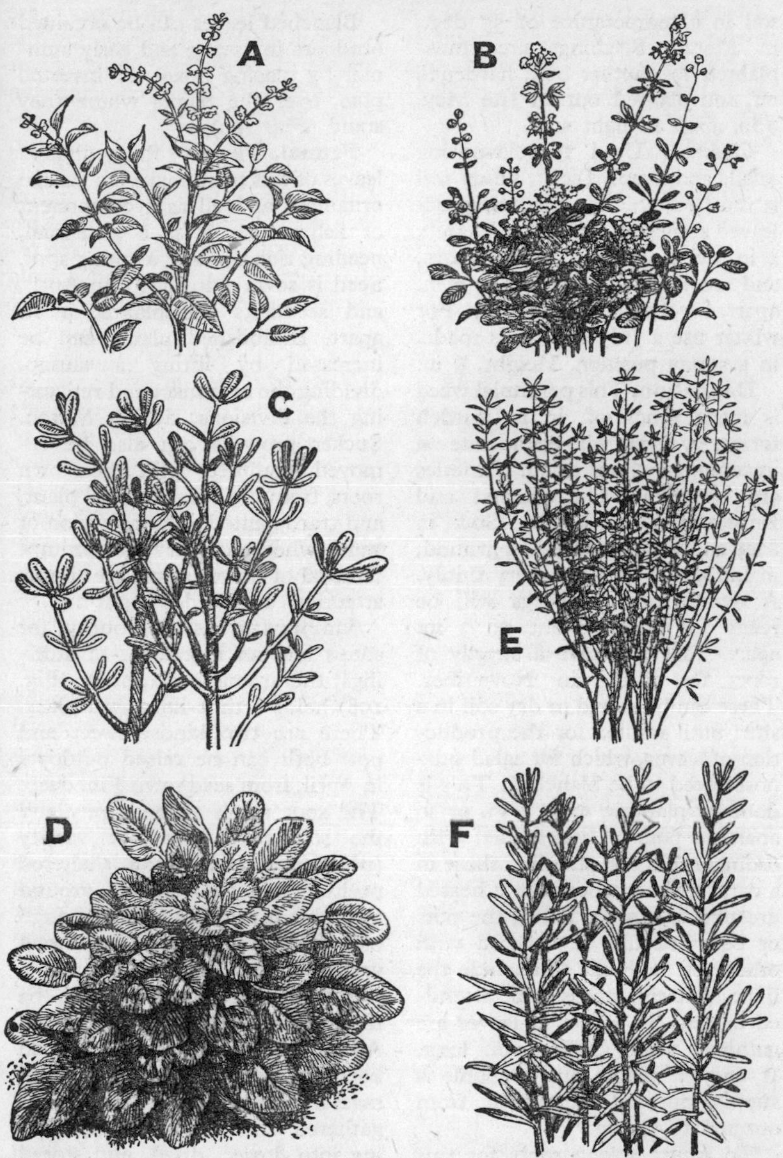

Fig. 198.—*Some of the less familiar but very useful garden herbs whose culture is detailed in the text. Basil* (A), *marjoram* (B), *purslane* (C), *rampion* (D), *savory* (E), *and tarragon* (F), *are all easy to grow*

soil in a temperature of 55 deg., in March. Seedlings are transplanted to another box, hardened off, and planted out in late May, 9 in. apart in light soil.

Chervil. Used for flavouring salads and soups. Light, sandy soil is most suitable for this aromatic-leaved annual. It is sown in March, ⅛ in. deep, where it is to remain, and seedlings thinned out to 6 in. apart, for the summer supply. For winter use a July sowing is made, in a sunny position. Height, 6 in.

Dandelion. This perennial weed is made much of, in its garden forms, by those who appreciate an uncommon winter salad. Varieties are Improved Thick-leaved and Improved Broad-leaved. Sow in May and June, in well-dug ground, in full sun, 1 in. deep, very thinly. A month later seedlings will be ready for thinning out, to 9 in. apart. This will give a supply of roots for lifting in November. These can be stored in dry soil in a shed until wanted for the production of leaves, which for salad purposes need to be blanched. This is done by planting roots 1 in. or so apart, in pots or boxes filled with ordinary soil, and standing these in a dark, warm cupboard or a heated greenhouse. In the latter, the pots or boxes should be covered with other pots or boxes to exclude the light. Watering needs to be attended to, and the blanched leaves are gathered when about 5 in. long. If enough plants are available a supply can be maintained from autumn to spring.

To secure strong roots for this forcing process plants should not be allowed to waste their strength by flowering; flower stems should be pinched out as they appear.

Blanched leaves can be obtained outdoors in spring and early summer by placing boxes, or inverted pots, over the plants where they stand (Fig. 199).

Fennel. The very finely divided leaves of this plant make it a garden ornament as well as a component of fish sauce. It is a perennial, needing rich soil and a sunny spot. Seed is sown ¼ in. deep, in April, and seedlings transplanted 1 ft. apart. Established plants can be increased by lifting a clump, dividing the root mass and replanting the divisions, during March. Sucker growths can also be removed, complete with their own roots, from the base of an old plant, and transplanted. The provision of water when necessary and prompt removal of flower stems are simple attentions required. Height 2 ft.

Marjoram. As a flavouring for soups and an ingredient of stuffings, the aromatic marjoram (Fig. 198) holds a time-honoured place. There are two kinds, sweet and pot; both can be raised outdoors in April, from seed sown ¼ in. deep. The spot needs to be sunny and the soil good, the pot variety (perennial) requiring a sheltered position and well-drained ground to enable it to come safely through bad winter weather. The sweet variety is treated as an annual.

Seedlings of both should be thinned out early to 9 in. apart. An old plant of pot marjoram can be increased by dividing the root mass in March or April. Shoots are gathered when the plants are coming into flower, dried, and stored for winter; leaves are also used straight from the growing plant. Pot marjoram grows 1 ft. high, sweet marjoram about 2 ft.

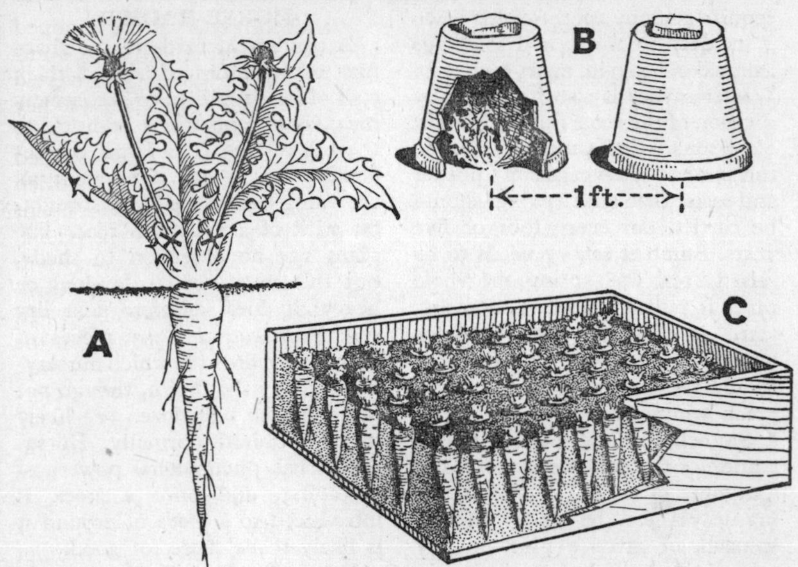

Fig. 199.—*Flower stems of dandelion should be pinched out at* X X (A) *as they appear. Leaves are blanched outdoors by covering with inverted pots* (B); *in winter by boxing roots* (C) *and placing in a warm cupboard*

Purslane. Leaves and shoots of green and golden varieties of purslane (Fig. 198) make excellent summer salading. Seed is sown where the plants are to remain (of one-year duration only) in May, and seedlings thinned out to 6 in. apart. Other small sowings, to secure a succession, can be made until August. Water is needed, when rain holds off, for the production of more leaves and shoots after each picking. Height, 6 in.

Rampion. Very little indeed of rampion is wasted (Fig. 198). The roots are cut up and used radish fashion, along with the leaves, in autumn salads; and in winter roots can be taken from store. Seed is sown in ¼-in. drills in rich soil and partial shade, in March to April for autumn supply, in May for winter use. Seedlings are thinned to 6 in. apart. Ample supplies of water are needed to plump up the roots. Those remaining unused in the ground in November should be dug up and stored in sifted dry soil in a cellar or frostproof shed for use as required. Height about 3 ft.

Savory. Shoots of savory (Fig. 198) have a very pleasing aroma, and for adding an extra touch of flavour to salads and soups the plant has long been renowned. It is customary also for those acquainted with savory to introduce a sprig or two into a boiling of peas or beans. There are two forms of this herb, known as summer savory and winter savory. The former is of one-year duration and grows about 7 in. high. Winter savory is evergreen and grows about 2 in. taller than the other. Neither is particular as to soil, but both require a sunny spot. Seed is sown ½ in. deep in April, and seedlings thinned out to 9 in. apart each way. Winter savory is also increased by division of the roots during March; old plants become unprofitable, so this method of propagation (quicker and easier than seed sowing) should be carried out every four or five years. Summer savory needs to be raised afresh each spring; the whole plant is pulled up when flowering starts in summer, and dried for winter use. Only parts of shoots should be removed from the evergreen winter savory.

Sorrel. The large-leaved garden edition of the field-weed sorrel has a number of uses. The sharp-tasting leaves can be dealt with as spinach, or given a place in any mixed salad, and they figure in sauces and soups. To make sorrel worth its ground space it must be given rich soil and be kept moist. Seed is sown in March, in ½-in.-deep drills, and seedlings thinned out to 1 ft. apart, or they may be transplanted. Roots of established plants (sorrel is perennial) may be divided and the portions replanted in March. Leaves are nipped from the plant as required, and flower stems should be removed early—they waste the plant's strength. Height about 18 in.

Tarragon. Leaves and ends of shoots of tarragon (Fig. 198) are used in salads and pickles. For winter use, tops are cut down during September and dried. The plant is perennial, and propagation is by root division during March, the small rooted pieces being replanted 9 in. apart in a 2-in.-deep drill, the drill then being filled in. Tarragon grows up to a height of about two feet.

HORSE-RADISH

A condiment made of the shavings or scrapings of a good thick root of horse-radish, to accompany meat, is an appetizing addition to the bill of fare. The large, coarse-looking leaves are not eaten; all the value lies in the long, straight, fat stick of a yellowish root. The plant has no objection to shade, but this must not be day-long or heavy; it does object to poor dry soil. Propagation is by pieces of root (sets or crowns) which nurserymen sell by the dozen, though not more than a half-dozen are likely to be required normally. Horse-radish has phenomenal powers of spreading, and once a stock is introduced to a piece of ground it is likely to be there for good.

Ready for Use. Roots are ready for lifting in October.

Soil Preparation. To secure worth-while roots the small patch of ground is prepared by digging to the depth of a foot at least and at that depth forking in some manure, or leaf-mould or decayed material from the vegetable refuse heap or pit. If the top soil is thin and poor, leaf-mould mixed with it will ensure satisfactory results.

When and How to Plant. Pieces of root of any length—as short as 3 in.—may be planted. If these have buds at the top only one should be allowed to remain to each piece. If they are broken pieces of root, the top should be cut across squarely and a bud will form after planting. They are to be planted upright, bud or square-cut end to the top, in holes 1 ft. apart, during February or March (Fig. 200).

The holes, about 10 in. deep, are made with a crowbar or strong

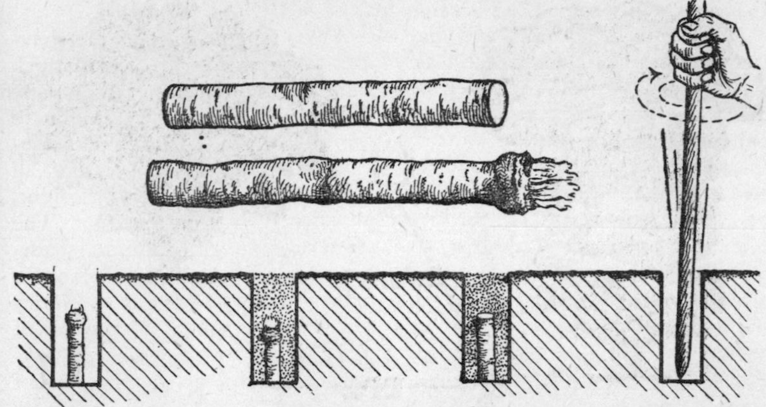

Fig. 200.—*Pieces of horse-radish root are dropped into crowbar-made holes, and the holes filled with soil. Only one bud should be left at the top of each. Broken pieces of root should have the top squared off, as shown at top*

stake, and into each a piece of root is dropped so that it goes right to the bottom. The root is then covered in with soil. In quick-drying ground it is advisable to make the holes at the bottom of a 4-in.-deep drill, so that no water (when it is given) runs to waste.

Watering and Hoeing. With plenty of moisture available the roots fatten up well to between 1 in. and 2 in. in diameter. Regular hoeing will keep down weeds, and the powdery surface which the hoe leaves will help the soil to retain moisture.

Lifting the Roots. All the roots should be dug up, unbroken, by November, the spade being used carefully. Broken pieces left in are likely to become a nuisance—spreading new growth where it is not wanted.

Storing for Winter. The ground cleared and the tops cut or twisted off, the roots are stored anywhere under cover in sifted fire ashes or sand slightly moist.

Preparing for Table. Washed or scrubbed, roots can be scraped as wanted. Surplus shavings can be dried in a slow oven and kept in a corked jar or bottle.

KALE (BORECOLE)

One of the most valuable and hardy of the winter greens, especially for late winter when other greenstuff is scarce, kale should be represented on every piece of vegetable ground. Vigorous in growth, hard frost actually improves the eating qualities of the generously produced leaves or sprouts, one plant giving many pickings over a long period. It thrives in rich, firm soil.

Varieties include Hardy Sprouting, Curled Scotch, Tall Curled, Drumhead (with solid cabbage top), Russian, Thousand-headed, Cottager's and Asparagus, the last two specially useful for late spring.

An ounce of seed yields about 1,000 plants. Seedlings appear in ten days after planting.

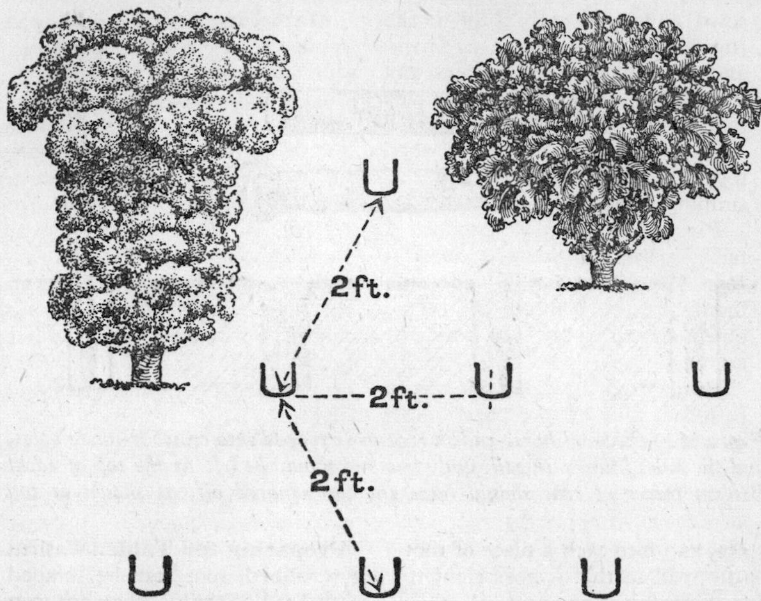

Fig. 201.—*Scotch kale (left) and asparagus kale (right) need plenty of space. They should be set out 2 ft. apart each way, and the trowel-made planting holes should be filled with water before the young plants go in*

Ready for Use. November and on to March or April.

Soil Preparation. Kale follows well after a crop of beans or peas for which the ground has been well dug and enriched. With rubbish cleared away and the top 2 in. broken up with the fork, no further preparation is necessary. Recent deep digging is not desirable, firm ground being an essential. With a loose root run growth is apt to be sappy and less resistant to frost. If the site is not in good heart deep digging cannot well be avoided. Plenty of decaying greenstuff should be mixed in 1 ft. down, and superphosphate of lime scattered over the dug surface, 2 oz. to the square yard, and raked in. Preparation is completed by treading or rolling the site (not when the surface is wet) until it no longer feels spongy.

When and How to Sow. To secure a supply over the longest possible period small sowings are made at intervals from March to May—the earlier sowings for early winter pickings, the later ones for the main winter and spring crop.

Seed is sown as thinly as possible, in $\frac{3}{4}$-in.-deep drills in the seed bed, this first being watered if dry. Seedlings are transplanted about 4 in. apart and later planted out, a few at a time, in the prepared row or rows. Or they may be thinned out in the seed bed to stand 4 in. apart, remaining there until wanted for planting out.

Asparagus kale and cottager's kale, for the production of numerous shoots in late spring, can be sown as late as early July in the rows where the plants are to remain, and there thinned out (without any transplanting) to 2 ft. apart. In this case, to save wastage of seed, three or four seeds should be dropped together at 2-ft. intervals, this also simplifying thinning out.

Planting Out. Kale occupies a fair amount of space, 2 ft. apart in rows 2 ft. apart, but as very little indeed of the plant is wasted no objection can be taken to it on that account.

Plants for final setting out should be lifted, with a trowel, from moist ground; this enables them to come away with plenty of soil adhering to the roots, a factor which is worth attention. They receive no check and get away at once in their new quarters.

If the planting site is at all dry, deep trowel-holes should be made and then filled with water (Fig. 201). When this has soaked away the plants are dropped in and the ground made firm around each by treading it with the boot heel (Fig. 202). The holes need to be of sufficient depth to take the whole of the bare stem, so that the lowest leaves are level with the surface.

Watering and Hoeing. The plants will take up a good deal of water if this is available; if it is not, growth suffers. The watering-can must not remain idle so long as rain holds off. The day after each watering, either the Dutch or draw hoe should be used to loosen the surface, even though there may be no weeds to uproot. If watering is not possible, the hoe will help by fining down the surface and blocking up air holes, thus preventing the evaporation of whatever moisture there may be in the soil.

Gathering Leaves and Shoots. A plant is not stripped of its green-stuff all at once. A few leaves and shoots are broken off at a time, and others taken as they develop, up and down the stem, until the plant has no more to offer. It has then done its job. Uprooted and burned on the rubbish heap, bare stem and roots will become wood ash—which is to be kept dry (so that the potash which it contains shall not be washed out) until wanted for raking or forking into a bit of dug ground previous to sowing or planting.

Preparing for Table. Leaves and shoots (or sprouts) should have thick stem ends removed, then be washed, and left in salt water for a few minutes before boiling. Since kale is available when other greens have been used up or have been ruined by hard frost, it is an invaluable winter food.

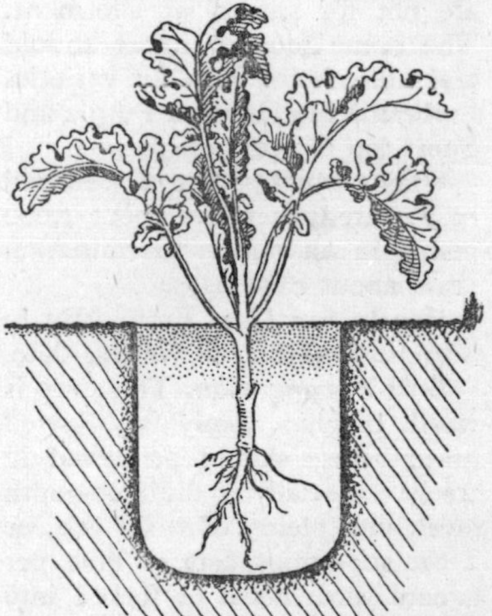

Fig. 202.—*The planting holes should be deep enough to take the whole of the bare stem, and the young kale plants be left very firm in the ground*

KOHL-RABI (KNOL KOHL)

An unusual-sounding name for an unusual-looking but very tasty vegetable. The plant looks like a turnip with cabbage leaves sprouting out of it here and there—hence its other name of turnip-rooted cabbage. But the cabbage has no heart. Though the young leaves may be cooked and eaten, it is the bulbous part (which sits on top of the ground) which constitutes the crop. In the kitchen this is dealt with turnip fashion, and its great value lies in the fact that kohl-rabi will succeed in light, dry soil in which summer turnips persistently fail.

Drought does not affect it, any more than does winter frost. But it grows best in good soil, and the tenderest bulbs are secured when water is given in dry summer.

The large-growing varieties of kohl-rabi grown for cattle feeding are not for garden or allotment. The home food producer should make his choice from the varieties Earliest White, Earliest Purple and Short-top Green.

Only a small packet of seed will be required; there are about 1,000 plants in an ounce. Germination takes about nine days.

Ready for Use. From July to March, according to sowing date.

Soil Preparation. This crop is worth digging deeply for. Rotted green refuse should be mixed in freely, especially at the foot-depth level; and plenty of wood ash, or 2 oz. superphosphate of lime per square yard, raked or forked into the dug surface, will give excellent results.

When and How to Sow. For a summer crop seed is sown in March, April or May—a small sowing each month securing a very useful succession of plants. For utumn and winter crops, seed is sown in late July. Drills should be $\frac{3}{4}$ in. deep and 18 in. apart.

If all space is otherwise occupied, the early sowings may be made on a moist seed bed. Seedlings are thinned out to about 3 in. apart, and lifted carefully with a trowel (from moist ground) and planted out before they become crowded. They must be watered in generously at once, in the absence of rain.

Thinning Out, Planting Out. Plants should stand finally at 10 in. apart in the row; rows to be 18 in. apart. Deep planting of the seedlings is to be avoided; reasonably shallow planting allows the stem bases to swell without hindrance (Fig. 203).

Watering and Hoeing. If water is scarce, kohl-rabi can get along without it better than most crops. But it will be the better for whatever water can be spared in the driest weather. After rain, and watering, work the surface finely with the hoe. Soil must not be worked up over the swelling stems; rather draw soil away from bases.

Gathering the Crop. The bulbs are in finest eating condition when the size of a cricket ball; if larger, they are likely to be tough. Plants are pulled up as wanted for use, and the bulbs taken to the kitchen.

Storing for Winter. Though hardy enough to be left in the ground all winter, it may happen that the space occupied is wanted for digging. In this case the entire crop may be gathered when the bulbs are large enough—in October or November—and stored in sifted ashes in a cellar or shed, any worth-while leaves being removed

Fig. 203.—*Kohl-rabi should be planted as shallowly as possible, to allow the stem bases to swell without hindrance;* 10 *in. apart in rows* 18 *in. apart*

for cooking as a separate vegetable.

Preparing for Table. The bulbs are washed, peeled, and then dealt with in the manner of turnips. Young leaves are boiled like cabbage. In the matter of food value, kohl-rabi is as nutritious as it is palatable.

LEEK

With a mild oniony flavour, the leek has a thick white stem—16 in. long in well-grown specimens, with a diameter of 3 in.—and long, green, strap-like leaves. The white stem is the part that is eaten. Leek soup is a very nourishing food; as a winter vegetable its value is undisputed.

Deep, rich soil is needed to give a good length of stem, and dryness has to be avoided.

Varieties include Musselburgh, Prizetaker, Monstrous Carentan, Ayton Castle Giant, and Flag (or London), the latter being specially suitable for an early crop.

An ounce of seed will give 1,000 plants. Average period of germination is nine days

Ready for Use. October, and on to April. The crop is available about 28 weeks after sowing.

Soil Preparation. Dry conditions at the root are ruinous to the leek. It is also a hungry plant. Soil is therefore prepared with these prime requirements in mind. It will be well provided for if it follows a row of peas or beans for whose benefit the ground was specially dug and enriched; if they failed because of drought or starvation it is no place for the leek.

Where there is a good depth of cultivated soil the plants will be most successful in a 1-ft.-deep trench, the width of a spade-blade. Stems will be longer and thicker if the bottom of the trench is forked up and rotted leaves added to it, or any decaying greenstuff available. If the trench bottom is dealt with

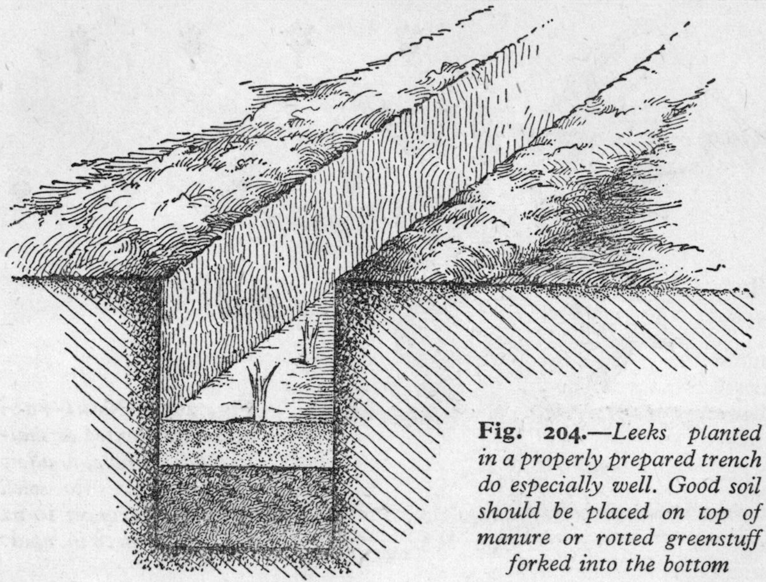

Fig. 204.—*Leeks planted in a properly prepared trench do especially well. Good soil should be placed on top of manure or rotted greenstuff forked into the bottom*

in this way, 4 in. of good soil should be placed on top of the food material for the reception of the young plants (Fig. 204).

They will thrive in clay if this is broken up deeply and made porous by the admixture of wood ash or sharp grit or sand or sifted fire ashes from the house, plus rotted greenstuff or manure at the bottom of the trench.

Where there is not much depth of good soil and where, because of unsuitable subsoil, it cannot be deepened by digging and manuring, the plants should be set out singly in holes made with dibber, trowel or crowbar after the ground has been enriched as deeply as is practicable.

When and How to Sow. Exhibition-standard leeks are given the necessary long growing period by being raised in a warm greenhouse or hotbed frame in January or early February. Seed boxes are lined with leaf-mould, filled with good soil (with sand or grit to make it porous), seed is sown thinly and covered with the merest sprinkling of sifted soil, and the seedlings are pricked out 3 in. apart into other boxes, and in due course hardened off for planting out in April.

For ordinary purposes seed is sown outdoors, on a seed bed in ½-in.-deep drills, in late February or March. The seedlings are thinned out—or moved to 3 in. apart into rich soil—and kept well watered until planted out in the prepared places in April. If cold weather or wet soil hinders outdoor sowing, seed can be sown in a shallow box in a cold frame—if a greenhouse or hotbed frame is not available—and dealt with as advised for exhibition-standard plants. Or the outdoor sowing may be made

Fig. 205.—*Pieces of glass, propped up with short sticks, give protection to leeks either sown in a seed bed or planted out early in a broad drill*

under the protection of pieces of glass, the tops meeting over the drill tent fashion with pieces of stick to support them (Fig. 205).

A Long Supply. If three small sowings are made at intervals, during February and March, outdoors, and the seedlings transplanted at intervals, the supply will be greatly prolonged. The earliest sowing and transplanting will provide an early crop, the next will secure the main crop, and the last will give a late crop.

Planting Out. Time to set out the young plants permanently is when they are about 6 in. long. If the trench system is adopted, they are spaced 9 in. apart down the centre of the trench. If they are to be planted in separate holes on the flat, the holes are made 9 in. apart, with dibber, trowel or crowbar. They should be not less than 6 in. deep—8 in. or 9 in. is better—and 3 in. across (to give the stems space to swell). A plant is dropped into each hole so that it falls to the bottom, and the hole filled up with water; enough soil will be carried down by the water to cover the roots. The complete filling in of the hole is left to subsequent waterings and hoeings. Meanwhile the

Fig. 206.—*Alternatively to the trench system of planting, leeks may be set out in separate holes. Water has been poured into the centre hole below and enough soil carried down with it to cover the roots. On the right, a fully grown leek*

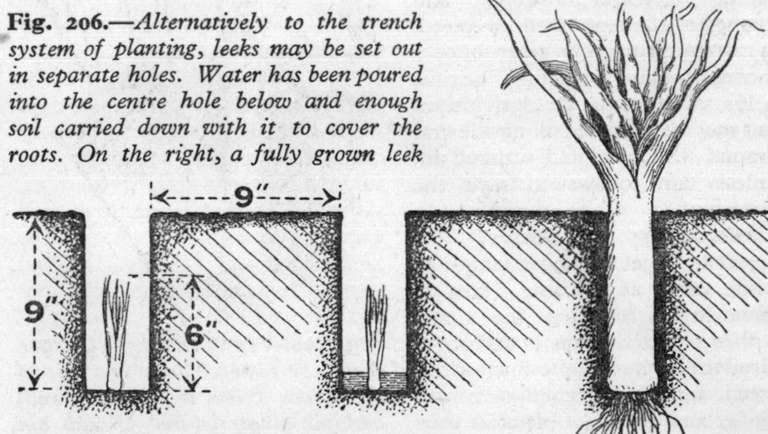

Fig. 207.—*Side view of a trench of leeks, the trench filled in and soil mounded well up. End view of a row is shown in the top sketch*

top growth will extend and push well up above the surface (Fig. 206).

Watering and Feeding. Trench plants and hole plants alike will rapidly increase in height and diameter if kept well watered. Weak liquid manure given once a fortnight, until blanching begins, helps still further, Or agricultural salt may be scattered alongside and around the plants and watered in, unless rain follows to save the watering.

Blanching the Stems. The object is to get as long a length of white stem as possible. This is done by surrounding the stems with soil so that light is excluded. Growth is then white instead of green, and the blanched stems are tender and tasty, not bitter as they otherwise would be (Fig. 207).

In the case of trench plants, the trench is gradually filled in with the soil that was taken out and placed at the sides, the soil level keeping pace with the base of the lowest leaves.

Plants in separate holes have soil drawn up to and around them, with the hoe, after the hole itself has been filled in.

Lifting the Crop. The plants can be dug out any time after blanching when they have reached a sufficiently large size. Soil is drawn carefully away with the spade or trowel, to expose one side of the stem; the spade is then driven slantwise beneath the root and the plant levered up and out (Fig. 208).

Storing for Winter. Leeks may be left in the ground until

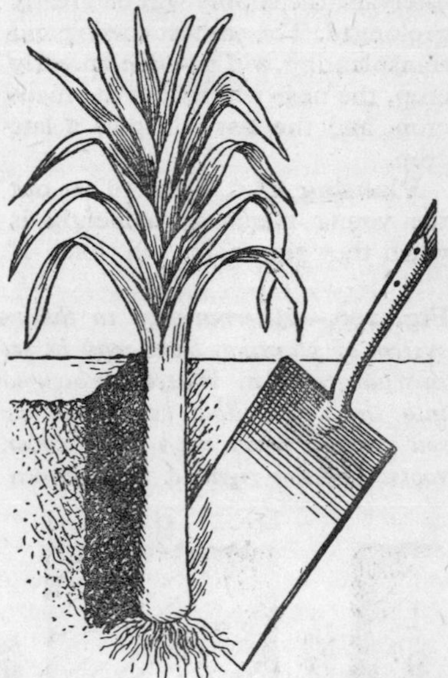

Fig. 208.—*In lifting big leeks, soil should be removed from one side of the trench (view is from one end) and the plants levered up and out with the spade driven in slantwise*

required, a few being lifted at a time. If the site is required for other purposes the whole crop may be lifted (when full growth has taken place) and stored in a damp-proof cellar or shed in a heap of sifted ashes or sand.

Preparing for Table. Remove roots, cut back the green tops almost to the white, and wash well, before cooking. There is real nourishment in a leek. Boiled young, it is a vegetable specially suitable for convalescents.

LETTUCE

The most important as well as the most popular salad plant grown in Britain, lettuce is not exacting in its requirements. It may fail in dry, poor ground. Given a reasonably rich and moist root-run it grows quickly—which is the secret of those crisp, tender hearts which make such delicious eating in hot summer. Its very desirable qualities make it worth growing the whole year round, and this can be achieved with the aid of warm greenhouse and frame.

Choice of varieties is largely a matter of taste, and most home food producers grow both the cos and the cabbage kinds. The cos lettuce has long leaves and grows upright, and needs to be blanched by having the leaves banded together near the top. The cabbage lettuce is squat—low-growing—and does not need that attention. If there is anything to choose between the two kinds it is that the cabbage lettuce stands the better chance in thin, quick-drying soil; whereas the cos kinds in similar circumstances are inclined to bolt, that is, rush up to flower.

Varieties of cabbage lettuce for sowing outdoors in spring and summer include Standwell, Continuity, Holborn Standard, All the Year Round (all four specially resistant to drought and disinclined to bolt), Drumhead, Favourite, Golden Ball, May King, May Queen.

Cos varieties for summer use include Paris White, Superb White, Mammoth White, Little Gem.

Cabbage lettuces for autumn outdoor sowing, to heart up the following spring, include Hammersmith Hardy Green, Imperial, Arctic, Stanstead Park, Commodore Nutt.

Cos varieties to stand the winter outdoors (autumn-sown) include Black-seeded Bath and Winter White.

For heated greenhouse and hotbed frame culture the following cabbage varieties are most suitable: Golden Ball, Commodore Nutt, Early Paris, Majestic, May Queen, Tom Thumb.

An ounce of lettuce seed should yield about 2,000 plants, and average period of germination is about nine days.

Ready for Use. From late spring or early summer on to autumn, from outdoor sowings. With the aid of a frame the period is extended. The full cycle of the year can be completed by raising plants in the early weeks of the year in a temperature of 65 deg. Lettuce is ready for use about ten to twelve weeks after sowing.

Soil Preparation. The ideal soil for lettuce is one that crumbles between the fingers—but is not dusty or sandy—and contains plenty of humus: that is, old manure or rotted vegetable matter. One of the proprietary brands of hop manure will transform thin,

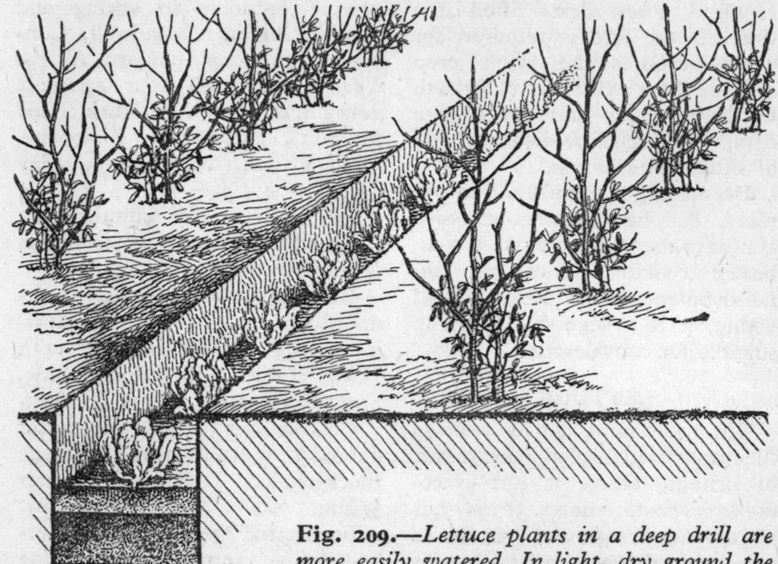

Fig. 209.—*Lettuce plants in a deep drill are more easily watered. In light, dry ground the shade afforded by peas, beans or other tall-growing plants is welcome*

light, hungry ground. Though the soil needs to be broken up at least 1 ft. deep it is no use burying these enriching materials at that depth. They should be mixed with the top few inches, or the roots will never get to the food.

If manure or manure substitute is very scarce, what little there is can be made to go farther by lining it into the bottom of 6-in.-deep drills, to the depth of 1 in. or 2 in., and covering it with 1 in. of soil (Fig. 209). Planted in this, young lettuce plants start well, and will continue well if the drill is kept well supplied with water in hot and dry weather. This is the best treatment for light soil.

Clay soil can be dealt with similarly, with sand, grit, ashes or crushed mortar rubble to break it up and keep it open. Wood ash raked plentifully into the surface—after the other attentions have been carried out—or scattered in the drill before planting is conducive to quick growth and leaf formation.

When and How to Sow. For ordinary, everyday use, lettuce is sown outdoors from March to August; and the contents of a small packet can be made to produce a long-drawn-out supply, by the simple expedient of sowing the merest pinch of seed every ten days or so. Thus plants are secured in all stages—a half-dozen plants ready for use, another half-dozen nearing that stage, and so backward to a row of seedlings waiting to be thinned out or transplanted, and a row of newly sown seed.

The sowing of an entire packet at once will mean a wasteful glut, unless there is a really large demand. Lettuce plants bolt if not used within reasonable time.

Seed can be sown very thinly in a ½-in.-deep drill and, duly thinned out to 9 in. apart, allowed to remain there and heart up. Or the seedlings can be lifted with a trowel and transplanted to where they are to finish. Or seedlings can be raised in a shallow box and then planted out. Whichever plan is adopted the soil should be moist at all stages: before the seed is sown and up to the time of pulling the mature lettuce for use.

Where to Sow. Earliest and latest sowings do best in a sunny, sheltered position; in the home garden a border at the foot of a fence or wall facing south is excellent. On an open allotment the earliest sowings can be protected (from heavy rain as much as from cold) and germination hastened by covering the sown drill with odd bits of glass (Fig. 210); or by sowing in a box and placing this in another box covered with a sheet of glass.

Summer sowings and plantings need shade from midday sun. The south-facing border is then unsuitable. Partial shade is secured by sowing or planting between rows of peas, runner beans or other tall-growing plants. Though this is of less importance in moisture-holding soils it applies in full measure to light ground that is always drying out.

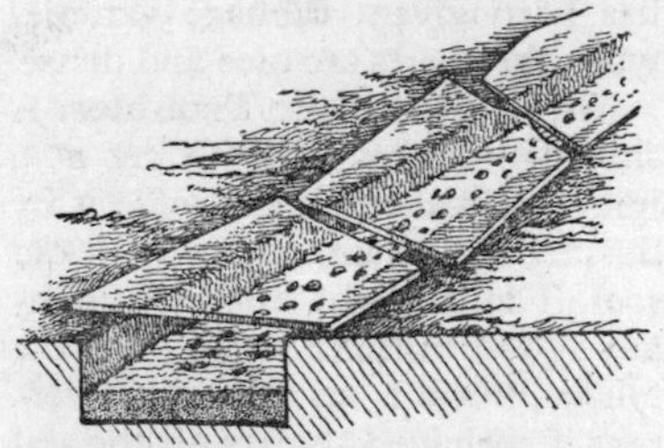

Fig. 210.—*Germination of lettuce seed sown in a drill is hastened by covering the drill with pieces of glass*

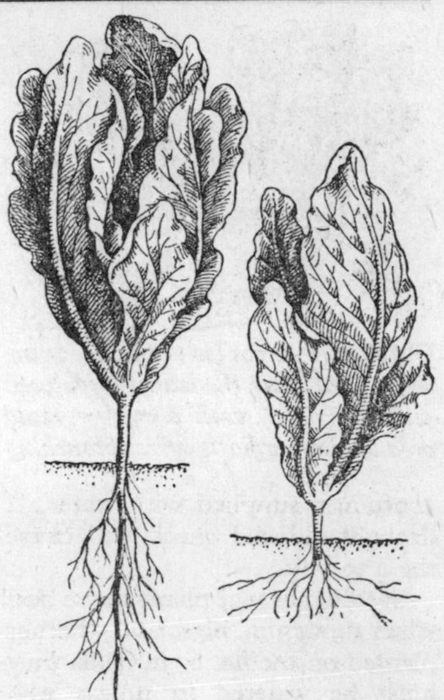

Fig. 211.—*Lettuce for transplanting should be lifted complete with all roots (left). Plants whose roots are broken (right) are apt to bolt*

Thinning Out, Planting Out. Plants sown in a permanent row need to be thinned out as soon as they can be handled to 3 in. apart. The first thinnings can be transplanted elsewhere if lifted complete with roots (Fig. 211), from moist soil to moist soil. At the next (final) thinning out—before the remaining plants touch—they will be withdrawn in pairs, so that those left stand at 9 in. apart. These final thinnings are very tender and tasty and should be used for salad purposes.

It is best to avoid transplanting from the time the weather warms up in May or early June, unless the moved plants can be kept

Fig. 212.—*A cos lettuce before tying (left), and after the leaves have been secured (right) with a rubber band or a loop of raffia to effect blanching*

constantly supplied with water. A drought-induced check will cause them to bolt.

Seedling lettuce plants move best when about 3 in. high, and whether planted on the flat or in drills they must be watered in unless rain precedes or immediately follows the move.

Unoccupied spaces such as the banked-up sides of a celery or leek trench should not be overlooked as a site for lettuce. Neither crop will interfere with the other, for the lettuce if sown or planted out early enough will be used up before the earthing up of the celery or leeks begins.

Watering and Feeding. Enough water should be given at a time to soak well down to the roots, and as soon as plants are out of the seedling stage they will respond to doses of nitrate of soda sprinkled along the row and between at the rate of 1 oz. to 3 yd. of row, this to be watered in, about once a fortnight.

When Lettuce Bolts. A plant that suddenly runs up loosely is going to flower, and nothing can be done to stop it. It should be pulled up and fed to the chickens or rabbits. Too much sun, not enough water or food—any or all of these will cause bolting. In areas where this trouble is persistent it will be found that it is nearly always the cos varieties that are the offenders. So far as drought is concerned, the cabbage varieties are far more reliable.

How Lettuce is Blanched. Cabbage varieties do not need to have the leaves bunched together to induce blanching. It is necessary only with the cos (upright-growing) kinds, the operation ensuring that hearts and inner leaves of these shall be made tender and crisp and more or less white by the exclusion of light.

The outer leaves are held together at the top with one hand whilst a piece of raffia is slipped around with the other, not tightly but securely, at a point well above the centre of the plant. The raffia is then tied. Instead of raffia a rubber band may be slipped over (Fig. 212).

The time to do this is when the plants are nearly full-grown and when the leaves are not moist with rain or dew or after watering.

Pulling for Use. Cos varieties are ready for pulling up about ten days after the tie (or rubber band) has been given; cabbage varieties when the hearts are nice and dense.

Slugs and Other Troubles. A slug will walk a mile to get at a juicy lettuce seedling. Baffle it by dusting the young plants with old soot. That straight from the chimney is too burning for use on the foliage, but it is an excellent deterrent if sprinkled thickly on the soil all around each plant. Or lime may be used as a surface dressing.

Leatherjackets also have a great

liking for this crop, in all stages. Deal with them, and with cutworms, as advised on page 409, where also will be found directions for dealing with greenfly and two diseases which afflict lettuce.

Winter and Spring Lettuce. Varieties previously mentioned for autumn sowing (late August and September) should be sown in a sunny, sheltered position where, thinned out, they can be covered with glass or given other protection during hard weather. Or the plants may be lifted and replanted at the foot of a south-facing fence or wall before winter sets in. In cold districts, or where the soil lies wet and heavy in winter, they will be safer transplanted to a cold frame, and given plenty of air in good weather, but only just enough water to keep them going.

They must have a depth of good soil in the frame, all light possible, and slugs should be watched for.

A sowing in a cold frame in October will give strong young plants for setting out in a sheltered spot in March.

Earliest Outdoor Lettuce. A greenhouse, or hotbed frame, with a temperature of about 55 deg. by night makes possible sowings in January, February, March, for setting out in the open in March, April and May respectively.

A Greenhouse Crop. Varieties previously mentioned for heated greenhouse and hotbed frame culture can be grown in boxes (from first to last under glass) for using young during mid-winter. The ordinary grower, however, will find all his requirements met by outdoor sowings.

Preparing for Table. Remove roots, soiled outer leaves, wash, and dry by enclosing in a cloth and swishing this to and fro in the air. Eaten raw, lettuce has laxative, antiscorbutic and cooling properties. It can also be boiled like spinach, and in this form it is a vegetable recommended by doctors for convalescents.

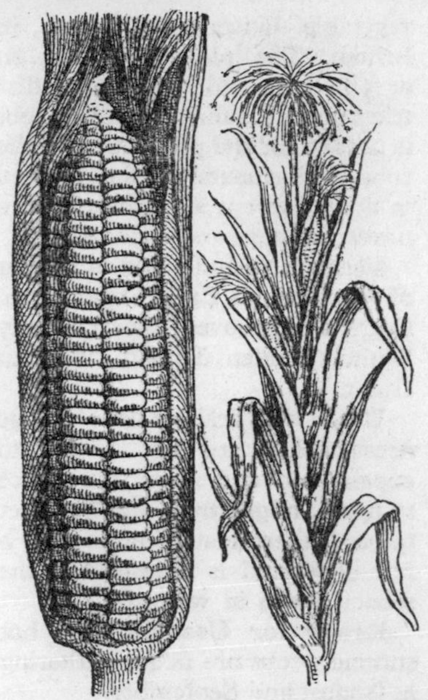

Fig. 213.—*Cobs of tight-packed seed of maize make a delicious boiled vegetable. The cobs come after the long flower-plumes (right) in summer*

MAIZE
(SUGAR CORN, SWEET CORN)

Looking like a thick-stemmed giant grass or sturdy bamboo, garden varieties of maize are grown for the sake of the delicious cobs of tight-packed seed which follow the long flower plumes (Fig. 213). These heads are gathered before the seed becomes hard, boiled, and eaten as "corn in the cob"—a highly nutritious, if uncommon, vegetable. Uncommon, that is, in Britain. The plant grows 4 ft. or 5 ft. high and is for warm districts only. A sunny, sheltered spot is needed for the production of the cobs. Unfortunately it is not suited to a wind-swept allotment. It also needs moisture and a rich soil.

Varieties include Sutton's First of All, Sutton's Early Sugar Corn, Carter's Improved Sweet, Early White, Golden Bantam, Golden Giant.

Those who desire a little change occasionally, are not afraid to experiment and have the space to spare, might try a small packet of seed. Germination takes only a few days, and is advanced if the seed is sown in warmth.

Ready for Use. Given a hot summer, cobs are fit for gathering in August and September.

Soil Preparation. A shallow soil is unsuitable. Ground needs to be dug 18 in. deep and packed with leaf-mould, rotted weeds and similar greenstuff, or manure.

When and How to Sow. Seed is sown outdoors in May, 2 in. deep, the seedlings to be thinned out finally to 18 in. apart. Thinnings can be transplanted if lifted with the trowel from moist ground. In a warm greenhouse or sunny frame seed may be sown in April, 2 in. apart and 1 in. deep, in pots or a shallow box filled with leafy soil; the plants to be hardened off gradually for planting outdoors in full sun.

Planting Out. Late May is early enough for planting out glass-raised seedlings. A depression 2 in. deep and 8 in. in diameter is left around each plant, for watering. Liquid manure given every ten days produces strong, quick growth.

Cutting the Cobs. The heads, ears, or cobs are gathered when the corn or seed is fully developed, but before it becomes hard—that is, when the cobs feel firm and not spongy when pressed. They are cut from the stems with a knife. The rest of the plant forms useful cattle fodder.

Preparing for Table. The outer sheath and fibres removed, the cobs are ready for boiling; they go to the table whole, usually on pieces of toast. Food value is considerable.

MARROW

Vegetable marrows will yield as big a crop (for cooking, jam making, and chutney) grown on the flat or on a sloping bank of soil as on the regulation heap of vegetable refuse or old manure, provided the plants are given rich living and frequent drinks. Full sun is necessary, away from trees.

Because these plants have a reputation for growing themselves, marrows are often consigned to any rubbishy corner of the ground, where they fail because of the shade and drip from tree branches, starvation, and never a sight of the watering-can. The crop is too valuable for haphazard treatment at any stage.

Where space is precious, the non-rambling bush varieties should be grown. These include Tender and True, Green Bush, White Bush (creamy-white fruits), Yellow Custard and White Custard. The last two bear smaller and more solid fruits than ordinary marrows, and are flat and broad instead of round and long.

Trailing varieties, which require more space, include Table Dainty,

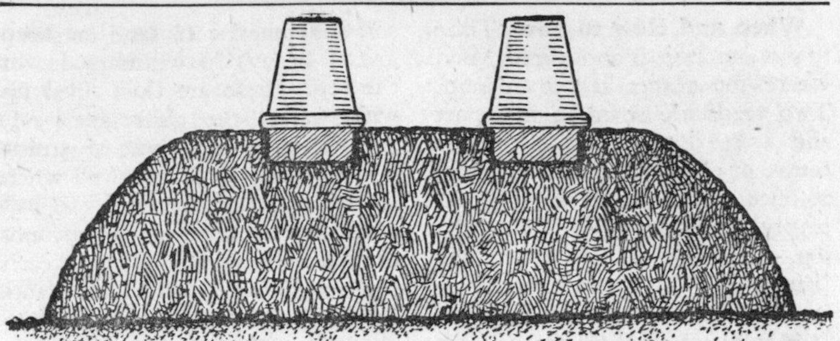

Fig. 214.—*Marrow seed sown outdoors, under inverted flower pots on a flat-topped mound of tightly packed decaying greenstuff mixed with soil*

Long Green, Long White, Long Cream, Moore's Cream, Pen-y-Byd (round-fruited, creamy white).

A small packet of seed will give all the plants likely to be required —150 plants per ounce. Germination takes about ten days.

Ready for Use. July to autumn. Marrows can also be stored for winter use.

Soil Preparation. If a mound of good material—old manure, or decaying greenstuff (not sticks and miscellaneous rubbish)—is available and not likely to be required for digging in or other purposes before late autumn, and is not under trees or too shaded by buildings, this should be made solid by beating with the spade, and given a flat top. Depressions (for watering) should be made 3 in. deep and 2 ft. apart; each will accommodate one plant (Fig. 214).

If marrows are to be grown on the flat, prepare positions by making for each plant a circular hole 18 in. deep and the same across (Fig. 215). Fill to within 6 in. of the top with decaying leaves or other vegetation (weeds, lawn mowings, etc.) and tread this material firmly. Cover with 3 in. of soil, leaving a 3-in. basin for watering; the positions to be not less than 2 ft. apart. On naturally sloping ground, or the side of a bank, leave each depression with a level surface (Fig. 216).

Where neither rotting greenstuff nor manure is obtainable, dig the site 1 ft. deep and rake into the dug surface superphosphate of lime—2 oz. per sq. yd.

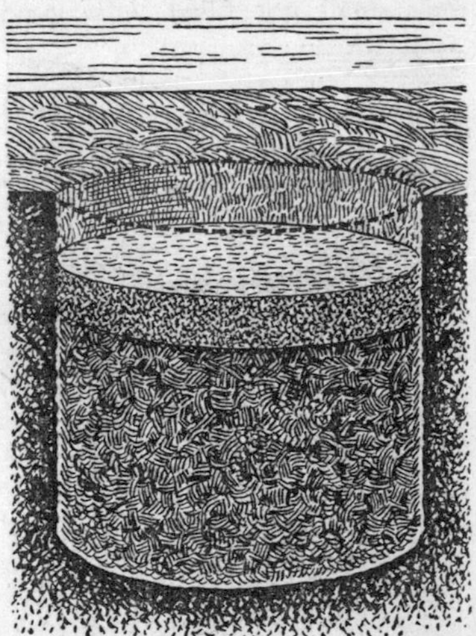

Fig. 215.—*Marrows to be grown on the flat should have holes prepared for each, with decaying greenstuff trodden in and covered with soil*

When and How to Sow. Time to sow outdoors is about mid-May, where the plants are to remain. Two seeds are sown, 2 in. apart and 1 in. deep, on edge, in the centre of each prepared place, and at once covered with an inverted empty flower pot 6 in. across the top, or a box, or piece of glass (Fig. 214). This covering remains in place until top growth appears. It is then removed by day (unless the weather is cold or very rainy, in which case the covering is propped up at one side to give air) and replaced at night until risk of frost has passed. If both seeds germinate the weaker of the two plants is removed in due course.

Sowing Under Glass. Earlier plants are obtained by sowing in a sunny, closed frame or in a sunny greenhouse, in mid-April, two seeds 1 in. deep and on edge in each small pot filled with good soil (lightened with sand or sharp grit if heavy) to within ½ in. of the top. These are then filled up with water (the chill taken off) and placed in the frame or greenhouse. Some air is required when top growth appears, and the soil needs to be kept moist but not sodden. The weaker plant of each pair is removed and the plants accustomed by degrees to outdoor conditions before being set out.

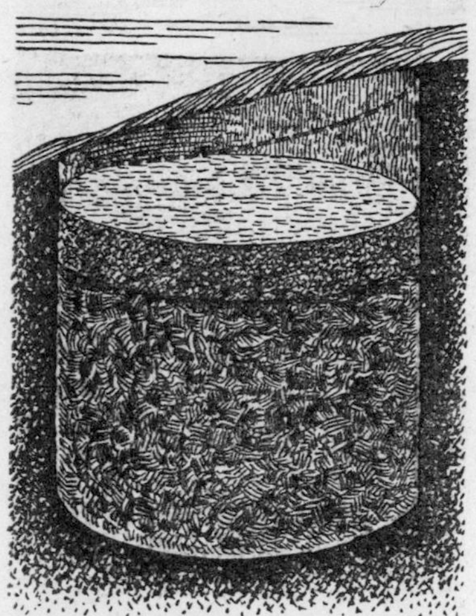

Fig. 216.—*In sloping ground, marrow holes prepared for sowing or planting should be given a flat top*

Bought Plants. If marrow plants are purchased these must not be leggy or pale-looking. They should have thick stems, short joints and substantial green leaves and plenty of roots. If greenfly is in evidence dip each plant, inverted (not the roots), in a liquid insecticide such as quassia and soft soap solution, leaves and stem being swished about in the liquid for a few seconds.

Planting Out. Those raised in frame or greenhouse should not be planted out until after mid-May, flower pot or box protection being given each night for a couple of weeks. Plant with a trowel, as deep as the lowest leaves; water at once.

Watering, Feeding. Fill each depression with water as often as the soil approaches dryness. Plants will fail if they go thirsty. As soon as fruit has formed, feeding with dried blood will help—a tablespoonful stirred into each 2 gal. of water, given once a week.

Plants are further strengthened if joints, where these make contact with the ground, are covered with 2-in.-deep mounds of soil pressed down. Roots form on those parts of the stem and assist in the swelling of the marrows.

The falling off of young fruits when about 2 in. long, or less,

Fig. 217.—*Pollen transferred from a male marrow flower (left) to a female flower (right) enables the fruit to set*

may be due to drought. More often it is due to lack of fertilization of the female flowers. Normally the necessary transference of pollen from male to female flowers is done by bees or other insects. Where no pollen is transferred the fruits cannot set and the immature swellings drop off. It can be done by hand.

Female flowers, which bear the fruit, have a distinct swelling behind the petals and are on very short stems. The male flowers, which do not fruit but provide the pollen, show no swelling and are on long stems (Fig. 217).

To effect fertilization, pick off a fully open male flower, bend back the petals and gently press the centre part into the fully open female flower—when sun is shining on the plants—and leave it there. The male flower will later fall away. Some of its pollen having been deposited where required, the swelling behind the female flower will increase and develop into a fine vegetable marrow.

Cutting the Marrows. Best cookers are those taken young before the outer skin has toughened to such an extent that it is not easy for the finger-nail to break it. Plants remain longer in bearing if their fruit is not allowed to become too large.

Storing for Winter. Marrows that are not over-ripe will keep in good condition for months if cut when dry and suspended, by the stalk end and string, under cover where they cannot be affected by frost, damp or too much artificial heat.

Preparing for Table. Peel the marrow, cut it open, take out seeds, and cut it into convenient sizes for boiling or frying. As a food it is very palatable and filling.

MINT

For adding flavour to new potatoes and the first green peas there is nothing to rival juicy, aromatic mint. Dried and powdered mint is a second choice for adding to vegetables while cooking and for making sauce; but green mint, picked from the open (or from a box of soil in warmth in winter) is vastly superior. Unfortunately, mint is so often left to take its chances in the ground, that instead of foot-high, juicy stems with big, wholesome green leaves the neglected mint bed offers only wiry, spindly stems and a few indifferent leaves.

It has its own requirements in the matter of soil and position. Though the roots travel mostly parallel with the surface they like the ground to be dug deeply before they are consigned to it, to be enriched with a little manure or plenty of leaf-mould or hop manure. They like plenty of moisture, and they hate to be sun-baked.

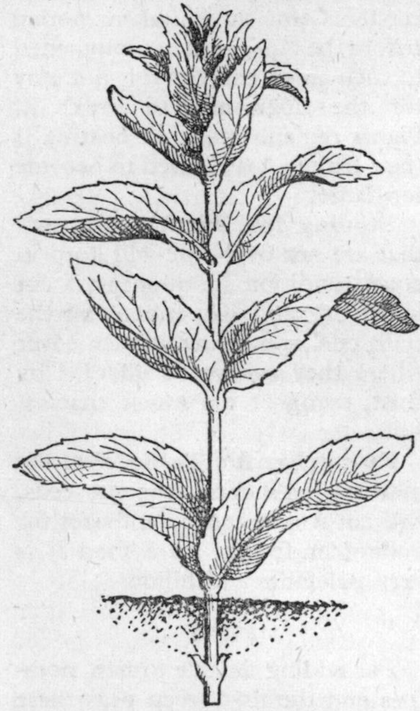

Fig. 218.—*Mint is easily increased by cuttings severed immediately below a joint and planted firmly*

Mint is propagated by division of root clumps and by cuttings of the top growth. A start can be made with one strong clump, purchased from a nurseryman, and a stock quickly worked up in the manner described below.

Ready for Use. Pickings of mint are available outdoors from April to September; the rest of the year from plants in a pot or box of soil in a warm greenhouse.

Soil Preparation. Mint will not grow under trees or a hedge or in full shade, but it requires some shelter from midday summer sun. The patch where it is to be planted might be a sheltered corner, dug 1 ft. deep and enriched with decayed vegetable matter, or animal manure or hop manure, and not beyond easy reach of the watering-can. To be profitable it must have one of these humus-providing materials; unfortunately no artificial fertilizer can be used as a substitute.

How and When to Plant. Roots are planted either in October or March—separate roots placed about 9 in. apart in a 2-in.-deep drill; or a clump, for working up a stock of plants, can be put into a trowel-made hole by itself.

Increasing the Stock. Cuttings taken in late June and planted in a shaded spot and kept watered root quickly. They consist of shoot ends 3 in. or 4 in. long, cut through immediately below a joint. The leaves at that joint should be cut off and the stem planted 1 in. deep (Fig. 218).

Also stems about 4 in. long can be eased up from around the outside of a clump, each with its few roots, and be replanted.

A row or bed of "rusty" mint,

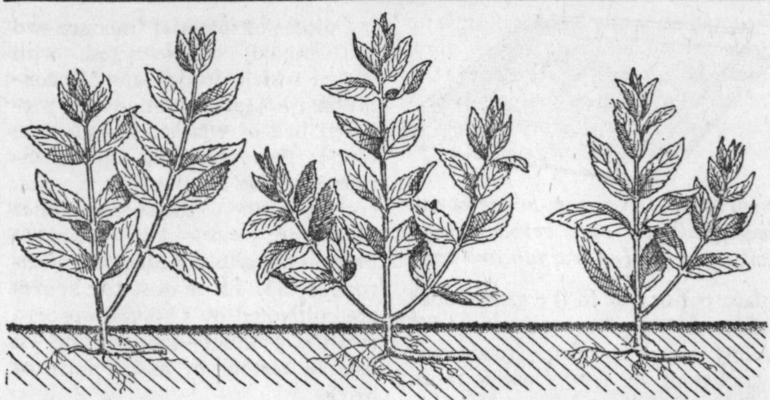

Fig. 219.—*Another method of increasing mint is by division of old root-clumps, separated pieces with roots attached being planted about 9 in. apart*

with stems and leaves that have a rusty appearance, should be scrapped. Plants and roots should be burned and a fresh start made, the new stock of plants being given some other position. The trouble is brought about by neglect and starvation. It seldom occurs if plants are dug up every third year and the best of the roots replanted in another part of the ground.

Replanting. Mint grows so quickly as a rule, especially in a moist summer, that a patch of it soon becomes a miniature jungle; and because the congested roots have exhausted all available food the plants deteriorate. On that account replanting in fresh ground, after the plants have been in occupation about three years, is practised. The tangled roots are dug up, the oldest and woodiest burned and the younger, vigorous ones planted 9 in. apart and covered 2 in. deep, in October or March (Fig. 219). Every piece of creeping root should be extracted from the old quarters, the spade being used deeply.

Watering and Weeding. Give water by the canful as often as the ground dries. Moist conditions will be favourable to the growth of weeds, so these should be looked for and pulled up before they become any size.

Winter Treatment. Take the shears to the old mint bed in late autumn and cut off all the stems close to the ground. Remove them, together with weeds and general rubbish, to the bonfire; then cover the bed or row 1 in. deep with sifted leaf-mould, or with soil mixed with broken-up hop manure. New growth the following spring will be worth having.

Green Mint in Winter. When there is no sign of mint outdoors recourse can be had to the dried and powdered product; but fresh mint is better in every way. To secure winter-green mint lift a clump from the ground in autumn and plant it in a flower pot filled with good soil. Or plant roots closely together in a box just deep enough to hold them with ½ in. of soil below and above (Fig. 220). Water the soil thoroughly, then

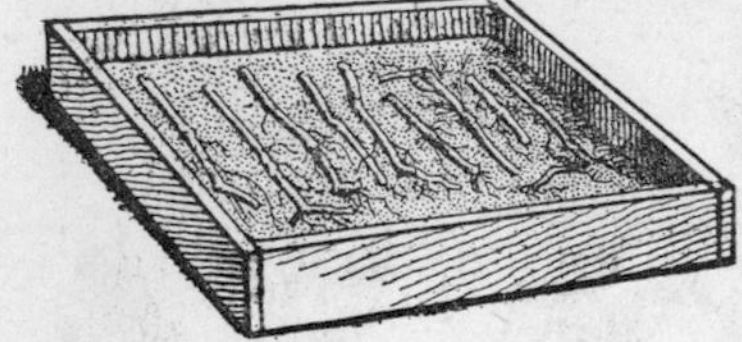

Fig. 220.—*Green mint in winter can be picked from roots boxed in good soil and placed in warmth and light*

place pot or box in the greenhouse where the temperature does not fall below about 55 deg. Inside the window of an always warm room will do. Full light, and moisture as required, will do the rest. Pickings will be produced abundantly.

Storing for Winter. Mint gathered in summer is easily preserved, as explained on page 416.

Gathering Mint. Nip off young shoot-tips, about 4 in. long, with thumb and finger, as required. New shoots will appear lower down on the stems for later use.

Preparing for Table. For making sauce, young stems should be stripped of their leaves (after washing) and the leaves minced finely. Young shoots can be placed whole in the saucepan along with potatoes, peas and so on, after being washed.

MUSHROOM

This delicious fungus, which grows as well in full darkness as in complete light, is equal in food value to such root crops as onion, turnip, carrot. Its requirements are heat and moisture, stable manure and soil. There are several ways of growing mushrooms, and the crop is always worth raising, at all times of the year.

Varieties include Brown and White.

Mushrooms are raised by planting pieces of material (manure and soil mixed) impregnated with spawn which, under suitable conditions, spreads through the prepared bed as whitish threads (the roots); these send up the mushrooms, which are the fruit. Spores, corresponding to the seeds of other plants, are produced in vast numbers on the gills beneath the mushroom's cap. These dust-like spores are cultivated by a special process, and the product—for planting—is sold in cartons or in the form of bricks.

A brick of mushroom spawn is 8 in. or 9 in. long, 5 in. or 6 in. wide and about 2 in. thick, and for planting is broken into about eight pieces. These pieces are inserted 8 in. or 9 in. apart and 2 in. deep in the prepared bed. The contents of a ½-pint carton are sufficient to impregnate 30 to 40 sq. ft. of bed.

Ready for Use. Mushrooms are obtainable all the year round—outdoors during summer and autumn, the rest of the year in a frame, greenhouse, shed or cellar. The first mushrooms appear six to nine weeks after planting in a bed of manure.

When and Where to Plant. Warmth being a prime consideration, mushrooms are raised with least trouble in summer and autumn in the open. Crops to be available in late autumn, winter and spring need the shelter of a frame or building where the temperature by night does not fall below about 55 deg.

Fortunately a bed is not essential, though very desirable, for growing a few mushrooms. The spawn can be planted in a corner of a lawn or in the turf of a meadow or

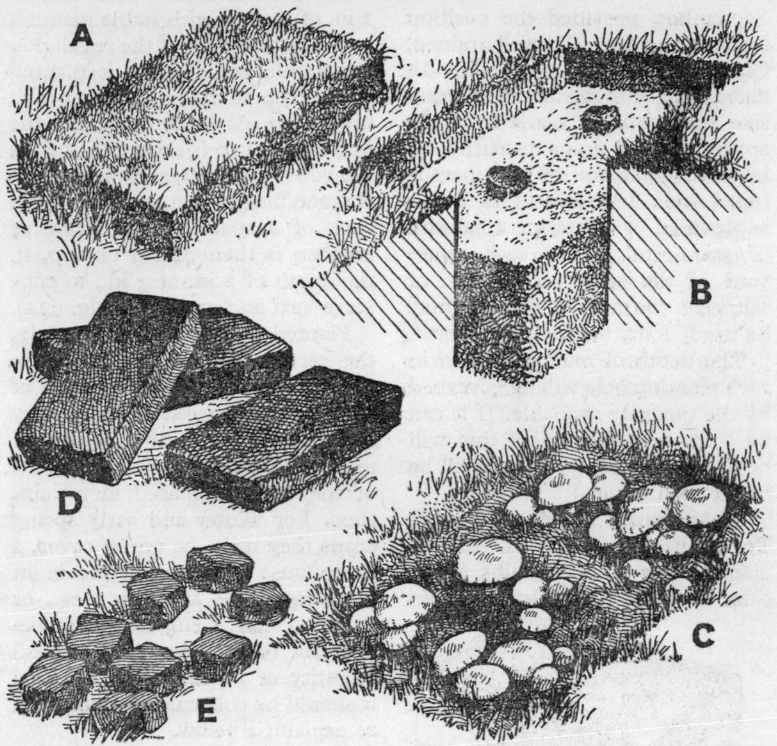

Fig. 221.—*Mushrooms can be grown in a lawn or meadow* (C) *by raising pieces of turf* (A) *and planting portions* (E) *of mushroom spawn bricks* (D) *as at* (B), *then replacing the raised turf and making it quite firm*

orchard, and in large flower pots and boxes and tubs.

Mushrooms in Turf. If a corner of the lawn is used for growing mushrooms it should be wired off to preserve it from trampling feet and the lawn-mower. Planted in orchard or meadow, mushrooms can be left to take their chance. The method of planting consists in raising pieces of the turf, 1 in. thick and of any convenient area—say the width of a spade-blade and 1 ft. long—at intervals of about 3 ft. Soil is taken out, and replaced with more or less fresh stable manure (horse droppings) trodden down firmly. In this a couple of pieces of spawn are planted, a few inches apart, so that these lie just below the surface of the manure.

The spawn is then covered with enough soil to bring the surface of the piece of turf, when this is replaced, level with the surrounding grass. The piece of turf should be firmed back into place by treading or rolling (Fig. 221).

Planted during May or June, mushrooms should make their appearance during August and

September, provided the position is sunny and the soil is well drained. Clay and chalk are unsuitable. In favourable circumstances successive years will be marked by the appearance of crops covering an increasing area, for the root threads travel well. Inducement to do so is provided by scattering a handful of agricultural salt over each square yard of the area, each June; or saltpetre (nitrate of potash) may be used, 1 oz. to the square yard.

The depth of manure placed in each planting hole will be governed by the quantity available. If it can be 9 in. or 10 in. thick this will be ideal; a couple of inches will be better than none.

Mushrooms in Pots, Boxes, Tubs. Flower pots of 10 in. diameter, or boxes or tubs about 9 in. deep, filled firmly to within 1 in. of the top with stable manure, will take the place of the regulation mushroom bed. Spawn is planted 1 in. deep in the manure (which must be made quite firm), and the pot, box or tub is then filled to the top with sifted soil, and this in turn is made firm by patting it with the back of a spade. Clean straw or bracken is then placed on top, to the depth of 2 in. or 3 in., to conserve heat and moisture (Fig. 222).

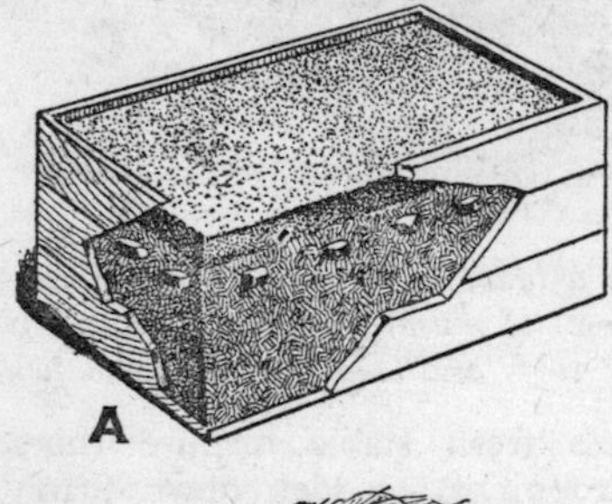

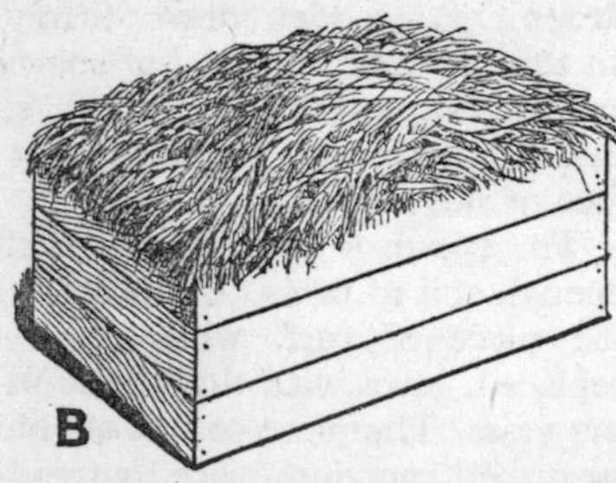

Fig. 222.—*Mushroom spawn can be planted in a box* (A), *the top then being covered thickly* (B) *with clean and dry straw or bracken*

Planted in May, June or July, the receptacles can stand out in the open, in the sun and out of cold winds, covered against heavy rain (when necessary) with old mats, sacks, or something similar; or they can be placed in an airy shed. For winter and early spring crops they must be under cover, a greenhouse with a minimum night temperature of about 55 deg., or a warm cellar, being most suitable.

When more than quite a small quantity of manure is to be used it should be collected and prepared as explained below.

Collecting the Material. If a cartload of fresh stable manure is available at one time this should be spread out under some sort of cover—in an open shed, or in a barn—or corrugated-iron sheets, old linoleum, etc., be used to roof it over. The object of this is to prevent its becoming sodden with rain or snow or being dried by sun or wind during the time the manure is being prepared for planting.

If road droppings have to be collected, a small quantity at a time, these should be stored as above until the desired bulk is secured.

Preparing the Material. The manure is to be forked over at two-day intervals for about a fortnight, if for use during late spring and summer; for about a week in the cold months. The object is to let out rank heat and gases. Long straws should be removed while the manure is being shaken out with the fork; straws less than 1 ft. in length can remain.

Proceedings begin with the piling up of the collected manure. This is then unpiled with the fork two days later, and turned inside out during repiling; that is, the shaken-out manure is piled up again with the material that was at the outside now in the centre. At the next forking the centre will become the outside, and so on until the end of the week or fortnight. By then the manure will have lost its strong odour, and should be just moist enough to bind together when pressed in the hand.

If it is too dry it must be moistened, with tepid water given from a can fitted with a fine rose, the heap being taken down again for this purpose. Water is then sprinkled over each layer as the heap is rebuilt. The manure must not be made so wet that moisture can be squeezed out.

These preparations satisfactorily completed, the manure can be filled into boxes or whatever receptacles are to be used; or packed into a frame; or made up into an outdoor or an indoor bed.

Adding Leaves to Manure. To make the prepared material go farther, slightly moist (not sodden) tree leaves can be added, the best for the purpose being beech or oak, the addition being made just before a bed is to be built up or a frame or box filled. Leaves may be mixed with the manure to the extent of about one-third of the latter's bulk.

Mushrooms in a Frame. A hotbed frame (*see* page 65) occupied in summer by a cucumber or melon plant will produce a few mushrooms at the same time if spawn is planted in the bed, here and there, near to the ends and sides, round about July. Spawn can also be planted in the area of manure outside the frame, covered with 2 in. of sifted soil and then a few inches of dry bracken or straw.

An ordinary cold frame (not placed on heating material) to be pressed into service for mushroom growing should have prepared manure (plus leaves if necessary) firmed into it, to receive the spawn. The material needs to be shaken out with the fork into the frame, in level layers, each layer being trodden down before the next goes in. Firming should be given special attention along the sides and ends. If the material is left loose, great heat will be generated and as quickly dissipated. After the final treading the material should be about 1 ft. deep—a few inches deeper if possible, especially if a winter or spring crop is aimed at. The spawn should not be planted until the temperature of the made-up material has been tested and found to be suitable (Fig. 223).

Taking the Temperature. It is important that the temperature of the bed should not be too high when the spawn is planted. For three or four days after making up, the heat will increase. When it is on the down grade—has fallen to about 80 deg.—is the time to insert the spawn.

Temperature can be taken with a thermometer pushed about 8 in. into the bed. Or it can be tested by plunging a stake into the manure, leaving it there a few hours, then withdrawing it and grasping the hot lower end. If it is too hot for the bare hand to continue gripping, spawning must be delayed until further daily tests proclaim the temperature to be on the decline. A temperature as low as about 50 degrees will do, but mushrooms will be longer in making an appearance.

Planting the Frame Bed. Holes are made in the manure, about 2 in. deep and 9 in. apart each way, and in each spawn is planted. Manure is replaced over the spawn, then the whole surface is covered with sifted soil, this to be 2 in. deep after being patted down with the flat of the spade.

Chalky, clayey or dusty soil is useless for the purpose. It must be good, fertile soil, free from stones and bits of rubbish, and just moist enough to ball up when a handful is compressed.

Those operations completed, the frame light is shut right down, to maintain a close and moist atmosphere, and covered over with sacking, matting, or straw or bracken to keep the heat inside the frame.

Outdoor Mushroom Bed. Backed by a fence or wall facing the south, with some shelter against winds from the north and east, an outdoor mushroom bed is ideally situated (Fig. 224). It can be of any dimensions, of course, but the depth should be not less than about 14 in. The bed to produce winter or early spring crops would be better if 2 ft. deep when firmed down. Usually the beds are about 2½ ft. wide, with either flat or sloping top. The object of the sloping top is to shoot off heavy rains or prevent snow (in winter) remaining long in position. The slope may be from the back down to the front; or back and front may slope, with a flat ridge about 6 in. wide.

The outdoor bed is made up in a similar manner to a frame bed, and when its temperature is satisfactory (as previously explained) spawn is inserted in the manure 2 in. deep and at intervals of 9 in., the surface then covered with 2 in. of sifted soil beaten firm, and a

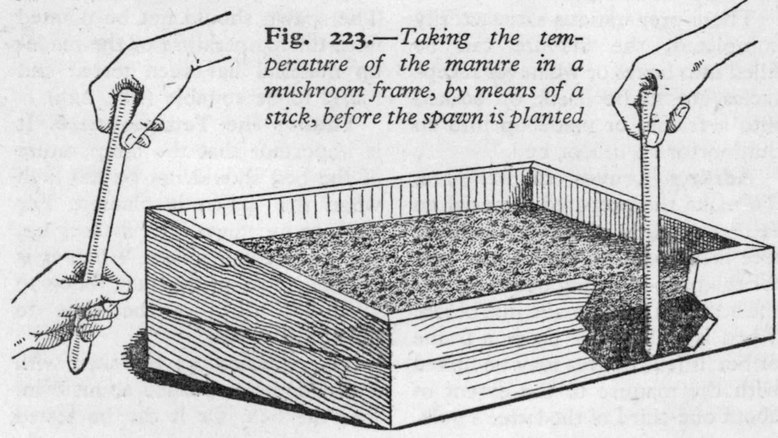

Fig. 223.—*Taking the temperature of the manure in a mushroom frame, by means of a stick, before the spawn is planted*

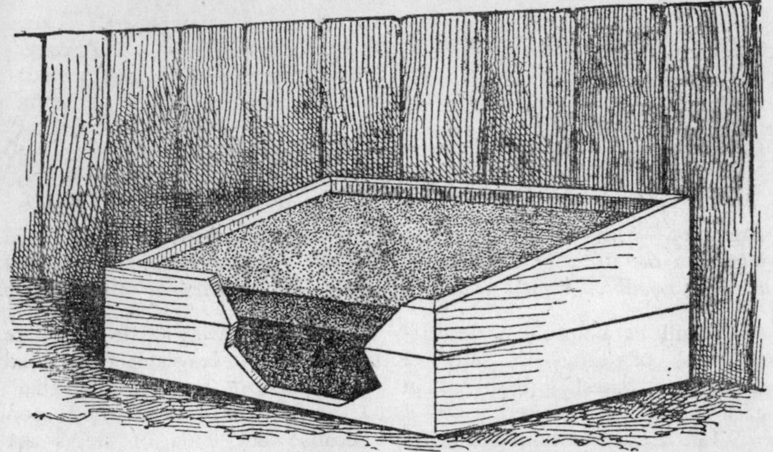

Fig. 224.—*A mushroom frame, or an outdoor bed, is ideally situated if backed by a fence (or wall) facing the south. The front of the frame is cut away to show firmed soil on top of manure in which spawn is inserted*

covering of straw or bracken put on to the depth of 1 ft. or so. Pieces of board should be placed on top to keep this covering material in place, with the addition of sacking, old lengths of linoleum or anything similar as winter protection.

The soil over the manure is put on from the bottom upwards if the bed has a sloping top, in 2-in.-thick layers 4 in. or 5 in. deep. There is then no difficulty in getting the soil to stay put.

Indoor Mushroom Bed. In making up a bed in cellar or greenhouse for a winter crop the aim should be a minimum depth of 9 in. of prepared manure, with an extra 3 in. or 4 in. if leaves are mixed in. The bed that is 2 ft. thick will naturally give earlier mushrooms and the supply will be more prolonged. The cellar or greenhouse should have a night temperature in winter of about 55 degrees. During summer the bed could be located in a draught-free shed—cold draughts being one of the things to avoid.

A convenient position for bed, pots, tubs or boxes in the greenhouse is under the staging, but precautions need to be taken against water given to pot plants on the staging dripping down on to the bed, etc. Dry heat is as bad as cold draughts. The necessary moist atmosphere can be maintained by syringeing walls and floors with tepid water whenever the air begins to smell dry.

Watering, Feeding. Not until the first mushrooms appear is it necessary, as a rule, to give any water. The soil covering should be watched, and occasionally tested by a poked-in finger. If the finger, inserted full length, registers a moist condition, the watering-can will remain idle. When the soil feels dry, or dryish, give water with the chill taken off. Whilst mushrooms are being produced, an occasional

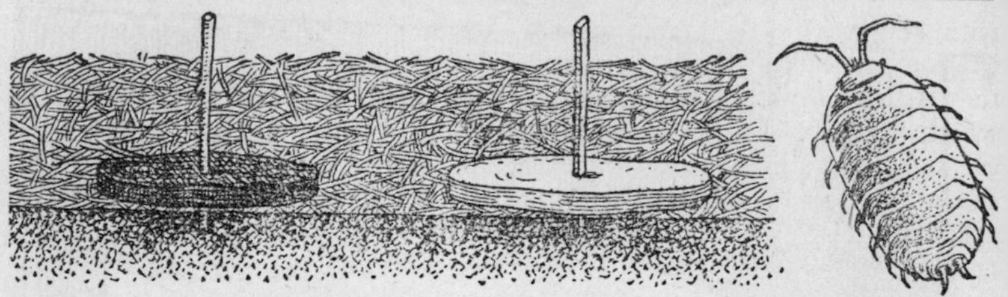

Fig. 225.—*Slices of carrot or potato skewered on stick for handle and buried in the straw or bracken covering the mushroom bed serve as bait to trap woodlice (right), which are sometimes troublesome to this crop*

tonic will be helpful—a dessert-spoonful of salt, or saltpetre (nitrate of potash), dissolved in each gallon of water used.

While those attentions are being given the straw or bracken covering will need to be temporarily removed.

Woodlice and Maggots. Quarter-inch-thick slices of carrot or potato (Fig. 225) placed here and there under the straw or bracken covering will serve as traps for woodlice, which sometimes abound and do their best to spoil a good crop. This bait should be examined every day, and the woodlice found below collected and disposed of. Maggots of a small fly are occasionally troublesome. These grubs burrow into the mushrooms and render them worthless—unless one can stomach cooked maggot. This is a hot-weather nuisance, and unfortunately nothing can be done about it.

Gathering the Mushrooms. To get at the crop, when it begins to appear, the straw or bracken covering has to be removed, then replaced. This needs to be done carefully, or some of the crop may be damaged. The method of gathering does not involve a knife. Each mushroom is gripped by the stalk, which is twisted and pulled so that it comes away at the base. The small hole it leaves is then filled with a little of the surrounding soil. Use of the knife is frowned upon because cut ends of stems are likely to decay, and that leads to considerable trouble.

Clusters of mushrooms will continue to appear for two, three, perhaps four months, according to circumstances. The material of the bed then serves another purpose. It is grand for digging into the vegetable ground and for making soil mixtures for filling seed pots and boxes, and for pricking out seedlings and for potting.

Preparing for Table. Cut off lower part of stalks and skin the top of the caps before frying, baking, stewing, pickling or making into ketchup.

Method of drying mushrooms for storing is described on page 416.

As a food the mushroom ranks with carrot, turnip, onion, beetroot, and can take the place of those vegetables in the diet of diabetics.

MUSTARD

This famous salad companion of cress (Fig. 226) should be sown about four days later than cress if the two are to be used together, its period of germination being that much less, otherwise they are dealt with similarly. The white variety (pale yellow seeds) is more favoured than the brown (brown seeds) which is very pungent. The seeds are also used for making the condiment mustard. Full cultural and other details are given under Cress (page 277).

ONION

An onion crop depends on the attention and care given to it to a greater extent than most other vegetables. The roots will go down 2 ft. or more if given the chance, and with something good to live on will produce bulbs of first-rate quality—for current requirements straight from the ground in spring, summer and early autumn, for the rest of the year from store.

Crops are obtained by (*a*) sowing outdoors in spring and autumn, (*b*) sowing under glass during January to February for later planting out, (*c*) planting purchased seedlings during March to April, (*d*) planting onion sets during February to March.

Varieties are numerous, most seedsmen including in their lists their own specialties. The following are some of the most dependable:—

Good keepers, noted for their storing qualities: White Spanish, Rousham Park Hero, James's Long Keeping, Bedfordshire Champion, A1, Selected Brown Globe, Improved Reading, Ailsa Craig, all suitable for spring or autumn sowing; Autumn Queen, Giant Zittau, specially for autumn sowing.

For pickling: Small Paris Silverskin, Improved Queen, White Queen, Covent Garden Pearl.

Spring onions—for pulling green for salad purposes—are of no particular variety, though one of the

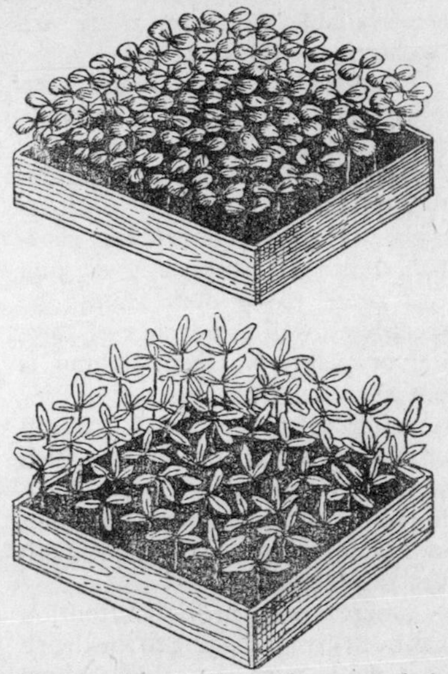

Fig. 226.—*A box of mustard is shown above, a box of cress below. The seedlings stand much more thickly, of course, than shown here. They have been spaced for the sake of clearness. Thick sowing is needed.*

most suitable is White Lisbon, sown outdoors in August. The thinnings of any variety can be used in this way.

About 2,000 plants are contained in 1 oz. of seed. Average germination period is about eight days.

Ready for Use. A crop sown outdoors in August is ripe and ready for storing the following late July or early August. Sown outdoors or under glass in early spring the crop is ripe for harvesting in August or September of the same year. Onions can, of course, be pulled for use before those dates; the crops reach maturity during those months. Sets, and purchased seedlings, ripen their crops during the current summer. Spring onions are available whenever there are seedlings to thin out.

From the open ground and from store onions can therefore be available all the year round.

Soil Preparation. In addition to rich soil and a sunny position a prime requirement is a firm root-run. For that reason any digging that needs to be done should be completed well in advance of sowing or planting. Deep digging is not essential if onions can follow on after celery or carrot, parsnip or peas, or beans or cabbage, which were provided for by a deep working of the soil and a certain amount of manuring, or enrichment with vegetable refuse.

Where no such previous attention has been given, digging to the depth of 2 ft. is very advisable, animal manure, or hop manure or decayed greenstuff being worked in deeply. If manure is used it should come no nearer to the surface than 6 in.

Ground that is stony, chalky, heavy and wet, or shallow, will have to be dealt with as explained in the section ALL SORTS OF SOILS (page 31).

Final preparations before sowing or planting consist in treading or rolling the ground quite firm (when not wet) if there is a suspicion of sponginess or looseness under foot, and forking or raking the surface so that this is left as powdery as possible (Fig. 227). During this forking or raking plenty of wood ash and soot should be worked in, or 1½ oz. sulphate of potash per square yard.

When and How to Sow Outdoors. The early spring sowing is largely dependent on weather and soil conditions; the seed should be got in if possible at the end of

Fig. 227.—*An onion bed should be rolled if the soil does not feel firm underfoot, then raked finely in preparation for sowing or planting*

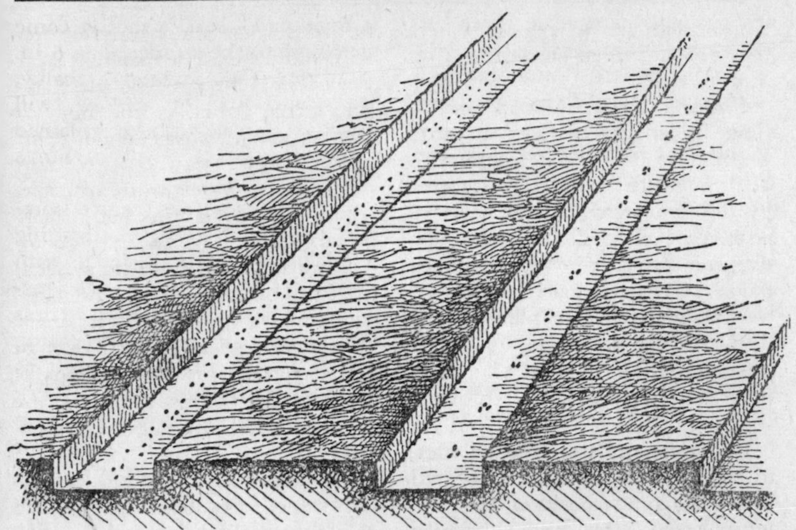

Fig. 228.—*Economy in seed and labour is secured if onion seed is sown in small groups in a drill (right) rather than continuously (left)*

February or early in March. The autumn sowing is carried out about mid-August, where the climate is suitable; in cold districts it is rarely successful and reliance has to be placed on an early-year sowing outdoors or under glass. August-sown onions have it in their favour that they usually escape the attention of the devastating onion fly.

Drills are made about ¾ in. deep and 1 ft. apart, and the seed is sown as thinly as possible, either continuously (this providing thinnings for use as spring onions) or three or four seeds are dropped together at intervals of 4 in. or 6 in.—the latter where larger bulbs are required (Fig. 228).

In the case of the spring sowing, a very little seed can be made to go a very long way if instead of being sown in the row it is sown in a pot or box and the seedlings dealt with as explained later.

Thinning Out. Spring-sown onions dribbled as a continuous line in the drill are thinned out as soon as they can be handled separately, so that they stand about ½ in. apart; a fiddling job but productive of profitable results. For at the next and subsequent thinnings out, withdrawn seedlings are usable as green spring onions. The final thinning leaves bulbs at either 4 in. or 6 in. apart.

Where the grouping system is adopted, one plant only is to be left where the three or four seeds were sown.

Autumn-sown onions remain unthinned (unless very crowded, the result of hurried and wasteful sowing) until the following March. Seedlings are then pulled out, as green spring onions, and others are trowelled up, with all their long roots, for transplanting to another row if this is required.

Those that are to remain where they are and ripen are left at 4 in. or 6 in. apart.

Sowing Under Glass. Seed is sown in January to February in a greenhouse or hotbed frame with a temperature of about 55 degrees by (*a*) those who, wisely, wish to economize in seed, (*b*) those who live in a district where the ruinous onion fly is particularly prevalent, the seedlings when planted out being too far advanced for attack by that pest, (*c*) those who want to grow big onions of exhibition standard.

Requirements can also be met, to some extent, with an unheated frame in a sunny position, the seed being sown after mid-February; though naturally these plants are later than those raised in heat.

A shallow box, or a pot, is filled with two-thirds good soil, one-third sifted leaf-mould, plus a sprinkling of sharp grit or sifted sand. Seed is sown thinly on the firmed surface and barely covered with sifted soil. The resultant seedlings, kept close to the glass, are transferred when 3 in. high to another box (or boxes), about 1½ in. apart. They are then gradually hardened off by exposure to cooler conditions for planting out in April or early May (Fig. 229).

Planting Out Seedlings. Seedlings can be set out in the prepared rows, which are to be 1 ft. apart, at intervals of 4 in. or 6 in.; or 2 in. apart to provide pullings of green spring onions, those that are to ripen being left at 4-in. or 6-in. intervals.

Growers who aim at big, exhibition standard bulbs in the 3-lb. to 4-lb. class allow 15 in. between rows and 14 in. between plants.

In any case it is desirable that a hole should be made for each young plant with a trowel, deep enough to take the roots full length, without

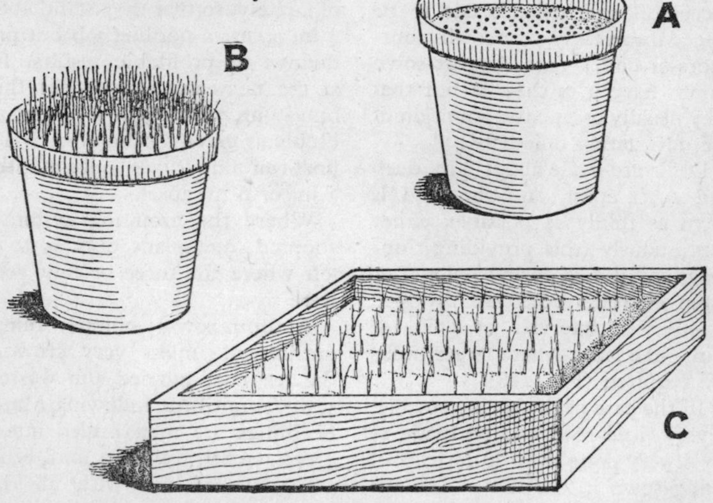

Fig. 229.—*Onion seed sown under glass in a small pot* (A). *The seedlings* (B) *are transferred to a box* (C) *for later planting out, after hardening off*

bending or folding. When the hole is filled in and the roots covered the merest portion only of the bulb end should be below the surface. If it can be managed, no part of the bulb end should be covered (Fig. 230).

The tops will fall over at first. If the tops drag on the ground and worms pull them in the tips can be snipped off; this will prevent the root-hold being loosened.

Even if the ground is moist at the time it will help the young plants if they are watered in at once.

Seedlings for planting out in March to April can be purchased from nurserymen; they should show no signs of yellow in the leaves and should have plenty of long root.

Onions for Pickling. The varieties specially suitable for this purpose (page 323) should be sown very thinly in drills 7 in. apart, in early April, and the ground need not be specially manured for them. The seedlings are not thinned out, as the bulbs are intended to reach only useful pickling size.

The variety Sutton's Improved Queen is a silver-skinned variety claimed to be the quickest-growing onion in cultivation, a March to April sowing producing an early summer crop of bulbs from 1 in. to 2 in. in diameter. It can also be sown in July, for a later crop in the same year. In addition to its qualifications for the pickle jar its delicate flavour makes it acceptable in summer salads.

Another excellent miniature onion is the pure white Pearl Pickler with a very mild flavour.

If there is no room for a pickling-onion sowing, small bulbs suitable for the purpose can be selected from the main crop when this is lifted.

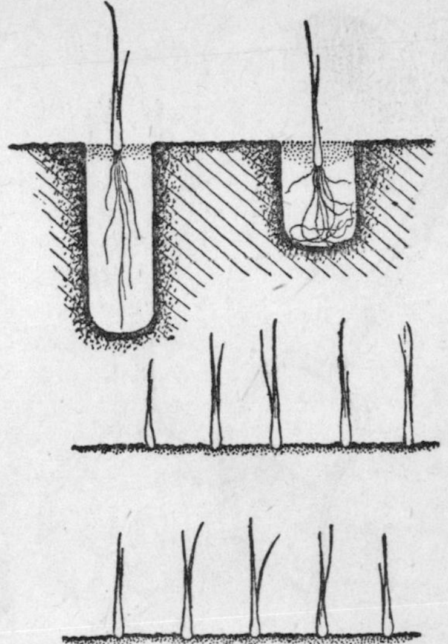

Fig. 230.—*Onion seedlings should be planted as on left (at top), as shallowly as possible, not as shown on right. They should stand about 4 in. apart in rows 1 ft. apart (below)*

Planting Onion Sets. Small bulbs up to the size of a hedge-nut are sold as onion sets, by the pound, for planting out in February to March. These are specially raised for the purpose. They grow rapidly and are generally immune to attack by the onion fly. Rich and firm soil, with a crumbled surface, is necessary. The small bulbs are planted 6 in. apart in rows separated by the same distance, with only half their depth covered. If the soil is very light, however, and wind disturbs them, the bulbs may be completely covered. In the latter case soil should be drawn away with the hoe when the plants are growing strongly so that each bulb is well exposed and freely expanding.

Fig. 231.—*Onions swell and ripen more easily if soil is carefully scraped from the bulbs with the Dutch hoe*

Watering, Weeding, Feeding. Whatever water can be spared will be put to good use if applied to the onion rows. Weeding close up to and around the bulbs should be done by hand. Apart from possible injury to them due to the use of a hoe, deep disturbance of the soil must be avoided. A scattering of dried poultry manure between the rows, followed by a good watering, may be given once a week, or 1 oz. of superphosphate of lime per yard run, or dried blood given in liquid form—a tablespoonful of the powder to each 2 gal. of water.

Feeding can start as soon as the plants are growing strongly. It should cease at the end of July, or keeping qualities may be impaired.

Running to Seed. A good strong onion plant in flower is a rather imposing sight. But it means a wasted bulb—unless this is specially intended to produce seed. As soon as a thick, circular, central stem is seen to be rising, nip it right out. The bulb that produced this flower stem should be used as soon as large enough.

Thick-necked Onions. Tops sometimes come bull-necked, especially when the summer is a wet one, the foliage at the base being nearly as thick as the bulb. To check this coarse growth the tops should be bent over forcibly as low down as possible. Such bulbs are of no use for storing and should be pulled for use as soon as possible.

Onion Fly and Other Troubles. For these see the chart Remedies Against Enemies of Vegetable Crops (page 407).

Harvesting the Crop. To assist ripening of the bulbs, soil should be scraped away from around them with the Dutch hoe (the blade turned over) so that they sit on the surface with only the roots covered (Fig. 231). When the tops show signs of browning—in late July or August where sown the previous autumn, in August or early September where spring sown—ripening is hastened by bending all the tops over so that they lie flat. This is done quickly with the handle of rake or hoe held horizontally low down across the rows and moved along (Fig. 232). Tops that bob up again should be firmly dealt with. Necks thus bent at right-angles, the upward flow of sap ceases and a few days later lifting can start.

If quite ready for gathering, bulbs should come out of the ground with very little resistance, showing withered roots. The presence of

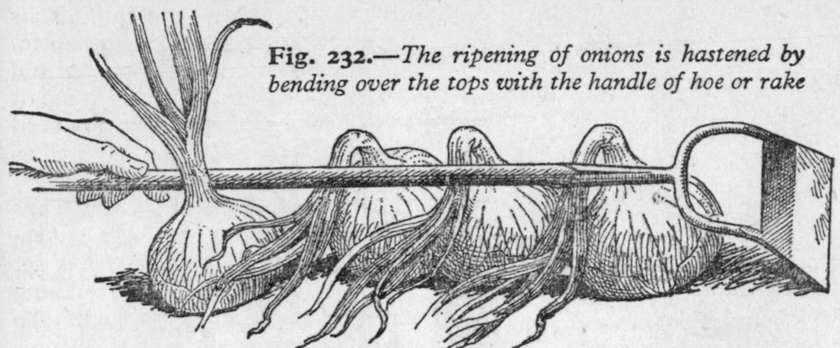

Fig. 232.—*The ripening of onions is hastened by bending over the tops with the handle of hoe or rake*

obviously new (white) roots among the old and withered ones indicates that growth is about to start again. This renewed growth must not be allowed. The plants should be lifted as soon as possible and the bulbs dried off by exposure to sun—or to a free current of air under cover if rainy conditions prevail.

The quickest way to get the ripened bulbs up is to loosen the soil alongside the row with the fork, grasp the tops and pull. They are then laid out (Fig. 233) on the ground, if this is dry, or on a hard path, or on the top of a shed, for sun and wind to dry them off thoroughly—with some sort of covering by night in case of rain. If the weather is too bad for that they must be dried off under cover.

Storing for Winter. Not until they are perfectly dry should the bulbs be placed in store—on shelves or a dry floor, not more than two or three deep, where they can be looked over occasionally. Bruised onions should not be stored, and any that later show signs of decay should be removed at once. It is not conducive to good keeping to store onions in a pile or sack or deep box.

If neither shelf nor floor space is available in shed, cellar or attic, a convenient way of disposing of them is to tie them with string by the necks to 3-ft. stakes (starting from the bottom) so that each stake is covered from top to bottom with a single-layer band of onions. These can then be hung on a wall or from a roof beam, and the onions pulled from a stake as required (Fig. 234).

Preparing for Table. Remove outer skins of bulbs and cut off the tops and any remaining roots. The method of pickling onions is explained in the section Easy

Fig. 233.—*Lifted onions laid out on dry ground* (*or a hard path*) *in the sun, to dry off before storing*

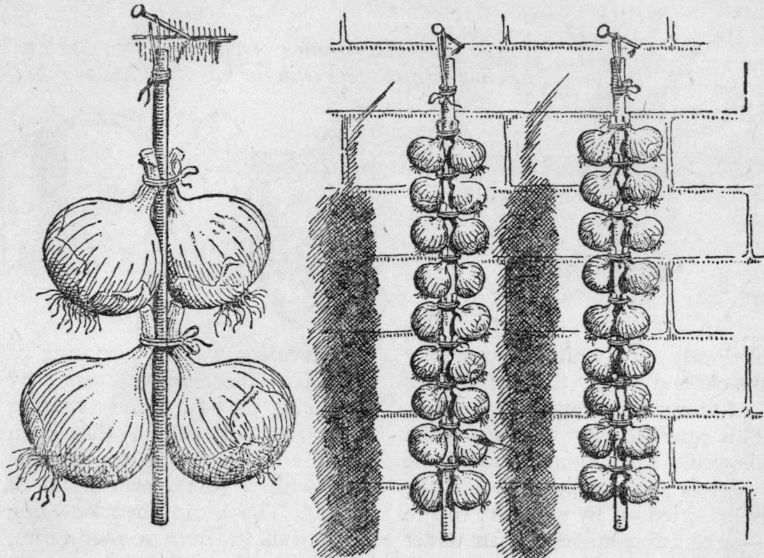

Fig. 234.—*A convenient way of storing onions is to tie them to stakes*

HOME PRESERVATION OF VEGETABLES (page 412). Green spring onions should have the outer skin stripped off, roots cut off, and the tops tipped back beyond any discoloration or injury. Appetizing and easily digested, onions have considerable nutritive value. There is more actual nourishment in mild onions than there is in those of a stronger flavour.

Onion, Potato or Underground. The potato or underground onion is of less interest to the home food producer than to the botanist. Small bulbs for planting in February to March are sometimes obtainable (sold by the pound) and their culture is the same as that of the shallot, described in detail on page 377.

PARSLEY

For flavouring and garnishing, for making sauce to go with boiled broad beans, cod, or other fish, parsley wins a place in every well-ordered vegetable patch. Give it moisture in spring and summer and a moderately good root run, and sprigs may be picked from it the year round.

Varieties include Double Curled, Giant Curled, Moss Curled, Hardy Winter Matchless.

From 1 oz. of seed about 2,000 plants could be raised. Seedlings are not, as a rule, in any great hurry to appear; time taken is from three to eight weeks.

Ready for Use. Sprigs are available for picking in summer from a spring sowing. A round-the-year supply is simple to maintain, with or without the assistance of the dried product.

Soil Preparation. The dwarf habit of parsley makes it an ideal edging to a border in the home garden. In the allotment it can be fitted in as a short row, or series of short rows, wherever there happens to be room for it and where it can remain undisturbed. In very light and quick-to-dry-out soil a little shade in summer will help it; which does not mean it will thrive under a tree or hedge or jammed close to a fence. In more substantial soil it can be in full sun. It appreciates leaf-mould below, and water when the ground dries.

If the soil is very heavy and inclined to lie wet in spring and winter it should be broken up 1 ft. deep and plenty of sand, road grit, or crushed mortar rubble or brick mixed with it.

As a finishing touch, before the seed is sown, rake in superphosphate of lime—2 oz. for 9 ft. of row.

When and How to Sow. Any time from March to July seed can be sown. A summer supply is secured by sowing in March or April, and if strong young plants are wanted for winter and spring seed can be sown in June or July.

Plants remain profitable for two years, when they run to seed (Fig. 235). If a small sowing is made every year there is no hold-up in supplies. Seed is sown in ½-in.-deep drills where the plants are to remain.

Parsley seed is capricious in its germination, sometimes coming up in three weeks, at other times taking as long as eight weeks. It can be speeded up by keeping the sown drill moist and by covering this with pieces of glass laid flat on small stones so that they are raised about 1 in.; the glass to be removed when the seedlings are visible.

The plants are to stand finally at 6 in. apart. If the thinnings are lifted with a trowel, complete with roots, when the ground is moist, they can be planted to extend the row or form another one. If watered in at once there will be no check to growth.

Fig. 235.—*When parsley runs up to flower the stem should be removed at the base to prevent seeding*

Watering and Weeding. In a hot summer even young parsley is apt to run to seed for lack of sufficient moisture. An occasional bucketful of water will prevent this and encourage vigorous, dense growth. As a rule weeds are not troublesome, these being choked at an early stage by the parsley's own spreading foliage. But they should be looked for, and removed, during the parsley's seedling stage.

Picking the Sprigs. Whatever pickings are required at any one time should be taken not from one single plant but from several.

If flower stems appear, these should be removed at the base. Unless picking is done constantly a plant here and there may become overgrown and the foliage will be coarse. In this case the tops should be cut back; a fresh crop of young, neat growth will result.

Winter Treatment. In some soils and localities there is no difficulty whatever in carrying parsley through the winter, no protection of any kind being needed. But where the ground is heavy and wet it is advisable to lift a few plants and winter them in good soil in a frame, or in pots in a greenhouse, so that picking may continue through winter and early spring.

Dried Parsley. The method of drying parsley is described in the section EASY HOME PRESERVATION OF VEGETABLES (page 412).

Preparing for Table. Remove stalks from the sprigs, wash, and dry by shaking in a cloth.

PARSNIP

One of the most important of winter vegetables, the parsnip gives a heavy yield in return for a sunny position in well-dug ground. The fat, tasty root likes to go to a good depth, but excellent crops can be got from shallow soil if the right varieties are chosen.

Where there is not much depth of good soil the most suitable kinds are Turnip-rooted (small, round roots) and Intermediate (midway between the round and the long-rooted varieties). Where there is a good depth, sow the long-rooted Tender and True, Hollow Crown, Student, Maltese, Jersey Marrow.

¼ oz. of seed is sufficient to sow about 75 ft. of row. Seedlings appear in from four to six weeks.

Roots are ready for lifting (as required) in November and are available until March.

Soil Preparation. If a row can be located where onions, leeks, celery, beans or peas did well as the immediately previous crop (thanks to deep digging and generous treatment) the parsnip is well provided for. Otherwise the piece of ground should be dug 18 in. deep (if the subsoil is of such a nature as to allow this) and enriched with really old manure or well-decayed leaves and other green-stuff placed mostly below the top 9 in.

Where the subsoil is chalk, clay, gravel or other obstinate material, dig to whatever depth is possible and sow the varieties previously named as best for this type of ground.

A generous dressing of wood ash, or 1½ oz. sulphate of potash to the square yard, forked or raked into the surface a few days before sowing, is advisable in all cases.

When and How to Sow. Because of slow germination, and slow early growth of the seedlings when up, seed needs to be sown as early in the year as possible; if not in February, then in March. But the weather must be waited on, and the soil be in such a condition that by vigorous forking or raking the surface can be broken down as crumbly as can be; for the seed requires to be covered with fine soil. Wood ash worked plentifully into the top, and a good drying wind, will help bring it into suitable condition.

Inch-deep drills 15 in. apart are made with the hoe, where the plants are to remain, and distribution therein of the confetti-like

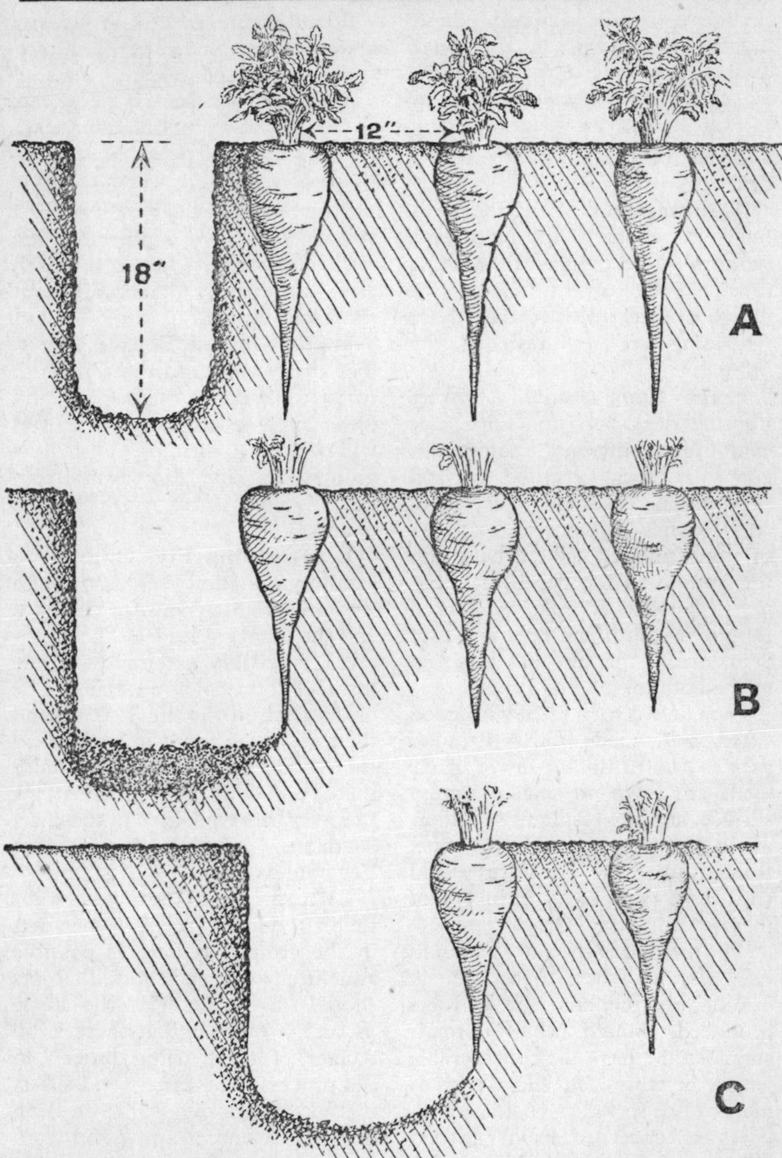

Fig. 236.—*Even the biggest roots of parsnip can be lifted without breaking if a start is made by digging a hole* (A), *then drawing the soil away from the first root* (B), *which is then withdrawn. Soil removed from the side of parsnip number two* (C) *is then used to fill up the first hole, and so on*

seed calls for a calm day; a wind may blow most of it away before it can touch the drill bottom. Five or six seeds are dropped together, to form groups, at 12-in. intervals, and the soil pushed back into the drill above them.

Thinning Out. When the seedlings are about 2 in. high each group is to be reduced to a single plant. The surplus should be drawn out carefully so that those remaining are left firm in the ground.

Extra Long Roots. Growers wanting very long parsnips, for exhibition purposes, sometimes adopt a special method of soil preparation. Holes are made, 15 in. apart each way, with an iron bar or stout, pointed stake driven into the ground to the depth of about 3 ft. The bar or stake is worked to and fro until the hole is about 8 in. across the top and tapering to the bottom.

Each hole is then filled with good sifted soil, made fairly firm to within 1 in. of the top. Five or six seeds are sown on each prepared surface, and the resultant seedlings of each group thinned to one. Roots thus have an unrestricted run down with every inducement to swell.

The method is specially useful in hard clay, or where there is chalk or other obstructions. But the roots produced, though usually broad-shouldered, have a considerable length of whip-lash end which is mere waste so far as cooking purposes are concerned. From the food view-point, medium-sized parsnips are the best.

Hoeing and Feeding. Regular hoeing along both sides of a row not only keeps down weeds but maintains a crumbled surface which, by preventing undue evaporation of moisture from the ground, reduces the need for watering in very dry weather. During the hoeing the roots will be helped to increase their bulk if superphosphate is worked in, 1 oz. per yard run of row. Two applications are sufficient—the first about a month after thinning out, the second about six weeks later.

Badly Shaped, Forked Roots. Too many stones in the soil cause roots to become misshapen, and lower ends of long-rooted varieties will fork and turn up in shallow ground. Forking also results from the digging in of fresh animal manure.

Leaf-mining Fly. Grubs of a small fly sometimes tunnel through the inner tissue (between the back and the front) of leaves. Their progress is visible externally in the form of light-coloured trails. The grubs feed on the inner tissue and their activities result in undersized roots. Methods of dealing with these, and with grubs that attack the roots, are explained in the chart Remedies Against Enemies of Vegetable Crops (page 408).

Lifting the Roots. Parsnips retain their full flavour when left in the ground as long as possible and lifted only as required. Roots should be got up with the spade in such a manner that there is no danger of these being broken in the process. The easiest and surest method is to dig an 18-in-deep hole at one end of a row and work the soil away from the first root until this is exposed full depth. It can then be loosened and, gripped by the crown or shoulder, drawn out. Subsequent roots are got at by working the soil back into the hole or small trench thus left by removal of the root that was last extracted (Fig. 236).

Storing for Winter. Roots can be left in the ground until February, when growth starts again. At first sign of that happening the remainder should be lifted and put into store. Meanwhile, when frost threatens to set the ground too hard for roots to be dug up for current use, a layer of bracken or straw scattered over the undug row will prevent them from being frozen in.

Alternatively, roots may be lifted in bulk, after November, and stored. This is always advisable if the ground lies wet in winter. Lifted, the top growth is cut off and the roots are allowed a day or two to dry (under cover, if necessary). They are then stacked in a heap in a cellar or dry shed; with a sack or old bits of carpet thrown over them if the shed is not too weatherproof. They should not be shot out of a wheelbarrow, but stacked neatly, to conserve space and prevent injury. The best way is to pack them head to tail (Fig. 237).

If under-cover storage space cannot be provided parsnips are safe enough outdoors clamped as described under beet (page 252).

Preparing for Table. Wash the roots, cut off a thin layer of the top (or crown) and cut out the hard central part there. Divide down the centre, or roots may be quartered if more convenient, for cooking. Apart from its nutritive value, parsnip aids digestion of other cooked foods with which it is mixed and is specially valuable in the kitchen on that account.

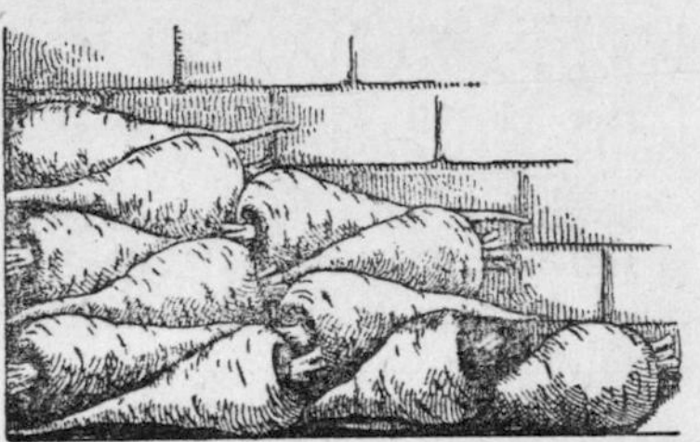

Fig. 237.—*Tops removed, the parsnips roots are stored head to tail in a heap in a corner of a shed or cellar*

PEA

If peas were valueless as food they would still be grown for the immense gastronomic pleasure of eating them. Fortunately their food value is very high. The plant's chief requirements are moisture, a good depth of soil, and plenty of well-buried material for the deep-probing roots to get hold of.

Varieties are numerous in the seedsmen's catalogues. Those named here (with approximate height) are among the most useful.

For earliest picking—late May and early June: English Wonder ($1\frac{1}{2}$ ft.), Peter Pan ($1\frac{1}{2}$ ft.), Kelvedon Wonder ($1\frac{1}{2}$ ft.), Pioneer (2 ft.), Hundredfold (2 ft.), Little Marvel (2 ft.), Market Gem (2 ft.), Thomas Laxton (3 ft.), Gradus (3 ft. to 4 ft.), Early Giant (3 ft. to 4 ft.).

Second early—first pickings ready a week or fortnight after the preceding: Rentpayer ($2\frac{1}{2}$ ft.), Admiral Beatty ($3\frac{1}{2}$ ft.), Evergreen (4 ft.), Duke of Albany (5 ft.).

Main crop—available a week or fortnight later than the second earlies: Fillbasket (3 ft.), Senator (3 ft.), Lord Chancellor (3 ft.), Alderman (5 ft.).

For the latest crop—a week or fortnight after the first main crop pickings: Veitch's Perfection (3 ft.), Veitch's Autocrat (3 ft. to 4 ft.), Latest of All (3 ft. to 4 ft.), Continuity (4 ft.).

Sown 2 in. apart, ½ pint of seed is sufficient for two 30-ft. double rows. Average germination time is about twelve days.

Ready for Use. First pods are plump enough for gathering from eleven to sixteen weeks after date of sowing, according to variety. Those listed for earliest picking come into bearing eleven to twelve weeks after the seed is sown; second earliest, about twelve to thirteen weeks; main crop, thirteen to fourteen weeks; latest crop, fourteen to sixteen weeks. Those periods are only approximate, much depending on soil, situation, and weather conditions.

A regular supply is maintained by successive sowings. Shelled peas can also be dried and stored for winter use.

Soil Preparation. If the ground has not been deeply dug and enriched and there is not time so to deal with it before sowing time arrives, each row should be provided for separately by taking out an 18-in.-deep trench at least 1 ft. wide and treading into the bottom of it rotted leaves or other decayed greenstuff, this to be about 4 in. thick when firmed. If animal or hop manure can be mixed with it the yield of plump pods will be greater.

Enough of the excavated soil is then returned to the trench, and stamped down, to bring the surface to within 6 in. of the general level. When the sown peas are covered in 3 in. to 4 in. of space will remain at the top which will serve to receive water later on.

In the case of dwarf varieties that will leave only a few inches of ground between rows untouched; for the little extra labour involved the whole breadth would be better deeply dug and enriched. It is worth bearing in mind that this generous preparation is not only for the benefit of the peas. The crop that will follow when the peas have yielded the last picking and been cleared away will also benefit considerably by the extra depth of good soil.

Where taller varieties are concerned greater space must be left between rows, and here the trench system is more justified. The method of preparing the trenches is explained in the next paragraphs (Fig. 238).

Trenches for Peas. Operations begin by pegging down the garden line to secure a straight row. The top 9 in. of soil is then dug out, from one end of the row to the other, to the width of 1 ft. or 18 in., and placed all on one side. The lower 9 in. comes out next and is all placed on the opposite side of the row.

Spade or fork is next used to break up the trench bottom, this to be left where it is. The rotted greenstuff goes in and is trodden down on top of the broken-up bottom. The soil that was taken out last is spaded back into the trench, and then some of the soil that was taken out first goes back on top of it. This top soil is to be returned last because it is naturally more fertile than lower soil.

The contents of the trench are then consolidated by moderate treading, and so that there shall be something to sustain the roots before they get down to the buried

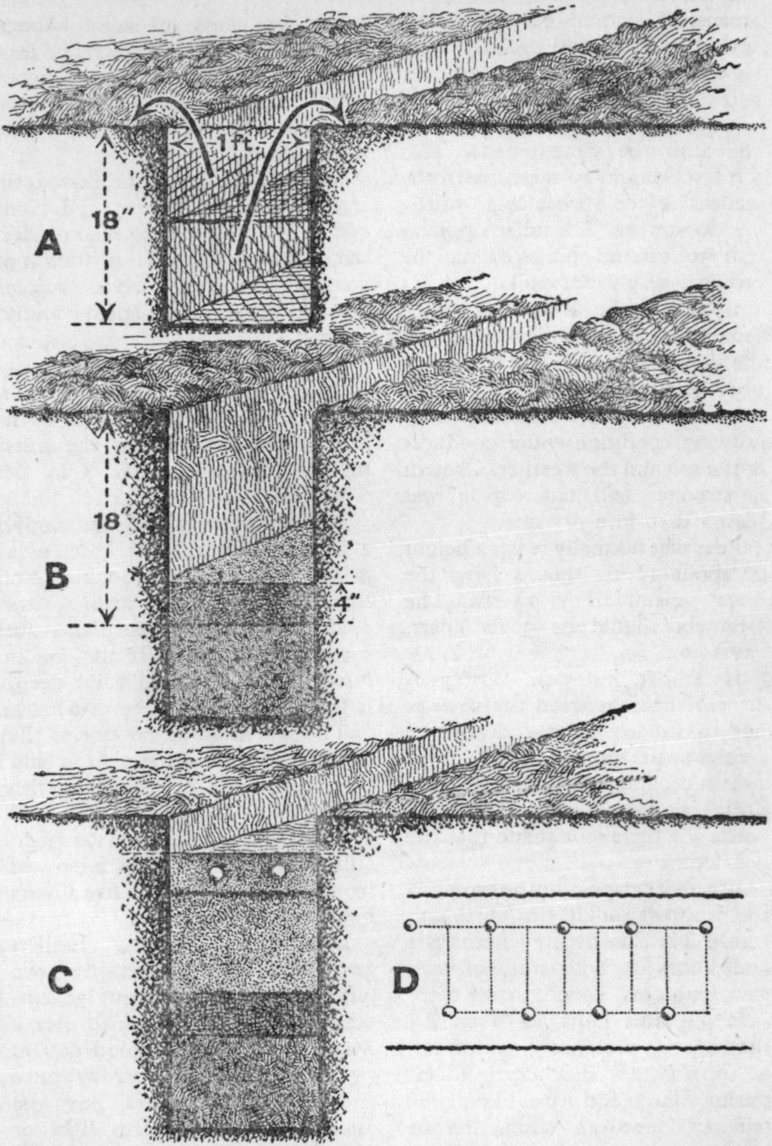

Fig. 238.—*In making trenches for peas, top soil is heaped on one side, the lower soil on opposite side* (A). *Subsoil is then broken up, and topped with 4 in. of rotted greenstuff* (B). *The trench is then filled with soil (the good top soil going in last) to within 6 in. of the top, seed is sown and covered with 2 in. of soil* (C). *Method of spacing the seed along the drill is shown at* (D)

greenstuff or manure the trench surface should be dressed with superphosphate of lime, 2 oz. per 6 ft. of row; if possible 1 oz. of sulphate of ammonia should be added to the same length. This top food should be mixed with the trench surface a week or so previous to sowing. A similar application to ground prepared in the ordinary way is advisable.

Spacing the Rows. Distance separating the rows depends upon the height to which the variety of pea normally grows, and this height is influenced to a certain extent by growing conditions—the goodness of the soil and the weather. Growth is stronger and taller in a wet season than in a dry one.

Peas that normally reach a height of about 1½ ft. should have the rows separated by 1½ ft. The 3-footers should be 3 ft. apart, and so on.

If a 4-ft. or 5-ft. variety is grown, space between the rows is put to use by sowing down the centre such quick-growing crops as lettuce, spinach, radish. In very bright weather these grow all the better for the slight shade that the pea tops cast.

Where it can possibly be arranged the pea rows should run north and south. The sun then gets between and shines on both sides of each row, with great benefit to the crop.

When and How to Sow. All the varieties previously named can be sown (where they are to finish) during March and April. To maintain an unbroken succession of pickings of any one variety rows should not be sown all on one date but at intervals up to May or early June—a second row when seedlings of the first show through, a third row when the second-sown show through, and so on. The last sowing, in May or early June, should be of the early varieties, as these mature more quickly than other kinds.

Rather than make the first sowing of the year in wet and cold soil in March, keep the seed packet unopened until the soil is drier and warmer in April; seed simply remains dormant in sticky, chilly ground.

Unless the trench system is adopted, drills will need to be made, with the draw hoe or with the spade held nearly flat; the drills to be flat-bottomed and 5 in. or 6 in. deep.

The seeds are spaced out singly, 2 in. apart, down both sides of a drill, thus securing a double row. Broadcasting in the drill wastes seed, and crowded pea plants are sorely handicapped. If the soil is heavy, cover the seed 2 in. deep; if light, 3 in. deep (Fig. 238).

The soil may be so dry at the time of a late sowing that it will be necessary to fill the drill with water overnight before the seed goes in; germination will be aided still further if the seed is soaked in water for four or five hours before it is sown.

Extra-early Sowing. Earliest cropping peas are sometimes sown outdoors in late October or November, though little is gained over a March sowing and a good deal of risk is taken—from sparrows, mice and slugs. It should only be attempted if the soil is light or sandy and if the position faces south and is sheltered from north and east, conditions which are not very frequently found outside a fortunately placed home garden.

Fig. 239.—*Short twiggy supports are placed to the peas, to give them a climbing start, then taller stakes according to the normal height of the variety*

For this sowing the ground need not be so generously prepared, and the drills—running north and south, to secure all possible sun—need be only 2 in. deep, the seed being covered to that depth.

Sowing in Boxes. Seed can be sown in boxes in February or early March and the seedlings planted out in April. Boxes between 2 in. and 3 in. deep are filled with good soil and the seed sown 1 in. apart and 1 in. deep. The boxes are placed in a sunny frame kept closed until the seedlings break through the soil, air then being given in increasing amount.

If enough boxes are available this is a plan worth adopting in a cold or wet district and where the soil is very heavy.

Planting Out. Box-raised seedlings must be kept close to the light or they become drawn and weak; no later treatment can make them profitable. Always sodden soil may cause them to perish. When things go right, strong and short-jointed plants are ready to be set out in rows in April. Planting is to be done with a trowel and at such a depth that the roots go down straight and the bare leg of stem is buried. Lacking rain, they need to be watered in at once.

It is essential that the plants be removed from the boxes complete; that is, with all their roots intact. Previous watering of the soil in the box assists this.

Staking the Peas. An advantage of dwarf varieties is that there is less trouble about stakes. All they need is short twiggy supports just long enough to hold them upright (Fig. 239). These should be pushed well into the ground about 1 ft. apart and a few inches out from the row, on both sides, soon after the seedlings appear.

Taller varieties need the short, twiggy pieces and, in addition, stakes a few inches longer than the average height of the variety being dealt with. The short pieces go in first, and then as soon as possible the main tall stakes, at intervals of 1 ft. and 6 in. out from both sides of the row. These will have a rather heavy burden to carry when the plants, full grown, are wet with rain. They should therefore be pushed several inches into the ground and the soil firmed around each, if necessary, with the boot heel; and they should be upright, not sloping inwards.

The plants need no tying. They do their own climbing, with the aid of numerous clinging tendrils.

Watering, Feeding, Mulching. It may not perhaps be possible to fill the depression at the top of each drill or trench with water, when water is needed, but every drop that can be spared will be used profitably by the plants in dry weather. Pods cannot plump up without it.

Poultry manure scattered along a row, every fortnight, before watering, will not only assist production but will prolong the useful life of the plants. Alternatively, superphosphate of lime may be given, 1 oz. to each yard of row, once a week, and watered in—unless rain saves that trouble. Feeding should not start until flowering is over and the tiny pods can be seen.

A good deal of watering can be saved by applying a surface mulch—that is, putting down a layer of lawn mowings, dead weeds, etc., so that the soil in the drill or trench, and on both sides for a few inches outwards, is covered. This prevents the rise and evaporation of moisture already in the ground. Subsequent waterings are given through the mulch, as also are applications of poultry manure or superphosphate, these being washed into the soil during watering.

Fig. 240.—*Bits of tin, etc., tied to a line will serve as a bird scare*

In hot, dry weather it is helpful to growth if water can be swished over the tops of the plants from a watering-can fitted with a rose. This is specially appreciated on warm evenings.

Mildew and Other Troubles. When mildew attacks pea plants the pods cease to develop. The best should be made of a bad job by gathering whatever usable pods there may be and then removing the attacked plants and burning them. This will at least prevent the disease spreading. Generally it is the result of drought, but sometimes follows a succession of hot days and chilly, rainy nights.

Birds should be scared away from the newly sown seeds, and the seedlings, of which they are extremely fond, by suspending loosely on string stretched above the rows pieces of tin or glass so that these rattle together in the wind and reflect dancing beams of light in the sun (Fig. 240).

Slugs lie in wait for the appearance of young plants. Mice may do their best to see that few plants come up. Weevils may eat pieces out of leaf edges, and green-fly suck sap from shoot ends. These should all be dealt with as explained in the chart on page 408.

Picking the Pods. These should be gathered whilst young—when the seed is bulging in the pods but before the latter begin to lose their fresh green appearance and the bloom that covers them. They must not be torn from the haulm (tops) or this will be damaged. The stem of the plant should be steadied with one hand at the point where a pod is to be gathered and the pod nipped off between thumb and forefinger. Or pods can be very quickly snipped off with scissors. If pods are left too long before picking, plants are weakened and production soon ceases.

Storing for Winter. Peas shelled and dried are a valuable winter standby. Methods of drying, storing and preparing for cooking are explained on page 416.

Preparing for Table. Shelled green peas should be washed in cold water before cooking. Nutritive value is considerable. Protein, fat and carbohydrate values are even higher in dried peas.

SUGAR (EDIBLE-POD) PEA

The sugar or edible-podded pea is well named, for the pods—soft and fleshy—as well as the seeds inside are eaten. Pods are gathered while the seeds are small, before they begin to bulge. Cooked like French beans—whole, without cutting—they can be served hot or used cold in a mixed salad. Flavour is sweet and delicious. Culture is the same as for the ordinary green pea. Sown during March or April, they are ready for use about twelve weeks later.

Varieties: Paramount, Melting Marrow, Giant Sugar (each 5 ft. high), Purple-podded (6 ft.).

POTATO

The heaviest crop of potatoes of the best possible quality is the attainable right of every home food producer, though it is commonly regarded as an achievement reserved for experts only. The first essential is really good planting tubers—technically, seed potatoes or sets. The second is correct cultivation, which means attention to a number of orderly, simple details quite devoid of anything extravagant in the way of labour or outlay.

Quantities to Plant. Fortunately it is possible to estimate approximately the yield from any given quantity of seed potatoes planted. If a total of about 4 cwt. is aimed at, eight 30-ft. rows—or the equivalent of a 240-ft. run—should be planted.

These eight rows could be made up of: one 30-ft. row of what is known as a first early variety and two rows of a second early variety, 4 lb. of seed potatoes being required to plant each row, this accounting

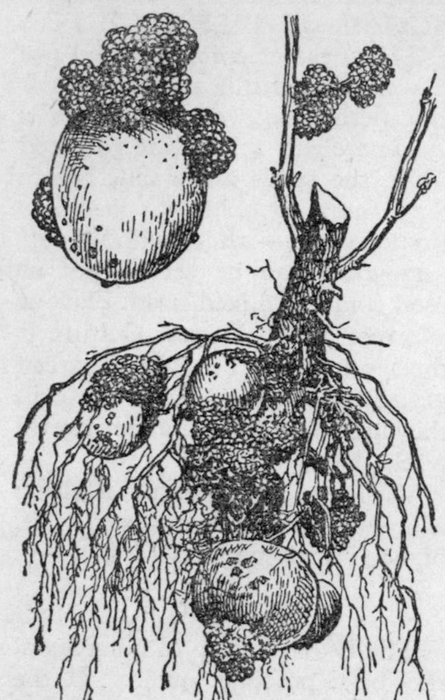

Fig. 241.—*Potatoes badly affected by the devastating wart disease*

for 12 lb. of seed; and five rows of a main-crop variety (or varieties), requiring 3 lb. of seed per row, this accounting for a total of 15 lb. of seed.

The yield of the first three rows can be reckoned as 1½ cwt., of the next five rows as 2½ cwt. So that from the planting of 27 lb. of seed a total yield of 4 cwt. can be expected.

Ready for Use. In normal circumstances the first new potatoes will be available some time in July, from the planting of first early varieties. In August the second earlies become available, and in late September the main-crop varieties, for storing, these being in sufficient quantity, in a normal season, to last out until the first of the next year's new potatoes can be dug up.

In selecting your varieties, and quantities to plant, the object should be to secure sufficient potatoes for current needs from as early in the year as possible and enough for storing later in the year for winter and spring use.

For July use, first early varieties include Arran Pilot, Epicure, May Queen, Sharpe's Express.

Ready for lifting in August, second early varieties include Great Scot, Ben Lomond, British Queen, Arran Comrade, Catriona.

Main-crop varieties, late September, include Majestic, Arran Banner, King Edward VII, Gladstone, Kerr's Pink, Redskin, Up-to-Date, Arran Victory.

Immune Varieties. The most devastating potato disease in the world is known as wart disease, on account of the small cauliflower-like, greeny-yellow growths that develop at the base of stems and on tubers of attacked plants (Fig. 241). The disease is so serious that it must be notified at once to the Ministry of Agriculture (address obtainable from local council offices or police station) and their instructions awaited. Affected tops and tubers must be burned, and, as the soil in which it occurs remains contaminated for years, only varieties of potato certified as immune may be planted therein. In this case immune refers only to the wart disease and not to any other of the troubles that afflict the potato; these are dealt with in a later paragraph and in the chart on page 408.

It is of the very greatest importance that this regulation be complied with. Of the varieties already listed the following are definitely immune and may be planted with every confidence in ground which has been infected by wart disease: Arran Pilot, Great Scot, Ben Lomond, Arran Comrade, Catriona, Majestic, Arran Banner, Gladstone, Kerr's Pink, Redskin, Arran Victory.

Buying Seed Potatoes. Odd lots of seed picked up at the greengrocer's without any official certificate to accompany them may prove to be a ruinous piece of shopping. To safeguard the home food producer's interests, the Ministry of Agriculture requires that all potatoes sold for planting shall have been officially certified as having been grown on land free from wart disease (for which a numbered certificate is given, certificate numbers being prefixed with the letters C.L., meaning clean land); or that they have been inspected officially and found to be free of wart disease (certificate numbers also prefixed C.L.); or that they are of an approved variety true to type (letters T.S. before certificate numbers signifying true stock).

The letter A preceding the C.L. or T.S. on the certificate means that the potatoes have been grown in an area infected by wart disease (though they are not themselves infected, of course), and these must not be moved or planted outside the scheduled infected areas.

If the number of the official certificate and various other official particulars are not enclosed in, or delivered with, any bag of seed potatoes the purchaser has a legal right to demand a written statement setting out these details: name and address of seller, the class, the variety, the size and dressing, and the number of the certificate.

Class of Potato. Seed potatoes are officially classified as follows: Class I (Scotch) signifies potatoes grown in Scotland; Class I (Irish), potatoes grown in Ireland. Potatoes grown in England or Wales under the provisions of a scheme authorized by the Minister of Agriculture are indicated as Class I (English Special Stock) or Class I (Welsh Special Stock).

Those referred to as Class I (English once grown) are potatoes grown in England or Wales which are either the produce of seed grown in Scotland or Ireland in the preceding year, or are the produce of seed included in the special stock classes in the preceding year, such produce not being in accordance with a scheme authorized by the Minister of Agriculture.

All other potatoes not included in the foregoing are referred to as Class II.

The significance of all this is explained below.

Name of Variety. Under these provisions of the Ministry it is required that a variety must be true to type to the extent of 97 per cent of the quantity of seed potatoes sold. If it is not so, the seed must be sold as mixed varieties.

Size and Dressing. The size of seed potatoes is important. Best results come from planting those about the size of a chicken's egg (Fig. 242). Dealers are therefore required to declare that their seed conforms to certain limits, size and dressing referring to the dimensions of mesh of top and bottom riddles (sieves) used in gauging the seed. The latter are required to pass through a 2¼-in.-mesh riddle but not through one of 1¼ in.

When the dealer states only the size of the bottom riddle (1¼ in.)

his seed is sold with the description "as grown."

Home-saved Seed. The potato deteriorates as to weight of yield and size of tubers if a crop is raised from home-saved seed for more than two years in succession. Seed potatoes raised in another district should therefore be obtained for planting (see under heading Class of Potato) to as large an extent as possible. A money-saving compromise can be effected satisfactorily by saving enough seed potatoes each year to plant half of the next year's potato area, the other half being planted with seed raised elsewhere. The following year seed potatoes can be saved from the new half, and so on. In that manner a vigorous stock is maintained, as free from disease as care can make it, and the home grower profits exceedingly.

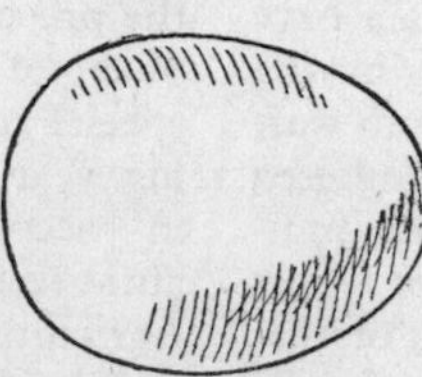

Fig. 242.—*Seed potatoes for planting should be about the size of a hen's egg (right). The rose, or crown, end of a tuber is shown at the left*

How to Save Seed Potatoes. Chicken-egg-sized tubers can be picked out from the crop when this is lifted in bulk, but—and this is of supreme importance—they should be picked out during the actual digging and not later from the potato heap. The reason for this selection on the spot is that suitable-sized seed must be chosen only from those plants which have a really big individual crop. A vigorous plant which is dug up with an excellent weight of big tubers will almost certainly have a few small ones attached, and these are the best seed.

Seed potatoes selected in that manner will, when planted the following year, produce a crop almost, if not quite, as good as the parent crop; because the seed inherits the good qualities of the parent.

Bad, or weak, qualities are as easily inherited. Small tubers saved from a plant that produced nothing but small ones will, when planted, yield even smaller potatoes. Disease is also passed on with equal facility.

The folly of planting any old seed needs no further stressing.

Suiting Variety to Soil. Some varieties of potato produce grand crops of magnificent eating and storing qualities in one district, yet prove far from satisfactory in another district. Soil and locality must therefore be considered.

Varieties that are known to do well in any one district should be adopted by the newcomer to potato growing. The names can be learned from local growers.

For soil described as fairly heavy, or medium, the variety King Edward VII is generally suitable. Soils ranging from medium to heavy suit Great Scot and Ben Lomond. All types of soil—properly cultivated—can be cropped with Majestic, Arran Pilot and Arran Banner; the latter is also generally suitable for light and dry ground.

When ordering seed potatoes it is advisable (*a*) to indicate a second choice in case the dealer has run out of the variety, or varieties, ordered, or (*b*) to state definitely that none other than the variety ordered shall be sent. That precaution may save a lot of trouble.

Soil Preparation. Potatoes will not grow satisfactorily in lumpy soil; it must be broken up as finely and to as great a depth as possible. If the ground is clay, or otherwise heavy, lighten it with wood ash, charred woody pieces from the bonfire, and leaf-mould. It is not advisable to attempt to lighten it with grit or ashes from the house fires, such material tending to scratch the tender skins of young tubers and induce surface scab.

If manure can be obtained, bury it below the top 9 in. It should not come in contact with the seed potatoes at planting time, more especially if the manure is raw—that is, new. Material from the soft refuse heap is invaluable for enriching potato ground, trodden in thickly at the 9-in. depth. So also is seaweed, straight from the shore or stacked and dried.

Material from a worn-out hotbed or mushroom bed or from the old marrow heap can be dug in with considerable profit; or it can be used to line the planting drills. If potatoes are planted with a trowel and not in drills, the material should be dug well in.

After the ground has been dug, further assistance can be given to the coming crop by raking, hoeing or forking into the surface one of the trade-name potato fertilizers; or this mixture—superphosphate of lime three parts, one part each of sulphate of ammonia and sulphate of potash, applied at the rate of 4 oz. to the square yard; or plenty of wood ash, which is obtained by burning woody garden or allotment refuse.

Wood ash provides the potash which potatoes require, as also does the ash of burnt bracken and of seaweed.

These powders can either be mixed with the dug surface or sprinkled in the planting trench or in the trowel-made holes, before planting.

Sprouting the Seed Potatoes. Growth starts from the small sunken buds or eyes scattered about the tuber. The best are at the broad end, which is spoken of variously as the rose or crown end. The plants get an earlier and better start if planted after these eyes have made about ½ in. of growth. Method of sprouting is as follows.

As soon as the seed potatoes become available (either purchased, or picked out from the home crop at lifting time) they are placed touching in shallow boxes (Fig. 243), on end, broad end at the top. Each box should be a shallow framework only; solid sides and ends obscure the light which is essential to the production of short, sturdy, green sprouts; and each should hold one layer only.

The filled boxes are at once placed under cover where frost cannot reach but where light is unhindered. Warmth is not required, but if the shed, attic or other shelter is not absolutely frost-proof the boxes should be covered with dry material (such as bracken or straw or sheets of paper) in very cold weather; the covering to be removed when there is no danger of the tubers being frosted.

From first to last they must be dealt with gently. Skins are easily bruised, and in that condition the tubers are apt to rot in the boxes. They should be looked at from time to time and any that by their appearance give rise to doubt should be removed and burnt.

No water should be given whilst they are set up in the boxes. If shoots show signs of developing long and spindly and white they are not getting sufficient light, and chances of getting a big crop are being reduced.

Limiting the Shoots. Shoots will develop at various points on the tuber, not only at the broad (top) end, but they are not all required. Remove the weakest first, then reduce the remainder to the two sturdiest. Those that are not wanted are easily rubbed off with a touch of the finger. Yield will be both bigger and earlier for this attention. More than two shoots, however, should be left if the sprouting tubers are on the large side and it is intended to divide them before planting.

Dividing Big Tubers. Chicken-egg-sized seed potatoes are planted intact. But larger ones give a bigger total yield when divided and the portions planted as though they were small whole tubers. The cutting should be done after sprouting, with a sharp knife, from top to bottom if possible, each portion to come away with at least one sturdy sprout.

If the cutting is done before sprouts develop there is a risk that some portions may fail to grow after planting, as all eyes do not necessarily send out shoots.

There must be no haste to divide the sprouted tubers. The time to

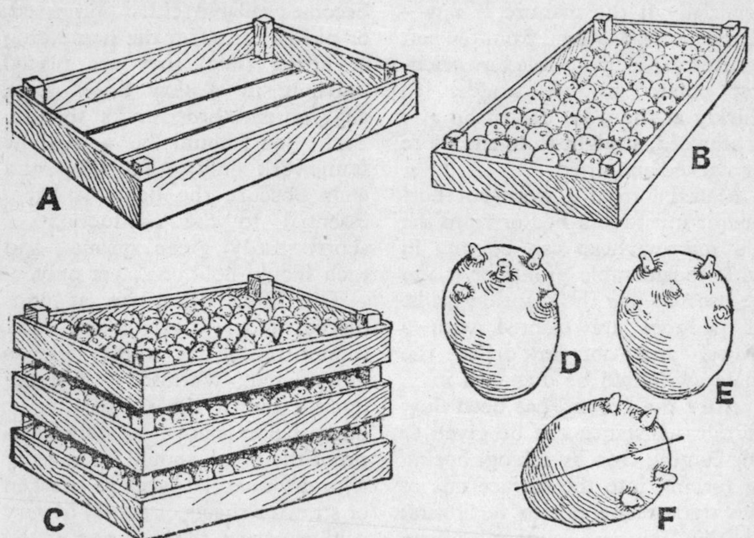

Fig. 243.—*A sprouting box for seed potatoes is shown at* (A), *filled with tubers at* (B), *and filled boxes stacked at* (C). *A sprouted tuber straight from a box is shown at* (D), *the same prepared for planting at* (E) *by removal of all but two sprouts, method of dividing a large tuber at* (F)

Fig. 244.—*Covering-in planted potatoes needs to be done carefully, to avoid breaking off the sprouts*

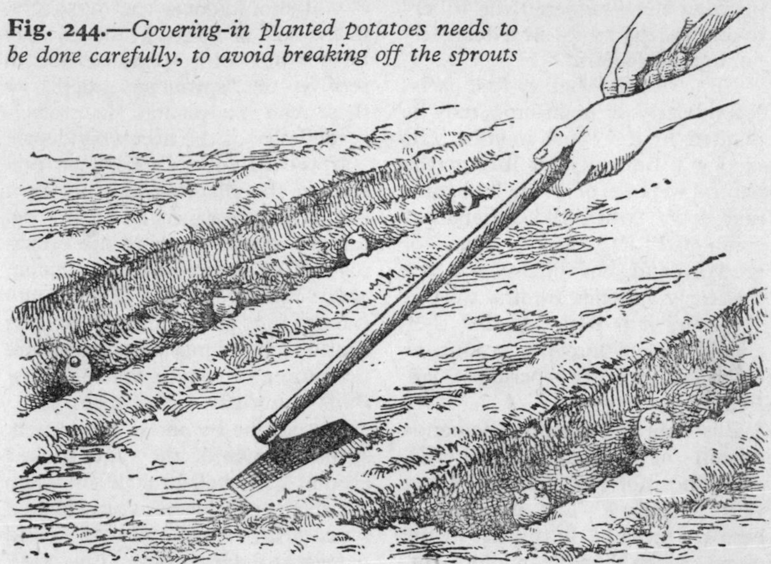

do it is immediately before planting. Should it be discovered, after cutting, that the ground is very dry, the divisions should be put back in the sprouting boxes (under cover where they came from) for five or six days, this giving the cut surfaces a chance to harden somewhat. After that they can be planted in the dry ground without risk.

The chief things to avoid are (*a*) the cut surfaces being dried by sun or wind, and (*b*) the breaking off of shoots by careless handling. The safeguard against the latter is obvious. Protection against wind or hot sun is given by doing the cutting in shade or in a shed and by covering-in the cut tubers as soon as they are planted.

There is nothing to be gained from powdering cut surfaces with lime, wood ash, or anything else, before planting.

Planting Unsprouted Tubers. The advantages of larger and earlier yield must be forgone if, because of lack of time or convenience, tubers have to be planted in an unsprouted condition. They should be placed in the trenches, or trowel-made planting holes, upright, and broad end to the top. If dropped in just anyhow they naturally fall on their sides, with the result that a larger number of shoots come up than would be the case if planted broad end up.

The plant that starts with two, or at most three, strong shoots will produce more good tubers than the plant that sends up half a dozen crowded growths to start with.

When to Plant. Late February to about mid-May covers the ordinary potato-planting period. It is governed by state of soil and weather. Cold, sodden ground is no medium for seed potatoes, sprouted or unsprouted. It is better to be a month later than the usual time (for the district) of planting than condemn the tubers to conditions that are most definitely not in their favour.

All varieties, whether first early, second early, or main-crop, may be planted in the same month. The crop will be ready for lifting (the natural vagaries of spring and summer apart) when the variety has completed its natural span of growth, and not before. As the first early varieties are first to start sprouting it is desirable that they should be got into the ground as early as possible—perhaps late February.

But February planting demands certain conditions, a sheltered, sunny position and light soil being very necessary. The possibilities here are more likely to exist in the home garden than on an allotment. A border of light (but good) soil at the foot of a south-facing fence or wall, unshaded by trees or a building, is ideal. There sprouted seed potatoes may be planted if not in February then in mid-March. In the Midlands, where conditions generally are colder, the end of March is safer. Farther north and in Scotland mid-April is the safest date.

Second earlies can be planted, in normal circumstances, during the first half of April, and main-crop varieties from then on to about mid-May.

How to Plant. First early and second early varieties will be planted 1 ft. apart, main-crop varieties about 16 in. apart, in rows 2 ft. distant from each other and running, where possible, north and south so that both sides of a row get full benefit of the sun.

Planting depth depends on nature of soil. If this is heavy, about 4 in. of soil should cover the tops; 6 in. if the soil is light. Trenches may be got out with spade or hoe to receive the sprouted tubers, or these can be planted in trowel-made holes of the necessary depth.

Sprouted tubers should be carried to the planting site not in a bag or sack or heaped in a trug, for this would result in the breaking off of many sprouts, but in single-layer boxes. Unsprouted tubers can be submitted to less cautious handling, but even here precautions must be taken against skins being bruised or torn.

Placed one by one in the trench, sprouts upward, they are packed around with well-broken soil when the row is completed, then covered over, with equal care to avoid damage to the sprouts (Fig. 244). Those planted in trowel-made holes are speedily covered in by passing the rake along and above the row.

Hoeing Between Rows. It is necessary to keep the surface soil between rows broken and loose, to keep down weeds and also in preparation for earthing up. If the surface is too hard to work with the Dutch hoe or draw hoe the fork is the tool to use. The soil should not be disturbed too close to the actual lines. These should be marked plainly, at the time of planting, with stakes or large wooden labels.

Earthing Up. Potato plants need to be earthed up by scraping soil with the draw hoe from between rows and piling it against the stems of the leaves, but without covering the leaves (Fig. 245).

The purpose of this is to keep the tubers, which are swelling just beneath the surface of the ground

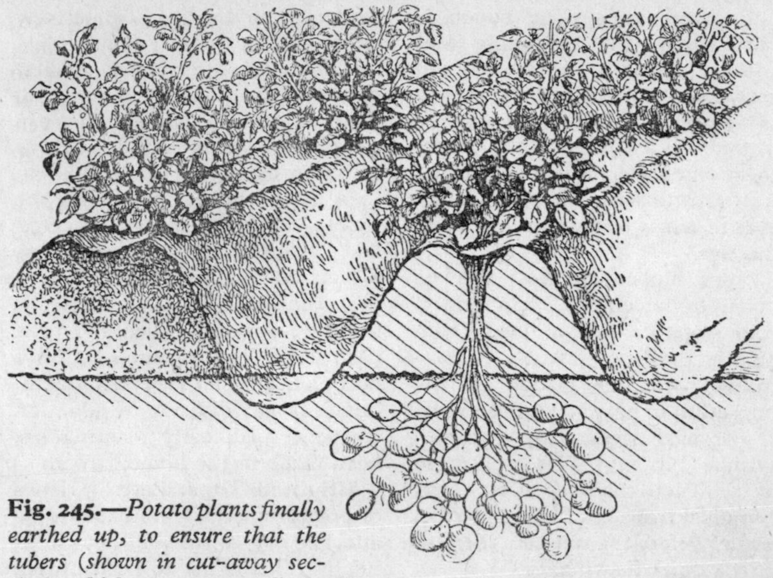

Fig. 245.—*Potato plants finally earthed up, to ensure that the tubers (shown in cut-away section) which grow naturally quite close to the surface are well covered*

and gradually working upwards, in complete darkness. Without this mound to cover them more deeply many would in due course become exposed to the light; the result of such exposure being a green tinge on the tubers, which gives them a bitter flavour and renders them most distasteful when cooked. Earthing up serves a secondary purpose in supporting the tops which otherwise would flop all ways.

Soil is first drawn up to the stems when the plants are about 6 in. high, again when stems have lengthened another 6 in., and again if there is more bare stem to cover. The result is a continuous bank of soil with sloping sides, with a V-shaped depression along the top, out of which the leaves stand up. The bank-top depression is to catch rain for the benefit of tubers and of the thirsty potato roots.

Easiest way to earth up is for the operator to straddle a row and, walking backwards, use the hoe on left and right sides alternately, the hoe held so that its cutting edge is at an angle of about 45 degrees with the ground (Fig. 246). The tool is used with a chopping motion to break lumps of soil, with a scraping motion to draw the broken soil into position. If necessary, the fork can be used to loosen the surface first. As the banked-up soil increases in height, so will the channel (from which earth is withdrawn) between each pair of rows deepen.

When the first earthing up is about to start, some wood ash, or superphosphate, sprinkled alongside the plants and between them, provides a tonic that will be put to good use by the vegetables.

Frosted Tops. The potato is not a hardy plant, so trouble from frost can always be expected. When early tops are blackened completely by frost that much growth is wasted, but unless the tubers themselves have been badly frosted later growth will push up from any eyes that may so far have remained inactive.

Tops nipped by frost can be saved from complete crippling if cold water is thrown over them before the sun reaches them—thrown over the foliage by the bucketful, or hosed over the plants, or applied generously with a syringe (Fig. 247). This application of cold (note the *cold*) water starts a gradual thawing of leaf-and-stem tissues before the sun gets there to start a quick thawing.

It is the quick thaw which causes disaster to frosted plants; a slow thaw leaves them comparatively unharmed.

Those that are planted earliest naturally run the greatest risk of frost. Any top protection that can be given them is useful, such as sticks pushed into the ground to hold up a low roof of sacking, or shoots of evergreen (laurel, etc.) laid flat along the row tops. This protection should be held ready in the event of frost threatening; it must be removed when the frost has passed. The scheme might not be practicable on every allotment, but it is not difficult of adoption where a small early planting has been made in the home garden.

Blighted Tops. Later varieties of potato especially are liable to be attacked by a disease known as blight. This is not to be confused with green- or black-fly, which are also sometimes referred to as blight.

Fig. 246.—*Potato plants can be earthed up by the operator straddling a row (left) or by using the draw hoe from one side to move the soil (right)*

Fig. 247.—*Potato plants nipped by frost can be saved from complete crippling by syringeing tops with water or scattering water over them from a bucket*

It is a fungus attack, assuming most serious proportions in a wet summer. It appears in the form of brown blotches on the upper surface of leaves and within a few days of this being noticed the tops may perish.

Though complete destruction of the tops is not inevitable, tubers may rot in the ground or, in spite of the fact that they may appear unaffected when lifted, they may decay in store. The safe plan is not to wait for those brown blotches to appear but to coat the leaves, back and front, with a fungicide in powder or liquid form whilst the foliage is still healthy—first in June, again three weeks later, and once more in August. Used in powder form the fungicide should be applied five or six times, at intervals of about a fortnight.

A preparation known as Bordeaux mixture, for either wet or dry spraying, can be purchased in tins, for this special protective purpose. It is sold with directions for use. Methods of dusting and spraying are explained in the PESTS AND DISEASES Section on page 397.

It must be noted that possible risk of injury to potato plants when thus dusted or sprayed must be accepted when the area is within ten or twelve miles of certain large industrial towns, on account of acid fumes which may be in the air interacting with the Bordeaux mixture to the serious damage of foliage. Where there is any doubt, useful advice on this point may be got from experienced growers in the locality.

Tubers often become infected at the time of lifting through contact

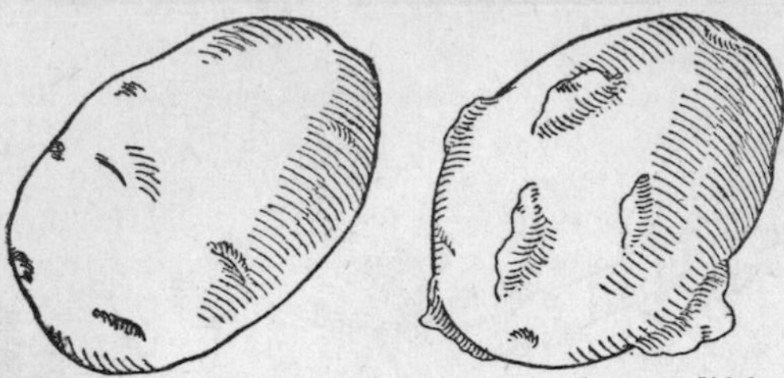

Fig. 248.—*Potato tubers are ready for lifting when the skins are tough* (*left*) *not when the skin is so soft that it flakes and tears easily* (*right*)

with spores (seeds) of the fungus washed from the leaves by rain; when that happens they will rot in store. Here the safeguard is to lift the crop a fortnight or so after the tops have died completely; or if it is time to lift and the tops are still green, cut these off and dig up the tubers a week or so later.

Other Troubles. Wart disease has been referred to in a previous paragraph; other troubles such as the Colorado beetle are dealt with in the chart, Remedies Against Enemies of Vegetable Crops, page 408.

Potato Plants in Flower. Some potato plants carry many flowers, others none at all. Whether flowers are produced or not the crop of tubers is in no way affected. Rows of plants decked out with white or lilac blooms, each about the size of a halfpenny, are certainly a most pleasing sight, but to the food grower they represent beauty and nothing more.

Those flowers which chance to be fertilized are followed by berries which are definitely poisonous; fatalities have occurred through eating them. Each potato berry contains from 100 to 300 seeds. Hence seed potatoes and potato seed are not interchangeable terms.

The professional grower seeking to raise a new variety effects the cross-fertilization of potato flowers of two different varieties, and sows ripened seed from the resultant berries. From that January sowing, under glass, are produced seedlings which are planted outdoors in May and then dealt with as though they were plants raised in the ordinary way from seed potatoes (tubers). For five or six years the stock thus raised is weeded out with the utmost care; weaklings, those with badly shaped tubers or bad cookers, and other undesirables being destroyed. The ultimate result may or may not be a new variety worth marketing.

When to Dig the Crop. First early varieties are due for lifting first, but haste to start on the new potatoes should be checked until tubers have reached a fair size. Indication that that stage has arrived is given by the tops when these start yellowing. A plant should then be lifted and skins of the tubers tested. If these are so soft that they tear easily it can be taken as a sign that the tubers have still to do some plumping up, and it would be a pity to lift too many at once. Skins should be fairly tough before digging up a whole row (Fig. 248).

Later varieties can be lifted when all the green colour has left the foliage; or tubers may remain in the ground until the tops have died right down—after which nothing but harm can come to the undug tubers, in the form of wireworms and other pests, and disease.

Ideal conditions for lifting are no rain and a dry soil. Something can be done to help wet soil dry out by cutting off the tops (the haulm) a few days before digging is to begin. This exposes the ground to wind and whatever sun may shine, and gives more chance that the potatoes will come up clean —not plastered with wet earth.

How to Dig the Crop. Lifting is carried out with a fork, and if its tines or prongs are long the job is expedited. A start is made at one end of a row, the fork, held upright, being jabbed into the ground 8 in. or 9 in. from the base of the mound. Pressure from the ball of the foot presses the fork in still farther whilst the handle of the tool is being levered towards the digger. In that manner the tines are coaxed beneath the mass of soil and tubers (Fig. 249).

Thus loosened, the tubers are brought up on the flat of the fork, the upheaval being assisted, if necessary, by the grip of the digger's free hand on the plant's stems (if the tops have not been cut off). The fork-load is then dumped a few inches to left or right, wherever there is a vacant space.

Plant number two is then lifted and the fork-load of potatoes dumped on the surface whence number one was lifted, and so on to the end of the row.

It is easier to work from left to right (or right to left) of a row than to dig at right angles to it. And the object of using a long-tined fork and pushing this in well away from the base of the mound is to

Fig. 249.—*Tines of the fork should not be jabbed through tubers when lifting potatoes. To avoid injury the fork should be thrust in at one side, then levered downward as indicated by dotted arrow*

avoid spearing some of the tubers and leaving others in the ground. It is always worth while going over a dug row later with the fork to ensure that no potatoes have been missed. Otherwise odd ones may send up unexpected growth in the midst of next year's crop of beans or whatever may then be located there.

Drying the Tubers. The lifted potatoes should not be picked up immediately but be left on the ground to dry (Fig. 250). On a hot or windy day a few hours' exposure will be sufficient; in damp, muggy weather a couple of days may pass before the skins are dry. If rain falls just after lifting, bracken or straw will be needed to cover them; it may even be necessary to gather them all up and put them under cover. Circumstances will dictate the exact proceedings, the object being to get the skins dry but not to expose the potatoes to light for so long that they become green.

Tubers of seed size, however, selected on the spot (see under How to Save Seed Potatoes, page 344) should be allowed to green before being put away on shelves or in sprouting boxes. These can stay out for four or five days, on

Fig. 250.—*Lifted potatoes left on the ground in orderly rows to dry*

the ground or on a hard path (providing it doesn't rain), and be turned over a time or two to facilitate the greening process.

Whilst the crop is drying, tubers that have been injured by the fork, diseased and undersized ones, should be picked out and the best of them set aside for prompt use. Very small ones and those not too badly diseased can be cooked and fed to chickens and other livestock; definitely unfit tubers should be burned.

Potato Tops Disposal. Before the potatoes go into store, or as soon as possible afterwards, the tops should be raked into small heaps and then carted away either for burning or adding to the soft refuse heap or pit. If they are diseased, the bonfire is the place for them; their ashes will return good potash to the soil. If they are clean they will rot down along with other vegetable matter in the compost pit or heap for later digging in.

Storing for Winter. Early potatoes for using up before the main crop is called upon can be stored in sacks, baskets, bags, barrels, anywhere under cover where they can be easily got at. They need ventilation (or they sweat, which induces decay), shelter from rain, protection against rats and mice; they must not be subjected to heat (which will shrivel the skins and start them sprouting), and they must be kept dark. These early varieties will keep in good condition (if not previously used up) until the end of the year, providing they are protected against frost and sorted over occasionally for the removing of tubers showing decay.

Potatoes for winter store need to be provided for similarly, with extra precautions against damp. The larder might accommodate a sack or two or a few boxes, and the cellar or attic the remainder. Paper, pieces of old sacking, bracken, anything of that nature placed thickly over the boxes, etc., will be an insurance against frost.

If the potatoes are to be heaped on the damp floor of a cellar or shed, the floor should first be covered with a layer of dry bracken, heather, straw, stout twigs or small branches of trees as a cushion between tubers and the damp base. The heap should not be more than about 18 in. deep, to decrease the risk of sweating, and it should be covered to keep out the light.

It may be necessary to store all or part of the crop outdoors. The procedure is as follows. A layer of sifted ashes from the house fire is put down, at least 2 in. thick, on the driest part of the ground. On that layer the tubers are placed (with care to avoid bruising) as a long heap, 3 ft. to 4 ft. wide and about 18 in. deep, the sides sloping as steeply as possible up to a narrow ridge (Fig. 251).

They are then allowed a few days to sweat before being covered with not less than 6 in. of bracken, heather or straw, this in turn being covered with 3 in. of soil made firm and smooth with the back of the spade—so that rain shoots off as fast as it falls. If rain threatens before the sweating period is over the heap should be covered without further delay.

There is no bother about finding the soil covering, for this can be dug from all round the base of the heap, the surrounding trench then serving as a runway for rain or surface water. It may be necessary to provide the trench with an outlet if water threatens to accumulate.

Ventilation is arranged for by providing the outdoor heap with two or more chimneys of tightly twisted straw or bracken, these to go into the ridge as far as the top layer of tubers and to stick out a few inches above the soil covering. Earth should be packed around these tightly so that rain cannot enter that way.

When the heap is drawn on, the covering is removed from one end, a supply of potatoes taken out and the covering replaced at once.

One further attention sometimes given consists in dusting the layers of tubers as these are placed in store, indoors or out, with lime or sulphur. This serves to check decay and acts as a deterrent to rats and mice.

Potatoes in Pots. Other methods of growing are worth consideration. With a greenhouse temperature of 55 deg. (by night) it is not difficult to get new potatoes well in advance of the earliest outdoor crop, sprouted tubers being planted singly in 10-in. or 12-in. pots (Fig. 252). These are half-filled with a mixture of good soil two parts, one part sifted leaf-mould. A tuber is placed upright in the centre of the surface and the pot then filled to within ½ in. of the rim with the same mixture, this to be pressed down, not too firmly, with the fingers. The pots are then placed close to the glass and the soil kept just moist.

When the tops have reached about 6 in. in height they should be held up by means of short twiggy sticks pushed carefully down the sides of the pot.

The crop is got at by inverting the pot and removing this from the soil mass, the upside-down tops being supported by one hand. Tubers of usable size can then be picked out and the soil mass returned to the pot to enable smaller tubers to complete their swelling.

First early varieties such as May Queen, Snowdrop, Eclipse, should be chosen for this purpose. If potted in January, useful potatoes should be ready by April. They can also be grown in a cold or hotbed frame, more successfully in the latter. The frame needs to be of ample depth, with 9 in. of really good soil. Sprouted tubers are planted 3 in. deep and 1 ft. apart each way. The frame light is covered with some protective material each night in case of frost, and no ventilation given until tops show through the soil.

Air is then admitted cautiously, as opportunity offers. Some extra soil should be introduced into the frame for mounding up around each plant when the tops are up about 6 in., and the root-run has to be kept uniformly moist. When 1 ft. of growth has been made a little groping with the fingers at the base of each plant will enable the size of tubers to be discovered. The largest should be taken first and displaced soil put back. The groping is repeated until all tubers have been gathered.

Preparing for Table. Tubers should be scrubbed, and deep eyes nicked out. Food value is greater if potatoes are cooked in their jackets; the skin then comes away very thinly, leaving much nourishment which is lost when potatoes are peeled before cooking. That

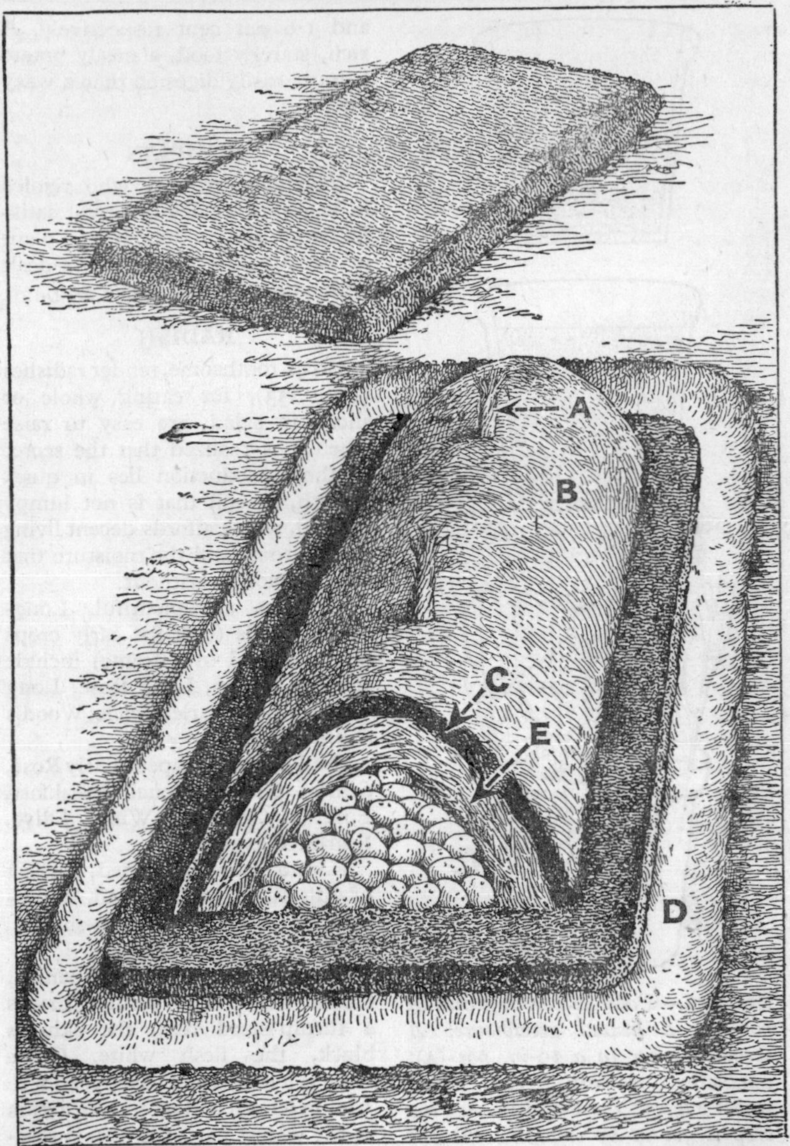

Fig. 251.—*Method of clamping potatoes outdoors. On a layer of sifted fire ashes (as at top) the tubers are piled, then covered with dry bracken, heather or straw* (E), *then soil* (C) *patted down to give a smooth surface* (B). *Ventilation is given as at* (A). *A drainage trench* (D) *surrounding the whole bed of ashes serves as a runway for rain or surface water*

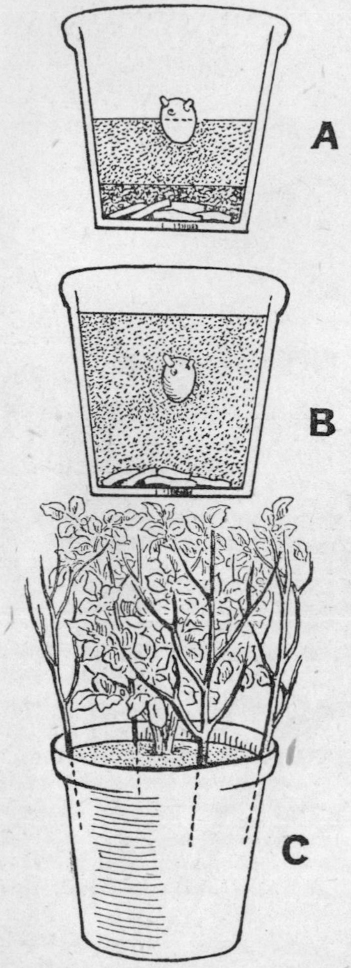

Fig. 252.—*Potatoes can be grown in pots in a heated greenhouse. A sprouted tuber in a 10-in. pot* (A); *completion of potting* (B). *Short stakes support the tops* (C), *and the crop is got at by emptying the pot*

loss represents 9 per cent of the nitrogen content and 17 per cent of the valuable salts. Boiled in their skins the losses are reduced to 0·8 and 1·6 per cent respectively. A rich, starchy food, a mealy potato is more easily digested than a waxy one.

PUMPKIN

Vegetable growers who rejoice in value for money get great satisfaction in the produce from a plant or two of pumpkin. This is dealt with under Gourd (page 290).

RADISH

Crisp, toothsome, tender radishes (Fig. 253), for eating whole or sliced in salad, are easy to raise when it is realized that the secret of their production lies in quick growth, in soil that is not lumpy or hard, which affords decent living for the roots and the moisture that they cannot do without.

Varieties are plentiful. Long-rooted kinds (best for early crops outdoors and in a frame) include Earliest Frame, Long Rose, Long White, Long Scarlet, Icicle, Wood's Scarlet Frame.

Oval or olive-shaped: Early Rose, Scarlet Globe, French Breakfast, Forcing Crimson, White Olive, Scarlet Olive.

Round or turnip-shaped: Earliest of All, Red Forcing, Red White-tipped, Scarlet Turnip-shaped, White Turnip-shaped.

For winter use: Black Spanish, China Rose. The former makes a turnip-sized root, the skin is black, the flesh white. China Rose is a long oval in shape, 4 in. to 5 in. in length and up to 2 in. across at the widest part; the skin is rose-coloured, the flesh white. These winter radishes sometimes grow even longer.

An ounce of radish seed is sufficient to sow a row of 100 ft.—

Fig. 253.—*Radish types: oval or olive-shaped* (A), *turnip-shaped* (B), *long* (C)

representing about 1,000 plants. Seedlings appear in about six days.

Ready for Use. The ordinary varieties, for spring and summer use, are available in from four to six weeks from the time of sowing outdoors. Sown in early spring in a hotbed frame, about two weeks; in a cold frame, about four weeks. Sown in heat during winter, about eight weeks. Black Spanish and China Rose, grown outdoors, are specially useful for storing for use from November to March.

Soil Preparation. The radish being a speedy crop, grown in only small quantities at a time, no special place has to be assigned it. Short rows can be scattered about wherever most convenient, followed always by the watering-can. Any piece of ground well dug and enriched, well broken on the surface, for any crop of longer standing, offers the right sort of living.

If the ground is clay-like, chalky, stony or dusty, the easiest way of ensuring the essential quick growth is to take out 3-in.-deep drills, line these with 1½ in. of sifted leaf-mould pressed down, cover with ½ in. of sifted soil, sow seed on top, cover with ½ in. of fine soil, and use the spare ½ in. for watering in dry weather (Fig. 254).

When and How to Sow. Chief outdoor sowings are made from March to September, a short row every three weeks or so; this ensures a steady supply without any wasteful glut.

Earliest outdoor sowing, in February, needs the warmth and shelter of a piece of ground well drained and facing south—a border in the home garden backed by a south-facing fence or wall being ideal. The sown row should be

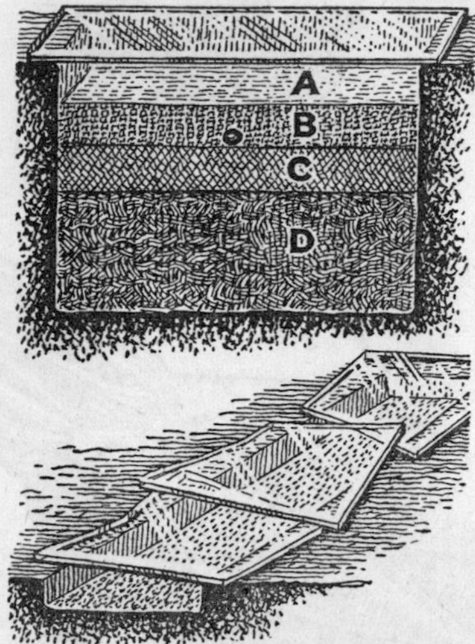

Fig. 254.—*In clayey or difficult ground radishes demand care. A sown drill is shown covered with odd pieces of glass and (above) in section. Space for watering* (A), *sifted soil covering seed* (B), *sifted soil* (C) *on top of sifted leaf-mould; the whole representing a 3-in.-deep drill*

covered with pieces of glass and paper or sacking until seedlings show, then protected every frosty night with similar material or sprigs of evergreen laid down to protect the tops (Fig. 255).

Seed should be dropped one by one at 1-in. intervals, rows to be 4 in. apart, and covered ½ in. deep. Dry ground, for spring and summer sowings, should be watered first. If deep drills are adopted these should be filled with water an hour or two previous to sowing.

The large varieties for winter use are sown outdoors from June to August, in drills 6 in. apart.

Protection for Seed. Pieces of glass placed flat over the drills serve not only to hasten germination and protect against bad weather but to foil hungry birds. Or sheets of paper (a stone at each corner to hold them down) can be used to keep feathered raiders at bay. Birds are not so interested in radishes in the well-up stage; it is the seed they go after most.

Radish in a Frame. A hotbed frame in which early carrots or lettuce, etc., are being grown will provide space also for a "stolen" crop of radish sown any time from December to February. Good soil in a cold frame in a sunny position will give an early crop if seed is sown in February.

Varieties: Forcing French Breakfast, Wood's Scarlet Frame, Earliest Frame, Forcing White Olive are among those specially suitable for this purpose.

Thinning Out. Seedlings must be thinned out, by hand, before any crowding takes place, to 3 in. apart (Fig. 256), the large winter varieties to 6 in. apart. The soil should be moist when this is done, to lessen disturbance to those that remain.

Watering. Applications of water in dry weather have to be generous, so that the ground is soaked.

Fig. 255.—*Sprigs of evergreen placed flat over the early radishes on frosty nights will save them from injury*

Without constant attention to this the radish crop cannot be really successful.

Pulling the Roots. Radishes are at their best when pulled young. They are then crisp, tender and not fiery. They become tough or woolly with age, though sometimes that can be accounted for by dry soil. Allowing them to become crowded before thinning out results in hollow roots, or else in abundance of leaf and not much else (Fig. 257).

Storing for Winter. The Large Black Spanish and China Rose can be used straight from the ground, but they are of greatest use when stored. They can be lifted in November and packed away in a heap of sifted fire ashes, or sand, in a shed or cellar, to be drawn on as wanted. Under this treatment they will keep in excellent condition until March.

Preparing for Table. Remove the leaves, wash the roots, and use whole, or slice and add to a mixed salad. The big winter varieties need to be thinly sliced. Radish is classed as an appetite encourager and aid to digestion, when eaten young.

RHUBARB

Stewed, jam, tart, pudding—in whatever guise rhubarb is served up it is a highly popular addition to the table's dainties. The stems (which are the only edible portion of the plant) come fat and plentifully from any clump correctly tended. It makes massive roots which need to go down deeply; it needs manure or decayed vegetable matter to keep it going, and plenty of moisture must be supplied to the growing plants during dry spring and summer periods.

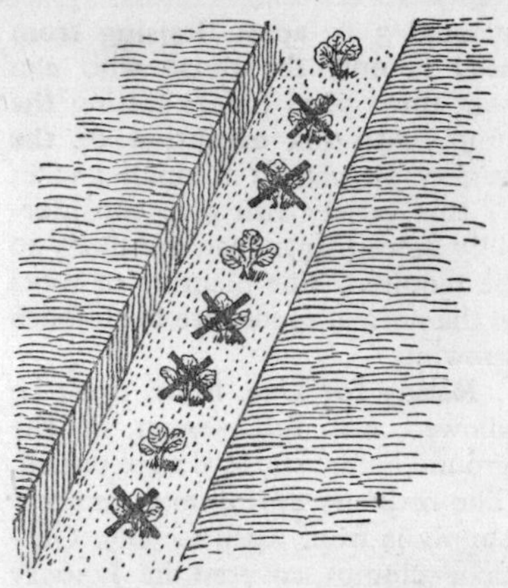

Fig. 256.—*Early thinning out of young radish plants is essential. Seedlings to be removed are indicated in this diagram by a* **×**

Varieties include The Sutton, for the main crop; Goliath, Reading Ruby, Champagne, Royal Albert, all providing pullings in advance of the main crop; Victoria, which comes in late and provides enormous sticks; Perpetual, which can be pulled in the same year as the seed is sown.

Roots, consisting of either one or two crowns (or buds), are

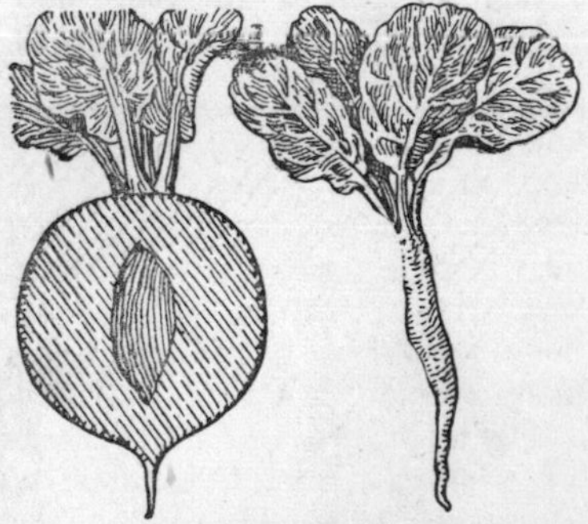

Fig. 257.—*Crowded radish plants develop hollow roots (left) or a lot of leaf and not much else (right)*

planted 3 ft. apart. Raising from seed is only for those who can wait three years before tasting the crop, with the exception of the variety Perpetual; a small packet of this variety will give considerably more plants than are likely to be required. The planting of roots is the normal procedure in rhubarb growing.

Ready for Use. Roots must be allowed one full season in the ground before any sticks are pulled. The ordinary spring and summer supply is from April to July. Outdoor clumps covered in January with inverted tubs or boxes give sticks fit for use two or three weeks in advance of the ordinary supply; with manure to cover the tubs or boxes, the supply is still earlier. Clumps lifted from the open in winter and forced in heat provide pullings of succulent sticks in about six weeks.

Soil Preparation. Rhubarb should be located handy to a water supply and where it can remain for years. It is a permanent, stand-still tenant. It can be planted between fruit trees provided these do not cast too much shade and the ground is dug at least 2 ft. deep and enriched before the roots go in. It is better off in the open than in constant shade.

Use of the spade or fork, and animal or hop manure, or rotted greenstuff, is amply repaid in future produce. Either of these rich materials should be mixed in very generously with the soil below the top foot; and a handful of bonemeal worked into the top soil around the root when planting will be well worth the little it will cost.

Soil that is heavy and wet can be brought to the right condition for rhubarb by mixing in throughout a depth of 2 ft. plenty of grit sand, sifted fire ashes or wood ash Soil light in nature and quick to dry out demands one of the rich materials (or a mixture of these) previously mentioned, in specially generous measure; they must serve the plant for years, so must be given in abundance.

Ground should be prepared well in advance, to give it plenty of time to settle down to the necessary firmness.

When and How to Plant. October and February are the best periods to get the roots in; February is preferable if the ground is heavy. A hole more than large

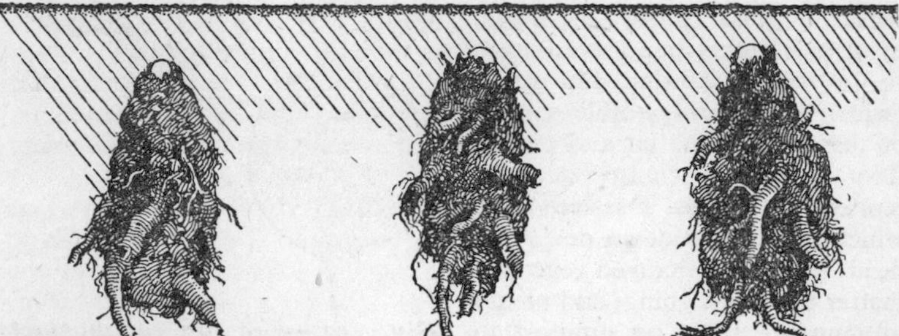

Fig. 258.—*Rhubarb roots should be planted deep enough for the tops to be covered with about 2 in. of soil, and set at distances of about 3 ft. apart*

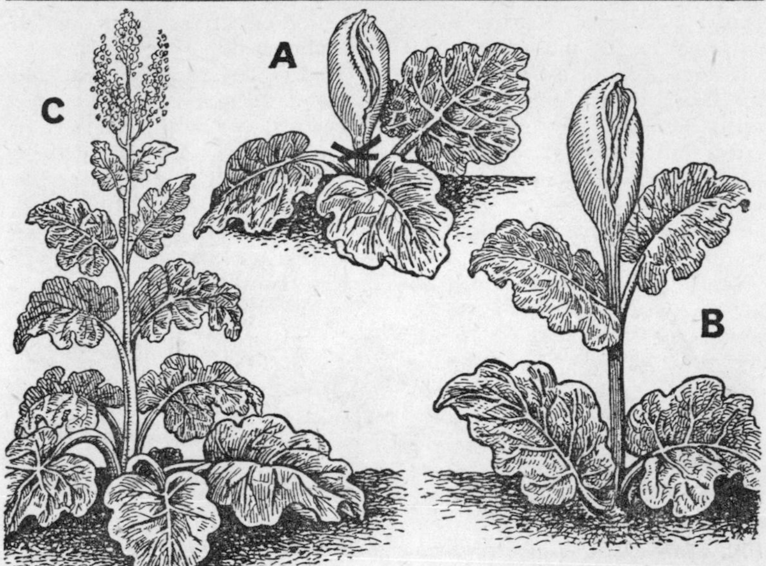

Fig. 259.—*Rhubarb weakens itself if allowed to run up to flower* (C) *and produce seed. The immature flower spike* (A) *should be removed before it gets to the stage shown at* (B). *It should be cut close to the ground*

enough to take the root should be made, the depth being such that when the hole is filled in the top of the fat, squat bud (there may be two, or only one, to each root) is covered with 2 in. of soil. Planting holes should be 3 ft. apart each way (Fig. 258).

When and How to Sow. Seed is sown in March, very thinly, in a drill 1 in. deep, and seedlings thinned out so that by the end of summer they stand about 9 in. apart. The following February they are lifted and replanted where they are to remain, 3 ft. apart. Growth at first is slow, and if they are to make really profitable clumps no sticks should be pulled until the plants are three years old. Exception to that is made in the case of the variety Perpetual, which gives sticks fit for use in six months. Seed of this can be sown outdoors in March, but stronger and earlier plants are obtained by sowing them in a shallow box, in a sunny frame or greenhouse, the seedlings being set out in rich ground in May, 3 ft. apart.

Watering and Feeding. Rhubarb will rub along, in a mediocre way, without any watering or feeding. But the difference in size and number of stems when the ground is soaked occasionally in rainless weather is remarkable. Weak liquid manure works wonders during the growing season.

Pulling the Sticks. First-year roots should be given a whole summer in which to become established, without a stem being taken. The temptation to ignore this rule is great, but for the sake of subsequent years it should be resisted.

Fig. 260.—*Out-of-season rhubarb can be produced outdoors by covering a dormant clump with sacking on a tripod of sticks (left) or an inverted box (right)*

Stems can be pulled when they attain useful size. It is wasteful to take them too young. Best stage at which to pull them is when the leaf is right open and flattened out. It is advisable to cease pulling at the end of July, each clump then being left with three or four stems to build up the plant's strength for next season.

Damage can be done by careless gathering. Best method is to grasp the stem low down, press it outward from the base, then twist it to left or right. It comes cleanly away then from the basal bud.

Rhubarb in Flower. The flowering stem of rhubarb (Fig. 259) is a startlingly massive affair, produced in summer, 4 ft. or 5 ft. high and crowned with creamy bloom. This is definitely wasted growth, so far as the home food producer is concerned, and weakening to the plant. The stem should be removed directly it is noticed, before it has reached more than a few inches in height. If seed is required, it is more profitable to buy a small packet than allow a strong clump to waste its substance in this manner.

Out-of-Season Rhubarb. The encouragement to produce early stems which a strong clump of rhubarb receives from a covering of some sort in January is considerable. A tub, barrel, or box not less than about 2 ft. deep up-ended over the clump is all that is needed to secure sticks two or three weeks earlier than the normal date (Fig. 260), which is advanced at least another fortnight if manure, or a mixture of manure and dead leaves, can be mounded over the covering.

Where this heating material is used, the tub, barrel or box should have a movable lid so that growth can be inspected and stems pulled without need for removing the covering. Out-of-season growth is brisker if the clumps are covered after a hard frost or two. Roots forced thus should not be cropped too severely the following summer.

Clumps lifted from the open and forced in heat in a greenhouse are so weakened that they are not worth replanting, but where the facilities exist a dish of rhubarb can be enjoyed at Christmas by beginning the indoor forcing about the second week in November. The clumps should be not less than three years old and should be dug up with as much root as possible. Place them under the greenhouse bench, close together, covered with soil (moistened with warm water) so that only the tips of the buds are visible, and sacking or other material hung from the bench to exclude light. In a temperature of about 55 deg. growth quickly begins and in six weeks or so there are fine pink stems to pull.

The roots may be packed closely in a box, with soil to fill the spaces, and then placed under the greenhouse bench, instead of being on the floor with soil packed around and between them. The same result is achieved if the box is placed in a cupboard in a room where the temperature remains steady at about 55 deg. by night as well as by day. Always the soil must be kept reasonably moist. Roots respond more readily to forcing if the clumps after being dug up are left exposed on the ground for about a fortnight for frost to get at them; it is no use exposing them in wet weather.

Cure for Thin Sticks. When stems begin to show sign of dwindling in size it is an indication that the clump is past its best. At the first hint of this the clump should be dug up, divided, and the strongest pieces replanted elsewhere, the new position to be dug and enriched well beforehand.

Time for this division and replanting is February. The old clump is got up, with all its roots, by digging deeply around it with the spade and then undermining. Hoisted on to the surface, the clump has then to be separated into suitable pieces, each piece to come away with either one bud or two, obviously worn-out pieces to be discarded (Fig. 261).

The mass is very woody, and it

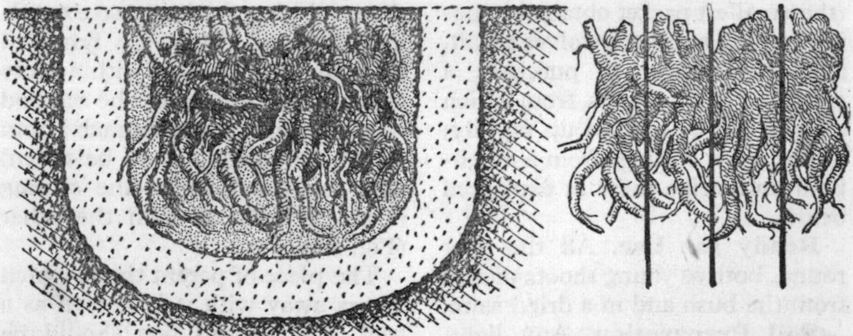

Fig. 261.—*A clump of rhubarb for division should be dug around and completely undermined* (*left*) *then hoisted to the surface and separated* (*right*)

may be necessary to use a saw to do the cutting—from top to bottom of the clump. It is possible to do it with a sharp spade held vertically and jabbed down forcefully, but seldom is division achieved in that way without one or two good buds being sliced and ruined.

The divisions are dealt with then as individual plants, and if the pulling of stems from these can possibly be avoided the following year they will make strong clumps.

Preparing for Table. Cut off leaf, and the base of the stem, and peel it from the bottom upwards if at all stringy. Then wash it, and cut into inch lengths for stewing, making puddings, tarts or jam.

SAGE

One of the most appetizing odours on any vegetable ground comes from sage, an evergreen shrub growing about 3 ft. high. The aromatic leaves are used for making stuffing and sauce. They can be picked any time of the year and can also be dried and stored. It is at home on chalk, in full sun, and its only fad is dislike of a heavy soil that lies wet in winter. This can be put right without difficulty.

Plants can be raised from seed (the smallest packet obtainable being ample), but that involves a wait, and it is better to purchase a couple of young plants, from which a stock can be worked up rapidly; or beg a few cuttings from a neighbour and strike these as explained below.

Ready for Use. All the year round, both as young shoots picked from the bush and in a dried state.

Soil Preparation. Any light, well-drained soil is suitable, well away from shade; in the latter position sage grows leggy and soon peters out. Clay or other heavy soil can be lightened with grit, sand, sifted ashes, wood ash, or chalk dug into it to the depth of about 18 in. Dusty ground will need old manure, hop manure, leaf-mould, or well-rotted vegetable refuse to give it body—not simply spread on the surface but mixed in throughout the top 18 in.

When and How to Sow. At the end of March or beginning of April seed can be sown about ⅛ in. deep in a well-raked bed, as thinly as they can be dropped, the seedlings to be trowelled up when they are big enough to handle and planted 4 in. apart. The following March or April they will be ready for planting where they are to remain.

When and How to Plant. Young plants can be purchased and got into the ground in late March or April, 12 in. apart, the roots to be covered in firmly. Settle with a good watering, and repeat this as necessary in dry weather. To give them a bushy foundation pinch off the ends of all shoots after planting; this causes other shoots to be produced, and a well-developed shrub results.

How to Take Cuttings. Side shoots about 4 in. long make excellent cuttings. They are removed from the parent plant with a piece of the latter attached. The method is to hold the stem or branch (from which the cutting is to be taken) with one hand whilst the cutting is gently torn off with the other (Fig. 262).

The piece of parent tissue which comes away with it is known as a heel. Any ragged bits should be trimmed from it with a knife, and the cutting is then ready to be

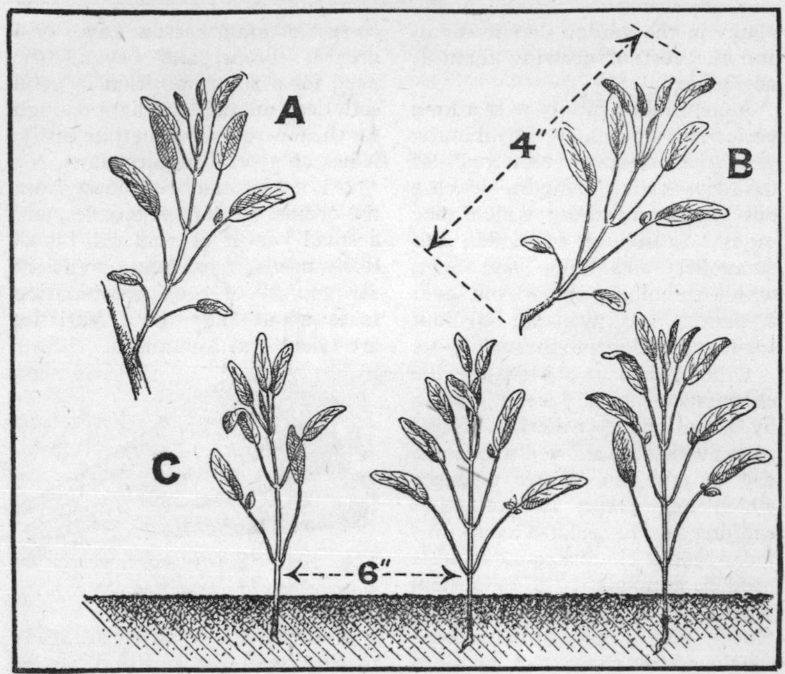

Fig. 262.—*Sage cuttings* (A) *are taken each with a heel* (B) *of the old wood, then planted as at* (C) *and made very firm in the ground*

planted. This is done in April or May, the prepared pieces being inserted in holes about 1 in. deep and then made firm at the base with the fingers. Set out about 6 in. apart in light soil where, shaded from midday sun, they quickly root, provided the ground is not allowed to become too dry. The following year they can be lifted and replanted where they are to stay; shoots to be nipped back, as previously explained, to induce bushiness.

Shapely Plants. Sage is not tidy in its habit of growth. Shoots are apt to straggle out from older shrubs. These need to be cut back about halfway, in September, and flower stems (the flowers are blue) removed at the same time.

Drying for Winter. The method is explained in the section EASY HOME PRESERVATION OF VEGETABLES (page 412).

SALADINGS

All plants commonly used for salad purposes—tomato, cucumber, lettuce, endive, mustard, cress, radish, onion, beet, etc.—are dealt with fully elsewhere in these pages under their respective names.

Apart from their tasty and refreshing qualities salads play a big part in maintaining general health. Eaten raw, nothing of the nutriment is lost, as it is in the case of cooked vegetables. Very little space is taken up by salad plants in the garden or allotment, and the cost of growing them is negligible.

A continuous supply over a long period is easily achieved by making very small sowings at intervals of ten days or a fortnight—leaving out of account those which take months to mature, as tomato and cucumber; and onion and beet, whose thinnings, spread out over a period, are available without sowings additional to the main crop.

Other points to observe are the encouragement of speedy growth by attention to watering. Salad plants which are allowed to become dry at any time suffer a check which may result in premature running up to seed. Given uniformly moist conditions no trouble need be anticipated. "Take them young" is a golden rule. Salad plants left to grow old become tough and lose those other qualities for which they are specially grown.

Early and late sowings of such things as lettuce, radish, mustard and cress should be in full sun in a position sheltered from cold winds; in a lightly shaded position during summer, especially if the soil is light and quick to dry out. Thinning out must never be delayed, and if seedlings are to be transplanted they should be moved from moist soil to moist soil, the watering-can taking the place of rain, if necessary.

SALSIFY

Salsify (Fig. 263) is a good food plant, with a most distinctive flavour reminiscent of oysters: hence its other name, vegetable oyster. The small parsnip-like roots are cooked and eaten in the manner of carrots or asparagus. The tops consist of long, narrow leaves of a greyish colour, and beyond the need for a sunny position in good soil, deep enough and light enough for the tap-roots to penetrate easily, it has no special requirements.

It is a welcome break-away from the ordinary run of vegetables, and a small packet of seed will fill all likely needs, 1 oz. being sufficient for 200 ft. of row. Germination takes about nine days. Varieties are Giant and Mammoth.

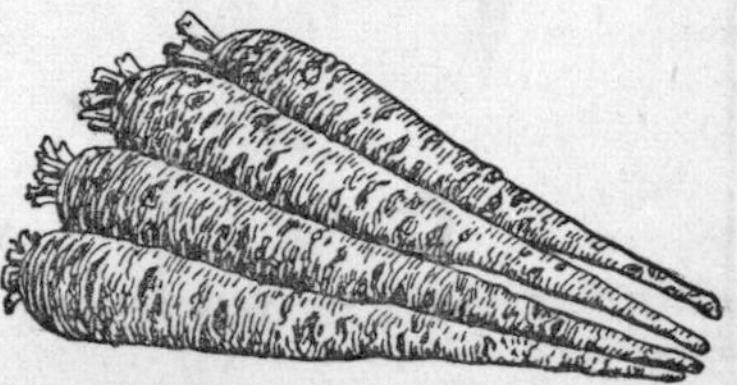

Fig. 263.—*Salsify roots ready for storage or to be prepared for cooking*

Ready for Use. Roots are ready for lifting in October and can be stored up to March.

Soil Preparation. Ground that is on the sandy side is ideal, especially if the seed can be sown where a deep-rooting crop such as peas or beans flourished. Poor soil should have old manure, or leaf-mould, worked in below the top 9 in., and leaf-mould or material from a worn-out hotbed or mushroom bed mixed with the top soil will help.

When and How to Sow. The time to sow is April and May, and the longish seeds should be dropped in threes at 9-in. intervals in a 1-in.-deep drill. If more than one row is required these should be 1 ft. apart.

Each cluster should be reduced to one plant when the grass-like seedlings are about 2 in. high. These may be transplanted if lifted carefully by means of a trowel.

Hoeing and weeding are the later attentions required.

Lifting the Roots. The fork should be used to get the roots up —without breakages—when the plants have completed their growth in October.

They can be left in the ground for lifting as wanted during winter if the soil is light and dry. Otherwise they will be safer put into store in November.

Storing for Winter. Freed of loose soil and the tops twisted off, the roots can be stored in a frost-proof shed, cellar or attic, in dry soil or sand.

Preparing for Table. Roots should be scraped gently to remove only a thin layer of peel, then placed in water containing a little lemon juice before cooking.

SAVOY

The savoy cabbage (Fig. 264) is noted for its hardiness and the fact that it will give satisfaction in soil not up to the rich standard required by the cabbage tribe generally. For cultural directions see Cabbage (page 258).

Varieties include—early: Best of All, Early Dwarf Ulm; maincrop: Dwarf Green Curled; late: Ormskirk Late Green, New Year, Rearguard, Late Drumhead.

Ready for Use. Heads can be cut as early as August, from an early sowing, but the crop is of greater value during autumn and winter—up to March.

Soil Preparation. Though just ordinary soil will suit savoy, the best heads are produced when the ground is dug deeply and enriched.

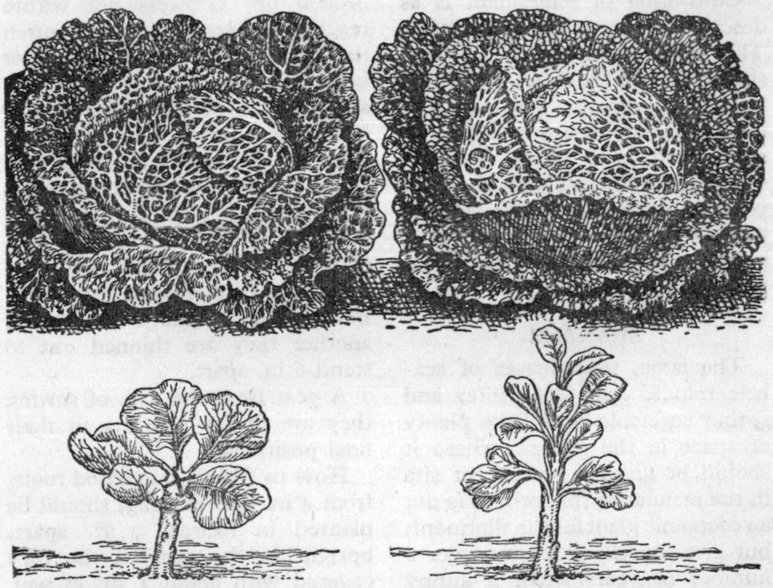

Fig. 264.—*Two fine savoy cabbages, as cut for the kitchen (above). Savoy stumps should be left with a few leaves and nicked across the top (below left) at the mark X, to produce sprouts (right) for later use as greens*

When and How to Sow. Seed may be sown from March to May; in the latter month if a late crop is wanted—transplanted seedlings being set out in July, 18 in. apart in rows 2 ft. apart. From the seed bed they should be shifted early to a nursery bed, 4 in. apart.

March-raised seedlings should be planted out finally in May; April-raised ones in June.

Cutting the Heads. Frost improves the flavour of savoy. If the loose outer leaves are left on the plant and only the compact head or heart is cut, useful sprouts will develop for use as greens (Fig. 264).

Preparing for Table. As under Cabbage (page 262).

SCORZONERA

Cultivation of scorzonera is as described under salsify (page 368). This plant has pointed, oblong-shaped leaves; the roots, for which the crop is grown, are long and black-skinned. The white flesh is sweet in flavour. If the roots do not reach sufficient size the first year the plants should be allowed to grow on a second year. Lifting, storing, preparing for table, as for Salsify (page 368).

SEAKALE

The large, thick leaves of seakale require that this winter and spring vegetable shall have plenty of space in the garden, where it should be given a permanent site in the manner of rhubarb. It is not an economic plant for the allotment, but gives excellent returns over a number of years when a sunny position and rich soil can be spared for it in the home garden.

Parts eaten are the stems and leaf stalks, which require to be blanched as explained below.

Varieties: Lily White, Ivory White, Ordinary.

Roots can be purchased for planting in March, and a stock can easily be worked up from root cuttings. Raising from seed is a slow business, plants not being profitable until they are two years old. A small packet suffices, and germination takes about twenty days.

Ready for Use. The blanched stems are available from February to June outdoors; earlier in heat.

Soil Preparation. Seakale in its wild form is a coastwise plant and accustomed to salty conditions. Seaweed is to its liking, buried thickly below the top 9 in., the soil below that depth being well broken up. Growers not within reach of free seaweed should enrich the ground with rotted manure or vegetable refuse well decayed. The soil needs to be well drained, clay or other heavy ground being brought to that condition by the digging in of mortar rubble, sand, grit or ashes.

When and How to Sow. Seed is scattered very thinly in 1-in.-deep drills in March or April. Before the seedlings jostle one another they are thinned out to stand 6 in. apart.

A year from the date of sowing they are fit for planting in their final positions.

How to Plant. Purchased roots, from 4 in. to 8 in. long, should be planted in March, 2 ft. apart, upright in the ground, the tops covered with about 1 in. of soil. Only one bud should be allowed to remain at each root-top, others being removed with a knife; the

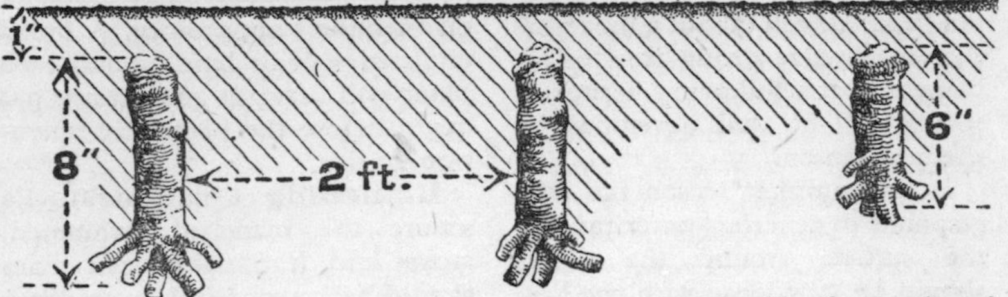

Fig. 265.—*Seakale roots are planted upright, covered with about* 1 *in. of soil, the ground to be well drained and rich, the position sunny*

object is to keep each plant single (Fig. 265).

Root Cuttings. Side roots can be taken from the main roots (or crowns) of older plants when these are dug up for forcing in a temperature of about 50 deg.; or they can be taken from a plant lifted for the purpose of increasing the stock.

The thin side roots, which will be about ½ in. thick, are cut away and divided into pieces about 5 in. long, for planting in March or April (Fig. 266). Each is dropped upright into a hole of sufficient depth and diameter to take it comfortably, the tops to be covered 1 in. deep. Space them out 2 ft. apart, and when top growth appears reduce the shoots to one per plant.

As a guide to which is top and bottom of these root cuttings they should each be cut square across at the upper end when removed from the main root, the lower end being trimmed slantwise.

Cuttings taken from roots lifted for forcing should be buried flat in a heap of soil, to await planting time (March).

Every properly planted root cutting is pretty certain to grow; those

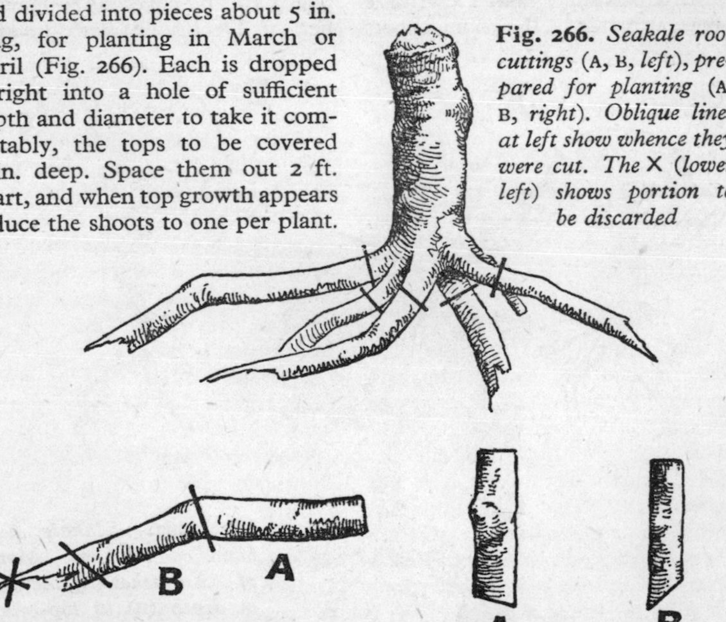

Fig. 266. *Seakale root cuttings* (A, B, *left*), *prepared for planting* (A, B, *right*). *Oblique lines at left show whence they were cut. The* X *(lower left) shows portion to be discarded*

not large enough (about 2 in. across the top) to give strong growths for blanching the following winter or spring will be well developed by the next season.

In the summer season the crop responds to generous watering, and the surface around the plants should be kept loose with the hoe. A big handful of agricultural salt per square yard should be hoed in during June and again four weeks later, the dressing to be followed by watering if it does not rain within a day or so.

Flower Stems. White flowers are produced in early summer, on 18-in. stems—if allowed to. Seeding will weaken the plants, so the stems should be broken out at the base before they have a chance to lengthen.

The only really troublesome pests which affect early growth are slugs, attracted by the young shoots on their first appearance. A broad circle of soot or lime around each plant will serve as protection, put down before the blanching operation begins.

Blanching Outdoors. To secure the blanched (whitened) stems and leaf-stalks, each plant should be covered in winter, when it is leafless, with an inverted box or tub; or, as soon as the first growths are visible above ground, with a 3-in.-deep mound of sifted fire ashes; or soil can be hoed up along both sides of a row of plants to cover the crowns to that depth. Before the growths push through the mound the depth of this should be increased to about 7 in. By the time the growths have reached that length they will be fit for cutting (Fig. 267).

How to Force Seakale. If plants can be covered, in November or December, with inverted

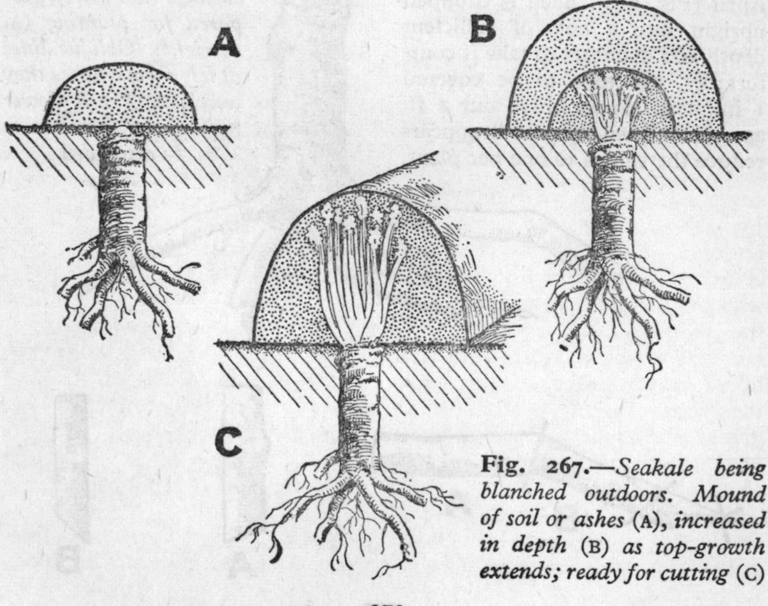

Fig. 267.—*Seakale being blanched outdoors. Mound of soil or ashes* (A), *increased in depth* (B) *as top-growth extends; ready for cutting* (C)

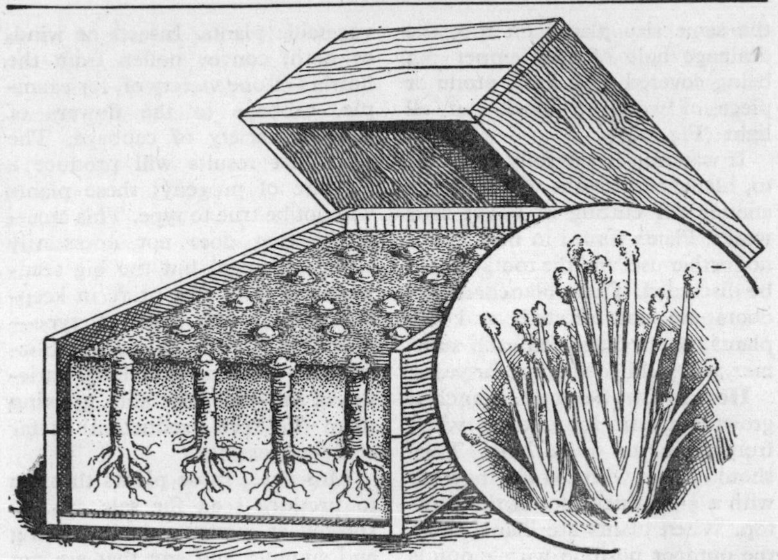

Fig. 268.—*Seakale ready to be blanched indoors, in a box of soil; one side removed to show the disposition of roots. The result is shown on the right*

boxes or tubs or large flower pots, and these in turn covered, a month later, with a mixture of fresh stable manure and dry leaves, production of blanched growths will be considerably hastened.

For forcing in a greenhouse, with a temperature of 50 deg. or more, strong roots should be lifted any time between November and January and planted—after the removal of side roots—close together in a box about 1 ft. deep, with soil between and around them, the root-tops just covered. The box is then placed under the greenhouse bench, water of the same temperature as the greenhouse is given, and light is excluded by placing an inverted box on top (Fig. 268).

Or prepared roots can be planted similarly in pots deep enough to hold them, with inverted pots of

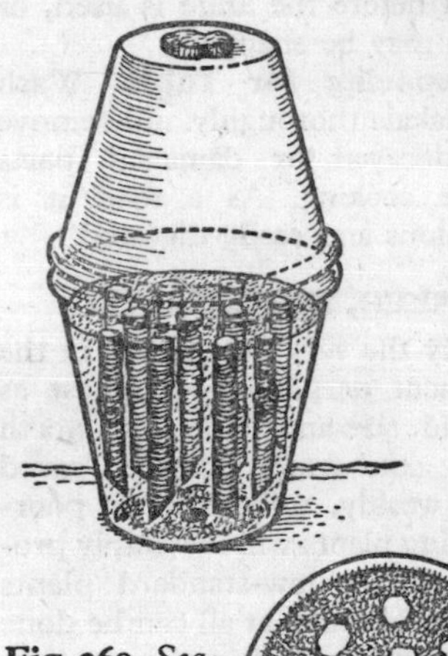

Fig. 269. *Seakale roots planted in a pot, covered with an inverted pot, for blanching indoors. Inset at lower right shows how the roots are spaced*

the same size placed on top, the drainage hole of each upper pot being covered with a flat stone or piece of wood to block out all light (Fig. 269).

If watering is carefully attended to, blanched growths will be large enough for cutting in about four weeks. Plants forced in heat are of no further use, and the roots should be discarded. Those blanched outdoors are not affected, and the plants, watered and fed each summer, will yield good crops for years.

How to Cut Seakale. Blanched growths are fit for cutting when from 7 in. to 9 in. long. They should be cut with a knife, together with a ½-in.-thick slice of the root-top. When plants are blanched in the outdoor position with mounds of soil or ashes, this material should be removed carefully from all round before the knife is used, or stems may be snapped.

Preparing for Table. Wash the seakale thoroughly and remove any decayed or damaged parts before cooking. As a food it is nutritious and easily digested.

SEED, HOME-SAVED

Only the very best plants in the allotment or garden—the best as to yield, size and so on—are worth saving seed from. For seed saved from weakly, unhealthy or poor-cropping plants will inevitably produce similar low-standard plants in turn. Nothing at all can be done in the way of cultivation to help poor-parentage seedlings build up into good plants. The result is inevitably a thoroughly unsatisfactory crop, wasted time, labour and ground.

Another point to be considered is the cross-fertilization of some vegetable plants. Insects or wind, or both, convey pollen from the flowers of one variety of, for example, cabbage to the flowers of another variety of cabbage. The seed that results will produce a mixture of progeny; these plants will not be true to type. This cross-fertilization does not necessarily always happen, but the big seed-growers—who take pride in keeping their stocks true to type—guard against chance cross-fertilization by isolating individual varieties of the same vegetable, growing them (for seed production) as far apart as possible.

Moreover, those plants that are to produce seed for sale are inspected at intervals during spring and summer and any that are not themselves absolutely true to type are pulled up and burned.

Saving Bean and Pea Seeds. The seeds most commonly home-saved for next year's sowing are those of beans and peas, and results are satisfactory providing the best pods, well packed with good, sound seed, are selected for the purpose.

The seed must be ripe when put away for the winter, or it will be useless. To that end the plants from which seed is to be saved must be left to grow on until the pods are yellow or brown. When that change of colour has taken place the seeds within the pods have become hard. To make certain they really are thoroughly ripened, the plants can be pulled up and laid out so as to expose the pods to all the sun that is going, until they are baked dry.

If there is more rain than sun the plants could be hung up under cover, where plenty of fresh air circulates, until pods are quite dry.

Marrow Seed. There is no trouble about harvesting seed of vegetable marrow or obtaining enough to fill the next year's needs, the fruit being packed tightly with big flat seed. A specially selected marrow should be left on the plant until as late in autumn as possible, to ripen completely. It is then sliced in half, lengthwise through the centre, and the seeds picked out of the pulp and dried in the sun for a day or two.

Next Year's Tomatoes. Where facilities exist for the home-raising of tomato plants it may be worth while saving a few seed from one or two of the finest fruits on a plant that happens to be outstanding because of its heavy yield and excellent behaviour generally. The selected tomatoes should be picked when quite ripe, opened, and the pulp rubbed in a folded cloth to remove the seed, this then being dried by exposure to sun.

Second-year Seeders. It is the nature of onion, beet, carrot, parsnip, and members of the cabbage tribe to flower and produce seed not during their first year of existence but when they are in their second. That makes it necessary for the grower who would get seed from them to make special provision for this second year of growth.

The few specimens that here and there in the rows run up to flower within a few weeks of being sown are behaving unusually, and this undesirable tendency to bolt would be passed on through their seed. These therefore should be shunned as seed producers. The extra year of growth that is necessary for the second-year seeders is arranged for by replanting one or two specimens of each kind after the crop has been lifted—or cut, in the case of cabbage.

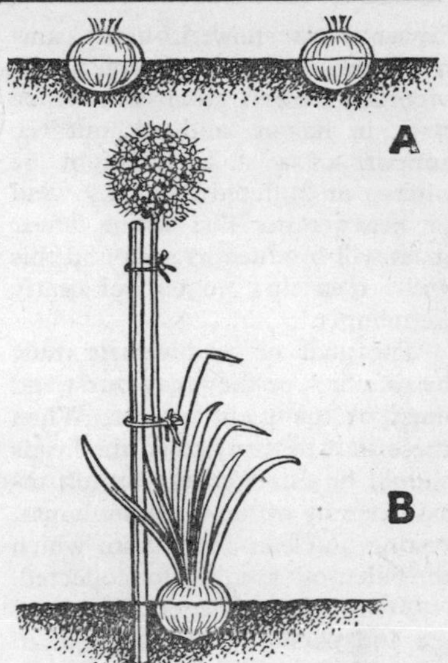

Fig. 270.—*Onions taken from store and planted* (A) *for the production of seed. In flower and staked* (B)

Onion Seed. The flower-head of an onion results in a large quantity of seed (Fig. 270), and the home food producer is not likely to want more than a couple of onion plants can produce. Bulbs selected from the general crop for their shape and size (both qualities to be typical of the particular variety) should be taken from store in February or March and planted about 12 in. apart in rich soil and a sunny, sheltered position. They should be just deep enough in the ground to remain steady in position, which means that the top half of each bulb will be exposed above the surface.

Water is to be given to the growing plants as needed, and when flower stems show, in early summer, each should be staked. A vigorous flower stem will reach 3 ft. in height, and without the support of a stake it might be broken or buffeted down by wind or heavy rain. The white flower mass will produce its seed and this will ripen in August or early September.

The pods or seed vessels must be watched, or they may burst and most of the seed be lost. When these start to turn brown the heads should be removed for drying inside a sunny window or greenhouse, resting on clean paper from which the fallen-out seed is later collected.

Other Root Crops. Beet, carrot and parsnip that are required to produce seed are planted out, from store, and dealt with in the same manner as onion bulbs (already explained). Flower stems of beet are safer if given a stake; carrot and parsnip do not need this.

The flowers of these, and of onion, can be safeguarded against the possibility of receiving pollen from other varieties of their kind by having muslin bags slipped over their heads. But that must be done before the flowers actually open (Fig. 271).

The Cabbage Tribe. Members of the cabbage family produce seed in plenty if, after kitchen requirements have been taken from them, old plants are lifted and replanted where they will not be in the way. New growth will be made from the stems or stumps, and from that new growth will arise in due course flower stems productive of seed pods; the seed is removed from them when the pods have ripened.

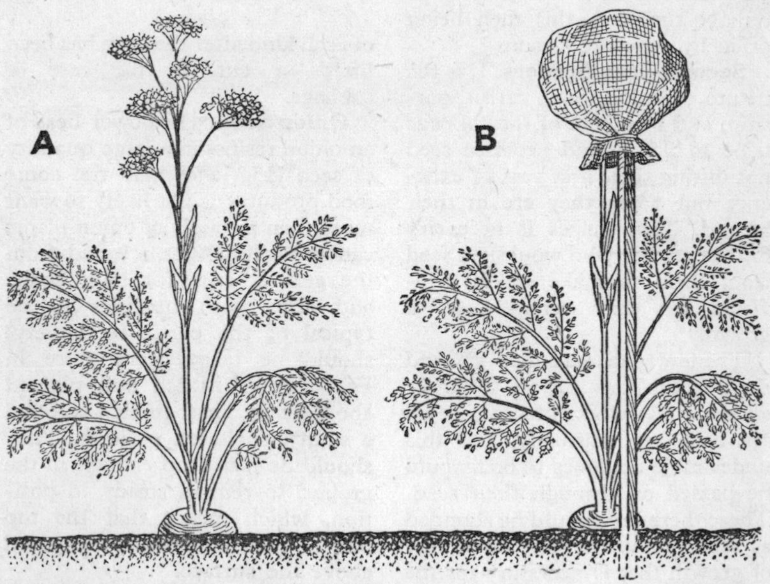

Fig. 271.—*A flower-head of carrot* (A) *enclosed in muslin bag* (B) *before flowers open, to prevent cross-fertilization. This ensures true-to-type seed*

How to Store Seed. Shelled out of their pods, or shaken from seed heads, the seeds should be examined and cleaned, so far as is possible. Large ones, such as peas and beans, can be rapidly looked over and any that have been pierced by grubs thrown out. Small ones can be scattered on the palm of one hand and blown at gently to remove grit, husks and other bits of rubbish.

They should then be put away in stout paper bags for winter storage beyond the influence of damp and heat and frost, and out of reach of rats and mice. A sure way of keeping seeds from these pests is to put them in tins with tight lids, or in jars or wide-mouthed bottles with screw-on caps or properly fitting corks.

Each bag, tin, jar or bottle should be labelled with the name and variety of the seed it contains.

New Seeds Best. Pea and bean seeds remain good for a couple of years, as also do onion and carrot; three years is the useful life of lettuce, parsley, spinach; and seed of the cabbage tribe is good for four years. Beet, cucumber, marrow have a span of five years, but parsnip seed is of no use when more than a year old.

The younger the seed of any kind of vegetable, the more numerous the seedlings that come up. The older the seed the more thickly it must be sown, because fewer will germinate. The unwisdom of relying on other than new seed is obvious.

Also it is not wise to rely entirely on home-saved seed of any particular vegetable crop that is to be grown more or less extensively. A portion of the crop should, if possible, be raised from purchased seed, just in case the home efforts are not rewarded with full success.

SHALLOT

Not only when onions are in short supply is the shallot useful. It is invaluable for adding flavour to stews and soups, and for making winter pickles. It gives a really big return for space occupied, and on ground without much good depth—where onions do not do well—shallots can be depended on.

Varieties include Mammoth Exhibition, Giant, Ordinary. The simplest way of dealing with this crop is to plant bulbs (sets or cloves), sold by the pound; $1\frac{1}{4}$ lb. is sufficient for a 30-ft. row. Each bulb produces a cluster of others like itself. Or seed—variety The Sutton—can be sown, to produce single bulbs; there are about 1,000 plants in 1 oz. They come up in about ten days, and can be pulled about six months after sowing.

Ready for Use. Harvesting time is July, and bulbs can be kept sound in store up to March.

Soil Preparation. If shallots can be prepared for as explained under Onion (page 324), they will be given ideal conditions. If the ground is light it should be improved by digging in old leaves, or decayed material from the soft rubbish heap or pit. It must be firm, any suspicion of looseness underfoot being an indication that treading or rolling is required.

Before planting or sowing, a good scattering of wood ash, or a sprinkling of superphosphate of lime, should be raked or hoed into the surface, or, where the soil is of the summer-thirsty kind, dusted over the bottom of a broad drill.

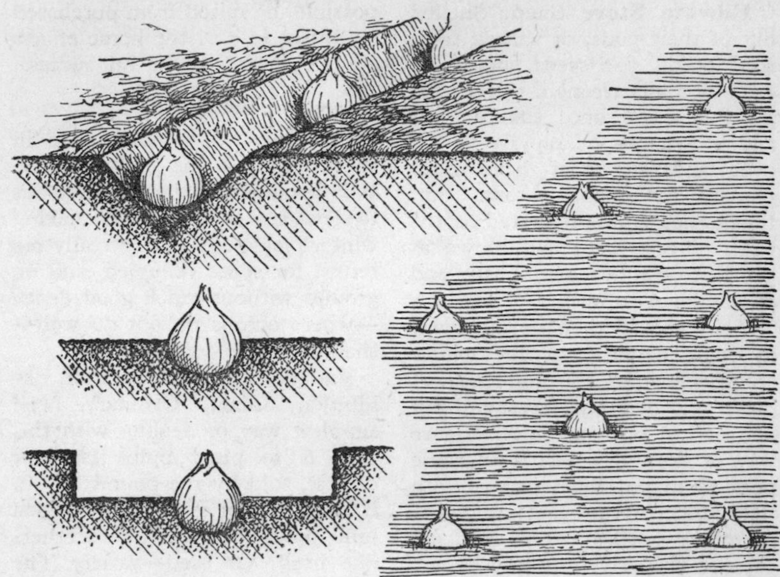

Fig. 272.—*Shallots planted on the flat (right, and middle left); in a wide drill (lower left); in a V drill (top left). These methods suit thin, dry soil*

The shallot is a sun-lover, so its position should be beyond any shade.

When and How to Sow. Seed is sown very thinly in rows about 8 in. apart, and covered with ½ in. of soil. Seedlings are thinned to 8 in. apart, and the thinnings can be transplanted.

When and How to Plant. Late January and February are the months for planting, though if the site has not been prepared by then or the weather is unsuitable the planting would be better delayed until March. The bulbs are set out 9 in. apart in rows 1 ft. apart, and are to be buried only half their own depth—that is, the top half is to be above ground.

Shallow planting holes can be made with a trowel, soil being pressed back around each bulb as it goes into place. Or a continuous shallow V-shaped drill can be made with a corner of the draw hoe and the bulbs pressed gently into position at 9-in. intervals. The best plan on dry ground is to make flat-bottomed drills the width of the draw hoe blade and about 2 in. deep, and plant the bulbs along the centre. Should water prove precious in late spring and early summer every drop poured into the drills will be put to good account and none run to waste (Fig. 272).

Wind, Worms, Cats. It is a common experience to find newly planted shallot bulbs dragged out of position by worms or scattered by wind or cats. It does not happen after the bulbs have anchored themselves with roots, but rooting is delayed by disturbance. Wind can be a considerable source of annoyance on light soil, but the bulbs are less at the wind's mercy if soil is pressed around them firmly. The trouble most frequently arises when the bulbs are merely pushed halfway in, not properly planted.

Worms and scratching cats both hate soot. If this—straight from the chimney, if possible—is scattered thickly between and outside the rows the pests are defeated. But more than one application of soot will be necessary, particularly after heavy rain.

Hoeing and Feeding. If the drill method of planting is adopted the drills must not be filled in during hoeing—if the latter proves necessary for keeping down weeds. The new bulbs which develop around the base of the old one want room to swell, so they should be allowed to sit on the surface.

Some time in June or July they will be approaching the ripening stage, and in this condition they will be assisted by the removal, with hoe or fingers, of any soil that is covering their lower parts. But this removal must not be overdone, to the extent of exposing roots.

A little poultry manure sprinkled in the rows now and again during April and May and watered in will assist the crop.

Lifting the Bulbs. Just when the bulbs are ready for pulling up depends on the date of planting and the warmth of the season or district. But July is the usual month. Yellowing of the tops shows that growth is completed, and any time after these start to wither the clumps of bulbs can be pulled up.

Each cluster should be broken up and the separated bulbs laid out in the sun, on hard ground, a clean path, or the roof of a shed, to dry. After two or three days they can be stored; if rain falls meanwhile the bulbs must be covered over or taken under cover.

Bulbs raised from seed sown in March may be a little later in ripening.

Storing for Winter. Any dry place where air circulates freely will carry shallots safely through winter to as late as March. Remnants of the tops should be removed and the bulbs placed in paper bags or not-too-deep boxes.

The best of the crop (from planted bulbs only) should be set aside for planting the following year.

Preparing for Table. Bits of root and outer skin should be rubbed off, before cooking or pickling. Shallot has the same nutritive value as its near relation, the onion.

SPINACH, SUMMER OR ROUND

The leaves of spinach are a most desirable vegetable, the summer varieties being classed as round because the seeds are round, winter varieties as prickly because the seeds are prickly.

Summer spinach is very apt to run up to seed (bolt) in light soil, but the risk is reduced where the ground is heavier, rich and moisture-holding.

Varieties include The Carter, Long Standing Round, Victoria. One-tenth ounce of seed will sow a 30-ft. row, and seedlings appear in about twelve days.

Ready for Use. First leaf pickings can be had in May from an early sowing, and with a succession of small sowings gatherings are available up to September. Time to elapse between sowing and picking is about twelve weeks.

Fig. 273.—*Summer spinach sown in seed-groups of three in flat drills between rows of peas. It helps germination if the seed is soaked in water*

Soil Preparation. A light soil is definitely not to the liking of summer spinach; even a short drought will cause the plants to bolt. But it can be made more substantial and moisture-holding by digging in rotted manure or decayed greenstuff; leaf-mould is very useful in this respect. Ground cannot be too rich for the crop.

The position should not be in full sun but where some shade falls, as between bean or pea rows. The full benefit of watering is secured if the plants are grown in 2-in. deep drills.

When and How to Sow. The earliest sowing is usually made in February, and small successive sowings continue up to August. Drills are made 12 in. apart and the seed covered 1 in. deep. Germination is assisted by soaking the seed in water with the chill off for about twenty-four hours, previous to sowing (Fig. 273).

Economy in seed and the trouble of later thinning out is effected by dropping the seed in threes every 8 in. along the drill, each group of seedlings being reduced to one. Frequent soakings with water will be needed to keep the plants going in the absence of sufficient rain.

Gathering the Leaves. The outside leaves are picked as they become large enough, a few only at a time from each plant. If a plant is stripped, it is finished. If two or three are taken at a time, it will continue to produce more until it is exhausted.

Preparing for Table. Wash the leaves and remove coarse stems before cooking. No green vegetable is more easily digested. It is rich in iron and in vitamins A, B and C.

SPINACH, WINTER OR PRICKLY

The prickly part of this spinach, which is for winter and spring use, is the seed. Varieties include Giant-leaved Winter and Long Standing Prickly.

Ready for Use. Leaves are ready for picking in October, and onwards to March.

Soil Preparation. Ground should be rich and well drained. If it lies wet in winter this spinach may fail.

How and When to Sow. First sowing may be made in July, and small sowings at intervals until August, in drills 1 ft. apart, the seed to be covered 1 in. deep, and seedlings thinned out to leave plants 6 in. apart.

Other details as for summer spinach.

SPINACH, NEW ZEALAND

Where summer spinach fails, because of dry soil, New Zealand spinach has a reasonable chance of success, however hot the summer may be. The thick leaves, triangular in shape, are carried on stems which creep close to the ground.

Ready for Use. First pickings in June, and on to September.

Soil Preparation. Ground needs to be dug well and enriched with whatever humus-providing material is available—old stable or farmyard manure, hop manure, leaf-mould and decayed vegetation generally. The position should be fully exposed to sun, in as warm a spot as possible.

When and How to Sow. It is not safe to sow outdoors until May, seed then being dropped in threes, the groups to be 18 in. apart, seedlings to be reduced to one at each position. It helps germination if the seed is first soaked for twenty-four hours.

Earlier plants, to provide the June pickings, are raised in a greenhouse, or hotbed frame, with a temperature of about 55 deg. The seed is sown, singly, well apart in shallow boxes filled with leafy soil. The plants are hardened off in a cold frame and planted out in late May. As these occupy more space than outdoor-raised plants (the longer season of growth helping them do so) they should be spaced 3 ft. apart.

Successional sowings are not necessary; one main sowing suffices.

Gathering the Leaves. Plants should not be stripped, but leaves picked here and there from the creeping stems, which continue to produce foliage until the autumn.

Other details as for summer spinach.

SWEDE

Boiled as a winter vegetable the roots of the swede (Fig. 274) are delicious; the young tops can be boiled, too. In districts where the winter is generally too severe for the ordinary turnip, garden varieties of the swede will stand up to any frost. And any reasonably good soil will grow a good crop.

Varieties include Purple-top, Crimson-top, Bronze-top, White. A small packet of seed will suffice, 2,000 plants being represented in 1 oz. Germination takes about twelve days.

Ready for Use. Roots reach useful size by October and are available until March.

Soil Preparation. Moisture is one of the chief requirements; in dusty ground the seedlings hang

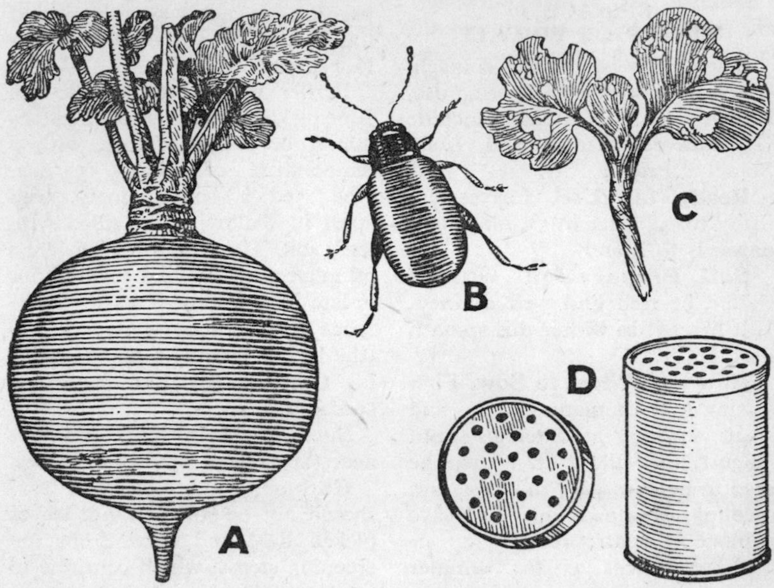

Fig. 274.—*Garden swedes* (A) *can be safeguarded against attack by the flea-beetle* (B, *greatly enlarged*), *which nibbles the seedlings* (C), *by dusting soot over the young plants from a tin with a perforated lid* (D)

fire. The crop is worth digging 18 in. for; and any rotted leaves that can be spared should be dug in, to improve the moisture-holding quality of the ground.

When and How to Sow. From March to June is the usual sowing period, the earlier date being chosen if well-developed roots are wanted by October. These take about seven months to reach useful size.

Seed is sprinkled very thinly in a 1-in.-deep drill; if more than one row is needed the drills should be drawn 15 in. apart. The seedlings need early thinning, so that plants stand finally at 1 ft. apart in the row. Labour in thinning out is saved if three or four seeds are dropped in groups 1 ft. apart, instead of being sprinkled in a continuous line. Thinning is then performed speedily, even though every seed produces its seedling.

Summer Hoeing. If water can be given to the seedlings in dry weather it will help them over the danger period—the young stage when the turnip flea-beetle and its grubs feed on the leaves (Fig. 274). Hoeing frequently close beside the rows will help considerably; it encourages quick growth. Soot dusted over the young plants (Fig. 274), when these are damp with dew or after rain, is beneficial, making the foliage distasteful to pests.

Pulling the Roots. Overgrown roots are tough; the swede is at its best when the roots are of medium size, young and firm and juicy. They should be pulled up as wanted for use in the kitchen.

Storing for Winter. Swedes take no harm left in the ground all winter, but if the ground is to be cleared for digging the roots can be taken up, the top growth cut off, and stored in a heap of sifted fire ashes in a shed or cellar. Or the roots can be clamped outdoors, as explained under Beet (page 252).

Swede Tops. The green vegetable part of this crop is extremely useful in winter. Three or four roots are pulled up from the open or taken from store—not the best, but the unshapely or undersized ones. Place them in a box, touching, top side up, and dribble soil in the gaps until it is level with the crowns. Place the box in a warm, dark cupboard, or under the greenhouse bench, with another box, inverted, on top to exclude light. Keep the soil just moist (not wet), and new top growth will be produced. The tender leaves can be cut when large enough, for boiling.

Preparing for Table. Roots should be peeled, with a knife, and cut into ½-in.-thick slices, before cooking. Tops should be washed, for boiling. Swedes contain vitamins B and C.

THYME

Refreshingly aromatic, the leaves of the dwarf (6-in.-high) evergreen herb called thyme (Fig. 275) are used in making stuffing and for flavouring soups and sauces. It grows well in any sunny spot, and it prefers dryish ground. Varieties are Common and Lemon Thyme.

Young plants can be purchased. Or a stock can be raised by means of cuttings or root divisions from an old plant—obtained by barter with a fellow gardener. The slowest method is that of sowing seed. Seedlings of the herb must be allowed a year of grace before sprigs can be picked. Established plants offer suitable small shoots all the year round, being evergreen. Shoots can also be dried for winter use.

Soil Preparation. Plants are apt to perish in winter if the ground is very heavy and water-holding. This type of soil should be made thoroughly porous by means of sand or sharp grit dug in before planting. Very light soil should be stiffened with hop manure or leaf-mould. The warmest corner of the piece of ground is the most suitable.

When and How to Sow. During March or April seeds can be sown in a ½-in.-deep drill, as thinly as they can be spaced, and the seedlings lifted three or four months later and planted where they are to remain, about 6 in. apart.

When and How to Plant. Either March or September is suitable for planting purchased plants. They should be set out about 6 in. apart, and at once watered in. Apart from keeping them free of weeds no other attention is required—except the replanting which is necessary every three years or so; they are apt to die out in winter when they become too woody.

Dividing and Replanting. The plants form straggling tufts, and at the end of three or four years need to be divided. Lifted with a trowel, a plant is pulled apart into as many pieces as will come away with roots. These divisions are replanted, as deeply as the lowest shoots, and the soil pressed firmly around them. Late March or April is the best time in which to do this.

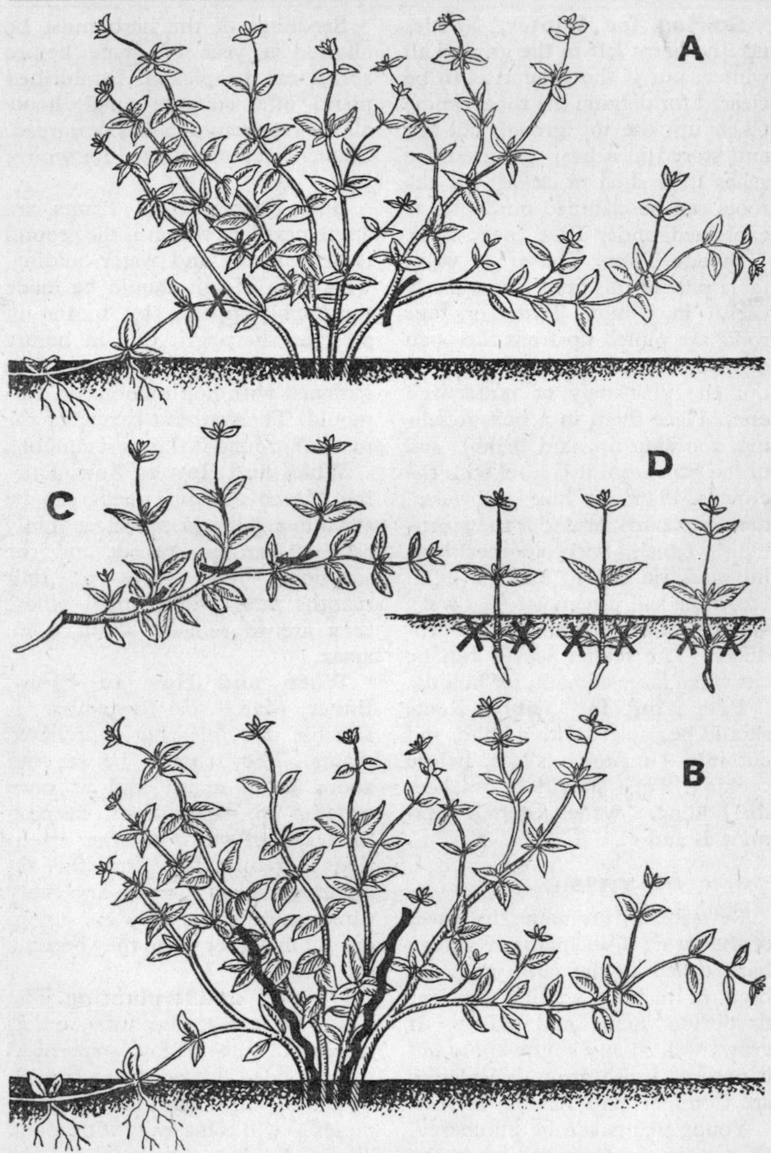

Fig. 275.—*A shoot of thyme layered* (A, *lower left*) *for transplanting; it will be severed at* (X). *The extreme right shoot will provide useful cuttings, as at* (C), *to be planted as at* (D) *after removal of lowest leaves* (X). *A plant can be divided for replanting as shown by thick wavy lines at* (B)

In order to take cuttings side shoots, or sprigs, are removed from the old woody main stems in such a manner that they have attached to them a piece of the parent bark —technically, a heel. Ragged edges of this are trimmed with a sharp knife, and the cuttings are ready for planting, 6 in. apart, where they are to remain. They may be anything between 2 in. and 4 in. long, and 1 in. of the stem should be below ground, which is afterwards firmed with the fingers or boot heel.

This may be done any time during summer. The cuttings must be kept supplied with water during dry weather, and if the soil is very light and thirsty they will take root more quickly in a lightly shaded spot; they can be transplanted to a more open position the following March or April.

Gathering Shoots. Shoots can be picked for use whenever required, but should not be removed complete; 1 in. of stem should remain where each sprig is taken, to send out fresh growth.

For Winter Use. Method of storing a supply of thyme is explained in the section Easy Home Preservation of Vegetables and Herbs (page 412).

TOMATO

One of the greatest of favourites for eating and cooking, the tomato is of special value on account of its health-giving vitamins. Splendid crops can be grown in the open as well as in an unheated or heated greenhouse, either from purchased or home-raised plants. Moderately good soil, warmth and a moist root-run are the chief requirements.

Early ripening varieties are necessary for outdoor culture. They include the following, which are also suitable for the greenhouse: Earliest of All, Princess of Wales, Abundance, Up to Date, Ailsa Craig, and, if yellow fruits are favoured, Golden Queen, Golden Nugget. If masses of large corrugated fruit are wanted, an excellent early outdoor variety is Open Air. Earliness in ripening is especially desirable when tomatoes are grown outdoors, owing to the comparative shortness of the summer.

The easiest method is to purchase young plants in late May (June in cold districts) for setting out 18 in. apart. A heated greenhouse or hotbed frame is needed for raising plants from seed. A small packet will suffice, 1 oz. of seed representing 2,000 plants. Seedlings appear in about ten days.

Ready for Use. Outdoors, tomatoes are ready for picking at the end of July and up to late September; in an unheated, sunny greenhouse in early July and up to late October; in a heated greenhouse winter and early spring crops are possible.

Outdoor Crops. For early and prolonged fruiting the ideal outdoor position is in full sun, shielded from cold winds, as at the foot of a fence or wall facing south or west. If that is not available plants may be set out in rows in the open, these to run north and south, thus securing an equal share of sun on both sides of each row.

Bought Plants. These should be about 9 in. high, close jointed, thick stemmed, dark green with a bluish tinge, and preferably showing the first flower truss. Avoid leggy plants with light green foliage; they have been rushed in considerable heat and not properly hardened off for planting out. If small white flies are present the plants will be dear at any price.

They should not be purchased before late May for outdoor planting. Those raised in pots give the best crops; plants from boxes have been cramped for root space and are not so suitable.

Soil Preparation. The site should be dug 18 in. deep, with leaf-mould or hop manure worked in 9 in. down, and plenty of wood ash (from the rubbish fire) mixed with the top soil. Stable manure may be used, but unless it is quite old it should not be nearer the surface than about 9 in. Manure near the top at planting time results in gross, unfruitful growth. If nothing of this nature is at hand for enriching the ground, dig in well-decayed material from the soft refuse collection.

When and How to Plant. The end of May is early enough to set out the plants. If the weather is specially favourable they might be planted as early as the middle of the month, but the possibility of destruction by late frosts must always be taken into account. In colder midland and northern districts the wise rule is to play for safety and defer planting a few days into June.

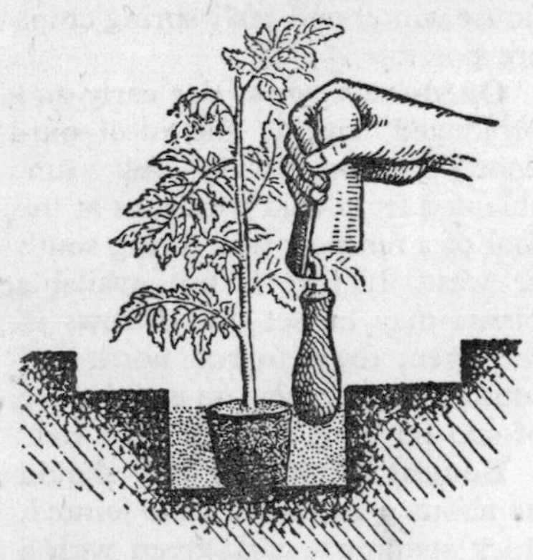

Fig. 276.—*A young tomato plant being firmed, with the end of the trowel, in its planting hole. The broad depression is for later watering*

If the soil in the pots or boxes containing the plants is other than moist, soak it right through an hour or two before planting. Remove them from a box with a trowel; from pots in such a way that the ball of soil surrounding the roots is not broken, and remove the drainage crocks.

Planting holes, made with the trowel, should be more than large enough to take the ball of soil and roots. When the plant is in position well-crumbled soil is worked down the sides of the hole, until this is filled, and firmed with the butt end of the trowel (Fig. 276). The plant should rest at such a depth that the top of the ball of soil is just covered.

The surface of the filled hole should be 2 in. lower than the surrounding level, to hold water when this is given. If this depression is about 1 ft. across, so much the better (Fig. 277).

Roots should be about 6 in. away from the base of fence or wall; in this position the depression would be semicircular and not round in shape. Plants to be 18 in. apart. If grown in rows the latter should be 3 ft. apart.

They should be started off with a good watering; and if the weather is very bright and the leaves show signs of drooping the plants should be shaded with paper whilst the sun is on them, at any rate for the first couple of days.

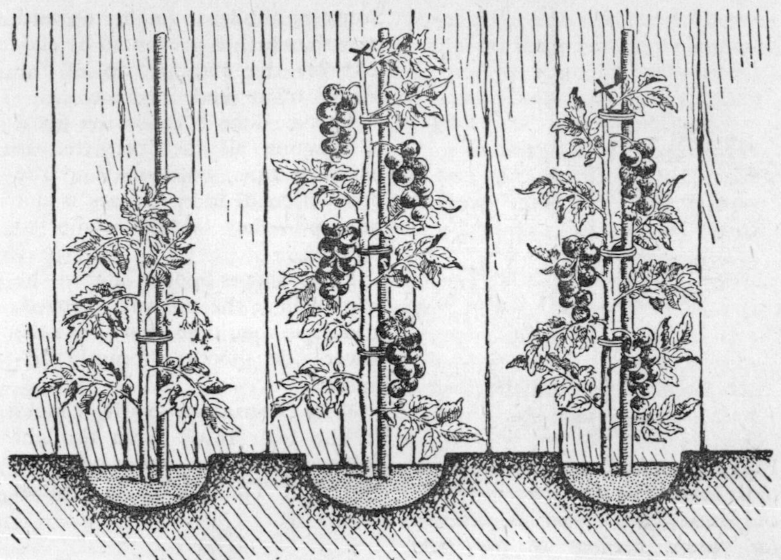

Fig. 277.—*Tomato plants at the foot of a fence, with depressions for watering. The young plant on the left has its first flower truss. Centre, top of plant removed* (X) *above fourth truss of fruit. Right, top removed above third truss*

For a week or so after planting tomato plants should have nightly protection, in the form of paper hoods, or inverted boxes can be placed over them, as a safeguard against frost, the covering to be removed by day.

Staking and Tying. Stakes are essential, whether the plants are against fence or wall or in an open bed, and should be put in place as soon as night protection ceases to be necessary. They need to be really strong, should be pushed deeply into the ground about 3 in. behind the plant, and should stand about 5 ft. above the surface.

Tie each plant to its stake with raffia or thick string, the loop to be loose enough to allow room for stem expansion, more ties to be given as the plant extends its growth upwards (Fig. 278).

Keep to Single Stems. It is the nature of a tomato plant to produce several stems, these beginning as small side shoots arising in the angles between leaves and main stem. All these should be removed as soon as they appear, leaving only the single main stem; the object being to divert all the energies of the plant to a few large trusses of fruit (Fig. 279).

A watch needs to be kept for these side shoots. They are produced lavishly, they lengthen very speedily, and some are apt to be overlooked among the general foliage. They can be broken out from their sockets with a push of the finger, or be nicked out with the point of a pocket-knife blade.

Watering and Feeding. Tomatoes are thirsty plants and in dry weather water ought not to

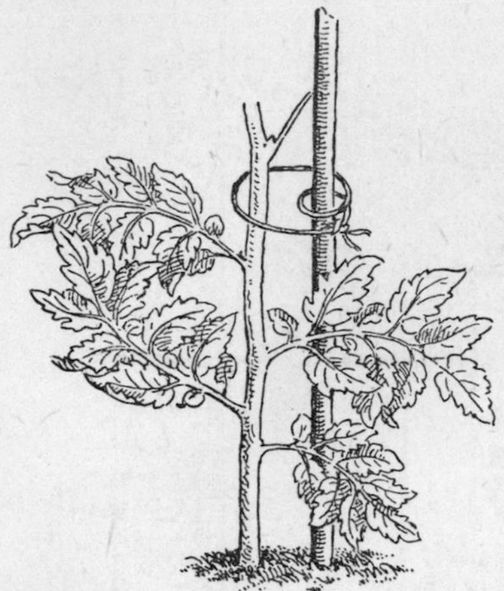

Fig. 278.—*How to tie a tomato plant to its stake. The tie is knotted behind the stake, and room is allowed for future swelling of the stem*

be stinted. They are hungry, too, but feeding from the surface should not begin until the first fruits on a plant are rather larger than marbles. One of the special tomato fertilizers can be used (sold by seedsmen and some chemists and at the big stores). A spoonful per plant once a week is sufficient, sprinkled on the soil above the roots and watered in.

If roots appear at the surface, cover with 1 in. of good soil with which a little of the special fertilizer has been mixed. Make this top dressing firm.

When to Remove Tips. In a hot summer plants set out early can ripen five trusses (bunches) of fruit, but four is the normal number; in cold and late districts three trusses are the limit of a plant's ripening capability. According to the local conditions, each plant should be stopped when its third, fourth or fifth truss has developed. Stopping alludes to further upward growth, which is prevented by cutting off the extreme tip of the plant's main (and only) stem.

This is done because the plant is carrying all the fruit that is likely to ripen outdoors, and the production of more trusses is not required—they would come to nothing.

Other shoots appear later at the point where the tip was removed, and these should be treated like the lower side shoots—promptly dismissed.

Why Tomatoes Split. Cracks in the fruit result from drought followed by heavy rain or generous watering. The trouble is avoided

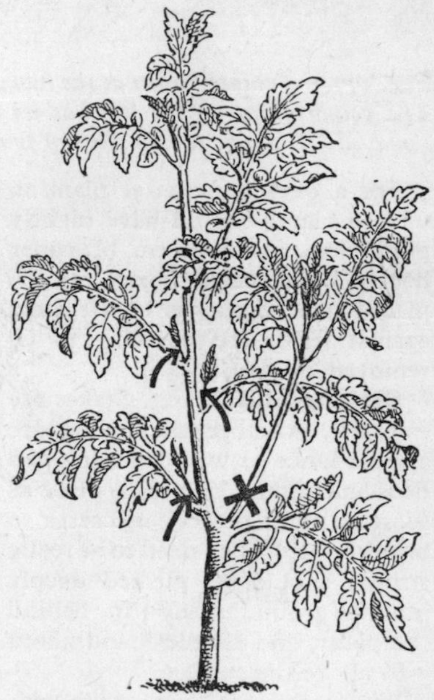

Fig. 279.—*A tomato plant is kept to a single stem by the early removal of side shoots (arrows). The shoot on the right, overlooked by the grower, should be broken out at its base* (X)

Fig. 280.—*Tomato seedlings raised in a pot (top left), for pricking out in a box (top right) or for transferring singly to small pots (below)*

by seeing that the soil never becomes actually dry; when it approaches that condition a bucket of water per plant is not too much.

Picking Tomatoes. Fruit should be gathered not by the complete truss but individually as they ripen. They are ripe when fully coloured all over. Break off each fruit, complete with a short piece of its stem, as soon as it is fit for taking. Gentle handling is necessary. The skin easily bruises.

Yellow Patches. Odd fruit here and there sometimes seem reluctant to colour all over; they are marred by yellow patches. Generally this is due to lack of sufficient potash in the soil. The cheapest source of potash is wood ash, and this should be worked plentifully into the top soil before planting. A spadeful per plant, followed by a good watering (without the wood ash being washed away), when the first trusses have formed will do a lot to prevent this yellowing.

Ripening Indoors. Late in the season, when it is obvious that remaining tomatoes will not ripen in the open, trusses or individual fruits should be cut off. The trusses may be hung up inside the sunny window of a warm room, odd fruits being placed in similar surroundings, to complete the ripening. A warm pantry or cupboard will do as well. The amount of light seems to have little to do with this artificial indoor ripening; it is temperature that counts.

Non-ripeners. There is a point beyond which unripe tomatoes sometimes refuse to go. Those that remain more or less completely green are still of considerable use, in the making of pickle or chutney for out-of-season use.

Tomatoes in Store. Ripe (but not over-ripe), unbruised, healthy fruits will keep satisfactorily on a shelf indoors, if picked dry or wiped dry with a clean cloth. They should be placed in a single layer and without touching, where there is a current of air, no dampness, and where the temperature neither rises nor falls unduly. A sheet of paper placed above them will protect them from dust. They must be looked over occasionally and

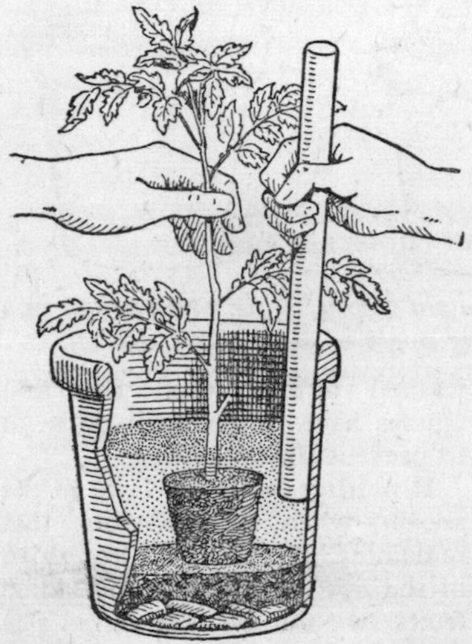

Fig. 281.—*How to transfer a tomato plant from a small pot to a larger one, in which it will be fruited*

those showing a wrinkling of the skin used up first. Any showing sign of decay should be ejected immediately.

Raising Plants from Seed. There is nothing specially difficult about this, apart from the chief requirement of a steady temperature of about 55 deg. (by night) combined with full light. The seeds germinate better in darkness than in full light, but the latter is absolutely essential from the seedling stage onwards—which rules out a warm room cupboard as a makeshift greenhouse (Fig. 280).

Tomato seedlings will come up quite satisfactorily in a warm living-room; the snag comes when the potted-on seedlings, still requiring those 55 deg. of warmth, cannot be given the maximum light.

To raise plants for fruiting outdoors or in an unheated greenhouse seed is sown in February or March, in a greenhouse or hotbed with a night temperature of 55 deg.; very thinly in small pots or a shallow seed box filled to within ¼ in. of the top with a mixture of good soil two parts and one part finely sifted leaf-mould. The seed is covered ½ in. deep, and the pots or box covered with glass and then paper—to keep moisture in and light out. This covering is removed directly seedlings are visible.

Transfer to Small Pots. To bring seedlings to the stage when they need shifting separately to small pots great care is necessary in watering. Water, of the same temperature as the hotbed frame or heated greenhouse, is to be given only when the soil is approaching dryness; otherwise many of the seedlings will damp off—flop over at the base—and that will be the end of them.

When they are between 1 in. and 2 in. high they are due for transference singly to 3-in. pots filled with the soil mixture as advised for sowing. They are fragile at this stage and need very careful handling. Bruising has to be avoided when pressing the soil down around the single stems.

Watered in, they are then stood close to the glass to be kept short and sturdy. If these pots become filled with roots by late April the plants will need to be shifted to larger pots, of 4-in. or 6-in. top diameter.

If pots are not available, seedlings can be shifted direct to shallow wooden boxes in which they are to stand 3 in. apart. But these never make such robust, fruitful plants as those given the more generous accommodation of flower pots.

Those intended for growing on in an unheated greenhouse must be gradually accustomed to the lower temperature. Those for planting outdoors must spend ten days or so in a sunny frame, with increasing exposure to outdoor conditions—which is known as hardening off.

Greenhouse Crops. Plants to be grown on and fruited in an unheated, sunny greenhouse are dealt with in much the same manner as those in a heated house, plants for the latter being raised earlier, of course. Planting can be done in the unheated house in late April.

Pots in which the plants are to finish, one plant per pot, should be not less than 12 in. across the top (Fig. 281); or boxes about 10 in. square and 1 ft. deep will be found quite suitable. Larger boxes can be used, and two or more plants be together, but there must be no crowding, or health will inevitably suffer. Each plant demands at least 12 in. of elbow room.

The pots or boxes are to stand on the greenhouse bench, as close to the front glass as possible. The crocks in the bottom of each pot, and the drainage holes in the bottom of each box, should be covered with a layer of leaf-mould or quite old manure, or hop manure. Roots will appreciate this when they get down to it. They are to be two-thirds filled with as good a soil mixture as can be contrived.

The ideal is fibrous loam—the top soil of a meadow after the good turf has been removed—pulled to pieces lumpily by hand, three parts, and one part leaf-mould; the next choice is fertile garden soil and leaf-mould mixed, with some fine sand or sharp grit added if it is on the heavy side. During the mixing a good scattering of wood ash should be worked in.

Warm the Soil First. Plants will be checked in their growth if potted or boxed with cold soil. This should be warmed first, with the aid of a hot brick, a tray over the kitchen fire, or the oven; or exposure of small heaps to the temperature of the heated greenhouse for a few days will achieve this object.

Supports in the Greenhouse. Each plant needs a stake long enough to carry it to within 9 in. of the sloping roof glass, to which it will then be trained parallel (on string or wire), at that same distance, if there is not sufficient space between pot and roof glass for the plant to be trained upright for its full length (Fig. 282).

The plants are to be kept single stemmed, and tied, as explained for outdoor plants.

Watering under Glass. Until the plants get hold of the soil in the final pots or boxes there will be no great call on the watering can. Whenever water is given it should be sufficient to soak right through the soil and drip out of the drainage holes. Then no more should be given until the soil is nearly dry again. Water should not be slopped around the floor or bench when tomato plants are in flower or fruit; they like the atmosphere to be drier then.

If water is given on sunny days, during the forenoon, the air has a chance to dry before evening; though in the height of summer the plants in pots, in full bearing, may need watering twice in the day.

Ventilation Needs Care. On hot summer days, with no wind blowing, it may be necessary to open wide the door and ventilators of the greenhouse; at other times the giving of air demands caution. Tomatoes hate the air to be still and muggy; they also hate cold draughts. The ventilators will have to be managed with discretion.

Cold nights in late spring are a special peril where the unheated greenhouse is concerned. Tomato plants a few inches from the glass are within the influence of outside cold, and will need additional protection in the event of frost. This can be given in the form of sheets of paper placed between the plants and the glass.

Setting the Fruit. Tomato flowers need to be fertilized to ensure the production of fruit. The fertilizing pollen can be distributed by tapping the stakes (or other supports) to which the plants are tied. A sharp tap or a jerk is sufficient, once or twice a day, whilst they remain in flower. But it is no use doing this when the atmosphere of the greenhouse is damp; it should be dry, and the sun shining.

Feeding Greenhouse Tomato Plants. The space that was left at the top of each box or pot (they were only two-thirds filled) when the plants were given their final shift should be filled in, to within 1 in. of the top, when the plants come into bearing. The same soil mixture should be used, enriched with a handful of wood ash per plant or a teaspoonful of one of the special tomato fertilizers. The latter should also be given once a week from then on, watered into the surface.

If any leaves in positions low down on the stems wither they should be removed. Foliage that shades trusses from the sun or is very crowded can also be shortened back to let in light and air. Otherwise, healthy foliage (apart from the unwanted side shoots, to be removed as explained in the case of outdoor crops) should be interfered with as little as possible.

White Fly and Other Troubles. White fly attacking greenhouse tomato plants must be got rid of by fumigating (see section PESTS AND DISEASES OF FLOWERS AND VEGETABLES, page 397) with one of the special preparations sold for dealing with this particular pest.

The presence of root knot disease is indicated by the foliage drooping and yellowing; the stem then becomes limp, and the plant collapses. Minute eelworms in the roots are the cause. Sleepy disease causes leaves to droop, and later on mildew appears on the lower parts of stems. Canker of the stem starts as gummy, moist patches, which become hard and dark and then whitish. Black stripe attacks the stem low down and works upward. In each of these cases affected plants should be uprooted and burned, and the soil should be treated with quicklime before it is used again.

Various forms of leaf-rust are

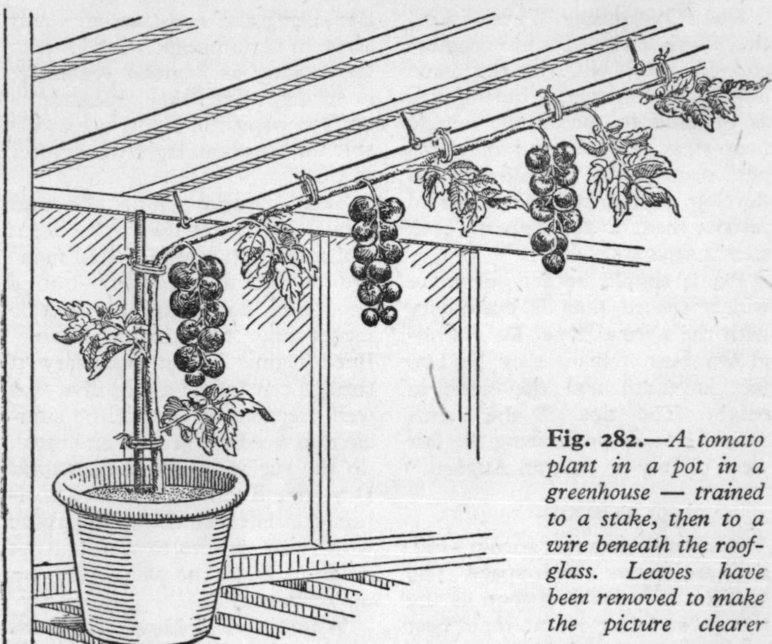

Fig. 282.—*A tomato plant in a pot in a greenhouse — trained to a stake, then to a wire beneath the roof-glass. Leaves have been removed to make the picture clearer*

sometimes troublesome, the leaf, in some instances, rolling up and dying. In early stages the disease may be prevented from spreading to healthy leaves by dusting these with flowers of sulphur, affected leaves being picked off and burned. Fruit itself is sometimes attacked by black spot disease; those so disfigured should be removed and burned.

Generally these troubles may be avoided by starting with clean, healthy plants, keeping the atmosphere of the greenhouse reasonably dry and giving plenty of air, ample space between plants, and all the light possible.

The disease that is most troublesome to outdoor tomato plants is that known as blight; it is the same as that which attacks potatoes. It appears in the form of brown blotches on the upper surface of leaves. It can be controlled by spraying with Bordeaux mixture, but this must not be used when the fruit is ripening. The mixture can be purchased, with directions for use. One other disease—septoria—is dealt with in the chart "Remedies Against Enemies of Vegetable Crops" (page 409).

Preparing for Table. Fruit should be cleaned by wiping with a damp cloth, and then, if for serving raw and whole, polished with a dry cloth. The tomato is particularly valuable as a source of vitamins A, B and C. As regards A and B, it is equivalent to lettuce and green beans; in regard to vitamin C it is equivalent to such fruits as oranges and lemons.

Bush Tomatoes. These varieties, which have come into prominence in recent years, as the name implies, are grown in bush form, as opposed to the normal single main stem. Any number of stems per plant may be allowed to develop, though it is advisable to restrict them to four, giving each stem a separate stake.

Plants should be set out more widely spaced than is customary with the normal type, for a well-grown bush tomato may be two feet in width and the same in height. The tips of the stems should be removed during the last week of July or early in August.

TURNIP

Garden varieties of turnip (Fig. 283) are always worth space. The tops are as valuable a food as the roots; the latter are at their best when about the size of a cricket ball. Soil of sufficient quality to produce a good potato crop will grow turnips, provided they never lack moisture. The latter is necessary to quick growth, without which turnips are unsatisfactory.

Varieties for early use include Snowball, White Milan; for winter, Chirk Castle Blackstone, Orange Jelly and Green Top White, which is one of the best for producing tops.

½ oz. of seed will sow three 30-ft. rows. Germination takes about twelve days.

Ready for Use. Turnips are most useful in late spring and early summer, and again in autumn and winter; tops, for cooking as a green vegetable, in spring, when other greenstuff is not too plentiful. Roots are available for use about eight weeks after sowing.

Soil Preparation. Ground should be dug at least 1 ft. deep, and some rich material—old manure or rotted greenstuff—buried about 8 in. down; and it should be made quite firm before sowing. But digging is not necessary if turnips can follow a crop that was well prepared for; it will be sufficient to weed the ground and break up the surface finely with a fork. Dry ground calls for a shaded position for later sowings; otherwise with full exposure to sun and not much moisture the plants may run up to flower.

When and How to Sow. Earliest sowing of the year, mid-

Fig. 283.—*Garden turnips are worth all the space that can be given to them. Above, Sutton's Early Snowball; below, White Milan*

March, is best made in a warm, sheltered spot.

Small successional sowings can be made up to the end of May. Sowings in June and July are risky; usually the weather is too hot to suit them.

Sowing period for the winter varieties is mid-August. A September sowing of one of the winter sorts will give a grand supply of tops the following March and April.

Seed is sown ½ in. deep in drills 9 in. apart; thinly for root production, fairly thickly for tops. Germination is hastened by soaking the seed for about 24 hours before planting.

Thinning Out. It will help the seedlings along tremendously if they are watered in dry weather. Growth then will be brisk, and thinning out will need early attention—first to 3 in. apart, then to 6 in., at which the plants finally stand. The intermediate thinnings will provide small but very useful roots.

If tops and not bulbs are wanted the plants are pulled up when they have produced enough leaves of sufficient size.

Gall Weevil and Other Troubles. These are dealt with under "cabbage tribe" in the chart "Remedies Against Enemies of Vegetable Crops" (page 406).

Storing for Winter. Roots not intended to stand the winter outdoors may be pulled up in November, the leaves cut off, and stored in a heap of sifted fire-ashes in a cellar or shed; or they may be clamped outdoors, in the manner explained under BEET (page 252).

If a late sowing fails to produce useful roots in winter the plants should be left to give a crop of tops when growth restarts in spring.

Preparing for Table. Peeled thinly, roots are cut into slices before cooking. Tops, for boiling, should be washed. Both are of greatest value in the diet when young and juicy.

WATERCRESS

There is a snap about fresh watercress that is entirely lacking in the shop-withered cress. Its value in salad making needs no stressing, and it is tasty and satisfying enough to stand alone, as a salad on its own. Running water is not essential for its cultivation; it can be grown in a moist trench.

Watercress (Fig. 284) can be increased by seed, by division of plants, and by cuttings. Pieces with a few thread-like roots attached (Fig. 284B) are frequently included in a purchased bunch; if planted and kept moist, these quickly grow and spread. Suitable pieces can also be taken from plants of watercress found growing wild in clean stretches of water.

Ready for Use. Gathering starts in June and continues to September, from an April to May sowing; in November and on to May from a sowing in August.

Soil Preparation. The ground needs to be capable of holding moisture to a reasonable extent, and the best way to ensure this is to take out a trench about 2 ft. wide and 1 ft. deep, in a not too sunny position. Rotted material from the vegetable refuse heap or pit is then trodden firmly into the bottom, to form a rich layer about 6 in. thick. Some of the soil that was taken out is returned, to the

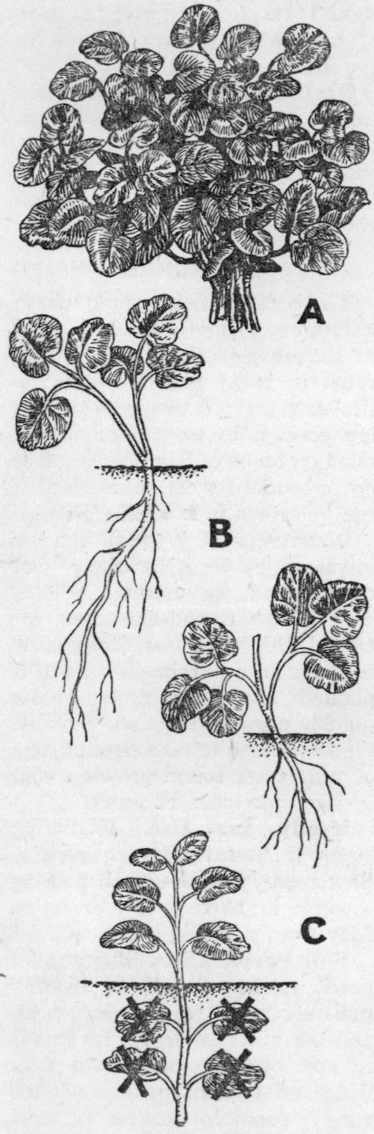

Fig. 284.—*Watercress* (A) *is easily increased by small rooted pieces* (B) *planted to the depth shown. Cuttings also root readily, lower leaves first being removed as shown at* (C)

depth of about 3 in., and that too is firmed. It should be soaked with water the day before.

When and How to Sow. Seed is sown during April and May for a summer crop, and in August for a winter–spring crop. It should be sprinkled thinly and evenly over the moist surface, then just covered with sifted soil. Paper placed over the top until the young plants are through will prevent too-rapid loss of moisture in hot, sunny weather. Then the plants can be kept more or less flooded by frequent waterings given from a can fitted with a rose.

Gathering Watercress. Plants are easily tugged up, so to avoid need for constant replanting gathering of the shoots has to be done with care. The safest and quickest way is to cut them off, leaving sufficient stems to provide new growth and further pickings.

Increase by Division. Plants should be given a change of site after a year in the one place, or fresh soil should be placed on top of the rich stuff in the trench bottom after the old soil has been removed. Also the plants may be given a fresh lease of life—pulled to pieces and the divisions, each with a few roots, replanted. This can be done at any time during spring or summer, when growth is active. And cuttings can be taken (Fig. 284C)—3-in.-long shoots cut through squarely just below a joint and planted firmly in the damp soil, 1½ in. of the stem to be buried.

Preparing for Table. Shoots should be washed very thoroughly, preferably in running water, then dried by shaking in a clean cloth. Bare pieces of stem and discoloured leaves should be removed.

SECTION XXIII

PESTS AND DISEASES OF FLOWERS AND VEGETABLES

SHUTTING one's eyes to trouble due to pests or diseases and hoping for the best is the short cut to serious losses. Trouble unchecked at an early stage increases in severity; results are spoiled growth and reduced yields. Because prevention is often easier than effecting a cure, attack should be expected and—where this is possible, as in examples given in the accompanying charts (page 402)—the first blow should be struck by the cultivator.

Look for First Signs. At the very first indication of activity by creeping, crawling, flying, sucking or biting enemies, or onslaught by disease, the appropriate remedy should be applied promptly and thoroughly.

Precautions against the spreading of trouble include the prompt burning of all removed diseased portions of plants (and affected roots), and all picked-off foliage covered with green- or black-fly. If it is consigned to the rubbish heap instead of to flames, the heap becomes a breeding ground for further afflictions.

No woody rubbish should be left lying about. Bits of old stakes and decaying wood do not actually breed woodlice, slugs and snails, but they provide an excellent lurking place and nursery for these pests. A plot that is weedy is an encouragement to all forms of animate and inanimate trouble.

An important precaution consists in buying plants and seed only from a thoroughly reliable firm, thus ensuring so far as is possible that trouble is not introduced to the plot from those sources.

No Cure-all Remedy. There are excellent proprietary remedies in seedsmen's lists, and purchasable from horticultural sundriesmen, but these must be expected

Fig. 285.—*Colorado beetle. A destructive pest among potato plants, this beetle is ½ in. long, yellow with black stripes. Its occurrence must be notified to the Ministry of Agriculture*

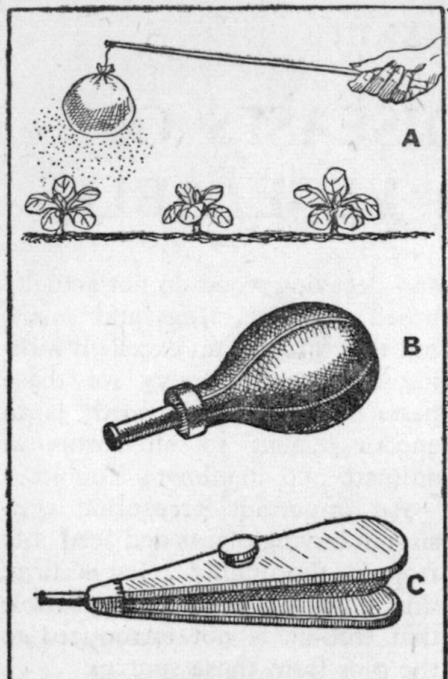

Fig. 286.—*Dusting plants with soot or other pest-defeating powder is done quickly with the aid of a muslin bag on the end of a stick* (A) *or with a special puffer* (B) *or blower* (C)

to do only what is claimed for them. It is necessary also that they should be applied according to the directions accompanying them.

The materials when not in use should be put away under cover and beyond the reach of children and animals. Even if not poisonous they might have serious effects if eaten in quantity.

Insecticides. As the word implies, insecticides are for use against insect pests, in the adult stage as well as in the caterpillar, grub or maggot stage. They should be applied, in powder or liquid form, direct to the bodies of the pests. Naphthalene and other soil insecticides, however, are for application to the soil. These soil insecticides drive away, or gas, pests that are below the surface, and also scare away egg-laying flies from cabbage, carrot and other plants.

The latter purpose is served also by calomel and fresh soot and similar powders. Soot is most efficacious applied to the soil fresh from the chimney; for dusting over plants it should not be fresh, or foliage will be scorched.

Paraffin-tainted sand or sifted fire ashes will scare away flies seeking to deposit eggs at the base of cabbage, carrot and other stems. Half a pint of paraffin is stirred thoroughly into a bucketful of fine sand or sifted ashes and the mixture spread around and alongside the plants to be protected.

Repeated Applications Necessary. Whatever is used, it cannot be expected to effect a complete clearance with one application only; a second or third dose is necessary. The purpose is not served by exceeding the recommended strength and hoping thus to avoid further exertion; indeed, there is danger in over-dosing.

Dusting with Powders. Small bellows or other puffing devices, with container attached, are useful for distributing insecticides in powder form. Or the powder can be shaken out of a small muslin bag jerked about over the plants or soil. The bag might be attached by about 6 in. of string to the end of a stick, with the advantage that the liberated powder is farther removed from the person doing the distributing (Fig. 286).

Choose a dull day, or a calm evening, for the job, otherwise there will be wastage due to wind. Also, to prevent waste, avoid dusting when rain appears likely to follow, or the powder may be

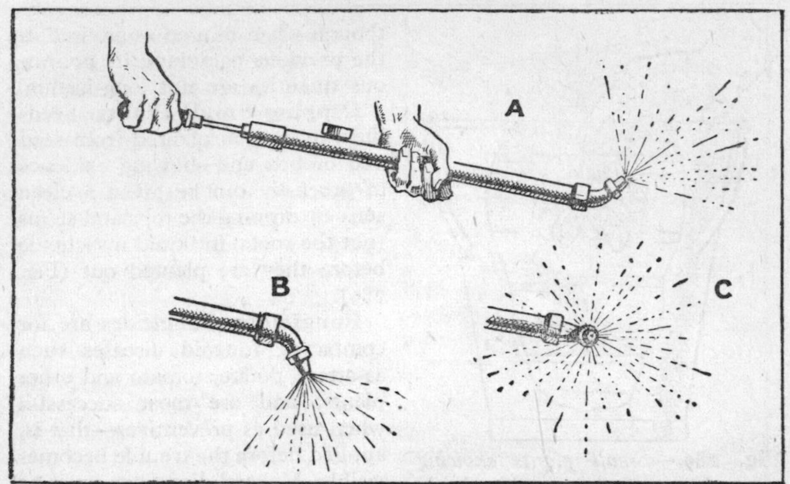

Fig. 287.—*A syringe with a bent nozzle enables the spray to be delivered easily in any direction: upwards* (A), *downwards* (B), *or sideways* (C)

washed from the plants. Soot and other powders applied to soil are ineffective when wet with rain, and need renewal.

Spraying with Insecticides. In liquid form an insecticide should be applied as a fine but very thorough shower, by means of a syringe—in any of the forms obtainable (Figs. 287 and 288). Get at the plants from all angles so that the liquid reaches everywhere. Early morning or evening, or some other sunless period, and when rain is not likely, is the best time.

A solution of quassia and soft soap (bought in concentrated form, in small tins) is a good all-round spraying liquid. A little of the contents of the tin should be dissolved in hot or boiling water, then diluted with clear water according to the directions. The liquid is most effective applied as hot as the hand can comfortably bear.

The paraffin emulsion mentioned in the chart (page 406) as a killer of fly on broad beans should be prepared first as a soapy mixture—a handful of soft soap stirred vigorously in just sufficient hot water to dissolve it, the quantity then being

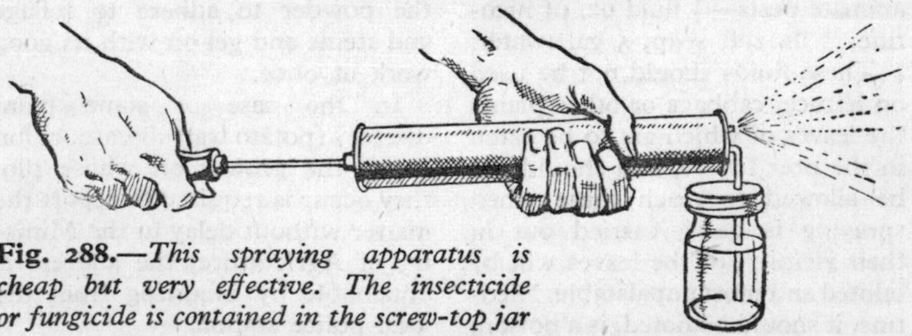

Fig. 288.—*This spraying apparatus is cheap but very effective. The insecticide or fungicide is contained in the screw-top jar*

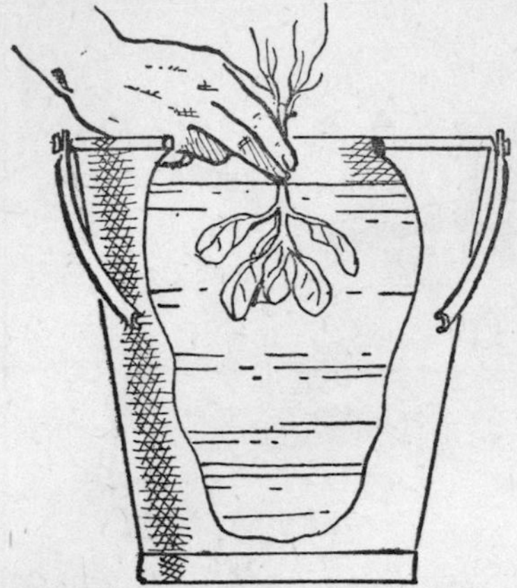

Fig. 289.—*Small plants showing signs of fly or other trouble should be inverted and dipped stem-deep in liquid insecticide before being planted out or potted*

increased to 2 gal. by the addition of clear water, the wineglassful of paraffin going in last. The mixture should be squirted backwards and forwards in the bucket, with a syringe, and agitated similarly, or stirred, during use.

Derris preparations that are to be used in liquid form are made up in these proportions: 1 oz. of derris powder, ¼ lb. soft soap, 3 gal. water: the soft soap to be dissolved first, in a little hot water.

Nicotine is a certain killer of green- and black-fly and other small animate pests—½ fluid oz. of nicotine, ½ lb. soft soap, 5 gal. water.

These fluids should not be used on lettuce, cabbage or other plants the leaves of which are to be eaten in the near future, and should not be allowed to reach these when spraying is being carried out in their vicinity, or the leaves will be tainted and most unpalatable. Nicotine, it should be noted, is a poison, though when diluted as advised in the previous paragraph its poisonous qualities are not long-lasting.

Dipping Small Plants. Seedlings to be transplanted from seed bed or box and showing evidence of green-fly can be given a clean start by dipping the tops and stems (not the roots) in liquid insecticide before they are planted out (Fig. 289).

Fungicides. Fungicides are for combating fungoid diseases such as attack potato, tomato and other plants, and are most successful when used as preventives—that is, applied before the trouble becomes visible. Makers' directions must be followed closely.

Every part of leaf and stem is to be coated with the spray (Fig. 290), delivered as a fine shower through a syringe, so that a film is deposited on the under as well as the upper sides of the foliage. A windless day and no rain fix the actual time of application.

In powder form, fungicides must be distributed with the same object.

One of the best general-purpose powders, especially where mildews are being dealt with, is sulphur, generally sold as flowers of sulphur. This should be dusted over the plants when these are damp with dew, in morning or evening, or after rain, the moisture assisting the powder to adhere to foliage and stems and get on with its good work at once.

In the case of some plant diseases (potato wart disease, onion smut) the grower on whose plot they occur is required to report the matter without delay to the Ministry of Agriculture; the address is obtainable by inquiring from the local police station.

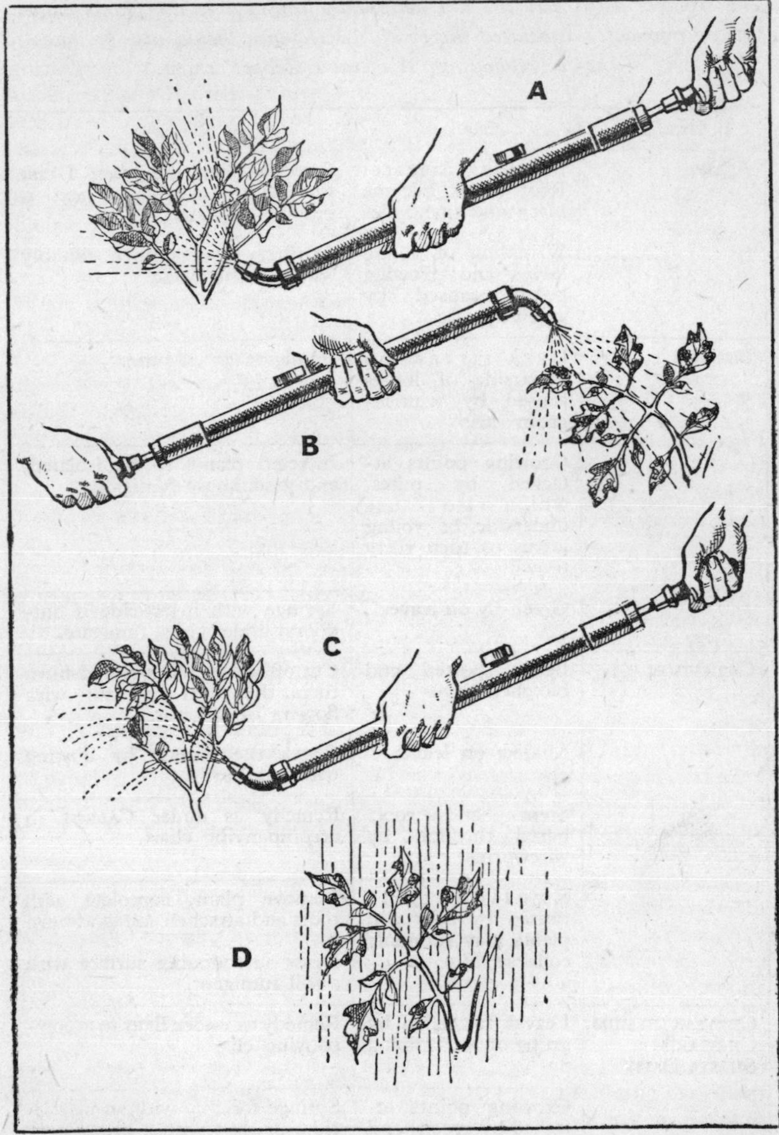

Fig. 290.—*Fungoid and insect troubles are most surely got at by spraying a plant from all directions* (A, B, C, D), *so that all parts are coated with as fine a film as possible. It should be done on a windless and rainless day, and when the sun is off the plants, and be repeated as often as necessary*

REMEDIES AGAINST ENEMIES OF FLOWERING PLANTS

The troubles listed here are not necessarily confined to the plants named, but are frequently associated therewith. Reference should also be made to the accompanying " Vegetable Crops " chart.

Attacked	*Attacker*	*Remedy*
ASTER	Blackleg disease. Root stems become black and plant dies	Remove plant and burn. Dress site with lime when next it becomes vacant.
	Wrinkling of young leaves and growing points caused by green-fly, etc.	At first sign, syringe forcibly with an insecticide.
BEGONIA	Dark streaks on underside of leaves caused by whitish-green thrip	Fumigate greenhouse.
	Growing points attacked by mites, which also cause underside of young leaves to turn rusty brown	Infected plants to be isolated, and greenhouse fumigated.
	Green-fly on leaves	Syringe with insecticide if outdoors; under glass, fumigate.
CARNATION	Badly spotted and blotched leaves	Cut off affected leaves and burn them, then dust the plants with flowers of sulphur.
	Mildew on leaves	Check the disease by dusting with sulphur.
	Stems and roots bored through by wireworms	Remedy as under CARROT in accompanying chart.
	Swollen stems caused by eelworm; plants may suddenly collapse	Remove plant, complete with roots and attached soil, and burn it. Dress surrounding surface with a soil fumigant.
CHRYSANTHEMUM, CINERARIA, SHASTA DAISY	Leaves tunnelled by grubs of leaf-mining fly	Remedy as under BEET in accompanying chart.
	Growing points attacked by green- and black-fly	Syringe forcibly with an insecticide; or dust with a proprietary powder.
	Small reddish circles of rust on chrysanthemum leaves	Pick off and burn diseased leaves, then dust the plants freely with sulphur.

REMEDIES AGAINST ENEMIES OF FLOWERING PLANTS

contd.

Attacked	*Attacker*	*Remedy*
DAHLIA	Buds and blooms eaten by earwigs	Trap the pests by placing inverted flower pots, stuffed loosely with dry crumpled paper, among the foliage; or empty matchboxes partly opened. Earwigs hide in these traps by day; shake out and destroy.
DELPHINIUM, LUPIN	Flower spikes eaten through by slugs and snails	These pests should be searched for among the foliage, and at base of plants, and destroyed.
	Damage to dormant plants and to young shoots in spring, by slugs and snails	Cover crown of plants with inch-thick layer of sharp, sifted coal or coke ashes during the winter. Soot gathered fresh from chimney and placed on soil-surface around the plants in early spring will keep slugs and snails at bay.
GLADIOLUS	Buds bored into, and blooms eaten, by caterpillars and small slugs	Inspect plants daily and pick off the pests.
	Bulbs holed by wire-worms	Trap these pests as advised under CARROT in accompanying chart.
HOLLYHOCK	Foliage made unsightly by rusty spots	Diseased leaves to be cut off and burned. To prevent recurrence the following year, spray the plants in March-April with Bordeaux mixture, and repeat when flower spikes begin to push.
MARIGOLD	Foliage eaten by caterpillars	Search for the pests on underside of leaves. To discourage the egg-laying butterflies and moths, spray foliage, above and below, with quassia and soft-soap solution; repeat, up to time of flowering.
NASTURTIUM	Green- and black-fly can quickly cripple and destroy the plants	The pests cluster thickly on underside of foliage. Spray forcibly there with an insecticide; this should be followed next day by a clear-water syringeing.
PANSY, VIOLA	Spittle-like blobs on foliage ("cuckoo spit")	Within the blobs lurk yellow or light-green grubs, consuming the plants' sap. Remove with piece of stick and destroy; or syringe with an insecticide. It is essential that the blobs be removed from above the pests to enable the insecticide to make contact with the pest itself.

REMEDIES AGAINST ENEMIES OF FLOWERING PLANTS

contd.

Attacked	*Attacker*	*Remedy*
ROSE	Green-fly	Syringe forcibly with an insecticide, when the sun is off the plants. Where they cluster thickly on shoot-ends, destroy between thumb and finger; or dip shoot-end in vessel of insecticide and swish it about.
	Nibbled flower-buds	Sacrifice the bud together with the small grub therein.
	Leaves showing white mildew	Dust with sulphur when leaves and shoots are damp.
	Orange rust on leaves	Spray in early spring with a fungicide sold for this purpose. Diseased fallen leaves should be picked up and burned.
	Black spots on leaves	Remedy as for orange rust.
SWEET PEA	Seedlings attacked by slugs	Young plants and surrounding soil should be dusted with old (not fresh) soot, or with dry wood ash, freely and frequently, to render them distasteful.
	Young shoots and flower buds pecked by birds	Bits of shiny tin or other metal suspended here and there among the plants, so that they sparkle and tinkle, are effective bird-scarers.
	Green- and black-fly	These must be fought with insecticide, liquid or powder, from the first appearance.
	Sickly-looking or suddenly wilting seedlings, caused by disease or underground pest	A seedling thus attacked should be uprooted and burned. Disturbance of the soil with trowel or piece of stick may reveal wire-worm or other pest for dispatch.
VIOLET	Leaves distorted or unhealthy looking, caused by minute red spider in numbers on underside	Spray underside of leaves forcibly with a nicotine solution or other insecticide. Attack by this pest is encouraged by hot and dry conditions; a safeguard is to water frequently and syringe liberally with clear water.
GREENHOUSE PLANTS IN GENERAL	Red spider, green- and black- and white-fly, mites, thrip, etc.	Too-dry conditions under glass are generally conducive to these troubles. The remedy is fumigation as described in the text. Plants, of course, should be inspected very closely for signs of trouble before you buy them.

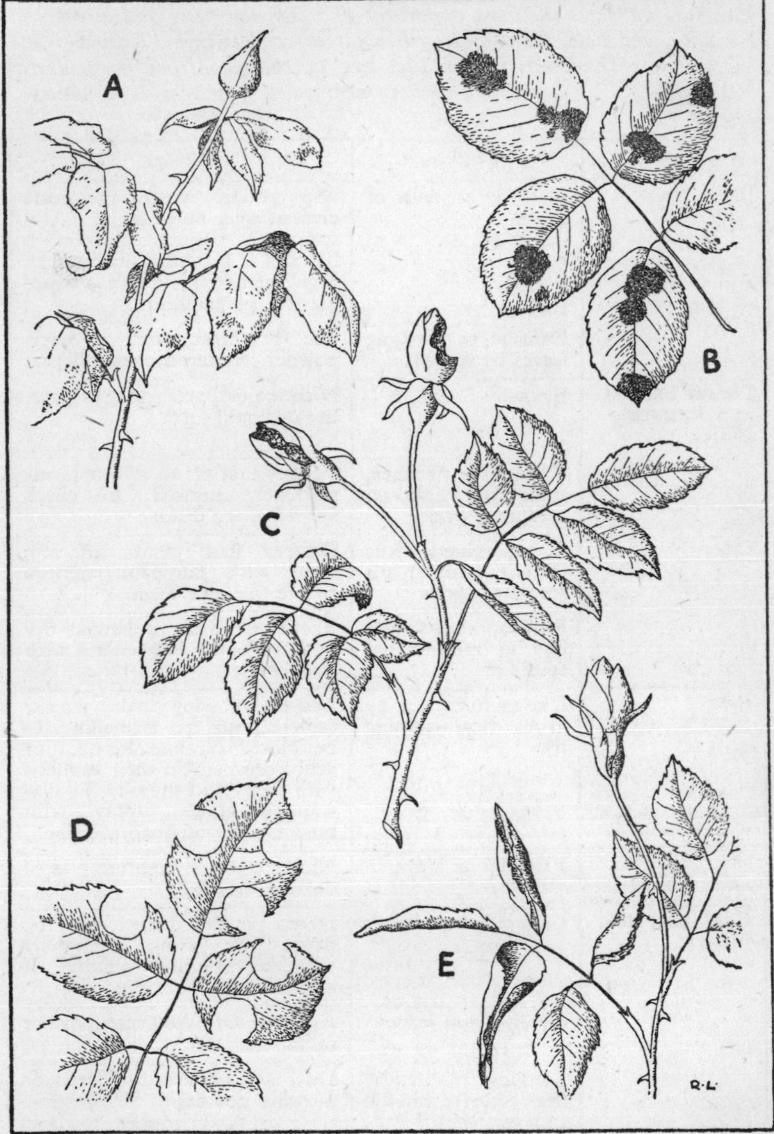

Fig. 291.—*Rose mildew* (A) *should be dusted with sulphur; black spot* (B), *sprayed two or three times at intervals with fungicide sold for the purpose. Pick off nibbled buds* (C). *The leaf-cutter bee lines her nest with circular pieces cut from rose leaves* (D). *Leaf-curl* (E) *may be due to thrips or to a small caterpillar using the curl as a hiding-place.*

REMEDIES AGAINST ENEMIES OF VEGETABLE CROPS

This chart indicates the most important and common pests and diseases of vegetables, and how, when and with what to combat them. Remedies and preventives, with directions for use, are purchasable from horticultural sundriesmen.

Attacked	*Attacker*	*Remedy*
BROAD BEAN	Black-fly on ends of shoots	Nip off tips, where the pests cluster, and burn them. Also spray with paraffin emulsion—a handful of soft soap dissolved in 2 gal. of hot water plus a wine-glassful of paraffin.
	Damage to seedling leaves by weevils	Old (not fresh) soot, or derris powder, scattered over foliage.
DWARF FRENCH AND RUNNER BEANS	Black-fly	Nicotine or pyrethrum, in powder or liquid form.
	Yellowish patches, spots (halo blight) on seedlings, pods	Destroy first plants affected, immediately noticed, to check spread of the disease.
	Red-margined spots (anthracnose) on seedlings, pods	Destroy first plants affected, spray with Bordeaux mixture before the pods form.
	Pale - spotted foliage due to minute red spider	Troublesome in prolonged dry weather; spray in evenings with clear water.
BEET	Leaves tunnelled by grubs (leaf - mining fly)	Leaves showing pale streaks (where grubs are tunnelling) to be picked off and burned; or grubs crushed (in their tunnels) with finger and thumb. To discourage attack, spray with quassia and soft-soap solution.
	Black-fly on leaves	Nicotine or pyrethrum, as a dusting or spray.
CABBAGE TRIBE	Caterpillars on leaves	Derris powder dusted over the pests. Or syringe vigorously with salt solution—handful of salt in a bucket of water.
	Green-fly on leaves	As above. Or pyrethrum, powder or liquid.
	Seedlings nibbled by flea beetle (turnip fly)	Dust with old soot, or derris or nicotine powder.
	Round swellings, or galls, at base of stem —and on turnips—caused by gall weevil grubs	As precautionary measure, lime the ground well before planting and reject young plants showing these swellings (each containing a white grub). Change the site for next cabbage crop.

REMEDIES AGAINST ENEMIES OF VEGETABLE CROPS

contd.

Attacked	*Attacker*	*Remedy*
CABBAGE TRIBE (*cont.*)	Roots greatly swollen and distorted—club-root disease ("finger-and-toe" in turnip)	Lime soil before planting, and raise seedlings in well-limed seed bed. Burn cabbage roots after crop cleared. Affected part of plot not to be cropped with cabbage tribe again for 3 to 4 years.
	Plants wilt — grubs attacking roots (cabbage-root fly)	Pull up and burn attacked plants. Sprinkle powdered calomel or naphthalene alongside rows to ward off egg-laying fly.
CARROT	Roots eaten by grubs of carrot fly (Fig. 293)	Naphthalene or powdered calomel dusted alongside rows immediately plants are thinned out, to ward off egg-laying fly.
	Round holes bored in roots by wireworm (Fig. 292a), (grub of the click beetle)	Portions of potato, turnip, old carrot, short lengths of cabbage stalk, buried 2 in. deep, will attract these pests; mark the buried pieces with sticks, disinter and inspect daily—and destroy the catch (Fig. 294).
CELERY	Leaves tunnelled by grubs (Fig. 296)	Deal with as under BEET.
	Rusty spots spreading over foliage	Spray early with Bordeaux mixture as a preventive. Badly diseased plants should be burned.
LETTUCE	Green-fly	Spray early with pyrethrum solution.
	Small holes in leaves (ring-spot disease)	Change the site for next lettuce crop.
	Stems rotting at soil level (grey-mould disease)	Destroy affected plants immediately noticed. Grow next batch elsewhere on plot.
ONION	White fluffy mould (white-rot disease) at base of bulb, which may rot	Remove and burn attacked plants at first indication.
	Young plants become yellow and wilt—due to grubs of the onion fly in the bulbs	Spray early, with paraffin emulsion (as under BROAD BEAN) to ward off, or scatter powdered naphthalene alongside and around rows. Pull up and burn the worst.
	Shrivelled foliage, sometimes showing a fine mould (downy mildew disease); does not attack the bulbs	Dust early and well with flowers of sulphur when foliage is wet with dew or after rain.

REMEDIES AGAINST ENEMIES OF VEGETABLE CROPS

contd.

Attacked	*Attacker*	*Remedy*
ONION (*cont.*)	Swollen stems, caused by eelworm	No remedy. Onions not to be grown on same bed subsequently.
	Black stripes on foliage (onion smut disease)	Must be notified to Ministry of Agriculture. Onions not to be grown on same bed subsequently.
PARSNIP	Grubs tunnelling inside leaves	As advised under BEET.
	Grub-eaten roots	As advised under CARROT.
PEA	Seedling leaves notched by weevils	As advised under BROAD BEAN.
	Green-fly	Nicotine or pyrethrum.
POTATO	Brown blotches on upper surface of leaves, also on tubers. Tops destroyed; tubers rot in the ground or in store (potato blight disease)	Spray with Bordeaux mixture (but not within about twelve miles of big industrial areas or foliage may be badly damaged) in early June and again three weeks later, as preventive.
	Distorted, cauliflower-like, greeny-yellow growths at base of stems and on tubers (wart disease) (Fig. 295)	Affected tubers and tops must be burned. Soil remains contaminated for years; only varieties known to be immune (*see under* POTATO in the alphabetical section) should be planted therein. Notify Ministry of Agriculture.
	Sickly-looking dwarfed top growth followed by withering of lower leaves. Tops die off early. Caused by potato-root eelworm	No remedy. Soil remains affected at least five years. Subsequent potato crops to be grown elsewhere on plot.
	Tubers scabbed, but fit to eat (scab disease)	Ground not to be limed where this trouble occurs. In soil of gritty nature line planting drills with leaf-mould; or sprinkle flowers of sulphur in drills.
	Leaves mottled, leaf edges curl upwards, black streaks on leaves; tops may perish (virus diseases)	Home-saved seed not to be planted. Where the trouble occurs plant best Scotch, Irish or other best-quality seed.
	Colorado beetle (½ in. long, striped) and its bright pink or red grubs on leaves	Presence of this pest must be notified at once to Ministry of Agriculture or local police. Crop must not be sprayed until instructions are received from the Ministry.

REMEDIES AGAINST ENEMIES OF VEGETABLE CROPS

contd.

Attacked	*Attacker*	*Remedy*
TOMATO	Green-black spots on foliage, which dies and rolls up. Stem and fruit also affected (septoria disease)	Spray with Bordeaux mixture immediately symptoms noticed; usually appears in June. Badly affected plants should be burned.
	Brown blotches on upper surface of leaves (similar to potato-blight disease)	Spray with Bordeaux mixture early—not when tomatoes are ripening. Other diseases are dealt with under TOMATO in the alphabetical section.
SLUGS, SNAILS	Soot fresh from the chimney scattered around (not on) lettuce and other plants will keep slugs and snails at bay. Orange-peel placed white-side down on ground will attract them for easy gathering and annihilation.	
CUTWORMS (Fig. 292b)	Sometimes known as surface caterpillars, the larvae of turnip and other moths eat through stems of cabbage, lettuce, etc., at soil level. Fork in naphthalene, 2 oz. per sq. yd. Also search for them in soil (just below surface) where they are obviously at work.	
LEATHERJACKETS	Destructive, underground grubs of the crane-fly (daddy-longlegs). Deal with as for cutworm. Specially numerous in newly dug grassland.	
WOODLICE	Destructive to top growth of seedlings. Put down pieces of old, rotting board and flat stones as attractive hiding places. Inspect daily and destroy the tenants.	
FIELD MICE	Trap in large jam-jars half filled with water and sunk rim-deep between rows of newly sown pea, bean, etc.	
WIREWORMS	Destructive underground larvæ of the click beetle. Deal with as for cutworms. Also as advised under CARROT.	

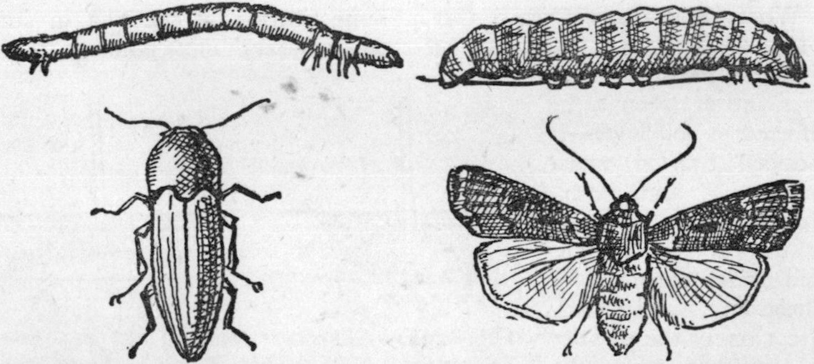

Fig. 292a.—*The wireworm (above) is the larva of the click beetle (below). It tunnels into carrot roots*

Fig. 292b.—*The cutworm or surface caterpillar (above) is the larva of the turnip moth (below)*

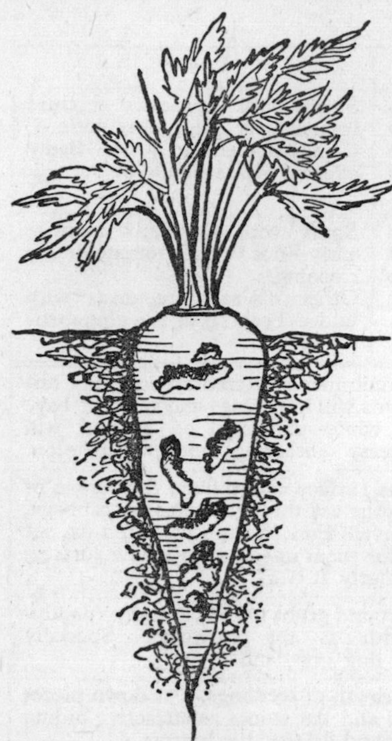

Fig. 293.—*This root destruction is the work of grubs of the carrot fly. To scare these scatter naphthalene alongside the rows as the young carrots are thinned out*

When Seedlings Damp Off. The condition of damping off —when seedlings flop over and are seen to be affected at soil level—is induced by too moist conditions and over-crowding. The fungicide to use in this case is sold under the name of Cheshunt compound. Use 1 oz. of the powder in 2 gal. of water, the powder being dissolved in a little hot water.

The solution should be applied, immediately after mixing, to the soil, the effect being to destroy the microscopic fungoid organisms which flourish in the conditions just mentioned.

The watering-can (or other metal vessel used for mixing or applying) should be well washed out afterwards.

Soil Fumigants. These are for gassing insect pests in the soil, flaked naphthalene being quite effective. When plants occupy the ground, the best that can be done is to fork or hoe the naphthalene into the surface. The real opportunity presents itself during deep digging, when crops are off the ground.

The naphthalene can then be mixed throughout the top foot of soil as digging proceeds, at about 3 oz. per sq. yd. The fumes rise, and penetrate sideways, and are very bad indeed for the health of wireworms, leatherjackets and other undesirables.

Crops Moved on. Soil pests and such diseases as club root can be dodged to some extent by following a system of rotation in cropping, no vegetable to occupy the same portion of the plot in successive years. Thus potatoes would

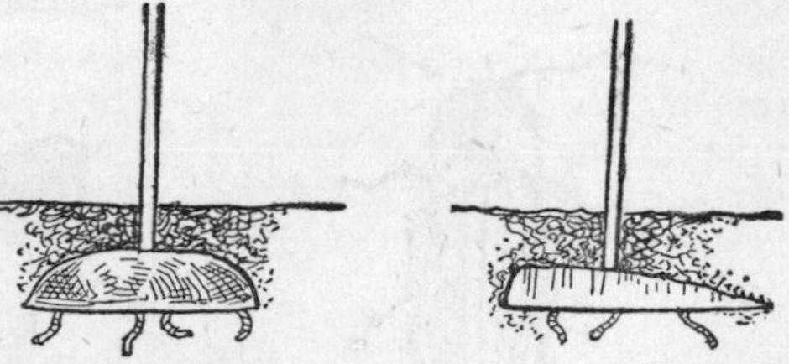

Fig. 294.—*Slices of potato (left) or carrot (right) buried, cut-surface downward, 2 in. deep, and speared with short sticks to mark their position, form effective traps for attracting wireworms where numerous*

not follow potatoes but be planted in the ground occupied the previous year by cabbage and others of the cabbage tribe. Cabbage crops would follow after onion, shallot, pea, bean, whilst these latter would occupy the site vacated by potatoes.

Fumigating Frame, Greenhouse. For the dispatch of insect pests in frame and greenhouse various excellent fumigating materials are on the market, with detailed directions for use; with the required burning apparatus in the case of liquid nicotine. Tobacco shreds or papers placed in a flowerpot on the floor of the greenhouse and lighted are equally effective. Flaked naphthalene can also be employed, burned over a lamp sold specially for the purpose.

The dose depends on the size of the structure; thus, naphthalene would be used at the rate of about 4 oz. per thousand feet cubic content. The latter is arrived at by multiplying length of the greenhouse by the breadth, then multiplying the figure that results by the height. The height is, for this purpose, the distance between the floor and a point halfway between the eaves and the top, or ridge. Figures are in feet.

When and How to Fumigate. A fine, calm evening is the time to carry out the operation, with all ventilators shut and any crevices covered with sacking. The material or lamp, as the case may be, is set burning and the operator retires without loss of time, locking the door behind him and placing wet sacking against its bottom edge.

Fig. 296.—*Grubs inside leaves of celery, etc., should be crushed in their tunnels between finger and thumb*

The vapour should be given twelve hours to do its work. Ventilators are then opened, the fumes are allowed a couple of hours to disperse, then the plants are syringed with warm water to clear them of debris. To make a good job of it the same procedure should be repeated three evenings later.

In dealing with a pest-infested frame, the simplest plan is to clear it of plants and to burn a saucerful of sulphur inside, the frame light to be closed and covered with sacking to imprison the fumes. The following day all inside parts of the frame should be syringed forcefully with very hot water containing as much soap and soda as can be dissolved in it.

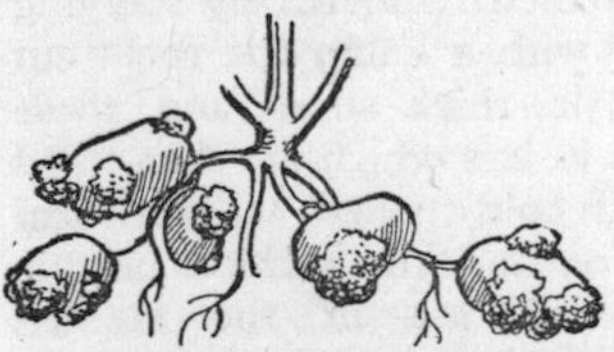

Fig. 295.—*Potatoes attacked by wart disease*

SECTION XXIV

EASY HOME PRESERVATION OF VEGETABLES AND HERBS

THE preservation of certain vegetable crops for use in winter (as distinct from root-crop storage methods, dealt with under vegetable names in the alphabetical section) entails little trouble, yet can add very appreciably to the family food reserves. Vegetables that can be dealt with as described in this section are not numerous, but they stand high in the nourishment list. The list can be extended by adopting bottling and canning methods, but unfortunately these require special apparatus and considerable care in the operation thereof. Only the simplest methods, which can be carried out by anyone without fuss or bother. are explained here.

Onions, Red Cabbage, Beet. These are the easiest to pickle, and though onions and beet can, of course, be stored in the natural state, a few jars of them in pickled condition are extremely welcome as well as valuable in winter.

Onion bulbs from 1 in. to 2 in. in diameter are just the right size for pickling. They can be picked out from any variety when the crop is lifted, or they may be of the special pickling type, such as Paris Silverskin and Queen.

The onion tops and roots removed, the bulbs next need to be peeled. This is less painfully carried out if the unskinned onions first spend about twelve hours in salt water—1 lb. of salt to the gallon. Skinned after this bath, they need soaking for about thirty hours in a fresh supply of salt water (same proportions).

At the end of that time they are washed in cold water, dried, then placed in jam-jars and covered with boiled spiced vinegar which has been allowed to become cold. Air must be excluded by tying over the top of each jar an airtight cover; these can be bought in packets from chemists' shops and the big stores. The pickled onions should remain in store about three months before being used.

Red pickling cabbage should be washed after the removal of discoloured outer leaves, then shredded with a knife (Fig. 297). The shreds are placed in a bowl or basin, in layers, and each layer sprinkled with salt before the next is added. There they remain for twenty-four hours, after which they are drained, then put into jars, covered with cold (spiced and boiled) vinegar, and the jars sealed with airtight covers.

Beet is also easy to deal with. The roots are boiled whole in salt water (not much salt) for about ninety minutes, then taken from the water and allowed to cool. The peel is then removed, by scraping gently with a knife, the roots cut into ¼-in.-thick slices and these placed in jars which are then filled up with cold (boiled) vinegar. Seal the jars, and the pickled beet is ready for use in the kitchen whenever it is required.

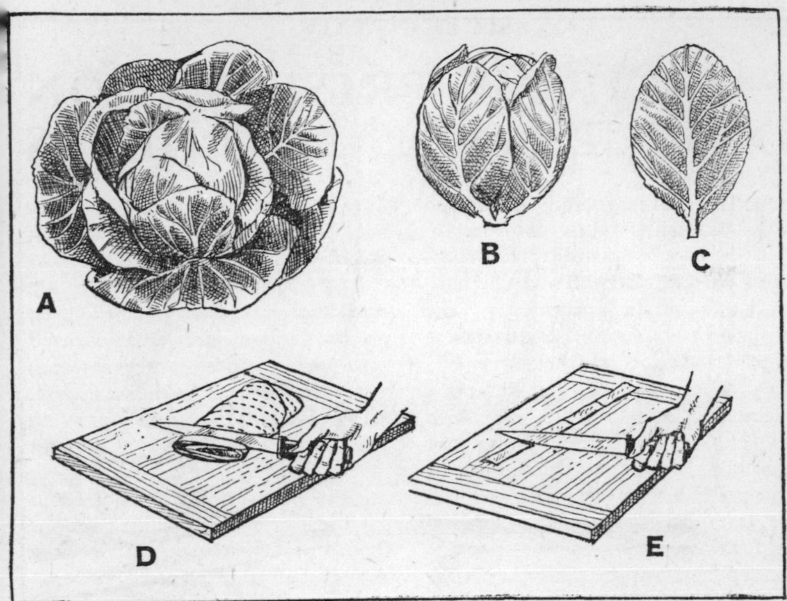

Fig. 297.—*Red cabbage for pickling* (A); *after removal of outer leaves* (B); *a leaf* (C) *folded over for cutting into strips* (D); *a strip being shredded* (E)

Beans Sliced and Dried. Runner and dwarf French beans can be dried as sliced pods. They should be young and tender, not old tough specimens gathered at the tag-end of the season. Old ones should be shelled and the seeds dried, as explained later (page 415).

Top and tail the young pods, remove the strings (Fig. 298), cut each into three slices (the smallest may remain uncut), and place in boiling water for about two minutes. Take them out, drain them thoroughly, then dry them until they are brittle enough to break easily.

The drying, which may take from four hours to as many days, according to the temperature to which they are exposed, is done in front of an open fire (not above, or they will be smoke-tainted), or in a warm airing cupboard, or in an oven which has just been used for cooking.

If the oven method is adopted the beans should be left in all night, the oven door slightly open. Rushing tactics must not be adopted. In a temperature higher than about 120 deg. the beans may scorch and be ruined. Drying need not be completed without interruption. The beans may go into the oven at intervals, as convenient, until they show by their brittleness that drying operations are complete.

During these proceedings they are most easily handled in shallow wooden boxes without tops and provided with bottoms of muslin

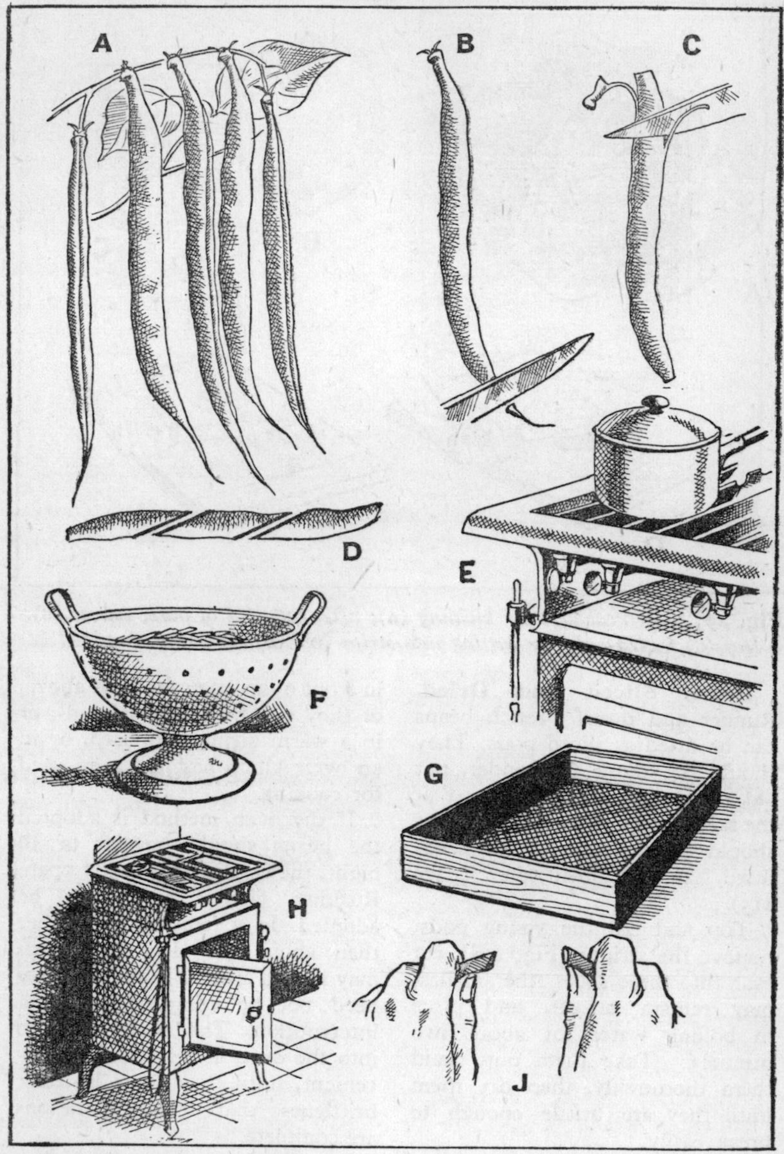

Fig. 298.—*Beans* (A) *for drying are prepared by topping and tailing* (B), *removing the strings* (C), *and cutting into three slices* (D), *and then placed in boiling water* (E) *for two minutes, taken out and drained* (F), *placed in a prepared tray* (G), *and dried in an oven* (H) *until quite brittle* (J)

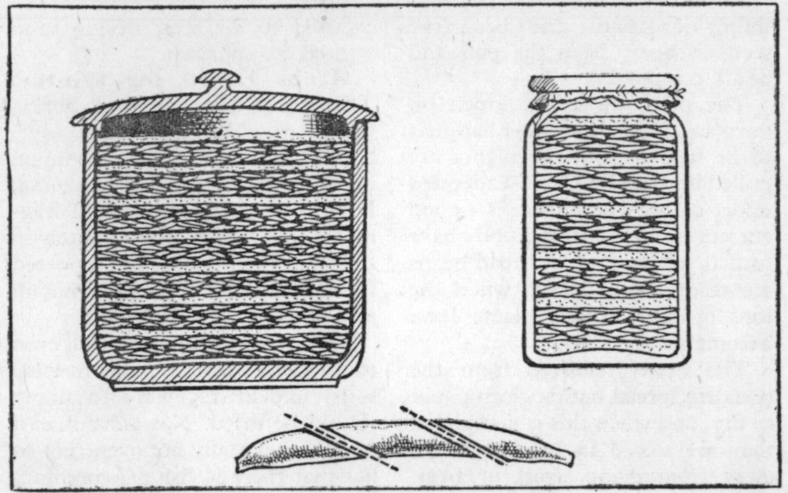

Fig. 299.—*Runner and dwarf French beans can be preserved for winter use by storing sliced young pods between layers of salt in sealed jars*

or canvas or wire gauze, the beans being turned over at intervals. When the job is finished and the beans have been given time to cool they can be stored in tins or jars provided with lids or covers, or in paper bags, in a dry cupboard.

Previous to cooking they should be soaked in water all night.

Salted Beans. An alternative method of preserving runner and dwarf French beans for winter use—for cooking them as fresh beans—is to place the sliced young pods between layers of salt in an earthenware or stoneware jar, or in large jam-jars, to be made completely airtight by sealing with one of the special covers (Fig. 299).

Economy in salt will result in failure; it should be used in the proportion of 1 lb. to every 3 lb. of beans. Start with a layer of salt in the jar, add a layer of sliced beans, then a layer of salt, more beans, and so on; the layers to be firmed down as filling proceeds, the final (top) layer being of salt.

The filled jar (covered) should be inspected a week later and another layer or two of beans and salt added to make up for the shrinkage which has taken place. It is essential that the final sealing shall leave the container absolutely airtight.

When the salted beans are required for use they should be washed in three or four changes of water, then soaked in warm water for two hours, then cooked in boiling water (no salt required) for about thirty minutes.

Haricot Beans. Without the use of either salt or heat shelled beans can be preserved for a very long period. Any kind of bean will do—broad, runner or dwarf French; though certain varieties of the latter, such as Green Gem and Lightning, are most generally suitable for use as haricots. That word simply denotes the dried bean (the seed) as apart from the pod and beans complete.

The pods are left to ripen on the plant, or if the weather happens to be wet or cold the plants are pulled up, bundled, and suspended under cover, where there is a good current of air, until the pods have turned yellow. Pods of broad beans are ready for gathering when the tops of the standing plants have become nearly black.

The beans removed from the pods are spread out on clean paper to dry, and when this is completed they are stored in bags or boxes away from damp, frost or heat.

Preliminary to cooking, pour boiling water over them and allow to soak for twelve hours.

Dried Shelled Peas. These also keep well, provided the peas—removed from the pods—are very thoroughly dried and then stored in large tins with tightly fitting lids to keep out the damp, or in bags or boxes in a damp-proof cupboard. The pods may remain on the plants until it is convenient to gather them, or the plants be uprooted and taken under cover for a time.

The shelled peas need to be exposed to the fire, or dried out in a slow oven with the door ajar, until there is no doubt of their dryness. Cooking should be preceded by twelve hours' soaking in water; this should be boiling when poured over them.

Mushrooms. Old or maggoty mushrooms will not keep satisfactorily; in any case only good ones are worth the trouble. Those selected for storing should be dried until quite crisp, after having the peel removed from the top and the stalks cut off. They should not be exposed to air after drying until wanted for cooking.

Herbs Dried for Winter. There is always demand during winter months for mint, sage, thyme, parsley and other common herbs for flavouring and seasoning. Dried and reduced to small fragments they will keep indefinitely in tightly corked bottles or stoppered jars in a cool dry cupboard—not on a shelf exposed to full light.

Parsley stands up quite well even to the worst winter weather in some soils and districts; even so, a supply should be dried. Not more than a minute in a really hot oven (not so hot that there is risk of scorching) will suffice. It can also be dried by slower methods, but does not retain its colour so well.

Old, woody sprigs of mint, thyme, etc., should not be gathered for drying. Clean young shoots, picked in summer when their first flowers are appearing, during early morning or evening and when there is neither dew nor rain upon them, are ideal.

Mint, sage and others with large leaves should be stripped from the stalks and dried to a crisp condition in a cool oven. In very hot, sunny weather it is possible to dry them sufficiently by prolonged exposure outdoors—spread out on sheets of clean newspaper and taken under cover in the evening.

Thyme and other small-leaved herbs can be hung up in bundles near a fire until they crackle and flake when touched. The leaves then part very readily from the stalks and can be powdered by rubbing between the palms of the hands or beneath the pressure of a rolling-pin; mint, parsley and sage to be broken up in the same way.

SECTION XXV

PLANNING THE FRUIT GARDEN

SOIL that produces good vegetable crops will do the same for fruit. Like some vegetables (such as the potato), some varieties of fruit have their likes and dislikes concerning locality and so on. Any such peculiarities can be learned from neighbours who have had a few seasons' experience of fruit growing in the neighbourhood. Considerations of space come next.

On the allotment, if tenancy is reasonably secure and the crime of produce stealing not too rife in the district, a row or two of small fruit, such as raspberries, gooseberries, currants, would be useful.

In the home garden the plan would be to scrap worn-out, unprofitable fruit bushes and trees and replace them with healthy, up-to-date types. Every fence, whichever way it looks—north, south, east or west—is capable of helping in the production of excellent pickings of blackberries and loganberries. The house walls should carry their own loads of fruit.

A single apple or cherry tree would give welcome summer shade on a grass plot, in addition to its fruit. If all other space were filled, room might still be found for a row or two of strawberries.

The Cost of It. The only fruit plants, bushes or trees worth buying are those offered by reputable nurserymen. They are true to name, thoroughly healthy, and will bear fruit when expected. Those

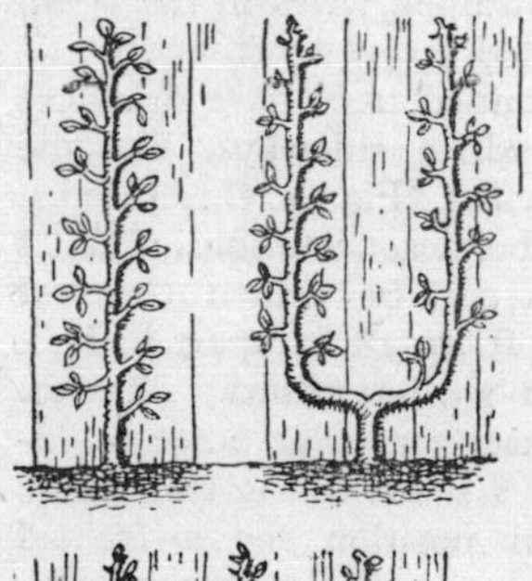

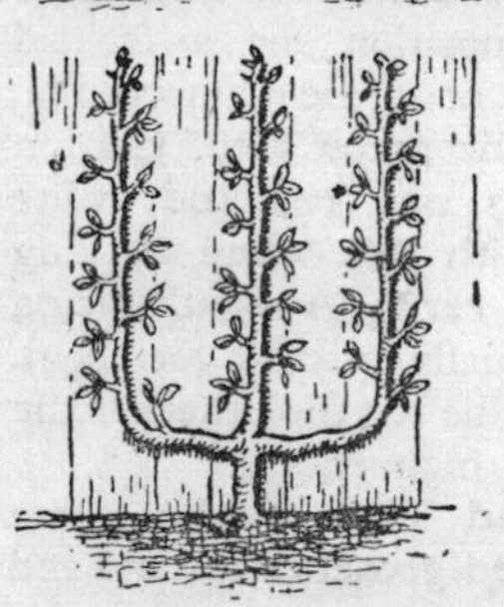

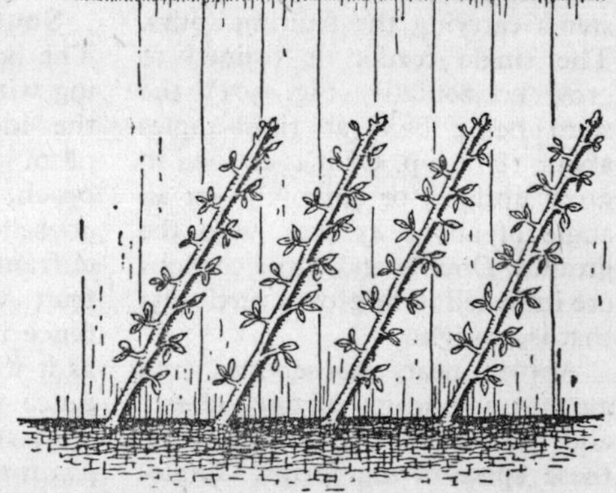

Fig. 300.—*Cordon-trained fruits save very considerable space. Single, double and triple cordons are shown on the left, oblique single cordons on the right*

Fig. 301.—*A horizontal cordon apple tree, trained to a low wire alongside a garden path, is novel and decorative as well as productive*

old enough to carry a little fruit naturally cost more than very young ones. The most expensive are those bought as job lots with no guarantee as to what they are.

With good plants the first cost is the last, apart from possible small expenses in connexion with spraying against disease or insect pests.

How to Save Space. Trees and bushes trained in the nursery to grow flat against a wall, fence or strained wires or other form of support, take up the very minimum of space. The simplest form of flat-trained tree is the cordon (Fig. 300). This has only one, two, or three stems—single, double, or triple cordon respectively.

The cordon has no other branches, only a main stem or stems carrying the fruiting spurs. The single cordon is trained to grow horizontally (Fig. 301), the stem being bent at right-angles about 18 in. up. Or it is trained to grow upright, or obliquely—at an angle of about 45 deg. with the ground. Double and triple cordons are intended to be grown vertically, that is, upright.

Apple, pear, gooseberry, red currant and white currant, cherry and plum, can all be grown in these space-saving forms. Single-cordon apple and pear trees can be planted as close as 2 ft. apart; single-cordon gooseberries and currants 1 ft. apart, double cordons 2 ft. and triple cordons 3 ft.

Espalier and Fan-trained. Espalier, or horizontal-trained, trees (Fig. 302) have a single central stem, with branches growing out horizontally to left and right—in tiers, about 1 ft. apart. This suits apples and pears especially, and the trees, in line against a wall, or against strained wires in the open, are planted about 10 ft. apart.

Fan-trained trees have branches which radiate sideways, like the ribs of a fan (Fig. 303). Apricots, plums, cherries, nectarines, peaches and figs can be grown thus, at from 15 ft. to 18 ft. apart in line.

South-wall-trained Trees. The house, garage or other building with a south-facing wall offers the ideal position for a trained plum tree or apricot, nectarine, peach, fig or grape vine. Cordon gooseberries and red and white currants with this warm backing fruit very early. A south-facing fence is equally suitable for them, as it would be for the others if the fence were high enough.

East and West Walls. Here again trained gooseberries and red and white currants are perfectly at home, also cherries, plums and early-ripening pears.

North-facing Walls. Gooseberries and currants in this position give a late crop of berries; thus, by varying the aspect, these fruits can be spread out over a long period. The north wall also suits morello cherries and early pears.

Fences with any aspect can be clothed with blackberries and loganberries, the growths fastened back fan fashion or horizontally, and planted about 8 ft. apart.

Small Fruits in the Open. Ordinary bush currants and gooseberries are planted in the open at about 5 ft. apart, preferably in rows; raspberry canes (these need supports) about 18 in. apart in a row, with 5 ft. between rows.

Strawberry plants are set out 15 in. apart in the row, 2½ ft. between rows.

Fig. 302.—*An espalier-trained fruit tree has tiers of horizontal branches, but has no front or back branches*

Fig. 303. *A fan-trained tree gives the maximum profit from a wall or high fence exposed to the sun*

Round Trees. The typical standard tree, with all-round branches (Fig. 304A), has an unbranched stem of about 6 ft. and is on the large side for the ordinary small garden, where it is less profitable than the smaller and quicker-fruiting bush and pyramid forms. Standard apple and pear and plum trees need to be spaced at least 18 ft. apart. That may seem an absurd waste of space when young standards are planted, but they need it all by the time full growth is attained. Standard cherries, and apples of more spreading growth, need to be separated by 25 ft.

Half-standard trees (Fig. 304B) have an advantage over full standards in that their branches are within easier reach; they have clean

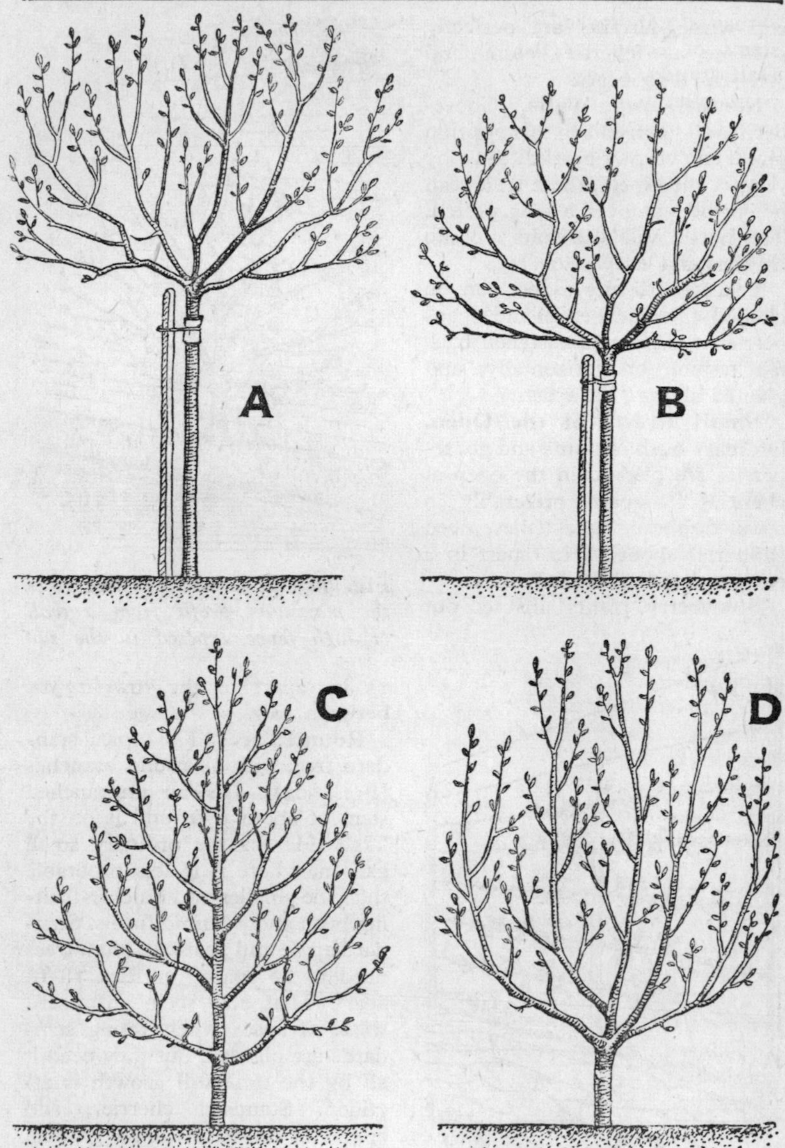

Fig. 304.—*A standard fruit tree* (A) *has an unbranched stem of about 6 ft. The half-standard* (B) *is a shorter edition of the standard. It has an unbranched stem of about 4½ ft. The pyramid-trained tree* (C) *has one main stem. The bush tree* (D) *has a number of stems rising from a very short leg*

—that is, unbranched—stems of about $4\frac{1}{2}$ ft. Half-standard apples, pears, plums and damsons are planted about 15 ft. apart.

The space-savers in the round tree class are bush and pyramid apples, pears, plums, cherries, at about 10 ft. apart. The pyramid form (Fig. 304C) has one main, central stem which goes straight up, with side branches radiating from it in all directions. The bush form (Fig. 304D) consists of half a dozen stems rising from a very short leg, with an open centre; there is no long main stem.

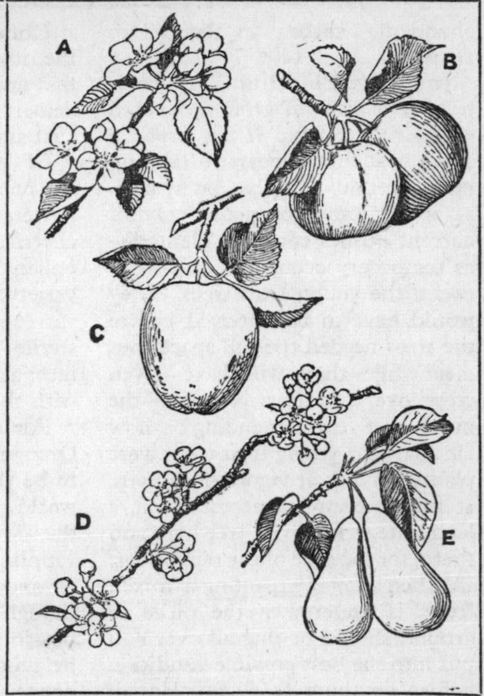

Fig. 305.—*Flowers of apple* (A) *in some cases need to be fertilized with pollen from another variety. Two varieties whose flowers are self-fertile are Bramley's Seedling* (B) *and Rev. W. Wilks* (C). *One of the very few varieties of pear whose flowers* (D) *are self-fertile is Louise Bonne of Jersey* (E)

Vegetables Among Fruit. Space that is vacant between young trees for the first three or four years after planting can be occupied by vegetable crops of a not-too-tall or vigorous nature. Rhubarb would not be out of place between standards or half-standards; between bush and pyramid trees salad crops could be grown. But to attempt any crowding is futile; neither fruit trees nor vegetables would succeed.

The same applies where flowers are concerned. A young fruit tree or bush planted during the dormant season when it has not a leaf upon it, in the mixed flower border, occupies nothing like the space it will require when in full leaf. And that space will increase from year to year. That is obvious enough, but it does not always receive sufficient thought at planting time.

The shade it will cast, the area which its extending roots will occupy and the demands it will make on neighbouring soil must be considered. If the young tree has got to fight for light and air and food with strong-growing herbaceous perennials it is likely to be a failure from the start. It is not advisable, then, to dot fruit trees or bushes about a vegetable or flower border unless they can have abundant space to themselves alone.

Intensive Planting. The ideal is to have a piece of ground devoted exclusively to fruit. If the essential spacing at first appears to take up more ground than can be spared, raspberry canes or gooseberry or currant bushes could be planted—as temporary occupants only—between the young fruit trees. They would have to be removed before the trees needed the full space, but meanwhile they will have given crops over a number of years—the number of years depending on how far apart the young fruit trees were planted and their vigour of growth. It might even be necessary at a later date to remove a tree here and there, for the sake of the remainder.

When intensive planting of mixed fruits is undertaken the piece of ground should be dug all over and put into the best possible condition before anything at all is planted. See ABC OF FRUIT PLANTING, commencing on page 425.

Extending the Fruiting Season. By selection of suitable varieties of any particular fruit, and planting these in varying positions (north, south, east or west) so far as any special requirements of that fruit allow, the season of ripening can be greatly extended.

There are, for example, varieties of dessert apple which ripen in early August and will not keep for more than a week or two, such as Beauty of Bath, and others which are not at their best until December and which keep well until February, such as Orleans Reinette and Laxton's Superb. There are cooking apples, such as Monarch, which are at their best as late as January and will store until April.

Choosing Varieties. To make the utmost of small space, varieties that are famed for their cooking or dessert qualities should be planted. Just any old sort will not do.

Of even greater importance is the necessity for ensuring that the flowers of apples, pears, plums, cherries are fertilized with the pollen from flowers of another variety of the same fruit. Many varieties of these four are self-sterile—that is, they are quite incapable of setting their fruit with their own pollen.

For example, the famous Cox's Orange Pippin, claimed by some to be the best dessert apple in the world, is self-sterile. Pollen from the flowers of one Cox's Orange Pippin cannot fertilize the flowers of another Cox's Orange Pippin, though the trees be the closest possible neighbours and the pollen be produced in the greatest abundance. To get this variety to fruit it is necessary to plant near to it another variety whose pollen is known to be capable of doing what is required; such as Bramley's Seedling, always a sure cropper, and said to be the best cooking apple in the world.

A few varieties of apple (Fig. 305) are self-fertile—they set their fruit with their own pollen, Bramley's Seedling being one. Among pears, Louise Bonne of Jersey is self-fertile. Victoria is one of the very few self-fertile plums (Fig. 306). Cherries are specially tricky in this matter of cross-fertilization, and two or more different varieties must be present near-by.

It is not essential that both mates should be present in the one garden; pollen is carried by bees and wind, and these will effect the

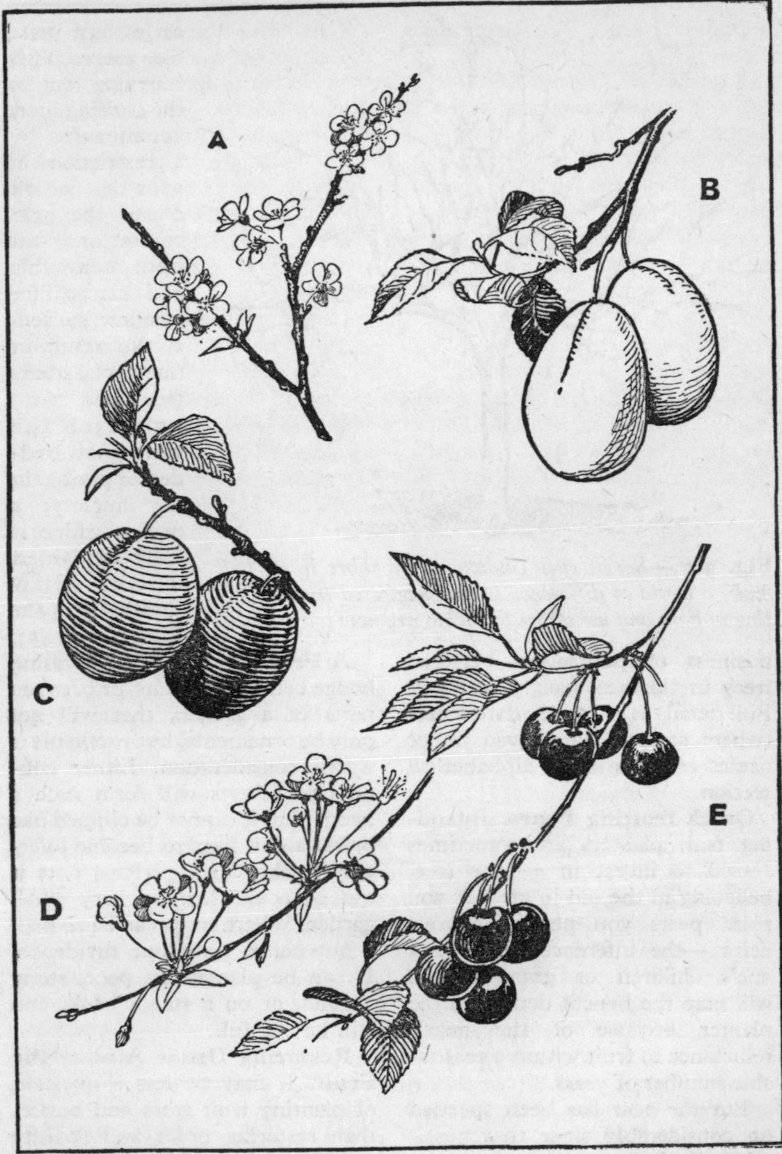

Fig. 306.—*Plum blossom* (A) *and two of the very few self-fertile plums—Victoria* (B) *and Monarch* (C). *Cherry blossom* (D) *and morello (sour) cherries* (E). *Only the sour cherries are self-fertile; flowers of all the eating varieties are self-sterile, needing pollen from a different variety*

Fig. 307.—*Seven cuts (indicated by short lines) will make a world of difference to this neglected tree, by letting in light and air where branches are now too crowded*

business of pollination between trees in the near neighbourhood. Full details as to appropriate mates (where essential) are given under names of fruits in the alphabetical section.

Quick-fruiting Pears. Intending fruit planters are sometimes scared to invest in a pear tree, believing in the old jingle "If you plant pears you plant for your heirs"—the inference being that one's children or grandchildren will reap the benefit denied to the planter because of the pear's reluctance to fruit within a reasonable number of years.

But the pear has been speeded up considerably since that pessimistic jingle was coined. Grown as a cordon or a dwarf bush, the pear will begin to carry fruit very shortly after transference from nursery to garden, especially if it is purchased as a four-year-old plant. This hurrying on of the fruiting date, accompanied by a restriction in growth, which makes the pear cordon or dwarf bush admirably suited to the smallest garden, is the result of the special stocks (root and stem) on which the varieties are budded or grafted in the nursery; a matter which is fully explained under HOW FRUIT TREES ARE RAISED, page 453.

A Fruiting Hedge. A dividing hedge between gardens, or between parts of a garden, that will not only be ornamental but profitable is worth consideration. Either cobnuts or filberts will form such a hedge; but it cannot be clipped like privet and it likes to become tolerably thick, which perhaps puts it out of count for the very small garden. Where space can be spared, a nut hedge gives fine dividends. It can be planted on poor, stony ground, or on a rough bank, and still be fruitful.

Restoring Order Among the Fruit. It may be less a question of planting fruit trees and bushes than restoring order and fertility among existing plants. Old standard apples and pears and plums may be improved by having their height reduced, and worn-out or crowded branches removed (Fig.

307). Other trees may have so suffered from neglect that they have become choked with unprofitable growths. Pruning may put this right and make them fruitful again. A jungle of raspberry canes or an almost unapproachable thicket of blackberries is not necessarily to be grubbed out. The congested shoots can be dealt with, and a general clean-up be put in hand.

Artificial fertilizers will help. Lime may be needed, especially by the stone fruits—the plums, cherries, etc. Grass may have been allowed to creep up to the base of trees and bushes and to rob the roots of air and warmth and moisture. They may be fighting a losing battle against diseases and pests. The planter may have been so generous with his trees and so niggardly of space that now the sky cannot be seen from between them.

All these things can be put right, as is explained in full detail in the following sections.

SECTION XXVI

ABC OF FRUIT PLANTING

A FLYING start for the plants, whether they be apple trees or strawberries, means not only bumper crops of fruit but less bother later on for the cultivator. What is done wrongly at planting time is not easily put right afterwards. Preparation of the ground, correct depth of planting, method of spreading out and covering in the roots, and staking and tying (where necessary) are simple items involving little trouble but of real importance.

Preparing the Sites. If the ground has been properly cultivated, all-over digging is not necessary. All that is required, by way of a start, is the preparation of adequate planting holes. These should be wide enough to allow of roots being spread out and deep enough to allow of the tree, bush, cordon, or whatever it may be, being planted at the same depth at which it stood in the nursery ground; that point is indicated in most cases by the soil mark on the stem.

The bottom of the hole should be broken up with the fork; but no manure should be worked in unless the ground is definitely poor, and then it must be so placed that it does not touch the roots when the plant is put in position.

Raspberry, black currant and strawberry like the ground to be rich, but most other fruits make too much wood growth if given manure at planting time. Artificial manure mixtures can be given as a top-dressing when trees, bushes, etc., first begin to fruit. Suitable mixtures are sold by the fruit nurserymen.

Unpromising Ground. If the subsoil is chalk and there are only a few inches of good soil on top, or if the ground is very stony, or sandy, the planting hole should be got out to the depth of about 18 in.

and the excavated material replaced by better soil, if possible. Chopped turves will do excellently for putting in the bottom of the hole, grass side down.

If the ground is clay, or otherwise heavy, it must be made porous by working into it sand, sharp road grit, mortar rubble, sifted fire ashes or small charred stuff and wood ash from the rubbish fire.

If the drainage is none too good, dig the hole 2½ ft. deep and line the bottom with broken brick, or stones, well rammed; this drainage material to be 6 in. deep when the ramming is finished. Turves spread above, grass side down, will be a further improvement, these to be covered firmly with enough soil to secure the correct planting depth (Fig. 308). Free drainage is of real importance.

Lime is Necessary. Fertility of soil is governed by the amount of lime in it. If the ground lacks lime it should be dressed with slaked or hydrated lime; or with ground limestone (powdered chalk) if the soil is light or sandy. How to test

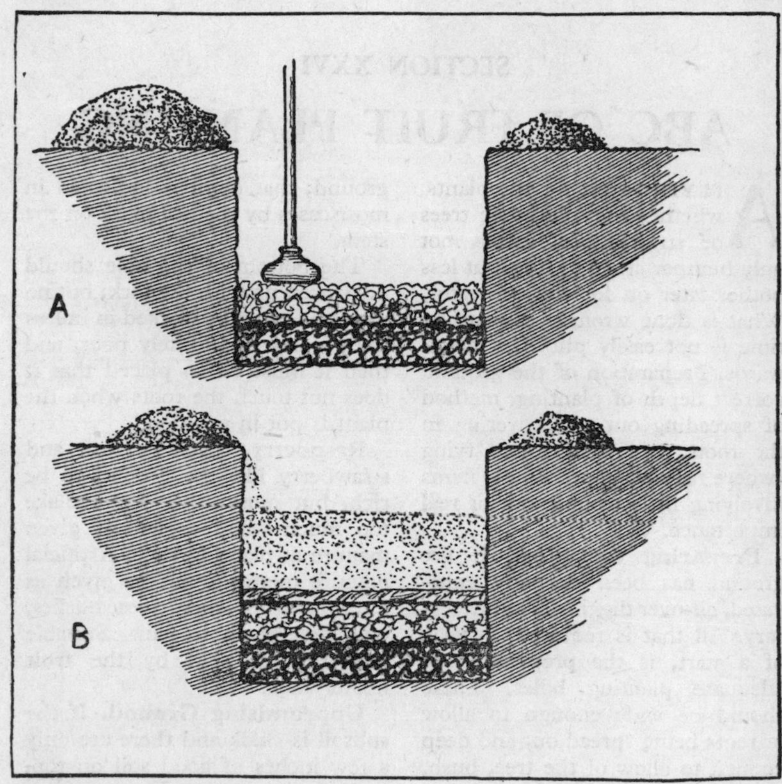

Fig. 308.—*Before planting fruit trees, poor drainage must be improved. Broken brick and stones are being rammed above broken-up subsoil in the planting hole at* (A), *which has been filled to the correct level at* (B)

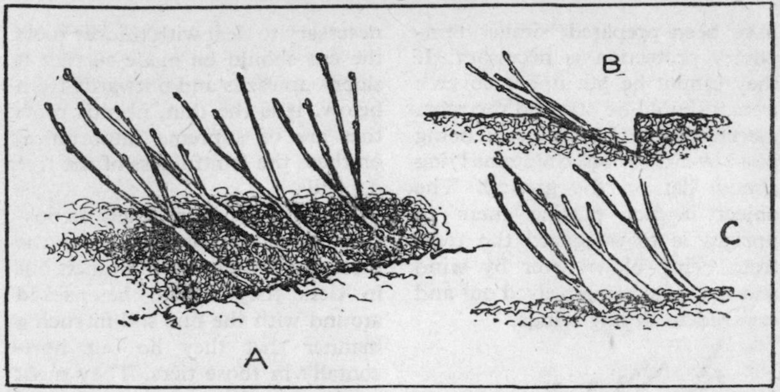

Fig. 309.—*As temporary protection for their roots these fruit bushes have been laid in an open trench* (A *and* B), *which has been filled in* (C) *so that the roots are completely covered. See also Fig.* 310, *below*

soil for lime is explained in the section FERTILIZERS AND MANURES, page 40.

There should be abundance of lime in the soil for all stone fruits —plums, cherries—and powdered chalk or hydrated lime should be mixed freely with the soil at the bottom of the planting hole and with the excavated soil before this is returned.

Old mortar rubbish crushed to particles with the garden roller is specially useful, in this respect, for adding to the soil; it also helps to drain heavy ground.

The same materials should be given as a top-dressing to fruit trees (whatever form these take) about every third year.

When to Plant. This can be done at any time while the plants are dormant; that is, between the end of October and end of March. But operations must be suspended during wet or frosty weather, and the holes should not be dug too far in advance of planting. The ideal is to dig them on the actual day that the trees, etc., are to go in; then sides and bottom will not dry hard or become pasty with rain. These latter conditions are all against the plants getting a good start.

Safeguard for Roots. If trees arrive for planting in bad weather they should remain unplanted and under cover, the roots covered with sacking or other material (Fig. 310), until they can be got into the ground under the best possible conditions.

If they arrive before the sites

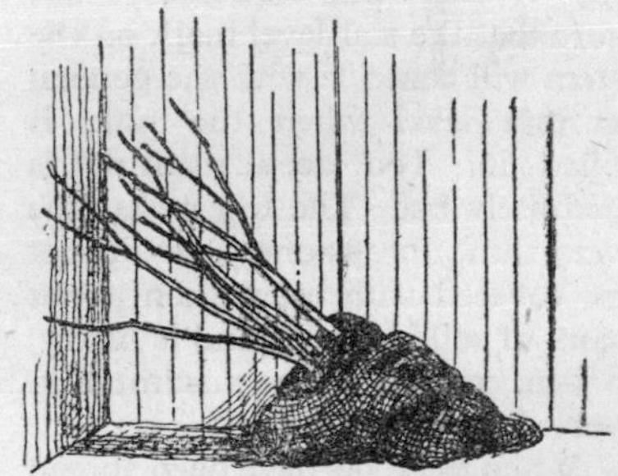

Fig. 310.—*Fruit trees or bushes whose planting must be delayed should have their roots covered in a shed, unless dealt with as in Fig.* 309

have been prepared, similar temporary protection is necessary. If they cannot be put under cover a trench should be dug and the roots placed therein (Fig. 309), soil being piled over the roots, the stems lying almost flat on the ground. The object in not putting them in upright is to safeguard the trees from being blown over by wind and the roots being heaved out and exposed to drying winds.

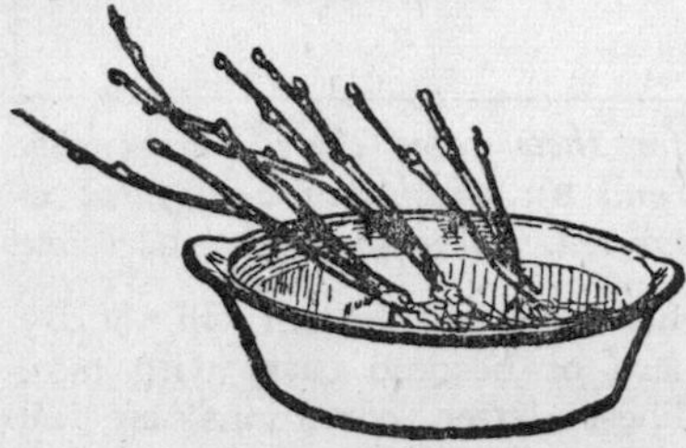

Fig. 311.—*Bushes which arrive with dry roots should be placed in water for a few hours before planting*

If roots are dry at planting time they should be soaked in water for a few hours (Fig. 311).

How to Plant. The tree should be placed centrally in the prepared hole and a piece of board, or handle of rake or hoe, placed across the top of this (Fig. 312A) to make sure that the soil-level mark on the stem will coincide with the general ground level when the hole is filled in. Too deep planting is definitely bad. The top roots (the very thin, fibrous ones) should not be covered with more than about 3 in. of soil if the ground is heavy; a 5-in. covering is the maximum in very light ground.

When the roots have been spread out, inspect them for bruised or broken ends. These must be trimmed cleanly back, with secateurs or sharp knife. Where it is necessary to deal with thicker roots the cut should be made so that it slopes upwards and outwards from below. It is the thin, fibrous roots that are of supreme importance; on these the fruitfulness of the tree depends.

Soil broken up as finely as possible should be used to cover the roots, and where these branch out in tiers they should be packed around with the fine soil in such a manner that they lie out horizontally in those tiers. They must not be curved upwards or bunched downwards (Fig. 312D).

The tree should be shaken gently as the filling-in proceeds (Fig. 312B), so that fine soil trickles down and fills all spaces among the roots. When these have all been covered the soil should be made firm above and around them by treading (Fig. 312C). But the top inch of soil which completes the filling-in of the hole should be left loose.

How to Stake and Tie. The tap root which held the tree upright in the nursery ground is no longer able to perform that function. It has been cut through and shortened and a stake must take its place in supporting the standard, half-standard, pyramid or bush-trained tree.

The stake should be put in place before the roots are covered in. It is then possible to see where to drive in the pointed end without injuring any of the roots. It should be long enough to reach up as far as where the branches begin, in the case of standards and half-standards. It should go up a foot or so among the branches of the bush-trained tree and farther still in the case of a pyramid.

No part of the tree should be

allowed to rub against the stake, or bark will be injured and disease may find a footing in the wound. To prevent any such injury, both stake and stem or branch where they are likely to make contact should be wrapped around with sacking or anything else that will prevent friction (Fig. 313A).

The tarred twine, or other strong tying material, should be passed around the padded stake twice (Fig. 313B), then crossed and the ends brought together around the padded portion of stem or branch, and finally tied behind the stake (Fig. 313C). In all cases some padding should be interposed between the tying material and the bark. The ties should be examined at least once a year, to ensure that the material is holding and the padding has not slipped. Ties will also need adjusting to keep pace with the swelling stem or branch.

In a very windy locality one stake may not be sufficient to support a tree. In this event a second stake should be driven in slantwise, the side away from the tree, its head pointing in the direction of the prevailing wind and tied to the first stake. It should be driven in at a point about 2 ft. out from the base of the tree (Fig. 313D).

Against Fence or Wall. The planting of trained trees against a fence or wall differs from open-garden planting only in that the hole takes a semicircular shape. The base of the stem should be about 6 in. out from the foot of the

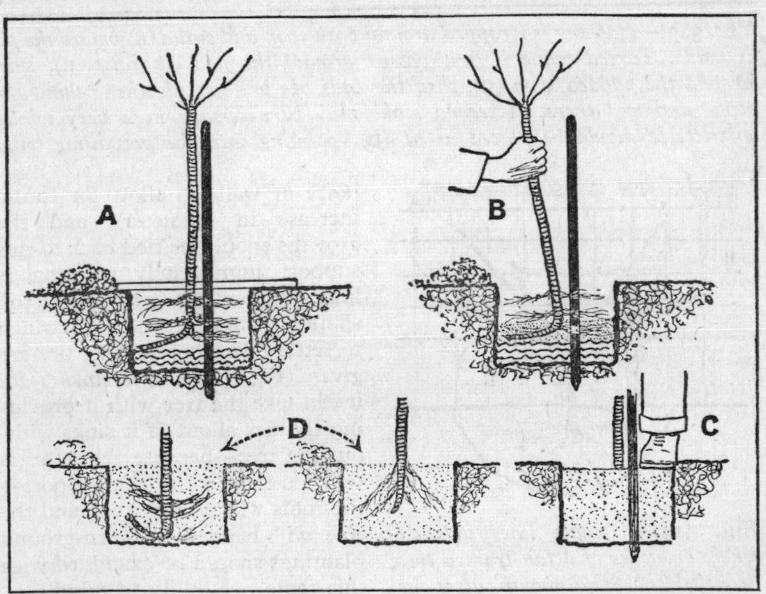

Fig. 312.—*A fruit tree with roots spread out in planting hole, and hoe handle placed across hole to test planting depth* (A). *The tree is shaken gently to settle soil among the roots* (B). *The soil is firmed above the covered-in roots by treading* (C). *Wrong methods of planting are shown at* (D)

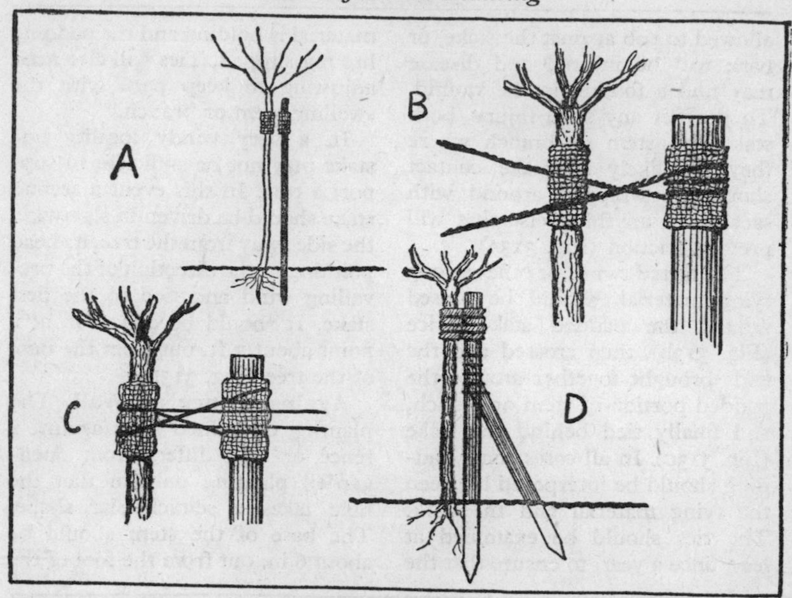

Fig. 313.—*Sacking is wrapped around both stem and stake* (A) *before the tie is made. Tarred twine is first passed around the padded stake* (B), *then around the padded stem* (C), *then the ends are brought together behind the stake and tied there. A second stake may be necessary in a very windy district; it should be placed as at* (D), *pointing into the prevailing wind*

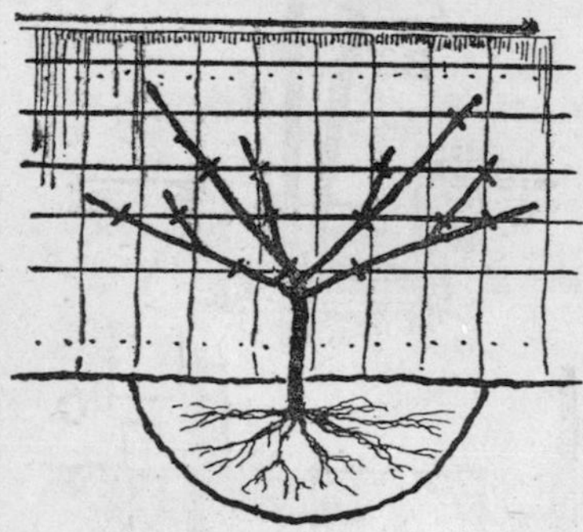

Fig. 314.—*Oblique lines indicate where branches of a fan-trained tree are tied, about a month after its planting, to the wire supports, which are fixed to the fence or wall. Note how the roots have been spread out in the semicircular planting hole*

fence or wall (to allow for future increase in diameter), and the growths should be tied back to this support immediately planting is finished—but not tightly. The soil should be allowed a month in which to settle down before final ties are given (Fig. 314). If it sinks 1 in. it can take the tree with it providing the ties allow. If it sinks without the tree—because the latter is tied too securely to the support—the roots will be disturbed and the tree will hang fire. Open-ground plantings should be examined with this same possibility in mind.

Soil at the foot of a house wall sometimes consists largely of builder's rubbish, and as no tree can be expected to grow in this the

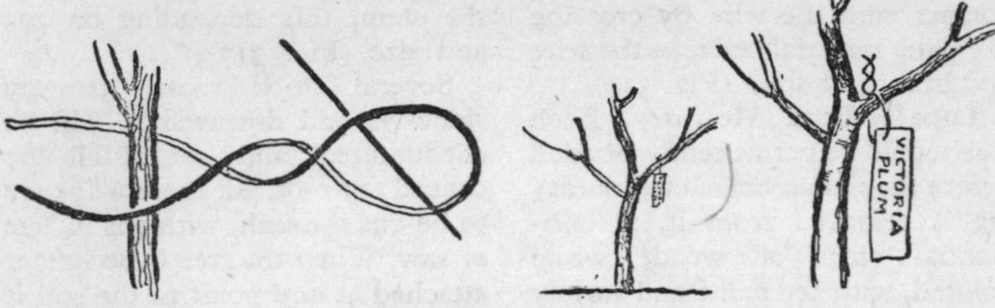

Fig. 315.—*Branches and stems of wall-trained trees are kept from close contact with the supporting wire by crossing the tying material*

Fig. 316.—*A label showing name and variety should be attached securely but not tightly to the inner end of a branch at the time of planting*

planting site may need special preparation. The bit of ground should be dug 2 ft. deep, to the length of 5 ft. to 6 ft. for one tree, and to the width of 3 ft. If a path happens to be in the way its foundation will need to be broken up to allow of the digging. Brickbats and other rubbish will have to be picked out and the site dealt with generally as explained in the case of open-ground plantings.

Trees that are to be tied to wire supports should be kept from close

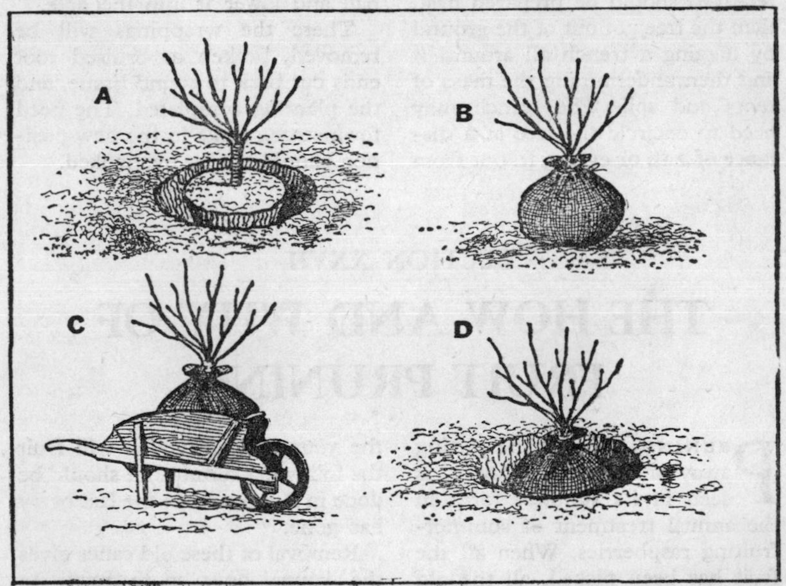

Fig. 317.—*A bush or young tree to be transplanted should be dug completely around and undermined* (A). *Sacking is then tied around the soil-mass and the plant lifted out* (B), *placed in a barrow* (C) *for easy transport, then lowered into the prepared planting hole* (D), *where the sacking is removed*

contact with the wire by crossing the tying material between the wire and branch or stem (Fig. 315).

Labels Beat Memory. Each tree should be permanently labelled before the nurseryman's temporary tag is removed from it. A substantial strip of wood, white painted, with the name and variety of the fruit written in bold block letters, is as good as anything, wired securely but not tightly to the inner end of a branch. The letters should be outlined heavily with pencil so that the latter bites into the wood (Fig. 316).

How to Transplant. Bushes and young trees are easily removed, during the dormant period, from one part of the garden to another. The hole to receive the tree to be removed should be prepared first, then the tree got out of the ground by digging a trench all around it and then undermining the mass of roots and soil. The trench may need to encircle the tree at a distance of 2 ft. or even 3 ft. out from the stem, this depending on age and size (Fig. 317).

Several thick roots, growing sideways and downwards, will be encountered, and last of all the central tap root. All these will have to be cut through, with spade, axe or saw. When the tree is no longer attached at any point to the soil it can be lifted up and out.

Sacking or something equally tough should be wrapped and tied around the mass of roots and soil so that the ball is completely and tightly enclosed before it leaves the hole. That will save much soil from being jarred away from the roots during its transference to the new quarters, with the aid of a wheelbarrow and an assistant who will help to unload the wrapped-up ball and lower it into the hole.

There the wrappings will be removed, broken or bruised root ends cut back to sound tissue, and the planting completed. The need for a strong stake in the new position should not be overlooked.

SECTION XXVII

THE HOW AND WHY OF FRUIT PRUNING

PRUNING, which is the cutting away of unwanted growth, is seen in its simplest form in the annual treatment of summer-fruiting raspberries. When all the fruit has been picked, all the old canes that carried the fruit are cut completely away as near ground level as possible. This can be done during winter, but for the sake of the young canes (which will fruit the following summer) it should be done in August when the last berry has gone.

Removal of these old canes gives the young ones more room to develop. The only pruning needed by the young raspberry canes consists in the cutting off, in late February, of any ends that may

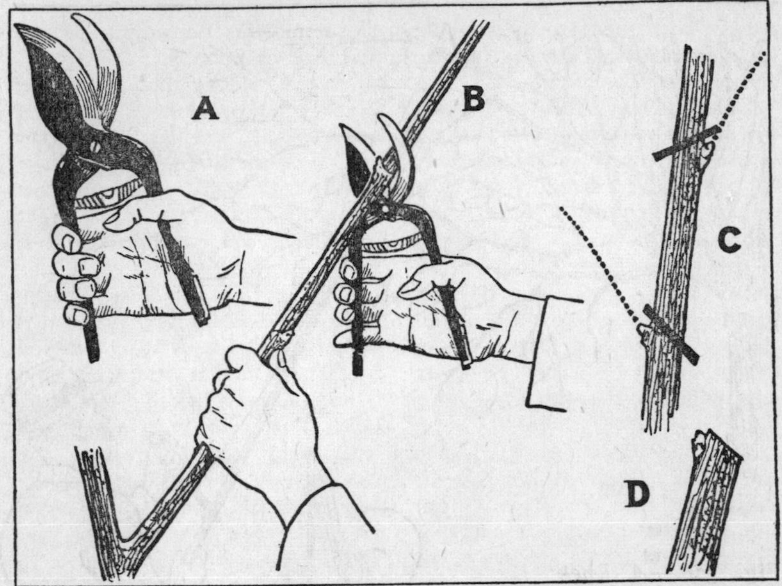

Fig. 318.—*Secateurs* (A) *are handled in this manner* (B), *cuts being made slantwise above buds* (C). *The cut end should appear as at* (D). *The dotted lines at* (C) *indicate the direction that growth would take from the bud*

bend over. The object of this is to enable the canes to carry a weight of fruit without the tops bending still farther. Here we have a rule-of-thumb method without any complications whatever.

In dealing with bush and tree fruits the pruner is met by certain complications. These, however, are smoothed out when the principles of pruning are understood.

More and Better Fruit. Left to its own devices any form of fruit tree or bush may become, in time, a mass of congested and unprofitable

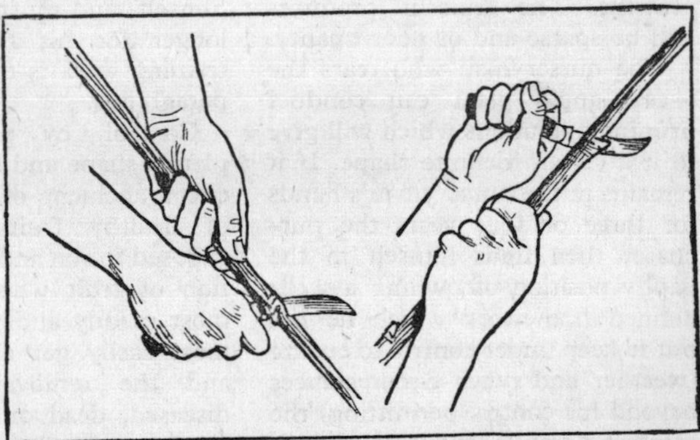

Fig. 319.—*The pruning knife should be held in such a way that the cut is made away from the operator, and quite close up to a wood bud but in a sloping direction*

Fig. 320.—*A long-arm pruner is invaluable for dealing with out-of-reach branches. The small sketch shows the mechanism of the cutting jaws*

growths. The fruit it produces will be sparse and of poor quality.

The nurseryman who rears the —say—apple plant can conduct pruning operations which will give to it a certain definite shape. If it remains in the nurseryman's hands for three or four years the purchaser then finds himself in the happy position of owning a well-defined framework which he has but to keep under control to ensure (weather and other circumstances beyond his control permitting) the greatest possible quantity of fruit of the best quality. If the purchaser buys it as a maiden (one year old) he has all the training work to do himself, and must wait that much longer for his fruit; this initial training work is explained in later paragraphs.

Control, by pruning, of the plant's shape and size includes the encouragement of the production of healthy fruiting wood fully exposed to sun and air; the production of fruit where it can ripen most readily and where it can be most easily got at for gathering; and the removal of damaged, diseased, dead or dying branches or shoots.

Tools for Pruning. An expert does most of his pruning with a sharp knife. The non-expert will do it most easily, and with less likelihood of damage to himself and the tree, with secateurs. The cut should be made just above (beyond) a wood bud, in a sloping direction, the slope carrying it above the bud; and the latter should point in the direction in which further growth is wanted (Fig. 318).

If a sharp knife and not secateurs is used the branch or shoot to be cut should be held below (not above) where the cut is to be made, and the blade should be directed away from the operator—who cannot then cut himself if the knife slips (Fig. 319). Torn edges that may remain after the cutting must be trimmed cleanly, or decay may start, and that may mean the death of the bud and the dying back of the shoot.

Growths that are out of reach from the ground should be tackled with the aid of steps or a ladder. Clambering about among branches can result in considerable destruction. The alternative to steps or a ladder is a tree pruner—a cutting device on the end of a long pole, worked by a wire (Fig. 320).

For cutting stout branches a saw will be needed. The first cut should be made from below, so that when the branch is sawn through from above it will come away without tearing the bark. If the branch is to be removed to its complete length the cutting should be done as close as the saw can be manoeuvred to the main stem or trunk, so that no stump is left to decay. The cut face should be as nearly upright as possible, and if the saw leaves it other than smooth a knife should be used to finish the job (Fig. 321).

Dealing with gooseberries, blackberries and other thorny subjects,

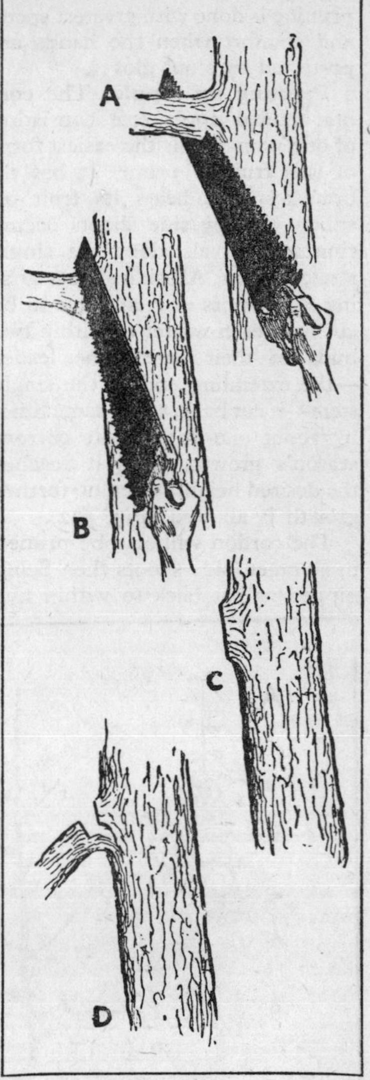

Fig. 321.—*A branch to be removed from a tree should first be sawn partly through from below* (A), *cutting being completed from above* (B). *The branch will come away cleanly* (C) *instead of tearing away* (D)

pruning is done with greatest speed and comfort when the hands are protected by stout gloves.

Pruning an Apple. The cordon-trained apple tree consisting of one stem only is the easiest form of this fruit to prune. It has no branches, but bears its fruit on spurs—stumpy side shoots occurring at intervals along the single straight stem. All side shoots arising from spurs or stem have to be cut back each winter to within two buds of their base. The leader—the extending end of the single stem—is cut back, at the same time, by about one-third of its current season's growth, until it reaches the desired height, when no further growth is allowed (Fig. 322).

The cordon will also be pruned in summer, side shoots then being nipped or cut back to within five leaves of their base (Fig. 322). This not only prevents the fruits being shaded but keeps growth within bounds and—of great importance—helps the development of fruit buds at the base of the shortened shoots.

This scheme of summer and winter pruning as outlined for a cordon apple applies also to espalier and fan-trained trees, to the branches of bush and pyramid, and to half-standards and standards in their early years.

Spur Pruning. Most varieties of apple produce their fruits on spurs (Fig. 323), exceptions including Lady Sudeley, Irish Peach and Mr. Gladstone, these latter carrying fruit mostly on the tips of shoots and making only a few spurs. Only very light pruning is needed for these, and they are never grown as cordons or espaliers. Otherwise an apple crop depends on the number and health of those stumpy side shoots, which are kept young and vigorous by being cut back when they become long and crowded.

A long spur due for revitalizing should be shortened by one-half the first year and cut back to two or three fruit buds at the base the second year (Fig. 324). Fruit buds are plumper and more rounded and prominent than wood (or leaf) buds and generally are found at or near the base of shoots. Leaf buds, which extend the wood growth, are slim and pointed (Fig. 324).

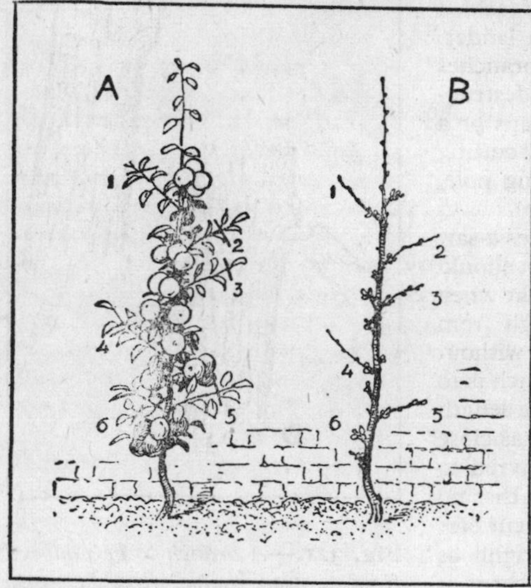

Fig. 322.—*A cordon apple will have side shoots shortened in summer as indicated by numbered strokes* (A). *The corresponding shoots as they appear in winter* (B) *before being spurred back*

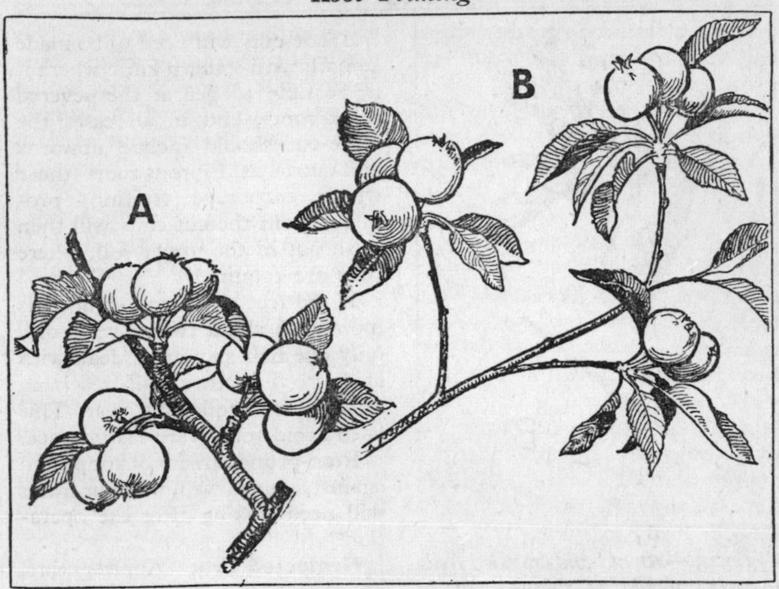

Fig. 323.—*A spur-fruiting apple* (A); *and a variety which bears its fruit mostly at the tips of longish side growths* (B), *making only a few spurs*

That distinction must always be borne in mind when pruning.

A further point to watch when dealing with any fruit trees trained against fence or wall is a tendency for some shoots to grow inwards to the support—that is, behind the tree. These should be removed completely as soon as they are noticed.

Shoots tending to grow in towards the centre of round trees—bush, pyramid, half-standard and standard—should be cut away completely, by way of summer pruning if small, during winter if they have become woody (Fig. 325).

Non-spur Fruiters. The production of spurs is not, of course, the rule among all kinds of fruit. The sweet cherry carries its fruit on spurs, but the sour varieties of cherry produce their fruit on shoots of the previous year's growth, as also do the peach, nectarine, apricot, black currant. With these non-spur fruiters the aim is to encourage strong new growths to take the place of shoots that have fruited. As many as possible of the fruited shoots are cut out each year to make way for the new ones that will fruit the following summer. Methods of pruning in such cases are explained fully under names of fruits in the alphabetical section.

Root Pruning. Trees in rich soil sometimes grow far too vigorously and either fail to produce any fruit at all or develop only very little. This over-production of unfruitful wood may result from too hard pruning, but more often from too rich living.

Where the trouble affects a young tree the rampant growth can be

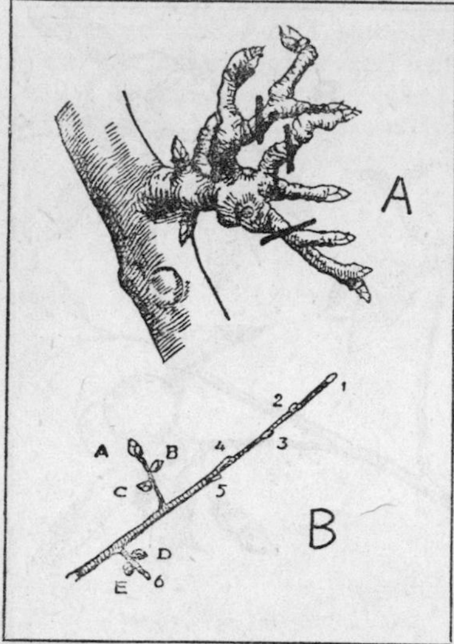

Fig. 324.—*An old and crowded fruit spur* (A) *should be thinned out as indicated by the black strokes. At* (B) *leaf buds are numbered* 1 *to* 6; *fruit buds are lettered* A *to* E

checked by lifting it completely, as soon as possible after the leaves have fallen, and replanting it. A trench should be dug around it, 2 ft. or so from the stem, to the depth of 2 ft., and the spade worked completely under it, all thick roots which anchor it in the ground being cut through. The tree is then lifted right out, with the least possible disturbance to the fibrous roots, and their severed ends cut back cleanly with a sharp knife (Fig. 326).

The tree is then replaced in the hole and the soil rammed back around it very firmly.

If the tree is too large for lifting, a trench should be made as already explained and all thick roots cut through with spade, saw or knife—including the central tap-root. The soil is then firmly rammed back.

Spade cuts will need to be made smooth with a sharp knife where it is possible to get at the severed thick roots, and in all cases the knife-cut should incline upwards and outwards. Fibrous roots (those which encourage fruiting) produced from the cut ends will then push out in the upper soil, where they are required.

If the tree to be root-pruned is more than about twelve years old, only one half should be dealt with at first, the other half receiving attention the following year. This is to avoid too severe disturbance.

Root-pruned trees not supported against a fence, wall, wires or trellis will need staking after the operation.

Neglected Trees. Apples, pears, plums or cherries grown as standards

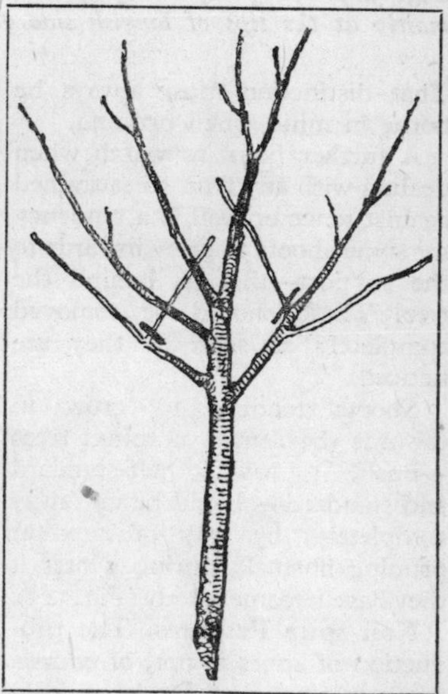

Fig. 325.—*Inward growing shoots or branches should be cut out as indicated above by the two short lines*

are sometimes allowed to get out of hand, and much of the fruit they produce is too high up for gathering. Part of the top should then be removed, so that the tree is reduced to a reasonable height,

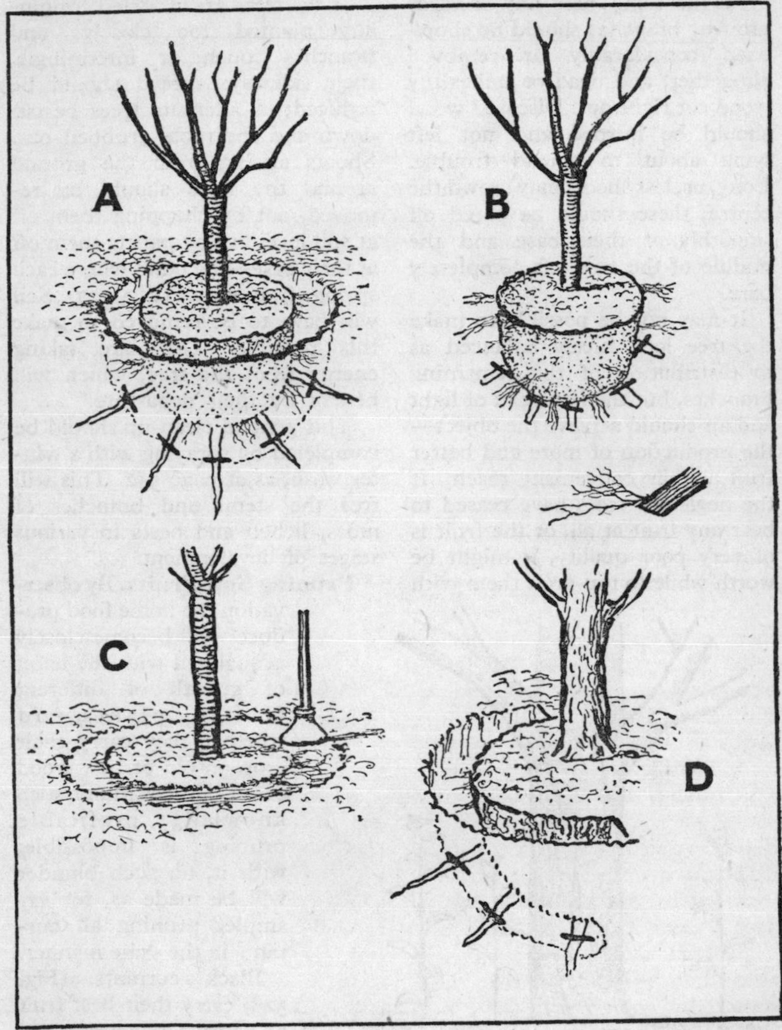

Fig. 326.—*A young unfruitful tree to be root-pruned should be dug around and under* (A), *lifted to the surface, thick root-ends cut back close* (B), *replaced in the hole and the soil rammed* (C). *An old tree should have only one-half of its root-mass* (D) *dealt with at one time. Method of cutting back thick roots with a sharp knife is shown in the small sketch (right centre)*

upright-growing branches being cut back to where horizontal ones branch out lower down.

At the same time any inward-growing branches should be shortened considerably or removed altogether, and dead or unhealthy wood cut right out. Diseased wood should be burned and not left lying about to spread trouble. Long, useless shoots may crowd the centre; these should be pared off smoothly at their base and the middle of the tree left completely bare.

It may not be possible to make the tree look nicely balanced as to distribution of the remaining branches, but the letting in of light and air should achieve the object—the production of more and better fruit within convenient reach. If the neglected trees have ceased to bear any fruit at all, or the fruit is of very poor quality, it might be worth while to top-graft them with pieces of a fruitful variety and thus revitalize them; the method is explained in the following section.

If the trees are crowded (originally planted too closely) and branches touch or intermingle, their sideways spread should be reduced; or alternate trees be cut down and the roots grubbed out. Shoots arising from the ground around the trees should be removed, not by chopping them off at soil level but by paring them off at their base—the point where each springs from a root (Fig. 327). Soil will have to be removed to make this possible. They are taking energy from the tree, which will benefit by their departure.

This general clean-up should be completed by spraying with a winter wash, as at page 552. This will free the stems and branches of moss, lichen and pests in various stages of development.

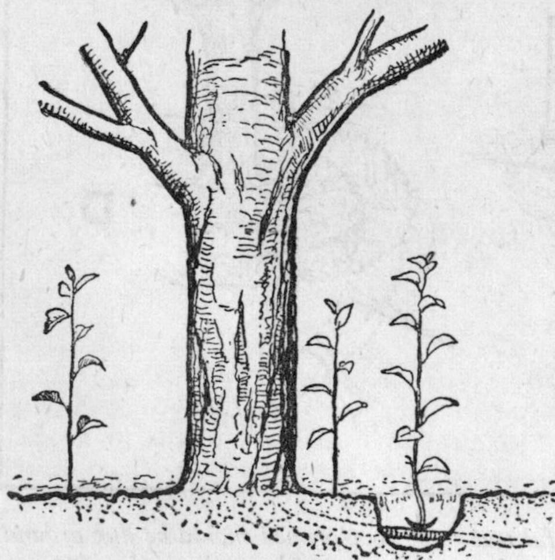

Fig. 327.—*Suckers should be removed by scraping away soil to the sucker's base and then paring it from the parent roots with a sharp knife*

Pruning Soft Fruits. By observation the home food producer will become closely acquainted with the habit of growth of different fruiting plants, and whether they carry their crop on old or new wood or on both. Without such knowledge profitable pruning is impossible; with it, no such blunder will be made as, for example, pruning all currants in the same manner.

Black currants (Fig. 328) carry their best fruit on new wood, whereas red and white currants produce chiefly on short spurs on old wood. In pruning black currants the object is to cut away each

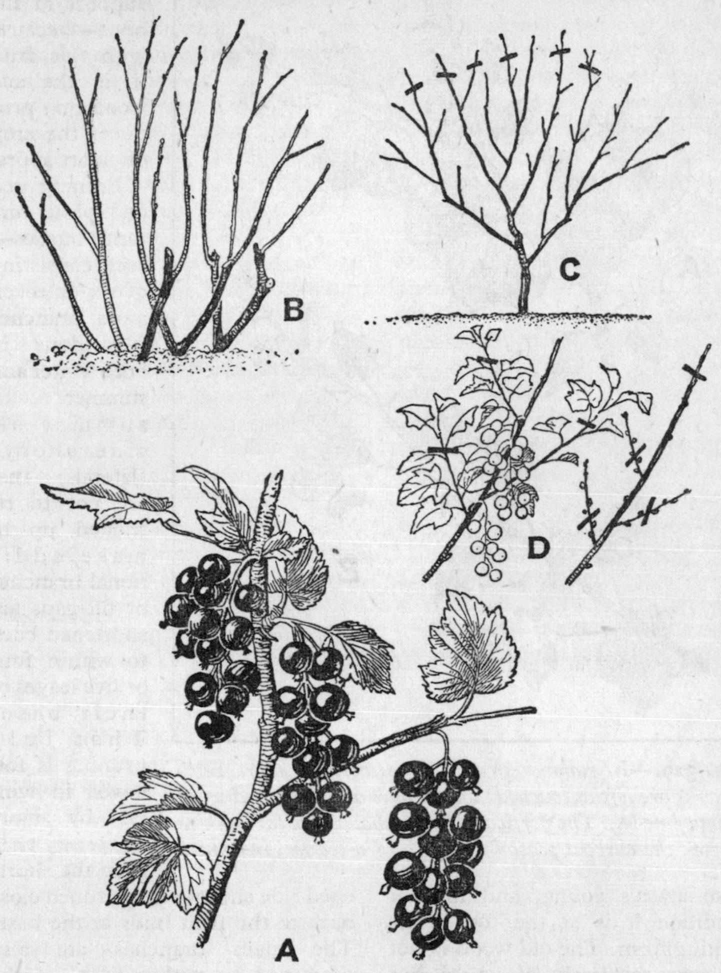

Fig. 328.—*Best black currants* (A) *are produced on young wood; old fruited wood (blacked-in,* B) *being cut back to young shoots annually. Red and white currants are produced chiefly on spurs on older wood, leaders of bushes being shortened in winter* (C); *side-growths are summer pruned as at* D, *(left), then winter pruned as at* D *(right), leaving short spurs for fruiting*

year all the old wood that can be replaced by young shoots that have grown up from or near the base during the same year. This is done in late August or early September, after the fruit has been picked. This cutting away of fruited wood each year keeps the black currant

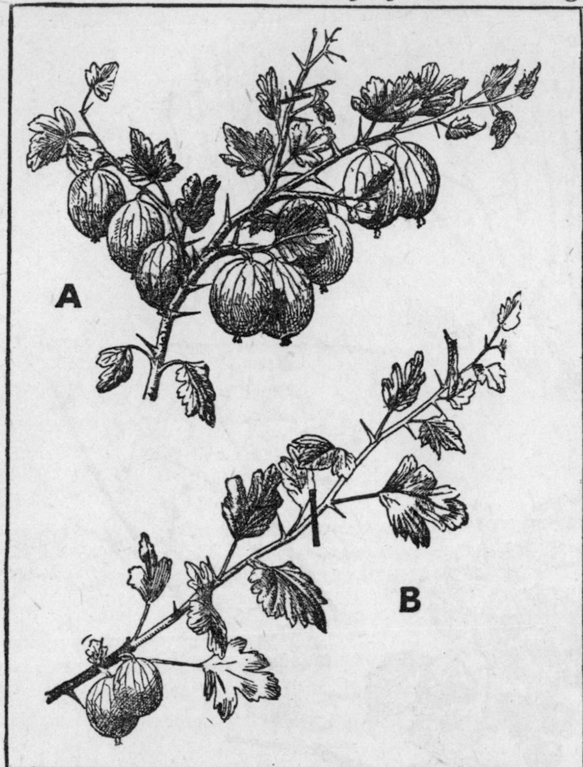

Fig. 329.—*In summer pruning gooseberries, short side-growths are left untouched; longer ones are shortened as at oblique line* (A). *The vertical line* (B) *shows how far back to shorten the current season's growth of a leader, in winter*

bush always young, and in that condition it is at the top of its fruiting form. The old wood is not cut away recklessly, of course, but only where there is strong new growth to replace it.

That habit of growth and fruiting makes the black currant quite unsuitable for training as a cordon. It is necessarily kept to bush form. Whereas red and white currants, though generally grown as bushes, make excellent cordons for planting against a wall or fence or a support in the open—because with this fruit it is the old wood that produces the crop on short spurs.

Pruning red and white currant bushes—each consisting of six or seven main branches—is done in both winter and summer. In summer all side shoots (laterals) that are not to be trained up to make additional branches or fill gaps are shortened back to within four or five leaves of their base. That July pruning is followed in winter by more cutting, this time the shortened side shoots being pruned close back to the fruit buds at the base. The main branches are also shortened to within 6 in. of the base of the same season's growth.

Gooseberries fruit on new growth as well as on spurs on the old wood. Short side shoots give the biggest fruit of the best quality. When dealing with gooseberry bushes, summer pruning consists in shortening the longest new side growths by one-half but leaving the short side growths untouched (Fig.

329A). In February the summer-shortened side growths are again cut back, to within 1 in. of their base, and the previous summer's extension growth at the end of each main branch (there should be not more than eight or ten of these) is cut back to within 6 in. of its base (Fig. 329B).

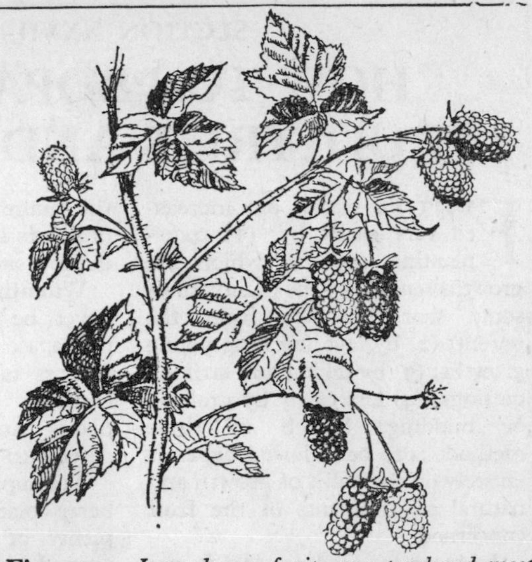

Fig. 330.—*Loganberry fruits are produced most freely on long canes of the previous season's growth*

The loganberry fruits on long canes (Fig. 330) produced the previous season, and pruning consists in cutting out old canes as soon as the fruit has been gathered (Fig. 331)—exactly as was explained in the case of summer-fruiting raspberries in the first paragraphs of this section.

The blackberry, by way of contrast, will continue fruiting from the old wood (on new side growths which the old wood will produce annually all along its length). But to keep the plants vigorous and 100 per cent profitable, as much as possible of the old fruited canes should be cut right away after the berries are gathered and long new canes arising from ground level or close to it trained up to take the place of the old ones.

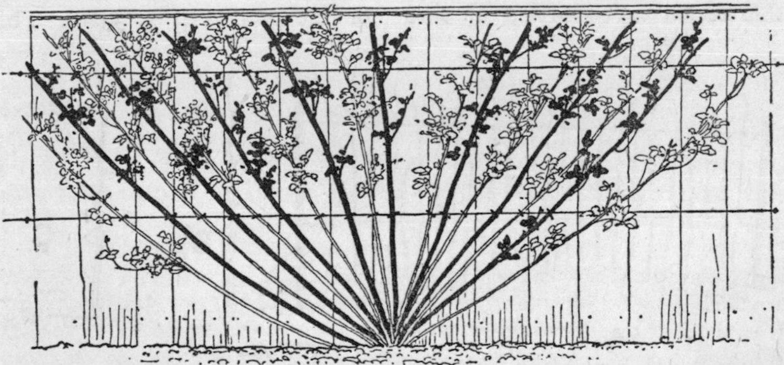

Fig. 331.—*The loganberry canes shown here with thick black stems are the ones that have fruited. They are to be cut right out, after fruiting, to make room for the new young canes—which will fruit the following year*

SECTION XXVIII

HOW TO PROPAGATE FRUIT TREES AND BUSHES

FRUITING plants are increased very easily by: (1) transplanting suckers, which are growths sent up by the plant's roots some short distance from the parent; (2) by layering long young growths; (3) by taking and striking cuttings; (4) less easily by grafting or budding. Which of these methods is to be followed depends entirely on the habit of growth and natural requirements of the fruit concerned.

Increase by seed sowing is not generally practised. Time taken for seedlings to reach the fruiting stage is far too prolonged. And in the case of apple, pear, plum, cherry and similar fruits the chances are hundreds to one against any seedling coming true to parent type.

With the exception of grafting and budding, which demand some skill, the operations described in this section can be carried out with the minimum trouble and the stock of plants increased considerably in number at no cost whatever.

Warning. The rule that should never be departed from is this: propagate only the best, the heavy fruiters of fine quality. The unfruitful, poor-quality, diseased plants can but hand down their defects to any progeny.

Transplanting Suckers. Raspberry plants (Fig. 332) produce plenty of young canes (suckers) around the clumps—out of line with the supports. These can be dug up with spade or trowel, between October and spring (October is the best time), complete with their own roots, and planted where they are to remain and fruit (Fig. 332B). The long root which connects sucker with parent has to be severed, of course, with a spade or a knife. After planting, these canes should be cut to within about 6 in. of the ground (Fig. 332C). This

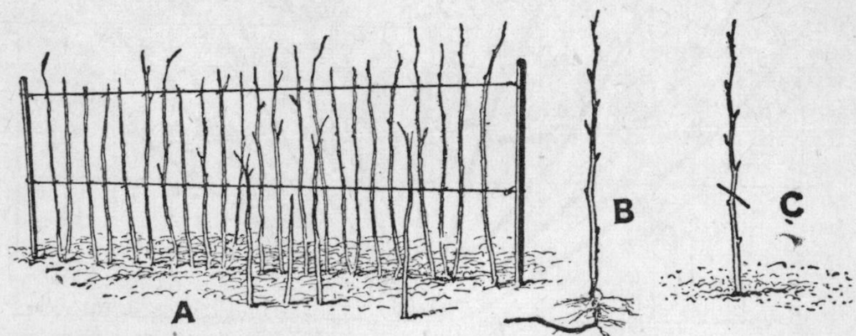

Fig. 332.—*Young canes or suckers* (A) *which spring up between the raspberry rows can be dug up complete with their own roots* (B) *and transplanted, and then be cut back to within a distance of about 6 in. of the ground* (C)

allows them a full season in which to establish themselves strongly before having to stand the strain of fruiting.

Loganberries and some varieties of blackberry sometimes produce suckers which can be transplanted in the same way. Where no suckers are produced, or they are insufficient in number, long young (unfruited) canes can be layered, as explained in the next paragraph.

Fig. 333.—*Cultivated varieties of blackberry can make any fence or trellis highly profitable*

Rooting Layers. The tips of long unfruited growths of blackberry (Fig. 333) and loganberry root very readily if the selected growths are bent over until the ends can be buried 5 in. or 6 in. in the ground. A hole is made with trowel or dibber where the tip makes easy contact with the soil, the tip is inserted 5 in. or 6 in. deep and the soil trodden back over it.

It is advisable to keep the buried tips in place by pegging them firmly with pieces of bent wire (Fig. 334). The operation is carried out in August, and the tips send out roots more readily if the soil is watered well in dry weather. The layers will be rooted by the following spring, and can then be dug up and transplanted after being severed from the parent plant. The parent stem of the layered blackberry should be cut through so that the new plant is left with only 3 in. or 4 in. of old stem. The layered loganberry can come away with a full length of parent stem, the cut being made at the top end.

The reason for this difference in early treatment is that the blackberry takes longer than the loganberry to become established as a new plant, and relieving the young blackberry roots of the old stem gives them the chance to make themselves strong and at home and fit for fruiting the following year. The loganberry is a much more vigorous plant, and is in no way handicapped by having to support some feet of the parent stem.

The fig can be layered, in the same way, in May, the rooted stem-tips being ready for transplanting in five or six months; that is, round about October.

Nuts are layered in autumn and given a full year before being transplanted; shoots two years old should be chosen for layering.

The strawberry (Fig. 335) is peculiarly adapted to layering. The parent plant sends out a number of runners which lengthen, and at intervals of a few inches produce young plants—one at each joint. These should be pegged down to the ground in early July with a wire pin or a stone close to each joint to ensure firm contact. If there are a sufficient number to choose from the first on each runner should be layered and the others cut away; the first makes the strongest plant. The rooted strawberry layers are severed in autumn and planted out in the fruiting bed, or potted up for growing under glass to give out-of-season fruit.

Gooseberry and Currant Cuttings. Even if no more gooseberry or currant bushes are required for space filling, a few cuttings should be taken to replace any bushes which may be showing signs of decreasing production because of advancing years. The time to do this is late September or early October, and the shoots to select for cuttings are growths that were made during the summer. These should be between about 10 in. and 15 in. long, strong and firm and free of disease. If they are not really firm and ripened at that time they should be left until November.

The need for a few of these should be borne in mind when summer pruning side shoots, enough to make cuttings being left unshortened.

They are cut through immediately below a joint and the tip of

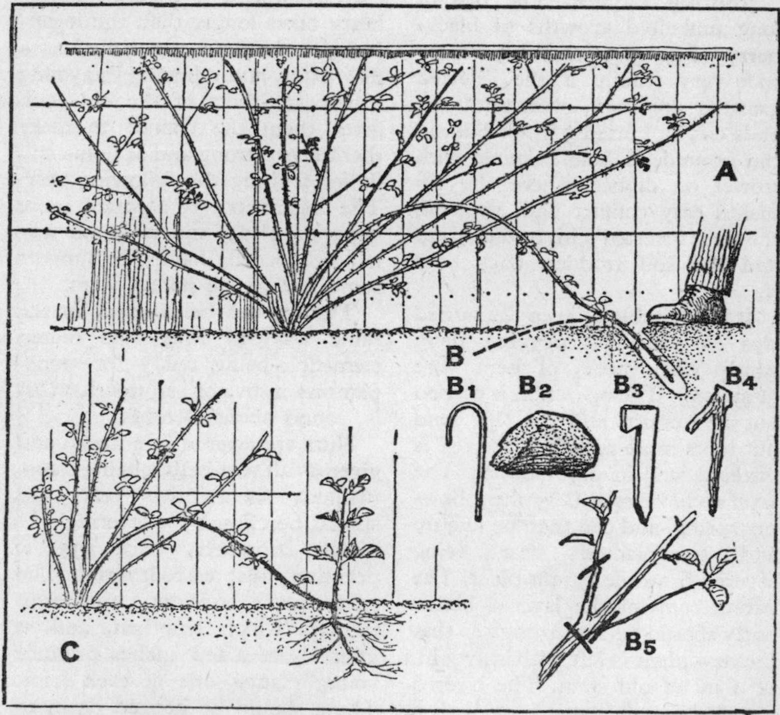

Fig. 334.—*Tips of blackberry* (A) *can be rooted as at* (B), *held in place by bent wire* (B1), *or a stone* (B2), *or notched wood* (B3), *or piece of branch* (B4) *cut from a tree or shrub as at* (B5). *The rooted layer is shown on right at* (C)

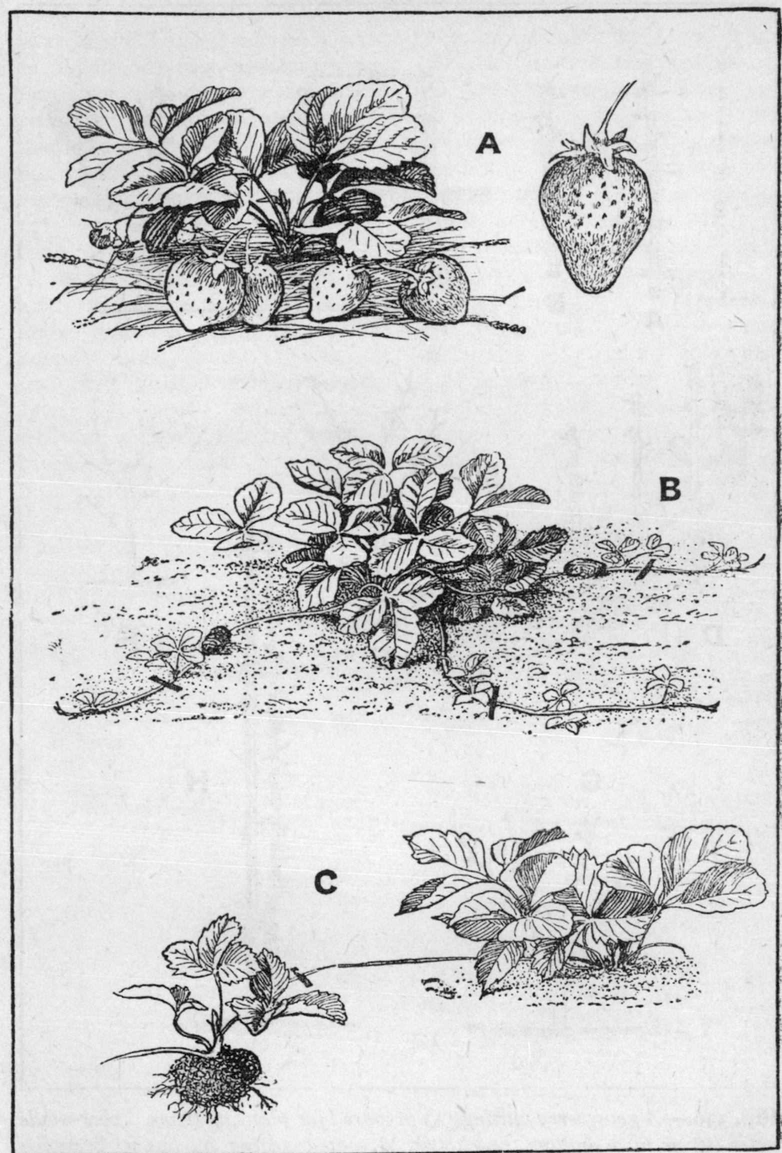

Fig. 335.—*A strawberry plant* (A) *sends out runners with young plants which take root readily if pressed to the ground with wire pins or stones* (B). *Thick strokes indicate point of cutting-back lengthy runners. A rooted layer* (C) *before being lifted is severed from the parent plant at the point indicated*

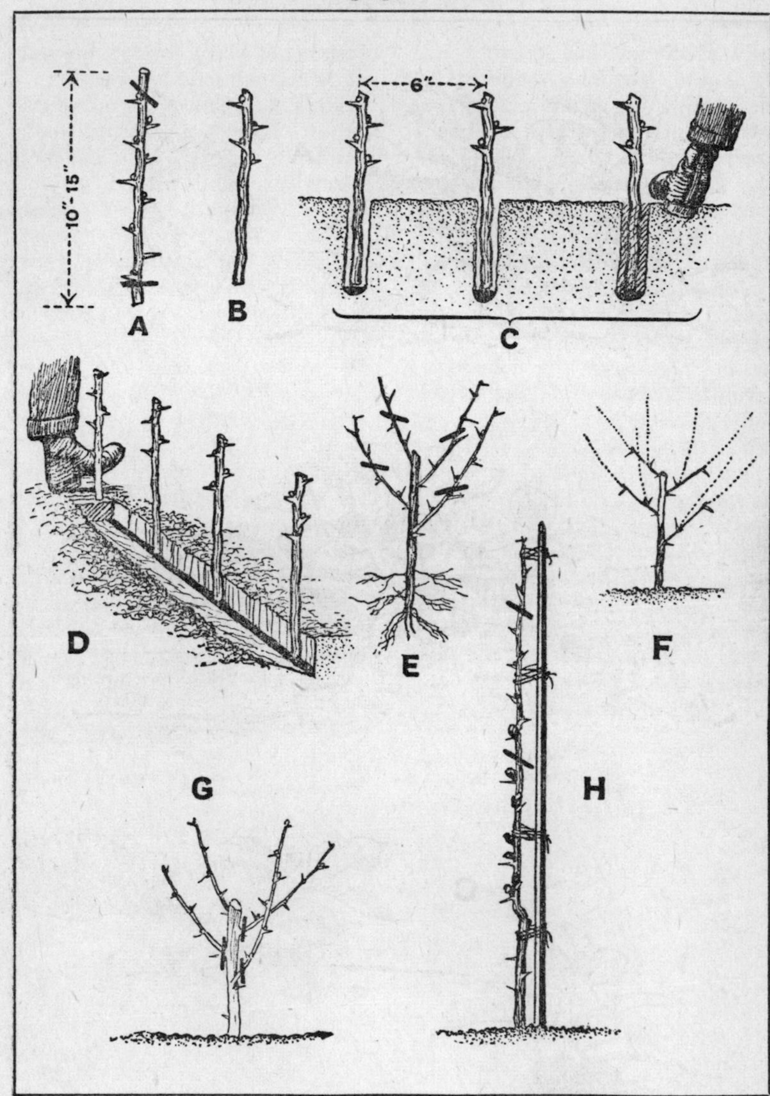

Fig. 336.—*A gooseberry cutting* (A) *prepared for planting* (B) *in dibber-made holes* (C) *or in a shallow trench* (D). *A rooted cutting* (E) *has its branches cut back to two buds each, the result being additional branches shown by dotted lines* (F). *Thus is a gooseberry bush made. A cordon* (H) *starts as a cutting whose growths are reduced to one* (G) *to provide a single stem. Oblique lines show subsequent cutting-back points, to induce strong growth*

each is cut off just above a bud (Fig. 336). Before gooseberry and red- and white-currant cuttings are planted, all but three or four of the top buds should be removed—with the tip of a knife, or they can be rubbed off with a finger. The length of stem which will be buried is thus free of growing points, which means that when the cutting is rooted it will send out either three or four branches.

The reason for this lower bud removal is that gooseberry and red- and white-currant bushes do best when they have a clean length of stem between soil level and head. Black currants, on the other hand, do best when they can send up suckers from below ground. With this in view all buds are left on the black-currant cutting (Fig. 337), which is planted to such a depth that only three or four of the buds are above the surface, the lowest of these being at soil level; some that are buried will send up branches.

Gooseberry and red- and white-currant cuttings are planted about 4 in. deep—that is, 4 in. of the stem is below ground. Above ground there will be some inches of budless stem and then three or four buds.

How to Plant Cuttings. Firm ground is wanted by these cuttings, so if it has been recently dug it should be trodden. They also need full exposure to light and air, so they must not be planted under trees. Best plan is to plant them 6 in. apart in a row where they will be in the way of nothing else until the next late autumn or early spring after that, when they will be ready for the final planting.

The cuttings can be planted in dibber-made holes; or the spade, held vertically, can be used to nick out a continuous narrow trench, the cuttings resting against the

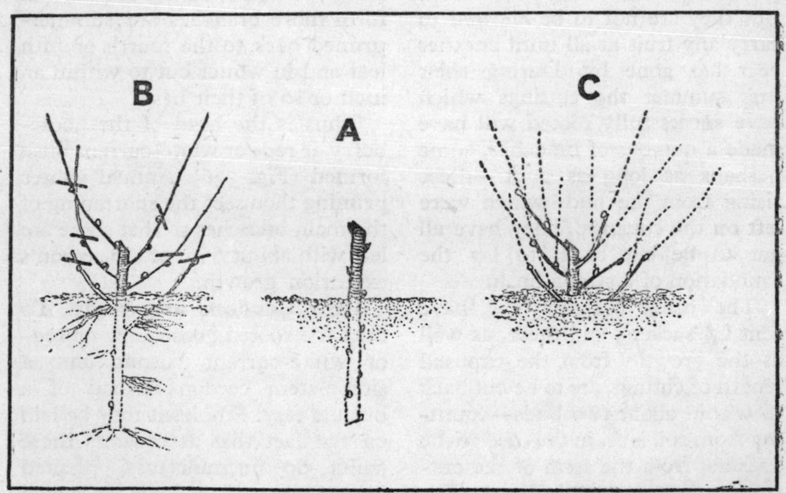

Fig. 337.—*A black-currant cutting has all its buds left on* (A), *the result being as at* (B), *where oblique lines show points of cutting back new growth, the result of this being additional branches shown by dotted lines at* (C).

upright side. If the soil is heavy, sand or sifted ashes or wood ash should be dropped into each dibber hole or sprinkled along the bottom of the narrow trench for the base of the cuttings to rest upon; this always encourages rooting.

The soil should be rammed back firmly around each cutting. When dealing with heavy ground it is particularly necessary to ensure that the base of the cutting is in contact with the prepared soil; if it is not, the cutting will die. Before the soil goes back into the dibber holes or the nicked-out trench it should be broken up as finely as possible; in trench planting it should be trodden back a little at a time.

If during winter and early spring frost loosens them—frost has a lifting action—firming with the boot heel must be done again.

How Bushes are Made. When the cuttings are a year old they are planted out where they are to fruit. But they are not to be allowed to carry any fruit at all until another year has gone by. During their first summer the cuttings which have successfully rooted will have made a number of branches, some perhaps as long as 2 ft.—these rising from the buds which were left on the cuttings. They have all got to be cut back, to lay the foundation of a strong bush.

The black currants will have sent up suckers, and these, as well as the growths from the exposed length of cutting, are to be cut back to within about two buds—counting from soil level in the case of the suckers, from the stem of the cutting in the case of top shoots. The end buds in all cases should point outwards, so that the currant bush shall be kept with an open centre.

In that manner is laid the foundation of a really vigorous black-currant bush. After that first cutting-back, pruning consists in an annual removal of as much old, fruited wood as can be replaced by new growths—the new growths of one summer carrying the fruit the following summer. In other words, one-year-old black-currant wood produces the best fruit.

Gooseberry, red- and white-currant rooted cuttings at the end of their first year need to have their shoots shortened to a bud within 5 in. or 6 in. of where they branch out from the cutting's stem. This will result in the production of still more branches, which at the end of the cutting's second year will be shortened by about one-third of the season's growth. In the third year fruit will be produced—on short spurs on the oldest wood and also on side shoots 4 in. to 5 in. long. Longer side shoots not required to form more branches are summer-pruned back to the fourth or fifth leaf and in winter cut to within an inch or so of their base.

Thus is the head of the gooseberry or red- or white-currant bush formed (Fig. 336). Annual winter pruning then sees the shortening of the main branches so that these are left with about 6 in. of the season's extension growth.

How Cordons are Made. To turn the rooted gooseberry or red- or white-currant cutting into a single-stem cordon instead of a bush is easy. Emphasis may be laid on the fact that as cordons these fruits do magnificently, planted flat against wall or fence, or staked in the open where a row of them occupies no more space than would be filled by a row of cabbages.

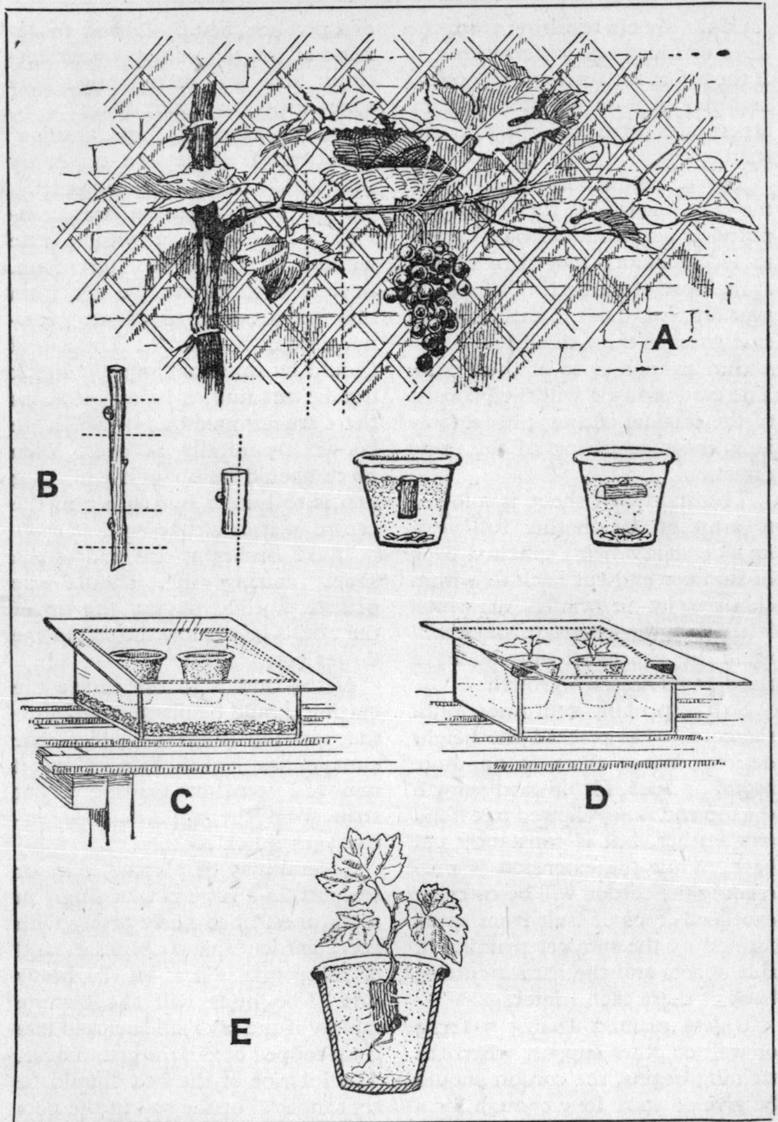

Fig. 338.—*Stages in the propagation of an outdoor grape vine* (A); *dotted lines enclose portion of stem which will provide one cutting. The length of shoot at* (B) *will provide two good cuttings. A cutting, after removal of one side, is planted upright in a small pot or on its side. Rooting takes place in a glass-topped box* (C), *air being given later* (D). *A rooted cutting is shown at* (E)

Of the shoots resulting from the three or four buds which were left at the top of the cutting, only one is required to form the cordon; the others are pared off close to the stem.

The chosen shoot should be in the best position for extension purposes and it should be cut back to within about a foot of its base—at the close of the cutting's first full year. If that shoot is carrying any side growths these should be cut to within an inch or so of their base. The cordon-to-be will then consist of the original cutting plus a foot-long shoot extending in the same direction.

The shortened shoot is allowed to grow on for another full year, its side shoots being pinched back in summer and cut back to within about 1 in. in winter, at which latter time the extension shoot will again be shortened—by about a third of its season's growth.

So the pruning continues, until the cordon has reached the height desired. When there is no more room, or need, for upward growth the top end is not allowed to extend any farther, but is constantly cut back. While the extension is proceeding the cordon will be carrying excellent crops of fruit from spurs formed by the summer pruning of side shoots and the harder cutting back of these each winter.

Unless planted against a fence or wall or other support when the training begins, the cordon should be given a stake long enough for a regular tying back of the extension growth, to ensure straightness and prevent accidents.

Double and triple cordons are built up in the same way, two or three shoots respectively instead of only one being allowed to remain at the top of the rooted cutting, and so staked that the stems grow up a foot apart.

Grape-vine Cuttings. Outdoor varieties of grape are as easily propagated by short cuttings (Fig. 338) as are glasshouse ones, providing a greenhouse with a little warmth is available to start them. Several cuttings can be got from one lateral—side shoot—at pruning time in November. The lateral should be firm (not sappy), and it can be cut into as many pieces as there are dormant buds—which are known technically as eyes. Each piece should be about $1\frac{1}{2}$ in. long and is to have a bud either in the centre of it or at one end.

If the bud is at one end of the short cutting this should be planted upright so that the tip of the bud is just below the soil in the flower pot.

If the bud is in the centre the cutting should be planted flat, after the opposite (budless) side of the cutting has had a slice of wood removed from it. Cutting a flat strip from the opposite side encourages quick rooting.

Several may be planted, 1 in. or so apart, in a large pot, or singly in small ones, filled fairly firmly with good garden soil containing sand or sharp grit if it is on the heavy side. The buds will shoot more rapidly if the pots are enclosed in a glass-topped box in the greenhouse. The interior of the box should be kept moist, but the soil in the pots should not be kept constantly sodden or the young growths might rot off.

The glass top of the box should be propped up about 1 in. at one side when growth has really started, and the pots can come out of the box when each cutting has made three or four leaves. The small plants need shifting then, singly, into 6-in.-diameter pots and each should be given a stake. Growth will be rapid in moist warm air, and when the pots are filled with roots the plants should be exposed more and more to open-air conditions (hardened off) for planting out against a warm wall—one facing south, south-east or south-west. Or the plants may be shifted into larger pots for eventual fruiting in the greenhouse.

How Fruit Trees are Raised. Apples, pears, plums, cherries, peaches, nectarines, apricots are propagated in the nurseries by grafting or budding the desired varieties on to special stocks. That is, the trees are not grown on their own roots. By joining (working is the technical term) pieces of the desired varieties on to specially selected young plants (the stocks) so that the latter provide in future only the roots and a very short piece of stem, whilst the desired varieties form the tops, a certain control is gained over the fruit trees thus formed.

That control is concerned with the size and the form or shape of the tree and the age at which it begins to bear fruit. Size and quality of the fruit may also be improved.

For example, standard and half-standard apples are grafted or budded on specially selected crab-apple stock which impart vigorous growth. Bushes, pyramids, cordons and other forms of trained tree intended to occupy less space than the spreading standard or half-standard are worked on what are known as paradise stocks, which have a dwarfing influence and result in earlier fruiting. Pears in standard and half-standard form are grafted or budded on the wild pear stock; other forms of pear are worked on selected types of quince stock.

The grafts or buds are taken from the best specimens of the varieties concerned, and the stocks that are to receive them are raised

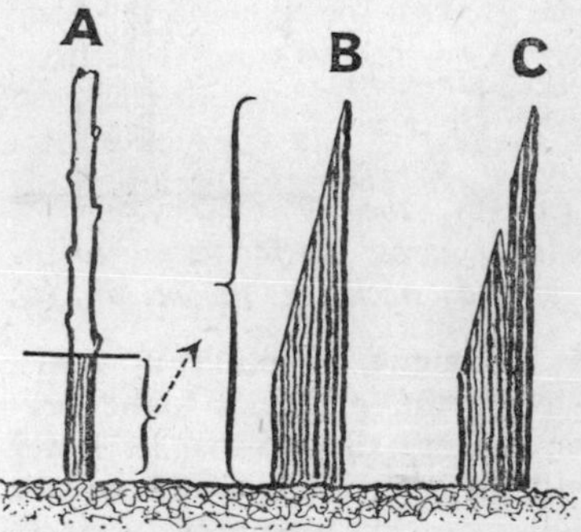

Fig. 339. *For tongue or whip grafting the stock is cut back* (A), *then cut with a long slanting face* (B), *then notched across where shown at* (C)

by means of cuttings, layers or seed. When these stocks have grown to suitable size grafting or budding can proceed.

The Art of Grafting. One method adopted by the nurserymen is known as tongue or whip grafting (Fig. 339). The young stock which is to receive the graft is cut down to within 2 in. or 3 in. of the ground. The knife blade is then used to make an upward-sloping cut about 1½ in. long on one side of the short stump. Again the blade is used, this time across the centre of the sloping cut surface, the blade being pressed down a short distance and then withdrawn; the result

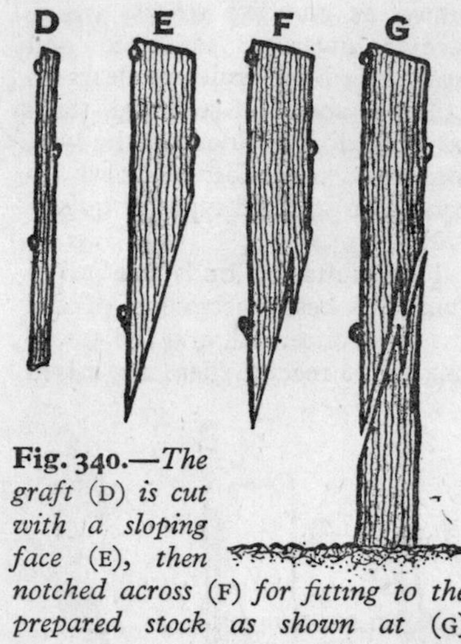

Fig. 340.—*The graft* (D) *is cut with a sloping face* (E), *then notched across* (F) *for fitting to the prepared stock as shown at* (G)

is a tongue, pointing upwards.

Next the graft has to be prepared (Fig. 340) so that its lower end has an opening which will fit tightly over the tongue of the stock, this opening being made across the centre of a slantwise cut about 1½ in. long; the latter to match, as nearly as possible, the sloping cut surface of the stock. The idea behind all this is that the cut surfaces of both graft and stock shall correspond as closely as possible over as great a length as possible, and that they shall join and become one after being fitted together and bound in place for a time with raffia.

This grafting is done during March or April, when the sap of the stock is active but the grafts themselves are dormant. So that the grafts shall be dormant at that time the shoots from which they are prepared are cut from the trees (which are to be propagated) before the real winter pruning starts. They are year-old shoots, well ripened by sun and about as thick as a pencil, and to keep them alive until March they are planted closely together outdoors with about half their length below ground.

When grafting time arrives these specially selected shoots are taken up and both ends are cut off each one so that each length is furnished with three or four good wood buds. The top cut is made just beyond a bud; the other end is cut about ¾ in. below the bottom bud.

It is at that lower point and on the side opposite to the bottom bud (nurserymen call it the stock bud) that the slanting cut with an opening across the centre is made—to fit the cut surfaces of the stock.

When the two have been interlocked (Fig. 341)—fitted neatly and tightly together—the union is secured with raffia bound around and tied, but the bottom bud of

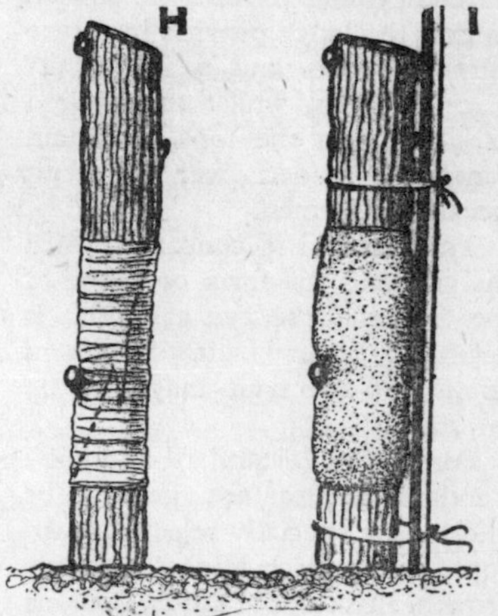

Fig. 341.—*Graft and stock fitted together and secured with raffia binding* (H), *which is then covered carefully with some moist clay* (I)

the graft is left exposed. Then, to prevent the cut tissues drying, the raffia binding is covered with special grafting wax, or moist clay worked up like putty and mixed with chopped hay or chaff.

A stake is necessary when the graft begins to grow, as it will soon do, as security against wind and to ensure a straight stem. The raffia should also be removed then, or it may cut into the swelling wood and damage the graft seriously.

The nurseryman now has a main stem on which to form the head of a standard or half-standard or bush or pyramid; or he can use it as the foundation of a fan-trained tree or an espalier; or he can train it as a cordon.

How a Bush Tree is Made. When the grafted plant is in its first year it is known as a maiden (Fig. 342). To give the young apple tree, for example, bush form, the elongated single stem is cut back during the winter that follows the first summer's growth to within 18 in. or so of the ground, the cut to be made just above a strong wood bud. This short leg will send out a number of shoots, which in early summer are to be reduced to four or five, any others to be removed by cutting or by rubbing off with the finger. Those retained should be best placed to form a well-disposed and balanced head.

Any growths that may be produced by the stock—below the point of grafting—must be removed as soon as they appear, and should suckers spring up they should be pared away from the roots from which they originate.

Late the following winter the four or five branches are cut back, strong ones to within 1 ft. of their base, weaker ones to within 9 in.—in all cases to a bud pointing in the direction which it is desired the branch shall take. If two good buds are left on each branch the number of branches will be doubled during the following summer, and in this way the bush tree will be provided with a good head.

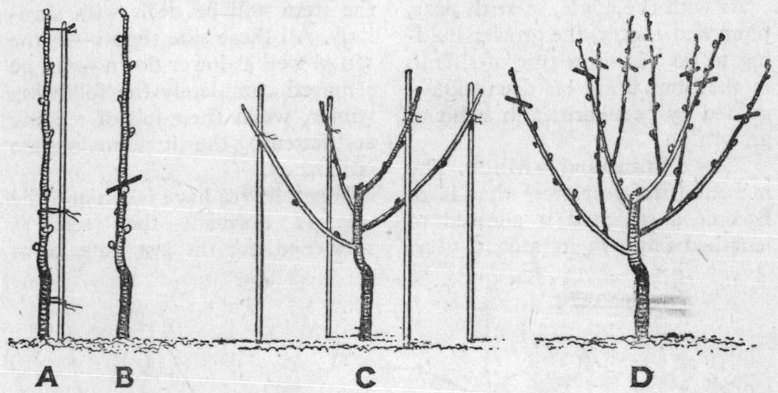

Fig. 342.—*The maiden* (A) *is cut back* (B), *the result being the production of four branches* (C) *which are staked out evenly. These are each cut back to two buds, to produce eight branches* (D), *the framework of the bush*

Side growths from these main branches are summer pruned, in August, so that each side growth is left with five or six leaves, and in winter they are spurred back to two or three basal buds; and the main branches (the leaders) are again shortened in winter. Pruning continues on much the same lines in subsequent years, but cutting becomes less severe as the bush settles down to regular fruiting.

As with the apple, so with pear, plum and cherry, the grower holding to no cast-iron rule-of-thumb method but using his discretion—guided by peculiarities in habit of growth.

How a Standard is Made. The maiden (first-year tree) that is to become a standard is allowed to lengthen until, in its second year, it is producing side shoots and is tall enough to be given a head. The standard's head is to begin at about 6 ft., the half-standard's at $4\frac{1}{2}$ ft.

The stem, which has been staked, is beheaded in June of the second year at a point 6 in. or 7 in. beyond the desired height. Side shoots will appear there, and when they have each made five or six leaves their ends are pinched off (Fig. 343). Other side shoots lower down on the stem will be dealt with similarly. All these side shoots—at the top as well as lower down—will be removed completely the following winter, when their job of feeding and fattening the single main stem is finished.

When leaves have fallen and the tree is dormant the stem is shortened, for the last time, to as

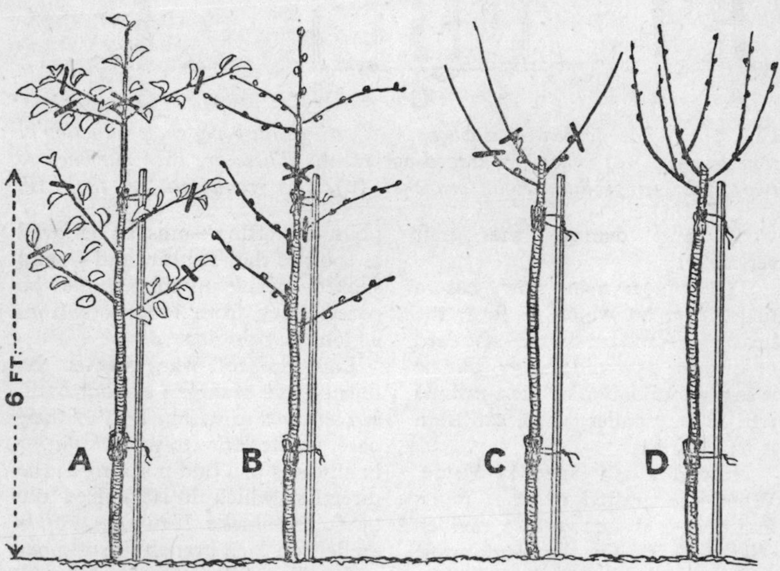

Fig. 343.—*Stages in the making of a standard fruit tree. Side growths and the top are cut back as at* (A), *as at* (B) *the following winter. The next winter branches are dealt with as at* (C), *a head of six branches* (D) *being the result*

near the 6-ft. or $4\frac{1}{2}$-ft. height as possible—that is, the top is cut off just below the upper side shoots and just above where three strong buds are fairly close together on the stem. These buds will grow in spring and become the foundation of the head. At the same time that the top is cut off all side growths lower down will be pared off completely; in future the 6-ft. or $4\frac{1}{2}$-ft. stem is to be kept bare.

During the third summer the growths from the three selected buds are allowed to extend as far as they will, and then in winter are cut back to within about 9 in. of the stem. When buds break on these the following spring the two strongest new growths on each of the three cut-back branches are selected and the others rubbed off; so that the fourth-year standard or half-standard consists of a branchless trunk either 6 ft. or $4\frac{1}{2}$ ft. in height, with a head of a half-dozen branches as evenly spaced as judgment and luck allow.

Thereafter a yearly extension of these leaders and a winter shortening thereof, and a summer pruning and winter cutting back of side shoots to form fruiting spurs, complete the cycle of operations.

How a Pyramid is Made. A central stem with branches coming out from it all around forms the pyramid tree, wide at the base and narrowing to the top. Shoots that develop from the stem of the maiden after this has been cut back in winter to about 18 in. from the ground form the first lot of branches; one of the shoots, best placed to form a new leader, is trained upright to a stake. Stakes may also be necessary at first to space out the branches so that these are evenly placed. In winter the upright leader is cut back so that about 18 in. of the season's growth is left to it.

The extension and shortening of the new leader and production of branches goes on each year, the branches being cut back as necessary to secure the pyramid form, and side shoots shortened in summer and cut back to basal buds in winter.

How a Cordon Apple is Made. As with other single cordons—such as gooseberry and red and white currant—the cordon apple or pear is one-stemmed from first to last. The winter-shortened maiden is left with a top wood bud to produce a shoot which (tied upright to a stake) will form an extension of the single stem. Other shoots which break out down that stem are shortened in summer and cut back to within about 1 in. of the stem in winter to provide fruiting spurs. The leader is cut back by 12 in. in winter, the side shoots it will produce in spring being summer pruned and then cut hard back in winter.

So the extension of the one stem, clothed with fruiting spurs, continues each year until the upward limit—as determined by the grower—is reached. Then the top is cut off at the required level and the end itself turned into a fruiting spur, by the summer shortening and winter cutting back of the side shoots there produced.

How an Espalier is Made. The horizontal-trained pear or apple is given its flat tiers of branches, spaced about 1 ft. apart on left and right of the single central stem, by an annual cutting back of the stem, shoots which

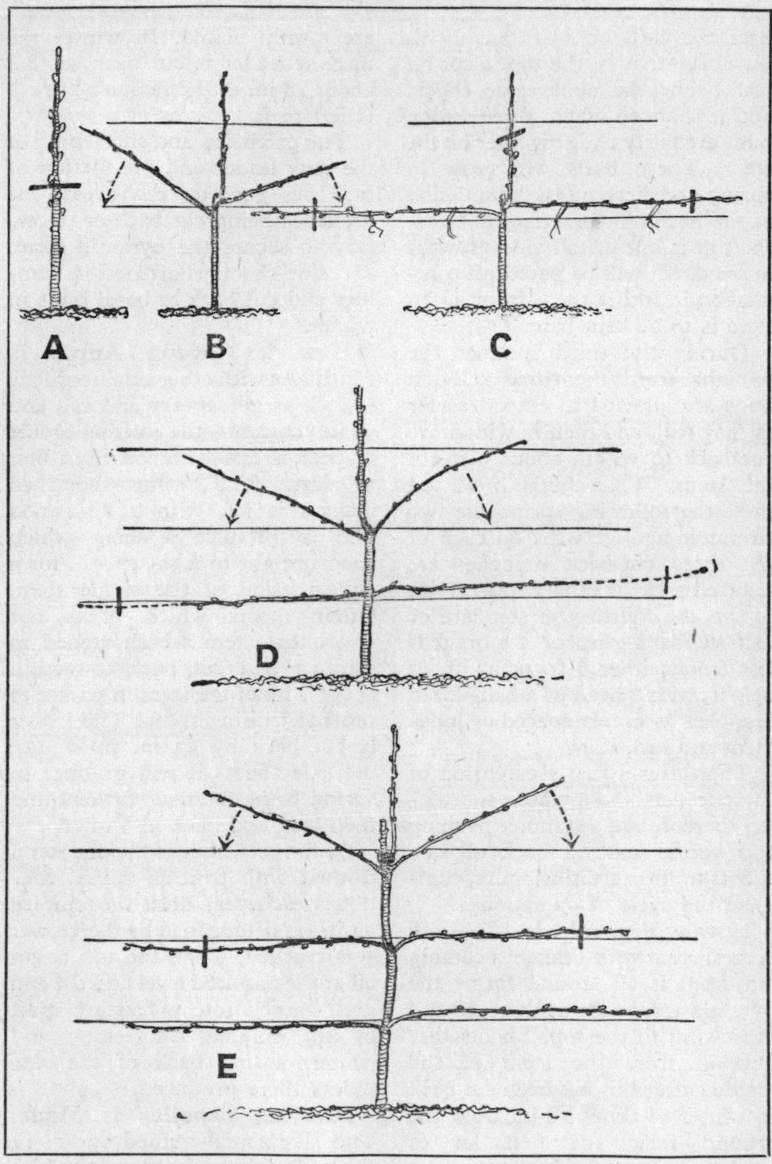

Fig. 344.—*How an espalier is made. The maiden is cut back* (A), *the resulting three branches dealt with as at* (B), *ends then being removed* (C). *Another tier of branches is tied down and extension growths shortened* (D). *A third tier has been produced at* (E). *A fourth can be made similarly*

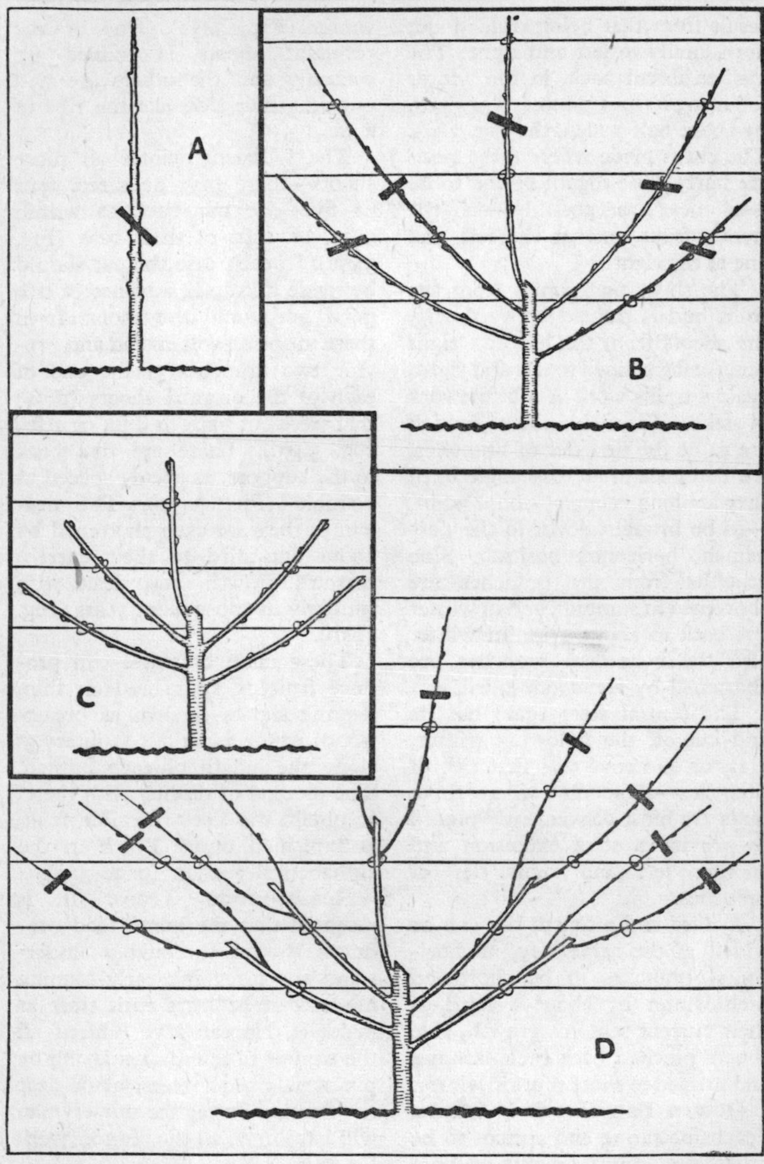

Fig. 345.—*A maiden, the foundation of the fan tree, is cut back as at* (A). *Shoots from the remaining buds are trained as at* (B), *and shortened, as shown by thick strokes, the result being as at* (C). *Two branches are trained up from each of the original ones, as at* (D), *these being shortened as shown*

result from that being trained out horizontally to left and right. The maiden is cut back, in the winter following its first summer's growth, by about half its length (Fig. 344). The cut is made where three buds are fairly close together; one to be —as near as possible—on the stem's front, one at the left and one at the right.

The shoot that comes from the front bud is trained up vertically, the shoots from the left and right buds being trained to left and right, against trellis work or a framework of stakes. These side shoots, which are to be the first tier of branches, are tied back at an easy angle until they are long enough—about 30 in. —to be brought down to the permanent horizontal position. Side growths from the branches are shortened in summer, and in winter cut back to about 1 in. In winter also the horizontal branches are shortened by about one-third.

The central stem again has its end cut off the following winter, 1 ft. or so above this first tier of branches—at a point where three buds are most conveniently placed to provide a stem extension and another left and right tier of branches.

A third and a fourth tier can be added in the same way, all horizontal branches to be shortened each winter by about a third of their current season's growth, side shoots pinched back each summer and pruned to short spurs in winter.

How a Fan Peach is Made. Peach, nectarine and apricot to be grown flat against a sunny wall are trained in the form of a fan. The first branches are obtained by cutting back the maiden to within 18 in. or 1 ft. of the ground, in winter (Fig. 345A). One of the resultant shoots is trained up centrally and the others are tied out on either side like the ribs of a fan.

The following winter all those shoots—there may be three, four or five—are cut back to within 9 in. or 1 ft. of their base (Fig. 345B). In each case the cut should be made a little in advance of two good buds, and the shoots from these in spring will extend and provide two branches at the end of each of the original shoots (those that were cut back to 9 in. or 1 ft., Fig. 345C). These are tied back to the support, as evenly spaced as possible (Fig. 345D). The next winter they are each shortened by about one-third of their current season's growth, and dealt with similarly in subsequent years (Fig. 345D).

These main branches will produce fruit on spurs and on thin, lengthy shoots (known as breastwood) which push out at intervals along the length of each branch. The method of dealing with these, to obtain the finest possible fruit, is explained under Peach in the alphabetical section (page 519).

Ready-made Trees. It is essential that the home food producer should thoroughly understand the foregoing early-training methods if he buys fruit trees as maidens. He can save himself all the trouble of foundation laying by purchasing older trees, at or near the fruiting stage; the nurseryman will have done all the pioneer work for him.

New Heads for Old Trees. How the nurseryman obtains his young trees in the first place is explained under The Art of

Grafting (page 453). The same art, on slightly different lines, can be applied in the home garden to apple and pear trees, up to the age of about twenty-five years, which have become unfruitful or whose fruit has proved to be of inferior quality. Such trees can be given another head. The old, unsatisfactory head can be removed and replaced by branches of a first-class variety of apple or pear (as the case may be), by a method known as crown or rind grafting.

Shoots of the desired variety should be cut from a selected tree—thoroughly healthy and producing fruit well up to the standard of the particular variety—in January. They should be between 9 in. and 12 in. in length, sturdy, well-ripened shoots of the previous season's growth. These will provide the grafts to be inserted in the outer ends of cut-back branches of the unsatisfactory tree. The latter, it should be noted, must be vigorous and the stem and lower parts of branches quite sound; a weakly tree is better chopped down.

Time to do this top grafting is in spring, when the sap is running freely. April is a good month for the job, the grafts meanwhile being buried half their depth outdoors, to keep them dormant but fresh.

Cutting Back the Branches. In winter, before the sap starts to rise, the main branches of the tree which is to receive the grafts should be cut back to within 2 ft. or 3 ft. of their base. A few smaller branches should be allowed to remain (shortened) in addition, to help draw up the sap until the inserted grafts are growing away well, but all twiggy wood should be cut clean away from the tree.

Then, when grafting time arrives, the winter-shortened main branches should be cut back another few inches, squarely, and the newly cut ends be smoothed with a sharp knife. A branch up to 4 in. in diameter will take one graft; larger branches will take two, perhaps three (Fig. 346A).

Preparing the Top Grafts. Taken from the soil where they were heeled in, the shoots that are to become grafts are cut into straight lengths containing either three or four buds; the top end being cut slantwise just above a bud, the lower end squarely about $\frac{3}{4}$ in. below the bottom bud.

Final preparation of the shoot consists in making a slanting cut upwards from the bottom, about $1\frac{1}{2}$ in. long, on the side opposite the bottom bud. It then resembles a shoot prepared for tongue or whip grafting, but is without a tongue; in top grafting the tongue is not needed (Fig. 346B).

Inserting the Top Grafts. Final preparation of the branch ends to receive the grafts is simple. A sharp knife blade is pressed into the bark at the extreme outer end of a branch, and then drawn lengthwise through it; the result is a cut about 2 in. long and the depth of the bark (Fig. 346C).

The cut edges of the bark are then raised at the top so that the graft can be slid in, with the graft's cut face pressing against the exposed wood of the branch. It goes in as far as the top of its own slant-cut surface, that top falling flush with the cut end of the branch (Fig. 346D).

All that remains to do then is tie graft and branch together, tightly, with broad raffia, but leaving the

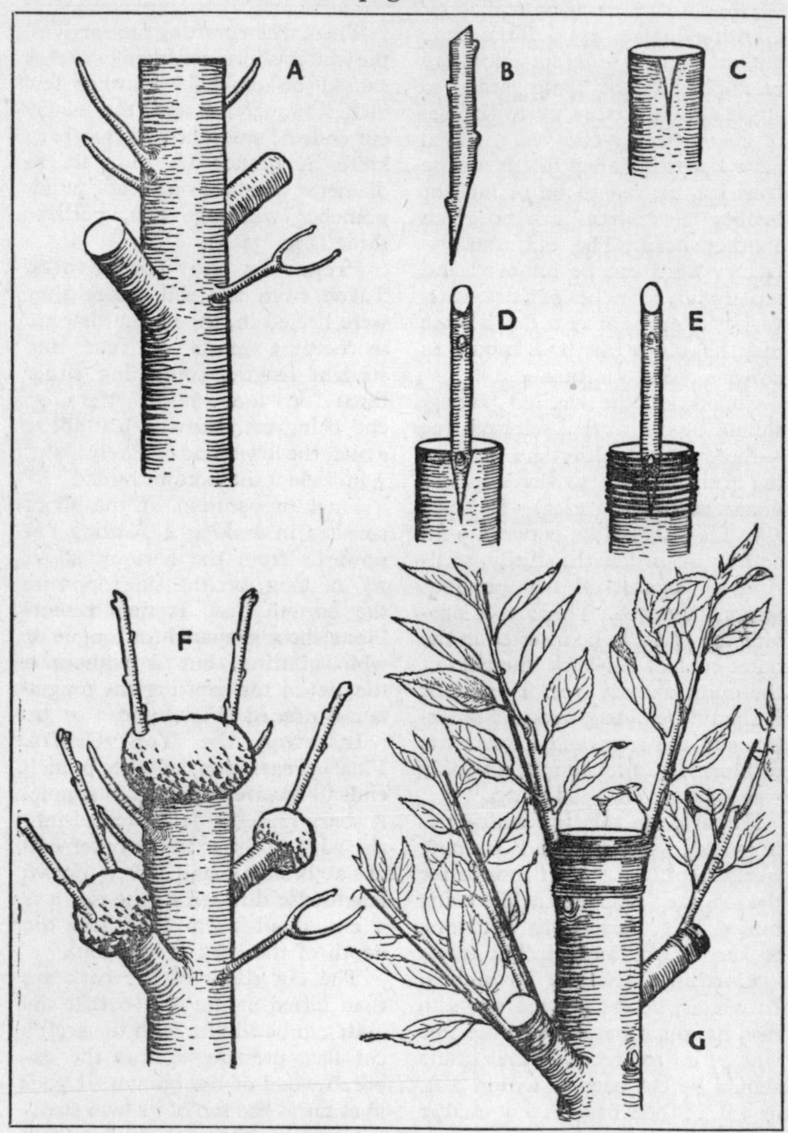

Fig. 346.—(A) *The first stage in top grafting—preparation of the stock;* (B) *a prepared graft;* (C) *a branch end with bark slit to receive a graft;* (D) *graft inserted in slit in bark;* (E) *graft bound in place with raffia;* (F) *the bindings and cut ends covered with wet clay;* (G) *clay and bindings removed, and each growing graft given a stake which is tied to the main branch concerned*

bottom bud of the graft exposed (Fig. 346E); the binding and exposed cut surfaces then to be covered with clay or wax (Fig. 346F), as explained under The Art of Grafting (page 453).

When the Top Grafts Grow. The buds left on the graft soon become active, if all goes well, and during May growth of the shoots begins to speed up. When they are a few inches long the grafting clay or wax should be removed and the raffia binding undone (Fig. 346G). If there seems any doubt as to the security of union between graft and branch, the raffia should be replaced for a time, but not too tightly; a natural swelling must be allowed for.

When the grafts have attained a length of about 18 in. they should be made secure against wind—which might otherwise loosen them or rip them right out—by being tied, not too tightly, each to a stick bound to the branch. They should remain so secured throughout their first year of growth. All branches other than those that have been grafted should be cut away at the time of staking, and no growth is to be allowed on any part of the tree except from the grafts.

The graft growths will in future be treated as ordinary branches, and these will not be long before they produce heavy crops.

The Art of Budding. Another way in which the nurseryman gets his trees is by budding selected varieties on to appropriate young stocks (up to three years old) during summer. Wood buds (not fruit buds) are cut, each with a piece of bark, from firm and well-developed (not thin and watery) shoots of the current year's growth and inserted in slits cut in the bark of the stock —one bud to a stock.

The bud unites with the wood of the stock and sends out a shoot which becomes the stem of the

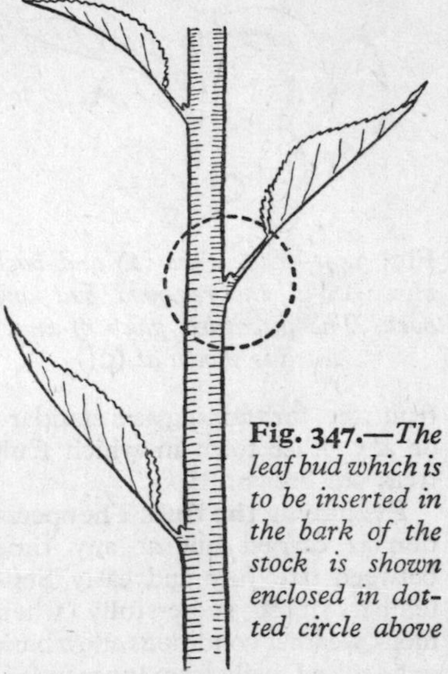

Fig. 347.—*The leaf bud which is to be inserted in the bark of the stock is shown enclosed in dotted circle above*

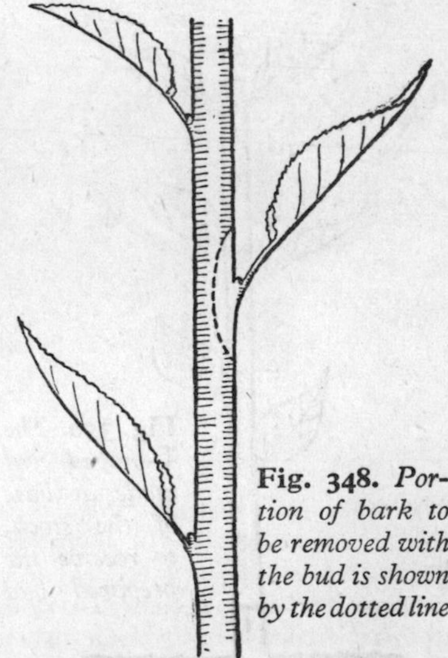

Fig. 348. *Portion of bark to be removed with the bud is shown by the dotted line*

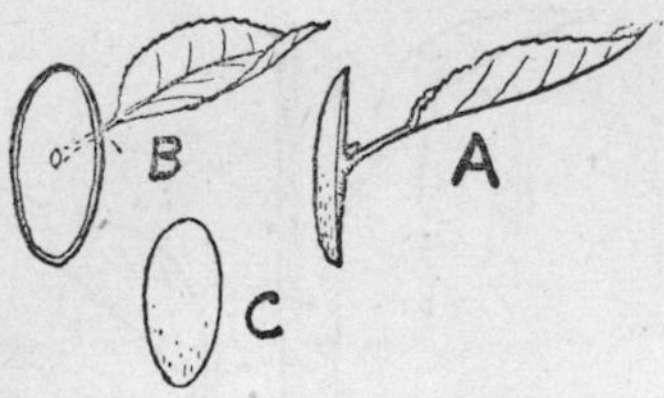

Fig. 349.—*Side view* (A) *and back view* (B) *of the removed bud and bark. The discarded piece of inner wood is shown at* (C)

fruit tree, for training as a standard or any other form in which fruit trees are grown.

Preparing the Bud. The operation is carried out at any time between late July and early September, most successfully when moist weather conditions allow bark to be raised easily from inner wood.

A shoot chosen to provide a bud is cut from the variety which is to be propagated (Fig. 347), and the bud is then removed by slicing it away. The knife blade that does the slicing goes into the shoot ½ in.

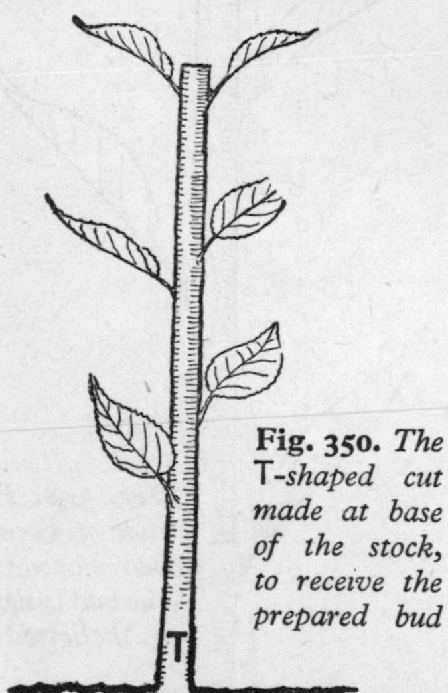

Fig. 350. *The* T-*shaped cut made at base of the stock, to receive the prepared bud*

below the bud (Fig. 348), and the cut is continued so that the blade comes out ¼ in. above the bud. The result is a shield-shaped piece of bark with a thin strip of wood attached to the underside of it, and with the bud on its outer side (Fig. 349).

The wood on the underside of the shield-shaped piece is then removed, without damage to the underside of the bud, by inserting the tip of the knife blade between the bark and the wood at the top of the shield and gently loosening the bark; the bark is then slipped off, without tearing any part of it.

The small strip of wood is thrown away and the bud is ready for insertion in the stock.

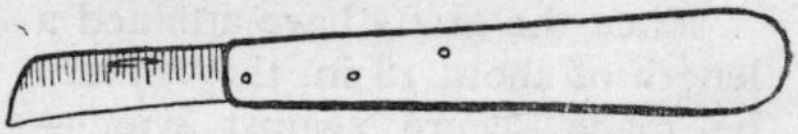

Fig. 351.—*The professional's budding knife makes the job much easier*

Preparing the Stock. The stock is not shortened in any way but left full length until the following spring. But any side growths nearer the ground than about 9 in. are cut off close to the stem.

The prepared bud is to be inserted in a T-shaped cut (Fig. 350) made in the bark of the stock as near to ground level as the kneeling operator can work. An inch-long cut makes the upright leg of the T; a ½-in.-long cut, at right-angles to the leg, makes the top of the T. The cuts are made to bark depth only. That completes the preparation of the stock.

Inserting the Bud. The leaf is cut off the bud piece, leaving about 1 in. of leaf stalk to serve as a handle. Held by that handle, in the operator's left hand, the bud piece (or shield) is gently worked down between the raised edges of the leg of the T—the left and right bark edges being raised with the tip of the knife blade (or the end of the thin bone handle of a proper budding knife, Fig. 351) held in the operator's right hand.

The bud piece goes in until its top edge makes a level join with the top edge of the T (Fig. 352). The raised edges of the T-leg are then pressed down over the bark of the inserted bud piece. Raffia is then bound around the short upper end of the bud piece (above the actual bud) and the stock, also round the

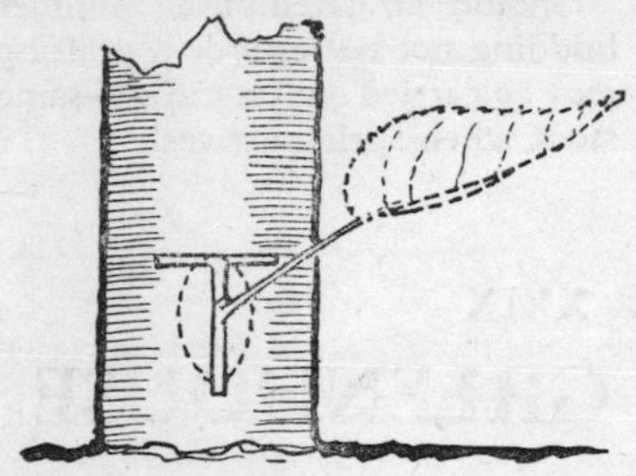

Fig. 352.—*The bud inserted. Dotted outline of leaf indicates portion removed, the leaf stalk remaining*

lower portion (below the bud), leaving the bud itself uncovered (Fig. 353).

The result is that the whole of the underside of the bud piece makes the closest contact with the inner wood of the stock, cut edges heal over, and the two become one.

When the Bud Starts Growing. In October or November the success or otherwise of the operation is indicated by what happens to the leaf stalk that was left on to serve as a handle. If that leaf stalk falls off, the bud has made the required join-up; if it withers and hangs on there is not much hope.

Fig. 353.—(*Left*) *Close-up of the* T-*shaped cut in the bark of the stock.* (*Right*) *Raffia is bound around, the bud itself remaining uncovered*

The raffia is removed, in October or November, from the bud that has taken.

During the general spring awakening of plant life the successful bud becomes a shoot, and when this is about 9 in. long the time has arrived to cut back the stock to within about 6 in. of where the bud was inserted. The growing shoot is tied to that 6-in. extension, not tightly, to steady it against wind, until early autumn (Fig. 354). Then the stock is cut back, finally, close to the extending shoot, and a proper stake becomes necessary.

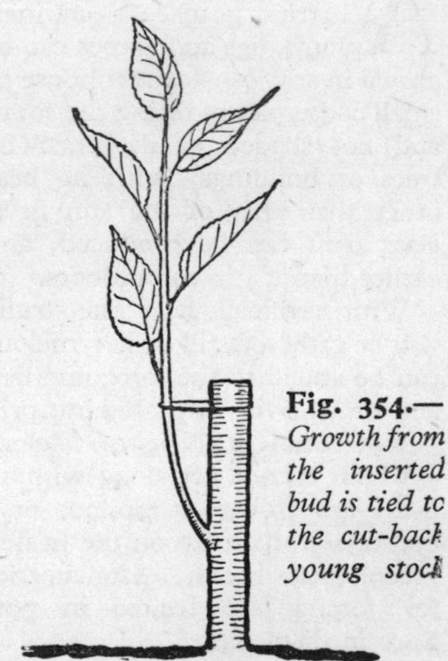

Fig. 354.—*Growth from the inserted bud is tied to the cut-back young stock*

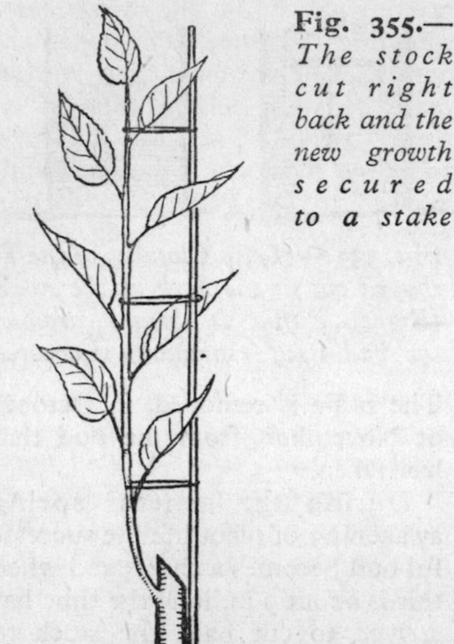

Fig. 355.—*The stock cut right back and the new growth secured to a stake*

A stake is pushed firmly into the ground in such a position that both stock stump and bud shoot can be tied to it (Fig. 355). The bud shoot becomes the stem of the fruit tree and provides the branches of the head, or the stem is trained as a cordon or in any other manner.

Amateur's Luck.—The home food producer who would try his luck at grafting or budding would do well to practise on a hedgerow shrub, with a sharp knife, steady hand, and not a little patience, until he feels confident enough to do it in earnest in his own garden.

Should an attempt at summer budding not be rewarded, grafting may be carried out on the self-same stock when spring arrives.

SECTION XXIX

FRUIT IN THE GREENHOUSE

APPLES, pears, apricots, cherries, peaches, nectarines, plums, figs and grapes can be grown in any lean-to greenhouse or small conservatory facing the south and not shaded or darkened by trees or buildings. With no heat other than that of the sun first-class fruit can be produced, and earlier than if grown outdoors.

With artificial heat the fruits will be gathered still earlier, melons can be added to the foregoing list, and strawberries be picked in April.

How They are Grown. Melons—which cannot get along without heat—are grown on mounds or a bed of soil made up on the heated greenhouse bench. Strawberries for forcing are fruited in pots 6 in. in diameter.

All the others listed in the opening paragraph can be grown and fruited in 12-in. diameter pots. Grapes, figs, peaches, nectarines and apricots can also be planted in a properly prepared border and trained either to the back wall or to wires running parallel with and about 9 in. distant from the front and roof glass.

Fruit Trees in Pots. Small trees grown on dwarfing stocks (as explained in the section HOW TO PROPAGATE FRUIT TREES AND BUSHES, page 444) and trained as compact pyramids or bush trees can be purchased in suitable varieties and of fruiting size, in 12-in.-diameter pots (Fig. 356), in which they will thrive for years.

When their fruit has been

gathered, in early summer, they are shifted from the greenhouse or conservatory to a sunny spot outdoors for the sun to ripen their new wood and get the fruit buds in condition for next year's crop (Fig. 357). There they remain—not neglected but tended according to their special requirements—until the following February, when they go under glass again. Exception is made in the case of indoor varieties of grapes and figs in pots; these need the winter protection of the greenhouse or conservatory.

Keeping Pot Trees Fruitful. Soil in a 12-in. flower pot is called on to do a lot. Some of it must therefore be renewed each autumn, when the leaves have fallen. To do that the plant has first to be removed from the pot. There are two ways of doing this. The tree may be gripped by the stem with one hand and lifted (together with the pot, of course) 1 in. from the bench or the ground, the rim of the pot then being given a smart rap or two with the handle of a trowel held in the other hand (Fig. 358). If the pot does not then come away the other method should be tried.

This requires an assistant. Tree and pot are inverted, and whilst the assistant steadies the tree the other operator raps the pot rim upwards—holding the pot with the other hand to avoid accident (Fig. 359).

When the parting has been effected, the tree is placed on one side whilst the pot is scrubbed thoroughly inside and out and the crocks (bits of broken pot covering the drainage hole) are dealt with similarly. Whilst these are drying the soil mass can be dealt with.

New Soil for Old. To allow of new soil being used some must be taken away from the mass surrounding the roots. The top inch or so can be removed first, with a piece of stick held as though it were a pencil. Then the soil surrounding the roots is loosened and allowed to fall away. Soil at the centre, around the larger roots, can remain (Fig. 360).

The tree is then to be replaced in the washed and dried and recrocked pot and the new soil filled in and made very firm. For this purpose the ideal soil mixture is old turfy loam (soil so filled with fibre it can be torn to pieces) three parts, and quite rotted stable manure one part; charcoal and a scattering of hydrated lime will

Fig. 356.—*Small apple trees on dwarfing stocks will thrive for years in 12-in. pots in the greenhouse*

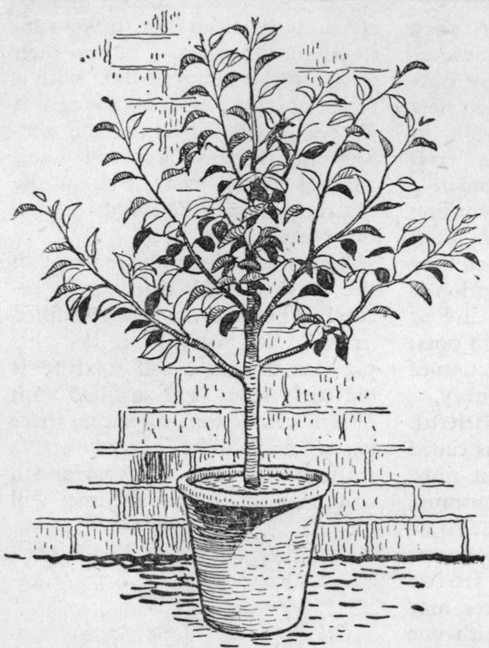

Fig. 357.—*A sunny spot outdoors is required, after the fruit has been picked, for the pot fruit tree to ripen its wood for the next year's crop*

improve the mixture. If there is difficulty about contriving this mixture at home the small quantity needed should be purchased from a nurseryman.

The mixture of the items should be thorough, and the whole should be warmed through, by exposure (in the greenhouse) to sun for a few days. It should therefore be ready before repotting is actually due.

How to Repot. A handful of old stable manure or leaf-mould should be placed over the crocks above the drainage hole, then a handful of the soil mixture placed on top of that and firmed down with the fist or the blunt end of a rammer—a piece of broomstick about 1 ft. long, one end cut square, the other wedge-shape (Fig. 361A).

The tree, held by the stem, is then placed centrally in the pot and soil trickled in with the other hand, quite loosely, until the pot is half-full. Roots should then be arranged so that they are not bunched (Fig. 361B) and more soil added—the pot being shaken vigorously on the bench to ensure that soil trickles into all crevices and that no small spaces between roots remain unfilled.

The soil is then rammed, first down the sides of the pot with the wedge end of the rammer (Fig. 361C), the square end being used above the roots. More soil is added, and rammed, until the surface stands finally within about 2 in. of the pot rim. The top ½ in. of surface soil should not be rammed but left loose (Fig. 361D).

That completes repotting, and the tree can be stood outdoors again until February. When that month arrives and the tree is due to go back into the greenhouse or conservatory the outside of the pot should be cleaned with a scrubbing brush, and the tree sprayed with winter wash to ensure that it goes in with a clean bill of health—as explained in the section HOW TO DEAL WITH FRUIT PESTS AND DISEASES, page 551.

Preparing a Greenhouse Border. If a grape vine, fig, peach, nectarine or apricot is to be planted

Figs. 358 and 359.—*Two ways of removing a bush apple from a pot. Above, the pot is raised an inch and the pot rim tapped smartly. Below, the inverted pot is rapped upwards, with an assistant helping*

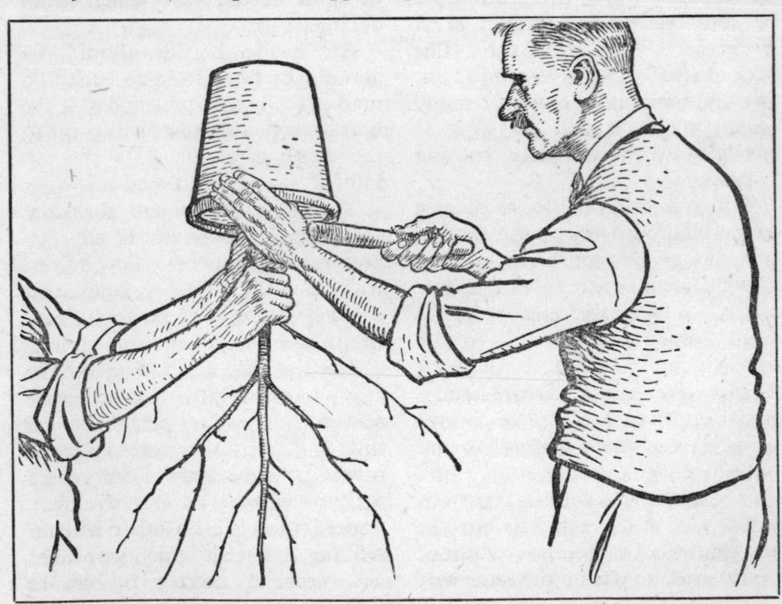

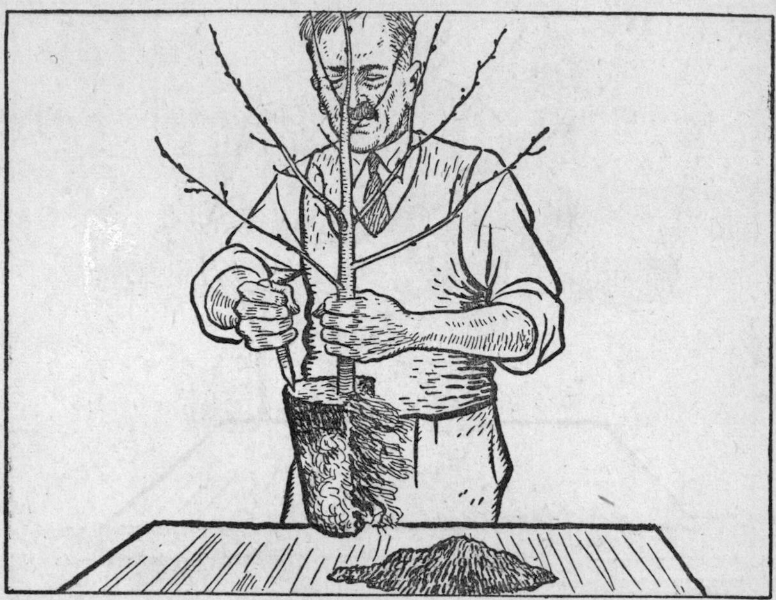

Fig. 360.—*Old soil should be teased away from the root-mass to allow of new soil being used in the repotting. The fibrous roots must not be injured*

permanently inside the greenhouse or conservatory the ground must be prepared with some care. The vine or tree will be expected to fruit heavily, without a break, for many years; which it will do if it is provided with adequate rooting conditions.

It is common practice to plant a grape vine outdoors at the foot of greenhouse or conservatory and lead the stem in through a hole low down. Provided the outdoor bed is well drained and the soil to the vine's liking, the method will serve. But the vine in those circumstances is not under such complete control as when the roots themselves are within the greenhouse.

The grape vine with its roots out in the cold and wet and its head in the warmth of a greenhouse cannot be expected to put up the same sort of show as the vine which is all enclosed.

An inside border should be about 4 ft. from front to back. To make a really profitable job of it the border or bed should be dug out to the depth of about 3 ft., the top foot of soil being placed aside—it is the most fertile and therefore should be returned last of all. The bottom of the hole should be lined with stones and broken brick, this drainage material to be about 9 in. deep after being rammed.

The hole should then be filled in again, preferably with good fertile soil taken from the open garden. If this is light in nature chopped turves or substantial loam mixed with it will be an improvement. Should there be no other soil for refilling than that which was taken out, crushed mortar rubble, or

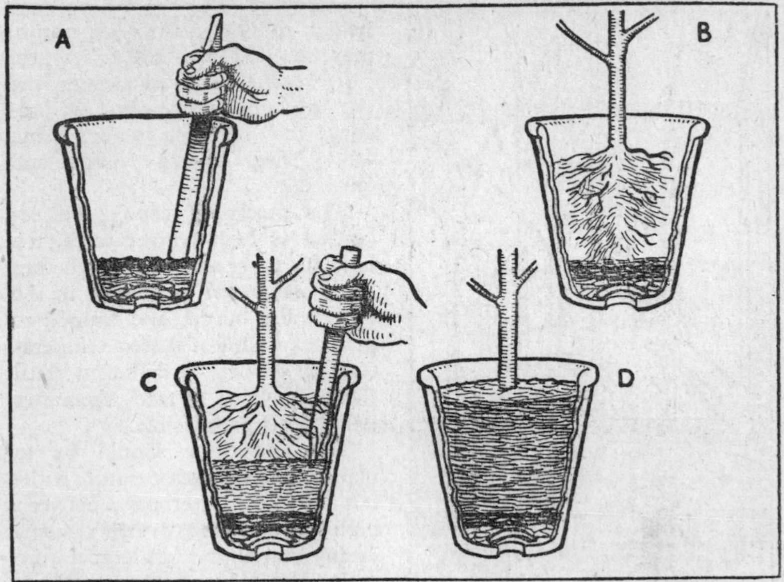

Fig. 361.—(A) *The blunt end of a rammer is used to firm a little of the soil mixture above the crocks in the bottom of the pot.* (B) *The plant in position, ready for soil to be dribbled in among the lower roots.* (C) *The wedge end of the rammer firms the new soil down the pot-side.* (D) *Repotting completed, ample space being allowed at the top for watering*

hydrated lime, should be mixed with it, plus bonemeal at the rate of a 6-in. potful per barrowload of soil; that which was the original top soil again being used as the top.

In any case the bonemeal should be mixed in, and for stone fruits (peach, etc.) mortar rubble or hydrated lime is essential. As the soil goes back into the hole it should be trodden firmly, so that there shall be no sinking to cause trouble to the roots later on.

Replacing Surface Soil. The inside fruit border is kept in order by a renewal of the surface soil every winter. The old soil should be scraped off carefully, in November, with a stick and the fingers, to the depth at which the topmost roots are exposed, and taken outside for disposal elsewhere. Its place is taken by fresh soil—fibrous loam if possible—enriched with a sprinkling of bonemeal or $\frac{1}{2}$-in. bones, with the addition of mortar rubble or lime in the case of stone fruits.

Fertilizing Indoor Fruit Blossom. The artificial conditions in which under-glass fruit trees are grown make it necessary that at blossoming time the flowers should be hand-pollinated. The transference of pollen is effected by twanging the wires to which plants are trained, or by dabbing or brushing the open flowers gently with a tuft of dry, loose cotton-wool tied to the end of a stick

Fig. 362. *The open flowers are gently dabbed or brushed to distribute the pollen. This ensures a good set of fruit* (Fig. 362). A rabbit's tail is sometimes used in the latter manner.

This should be done when the atmosphere is dry and the sun shining; pollen travels then most readily. If this is repeated on three or four successive days, a good set of fruit should be ensured.

Temperatures. Where artificial heat is available it must be used cautiously. One may force grapes and peaches to a greater degree than is possible with indoor-grown plums and pears. A grape vine may be started into growth in a temperature of, say, 60 deg., not to be exceeded until the buds unfold, when an additional 5 deg. may be allowed. When the vine begins to flower the temperature may be allowed to rise to 75 deg. For peaches and nectarines the starting temperature—in, say, January—may be up to 50 deg., rising to 65 deg. during March and onwards.

The foregoing should be regarded as high temperatures, too high for pears and plums, whether these are grown in pots or in the greenhouse border and trained to the back wall. For these a temperature of 50 deg. is sufficient until the fruits have formed; thereafter up to 60 is permissible.

The endeavour should be to maintain average temperature without any violent alternation between high and low. It is worth remembering that a too high temperature with dry air can do as much damage to the indoor fruit prospects as a low temperature with too moist air. And when the plants are having their essential period of rest—when leafless and dormant—they need no artificial heat, but abundant fresh air and exposure.

Summer and Winter Pruning. These and other attentions, and names of the most suitable varieties for fruiting in pots and in the indoor border, are detailed under names of fruits in the alphabetical section. Ventilation and general management of a greenhouse are explained in the section entitled FRAME AND GREENHOUSE starting on page 61.

Pest Troubles. The microscopic red spider, which sucks the sap from leaves, can be kept down by constant syringeing with plain water. But this syringeing must be temporarily discontinued when the trees are in flower, and again when fruit is approaching the ripening stage. A dry, close atmosphere encourages this pest, so whenever it is possible the air, the greenhouse bench, and path and walls, should be kept moist.

Green-fly can be got rid of by fumigating the greenhouse or conservatory, as explained in the section PESTS AND DISEASES OF FLOWERS AND VEGETABLES (page 411).

Keep the Greenhouse Clean. A fertile source of trouble in the greenhouse is miscellaneous rubbish allowed to accumulate on the floor beneath the staging. Woodlice and other pests lurk among the discarded flowerpots, seed boxes and similar items, which may have been carelessly cast aside there.

The greenhouse should be maintained in as cleanly a condition beneath the staging as elsewhere. A further precaution consists in scrutinizing most carefully every pot before it is introduced to the greenhouse. Any plant showing traces of pests or disease should be treated before it comes under glass.

Sheltered from their natural enemies—birds, frogs, etc.—by greenhouse conditions, pests have the chance of an easy life and rapid breeding. The vigilance and care of the grower must be directed to the complete cancelling out of anything which is in their favour.

SECTION XXX

FRUIT IN DETAIL

APPLE

THE value attached to apples as a food is evidenced by the number of varieties listed in fruit-growers' catalogues. These offer extensive scope for indulging in one's own particular fancies, and make it possible to select varieties that ripen in succession.

Selection should be made with an eye to definite purposes. Some varieties excel as cookers, others as dessert. Some will not keep—they need to be eaten off the tree, or within a week or two; these are the earliest kinds to ripen. Others are not at their best until late in the year and will keep for many weeks.

Ready for Use. Earliest ripe apples are available in July. Some varieties will keep until April.

Cooking varieties include: Arthur Turner, July to October; Early Victoria, July to August; Pott's Seedling, August to September; Stirling Castle and Rev. W. Wilks, October to November; Bramley's Seedling, October to March; Crawley Beauty and Edward VII, October to April; Lord Derby, November to December; Lane's Prince Albert, November to February.

Dessert varieties include Beauty of Bath and Irish Peach, early August; Laxton's Epicure and James Grieve, September; Ellison's Orange, September to October; Lord Lambourne, October to November; Cox's Orange Pippin, October to December; Ribston Pippin, November to December; Rival, December; Laxton's Superb and Orleans Reinette, December to February.

Certain varieties of apple are not

self-fertile; they are incapable of bearing fruit, or they produce but a very poor crop, unless the flowers are pollinated by a different variety. This is explained under Choosing Varieties in the section PLANNING THE FRUIT GARDEN (page 422).

A dozen good varieties of apple without this obstinate peculiarity comprise Stirling Castle, Pott's Seedling, Rev. W. Wilks, Bramley's Seedling, Lord Derby, Early Victoria, Lord Lambourne, Laxton's Epicure, Ribston Pippin, Laxton's Superb, Irish Peach, Rival. Each one of these is capable of cropping well even though there be no other apple tree in the garden. They are included in the lists given under Ready for Use (page 473).

An apple tree that is persistently non-fruitful, in spite of producing abundance of blossom, should have planted near to it a different variety that is known definitely to flower at exactly the same time; bees or other insects will effect the necessary transference of pollen. If there is any doubt the fruit grower from whom trees are purchased should be consulted.

Forms of Tree. In a small garden apples can be grown most profitably as cordon trees, or as small bush trees or pyramids, or as espaliers (Fig. 363). Where consideration of space is not so pressing, trees trained as standards or half-standards can be planted. These terms are explained in the section PLANNING THE FRUIT GARDEN (page 417).

The length of time the planter must wait for fruit depends on the form of tree and its age. It is advisable to purchase, at a small extra cost, trees of fruiting or near-fruiting size, to reduce this wait.

Choice varieties of fruiting size, trained as pyramids and dwarf bushes, for fruiting in pots in an unheated greenhouse or conservatory, can be purchased, and dealt with as explained in the section FRUIT IN THE GREENHOUSE (page 466).

When and How to Plant. As soon as possible after the leaves have fallen is the most suitable time to plant. The season extends from late October until late March, but it is not advisable to plant in wet or very cold ground or when frost or snow is about. Should trees arrive from the nursery when conditions are unfavourable they should be placed under cover, with sacks or other dry material over and around the roots.

Trees should be spaced so that later growth does not lead to overcrowding. Standards should be planted at least 18 ft. apart, half-standards about 15 ft., bush trees and pyramids about 10 ft. apart, espaliers about 10 ft. apart in line, and single-stem cordons 2 ft. apart.

For each tree a hole should be taken out of such a size that roots can be spread horizontally, and the soil mark on the stem should coincide with the soil level when the hole is filled in.

A strong stake should be driven in before the roots are covered with soil, unless it is a flat-trained tree—espalier or cordon—with a fence, wall or strained wires as support. The tree should be tied only loosely to the support at first, to allow of settlement of the disturbed soil. If a stake is used, a cushion of sacking or other material should be so placed between stake and tree that friction from the action of the wind is not possible.

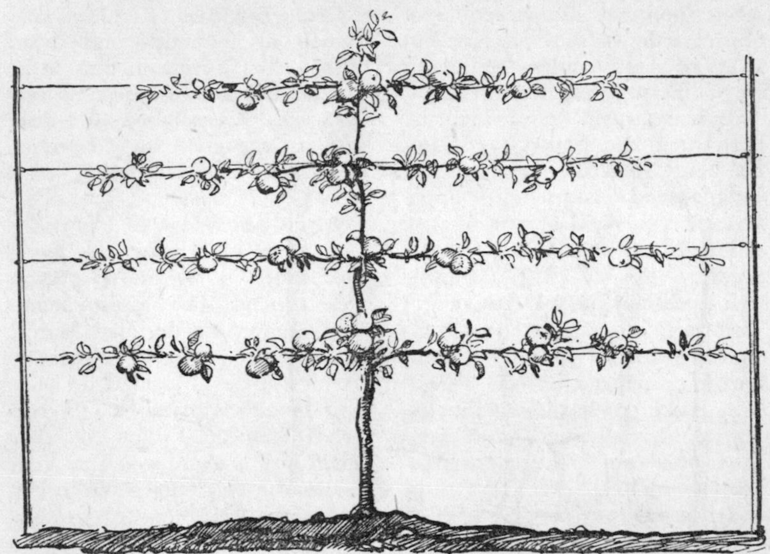

Fig. 363.—*The espalier form of apple tree is ideal for the small garden and wherever space is scarce. This one is trained against wires*

These and other points, including the preparation of planting sites, are fully explained in the section ABC OF FRUIT PLANTING (page 425).

Watering and Feeding. The first spring and summer after planting, trees will be in especial need of watering unless the season is a wet one. The soil must not be allowed to dry out or crack. At least a bucketful of water should be given to a tree at each watering, and so that it shall run in and not run away holes should be made in the surface with a garden fork (Fig. 364). Or a basin may be formed around the stem by building up a 3-in.-deep ridge of soil, this to extend 18 in. or so outwards and encircle the tree. The ridge should be wide enough and solid enough to hold water until it has soaked down to the roots (Fig. 364).

Wall and fence trees are generally the worst sufferers from drought, the soil at the foot of a wall or fence drying out more rapidly than open ground. In this case a water-containing ridge is invaluable, though here it will be not circular but shaped as a half-circle.

A surface covering or mulch of lawn mowings, weeds, or strawy manure placed over the area occupied by a tree's roots slows down the drying-out process. The covering should be 2 in. to 3 in. thick, and if considered unsightly it can be covered with a thin layer of soil. Where a ridge has been built up the mulch can be placed in the basin, subsequent waterings being given through the mulch—that is, without removing the material.

Established apple trees benefit just as much from these attentions.

Fig. 364.—*Before watering a fruit tree, holes should be made above the roots with a fork* (*left*). *Or soil should be ridged up* (*right*) *to form a basin*

Commercial growers on a large scale may not be able to fuss to such an extent, but the small grower gets more and bigger and better fruit when he adopts these methods.

Until trees have developed the fruiting habit they should not be fed. Then liquid farmyard or stable manure, or one of the special fruit-tree fertilizers sold under trade names, may be given at any time. A surface dressing of lime every three to four years does good—hydrated lime at the rate of about ¼ lb. per square yard being effective. It should be scattered on the soil during winter.

Too Rampant Growth. Over-production of unfruitful wood may result from too severe pruning in the case of older trees. Where it affects a young tree this can be brought into bearing by giving the wood growth a check. This is done by lifting the young tree completely, cutting back the long, thong-like roots to where thin fibrous roots branch out and re-planting it very firmly.

Trees too large for this treatment have their roots pruned without the tree being lifted. A trench is dug completely around it, 2 ft. or more out from the stem and 2 ft. deep, at which depth it is undermined. All thick roots encountered, including the central tap root, are severed with the spade, saw or sharp knife. The excavated soil is then rammed back into the trench.

This is explained fully under Root Pruning in the section The How and Why of Fruit Pruning (page 437).

Windfalls, and Other Troubles. Drought is sometimes responsible for the wholesale dropping of small apples. A high wind may rip many from the branches when the tree is carrying more than it should. When the windfalls are maggoty, grubs of the codlin moth or of the apple sawfly are responsible. These pests cause immense fruit losses and they should be dealt with as explained in the section HOW TO DEAL WITH FRUIT PESTS AND DISEASES (page 554). Other common apple-tree troubles are included in the chart accompanying that section.

Thinning the Fruits. In a disastrous year the phrase "thinning the fruits" may have a sardonic sound. A cold spring keeps bees in the hive when otherwise they would be effecting the distribution from tree to tree of the essential fertilizing pollen. A dry late spring and early summer brings young apples tumbling to the ground. Pests are accountable for still more. A too bounteous year is nearly always followed by a lean one.

A cold spring must be accepted with a resigned shrug. Drought, however, can be fought with bucket or hose and mulch. Pests can be reduced by spraying and trapping and soil cleaning, so that for all practical purposes they cease to amount to anything. And the off year that follows the too bountiful apple harvest can be prevented—by the grower refusing to allow such a thing as a too bountiful harvest.

This is done by removing some of the crowded fruit—after winds, early drought, and those pests which have chanced to escape annihilation, have taken their toll of the crop (Fig. 365).

When young apples are seen to be pushing each other off a spur it can be taken for granted that the grower who holds his hand instead of extending it and thinning out the fruit is piling up for himself, this year and almost certainly next, no small trouble.

Good removed ones need not be wasted; the kitchen department will know what to do with them. Those finally left on the tree will develop into full-sized specimens of first-rate quality; none will be undersized or misshapen. And because the tree has not been allowed to overtax its strength the chances of an equally good crop next year are much increased.

First to be removed are any showing a maggot hole in the skin. In any case these would fall later and perhaps be wasted. Taken from the tree, and the maggot removed, they can be put to use. Next to go are misshapen apples, then any showing signs of disease. The final thinning should see not more than two good fruits left to each spur. Apart from increase in size, shapeliness and quality, ripening of these will be thorough and complete.

Big standard trees and half-standards present a problem, and in their case thinning of the fruit may not be practicable. No such trouble occurs where bush trees and pyramids, espaliers and cordons are concerned.

Anxiety to get a big crop from a young tree during its first year of fruiting must be checked. It must be given time to establish itself completely. A few more apples can be left to ripen the second year,

Fig. 365.—*This overcrowded spur should have two of the apples removed—twisted off between the finger-tips* (*right*) *without injury to the spur*

and thereafter in increasing quantity.

About mid-July is the time to begin fruit thinning, when Nature has taken its course in the matter of windfalls.

Summer and Winter Pruning. Most varieties of apple produce their fruit on short spurs, which are stumpy side shoots occurring at intervals along the main branches. One of the objects of pruning is to increase the number of these, keep them short, and keep them evenly disposed about the tree. A few varieties, including Mr. Gladstone, Irish Peach, Lady Sudeley, carry their fruit at the tips of growths which were made the previous year; these must not be shortened—only kept thinned out—or there will be no fruit.

Summer pruning consists in shortening side shoots back to within five or six leaves of their base, in July. In winter these are cut back to their lowest bud or two buds. Leaders—the extending ends of branches—should be cut back in winter by about a third of their current season's growth.

The pruning of all forms of apple trees is explained in detail in the sections THE HOW AND WHY OF FRUIT PRUNING (page 432) and HOW TO PROPAGATE FRUIT TREES AND BUSHES (page 444).

Propagation. Apple trees are easily raised from seed sown outdoors in March, 3 in. deep. But trees thus produced cannot be expected to bear fruit for several years; and then the chances that their fruit will in any way resemble that of the parent tree are remote. It may be of very inferior quality, not worth the space it occupies.

The method is by budding a

selected variety on to a specially chosen stock, in July; or by grafting in March. Operations are fully explained in the section HOW TO PROPAGATE FRUIT TREES AND BUSHES (page 453).

When and How to Gather Apples. Not all the fruits on one tree will ripen at the same time. When a few ripe ones are picked, or some full-size ones fall, it does not mean that all the others on the tree are fit for gathering.

An apple is ripe if it comes away readily when gently raised on the palm of the hand (Fig. 366). This test cannot be applied to all the fruit on a standard tree, but where dwarf bush trees, espaliers or cordons are concerned the trouble of applying the test is handsomely repaid.

Varieties which naturally ripen late should be the last to be gathered. But picking should not be so long delayed that the ripe apples fall off or are wind-blown off; that is, if the fruit is wanted for storing. Apples that are bruised will not keep in store, and in decaying they are likely to spread trouble among the sound ones.

Shaking fruit from a tree is permissible if it is to be used at once. But otherwise hand-picking is essential. Grabbing or tugging the fruit results in loss of fruit the following year—the tugged apple generally bringing away with it the spur (or part of the spur) which produced it. The apple may come away with its own full length of stem, but nothing else.

Clambering among branches to gather the fruit is too destructive of spurs and bark. Steps or a ladder should be used to get at all apples out of reach from the ground. The top of the ladder should be padded with old carpet, sacking—anything that will allow the ladder to be lodged against branches without bruising the bark.

Apples gathered from a ladder should not be thrown down to a catcher. He sometimes misses; even if he does not, such treatment may result in bruising. If a bucket is hung by a hook from a rung of the ladder it can be filled by the picker and never a fruit spoiled (Fig. 367). But the bucket should not be emptied into a clothes basket or wheelbarrow or sack. The idea is to handle the fruit from first to last as few times and as gently as possible, and if the apples are to be stored it is essential that they be picked when dry.

Fig. 366.—*An apple is ready for gathering if it comes away from the spur readily when raised gently on the palm of the hand*

Storing for Winter. Only perfectly sound fruit, free of blemish, should go into store; the others should be put aside for current consumption.

The store may be a cupboard, pantry, attic, shed, garage or an outdoor clamp. A very dry place, such as a cupboard, is not altogether favourable; apples there are apt to shrivel. To prevent this it is worth while wrapping the best of them, separately, in clean dry greaseproof or tissue paper.

They may be stored in barrels or boxes so long as the apples are placed in one by one and not roughly tumbled in. A much better plan is to use shallow boxes that take no more than two layers of fruit, each box to have a piece of wood nailed at each of the four corners so that the boxes can be piled one on the other (Fig. 368). The corner pieces of wood should be long enough to give an inch or so of clearance between the top of the apples in a lower box and the bottom of the box immediately above. The filled boxes should be placed away from artificial heat and beyond the reach of frost and damp.

Stored apples that are in danger from frost can be safeguarded by covering them with a thick layer of dry straw, heather or bracken; sheets of dry newspaper are better than nothing. This precaution is likely to be necessary when apples are heaped in a shed, cellar or garage. In each of these cases the floor space which the heap is to occupy should first be covered with straw, heather or dried bracken, and the heap should be as shallow as possible.

A current of air passing through the store is all to the good, so long as it does not bring biting frost with it. It is essential that the storage place should be as airy as possible for at least the first fortnight, in order that the moisture sweated out by the newly stored apples shall be carried away.

If no under-cover storage can be found for a surplus of apples they can be clamped, outdoors, exactly in the manner explained in the

Fig. 367.—*A ladder-top should be padded, to prevent injury to the bark, and a bucket may be hooked to a rung (right) to receive the fruit as picked*

vegetable section under Potato (page 355).

Where stored apples are easy of inspection—as in piled shallow boxes—they should be looked over when opportunity offers, those that have developed bruise patches or other blemishes being picked out for prompt use.

The greater the trouble taken over this apple-storing business the greater the profit that accrues to the home food producer.

Other methods of carrying apples far beyond the season of gathering are explained in the section EASY HOME PRESERVATION OF FRUITS (page 565).

Preparing for Table. Apples to appear at table raw should be polished with a dry, clean cloth.

Their carbohydrate content gives apples a definite food value; also present is the vitamin which prevents scurvy. And they not only cure but also prevent constipation.

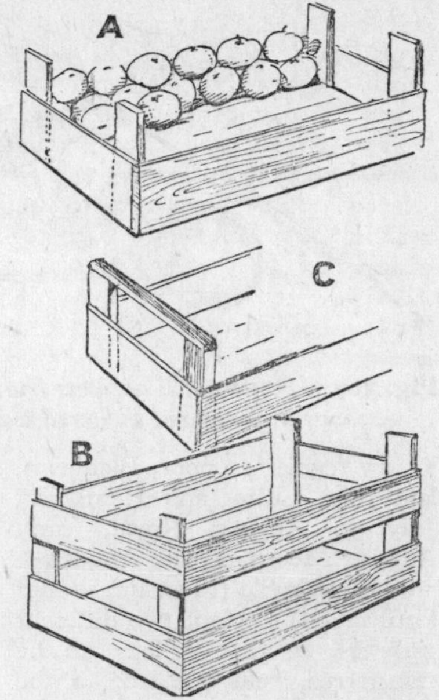

Fig. 368.—*Boxes for storing apples can be made as at* (A) *and* (C); *deeper ones are made as at* (B)

APPLE, CRAB

Excellent jelly can be made from the fruit of the crab apple. Garden varieties include Dartmouth (crimson fruit), John Downie (orange and scarlet), Yellow Siberian (orange).

The trees are very decorative with ripening fruit in autumn, and for that reason alone are often planted among ordinary trees and bushes in a shrubbery.

They can be obtained as standards, half-standards and bushes, and should be planted in autumn. Little pruning is needed after the head of the tree has been formed, apart from the removal of weak shoots, dead wood, growths working inwards and the prevention of overcrowding generally.

APRICOT

Many who would be glad to harvest a crop of delicious apricots are scared of planting a tree, labouring under the delusion that the apricot demands conditions which cannot ordinarily be given to it. The apricot is hardy enough, and given the shelter and warmth of a sunny wall it is capable of ripening excellent fruit in the open (Fig. 369).

Ready for Use. The season is not a long one, but fruits can be stored for a limited period, can be preserved, and made into jam. Apricot pudding, or tart, needs no boosting.

Varieties include New Large Early, ripening in mid-July, perhaps the hardiest of all apricots and

Fig. 369.—*Fan-trained apricots fruit readily against a sunny and sheltered wall*

a very regular cropper; Blenheim, late July; Luizet and Hemskerk, July to August; Royal, early August; Moorpark, late August.

It is advisable (to ensure proper fertilization) to plant two different varieties, so that pollen can be transferred from one tree to the other.

Forms of Tree. Fan-trained trees are obtainable for growing flat against a sunny wall. Pyramids and bushes, of fruiting size, can be purchased in pots for fruiting in greenhouse or conservatory; these to be dealt with as explained in the section FRUIT IN THE GREENHOUSE (page 466).

Soil Preparation. Free drainage is essential, and the soil must contain plenty of lime. If the ground is clay, or otherwise heavy, it should be broken up to a depth of 3 ft., plenty of mortar rubble and sand or sharp grit being mixed in throughout that depth. Any doubt as to drainage should be removed by taking out the soil to the depth of 3 ft. and in the bottom of the planting hole ramming a 9-in. layer of broken brick or stones. Soil that lacks sufficient lime should have lime rubble mixed with it, or be given a dressing of slaked lime well in advance of planting.

When and How to Plant. October is the best month for planting. Roots then have some encouragement to get hold of the ground before the dead days of winter. Soil must be made very firm around and above the roots, and fan-trained trees should be planted about 18 ft. apart. Further details, including instructions for staking and tying, are given in the section ABC OF FRUIT PLANTING (page 425).

Watering and Feeding. Dry periods lead to fruit splitting and fruit dropping; plenty of water should be given to avoid these and other troubles. Young trees especially must be nursed with the watering-can, 3 gal. to 4 gal. being given at a time. Loss of moisture can be prevented in hot dry weather by covering the area occupied by the roots with a surface dressing, 2 in. thick, of lawn mowings or weeds, water being poured, as required, through this mulch.

Young trees should not be fed until they begin to fruit. Rotted manure put down wet, as a surface mulch, in early June, is then of great assistance.

One of the special artificial mixtures sold for this class of tree can be hoed into the surface in March, at the rate of about 2 oz. per square yard.

Where lime is not present in any quantity, slaked lime should be put down every second or third winter, applying it at the rate of one pound to each square yard of soil.

Aid to Fruiting. Frost is always to be expected when the apricot is in flower, because the blossom is produced so early in the year. A double thickness of old fish netting hung from the top of the wall and reaching to the ground, shutting in the flowers, prevents frost affecting them (Fig. 370). Unfortunately that is not always practicable. But what can be done with little trouble to ensure a good set of fruit is hand-pollination of the flowers.

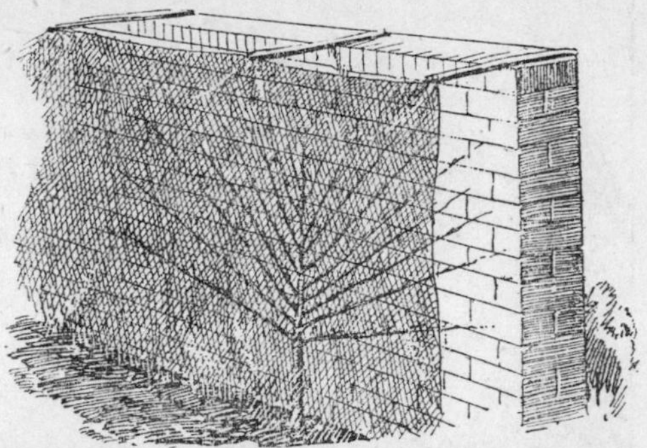

Fig. 370.—*Old fish netting hung from the wall top and extending down to the ground protects the early apricot blossom against frost*

Hive bees will not work in the cold, and bumble bees are no more inclined to do so. In bad weather, then, no bees will be available to transfer pollen from flower to flower. The grower must do it himself, with a fluffy piece of dry cotton-wool, or a rabbit's tail, tied to the end of a stick. This is brushed gently over the flowers, three or four times at intervals whilst the flowers are open. It should be done when the air is dry, preferably when the sun is shining.

The set of fruit will be more certain—and fewer will fall off when formed—if pollen is transferred between two different varieties of apricot. In this case the cotton-wool or rabbit's tail should be brushed over several flowers of the one tree and the brushing be repeated at once over flowers of the other tree, the operation being continued until all the bloom of both trees has been dealt with. It takes much less time than might be imagined.

Thinning the Fruits. If the apricots stand finally at about 5 in. apart—no closer—that will be as many as the established tree can bring to perfection. There should be no hurry to do this. A proportion will fall naturally, whilst the stone is forming in the fruit, and it will be time enough to do the final thinning when no more fall.

Why Apricots Split. If a tree is allowed to carry an extra-large crop many of the apricots will split, which is one reason for thinning out the fruit. A prolonged spell of very wet weather will result in the same trouble—as also will prolonged drought. Wet weather cannot be avoided, but drought can—or rather, it can be fought with watering-can or bucket.

Why Branches Suddenly Die. An apricot tree in badly drained ground is specially liable to the complaint known as die-back. A branch in full leaf and apparently in full health will suddenly wilt throughout its whole length and die. Lack of sufficient lime has also been blamed; and too much pruning with knife or secateurs.

If the drainage is suspected the tree should be lifted and replanted after the site has been dealt with as explained in the paragraph

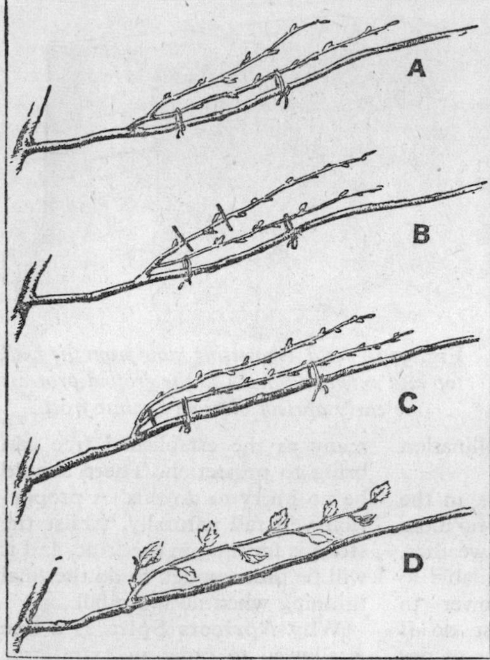

Fig. 371.—*A fruiting lateral of apricot tied in to a main branch* (A), *with a new lateral on the outside. The new lateral may be summer pruned as shown by the top line* (B) *and winter pruned at the lower line. Or the fruited lateral may be cut right back* (C) *and its place taken by the new lateral. When growth starts side shoots between extremities of the lateral* (D) *will be rubbed off*

headed Soil Preparation (page 482).

If lack of lime is suspected, add this in the form of plenty of old, crushed mortar rubble, or slaked lime, forked shallowly into the surface.

How the use of knife or secateurs can be largely avoided is explained under Winter Pruning (page 485).

Method of Fruiting. The apricot produces its fruit on spurs, on stubby side shoots, and also on laterals—which is the technical name for slender side shoots from the main branches. These laterals, or breastwood, will mostly need to be shortened during summer and later shortened again. Some can be tied in to fill any vacant wall space there may be to produce fruit the following year (Fig. 371).

Summer Pruning. Preliminary to summer pruning is the removal in spring—as soon as new growth starts—of all unwanted shoots, which will be numerous. These are rubbed off with the finger. They will include shoots on the front of branches, which if allowed to remain would project outwards from the wall. This disbudding, as it is called, is to prevent crowding.

In addition to fruiting spurs, short side shoots will develop during summer. These should not be interfered with if they remain at 4 in. or 5 in. in length; if they exceed that the ends should be pinched off, between thumb and finger, to reduce them to about 5 in. These will develop fruit buds and produce fruit the following year.

Longer side shoots (laterals or breastwood) should be tied in, where this can be done without crowding, to bear fruit the following year. Where space is lacking for this, these longer summer laterals should be summer pruned back to the fourth leaf, and later to two or three buds—to form fruiting spurs.

Pruning After Fruiting. After stubby side shoots (which were left untouched) have fruited they should be shortened back to a shoot at their base.

Each longer lateral which was left to fruit should be shortened, after the fruit has been gathered, to a new shoot arising from its base. These new shoots, which will carry the following year's fruit, should be tied in; they in turn will send out new shoots of their own, but these should be rubbed off with the exception of one at the outer extremity and one at the base. The latter will in due course take the place of the fruited shoot; if it exceeds 2 ft. in length the tip should be pinched off. The upper shoot which was left on the long lateral is there to draw up sap and so assist in the swelling of the fruit, and it should not be allowed to extend beyond about the third leaf.

The spurs should be kept young. When a spur is obviously ageing it should be cut back to a strong shoot at its base (unwanted wood shoots from spurs are rubbed off in summer), this shoot being summer pruned and shortened back later to about two buds—to make it a new fruiting spur.

Winter Pruning. Use of pruning knife or secateurs should be avoided as far as possible, removal of unwanted growths being done by pinching between thumb-nail and first finger-nail before wood becomes too hard. Wounds left by knife or secateurs, used when the apricot tree is leafless, provide an opportunity for infection to enter —including silver-leaf disease (see under PLUM, page 530), and die-back trouble is also encouraged.

A branch that has suddenly wilted and died, or one that shows the typical silvery colour (in the foliage) of silver-leaf disease, should be cut out during summer, if possible—round about June. Disease is then far less likely to enter the cut surface. An additional safeguard is to cover the cut surface at once with thick paint, so as to seal it.

Further pruning details are contained in the section THE HOW AND WHY OF FRUIT PRUNING (page 432).

Propagation. Nurserymen obtain their apricot trees by budding selected varieties on to special plum stocks, during summer. How this is done, and how a fan-tree is made, is explained in the section HOW TO PROPAGATE FRUIT TREES AND BUSHES (page 444).

When to Gather the Fruit. Ripening is hindered in the case of individual fruits when a leaf or two blocks out the sun. The cause of the shade should be pinched off. A fruit otherwise hidden from the sun can often be coaxed into a more prominent position by means of a piece of smooth stick placed lengthwise behind the shoot carrying it (Fig. 372).

Apricots are at their best, so far as flavour is concerned, when only slightly soft; over-ripe, they lose something of their quality as dessert fruit—for eating raw, that is.

Storing Apricots. The fruit can be stored for a limited time if taken from the tree before it is ripe, the ripening being completed in a cool shed or similar place.

How apricots can be preserved, without the use of sugar, is

Fig. 372.—*Fruit on a wall-trained apricot, nectarine or peach tree can be brought forward to catch the rays of the sun by means of a piece of flat wood*

explained in the section EASY HOME PRESERVATION OF FRUITS (page 565).

Preparing for Table. A dish of apricots for raw dessert can be made even more attractive if the dish is lined with clean leaves of Virginia creeper, ivy or blackberry. The fruit itself needs no preparation. Doctors describe the apricot as "wholesome and most agreeable"; most people will agree that this is an understatement.

BLACKBERRY

Garden varieties of the blackberry are superior in every way to the wildling. The berries are considerably larger, of even better flavour, and the yield can be tremendous. All this apart from ease of gathering, for the cultivated kinds are not allowed to develop into formidable thickets.

Though eating the fruit raw may be regarded as a somewhat messy business, its value only begins there. Jelly, jam, pudding, tart—its several uses make it an indispensable fruit wherever there is a vacant patch of wall or fence. Blackberries can also be grown in a row in the open, supported against strained wires or some suitable form of trellis.

Ready for Use. Earliest blackberries are ripe in July and the season continues until autumn—sometimes until the first frosts.

Varieties include Bedford Giant (the first to ripen, in July), John Innes, Himalaya Giant and Parsley-leaved.

Soil Preparation. The blackberry will grow in clay, sand and most other kinds of soil, but the finest crops are obtained when there is animal manure, hop manure, or plenty of leaf-mould in the ground and the roots can find all the moisture they need in spring and summer.

Clay should be made thoroughly porous by digging it deeply and at the same time working in sand, grit, wood ash or old mortar refuse, together with whatever manure or leaf-mould (or other decayed vegetation) can be secured. Sandy or light soil is porous enough; it should be enriched, and made more capable of holding moisture, by mixing in manure or leaf-mould or material from the soft rubbish heap.

When and How to Plant. Roots should be planted in late autumn, or early spring, 10 ft. to 12 ft. apart. Vigorous garden varieties require all that space, which will soon be occupied by long canes tied back fan fashion to the support.

Before planting, whatever top growth the root has should be sacrificed—cut back to 6-in. stumps, all of them (Fig. 373). This is to relieve the roots for the first year of a burden which, because of the transplanting, they are not strong enough to carry. It means that no fruit will be produced the first year after planting; but the roots during that time will be extending sideways and downwards and building up strength for the following year's big crop and future crops.

The alternative to this drastic cutting back is acceptance of the fact that first-year blackberry plants allowed to carry their long growths and produce a few fruits will never become strong and profitable.

If plants can be given different aspects—some planted against a south-facing fence or wall, others against east-, west- or north-facing supports, a long succession of pickings will be obtained. A southerly aspect is warmest, and a blackberry plant in such a position is likely to ripen its fruit first. A plant facing north is likely to ripen last.

Training. If there are no garden walls or fences available, a house wall or sides of a shed or garage will do as support. If blackberries are to grow in a row in the open, wires strained between end stakes should be provided.

As the canes extend they should be tied or nailed back neatly, radiating like the ribs of a fan (Fig. 374), or horizontal (or nearly so); whichever method is found the more convenient may be used.

Watering and Feeding. Water should be given in quantity whenever rain holds off for any length of time in spring and summer. A regular supply of moisture not only helps the berries to swell but assists

Fig. 373.—*The young blackberry plant should be cut back to within 6 in. of the ground before planting*

in the production of new canes to carry the next year's crop. If a dose or two of liquid manure can be given, in early summer, it will be far from wasted.

Whatever the liquid—plain or rich—every drop should be enabled to soak right down to the roots. This will be ensured if the soil is first hoed so that the loosened surface sucks in all that is given.

Pruning the Blackberry. A blackberry plant left to its own devices will go on producing fruit

Fig. 374.—*The side of a shed can be put to excellent use by training a blackberry, or a loganberry, against it, the growths spaced out widely*

from side shoots (laterals) that spring each year from old wood, until that old wood is exhausted and dies. It will also produce a new cane or two; and its finest berries will be on the latter.

In pruning the blackberry the object is to get rid each year of as many old (fruited) canes as can be replaced by new (unfruited) ones. Any time after the fruit has been gathered this can be carried into effect. New canes spring up from the base of the properly cultivated plant (a few suckers sometimes appear at a short distance from the plant) and these straight from the root growths are fastened close back to the support after fruited canes have been cut right out to make room. No more than five or six canes should be left to any one plant.

Propagation. Blackberries growing wild extend themselves by a self-layering method. A long rambling growth dips its tip, by its own weight, to the ground, and there the tip takes root. The same method of propagation is practised by the grower. Long, young (unfruited) canes are bent over until the tips can be buried in the soil. The tips are rooted by the following spring, and after being severed from the parent plant these are dug up and planted elsewhere. Further details appear under Rooting Layers (page 445).

Gathering the Berries. These should be picked before they become squashy, and it is worth while going over the plants every day or so during the season so that berries are secured in tip-top condition.

Preserving Without Sugar. How blackberries can be stored for future use is explained on page 566.

BLACK CURRANT

Large bunches of big black currants, rich in flavour, command fantastic prices even in the cheapest times; which is only one reason why a few bushes should figure in every bit of private ground where room can be found, or made, for them. The fruit is always in demand for pies, puddings, wine, jelly, jam—the latter an old-fashioned but sound remedy for sore throat.

Ready for Use. First black-currant pickings are made in July, and the season extends into September.

Varieties include, in order, approximately, of ripening: Boskoop Giant, Raven, Davison's Eight, Seabrook's Black (less prone to big-bud trouble than most others), Victoria, Edina, Baldwin, Daniel's September.

The black currant is available in bush form only; its fruiting habit renders it unsuitable for training otherwise.

Soil Preparation. A dry root-run has to be avoided. Any ordinary fertile soil will produce good crops so long as water can be given in dry summer spells. The ground should be dug 12 in. to 18 in. deep and rotted manure mixed in freely, or leaf-mould or decayed weeds; this is specially necessary if the ground is sandy or thin.

When and How to Plant. As soon after the leaf-fall as possible is the best planting time, though bushes may be got in throughout the winter when the ground is not very wet. Planting should not be attempted in periods of snow or frost.

A sunny, sheltered spot is appreciated. The bushes should be set out 4 ft. apart, a little deeper than the soil mark on the stems, and the soil should be firmed around and above the covered-in roots by treading.

Either before or just after planting the young bushes should be cut down to within about 5 in. of the ground. This means a total loss of fruit the following summer; but the plants gain strength, and without the burden of having to support much top growth are able to build up a sturdy root system. Plenty of fruit will be produced the year after and subsequently.

Pruning. The best fruit is carried on young shoots which were produced during the preceding summer. Older wood will also fruit, but the pruner's aim is to get rid each winter of as much of the old wood as can be replaced by existing strong new growths. The old wood should be cut out, after the fruit has been gathered, as low down as possible. The result of this treatment is a more or less new black-currant bush for the following year's fruiting. An open centre is maintained by making all cuts back to buds which point outwards.

Watering and Feeding. First-year plants are in particular need of water during a dry spring and summer—a bucketful per bush, poured on to the soil after the surface has been loosened with the hoe. The soil should always be kept stirred around the plants, but neither spade nor fork should be used or the shallow roots will suffer; the hoe is the tool to use. A surface covering of rotted manure put down in late spring is excellent. This keeps the soil moist, and provides food when water is given through the rich mulch.

Big-bud Trouble. The mites that cause some buds of black currant to swell abnormally are tremendous little pests. This big-bud trouble is noticeable in winter, mite-infested buds being double the size of normal ones and round in shape; unattacked normal ones are long and pointed. There is no possibility of mistaking buds which the microscopic mites have occupied.

Undersized, crumpled leaves may be produced by these buds, or the leaves may dry up and perish during early summer. The trouble becomes worse each year, until the bush is fit only for the bonfire. The way to fight it is to pick off all abnormally swollen buds in winter and burn them; and then, before flower buds are open and when leaves are about the size of a shilling, spray the bushes with lime-sulphur solution. This is made by mixing ¼ pint of lime sulphur, purchased from a garden supply shop, with 3 gal. of water.

The solution is to be applied as a very fine spray so that upper and under sides of leaves and all the wood are wetted. This catches the mites when they are on the move to other and so far healthy buds.

Birds and Caterpillars. If caterpillars are troublesome they can be got rid of by dusting or spraying the foliage with derris insecticide just after flowering.

To keep birds from sampling the fruit, a persistently active dog or cat is invaluable; otherwise old fish netting, or discarded muslin curtains, should be draped over the bushes after the black currants have finished flowering.

Unfruitful Bushes. A cold spring may render bees so inactive that only an odd insect or two may crawl about the flowers and so effect transference of fertilizing pollen. The setting of the fruit is not entirely dependent on visits of bees and flies, but when insects are not active at flowering time the trusses of fruit may be very poor indeed. Unfortunately, nothing can be done about this.

When black-currant bushes flower well yet fail to produce fruit, and neither big-bud nor a cold spring is to blame, it is almost certain that the unfruitful bushes are victims of a disease known as reversion or nettlehead. Not all shoots on a bush will be affected at once, at the beginning. But the disease spreads, until after a couple of years or so the attacked bush is incapable of producing a berry.

Obvious signs that reversion is to blame appear in the leaves of attacked shoots, these leaves being narrower than normal ones and with fewer indentations of the edges. Also, side shoots with narrowed leaves are sometimes produced in a cluster, giving the effect of a bunch of nettles. These bushes should be dug up and burned.

Propagation. Black-currant bushes are easily increased by means of cuttings taken during September or October, from thoroughly sound bushes only. The method is fully explained on page 449.

Gathering the Fruit. Picking should begin as soon as there are enough ripe berries available and continue, at intervals, until the bushes have been stripped. Bunches—or strigs—are taken complete, to save unnecessary handling of the fruit, which bruises very easily.

BULLACE

A small and sour plum, the bullace is not a small-garden fruit; though the produce of a bush tree, standard or half-standard would be welcomed by any knowledgeable cook—for mixing with apple to make jam, and for making tarts and wine.

A good variety is Langley. It has the advantage of being self-fertile —that is, its own pollen is sufficient to secure a good set of fruit—and it ripens in November. Bullaces are always improved, as to flavour, by a touch of frost. Planting and other details are as given under Plum (page 528).

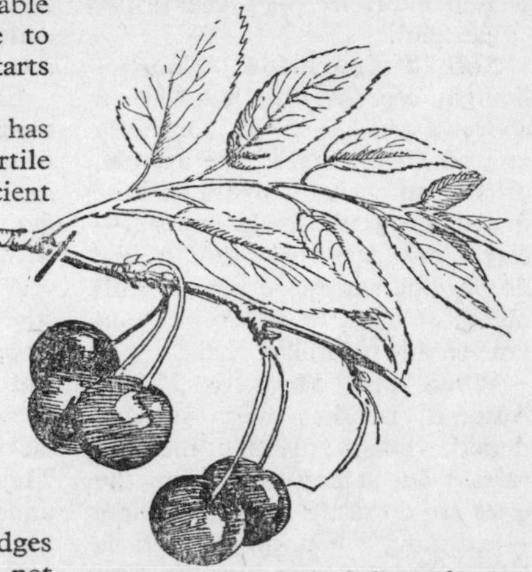

Fig. 375. *The fruited shoot of a sour variety of cherry may be cut back as shown above by the oblique line*

CHERRY

Birds are always excellent judges of fruit, and their judgment is not at fault where cherries are concerned. A healthy tree will produce a huge crop unfailingly, year after year. In spring it is a magnificent sight, with its dense masses of flowers. In early summer it is handsome and highly profitable—with its masses of fruit. It gives little trouble.

Ready for Use. Ripening dates vary between June and August, according to variety. Fruit hangs well for some time after it is ripe.

Varieties. For cooking, the sour or acid varieties Morello and Kentish Red are the best; for eating raw, the sweet varieties.

Though the acid Morello and Kentish Red are self-fertile, all the sweet varieties are self-sterile—they must receive pollen from a different variety for their fruit to set. This means that more than one variety should be present in the garden—unless other varieties are growing in the immediate neighbourhood. Even with Morello and Kentish Red it is not altogether advisable to plant either variety alone.

Sweet varieties which make appropriate mates are: Bigarreau Jaboulay and Early Rivers, ripe in mid-June; Bigarreau Frogmore and Kentish Bigarreau, early July; Noble and Bigarreau Napoleon, mid-August. Acid mates are Morello and Kentish Red, July to August. There are, of course, several other varieties of cherry, and before purchasing trees not included in the foregoing short list it would be advisable to seek the nurseryman's advice as to suitable mates.

Forms of Tree. Standards naturally give the largest yield. Where space for these cannot be afforded, fan-trained trees can be obtained for planting against a wall. Cherries are also grown as bush trees and pyramids, in which form they can be purchased as pot trees of fruiting size for the greenhouse or conservatory; their general treatment is explained in the section FRUIT IN THE GREENHOUSE (page 466).

Soil Preparation. Cherries flourish especially in good earth above a chalk subsoil. Ordinary ground should have lime rubble, or crushed chalk, or hydrated lime mixed freely with it. Heavy soil—clay, or near-clay—should be deeply dug and made porous with plenty of sand, or sharp grit, and lime rubble or broken chalk.

When and How to Plant. Autumn is the most suitable period, though planting may be carried out at any time when the trees are dormant—that is, leafless —excepting when the ground is wet, or frost or snow is about. Full instructions are given in the section ABC OF FRUIT PLANTING (page 425). Standards need to be 25 ft. apart, bush trees and pyramids 10 ft., wall trees (fan trained) 15 ft.

Watering and Feeding. Young trees need frequent soakings with plain water, particularly those against a wall, during dry spring and summer spells. Young and old alike benefit from dressings of lime, in the form of hydrated (water-slaked) lime or crushed chalk, every second or third year, during winter.

Birds and Other Troubles. Old muslin curtains or fish netting flung over the trees will save most of the ripening fruit from starlings and other birds.

Black-fly has a great liking for the young growths. These pests should not be left to get a hold. They breed at a tremendous rate and are most easily dealt with, when the advance guard first appears, by spraying with quassia solution; the concentrated preparation can be bought with directions for mixing. Fly-clustered shoot ends within reach should be dipped into the solution.

Exudation of gum from the trunk may result from bruising; from branches, by too much pruning, especially of older wood. If gumming is extensive the tree is weakened, and may die.

A silvering of the leaves indicates silver-leaf disease. Diseased or dead wood must be cut out, in summer, and burned at once, and the cut surfaces dressed with any thick, tacky paint, to seal the wounds. This disease is fully dealt with under PLUM (page 530), which is the most frequent sufferer.

Pruning. The sour, or acid, varieties—Morello, Kentish Red—produce their fruit on side shoots of the previous year's growth, the shoot generally being covered with fruit from end to end. When the fruit has all been picked, the shoots from which it came should be cut close back; the new ones are left unshortened, and they will bear the next summer's fruit (Fig. 375). Grown flat against a wall, the new shoots should be tied back as neatly as possible.

The sweet varieties fruit differently—on short spurs produced by older wood. These spurs are formed in great abundance, and little pruning is needed. Wall trees should not be allowed to become crowded with side shoots; surplus ones should be removed when quite small—rubbed off with the finger. Side shoots for which there is space should be pinched back to four or five leaves in summer, and cut back to within a couple of buds of their base in winter to form additional fruiting spurs (Fig. 376).

As standards, the sweet cherries

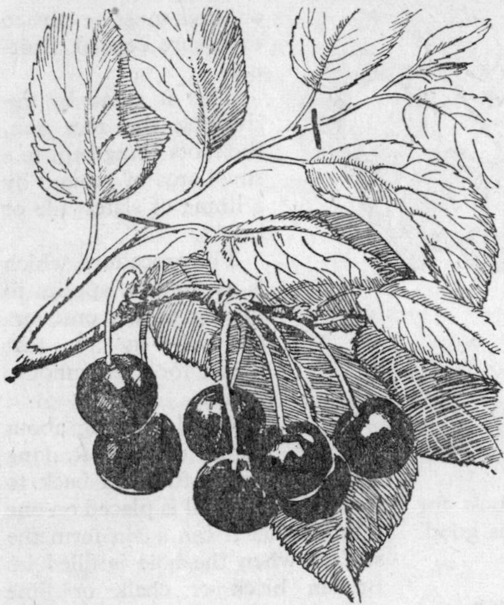

Fig. 376.—*Sweet varieties of cherry may have new side shoots pinched back in summer (upper line) and cut hard back in winter (lower line)*

can be left to look after themselves when a good head has been formed. If it becomes necessary to remove an old branch in order to keep the centre open, it should be cut back, as far as may be necessary, with a saw, not in winter but in summer. The cut surface should then be pared smooth with a sharp knife and the wound painted over with thick paint. This prevents gumming, and is a safeguard against silver-leaf disease, as explained under Birds and Other Troubles (page 492).

Pruning in general is further explained in the section THE HOW AND WHY OF PRUNING (page 432).

Propagation. Cherry trees are increased by budding or grafting selected varieties on to suitable stocks, as explained in the section HOW TO PROPAGATE FRUIT TREES AND BUSHES (page 444).

Gathering the Fruit. Ripe fruit will continue to hang on the tree for a considerable time, if it is protected against birds. Out of reach from the ground it should be picked from steps or a ladder with the top padded to prevent injury to the bark of the branch against which it rests.

Surplus Fruit. Cherries not required for immediate use can be preserved as explained in the section EASY HOME PRESERVATION OF FRUITS (page 565).

DAMSON

A variety of plum, the damson (Fig. 377) is particularly hardy. It makes a good windbreak, and can be purchased as a bush tree, standard, or half-standard. Planting and other requirements are as under Plum (page 528). The least possible pruning is needed when the fruiting stage is reached, all that is necessary being the removal of any old branch that threatens to spoil the shapeliness of the tree or for which there is no longer sufficient room.

Varieties include Bradley's King; this can be planted without a companion tree, as it is self-fertile. It ripens in September. Merryweather, ripening in September or October, produces the largest fruit. The earliest is Rivers' Early, ripe in August. The latest is Shropshire Prune, ready for use in

Fig. 377.—*The damson is a very hardy variety of plum. It makes a good windbreak*

October, and one of the best for preserving. Damson wine is good.

FIG

Given the shelter of a wall facing south or south-west, in a reasonably mild district, the fig can produce plenty of ripe fruit. It can be grown in bush form (Fig. 378), but it is more satisfactory when trained fan shape against a warm wall. Exposure to warm sun is essential for the ripening of the young wood that produces fruit.

Where outdoor conditions are unsuitable it can be grown and fruited as a dwarf bush in a 12-in. pot in greenhouse or conservatory or trained to the back wall; general management as explained in the section FRUIT IN THE GREENHOUSE (page 466).

Ready for Use. Outdoor figs ripen during August to September. The best wall variety is Brown Turkey (brownish-purple fruit). White Marseilles (greenish-white when ripe) is also suitable.

Soil Preparation. Growth of the fig is naturally brisk and lush, and this must be curbed to ensure regular fruiting.

This is done by restricting the root run, the roots being kept to a small area of ground by a lining of slates, tile or bricks.

The procedure, which is as follows, applies to the fig grown outdoors as well as to that meant for a greenhouse border.

A hole is dug about 2½ ft. deep, 5 ft. long and 3 ft. from back to front. The top soil is placed on one side, so that it can again form the surface when the hole is filled in. Broken brick or chalk or lime rubble is rammed down at the bottom of the hole to provide a drainage foundation about a foot thick. The sides of the hole are then lined, with brick or whatever else is available, to prevent the roots spreading, and soil is filled in.

The soil should contain plenty of lime, in the form of mortar rubble or broken chalk, and as soil is filled into the hole it should be rammed or trodden firmly so that it is solid throughout.

When and How to Plant. Late March or April is the most suitable time. A hole large enough to take the spread-out roots and deep enough to allow the soil mark on the stem to coincide with the new level is made in the prepared place, soil is worked between and over them with the fingers, then trodden firmly. The top inch should be raked over and left loose. No manure or artificial fertilizer should be added. If more than one fig is planted against a wall they should be 18 ft. apart.

Training. Main branches are tied or nailed back to the wall, radiating like the ribs of a fan (Fig. 379). When all available space is covered these should be not closer than about 1 ft. apart.

Watering and Feeding. Figs are thirsty plants in late spring and summer and water must not be stinted. The greenhouse fig, in a pot or against the wall, should be syringed with lukewarm water twice a day when the weather is bright and warm. In early summer the plant carrying a satisfactory crop (not otherwise) will be helped if the surface soil is covered with a 2-in. layer of old manure, or given a dressing of one of the special fruit-tree fertilizers that are on the market.

Method of Fruiting. With the fig there is no trouble in connexion with fertilization. The flowers are never visible—they are inside the immature fruit—and Nature can be left to its own devices. Fruit is produced on shoots of the previous year's growth, also on two-year-old shoots.

Pruning. When the figs have been gathered the shoots that produced them should be cut out and the sturdy young growths that have appeared during the summer trained in to take their place, where there are enough of these new ones. Provided they are well ripened by sun these will fruit the following season. Shoots that threaten to crowd should be removed whilst quite small. Young shoots that are very vigorous should have their tips pinched off in July.

In autumn the tree should be carrying the beginnings of the next year's crop—miniature figs, each nestling in the angle formed where a leaf joins a stem. If these miniature figs are larger than a big pea by the beginning of winter they are almost certain to drop off sooner or later; all above that size should be picked off in autumn.

Root pruning may have to be adopted in the case of a fig making too vigorous growth and producing too little fruit. The time to do this is as soon as the leaves have fallen; the method is explained on page 437.

Winter Protection. Before winter frost arrives the outdoor fig

Fig. 378.—*Planted in a border facing south and sheltered from cold winds a bush fig should be able to produce a goodly supply of ripe fruit*

Fig. 379.—*A wall-trained fig should have its main branches fastened back so that they radiate well apart like the ribs of a fan*

can be made safe by giving it the protection of dry matting, or straw, or slim branches of an evergreen, the material being tied loosely to the fig's branches or tucked round them and left in position until the following late March. This may not be necessary in a very mild district, but there is never any harm in playing for perfect safety.

Propagation. The easiest way to multiply a fig tree is by means of layers—shoots bent down until the tips touch the ground easily. A hole 5 in. to 6 in. deep is made at the point of contact, the tip inserted and the soil firmed back over it. Roots are sent out by the buried portion of stem, which meanwhile should be held secure in the ground by means of a peg made of bent wire. If watered well in dry weather, the new plant thus produced will be ready for transplanting in about six months. Before being dug up it must, of course, be severed from the parent plant. This layering operation can be carried out in May.

Gathering the Figs. These should not be left to become over-ripe, but be picked when appearance and feel indicate that the appropriate time has arrived. Doctors place value on the fresh fruit by reason of its mild laxative action.

GOOSEBERRY

Really heavy crops of gooseberries, the earliest of the berries, can be obtained from most soils even where chalk lies near the surface. For bottling, wine making, stewing, jam making, puddings and tarts this fruit is as famous as it is easily grown.

Plants purchased as young bushes are capable of fruiting well for many years, and when they show signs of wearing out they can be replaced at no cost by young ones quite easily raised as cuttings. From a single bush a large stock can be worked up.

In the form of cordons—single-stemmed plants — they can be grown against low fences, or walls, or wires in the open. They can also be grown as double and triple cordons, two and three stems respectively.

In this form, gooseberry plants occupy the least possible ground space and give the largest possible berries.

Ready for Use. The season extends from early May onwards. It can be prolonged considerably by planting cordons in various positions: some against a fence facing south, some north, some east, some west. Earliest to ripen will be the south-facing ones, the latest those facing north.

Varieties. These are numerous, but can be classified according to colour of the ripe berries.

Red ones include May Duke, very early; Lancashire Lad, mid-season; Winham's Industry, mid-season, a very profitable all-round variety for picking green and for jam making and dessert.

Yellow berries include Broom Girl, early; Leveller, mid-season, very large when ripe; Cousen's Seedling, late, an excellent bottler.

Green berries include Keepsake, very early for picking unripe but late in ripening; Lancer, late.

White berries include Careless, mid-season, excellent for jam; White Lion, large and very late.

Soil Preparation. It is worth digging the ground 18 in. deep, without bringing the lower soil to the top, and burying whatever manure is available. A good surface dressing of slaked or hydrated lime, in advance of planting, is advisable if it is suspected that the ground lacks lime. Special attention should be paid to this preparation where planting is to be done at the foot of a fence or wall, for there the soil is too often poor in quality and apt to dry out very speedily in rainless periods. Old stable manure worked in, or hop manure at the rate of a double handful per square yard, will give the soil body and help it hold moisture.

When and How to Plant. If planting can be done at the end of October the bushes or cordons will have a chance to establish themselves before winter sets in. It can, however, be done at any time up to February when the soil is free of frost and not too wet to work comfortably.

Planting holes should be wide enough to take the spread-out roots without cramping, and roots are to be covered to the depth shown by the soil mark on the stems. Soil should be trodden firmly round and above the covered-in roots. If, however, the ground is too wet for treading, the firming should be completed later, when the soil has become reasonably dry. The top inch of soil should be raked or hoed, after the treading, and left loose. Bushes should be 4 ft. or 5 ft. apart, single cordons 12 in., double cordons 2 ft., treble cordons 3 ft.

Supports. Bushes do not need staking, but cordons should be secured back to fence or wall with loops of sacking or stout cloth and nails, with tarred twine to wire supports in the open. These wires should be strained between stout end posts, one wire a foot up from the ground, another at 2 ft.

Watering and Feeding. Generous watering in dry weather (spring and summer) assists berries to swell and ripen and helps new growth. Planted against fence or wall, surface soil should be loosened shallowly with fork or hoe to ensure the water running in. Old manure, or wet hop manure, put down around plants keeps moisture in the soil and provides food for the roots. One of the special bush-fruits complete artificial fertilizers may be given in March, 2 oz. per sq. yd., and hoed in, with great advantage to the coming crop.

Weeds should be hand-picked, or uprooted with the hoe; deep

forking is likely to do injury to the shallow roots.

Keeping Birds at Bay. Considerable damage can be done by birds, sparrows chiefly, pecking out young leaf buds before these open. This trouble is prevented if the buds are made distasteful by dusting the bushes with old soot. So that this shall adhere it should be scattered over them whilst the bushes are damp with dew, or immediately after rain. Or quassia solution, bought in small tins with directions for mixing, should be applied as a fine spray. Either treatment will need repeating after a downpour of rain.

Later, fishing nets or old lace curtains thrown over the bushes, or draped down the front of fence cordons, will keep birds from the ripe fruit.

The Caterpillar Plague. Gooseberry bushes are sometimes stripped of leaves by caterpillars. If cordons are attacked, hand-picking in the very early stages is effective. Or these may be dealt with in the same manner as bushes—dusted or sprayed with derris insecticide just after flowering, or with hellebore powder (poison) up to within about three weeks of picking the fruit.

Mildew. American mildew is very destructive and spreads rapidly. It appears in early May as powdery white mildew on shoot-tips and the undersides of leaves, later on the berries. Immediately it is noticed, bushes should be sprayed with lime sulphur—one part of lime sulphur to 100 parts of water. An alternative spray consists of 1½ lb. of ordinary washing soda and ½ lb. of soft soap dissolved in a little hot water, more water then being added to make a 10-gal. solution.

European mildew is less destructive than the American. It appears in late summer, on the upper side of leaves and not on the fruit. As a preventive, where it has been troublesome the previous year, use either of the sprays already mentioned.

Other Troubles. Black-knot disease appears as black warts, or knots, on stems after these have been killed by the fungus concerned. This particular complaint is first apparent in the wilting of leaves. Affected branches should at once be cut off and burned. Coral spot, which shows as pink warts on live as well as dead wood, should be dealt with similarly. Cluster-cup disease shows as bright orange patches on leaves and fruit, which should be collected and burned without undue delay.

When growths die back, botrytis disease is present. It will sometimes kill entire bushes. Leaves attacked become yellow at the edges. The fruit may be affected—the skin browning, an ashy-grey mould appearing later, followed by the rotting of the berry. All dead growths and affected fruit should be removed and burned.

Wood of this description must never be left lying about. It should be consigned to the flames before the day is out.

Winter Clean-up. Spraying with tar-oil winter wash, between early December and the middle or end of January, will clean the bushes very effectively of all manner of dormant pests. Details are explained in the section HOW TO DEAL WITH FRUIT PESTS AND DISEASES (page 551).

Pruning should be carried out in February. Centres of bushes are to be kept clear of growths, and weakly, exhausted and dead or diseased branches cut out.

Berries are produced not only on spurs but on short young side shoots; the latter should be left untouched. Longer side shoots should be cut back to within about 1 in. of their base, to become fruiting spurs. Strong growths required to take the place of missing or worn-out branches are to be shortened by a third of their current season's growth.

The summer's growth at the end of each main branch—there should not be more than eight or ten of these to a bush—should be shortened back to within about 6 in. each spring until the bush has reached the desired size, when no further extension should be allowed.

Summer pruning consists in shortening the longest new side shoots by one-half.

Cordons are to be kept unbranched. In summer, all side shoots should be cut back—or severed between thumb-nail and first finger-nail—halfway, then pruned back to 1 in. or so in February.

Propagation. Strong, disease-free shoots of the current year's growth are taken as cuttings in late September or early October. Full details are explained in the section HOW TO PROPAGATE FRUIT TREES AND BUSHES (page 444).

Gathering the Gooseberries. One advantage in keeping the centre of a gooseberry bush open—clear of growths—is experienced when fruit is to be picked; produced on the outsides only, it is an easy matter to get at it. Berries should be picked from a number of plants at once, sufficient for immediate requirements. A bush should not be stripped at one go. If a little time is taken over the job some useful thinning out of crowded fruit will be achieved. If extra large berries are required, thinning out should be done early and rather severely—all the thinnings being used, of course; those that remain gain by exposure to light and air.

How to Keep Gooseberries. Methods are explained in the section EASY HOME PRESERVATION OF FRUITS (page 565).

Preparing for Table. Berries for dessert should be topped and tailed, with scissors, washed in cold water, and dried with a clean cloth. The gooseberry is of special value in the diet of dyspeptics and those with bilious tendencies.

GRAPE

As a profitable wall or fence coverer a grape vine is worthy of consideration. Any one of the outdoor varieties is capable of producing many fine bunches of fruit. The plants are so hardy they resist any frost, and growth is brisk and vigorous against a warm, sunny fence or wall.

Warmth and sun are essential to ripen the fruit, so the fence or wall that is to support the plant, or plants, should face south, or south-east, or south-west; and not be shaded by trees or buildings.

Late summer should see the bunches nicely ripened and ready for use, of such outdoor varieties as Buckland Sweetwater (pale amber berries), Miller's Burgundy (black), Reine Olga (reddish), and Royal Muscadine (white).

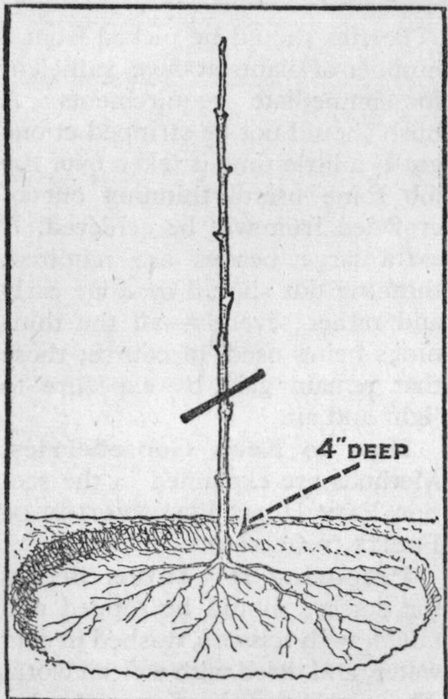

Fig. 380.—*The young outdoor grape vine should have its roots well spread out, and its top cut back to about 12 in. at the time of planting*

One of the most important points in soil preparation is good drainage. Ground that is water-logged in winter, or after heavy rains at any time of year, can be put right by taking out a hole 6 ft. to 7 ft. long, 4 ft. wide and about 3 ft. deep, ramming 9 in. of broken brick, stone, or lumpy lime rubble into the bottom, then filling up with good garden soil. This will make a suitable bed for one vine.

If the soil is thin and dries out easily it will need to be stiffened by mixing with it chopped turves or a barrow-load of quite old manure. Rich soil is not wanted, but there must be adequate food in the ground.

A border at the foot of a house wall is not infrequently a mass of brickbats and other rubbish 1 ft. or so down. This will have to be made good to the depth of 3 ft.

When and How to Plant. The best time to plant an outdoor grape vine is late October. Soil should be shaken from the roots (the plant will arrive from the nursery in a pot, or the nurseryman will have removed the pot and made a bundle of the roots) and these should be spread out in the planting hole; the latter to be of such a depth that when the hole is filled in the roots are covered with about 4 in. of soil (Fig. 380).

Soil should be worked between the spread-out roots with the fingers and made firm above and around them by treading.

If more than one vine is planted they should be not less than 4 ft. apart, grown as single main stems —that is, on the cordon principle. Or one vine can be made to cover a good deal of sideways space by training it as explained on page 501.

Training a Cordon Vine. The fence or wall needs to be covered with wooden trellis, or with horizontal wires spaced about 9 in. apart, to allow of the growths being tied back neatly and without any crowding.

The vine may be several feet long when received, a single rod or cane studded with buds. It is to be cut back to within 1 ft. of the soil. Given a warm summer, growth will be rapid. The cut-back rod will extend upwards, and side shoots will be trained out horizontally to left and right.

But not all side shoots are to be allowed to develop. The single-stem (cordon) vine is to be furnished with fruiting spurs on its left and right sides, 18 in. apart.

These are not to be in level pairs; each one is to be 9 in. lower (or higher) than its opposite side shoot. This arrangement enables all available space to be profitably covered without crowding.

Side shoots in excess of the required number are to be rubbed off when quite small. Those that remain (at 18 in. apart each side) are allowed to grow full length, being tied back horizontally to the trellis or wire background as they extend.

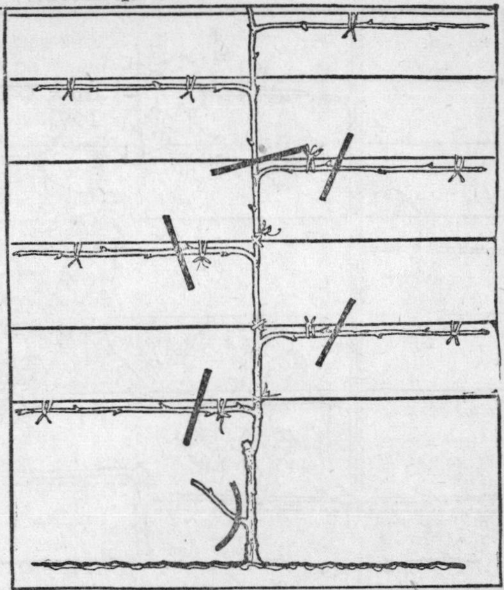

Fig. 381.—*The young cordon vine, trained to wires, should have its top and side shoots cut back, as shown by thick lines, twelve months after planting. Fruiting spurs are thus formed*

At the end of the first full twelve months—that is, the following November—the tied-in side shoots are each to be cut back to within two buds of their base (Fig. 381). Thus are the fruiting spurs formed. At the same time, the main stem is to be shortened to within about 4 ft. of the ground—that is, only 3 ft. of the summer's growth is to remain. The young vine is now 4 ft. or so high, with a couple of fruiting spurs on its left and one—possibly two—on its right.

Each year the side growths from the established spurs will be cut back, and the main stem shortened so that not more than about 3 ft. of that summer's upward extension growth is left to it. It thus increases its height each year by about 3 ft., until the top of the wall is reached, when no further extension growth is allowed. As its height increases, so more fruiting spurs are found room for at 18 in. apart on each side of the main stem.

A Horizontal-trained Vine. The cordon vine is more suited to a house wall than to a low dividing wall or garden fence. Against either of the latter the cordon vine must of necessity be kept short. In these circumstances the horizontal-trained vine is more profitable in that left and right extension is encouraged and therefore a greater number of fruiting spurs can be produced (Fig. 382).

For this system of training, a single rod or cane is planted, and cut down to within 1 ft. of the ground, exactly as is done with the vine which is to become a cordon. But no upward extension is allowed from the foot that remains. Instead,

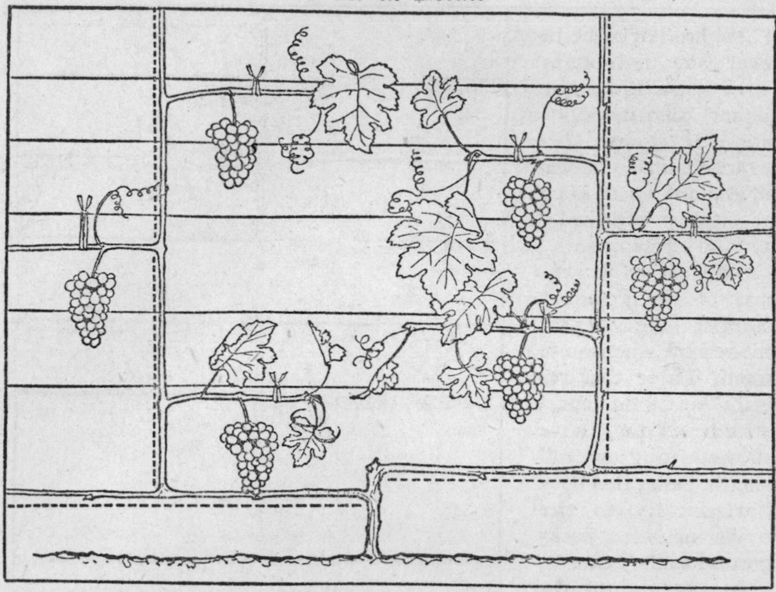

Fig. 382.—*A horizontal-trained grape vine. Main (permanent) branches or canes run parallel with the dotted lines; the others are fruiting growths*

the two top buds are allowed to shoot and any others on the 12-in. stump are rubbed off. The two top shoots are trained out to left and right, respectively, to form horizontal main stems from which side shoots are allowed to grow up vertically at intervals of about 3 ft.

These vertical side shoots become main stems. They are allowed to retain 3 ft. of the current season's growth at each winter pruning, and fruiting spurs are formed on them at 18-in. intervals on their left and right sides. The two horizontal main stems are each also allowed to increase in length by about 3 ft. each year, which allows of the annual addition of one more fruiting rod (vertical main stem, each with its spurs) at the left and right extremities respectively. The sideways and upwards extension goes on until all available space has been filled.

Method of Fruiting. Bunches of grapes are produced on young shoots which develop from the short spurs in spring; that is, the fruit is borne on shoots of the current year's growth.

Pruning the Side Shoots. The single side shoot from each spur is cut back each November or December, whether it fruited or not, to within two buds of the base of the past summer's growth (Fig. 383). The spur thus increases in length by not more than about ¾ in. each year.

All cutting should be done with a sharp knife, the blade directed away from the pruner, whose other hand grips the rod firmly just below the point at which the cut is intended to be made.

When Spring Growth Starts. Sometimes both buds left to a cut-back spur will start into growth in spring; sometimes only one. A single shoot only is required from a spur, so if both grow one must be rubbed off when it is not more than about 2 in. long (Fig. 384).

The tiny bunches of immature grapes, or rather flowers, can be seen when that much growth has been made. If only one of two shoots from a spur shows a bunch, that one will be left and the other rubbed off. If both shoots show a bunch, the stronger of the two will be left. If neither shows a bunch, the stronger shoot will be allowed to extend and the other be removed at once.

When the shoot with the bunch has extended and produced three leaves beyond the bunch, its end is nipped off so that only two leaves remain beyond the bunch (Fig. 384). Side shoots produced by this stopped shoot are left with one leaf only; the stem of the small side shoot is nipped off just beyond this.

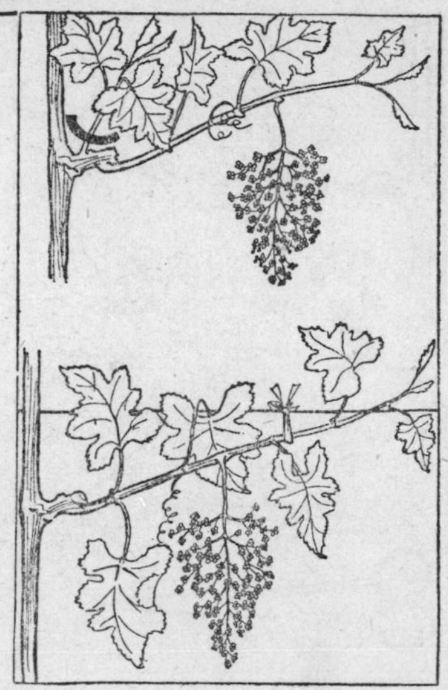

Fig. 384.—*One shoot only is required from a spur; a second one should be removed (top). A shoot should have its end nipped off after the second leaf beyond the bunch (bottom)*

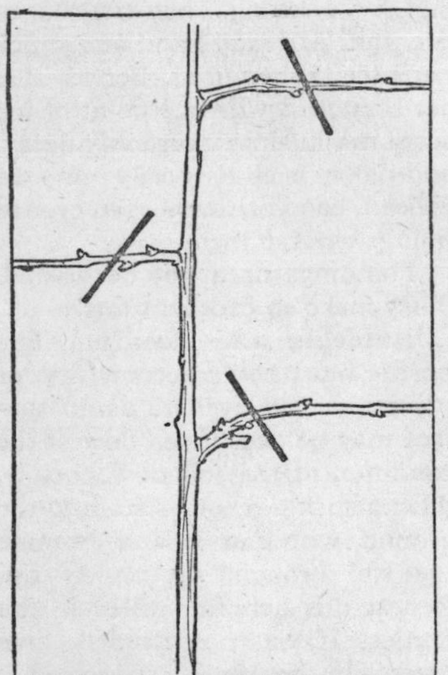

Fig. 383.—*Side growths of the vine are spurred back each winter, as shown by the thick black lines*

The spur shoot that shows no bunch should be allowed to extend to five leaves, the end then being nipped off.

Tying the Shoots. The spur shoots need to be tied down or back to the trellis or wires, with raffia, when 9 in. to 12 in. long. The piece of raffia is passed around the shoot, near the outer end, then around the support and tied there. But as the shoot is very brittle at its base it cannot be brought to the horizontal position at once. It should be drawn only part of the way down (or back) at the first tying, and brought carefully to its final position some two or three days later.

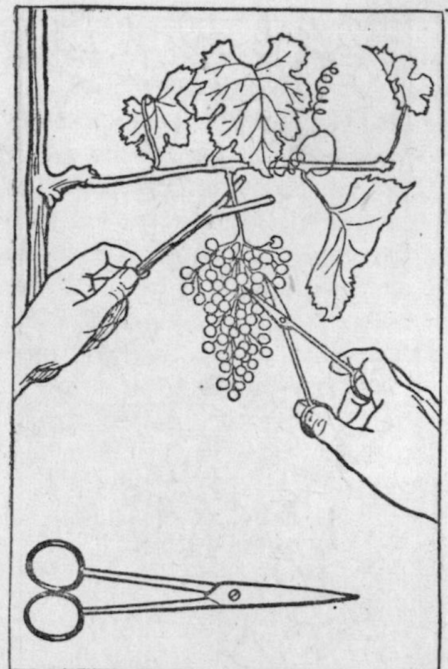

Fig. 385.—*Grape thinning scissors (below), and thinning proceeding (top) with the aid of a forked twig*

Pollinating the Flowers. Outdoors, bees and other insects will distribute the pollen on which the set of fruit depends. But if insects do not appear to be visiting the vine in any number it is safer to brush the fully expanded greenish-white flowers with a small fluffy wad of dry cotton-wool, or a rabbit's tail, tied to a stick or cane. This should be done when the sun is shining strongly on the vine and should be repeated daily for three or four days. This procedure is essential in the case of a greenhouse vine.

Thinning the Bunches. If more than one bunch appears on a spur shoot the weaker should be removed. The remaining one needs all the nourishment it can get.

Thinning the Berries. The berries are always thinned in the case of greenhouse vines, and this can be done outdoors if really first-class bunches of well-ripened berries are desired.

Thinning is done with long, thin, pointed scissors (Fig. 385), and to avoid handling the berries—and rubbing off their bloom—the bunch is manipulated with the aid of a forked twig about 8 in. long, held in the left hand. The bare upper stem of the bunch is held in the crutch of the forked twig and thus steadied, or pushed sideways or forwards (Fig. 385). First to be snipped out are berries in the centre of the bunch, then any very small ones on the outside, then any that crowd. The object is to leave berries spaced evenly at about ½ in. apart all over the bunch. Thinning should start when berries are about the size of small peas.

The job is done most comfortably early in the day, before the sun is too strong, or in the cool of evening. A steady hand and much patience are required. Berries that are scratched with the point of the scissors will almost certainly decay, and bloom is all too easily removed if head, hand or sleeve rubs ever so lightly against them.

Thinnings need not be wasted. They make an excellent tart.

Watering and Feeding. The border must never become dry, or berries may shrivel. A damp surface may be deceptive. To test the condition of the soil down below, push a stick 1 ft. or 18 in. into the ground, withdraw it, and examine the soil brought up on its tip. Repeat this here and there in the border. If water is needed, give several bucketfuls.

For feeding, when the berries begin to swell, one of the special vine fertilizers should be used; or poultry manure, a trowelful stirred vigorously into each bucket of water used. Or poultry manure may be mixed with an equal bulk of soil and spread over the border; subsequent waterings will carry the food down to the vine's roots.

Wasps. These are the greatest enemy of the outdoor vine. They can be dealt with as explained in the chart Remedies Against Enemies of Fruit Crops (page 564).

Storing Grapes. Ripe bunches can be kept fresh until the end of the year if cut with about 9 in. of the shoot to which the stem of the bunch is attached. The piece of shoot is inserted in a narrow-necked bottle—a wine bottle serves well—containing fresh clear water, and the bottle is placed on a shelf so that the neck slopes upward at an angle of about 45 deg., the bunch hanging clear (Fig. 386). The bottle should be held in place with heavy books or anything else that will keep it steady and inclined at an angle. The water should be replaced with fresh, at intervals. Grapes thus dealt with keep best in a dark room, well ventilated and cool. Any berries that show signs of decay should be snipped out.

Propagation. The grape vine can be increased by means of short lengths of side shoot, each length carrying a dormant bud. The method is explained under Grape Vine Cuttings in the section HOW TO PROPAGATE FRUIT TREES AND BUSHES (page 452).

Unheated Greenhouse Grapes. Outdoor varieties grown in an unheated greenhouse or conservatory ripen some time in advance of those outdoors. The vine may be trained up the back wall, though a better position is parallel with the roof glass, with the growths tied to horizontal wires supported 18 in. below the glass.

The vine may be planted outdoors and the main stem led into the greenhouse through a hole in the brickwork at the front. If the greenhouse is large and heated the border can be inside, and prepared as explained under Preparing a Greenhouse Border in the section FRUIT IN THE GREENHOUSE (page 468).

Fig. 386.—*Thick lines at top show where to cut a bunch of grapes for storing. The stem end is then placed in a bottle of fresh clean water*

During the time that the indoor vine is dormant—in winter, when leafless—it needs all the fresh air it can get, ventilators being open except during frost. This must be remembered—for the sake of other plants that the same greenhouse may be required to accommodate in winter. Plants needing to be coddled will not be happy in those hardier conditions which the vine demands in winter.

Training the Indoor Vine. The cordon system is most convenient under glass, a single rod being taken up until the limit of height is reached. At planting time the vine should be cut back to the point at which the front glass starts, or to within 1 ft. of the ground if planted against the back wall. Training, pruning and other details are then as explained in the case of the outdoor vine.

When growth starts in spring it may happen that the top buds on a rod push before the lower ones. In that case, to equalize growth, the rod should be untied and the top part allowed to hang down. That checks the upward flow of sap and encourages the lower buds to move; when the lower shoots are extending, the vine is tied upright again.

Ventilating and Syringeing. Warmth of the sun is trapped by careful manipulation of the ventilators. Before the sun goes off the greenhouse in the afternoon the vine, walls, glass and surroundings generally should be syringed with water of the same temperature as the house and the ventilators almost closed. The result is a sudden increase in temperature which will last throughout the night. The vine should also be syringed during the morning and the surroundings made damp, except during the time the vine is in flower and when the grapes are colouring.

Red Spider, Mealy Bug. These pests can always be expected under glass. Treatment is as explained in chart Remedies Against Enemies of Fruit Crops (page 563).

Leaf and Berry Troubles. However dull and cold the weather might be there should always be sufficient ventilation given to keep the air inside the greenhouse on the move—without draughts, of course. If the sun comes out suddenly after a dull spell and the ventilators are almost closed, the foliage may scorch: that is, turn brown in places and shrivel. It happens perhaps most frequently on early summer mornings, before the grower has increased the ventilation which was decreased for the night.

The same thing may happen to berries. Moisture deposited on these is suddenly dried up by the sun, and the berries are scalded. It does not happen if the atmosphere is moving, as it will be if the ventilators are open sufficiently.

Berries may split, or the stalks (shanks) of the berries shrivel, if watering is neglected for a time and the dry soil suddenly made sodden. Same results are experienced if the border is not properly drained, or if the vine carries a too heavy crop and is not being fed.

Preparing for Table. The bunch of grapes should be placed (without unnecessary handling, to avoid rubbing off the attractive bloom) on a fruit dish lined with vine leaves—autumn-tinted if possible—with grape scissors by the side. As a food, grapes are as nourishing as they are delicious.

GREENGAGE

The gage plums are among the most tasty of all fruit for dessert and preserving. Best known is the old Greengage, ripe in late August, and still holding its own with modern varieties. Culture is explained under Plum (page 528).

Fig. 387.—*Loganberries trained up a tall pole (left), up a tripod of poles (centre), over an archway (right), are capable of giving abundant crops*

LOGANBERRY

If there is a rubbish heap or other unsightly view to be blocked out, the loganberry will do it swiftly and very profitably. Trained against some sort of rough trellis, or against two rows of wire strained between strong end posts, it will form a dense screen, producing every year new shoots up to 15 ft. or so long. It can be trained up a pole or tripod of poles (Fig. 387, left), up a trellis archway (Fig. 387, right), or be fastened back to a fence or wall, or be grown in a row across a patch of ground, with wire supports.

The berries, generally produced in pairs, dark purplish-red when ripe and about 1 in. long, have an acid and very refreshing flavour. They can be eaten uncooked as dessert; mixed with currants, gooseberries and other fruits to make jam, with considerable improvement to the latter's flavour; mixed with other soft fruits to make tarts; made into jelly; and also be bottled or canned. The crop is large, and never fails in ground good enough for other fruits and vegetables.

Ready for Use. First pickings are ready in late July, and the canes continue to produce fruit up to mid-August. There is only the one variety.

Soil Preparation. The loganberry will grow in heavy ground over a clay subsoil, so long as it is ordinarily well drained, and in soil above chalk. Thin, dry soil can be made to the plant's liking by digging it deeply and mixing in animal manure, hop manure, or plenty of good leaf-mould or other varieties of rotted greenstuff.

A foremost requirement is full exposure to sun. This is necessary to ripen and harden the new fruiting canes that spring up from the base each year.

When and How to Plant. Autumn is the best time to get loganberry plants into the ground. If that is not possible, early spring will do. Roots should be spread out to their full extent in the planting-hole and then covered with well-broken soil so that they are buried as deeply as they were in the nursery ground—as indicated by the soil mark on the stems.

Plants do not need cutting down the first year. The canes can be left full length, except for the removal of any damaged tips, and they will produce fruit next summer, and thereafter be annually productive.

Training the Loganberry Canes. To keep the fruit within reach the long canes should be tied out diagonally, fan rib fashion, if grown against fence, trellis, wall or wires; upright if grown against a tall post.

Watering and Feeding. In thin ground a lot of water will be needed, from spring onwards, to support the strong growth and ensure plenty of large, plump fruits. This will have to be given by the bucketful if rain does not fall. A top dressing, or mulch, of old manure, or hop manure, will shut up the moisture in the soil. It should be put down wet, after weeds have been removed and the ground itself is wet, and will serve the further purpose of supplying much-needed food to the roots. These are not far below the surface, and to avoid injuring them neither spade nor fork should be used within 2 ft. or 3 ft. of the plants. Weeds should be removed by hand or with the hoe.

In the absence of manure, weeds or lawn mowings, or both, will serve as a moisture-holding top dressing, put down in spring or early summer, this to extend 18 in. or so out from the canes.

Pruning. Canes produced one summer will bear fruit the next, and as many fruited ones as can be replaced by new canes should be cut right out as soon as the fruit has been gathered. The new and unfruited canes should then be tied back in place. Meanwhile, the new canes should not be allowed to flop about anyhow; they should be tied in, loosely, whilst completing their growth.

It is not necessary to remove all the fruited canes in autumn. The strongest of them can be left to fruit again if there is room for them without crowding.

Propagation. Young canes in excess of the number required take root with extreme ease if they are bent over so that their outer ends can be buried 5 in. to 6 in. deep in the ground, during August. A long wire staple should be passed over the shoot to hold it down, or a brick or similar weighty object be laid on the shoot just short of where the tip enters the soil. It can be severed, with full length of layered stem, from the parent plant in February or March, lifted with all the roots that have formed at the buried tip, and transplanted where it is to remain and fruit. The soil around the buried tip should be kept moist in dry weather.

Maggoty Berries. Grubs of the raspberry beetle spoil the fruit by entering it and feeding on the interior. This pest can be controlled by spraying or dusting the plants with derris insecticide three weeks after the flower petals have fallen. It is advisable to take this precaution whether or not the loganberries have been attacked the previous year. This is a valuable fruit, and grubs should not be given the chance to embark on their work of destruction.

Fig. 388.—*Fruit of the medlar tree, hard and green when picked in November, needs to be over-ripened in store. This takes a few weeks*

Gathering the Fruit. Berries wanted for dessert should be picked, when dark purplish-red, with the stalk attached; for other purposes the stalk can be left on the plant. Loganberries are easily crushed, and care is called for in their handling.

Picking should be done only in dry weather—not when the berries are wet with dew or rain—and only those that are quite ripe should be taken. The plants should be gone over every second day until the crop has been cleared.

Preparing for Table. The berries need no preparation for dessert purposes. Over-ripe ones should be eaten on the spot or put to other use.

Preserving Loganberries. Methods are explained in the section EASY HOME PRESERVATION OF FRUITS (page 565).

LOWBERRY

The fruit of the lowberry resembles that of the loganberry, but when ripe is jet black. Roots should be planted 7 ft. apart. After the fruit has been picked the canes that bore the crop should be cut right down and the new ones, produced during the current summer, tied back in place. General treatment is as explained under Loganberry, though the latter is a more vigorous plant than the lowberry.

MEDLAR

The slightly acid taste of the fruit of the medlar tree (Fig. 388) is not brought out until the fruit—which is hard and green when gathered—has been stored for two or three weeks and allowed to become over-ripe. Indeed, it is off the eating list until that stage has been reached. The medlar is also used for making jelly.

It is easy to grow, its chief requirements being shelter from piercing winds and soil that is well drained.

Ready for Use. Fruit is ready for eating in late November or December. Varieties are Royal (this begins to bear fruit when quite young), Dutch, Nottingham. Plants are obtainable as standards, pyramids and bush trees.

Soil Preparation. The medlar is not particular as to soil, though this must be well drained. If the ground loses moisture easily in dry weather the site should be prepared by deep digging, plenty of old manure, or rotted vegetation, being worked in throughout the full dug depth. A surface covering of manure, or lawn mowings (put down wet and thickly), over the area occupied by the roots, is of considerable assistance on light soil in dry spring and summer weather.

When and How to Plant. Trees get away readily when planting is done in February or March. Method of planting, staking, etc., is explained in the section ABC OF PLANTING (page 425).

Pruning. The medlar should be shaped and pruned as described under Apple (page 478).

Propagation. Increase is by grafting on a pear stock, as explained in the section HOW TO PROPAGATE FRUIT TREES AND BUSHES (page 444).

Gathering the Fruit. The hard and green fruits should be picked round about mid-November, or earlier if frost comes, and placed in store for ripening as explained below.

Storing Medlars. The fruit needs protection against damp or it will go rotten. It should be placed on a shelf, in single layers only, with the wide eye downwards until the medlars have become brown and soft. They are then fit for use. The indoor ripening process usually occupies a fortnight at least before it is completed.

MELON

This succulent fruit is high up on the luxury list and needs warmth and moisture to produce a satisfactory crop. It can be grown in a heated greenhouse (Fig. 389), in the manner advised under Cucumber (page 286); with less trouble in a hotbed frame, also as advised for cucumber. Where details differ they are explained below.

Ready for Use. Sown in March, melons are ripe four to five months later. Varieties most suitable for hotbed frame culture include Sutton's Half-hardy, Cantaloupe, Hero of Lockinge. The first and second can sometimes be ripened in a cold frame, given a hot summer.

Hotbed Frame Melons. A hotbed, on which a frame is to be placed, is made up and managed as explained in detail in the section FRAME AND GREENHOUSE (page 65).

Seed is sown in March and plants dealt with as explained for cucumbers. A single-light frame will accommodate one plant.

The main shoot should have its tip nipped off when about 2 ft. long. Side shoots are produced as a result, and four of these (any others should be removed when quite small) should be taken to the corners of the frame, one to each corner (Fig. 390). Main shoot and side shoots should be pegged down to the soil. When a number of flowers appear on the side shoots the ends of the latter should be nipped off (Fig. 391).

Fertilizing the Flowers. To enable the female flowers to produce fruit they must be fertilized with pollen from the male flowers. Female flowers are distinguished by a distinct swelling immediately

Fig. 389.—*Melons grown in a greenhouse need to be supported individually in loose netting bags, to take the weight of the fruit from the stem*

behind the petals; male flowers have no such swelling. When several female flowers are fully open, a male flower should be picked, the petals removed, and the pollen-bearing organs pressed gently into each female flower in turn so that some of the pollen is left behind on the receptive stigmas.

Or the pollen can be transferred with the aid of a small fluffy wad of dry cotton-wool. This should be passed gently over the male pollen-bearing anthers and then over the stigmas of the female flowers.

The time for this is when the atmosphere of the frame is driest—in full sun, at midday.

The female flowers should be fertilized on one day, so that the resultant melons shall be evenly sized.

The soil must be kept evenly moist—never sodden, never dry. The water should be of the same temperature as the interior of the frame.

Water should not be poured at the foot of the plant; over-moist conditions there may cause the main stem to rot at soil level.

Syringeing is called for twice a day in bright weather, the leaves being dewed over with a fine spray above and, as far as possible, below, with clear water of the frame's interior temperature.

One of the general-purposes artificial fertilizer mixtures should be given once a week from the time the melons have reached the size of a tennis ball. Roots appearing at the surface should be covered with good soil, pressed down.

Ventilation. The frame should never be completely closed. The

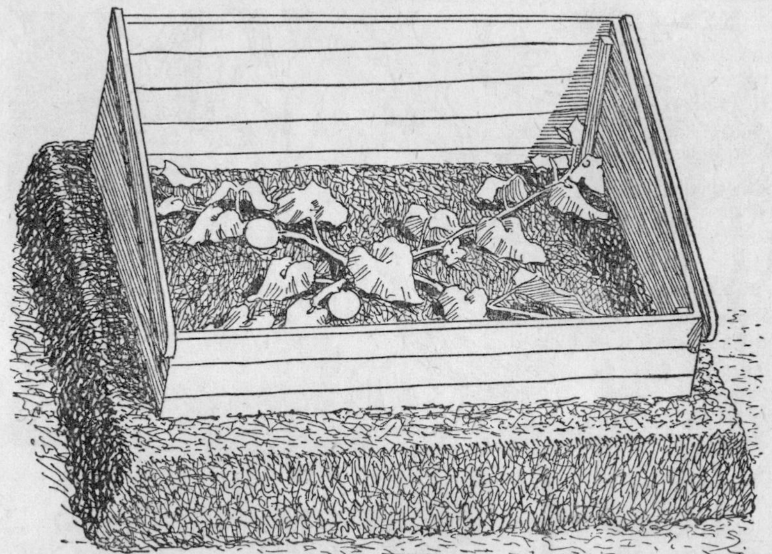

Fig. 390.—*A melon plant in the centre of a hotbed frame has a shoot trained out to each corner. They should be pegged down to the soil*

amount of air given will be governed by the weather. The object is to keep the atmosphere of the frame gently moving, moist and warm.

As much air as possible needs to be given when the melons are beginning to ripen. And to bring out the full flavour of the fruit the soil and the atmosphere should then be kept rather less moist.

Red Spider. Vitality is sucked from the leaves by microscopic red spiders, which appear and make their attack on the underside of the foliage when the atmosphere is too dry. Frequent syringeing with clear water will hold the pest well in check.

The Fruiting Stage. One fruit to each shoot is a safe rule; others should not be allowed to develop. If a smooth piece of wood, or a tile, is slipped under each fruit, contact with the soil is prevented. A melon

Fig. 391.—*Ends of side shoots of the melon plant should be nipped off (thick black lines) when flowers appear.* (A) *male,* (B) *female flowers*

resting on damp soil is apt to decay at the spot where contact is made.

Gathering the Fruit. A melon is ripe when a crack begins to form at the junction of stalk and fruit. It should be cut with a piece of stalk. If not wanted for immediate use it should be stored in a dry, airy place—and watched, to see that it does not become over-ripe.

Preparing for Table. The ripe melon should be placed on a fruit dish lined with clean leaves of any attractive kind, with a melon knife by the side.

Fig. 392.—*Good crops of mulberries can be had where other fruit trees fail because of smoky conditions. It makes a very good lawn tree*

MULBERRY

The mulberry (Fig. 392) has the distinction of being a thoroughly satisfactory town fruit tree. It will produce good crops of mulberries where other trees fail on account of smoky conditions. In bleak districts in open country it needs shelter, to break the blast; a sunny position is to its liking.

The fruit is excellent for dessert and for preserving, and as it has a habit of dropping when ripe the tree might well be planted on a lawn, ripe mulberries coming to less harm when they have grass to fall on. It is commonly grown as a standard.

Ready for Use. Ripening date varies between late August and late September.

Soil Preparation. A moist but well-drained soil suits the mulberry best. If the ground is thin and dry, or chalky, stony or clay-like, a large planting hole should be got out and filled with two or three barrow-loads of more suitable soil. If this is not possible, the ground should be dug deeply and old manure, or leaf-mould, or rotted material from the soft rubbish heap, mixed in very plentifully. If the ground is clay-like, in addition to one of these enriching materials old lime rubble, or sand, sharp grit, or small charred woody stuff from the garden bonfire, should be worked in to make the heavy ground more porous.

When and How to Plant. March is the best period to plant a standard mulberry. The roots are brittle and have to be handled carefully when being spread out in the planting hole. Fine soil should be worked between them, and when they have been covered with a good layer this should be trodden firm. Planting, staking, and other details are explained in the section ABC of Planting (page 425).

Until it becomes completely established a young tree must be watered liberally whenever rain holds off in the period between early spring and late summer.

Pruning. To encourage the formation of fruiting spurs in a young tree, side shoots not wanted to form additional branches should be nipped back to five or six leaves in summer and winter pruned to within about four buds of their base. Fruit is also produced on short young side shoots. The older tree will look after itself, though it may occasionally be necessary to cut back an awkwardly placed branch or remove a bit of dead wood. Explanation of pruning and training operations is given in the section The How and Why of Fruit Pruning (page 432).

Propagation. The mulberry is most easily increased by cuttings, 1 ft. or so long, planted half their depth, in the open, in October. Shoots for this purpose should be cut through immediately below a joint, and may be planted in dibber-made holes each with a good pinch of sand or sharp grit at the bottom to encourage rooting. Soil should be rammed hard around the planted cutting, with the boot heel. At the end of twelve months it should be well rooted. Growth is, however, very slow, and to obtain fruit in a reasonable time a well-formed tree should be purchased.

Gathering the Fruit. Mulberries should be gathered before they become squashy ripe—before they are quite black. The quickest method is to shake the fruit off by jerking the branches, with clean sheets of newspaper laid out on the ground to catch the mulberries as they fall.

Preparing for Table. For dessert purposes the stalks should be removed and the fruit piled on a dish lined with mulberry leaves.

MULCHING

This is the technical term for the operation of putting down a mulch —which is a surface layer of old manure, hop manure, leaf-mould, wilted weeds, lawn mowings or anything similar.

To be really effective the covering should be spread out over the area occupied by the roots of bush and cane fruits (Fig. 393), and over as wide an area as is practicable for tree fruits. It should be made sodden before it goes down, and if it can be 2 in. thick it is so much the more effective. Weeds should first be removed from the area to be covered and the soil loosened with the hoe or lightly pricked over with the fork; and if the ground is dry it should be soaked with water.

A mulch serves the purposes of hindering evaporation of moisture from the soil that is covered; of preventing shallow roots being overheated by strong sun; and, when manure forms the mulch, providing additional food, this being carried down below by rain or by subsequent waterings.

This attention is specially desirable where the soil is light or otherwise very freely drained. All trees and other fruiting plants, whatever the nature of the soil, recently planted and not yet having a proper hold on the ground, will be encouraged to go ahead briskly if a wet mulch is given them before dry spring weather causes the soil about their roots to lose its moisture.

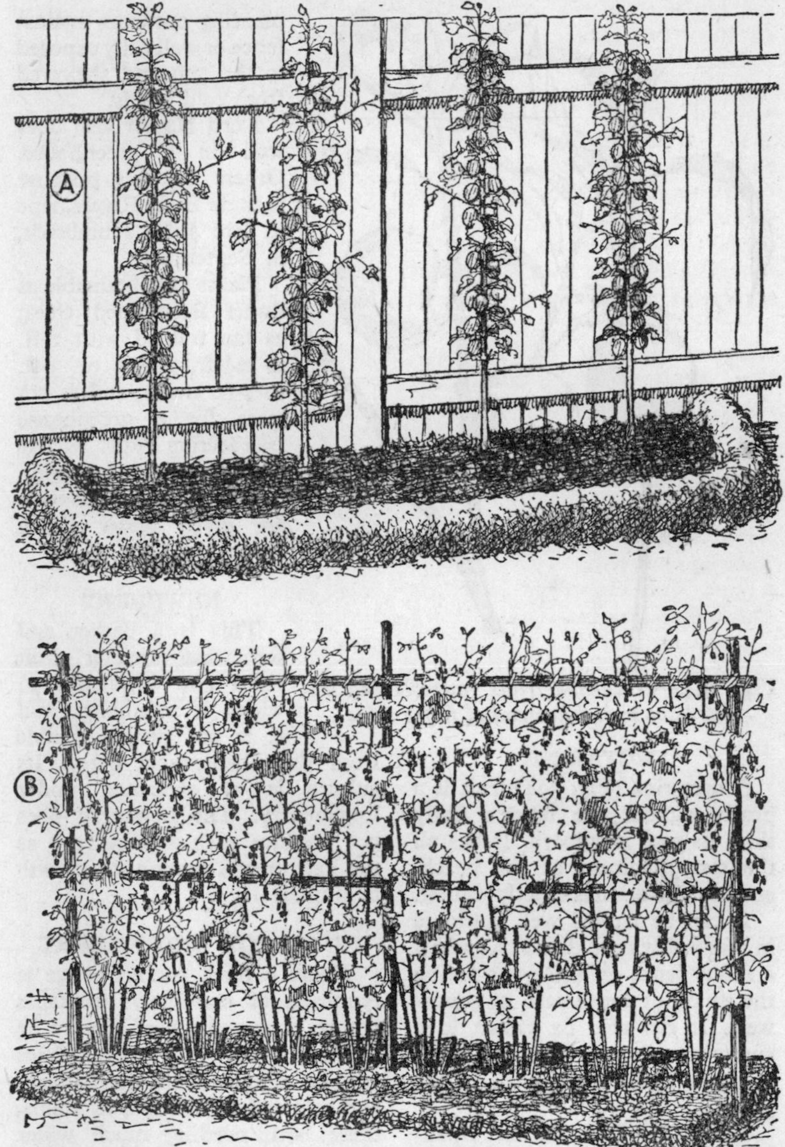

Fig. 393.—*Two methods of mulching:* (A) *inside a mound of soil forming a basin;* (B) *over an unconfined area. Cordon gooseberries against a fence are shown above; a row of raspberry canes, in the open, below. The mulch may be of manure, lawn mowings, leaf-mould, or anything similar*

Fig. 394.—*Nectarine fruits resemble peaches, but have smooth instead of fluffy skins*

NECTARINE

A nectarine (Fig. 394) fruit is a peach without the latter's fluffy skin; its peel is smooth. It has all the tasty juiciness of the peach, and its cultivation is exactly similar.

It can be fruited well outdoors in reasonably mild districts, against a sunny fence or wall—one facing the south, or south-east, or south-west. It can also be grown in a sunny greenhouse, provided there is ample space for it close to the glass.

Ready for Use. Earliest ripening date outdoors is mid-July, variety John Rivers. Variety Lord Napier ripens in early August, and Rivers' Orange in early September. These are the most suitable for planting outdoors against fence or wall fully exposed to the sun and sheltered from cold winds.

Lord Napier also does well in a greenhouse. Others for this purpose include Early Rivers, ripe in late July; Humboldt, in September.

Plants are obtainable as dwarf fan-trained trees; as fan trained with 2-ft. to 2½-ft. stems or 3-ft. to 4-ft. stems; and as pot trees for a greenhouse (see section FRUIT IN THE GREENHOUSE, page 466).

Details of cultivation are given under Peach (page 519).

NEWBERRY

This is a darker and somewhat sweeter fruit than the loganberry, which it resembles, and it is not distinguishable from the phenomenal berry. Its culture is as explained under Loganberry. The newberry does not produce such a large crop as the loganberry, though its growth is similar.

NUTS, COB AND FILBERT

Where a thick garden hedge is required, of extremely profitable nature, cobs and filberts should be planted, about 3 ft. apart. Trees can be obtained in bush form, and as standards with 4-ft. stems, these both needing much wider spacing, of course, than the hedge plants.

These are among the most obliging of all fruits, giving good crops on even poor stony ground.

Ready for Use. Ripening date is, as a rule, October. The nuts will keep in good condition, in store, for a lengthy period.

Varieties. Cob nut and filbert differ in shape and in husk covering (Fig. 395). The cob is roundish-oval, and its short husk barely covers the nut. The filbert is oblong, and the husk is long and tapering.

Cob varieties include Kentish Cob, the largest and a most prolific bearer; Cosford, very thin shelled; Cannon Ball, and Duchess of Edinburgh.

Filbert varieties include Red Filbert (dark pink skin), White-skinned Filbert, Garibaldi (frilled husk).

Soil Preparation. Ground of a naturally damp nature needs to be made thoroughly porous by really deep digging, sand or grit being worked in very liberally. These nuts do best in dryish soil and without any manure, but preparatory digging must not be omitted. Though a sunny position is preferable, good crops can be had in light shade.

When and How to Plant. October is the customary date for planting. Bush trees, which are the most profitable, should be planted about 12 ft. apart. General directions are given in the section ABC OF FRUIT PLANTING (page 425).

Method of Fruiting. The nuts are produced on short spurs, and on short twigs which grew the previous year, both spurs and twigs coming from the main branches which form the permanent framework.

Most prominent feature of nut

Fig. 395.—*The catkins of cob and filbert nuts, and the little tufted nut-producing flowers. A cob* (A), *variety Cosford; a filbert* (B), *variety Garibaldi*

bushes and trees in February is the display of catkins—2-in.-long tassels. These are the male flowers. They started as stumpy, tight, cylindrical objects pendulous from shoots here and there. In February, having increased in length, they loosen up and on the first sunny day are ready to get rid of their loads of pollen.

This pollen is wanted by the female flowers; without it these cannot form nuts. The female flowers are utterly unlike the long male catkins. They are tiny crimson tufts and go unnoticed unless one looks for them on the spurs and last year's short twigs. Wind carries the yellow pollen from the long catkins to the tiny female tufts, and the nuts are born.

To help Nature in this work it is worth while to shake, gently, the branches, this having the effect of distributing the pollen, some of which will settle where it is essential. If there happens to be a scarcity of long (male) catkins when the crimson-tuft female flowers are open, a good set of fruit can be ensured by hanging among them one or two catkin-bearing branches cut from the wild hazel (hedge nut) if these are available.

Male catkins are borne very plentifully by the variety Cosford, and if a bush of this kind is planted among other varieties there is seldom lack of sufficient fertilizing pollen.

Pruning Cobs and Filberts. The method of fruiting understood, pruning can be carried out in a manner which ensures the largest possible crop.

Not until the pollen of the long yellowish catkins has been distributed, and the nut harvest thus made sure, should pruning start. Then, in early March, the end shoot (extension shoot) of each of the eight or so main branches is cut back by about one-third of the growth which it made the previous year.

Long side shoots showing no signs of small green nuts are at the same time shortened back to within 3 in. to 4 in. of their base, to develop into fruiting spurs. But any such shoots needed to fill vacant space (without crowding) can be allowed to extend, being cut back by about one-third of their previous season's growth each March. In this way old and exhausted branches can be replaced, or additional branches formed. Short side growths should be left untouched.

Fruiting spurs are kept short by cutting back their new growth annually, the knife or secateurs stopping short at the immature nuts, of course. Growths inclined inwards should be cut hard back, so that the bush tree keeps its open centre. Weakly and worn-out wood, and any sucker growths at the base, should be removed. Standard nut trees are pruned similarly. A closely planted nut hedge will not be cut to the same extent, but the same pruning principles should be followed.

The ideal bush tree carries a main framework of eight or so branches on a single stem of 12 in. to 15 in. in length. A young plant is trained to the desired form in the manner explained for bush apples in the section HOW TO PROPAGATE FRUIT TREES AND BUSHES (page 444). General pruning work is detailed in the section

THE HOW AND WHY OF FRUIT PRUNING (page 432).

Propagation. By layering two-year-old shoots, in autumn, a true-to-variety stock of plants can be worked up without much trouble. A selected shoot, purposely left unshortened, conveniently placed for bending over to the ground, has its tip inserted in a dibber-made hole 5 in. to 6 in. deep and pegged there with a notched stick or long wire staple. Soil is rammed with the heel around it, and the layered shoot is left undisturbed for a full year. The tip will have rooted by then, and the shoot can be severed from the parent plant and be dug up complete with roots for planting elsewhere.

Sucker growths can be dug up, with roots, if any of these are present, and be replanted, in autumn. Nuts can be sown, when ripe, 2 in. deep outdoors, and the seedlings replanted after a couple of years. It should be noted that plants raised as seedlings or as suckers do not necessarily come true to name, as do layers. Standard nut trees are grafted on selected stocks. The operation of grafting is explained in the section HOW TO PROPAGATE FRUIT TREES AND BUSHES (page 444).

Gathering the Nuts. These are usually ripe by late September or October. Both husk and shell should be quite brown before gathering begins and the husk should come away readily from the nut. After being picked they should be sun-dried for a few days—spread out on sacking or other material so that they can be easily placed under cover at night, or by day in the event of rain.

They store best if picking is delayed until some of the nuts begin to fall.

For winter storage, the dried husks should be removed and the nuts stored in boxes or any other receptacles in which mice, rats or squirrels are unable to get at them, and where they will be safe from frost.

Preparing for Table. If nuts are heaped on a fruit dish, no preparation is needed other than the provision of one or more pairs of nut-crackers. Food value is very considerable, as vegetarians are well aware. Nuts are especially rich in fats and proteins, and also contain some starch and sugar.

PEACH (AND NECTARINE)

Peaches (Fig. 396) and nectarines are not hardy fruits, in that the trees will not thrive in a bleak district. But given a milder locality good crops of outdoor varieties can be ripened on a south-facing wall fully exposed to sun—unshaded by buildings or trees—sheltered from cold winds and draughts. The wall needs to be not less than 6 ft. high. If no garden-dividing wall of this description is available, a house wall, facing south, might well be made profitable and beautiful with a fan-trained peach or nectarine tree.

A sunny greenhouse whose front glass could be given up entirely to a fan-trained tree would also ripen plenty of fruit. Peaches and nectarines can be purchased as small pot trees, of fruiting size, for the greenhouse where the larger and more profitable fan-shape cannot be accommodated. Details of pot-tree culture are explained in full detail in the section FRUIT IN THE GREENHOUSE (page 466).

The outdoor ripening season of peach and nectarine varies between mid-July and late September, according to variety, locality and weather. Ripening in an unheated greenhouse is a little in advance of outdoor dates.

Varieties of peach for the sunny wall outdoors include Duke of York (ripe in mid-July), Peregrine (early August), Dymond (early September), Sea Eagle (late September). Duke of York and Peregrine are also suitable for the greenhouse.

Varieties of nectarine are given under Nectarine (page 516). The culture is the same as for peach.

Soil Preparation. Like all the stone fruits, these trees should have plenty of lime in the soil. If the ground is not naturally chalky, crushed chalk or old mortar rubble should be dug into the planting site. The border, or bed, for one tree should be at least 6 ft. long and 3 ft. wide, and be dug not less than 2 ft. deep. If the soil is poor, rotted manure should be mixed in; if heavy, it should be lightened with mortar rubble, charred woody pieces from the garden bonfire, sand or sharp grit, worked in throughout the full dug depth. A generous dressing of slaked or hydrated lime should be given to the surface of the border during every subsequent winter.

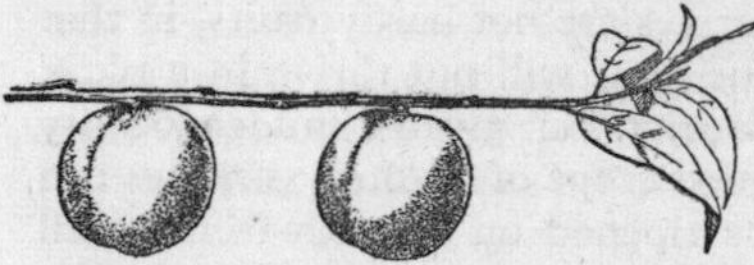

Fig. 396.—*A vigorous peach tree may carry two fruits per side shoot. A younger tree should have the fruits reduced to one per shoot*

When and How to Plant. A fan-trained tree needs 18 ft. of space, and planting should be done in autumn as soon as possible after the leaves have fallen. Roots should be spread out carefully in the planting hole, and they should be covered to the depth indicated by the soil mark on the tree's stem. The base of the stem should be 4 in. to 5 in. out from the wall, to allow of future swelling, and the tree must be left very firm in the ground; soil being consolidated around and above the covered-in roots by treading, the top inch to be left loose.

Training. Wooden trellis, or wires, should be fixed to the wall so that main branches and other growths of the fan tree can be tied back and spaced neatly. Immediately after planting the main branches should be tied only lightly to the supports, to allow of the tree sinking with the soil until the latter has finally settled down after the deep digging.

Method of Fruiting. The fruit is produced on young side shoots (referred to technically as laterals or breastwood) (Fig. 397). These are cut away after the fruit has been gathered, and shoots produced the same summer are tied back for fruiting the following summer. The ideal arrangement is to have these spaced at intervals of about 1 ft. along the length of each branch. They should be looped with raffia to their own branch and parallel with it, or be tied back to wire or trellis in the gaps between branches.

The Tree in Flower. Blossoms appear before the leaves, and the side shoots are as a rule thickly studded with them. The fruit that follows will need to be thinned out

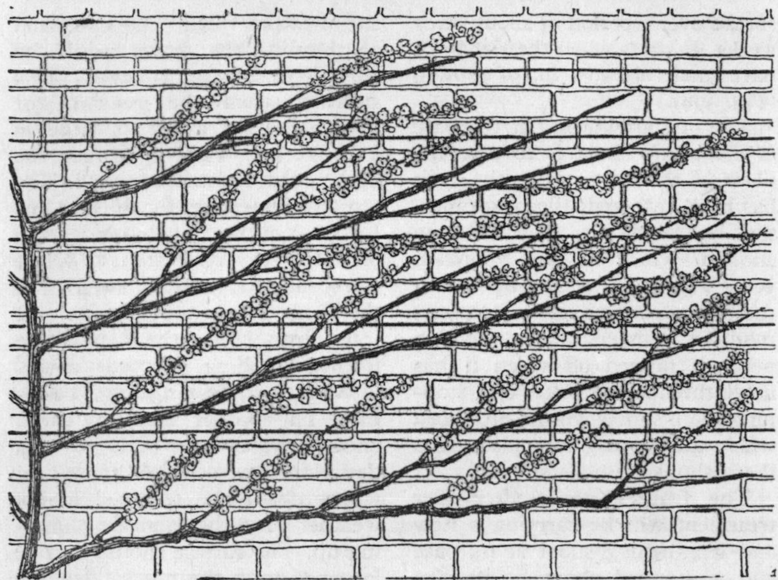

Fig. 397.—*Young side shoots (laterals, or breastwood) of the peach, shown here studded with blossom, produce the fruit. Note how evenly the growths are spaced. Here they are tied back to wires against a wall*

drastically later on, but the immediate object at flowering time is to get the blossom fertilized so that plenty of fruit shall set. Peach and nectarine are self-fertile; the fruit sets without requiring pollen from a different variety.

Normally, bees and other insects effect the transference of pollen from flower to flower. But to make quite certain this job is done, the grower should rub the fully open flowers gently with a wad of fluffy cotton-wool, or a rabbit's tail, tied to the end of a stick—this being carried out on dry days, preferably when the sun is shining, from the opening of the first flowers to the falling of the petals.

Night frosts may injure the blossom. To prevent this it is customary to hang old fish netting or muslin from the wall top down the front of the tree to the ground; the material to be far enough from the front of the tree to keep it from rubbing the flowers. The covering should be removed by day, in the absence of frost, to allow bees and other insects easy access to the blossom.

Thinning the Shoots. After the flowers come the leaves. As well as flower buds, leaf buds stud the side shoots thickly. These would cause very considerable crowding unless most of them were removed. Only two leaf buds should be left to each side shoot, one at the shoot's base, another at the shoot's tip. The others are rubbed off, one or two at a time from each side shoot, the operation, known as disbudding, being spread over a period of about three weeks. It starts when the leaf buds have made about 1 in. of growth (Fig. 398).

The one growth left at the base of a fruiting shoot is to take the place of the latter when the fruit has been gathered; the newcomer, tied in neatly as soon as long enough, will fruit the following year. The shoot at the tip is left there to draw up sap; it is not required to extend, so its growing point is nipped off when it has made three leaves. After that stopping more shoots will be produced where the nipping took place, and these should also be stopped.

The fruiting shoot after that treatment will be carrying a new and lengthening shoot at its base and a stopped shoot at its tip, with several fruits between those extremes. It will send out intermediate shoots, and these must be shortened back to one leaf each. The new shoot at the base should be allowed to extend, but not beyond about 20 in.; if it exceeds that length the tip should be nipped off, and any side shoots it may produce after that stopping should be nipped back to one leaf.

Any shoots produced in awkward positions—growing outwards from the front of the tree instead of from the sides of branches—should be rubbed off when quite small. Shoots needed to fill gaps or to extend branches should be allowed to grow on.

Thinning the Fruits. Overcropping has a very weakening effect on the tree. The grower should be satisfied with one well-ripened fruit on each second-year shoot—that is, one to each side shoot that was allowed to remain the previous year. The operation of thinning the fruits should be spread over six or seven days, starting when the peaches (or nectarines) are about as large as a hedge nut. First to go are the undersized and the crowded. The remainder—except for the best one (or two) on the shoot—are picked off after they have stoned. While the stones are forming, swelling of the fruit temporarily ceases and some drop. When the stones have formed swelling proceeds apace.

Watering, Syringeing, Feeding. The border must be given enough water at a time to soak down to the roots. A great deal will probably be required in hot weather when the fruits are plumping up. The surface should first be loosened with the hoe so that the moisture runs in easily.

The foliage should be syringed morning and afternoon on bright days, with sun-warmed clean water, to encourage growth and keep down red spider. The water must be quite clean; if there is chalk or lime sediment in it a deposit will be left on the fruit. This disfigurement can be washed from nectarines, but not from the woolly skin of a peach.

The tree that is fruiting satisfactorily can do with the assistance of weak liquid manure poured on to the soil once a week from the time the fruits begin to swell. Or one of the special fruit tree artificial fertilizer mixtures may be used.

Wasps and Other Troubles. Wasps find ripening peaches and nectarines an irresistible attraction. These should be fought at their home base, as explained in the chart Remedies Against Enemies of Fruit Crops (page 564). Red spider, which sucks sap from the

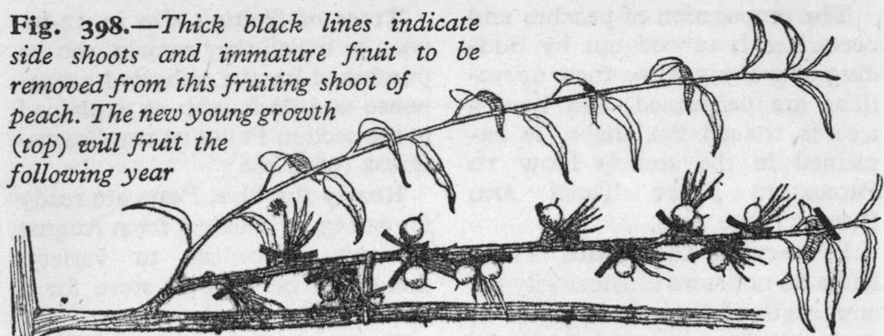

Fig. 398.—*Thick black lines indicate side shoots and immature fruit to be removed from this fruiting shoot of peach. The new young growth (top) will fruit the following year*

undersides of leaves, can be kept down by regular syringeing. If black- or green-fly put in an appearance, quassia solution sprayed as a fine, penetrating shower over the foliage, on two successive days when the sun is off the tree, will effect a clearance; but this should not be used after the fruit is any size.

A silvering of the foliage may occur on a branch. This is a sign of the destructive silver-leaf disease. It should be dealt with as explained under Plum (page 530). A blistering of the leaves may follow cold winds or cutting draughts; hence the need for a really sheltered and warm position.

Gathering the Fruit. Individual fruits may be hindered from ripening by leaves that shade them. If the removal of one or two such leaves does not expose the peach or nectarine sufficiently, it should be brought to the right position by means of a short, smooth piece of wood passed behind the shoot so that this is pushed forward. Or the purpose may perhaps be served by tying a shade-casting shoot a little more to one side.

Depth of colouring is one guide as to condition. If there is any doubt the fruit should be very gently pressed at the stalk end. If it feels hard there the fruit should be left on the tree a little longer, until the stalk end softens. If it is perfectly ripe the fruit will come away from its stalk quite easily.

This handling must not be overdone. The bloom is very easily removed from the fruit, and the latter's appearance spoiled. Also the skin bruises only too readily.

Pruning After Fruiting. When the fruit is all gone from the tree the side shoots which carried the fruit can go, too. Each should be cut out, with a very sharp knife or with keen-edged secateurs, just short of the point where the new shoot, which is to fruit next year, at its base originates.

These new shoots will complete their hardening or ripening under the influence of sun, to the great benefit of the fruit-to-be. They should be tied—none crossing—where most convenient, loosely back to the trellis or wire or to the branch bearing them.

Syringeing should be continued, vigorously, after the fruit has been gathered, until all the leaves have fallen.

The correct use of knife and secateurs as pruning tools is explained under THE HOW AND WHY OF FRUIT PRUNING (page 432).

The propagation of peaches and nectarines is carried out by budding or grafting. How these operations are performed, and how a tree is trained fan shape, is explained in the section HOW TO PROPAGATE FRUIT TREES AND BUSHES (page 444).

Preserving the Fruit. These fruits do not store satisfactorily for any length of time. It is better to deal with them as explained in the section EASY HOME PRESERVATION OF FRUITS (page 565).

Preparing for Table. With the minimum of handling the fruit for dessert should be placed on a dish lined with virginia creeper or other attractive leaves. Peaches and nectarines are mildly laxative, and of value in the diet of those suffering from diabetes.

PEAR

A standard pear tree takes up rather a lot of room and is not too eager to embark on its fruiting career, though when it does so the size of the crop continues to increase with passing years. Better suited to the small garden are pears in cordon form. Single stemmed, these can be planted 2 ft. apart against any sunny fence or wall; or against horizontal wires strained between end posts in the open; alongside a path is an excellent position for them. They come into bearing quickly and their fruit is of the largest size and best quality.

Also useful for the small garden is the espalier-trained tree, with horizontal wires to support the tiers of horizontal branches. These, too, fruit speedily and heavily. Planted in line they should be 10 ft. apart. Dwarf bush trees, at the same distance, are as profitable.

Trees of fruiting size in 12-in. pots, in which they remain, can be purchased for the unheated greenhouse and dealt with as explained in the section FRUIT IN THE GREENHOUSE (page 466).

Ready for Use. Pears are ready for eating, or cooking, from August onwards, according to variety. Some can be kept in store for a considerable period.

Varieties. Dessert pears include Laxton's Superb, ripe in August, its only drawback being that it will not keep; Williams' Bon Chrétien, in September, to be picked before it becomes yellow and allowed to ripen indoors; Conference, ready October to November, one of the easiest to grow and most satisfactory in all ways; Emile D'Heyst, October to November, easy to grow on practically any soil; Louise Bonne of Jersey, a big fruiter and regular cropper, ripe in October; Winter Nelis, which starts to ripen in November and will store to January or later; Josephine de Malines, starting to ripen in December and on to January in store.

Cooking varieties include Fertility, September to October; Catillac, October till April; Vicar of Winkfield, November to January. These all carry heavy crops.

Pollination. Most pears require to be fertilized by the pollen from a different variety—they are self-sterile. It is therefore advisable to plant two different kinds, unless there are other pear trees in the near neighbourhood.

Self-fertile varieties (set fruit with their own pollen) in the foregoing list are Conference, Laxton's Superb, Louise Bonne of Jersey, Williams' Bon Chrétien.

Bees can be assisted to spread the fertilizing pollen by the grower using a tuft of dry cotton-wool or a rabbit's tail tied to the end of a stick. This is fluffed over the fully open flowers on successive days when the atmosphere is dry and the sun shining.

Soil Preparation. Pears are not faddy as to soil, so long as it is not waterlogged in winter. The ground should be dug 2 ft. deep and the soil below that broken up. If the subsoil is heavy it can be lightened and made more porous by mixing with it plenty of sand or sharp grit. Some old manure may be worked into the top 6 in. if the soil is poor, but too rich ground causes over-vigorous growth, which results in unfruitfulness.

When and How to Plant. Roots should be spread out horizontally at the levels they have naturally taken, in an ample planting hole, and fine soil worked between and under them with the fingers. When the roots are covered, to the depth indicated by the soil mark on the stem, the soil should be made firm by treading. Cordons should be planted with the stem base about 4 in. out from the fence or wall.

Trees should be got in as soon as possible after leaf-fall, or during mild weather up to March.

Planting details are fully explained in the section ABC OF FRUIT PLANTING (page 425).

Watering and Feeding. At least a bucketful of water should be given to young trees, whatever their form, whenever necessary in dry weather. A surface covering of quite old manure, or hop manure, leaf-mould, or lawn mowings, will serve to keep the shallow roots cool and the surface moist in hot weather.

Feeding should be postponed until trees are in bearing. Weak liquid manure given once a week from the time the fruit starts to swell will have considerable influence on the crop; or a fruit tree mixed fertilizer can be used, according to directions accompanying it.

Birds, Wasps, Other Troubles. Birds and wasps will go for the choicest fruit when it begins to ripen. If birds cannot be scared away, they can be kept from the fruit by covering this with muslin draped loosely over the espalier or dwarf bush tree or cordon. Wasps should be tracked to their nests and there killed *en masse,* as explained in the chart Remedies Against Enemies of Fruit Crops (page 564). Remedies are also given there for the scabbed and cracked fruit trouble, and for scale on shoots and branches. Pear midge is dealt with under Thinning the Fruits (page 526).

Unfruitful Trees. Lack of fruit may be due to youthfulness, or to incomplete pollination (dealt with above), or to excessive wood growth. The latter is frequently the result of planting in too rich soil, or feeding the tree before the fruiting habit has been formed; the remedy is root pruning. This operation is fully explained in the section THE HOW AND WHY OF FRUIT PRUNING (page 432).

Summer and Winter Pruning. The fruits are produced on spurs on the old wood, and the spurs themselves are produced very abundantly. A well-managed cordon, espalier or other form of pear tree will be thick—but not too thick—with fruiting spurs. Pruning is simple enough. Side shoots are cut back by half their length in summer (August) and then shortened in winter so that they are left as stumps each with two buds; these become fruiting spurs.

Ends of main branches of a bush tree are shortened in winter by about one-third of the past summer's growth. A cordon is allowed to prolong itself by about two-thirds of its current season's growth each year, until it has reached any height desired; the tip is then treated as a spur. An espalier is treated similarly. If another tier of horizontal branches is required they are formed as explained in the section HOW TO PROPAGATE FRUIT TREES AND BUSHES (page 444).

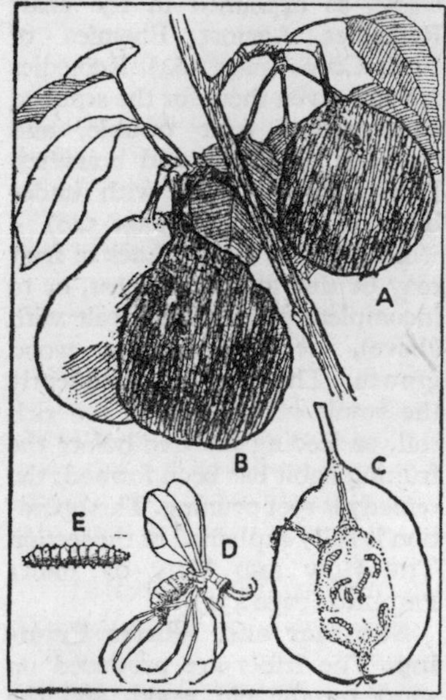

Fig. 399.—*Pears* (A, B, C) *attacked by grubs of the pear midge* (D), *and grub* (E), *both enlarged*

Shoots produced by the fruiting spurs are summer shortened by about one-half, and in winter cut back to within two buds of their base. When spurs become too long, and crowded with fruit buds and leaf buds, it is time to shorten them by cutting away half their length in winter.

A standard pear grown so tall that the fruit is difficult to get at can have some of its head removed in winter. Other than that, little if any pruning is required.

Operations are explained in full detail in the section THE HOW AND WHY OF FRUIT PRUNING (page 432).

Propagation. Pear trees are increased by budding or grafting desired varieties on to special stocks. Methods are explained in the section HOW TO PROPAGATE FRUIT TREES AND BUSHES (page 444). How young trees are formed to any desired shape is also explained there.

Thinning the Fruits. A too heavy crop one year may be followed by scarcity of pears the next year. To avoid this, and to increase the size and quality of individual fruits, some thinning must be done. Some of the pears will drop off when quite small, the tree being unable to carry them all. Some will fall, in June, as the result of attack by grubs of the pear midge if this pest happens to be in the locality.

Thinning should be deferred until this dropping is over, which is usually about the end of June. If extra-special fruit is required, dessert varieties should be left with one pear where there was a cluster of them; cookers can remain a bit closer. The fruit that is left on the tree to ripen should be the best-shaped and the healthiest.

The presence in any pear of midge grubs is indicated by discoloured patches, by over-early swelling and irregular shape (Fig. 399). These signs should be looked for, and the affected fruit picked off during the thinning and burned. All fallen pears not fit for use should also be burned, to ensure the destruction of any grubs that might be in them. Grubs wriggle out of the attacked fruit when this is on the ground and bury themselves in the earth, there to undergo the transformation to adult midge flies. These should be dealt with by cleaning the soil at the foot of trees as explained at page 559.

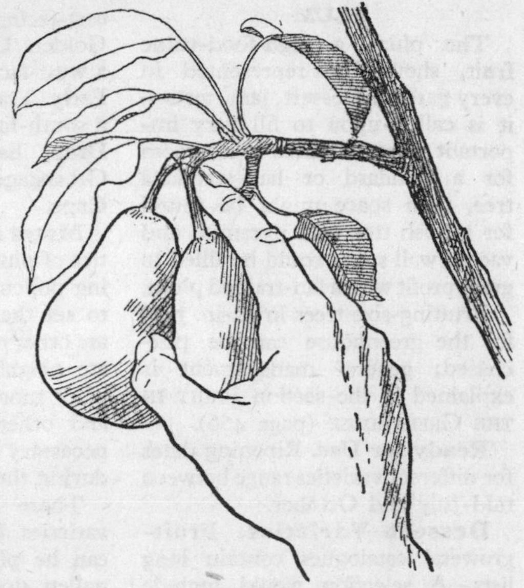

Fig. 400.—*A pear is ready for taking when it comes away at gentle pressure at the upper end of the stalk. Tugging may break the spur*

Gathering the Fruit. Varieties that naturally ripen late should be gathered late; quality is adversely affected if they are picked too soon. Ripening will be completed in the store. Varieties that ripen earlier, on the tree, are ready for immediate gathering (Fig. 400) when the fruit comes away almost at a touch, or gentle pressure at the spur end of the pear's stalk. Bruised fruit will not keep. Gathering should therefore be carried out with care.

Storing for Winter. A damp storage place is bad for pears, and they must be safe from frost. The store should be airy, and preferably dark, and the pears laid out singly—not in layers. Late varieties will ripen, according to their class, a few at a time, and they must be watched; the psychological moment can be determined by feel. Often there is only a borderline of a day or two between a fully-ripe pear and an over-ripe one.

Pears can be preserved as explained at pages 565–566.

Preparing for Table. Dessert pears should be carefully wiped and polished with a soft clean cloth. The fruit is advised by doctors in cases of constipation, gout, dyspepsia, anæmia; it should be eaten ripe.

PHENOMENAL BERRY

The berries of this cane fruit resemble those of the loganberry, but the crop per plant is smaller. Canes should be planted 7 ft. to 8 ft. apart. Treatment is as advised under Loganberry (page 507).

PLUM

The plum, a high-food-value fruit, should be represented in every garden. Dessert, jam, tarts—it is called upon to fill very important roles. If there is no room for a standard or half-standard tree, then space might be found for a bush tree or a pyramid, and vacant wall space could be filled to great profit with a fan-trained plum.

Fruiting-size trees in 12-in. pots for the greenhouse can be purchased; general management is explained in the section FRUIT IN THE GREENHOUSE (page 466).

Ready for Use. Ripening dates for different varieties range between mid-July and October.

Dessert Varieties. Fruit-growers' catalogues contain long lists. A selection would include Early Laxton, excellent also for cooking, and the earliest to ripen—in mid-July; Oullin's Golden Gage, early August; Purple Pershore, mid-August, useful also for cooking; Denniston's Superb Gage, mid-August; Early Transparent Gage, August; Greengage, excellent also for preserving, late August; the famous old favourite and always dependable Victoria, giving immense crops as useful for cooking as for dessert and ripe in early September; Coe's Golden Drop, October.

Cooking Varieties. These include Czar, mid-August; Belle de Louvain, late August; Pershore Yellow, August to September; Monarch, for dessert also, late September.

Wall Plums. Grown as fan-trained trees against a north-facing wall the following give magnificent fruit: Czar, Victoria, Monarch, Oullin's Golden Gage. Against an east-facing wall: Victoria, Coe's Golden Drop, Monarch. Against a west-facing wall: Czar, Victoria, Early Transparent Gage. Against a south-facing wall: Coe's Golden Drop, Early Transparent Gage, Greengage, Denniston's Superb Gage.

Mates for Plums. Many varieties of plum are self-sterile, requiring pollen from a different variety to set their fruit. So unless there are other plum trees in the immediate neighbourhood it is safest to plant more than one variety; bees and other insects will effect the necessary transference of pollen during their busy rounds.

There are, however, certain varieties that are self-fertile and can be planted singly; their own pollen does all that is required. This applies to most of those in the foregoing lists. The self-fertile ones include Early Transparent Gage, Oullin's Golden Gage, Denniston's Superb, Purple Pershore, Pershore Yellow, Victoria, Czar, Belle de Louvain, Monarch.

Soil Preparation. A chief requirement is sufficient lime in some form. If this is lacking it should be worked into the ground as broken chalk, or mortar rubble, or slaked or hydrated lime. Ground inclined to lie wet in winter needs to be dug at least 2 ft. deep over as large an area as is practicable for one or more trees, and plenty of mortar rubble or broken chalk, and sand or grit worked deeply into it. This will improve the drainage and provide the necessary lime; or the latter can be added as slaked or hydrated lime.

If the ground is sandy or gravelly it must be given body by the addition, during deep digging, of

Fig. 401.—*Plums are borne on spurs (left), produced by old wood, and on short semi-ripened shoots (right) of the previous summer's growth*

quite rotted manure or plenty of thoroughly decayed greenstuff from the garden refuse heap. And lime must be added—not dug in with the manure, but forked shallowly into the surface.

When and How to Plant. The dead of winter is not a good time to plant a plum tree. The best time is late October or early November; the next best, February. The soil mark on the stem should be taken as a guide to planting depth, the spread-out roots being covered with well-broken soil and this trodden well around and above them. A fan-trained tree needs to have its base about 4 in. out from the wall, and the branches should be tied only loosely to the support until the disturbed soil has settled thoroughly. Branches can be secured back to the wall with strips of sacking and nails; or horizontal wires, or wooden trellis, can be fixed to the wall to make training a neater job. Standard or half-standard trees will need staking. Standards should be 18 ft. apart, half-standards 15 ft., pyramid and bush trees 10 ft., fan-trained trees arranged in line 15 ft. apart.

Full working details are given in the section ABC OF FRUIT PLANTING (page 425).

Watering and Feeding. A mature standard or half-standard plum will get along without watering, even in the driest spells. But the crop will be improved if a 2-in.-thick layer of old manure, or a similar thickness of lawn mowings or dead weeds, is put down on the surface as a mulch, the material to be made sodden either before it goes down or immediately afterwards. Weeds should first be removed and the surface broken with the hoe.

The manure mulch will provide welcome additional food. In the absence of manure, a special plum tree artificial fertilizer mixture may be given in spring and watered in, but only to trees that have reached the fruiting stage.

Trees against walls may suffer seriously in the absence of rain, the position being a naturally dry one. Water must be given to them plentifully and as regularly as it is required, or many plums will drop. Feeding is specially beneficial when a good plum crop is being carried.

The plums are borne on spurs produced by old wood, also on short shoots of the previous summer's growth (Fig. 401).

Pruning. When the framework of the tree has been made, as explained in the section HOW TO PROPAGATE FRUIT TREES AND BUSHES (page 444), and is giving crops, only a little pruning is needed, and this should be done, so far as is possible, during summer—by the rubbing off of unwanted young shoots (badly placed, or likely to lead to crowding) and by shortening back longer shoots by pinching them between thumbnail and first finger-nail. Knife or secateurs should be used as little as possible.

End shoots of the main branches of a bush tree or pyramid should be nipped back, during July or August, so that the current season's extension growth is left with five or six leaves only—that is, about one-third of the current season's extension growth is removed in each case.

A fan-trained tree should have the longer side shoots nipped back in summer so that these are left about five leaves long, and the extension growths (branch ends) shortened by about one-third. Shoots springing from the front of the branches should be rubbed off when quite small.

Sucker growths sometimes spring up from the ground at a considerable distance from a plum tree. These shoots arise from the tree's roots and are robbing it of nourishment. They should be removed, by scraping away the soil around them until their junction with the roots is exposed and then paring them off closely at that point.

General pruning methods are explained in the section THE HOW AND WHY OF PRUNING (page 432).

Silver-leaf Disease. This disease, which attacks other fruit trees as well as the plum, causes foliage to assume a silvery colour. The death of the branch follows. Only one branch, or part of a branch, may be affected at first. But the trouble soon spreads, and it is of such a serious nature that the law requires all diseased or dead wood to be cut back to healthy tissue and promptly burned, on the spot.

The sawing-out of unnecessary branches, alive or dead, should be done in June, because then there are fewer of the silver-leaf disease spores about to gain lodgment in the cut surfaces of healthy wood; in that month the disease is at its lowest ebb.

Cut surfaces should at once be covered with any thick, tacky paint, to exclude any spores that may be about. Any ordinary pruning, such as can be done with knife or secateurs, should be carried out not later than September, and all prunings burned.

It is from dead wood that the silver-leaf disease spreads to live shoots and branches, and shoots or branches showing the ominous sign of silvery foliage instead of healthy green must not be left to die. They must be cut out promptly and burned, and thick paint applied to the cut face of the healthy wood that remains (Fig. 402).

The Too-vigorous Plum Tree. A young tree sometimed produces far too much, or too strong, wood growth. The result is that it fails to fruit, or bears but a very small crop. This excessive growth may

Fig. 402.—*A plum branch attacked by silver-leaf disease should be removed as shown at* (A) *and the cut surface sealed over with thick paint* (B)

be caused by too rich soil, over-feeding, or feeding before the fruiting habit has been properly formed, or by a too loose root-run. The remedy is to prune the roots, as explained in the section THE HOW AND WHY OF FRUIT PRUNING (page 432). The check thus given induces the formation of fruiting wood and lessens the production of mere wood growth.

Propagation. Plum trees are increased by budding or grafting chosen varieties on to specially selected stocks. How this is done, and young trees trained to the desired form or shape, is explained in the section HOW TO PROPAGATE FRUIT TREES AND BUSHES (page 444).

Insect Pests. A general clearance of pests can be made by spraying the trees with a tar-oil winter wash, any time between early December and late January, 1 pint of the wash to each 2 gal. of water. This clears stems and branches of hibernating insects, insects' eggs, moss and lichen. In the case of wall plums the spraying should be done before the end of the year, the buds generally being in a more advanced stage in that sheltered position than on trees in the open. This treatment is to be carried out only when the buds are completely dormant, or they will be injured.

Trees that were attacked by red spider during summer should be sprayed the following spring, after the petals have fallen from the flowers, with lime-sulphur solution, $\frac{1}{4}$ pint of the lime-sulphur to 3 gal. of water.

How these sprayings are carried out is explained in the section HOW TO DEAL WITH FRUIT PESTS AND DISEASES (page 551).

Thinning the Fruits. Plum clusters within reach are all the better for thinning out. If best-quality fruit is wanted the plums should remain not closer than about 2 in. apart. If the grower of choice dessert plums is satisfied with something less than the best the clusters should be thinned out so that, at the very least, no two plums touch one another.

If bulk is the main consideration clusters may be left somewhat thicker, but it must be remembered that a very heavy crop one year nearly always demands its price the next. That price is a next-year crop as small as its immediate predecessor was large.

Even after a moderate thinning the branches of some varieties of plum—the more straggly growing standards and half-standards—may be so weighted down with fruit that some support is necessary. These bowed-down branches should be held up with notched props placed in position before—not after—bark cracks (Fig. 403).

Weighted shoots that cannot be thus propped should be supported in some other way. Generally it is possible to tie them to canes or stakes secured to adjoining branches; or thick string or tarred twine can be passed from branch to branch and the too-heavy shoots looped to these lines (Fig. 404).

Plum wood is brittle and surprisingly ready to break (Fig. 403).

Gathering the Fruit. Harvesting plums is a dry-weather job, less for the comfort of the picker than for the sake of the fruit, especially if this is to be kept for any length of time.

To expedite the work, cooking varieties might be shaken from the branches. But their value is lessened by rough treatment, and careful picking from a pair of steps, or from a ladder (the top part padded with sacking to avoid injuring bark where the ladder rests), has its own reward.

Dessert varieties should always be hand picked, and so that the attractive bloom shall not be rubbed from the skins they should be handled by the stalks only.

Storing for Winter. Some late varieties, such as Coe's Golden Drop, keep well if put away dry in a dry and sunless room or other place, in shallow boxes, single layers if possible. None should be over-ripe and all should be thoroughly sound. They must be watched for signs of decay.

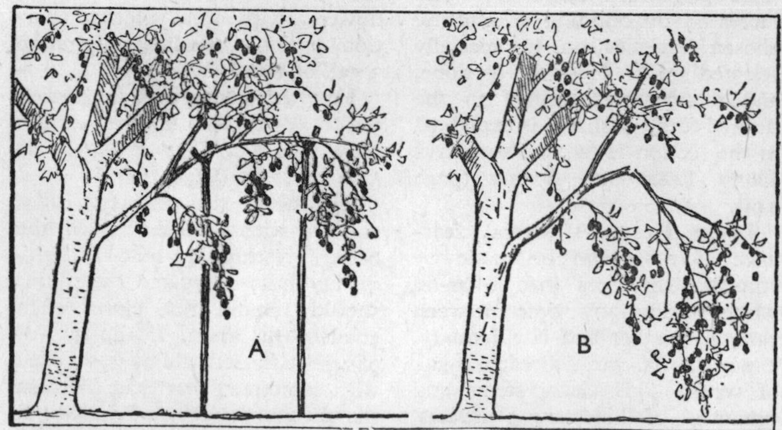

Fig. 403.—*Branches heavily laden with plums should be propped up* (A) *before the bark cracks, to prevent breakage* (B)—*a common occurrence*

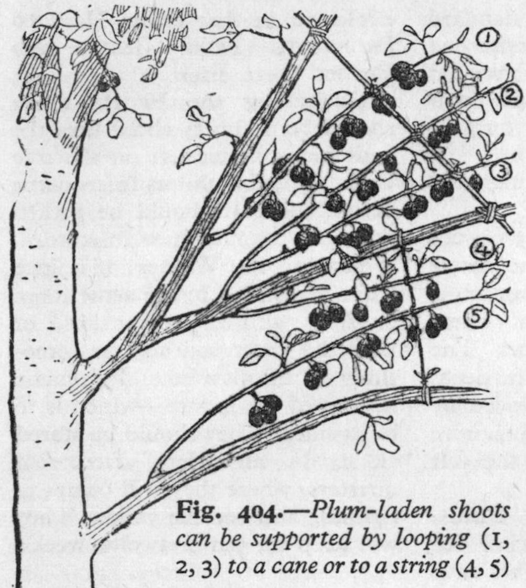

Fig. 404.—*Plum-laden shoots can be supported by looping* (1, 2, 3) *to a cane or to a string* (4, 5)

Plums can also be dealt with as explained in the section EASY HOME PRESERVATION OF FRUITS (page 565).

Preparing for Table. Plums for dessert should retain their stalks and be placed on a leaf-lined fruit dish. Their attractive appearance depends largely on the bloom on their skins; this should not be spoiled by hurried, last-minute handling. Their food value is considerable and they have a laxative effect. They should not be eaten raw when over-ripe—a warning too often disregarded, especially with regard to greengages—and it is well to remember that the uncooked skins are by no means easily digestible.

QUINCE

The fruit of the most commonly grown variety of the quince (Fig. 405) might be mistaken at first glance for a pear, of which the quince is a close relative. It is yellow when ripe, aromatic, and has a very distinctive flavour. Too bitter for eating raw or for cooking by itself, it is used for flavouring apple tarts and stewed apples — one quince (grated) to half a dozen apples—and for making jelly and jam. The fruit should be stored by itself, for reasons explained on page 534.

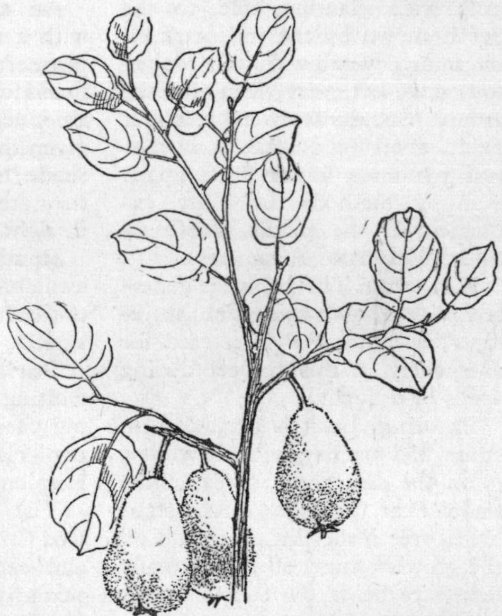

Fig. 405.—*Quince fruits are used for flavouring apple tarts and stewed apples, and for jelly and jam. They are too bitter for eating raw*

The tree is grown as a standard (reaching about 12 ft. in height) and in pyramid and bush form. Varieties include Pear-shaped (most commonly grown), Portugal, Smyrna and Vranja.

Ready for Use. November, and onwards in store.

Soil Preparation. The quince is not over-particular in the matter of soil, though if the ground is light it will need abundant watering in dry growing weather. The position should be dug 2 ft. deep, and light soil can be improved by the addition of some rotted manure or decayed material from the soft rubbish heap.

When and How to Plant. Autumn is the best period for planting, soon after the leaves have fallen. Roots should be spread out in a wide planting hole, to the depth shown by the soil mark on the stem, covered with well-broken soil and left very firm in the ground. Standards should be about 12 ft. apart (and staked), bushes and pyramids about 8 ft. apart. Planting methods are fully explained in the section ABC OF FRUIT PLANTING (page 425).

Watering. The quince is generally credited with being a moisture-lover; it crops well if catered for adequately in this respect during spells of drought.

Pruning. Fruit is produced on spurs, and pruning, in early winter, is on the same lines as explained under Pear (page 525). An established tree makes little demand on the grower's time, all that is really necessary being the shortening or cutting out of crowded growths.

Propagation. Increase is by budding or grafting, or by layers or cuttings. These operations are explained in the section HOW TO PROPAGATE FRUIT TREES AND BUSHES (page 444).

Gathering the Fruit. There should be no hurry about this, the fruit being better left on the tree until November unless frosts occur before then. It should be picked on a dry day, to ripen in store.

Storing for Winter. If quince fruits are stored in the same room or shed with any other kind of fruit the latter will acquire something of the flavour and aromatic quality of the quince—which is to be avoided. They should be stored alone, in any dark, frostproof quarters, where they will complete ripening and become yellow. They will keep for ten or twelve weeks.

RASPBERRY

An altogether delightful fruit, with a refreshingly acid taste, the raspberry (Fig. 406) is always in demand for dessert, jam and tarts. The chief need of the plants is moisture; given that they crop heavily. Some shade is not objected to; indeed, they are the better for it if planted in light and naturally thirsty soil.

Ready for Use. Ripe fruits are available from late July onwards, until frost comes, according to variety and weather.

Varieties. There are autumn-fruiting as well as summer-fruiting varieties, and treatment of the two classes differs as explained later under pruning.

The summer fruiters include Red Cross, one of the most reliable, and early; Lloyd George, a particularly strong grower; Norfolk Giant, a very heavy cropper, specially suitable for preserving; Pyne's Royal, big berries excellent for dessert. These are all red fruited. Yellow varieties include Yellow Antwerp, Magnum Bonum, Lord Lambourne.

The autumn fruiters include Hailsham, big, sweet and a heavy cropper; October Red; November Abundance; Queen Alexandra. These are all red. A good yellow variety is October Yellow.

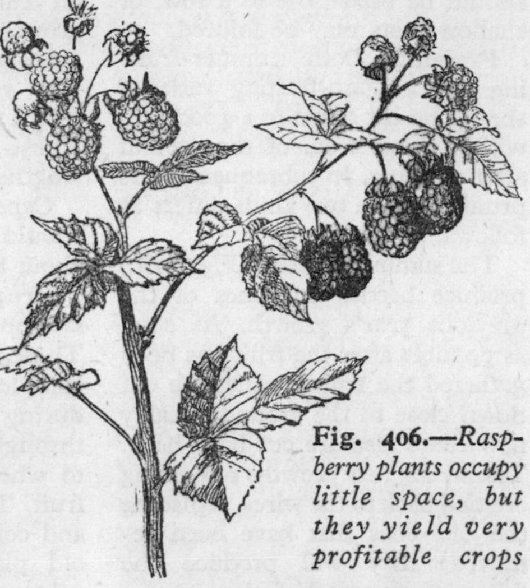

Fig. 406.—*Raspberry plants occupy little space, but they yield very profitable crops*

Soil Preparation. The site of a row should be prepared by digging a yard-wide strip 18 in. deep, working in old stable or farmyard manure or hop manure or rotted greenstuff into the top 9 in. (not deeper, the raspberry being a shallow-rooting plant) if the soil is poor and light.

If the ground is very heavy it should be lightened by digging in plenty of sand, sharp grit, or charred woody material from the garden bonfire, and strawy manure if available.

When and How to Plant. October is the most suitable period, but planting may be done up to March in the absence of frost and when the ground is not too wet.

Rows should run north and south, if possible, to ensure both sides of each row receiving maximum sun. The quickest method is to take out a continuous trench, spade-blade wide and about 6 in. deep. Roots are placed about 1½ ft. apart in the shallow trench, and covered with the excavated soil, this then being made firm by treading (Fig. 407). The rows should be about 5 ft. apart.

Wires strained between end posts should be provided for support, lower wire 2 ft. from the ground, upper wire 4 ft. The canes (shoots) can then be spaced out evenly and tied securely.

Watering and Feeding. As size and quality of the crop depend largely on an adequate water supply, rows should be soaked thoroughly once a week in dry weather from spring onwards. A layer of old manure, or hop manure, put down wet over the area occupied by roots, will supply extra nourishment and help to retain moisture down below. Or lawn mowings or any rough cut grass can be used, not as a food but to prevent the shallow roots being dried in hot weather.

Food can be given through the grass mulch in the form of liquid manure made with one of the general-purpose artificial fertilizers, this feeding to start from the time the berries begin to swell.

Weeds should be hand picked or hoed up. Neither fork nor spade should be used close to a row, or shallow roots may be injured.

Pruning. Both summer-fruiting and autumn-fruiting varieties should be cut down to a good bud within about 6 in. of the ground after planting. In subsequent years pruning of the two kinds differs as follows.

The summer fruiters (Fig. 408C) produce berries on canes of the previous year's growth. As soon as possible after the fruit has been gathered the fruited canes are cut down close to the ground; weakly new canes also are cut hard back. The strong new growths remaining are tied back to the wires, replacing the old ones that have been removed; they will produce the following summer's fruit.

The autumn-fruiting varieties (Fig. 408D) produce their berries on canes of the current year's growth, and each February *all* canes are cut to near ground level. The roots throw up new canes which will bear fruit in the autumn. These are tied to the wires as they lengthen.

Canes of established plants should be thinned out yearly to about 8 in. apart in the row.

Propagation. Sucker growths are thrown up freely between rows. These can be dug up with a spade, complete with their own roots, during October and onwards through winter, and transplanted to where they are to remain and fruit. This is a particularly easy—and costless—method of replacing old plants which show signs of exhaustion. But suckers should be taken only from thoroughly healthy plants. To propagate from any

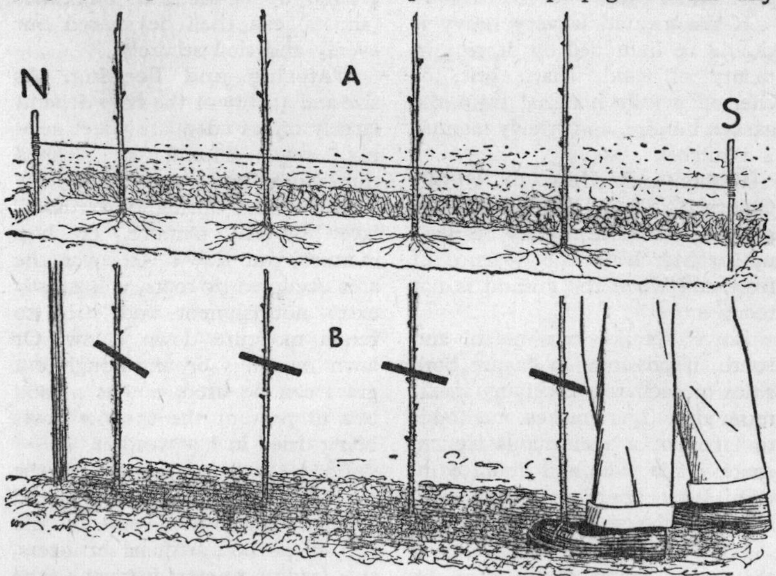

Fig. 407.—*Raspberry canes planted in a shallow trench, running north-south* (A), *and the soil made firm above the roots by treading* (B). *The black lines indicate points of cutting-back, immediately after planting*

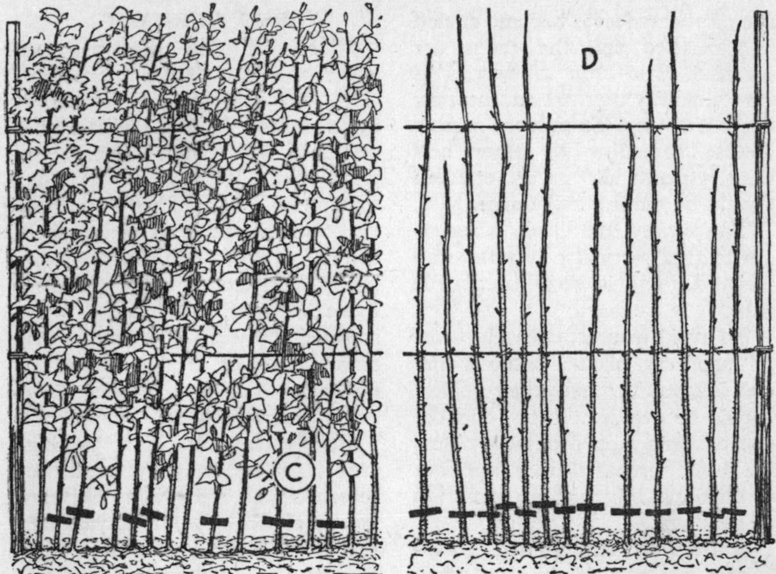

Fig. 408.—*Summer-fruiting varieties of raspberry should have the fruited canes removed as shown by lines* (C) *after the fruit has been taken. Autumn fruiting varieties should have all canes cut down* (D) *each February*

unhealthy plants is to propagate trouble.

Maggoty Berries. Grubs of small beetles (the raspberry beetle) sometimes infest the fruit. The egg-laying beetles can be collected by shaking the foliage, on a dull day or during evening, over a board smeared with grease or old motor oil. The beetles which fall on to the sticky surface can then be disposed of. This should be repeated at intervals during May and June. A quicker plan is to spray or dust the plants thoroughly with derris insecticide three weeks after the flower petals have fallen.

Withered Shoot Ends. Small red grubs of the raspberry moth may burrow into the tips of shoots and cause these to wither and die in early May. Affected shoots should be picked off and burned, with the grubs inside.

Another trouble which is known as blue stripe wilt disease sometimes attacks the fruiting canes, buds either failing to open or producing little growth. Wilting and death of affected canes follows. Inspection shows them to be studded with black specks—one stage of development of the fungus responsible. The new, unfruited, canes show blue stripes, which appear also on the leaves. The latter wither and die, and the attacked canes follow suit later on. They should be grubbed out and burned, roots and all—every piece of root that can be found—and their places filled, after the soil has been deeply dug, with healthy plants.

When mosaic disease is present

the raspberry leaves become curled and mottled and the canes are dwarfed. The crop of berries is very seriously reduced and no new canes shoot up. To prevent mosaic disease spreading to other and healthy plants all that are affected should be dug up and burned.

The variety Red Cross is resistant to this particular trouble, and Lloyd George is very susceptible to it.

To avoid trouble, cheap job-lots of raspberry plants, without any sort of guarantee as to their health, should be avoided. In the end the cheapest and most profitable plants are those purchased from a grower of high standing with a reputation to maintain.

Gathering the Fruit. Raspberries are completely ripe when they part readily from the small plug or core. They may be left until that stage is reached if required for kitchen purposes. But for dessert purposes they should be picked just before they are completely ripe, with short stalk attached. Picking should be done on a dry day. Berries soon go off if gathered wet.

Preserving Raspberries. There is no method of storing the berries in the natural state, but they can be dealt with very simply as explained in the section EASY HOME PRESERVATION OF FRUITS (page 565).

Preparing for Table. Berries gathered as advised—dry, clean, with stalk attached and not yet at the squashy stage—need no preparation for dessert. This is an acid fruit, very welcome as a cooling dessert and excellent for those with rheumatic or gouty tendencies. It contains some vitamin C.

RED CURRANT

Whereas black currants are sweet, the fruit of the red currant (Fig. 409) has an acid flavour. It makes a tasty dessert, and is highly esteemed for making tarts, jam, jelly, wine. It is grown in bush form, and as cordons with one, two or three stems. In cordon form the red currant occupies the minimum of space, planted against a fence or wall or against wires strained between end posts. As either bush or cordon it can be depended on to produce heavy crops year after year.

Ready for Use. First pickings are available in July, and the season can be extended to September by choice of suitable varieties. For early pickings the most suitable site for cordons is a fence or wall facing south; later crops can be secured from a north-facing fence or wall.

Varieties. These include Earliest of Fourlands (very early); Laxton's No. 1 (mid-season); Laxton's Perfection (late), producing specially large bunches of excellent fruit.

Soil Preparation. Very heavy, damp ground needs to be lightened by digging in deeply plenty of sand, sharp grit, or mortar rubble. Very light soil needs the addition of old manure, or decayed material from the soft rubbish heap. This currant will flourish in any ordinarily fertile garden soil.

When and How to Plant. November is the best planting time, though this can be done during mild weather, when the ground is not too wet, up to February. Bushes should be spaced 4 ft. to 5 ft. apart each way, cordons 12 in. apart. Full details are given in the section ABC OF FRUIT PLANTING (page 425).

Watering and Feeding. First-year plants need special attention with the watering-can; soil must not be allowed to dry out during spring and summer. Established plants also appreciate plenty of moisture at the roots, and a surface dressing of old manure, or wet hop manure, put down in late spring helps the production of a fine crop.

Pruning. Fruit is produced from short spurs, and a framework of vigorous older wood must be maintained. In summer (June or July) side shoots formed the same year should be nipped back to within four leaves of their base, and again shortened in winter—cut back close to the basal fruit buds; this applies both to bushes and cordons. An old, worn-out branch should be removed from a bush in winter, its place being taken by a conveniently placed younger growth, the latter not to be summer pruned but shortened back to 6 in. or 8 in. when the old branch is removed. Main branches should be slightly shortened in winter so that about 6 in. of the summer's extension growth is left.

Propagation. Red currants are very easily increased by means of cuttings as explained in the section HOW TO PROPAGATE FRUIT TREES AND BUSHES (page 444), where also is a step-by-step explanation of how bushes and cordons are made.

Caterpillars, Other Troubles. Grubs eating the leaves can be dealt with by dusting or spraying with derris insecticide just after flowering. Fly—black or green—should be attacked on their very first appearance with quassia solution. Scale on branches, stems and shoots can be countered by spraying with a tar-oil winter wash when the buds are completely dormant. Methods of using these remedies are explained fully in the section HOW TO DEAL WITH FRUIT PESTS AND DISEASES (page 551).

Fig. 409.—*Red currants are produced from short spurs; first pickings are available, as a rule, in July*

When gathering the fruit, complete bunches should be picked when the berries are dry and before they become squashily over-ripe. The currants soon reach the latter stage when in full sun; bushes and cordons in a position shaded during the hottest hours keep the fruit longer in prime condition. The less handling the bunches receive, the fewer currants will be spoiled.

For Winter Use. Red currants can be enjoyed after the fresh season as jam, jelly or wine.

In the dining-room biggest bunches of the largest currants make a fine show if piled on a leaf-lined dish and presented at table for dessert.

STRAWBERRIES

At the top of the list of soft fruits for dessert comes the strawberry; and there are those who consider strawberry jam as the best of its class. It is an easy plant to grow, and deserves to be represented, if only by a short row, wherever space can be found for it. It is only too eager to lend itself to quick and profitable propagation, so that a half-dozen plants to begin with will provide the foundation for an extensive strawberry bed.

Ready for Use. Outdoor strawberries are ready for picking in late June, in a favourable year. The shortness of the season during which this fruit is in is allowed to weigh against its cultivation by many who would grow a row or two of plants if picking were not so soon over—and who are not aware that the season can be considerably prolonged by planting for early use on a south-facing border and for later use on a north border. Also, different varieties ripen at varying dates. And if a greenhouse is available pot plants can be fruited out of season.

Varieties. These include: The Duke, very early, can be depended on in heavy ground; Early Cambridge, very early, vigorous enough to put up a good show even in poor ground; Royal Sovereign, early, generally regarded as the finest strawberry grown; Sir Joseph Paxton, mid-season, hardy and prolific; Tardive de Leopold, late, needs to be planted near a variety which produces pollen very freely, such as Royal Sovereign; Waterloo, the latest strawberry of all.

Soil Preparation. Nothing very special is needed in the way of soil so long as it is good enough to produce other crops. Whatever manure or leaf-mould or other rotted greenstuff is available should be dug into the planting site as long as possible in advance of planting, so that the ground can settle again, the strawberry needing a firm root-run. If the ground is heavy and lies wet in winter, or is waterlogged in spring or summer rain storms, it should be made porous by digging at least 18 in. deep and working in plenty of sharp grit, sand, or broken mortar rubble throughout the full depth. A position in full sun is essential for early crops.

When and How to Plant. From August to October, and March to April, are the planting seasons. The earlier period is the better, as plants have time to become established before winter and can be allowed to fruit the following year. Plants set out during March to April should not be allowed to fruit that year; flowers should be picked off, otherwise the plants are sorely weakened.

Plants are obtainable in small pots, or knocked out of pots (in which the runners were rooted), or as runners rooted in the open ground. Those in small pots are the dearest—and the strongest.

Unless the dug soil has settled down fairly firmly it should be rolled or trodden before the plants go in, but this consolidating must not be done if the soil at that time is so wet as to cling to the boots. The plants should be spaced 1½ ft. apart in rows 2 ft. apart, and the

Fig. 410.—*Straw placed around strawberry plants keeps the berries clean. It prevents their being soil-splashed during watering or heavy rains*

roots should be disturbed as little as possible—they move best with plenty of soil clinging to them. If pot plants are dry at the time, soak them with water an hour or two before setting out.

Generous-sized holes should be made with a trowel, deep enough to allow the plants to rest with their lowest leaves level with the surface. Soil should be returned to each hole and firmed over and around the roots with the fingers or the butt end of the trowel. The plants should then be watered in, unless it happens to rain as planting is concluded.

Watering and Feeding. A large part of the contents of the strawberry is water, and plants can scarcely have enough of it in dry weather. Ground can be prevented from drying out too rapidly in hot spells by spreading old stable manure containing short straw around the plants—between the plants in a row and between the rows. This should be put down in early spring. Rains (or watering) will wash the straw clean, the manure going down to the roots and the clean straw then preventing the berries from being splashed with soil (Fig. 410). If that cannot be done the plants will profit from occasional feeding, whilst the berries are swelling, with a special strawberry fertilizer or weak liquid manure.

Removing Runners. Plants will send out slender stems, flat with the ground, these producing at intervals baby plants. Only those required for propagation purposes, as explained in a later paragraph and in the section How to Propagate Fruit Trees and Bushes (page 444), should be allowed to remain; the others should be cut off as soon as noticed.

Protecting the Berries. If strawy manure is put down early, as a mulch, this will safeguard berries against soil-splashing. In the event of hard, late frosts some of the straw should be picked up and lightly placed over the blossoms. Frost not infrequently spoils the prospect of a bumper crop, and this flower protection is therefore worth every attention. Clean, short straw, or even dry leaves, can be used for the latter purpose, and removed from over the blossoms when frost has gone and then placed on the soil around the plants.

Where only a few plants are grown the berries can be kept

above the soil (lacking a surface covering) by means of small forked twigs (Fig. 411) pushed into the ground, the stem of a berry spray being lodged in each fork. This method is adopted in the case of indoor-grown pot strawberries.

Propagation. A strawberry bed well made in the beginning should remain profitable for about five years. A bed may cease to bear properly before that. It is easy to provide a stock of young plants for replacement purposes by layering the stronger runners from the most fruitful plants. Method of layering direct into the soil is explained in the section HOW TO PROPAGATE FRUIT TREES AND BUSHES (page 444). The best plan, however, is to layer direct into small flower pots (Fig. 412). These need not be more than about 3 in. in diameter (across the top).

Fig. 411.—*Strawberries can be kept from the soil by means of small forked twigs pushed into the ground*

The small pots are filled firmly, but not too solidly, to within ¼ in. of the top, with good soil, and then sunk full depth in the ground wherever there are strong young plants on runners. The runner plant nearest the parent is always the strongest. This is pressed into the soil in the pot and its runner stem pegged there with a piece of bent wire. The runner stem beyond is cut away, but the connexion with the parent is not interfered with yet.

This is done as early in summer as possible, generally during the first few days of July. The soil in the pots is kept watered, as necessary, and the young plants are sufficiently well rooted to be severed from the parents and planted out in their fruiting places in August or September—or shifted to larger pots for fruiting in the greenhouse as explained later.

If there are not sufficient young runner plants to allow of these being singled—that is, one plant only on each runner being rooted—two or more per runner can be used. But where possible a runner should be restricted to the first young plant that is produced.

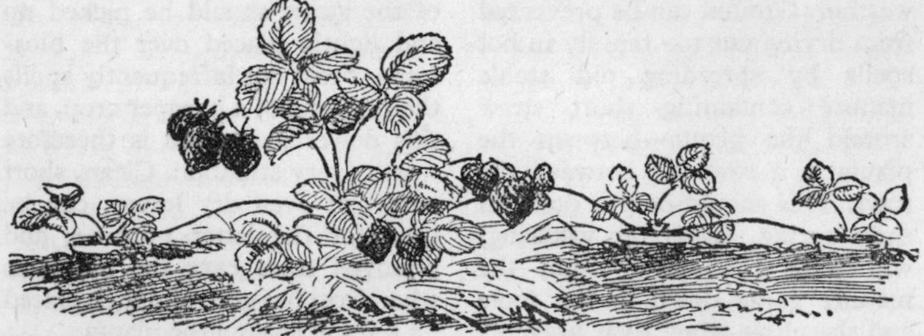

Fig. 412.—*Strawberry runners pegged down into small sunken pots make specially good plants for replacement or stock increasing*

Some of the young runner plants may be blind—lacking a firm heart (Fig. 413). These are incapable of fruiting and should be rejected for propagation purposes.

Birds, Other Troubles. Netting, propped up on sticks (Fig. 414), will keep birds from the fruit, but ends of rows must be covered in, too, or birds will find entry that way. It should be placed in position before the onslaught begins. The netting should not lie flat on the plants or birds will simply stand on it and peck through the meshes (Fig. 414).

Slugs and snails can be kept at a distance with soot sprinkled freely around the plants; but it must be kept from the berries.

A pet tortoise with access to the strawberry bed can do as much damage as the foregoing combined.

Mildew may be troublesome in dry weather, but it gets no real hold if the soil is kept reasonably moist and the plants are fed with an artificial or with liquid manure. It appears first on the undersides of leaves, usually during May, and if not checked may spread to the berries and cover these with a white mould. Flowers of sulphur or black sulphur should be dusted over the plants at the first sign of attack. It may be applied through small bellows or shaken out of a small muslin bag tied to the end of a stick and jerked, whilst held down low, over the plants.

Strawberry leaf spot (Fig. 415) considerably weakens plants if the disease is neglected, and both quality and quantity of fruit may be seriously affected. The variety Royal Sovereign appears to be specially liable to this trouble. At the first appearance of the spots the plants should be sprayed with Bordeaux mixture, according to maker's directions, spraying to be repeated at intervals until the flowers begin to open. Where the trouble has been experienced in a previous year the same programme should be followed as a preventive of its recurrence, spraying beginning whilst the leaves are still young. Mildew is also prevented from appearing by this early spraying.

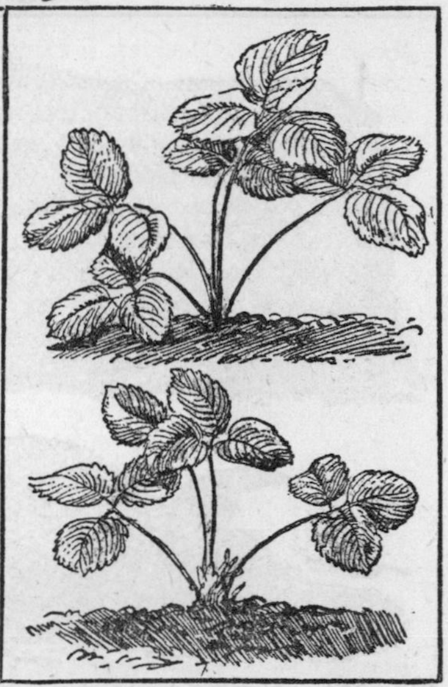

Fig. 413.—*A "blind" strawberry plant (at top) is useless. Notice the central growth, or heart, of the healthy young plant (bottom)*

Weevils may give trouble, the adult beetles attacking shoots and runners in spring, the grubs burrowing into roots and hearts (or crowns) from September until March. Egg-laying activities of these weevils can be interfered with by allowing no rubbish to lie around plants, eggs usually being deposited in such hiding places.

Fig. 414.—*Netting propped up on sticks may be needed to protect the berries from birds. It should not lie flat or birds will peck through the meshes*

The straw or other mulch should be removed from around the plants directly the berries have all been gathered; this material should then be dug in or buried elsewhere.

Digging is not advisable between strawberry rows—the roots lie shallow—but the hoe should be used vigorously. This tool will reveal pests to the keen eyes of birds, the latter not needing to be kept at bay after the fruit has gone.

Fig. 415.—*Strawberry leaf spot disease can be dealt with by spraying promptly with Bordeaux mixture*

Picking the Berries. Strawberries should be gathered when they assume full colour, but before they become too soft. They should be dry, and as they are easily damaged careful handling is necessary. For dessert they are picked with the plug and a piece of stem; without the plug, for jam making.

When a row has been cleared the straw or other mulch should be removed, along with any weeds, the oldest of the leaves picked off and runners that have escaped previous notice (Fig. 416)—with the exception of those runners that are to be rooted. Top soil should then be well stirred with the hoe.

Preparing for Table. Pile the finest of the berries, stalks inwards, on a leaf-lined dish, pyramid fashion. The stalks should be removed if strawberries are to be served with cream.

Indoor Strawberries. Runner plants that were rooted in small pots should be shifted into 6-in. pots, some time in August, for fruiting in the greenhouse. The drainage hole in each clean pot is covered with crocks and, if possible, a layer of leaf-mould or old manure. Then the plants can be removed from the small pots one at a time and transferred.

The potting soil needs to be substantial, not fine. Turfy loam pulled to pieces by hand is best, the pieces being about as large as a walnut. Some old manure or good leaf-mould and a sprinkling of wood ash should also be added.

The plant in position in the larger pot, the prepared soil is worked down around it with the fingers, the pot being shaken a time or two to assist the soil to settle. This needs to be left firm, by moderate ramming, but the firming must not be overdone. The leaves should rest flush with the soil surface, and the latter should be about ½ in. from the pot rim. The heart of the plant must not be covered.

Potting completed, the pots should be placed outdoors, where shaded from the hottest sun for about ten days, then in full sun. Water will need to be given as required, and the plants should be syringed with clear water every day in the absence of rain; undersides of leaves receiving special attention with the syringe, to check red spider. If any runners form on these plants they should be nipped off when quite small.

After October they will be safer

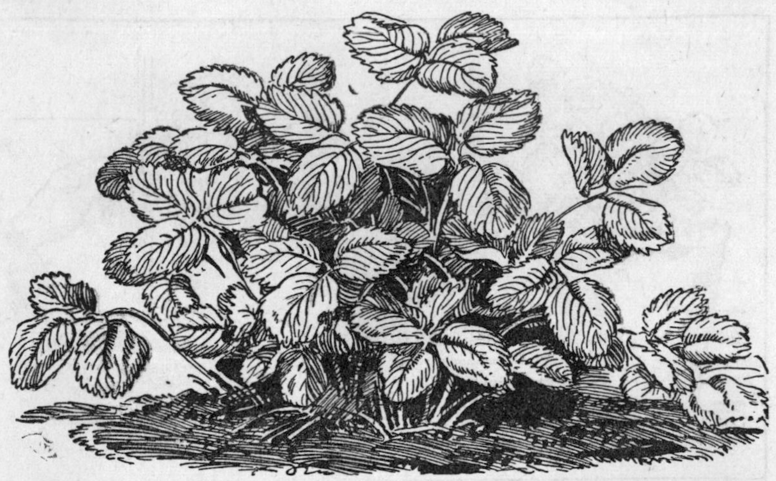

Fig. 416.—*This strawberry plant has been cleaned up, after fruiting—straw, old leaves, weeds and other rubbish removed, also unwanted runners*

Fig. 417.—*Strawberry plants in 6-in. pots plunged rim deep in sifted ashes, outdoors, for later removal to the greenhouse for early fruiting*

in a frame. If this accommodation cannot be spared the pots should be sunk rim deep in sifted fire ashes (Fig. 417), and in periods of very heavy rain or frost the plants should be covered with sacking or light mats. They can go into the greenhouse, after removal from the ashes and after the outsides of the pots have been scrubbed, in January or later. For early forcing a temperature of 45 deg. (by night) is necessary.

The plants should be in full light and be watered only when the soil is drying out. Over-watering ruins them. They should be syringed on fine, bright days, and

Fig. 418.—*The strawberry flowers should be dabbed with a wad of cotton-wool (left) or touched with a camel-hair brush (right) to distribute the pollen*

Fig. 419.—*Strawberries in pots in the greenhouse should be supported with small forked twigs*

when the flowers open they should be lightly brushed with a loose wad of dry cotton-wool, or a camel-hair brush (Fig. 418)—this to distribute the pollen and ensure a good set of fruit.

Not more than eight berries should be allowed to a plant, and when these start to plump up the plants should be fed once a week with weak liquid manure or an artificial fertilizer; feeding to be discontinued when the berries begin to colour. The fruit should be propped up with small forked twigs (Fig. 419) pushed into the soil, as explained in the case of outdoor strawberries.

Fruiting over, plants may be removed from the pots and, after the crocks have been picked away from the bottom of the soil and root mass, be planted out for fruiting (outdoors) again in due course.

It should be noted that strawberries take a great deal out of the soil, so if an exhausted row is to be discarded and replaced with these fruited plants—or with young, unfruited ones for the matter of that—and a fresh site cannot be provided, the old site must be deeply dug and enriched with manure, or hop manure, or plenty of good leaf-mould.

VEICHBERRY

This heavy-cropping cane fruit is a cross between a blackberry and a raspberry. The fruit, which is double the size of a raspberry and red in colour, ripens in August. Stakes are needed for support, and planting should be done in autumn or spring, on the lines explained in the section ABC OF FRUIT PLANTING (page 425). Fruited shoots should be cut out in autumn and strong young ones of the same year's growth be tied up in their place—for fruiting the following year.

WALNUT

To appreciate a walnut (Fig. 420) one need not necessarily be a vegetarian, though perhaps the latter realizes more fully its great food value. For dessert, for making walnut cakes, and for pickling, unripe, these nuts are a really valuable crop. The tree flourishes in towns, which is a big point in its favour, though it needs to be away from the shade of houses.

Trees can be obtained in standard or in bush form.

Ready for Use. Walnuts are ripe in late September or early October, and keep well in store.

Soil Preparation. The ground where a tree is to be planted should

Fig. 420.—*Walnuts in their green husks are esteemed for pickling. The husk is brown when the nut is ripe and splits (right) from the hard shell*

be broken up 2 ft. deep, and if heavy it should be lightened with sand, grit or mortar rubble. Manure is not needed.

If planted as a shade tree on a lawn, where it is decorative at all seasons, it should be in the centre of a 3-ft. circle free of turf.

When and How to Plant. Either October or November is the most favourable time to plant, and the roots should be covered to the depth indicated by the soil mark on the stem. A stake should be provided, until the tree or bush has a firm hold of the ground. Details are given in the section ABC OF FRUIT PLANTING (page 425).

Watering and Feeding. An established walnut tree will manage with the minimum of attention. But if a good yearly crop is appreciated the little extra labour of watering in dry weather, and feeding with weak liquid manure during spring and summer, helps it along considerably.

Pruning. From the time the tree first produces nuts, pruning can be forgotten. It may perhaps be desirable to cut back or remove entirely an awkwardly placed branch; but other than that, no cutting is required. The nuts are produced, usually in pairs, at the ends of the previous year's shoots. If much shortening is done there is that much less fruit.

The stumpy little female flowers which produce the nuts (Fig. 421) are so inconspicuous as to go unnoticed; one has to look for them. The male (pollen-producing) flowers take the form of longish catkins. The male and female flowers (a tree produces both) open at the same time, early in the year, and fertilization is effected by the wind which blows pollen from the one to the other.

In the course of centuries a walnut tree develops a huge spread of branches, with a height of 60 ft. or more and a trunk 20 ft. round.

Propagation. Walnut trees can be raised by sowing the nuts (still in their shells) outdoors during November. They should be buried 2 in. deep, the seedlings being lifted and transplanted twelve months later. Fruit has to be waited for patiently from a tree thus raised. Its production is speeded up considerably by grafting or budding on to a suitable stock. Methods are explained in the section HOW TO PROPAGATE FRUIT TREES AND BUSHES (page 444).

Fig. 421.—*Nut-producing flowers of the walnut are shown in the upper part of the sketch; the long pollen-producing catkins in the lower*

Gathering the Nuts. For pickling purposes the nuts are gathered whilst their thick outer covering is still green and the nuts themselves are small and soft, round about July. Not until late September or early October are the nuts ripe. The outer covering of the hard shells is then brown.

A vigorous shaking of the tree or its branches then brings the fruit tumbling down. There is an old-fashioned notion that the nuts should be dislodged by thrashing the branches with a pole, the belief being that this ill-treatment does the tree good. That folly has been perpetuated in the saying: "A woman, a dog, and a walnut tree, the more you beat them the better they'll be." Due regard for the walnut tree's bark, and of the young terminal shoots which will bear the following year's nuts, is as necessary as is careful treatment of any other fruit tree.

Storing for Winter. The gathered fruit should be spread out in layers, under cover, until the husks—the outer coverings—have fallen away. The nuts should then be stored in jars or tins, these to be made quite airtight and placed in any dry, frostproof shelter. Or they can be kept in a barrel or boxes, with layers of dry sand covering the layers of nuts.

Preparing for Table. The nuts are simply heaped on a dish, with nut-crackers by the side. The food value is high, walnuts being rich in mineral salts and vitamin B.

WHITE CURRANT

The culture of this fruit is exactly the same as explained for Red Currant (page 538). It is sweeter than the latter, and is used for dessert and for mixing with other soft fruits for making jams and tarts. Varieties include White Versailles, a strong grower producing very large bunches of richly flavoured currants, White Dutch, and White Transparent.

White currants do well in a town garden, though the fruits may be rather badly soiled by sooty deposits from the air. Their season may be lengthened somewhat by planting in special positions: fully exposed to sun for early ripening, against a fence or wall facing north for later maturity.

In the matter of pruning, one object is to keep really old wood down to the minimum. That which has obviously worn itself out should be cut right away, along with shoots which may be crowding the centre of a bush. These inner shoots are always unproductive and, like worn-out wood, seem to attract the pest known as scale.

It pays to practise summer pruning as well as winter pruning. In this way utmost encouragement is given to the production of those short, well-ripened growths ("spurs") which carry the bunches of fruit. The latter is not borne on shoots younger than the previous year.

WINEBERRY

The berries of wineberry are small, bright orange, and pleasantly acid in flavour. Planted 4 ft. apart, against a fence or wires, culture is as explained under Raspberry (page 534). Fruited shoots should be cut out, as soon as the fruit has been gathered, and the new summer shoots secured to the support.

WORCESTER BERRY

Used for making jam and jelly, the fruit of the Worcester berry is purplish-blue and produced in bunches, or trusses, black currant fashion. The plant is a cross between black currant and gooseberry and the fruit partakes of the flavour of both parents. Habit of growth resembles that of the gooseberry, and treatment is the same.

YOUNGBERRY

This fruit, the result of crossing an American dewberry and the phenomenal berry, is used for stewing, and it makes an excellent preserve. Large, juicy, acid, and deep red, it is ripe in July. Culture is the same as explained under the heading Blackberry (page 486).

SECTION XXXI

HOW TO DEAL WITH FRUIT PESTS AND DISEASES

It pays commercial growers of fruit to fight pests and diseases from one year's end to the other. They carry out preventive, trapping and killing operations on a very large scale. The home fruit-grower's produce seldom comes up to the best shop standard for the simple reason that he does not engage in a similar conflict on his own; or he does it only half-heartedly.

The cost of materials is insignificant compared with the value of crops from clean trees and bushes. Not only are such crops bigger, but they are far better in quality.

No spraying solution, dusting powder or other device will make a clean sweep of every fruit pest and disease, but each does a very great deal towards reducing the total number of troubles. The accompanying chart, Remedies Against Enemies of Fruit Crops (page 562), gives a concise survey of methods of dealing with specific troubles.

These methods are to be applied at the times and seasons indicated, and the home grower should realize that preventive measures can be carried out more effectively than operations during the height of the attack. Where preventive action is not possible remedies should be used at the very first indication of trouble. This saves expense.

Programme of Attack. Winter is the period for a general clean-up, to follow pruning. All rotting or

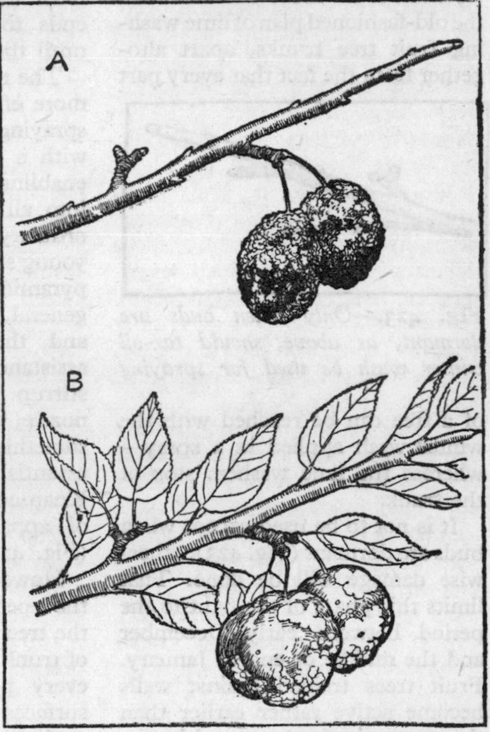

Fig. 422.—*Fruits "mummified" by brown rot disease* (A) *should be burned or buried after gathering. The appearance of the fruits in the summer stage of the disease is shown at* (B)

mummified fruits (Fig. 422), whether on the ground or still clinging to the trees, should be collected and either burned or buried deeply.

Trees or bushes should then be sprayed, forcefully, with a tar-oil winter wash (bought in tins) used according to the maker's directions. This rids the bark of moss and lichen and largely smashes the grand spring assault—before it can start—of quite a number of different insect pests by destroying their eggs, pupæ and hibernating grubs.

Winter Spraying. Tar-oil winter wash is far more effective than the old-fashioned plan of lime washing fruit tree trunks, apart altogether from the fact that every part

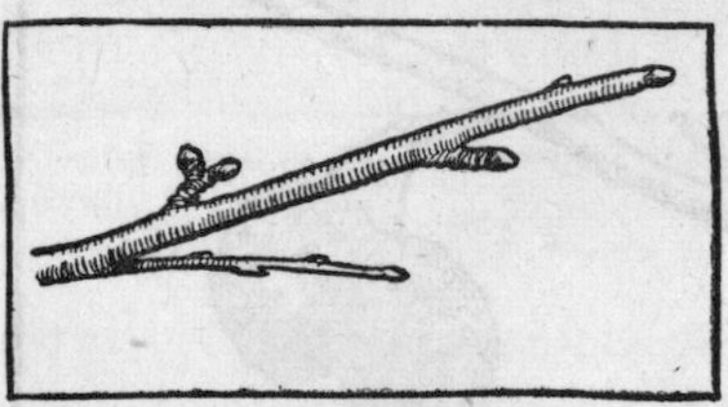

Fig. 423.—*Only when buds are dormant, as above, should tar-oil winter wash be used for spraying*

of a tree can be reached with the winter wash applied as a spray—whereas the lime washers stop at the trunk.

It is not to be used except when buds are dormant (Fig. 423), otherwise damage will be done. That limits this phase of the fight to the period between early December and the middle or end of January. Fruit trees trained against walls become active rather earlier than those away in the open, and it may be necessary to spray these with the tar-oil wash during the last weeks before the end of the year.

There is no point in leaving this spraying to the last possible moment. Round about Christmas or the first week of the New Year one bout of spraying could take in all the bush and tree fruits in the garden.

Preparing and Applying the Spray. Only as much of the liquid should be prepared at any one time as may be required for immediate use. It is to be mixed with water according to directions accompanying it. Quantity needed depends on the number and size of trees and bushes. These are to be coated from top to bottom, from shoot ends to base of trunk or stem, until the liquid starts to drip off.

The more forceful the spray the more effective it is, so the winter spraying apparatus should be fitted with a rather coarse nozzle—this enabling the solution to be driven into all crevices in the bark. An ordinary garden syringe serves for young standards, dwarf bush trees, pyramids, and trained trees in general, for gooseberries, currants and the like. Where pumping assistance is available the ordinary stirrup pump, given a coarse nozzle, will do the job still better; something of that sort is really essential in dealing with tall trees. Knapsack sprayers and other forms of apparatus may be purchased (Fig. 424).

However the spray is applied, the operator should move around the tree or bush so that every part of trunk and limbs is covered from every possible angle, the upper surfaces of top growth to be wetted as thoroughly as the undersides. It should be noted that no spray can be under control in windy weather, and the job should not be embarked

Fig. 424.—*The sprayer should get well down to the job—and wear old clothes, gloves or gauntlets, and a cap. Nearby plants are covered over*

upon during frost or when rain is likely to follow within a couple of days. A downfall of rain can wash practically all the liquid off.

Spraying Precautions. Old clothes should be worn, and gloves if possible, and a cap pulled well down will protect the operator's face and eyes. It is no use denying that spraying is a messy job.

Vegetables or other plants under or near to the trees should be covered over—sheets of newspaper are effective—whilst operations are in progress. If the liquid reaches them (or a nearby hedge) it should be hosed off at once with water.

These precautions apply in all cases, whatever the nature of the spray. Also the work is made easier if the solution, whatever it may be, is strained through coarse muslin before operations begin, to prevent the nozzle clogging (Fig. 425).

Last stage in the operations consists in cleaning the apparatus thoroughly, inside and out, with clear water, then drying it before it is put away.

Spring Spraying. Lime-sulphur solution is an excellent spring wash for applying to apple and pear trees whose fruits the previous season were attacked by scab, the spray to be applied just before the flower buds open (Fig. 426). It is used also against black-currant big bud mite, American gooseberry mildew, and fruit-tree red spider. Details are given in chart (page 562).

Lead arsenate (poison) is a spray for killing spring grubs by poisoning their food. This must not be allowed to make contact with any vegetables in the vicinity. Sprayed over apple trees as soon as the flower petals have fallen it will greatly reduce the number of maggoty windfalls (Fig. 427).

Derris insecticide and quassia solution each has its uses in connexion with other pests, as indicated in the chart.

Early Windfall Apples. Small and early windfall apples are often due to the core-eating activities of the grub of the codlin moth. This grub originates from an egg laid in the centre of the flower (Fig. 428A). It enters through the eye of the small fruit, eats the core, gnaws its way out through the side (Fig. 428B) and climbs down the tree trunk to the ground. There it buries itself, becomes a pupa and eventually emerges as a full-size codlin moth (Fig. 428C).

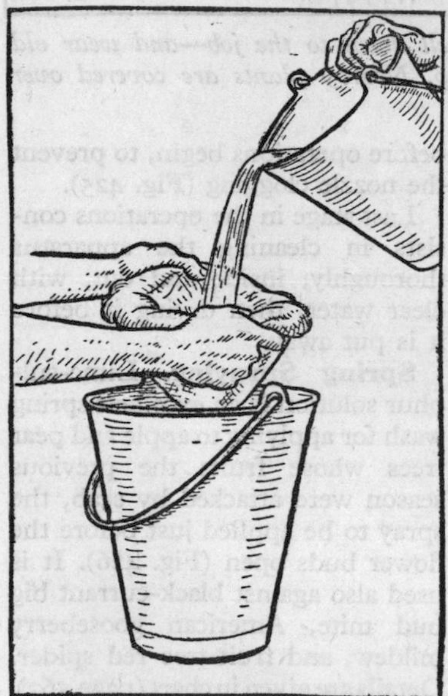

Fig. 425.—*The solution should be strained through coarse muslin before operations begin. This is to prevent the spraying nozzle becoming clogged*

To prevent these codlin moth grubs entering the apples the trees should be sprayed with lead arsenate—when bees have finished with the blossom, so that these shall not be poisoned, too. As soon as the petals have fallen the lead arsenate solution is sprayed through a fine nozzle over the bloom trusses so that the poison lodges in the eye of each forming fruit.

Grubs attempting to eat their way in have also to eat the poison, and that is the end of them.

Band Traps on Fruit Trees. There is another way of defeating the codlin moth grub, without spraying; though both methods might well be adopted, to make assurance doubly sure. This second plan is to tie a 6-in.-wide band of old frayed sacking, or else of thick crumpled paper (Fig. 429), around the tree trunk in June—in readiness for the downward procession of full-fed grubs. The latter halt at the obstacle and either die in its folds or enter the pupa stage.

When the fruit has been gathered in autumn these dry bands are removed and burned with all pests lodging therein.

Grease Banding. When the dry bands are removed with their codlin moth grubs and other incidental lodgers they might well be replaced by grease bands.

These sticky traps are to catch the feet and bodies of the parents of another type of grub—those which loop about the foliage and eat it (Fig. 430). These looping grubs, progeny of certain winter moths, attack not only apple but plum, damson, cherry, nut trees, gooseberry and currant bushes

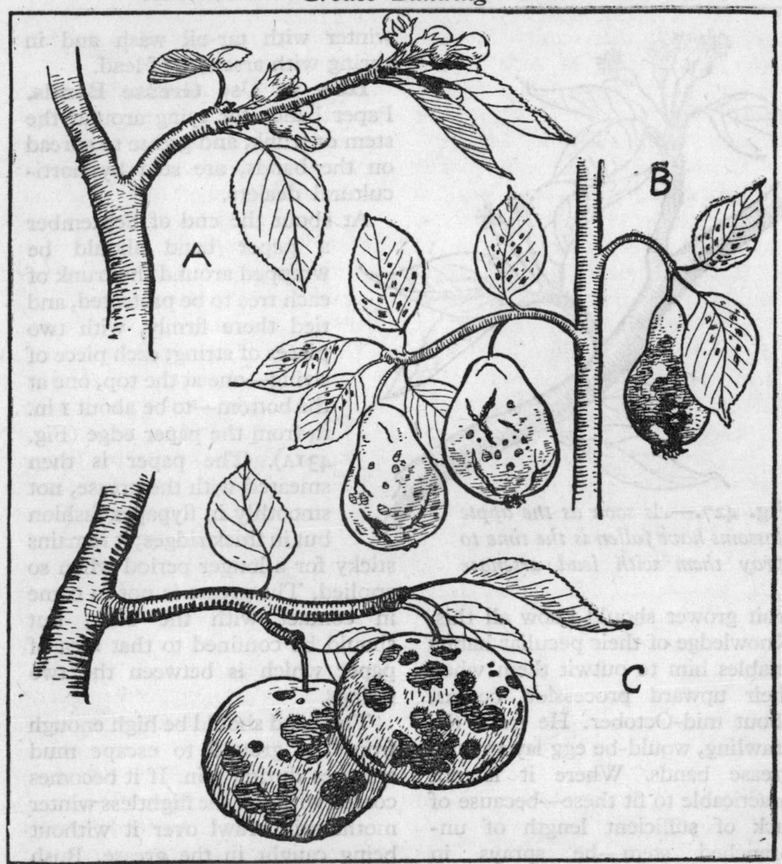

Fig. 426.—*Before the flower buds open* (A) *is the time to spray pear* (B) *and apple* (C) *trees whose fruits during the previous season were scabbed*

They eat buds, blossom and young fruit as well as leaves. They spin leaves together and lurk therein between feeds, and they do the same with flower heads.

For the sake of the fruit they must be killed by spraying with lead arsenate after the flower petals have fallen. Any of these looping grubs that manage to survive and eat their fill let themselves down on self-spun threads, during May to June, and bury themselves in the soil or any rubbish at the foot of the tree or bush. There they pass through the pupa stage and become moths.

The female winter moths desire to lay eggs on the shoots and branches. But they are unable to fly; their wings never develop sufficiently to lift them from the ground. So they crawl up the stems or trunks, to set the whole cycle of trouble going again.

It is important that the home

Fig. 427.—*As soon as the apple blossoms have fallen is the time to spray them with lead arsenate*

fruit grower should know all this. Knowledge of their peculiar habits enables him to outwit them when their upward procession begins, about mid-October. He traps the crawling, would-be egg layers with grease bands. Where it is not practicable to fit these—because of lack of sufficient length of unbranched stem—he sprays in winter with tar-oil wash and in spring with arsenate of lead.

How to Use Grease Bands. Paper bands for tying around the stem or trunk, and grease to spread on the bands, are sold by horticultural dealers.

At about the end of September a paper band should be wrapped around the trunk of each tree to be protected, and tied there firmly, with two pieces of string; each piece of string—one at the top, one at the bottom—to be about 1 in. in from the paper edge (Fig. 431A). The paper is then smeared with the grease, not smoothly in flypaper fashion but in thick ridges; it remains sticky for a longer period when so applied. The grease is not to come in contact with the bark, but should be confined to that area of paper which is between the two strings.

The band should be high enough from the ground to escape mud splashes during rain. If it becomes coated with soil the flightless winter moths will crawl over it without being caught in the grease. Bush

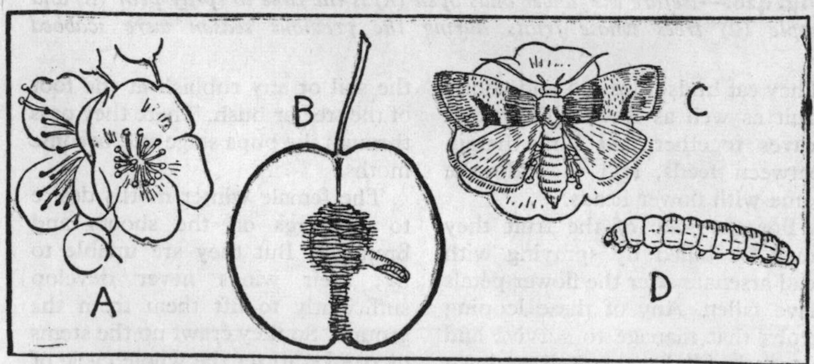

Fig. 428.—*From an egg laid in the centre of an apple flower* (A) *by the codlin moth* (C) *comes a grub* (D) *which eats the core* (B) *and then leaves by one side*

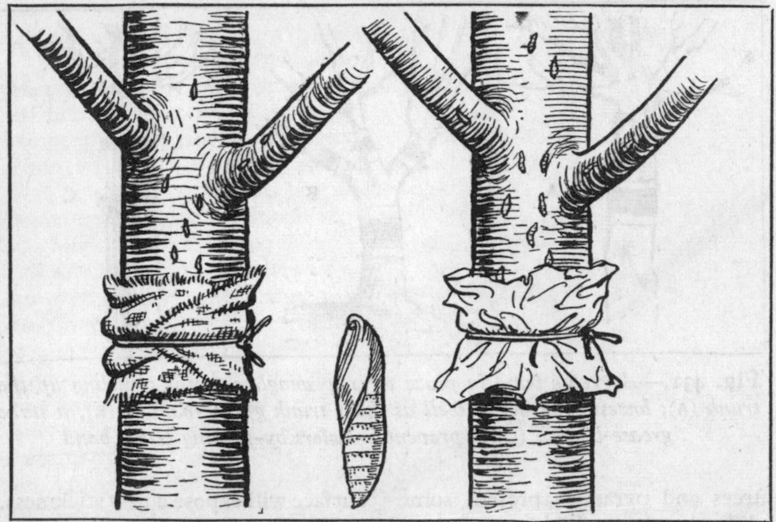

Fig. 429.—*A piece of ragged sacking or crumpled paper tied around the trunk will trap descending codlin moth grubs. A codlin moth pupa is shown*

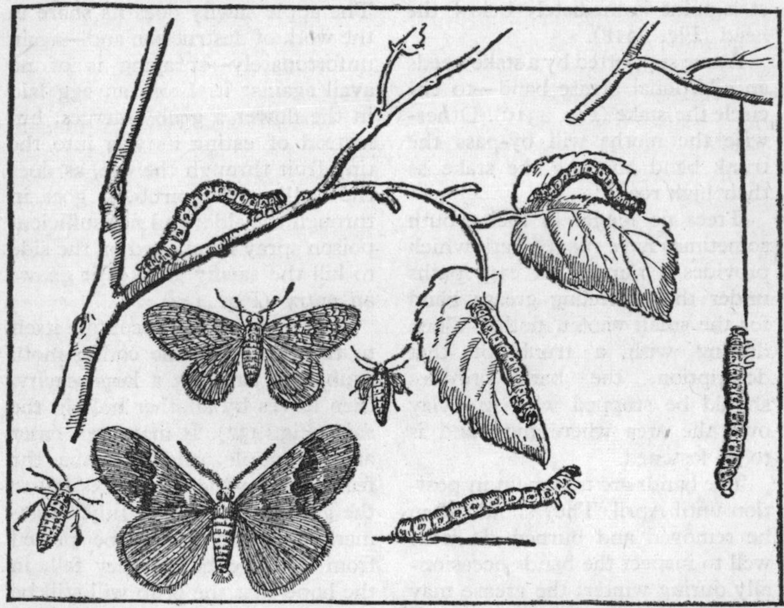

Fig. 430.—*Two varieties of winter moth and the flightless females. Their caterpillars are known as loopers. When these are full-fed they lower themselves to the ground as shown on the right. Grease banding is a remedy*

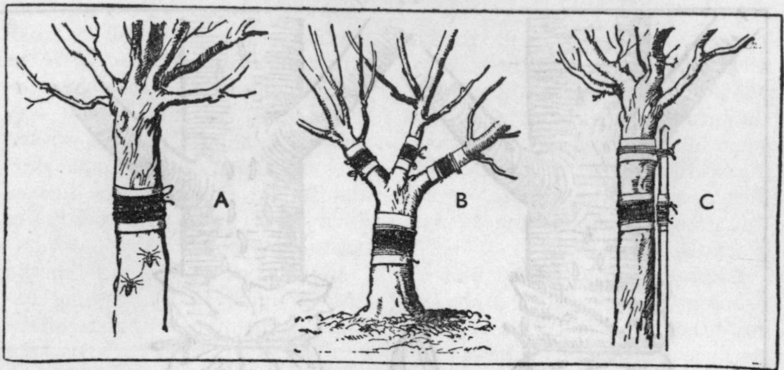

Fig. 431.—*A grease band in place to trap wingless moths crawling up the trunk* (A)*; lowest branches as well as short trunk grease-banded* (B)*; a stake grease-banded* (C) *to prevent crawlers by-passing trunk band*

trees and pyramids present some difficulty here. This can sometimes be met by banding the lowest branches, as well as the short stem at a point immediately below the head (Fig. 431B).

A tree supported by a stake needs an additional grease band—to encircle the stake (Fig. 431C). Otherwise the moths will by-pass the trunk band and use the stake as their high road.

Trees no longer in their youth sometimes have rugged bark which provides a number of easy paths under the encircling grease band for the small winter moths. When dealing with a trunk of that description, the bark crevices should be stopped with wet clay over the area where the band is to be fastened.

The bands are to remain in position until April. They should then be removed and burned. It is as well to inspect the bands occasionally during winter; the grease may have hardened, or become soil splashed, or studded thickly with its captives. A little scraping of the surface will expose a new stickiness.

The Apple Sawfly. The codlin moth is not, unfortunately, the only pest responsible for windfall apples. The apple sawfly does its share in the work of destruction and—again unfortunately—spraying is of no avail against it. From an egg laid in the flower a grub emerges, but instead of eating its way into the tiny fruit through the eye, as does the codlin moth grub, it goes in through the side; and not sufficient poison spray is retained on the side to kill the sawfly grub as it gnaws an entry (Fig. 432).

This grub does not confine itself to the core (like the codlin moth grub) but eats out a large cavity, then leaves by another hole in the side (Fig. 432). It may then enter another apple, and continue the feast. Fruit which it attacks fall to the ground in June or July. Hole-marked apples should be picked from the tree before they fall, in the hope that the grub will still be within; though it may already have made its way to the ground. Fallen fruit should then be collected to prevent any grubs still therein making their way into the soil.

More or less safe in the ground, the grubs go through the pupa stage of transition and the following spring emerge as mature sawflies. Much can be done to prevent this transition by cleaning the soil, as explained below.

Cleaning the Soil. Bits of prunings, leaves, fallen fruit and any other rubbish accumulated at the base of trees and bushes should be gathered up and burned in winter. A number of pests of various kinds will be destroyed in the process. If chickens can be allowed to run in the fruit quarters for a time they will scratch over the surface soil and disinter and eat many pupæ and grubs wintering there (Fig. 434).

An alternative plan is to remove 1 in. or so of the surface soil and replace it with soil taken from the vegetable ground; the removed soil to be buried in the bottom of a trench during digging. If the old surface soil must remain, soot or lime or both might be raked into it; or naphthalene forked into the top 2 in. at the rate of about 2 oz. per square yard.

Cleaning Vines or Peaches. In dealing with under-glass vines, peaches or nectarines when their leaves have fallen in winter, the after-pruning, pest-abolishing programme consists in painting or lightly washing all the wood—every bit of it—with Gishurst compound.

The vine or tree should be unfastened from the wires or trellis or whatever supports it and treated with the compound—made into a solution according to the directions accompanying it. The liquid is then applied with a stiff brush, or small scrubbing brush, worked from the bottom upwards so that the dormant buds are not in any way injured. It should be well worked into the spurs of the grape vine, and should extend to the tips of every side shoot of peach or nectarine.

Loose bark on the vine should first be removed by rubbing between the palms of the hands; all the

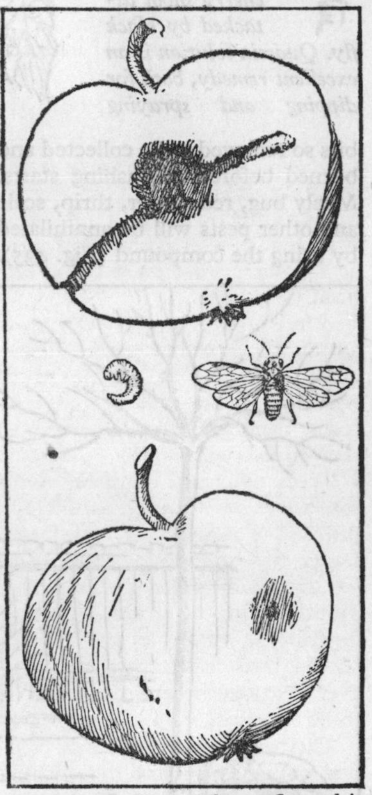

Fig. 432.—*The apple sawfly and its destructive grub. The latter enters an apple through a hole in the side (below), eats away the centre, then makes its way out. Top sketch shows grub tunnelling its way to the right*

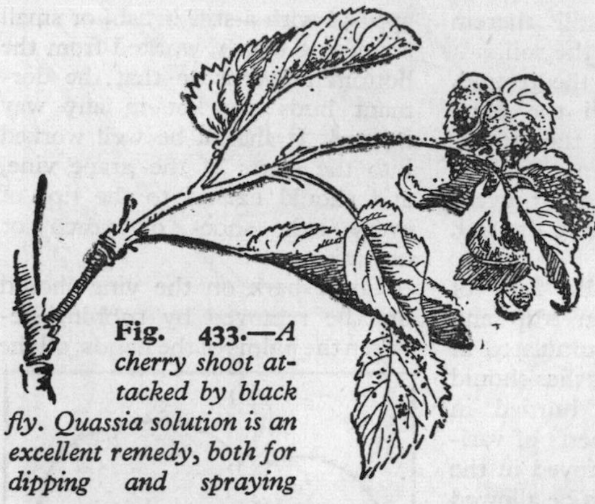

Fig. 433.—*A cherry shoot attacked by black fly. Quassia solution is an excellent remedy, both for dipping and spraying*

Whilst the plants are down from their supports all glass, woodwork and metalwork should be scrubbed with hot water containing as much soap as it will take up; and to each pailful of water a cupful of paraffin should be added. To ensure thorough mixture the liquid should be stirred vigorously and pumped backwards and forwards several times with a syringe.

bits so removed to be collected and burned before the washing starts. Mealy bug, red spider, thrip, scale and other pests will be annihilated by using the compound (Fig. 435).

To prevent the soil being trampled and becoming sodden during these operations it should be covered with planks or sacking.

Fig. 434.—*Chickens can be allowed to run in the fruit quarters in winter*

Fig. 435.—*Most efficient way to clean a greenhouse vine in winter is to lower it from its supports, remove loose bark by rubbing, and scrub stem and spurs (from the bottom upwards) with a pest-abolishing solution. To protect the soil from trampling and "drip" it should be covered over with sacking*

REMEDIES AGAINST ENEMIES OF FRUIT CROPS

This chart indicates the most common fruit pests and diseases, and how, when and with what to combat them. Remedies and preventives, with directions for use, are purchasable from horticultural sundriesmen.

Attacked	*Attacker*	*Remedy*
FRUIT TREES AND BUSHES GENERALLY	Insects' eggs, moss, lichen	Spray with a tar-oil winter wash, 1 pint to each 2 gal. of water, early December to late January. This is a general cleanser.
APPLE	American blight (woolly aphis) on branches, trunks	Dab the bits of white "fluff" (these conceal sap-sucking aphides) with a stiff brush dipped in methylated spirit, petrol, paraffin or tar-oil winter wash, as soon as noticed (Fig. 436).
	Fruit grub-eaten	Spray with arsenate of lead (poison) mixed according to maker's directions, directly the flower petals have fallen. Band the trunks with folded sacking or paper, late June–early July, to trap grubs; remove and burn bands and grubs when the fruit has been gathered.
APPLE, PLUM, CHERRY, GOOSEBERRY, CURRANT	Grubs "loop" about on foliage and eat it	Spray with arsenate of lead, as above. Also grease-band trunks, late September, to trap the wingless moths responsible for the grubs. Remove and burn the grease bands, together with the wingless moths and other pests trapped in the grease, in early spring.
APPLE, PEAR	Fruit scabbed and cracked	Burn or bury attacked fallen fruit. Spray with lime-sulphur, ½ pint to every 3 gal. of water, just before the flower buds open.
	Canker of the wood. Patches of bark on branches and spurs eaten away	Dead and diseased wood must be cut away as completely as possible, though it may mean sacrificing most, or all, of a branch.
APPLE, PEAR, GOOSEBERRY, CURRANT	Scale on stems, branches and shoots	Spray with tar-oil winter wash, when buds are completely dormant.
BLACK CURRANT	Big-bud mite	Spray with lime-sulphur solution, ½ pint lime-sulphur to 3 gal. of water, when leaves are as large as a shilling and before the flower buds are open (Fig. 436).

REMEDIES AGAINST ENEMIES OF FRUIT CROPS
—Contd.

<table>
<tr><th>Attacked</th><th>Attacker</th><th>Remedy</th></tr>
<tr><td>CHERRY</td><td>Black fly thick on leaves and shoots</td><td>Spray with quassia solution immediately the attack is noticed. Dip shoot ends that are within reach into the solution (Fig. 433).</td></tr>
<tr><td>GOOSEBERRY</td><td>Birds (sparrows chiefly) destroy young buds</td><td>Dust the bushes very freely with old soot, when bushes are damp with rain or dew; or syringe with quassia solution. Either makes the buds distasteful.</td></tr>
<tr><td></td><td>Caterpillars devour the leaves</td><td>Dust or spray the bushes with derris, after flowering; or with hellebore powder (poison) within three weeks of picking fruit.</td></tr>
<tr><td></td><td>Mildew on leaves and shoots</td><td>Spray against the American form of gooseberry mildew with lime-sulphur in early May; one part of lime-sulphur to 100 parts of water (Fig. 436).</td></tr>
<tr><td>PLUM, CHERRY, APRICOT, PEACH, NECTARINE</td><td>Silver-leaf disease (see also under Plum in the alphabetical section)</td><td>Growers are under a legal obligation to cut out and burn diseased or dead wood; this must not be left lying about. There is no cure.</td></tr>
<tr><td></td><td>Maggots in fruit</td><td>Burn all fallen plums not usable.</td></tr>
<tr><td>RASPBERRY, LOGANBERRY</td><td>Maggots in fruit</td><td>Spray or dust with derris insecticide three weeks after the flower petals have fallen.</td></tr>
<tr><td>RED SPIDER</td><td colspan="2">This very minute sap-sucking pest attacks plum, damson, gooseberry, etc. These should be sprayed, after the flower petals have fallen, with lime-sulphur solution—$\frac{1}{4}$ pint lime-sulphur to 3 gal. of water. Where it occurs in greenhouse or conservatory it can be kept down by frequent syringeing with clear water, a damp atmosphere being distasteful to it.</td></tr>
<tr><td>MEALY BUG</td><td colspan="2">A great pest under glass, especially on grape vines. Loose bark should be rubbed from the latter (not peeled off) in winter when leafless and vines and spurs painted with Gishurst compound. The latter should also be painted on branches and shoots of peach and nectarine under glass, in winter. This compound destroys red spider, scale, thrip, etc., as well as mealy bug.</td></tr>
<tr><td>RABBITS</td><td colspan="2">Rabbits and hares have an especial appetite for the stems of young fruit trees. These should be protected from ground level to about 18 in. up with small mesh wire netting encircling each stem and held in place, a couple of inches out from the stem, with stakes. Or the stems may be protected by means of spiny branches of gorse (furze) or hawthorn tied thickly round the base. The time to apply these protective measures is before the damage is done.</td></tr>
</table>

REMEDIES AGAINST ENEMIES OF FRUIT CROPS —*Contd.*

Attacker	*Remedy*
WASPS	Ripening fruit is a great attraction for wasps. Fruit on walls, fences, should be netted over with old muslin curtains; this will at least baffle the majority of the raiders, and it will scare away fruit-pecking birds. Best plan is to attack their base—watch where the homing wasps fly at dusk, search for the entrance hole and pour into it ½ pint of paraffin, then immediately plug the hole with a lump of turf. A piece of cyanide of potassium (poison) the size of a walnut dropped into the hole and followed quickly with a little water and then a plug of turf is also effective. Wasps can be kept from ripening grapes and other fruit in greenhouse or conservatory by covering open ventilators with muslin.

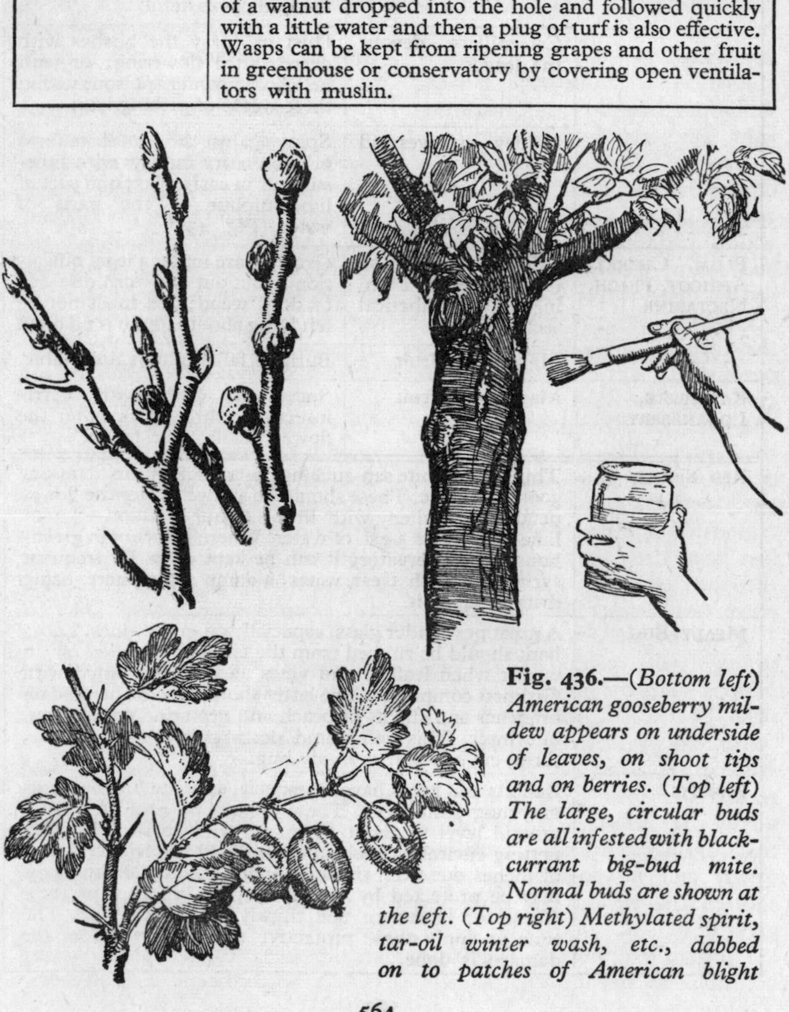

Fig. 436.—*(Bottom left) American gooseberry mildew appears on underside of leaves, on shoot tips and on berries. (Top left) The large, circular buds are all infested with black-currant big-bud mite. Normal buds are shown at the left. (Top right) Methylated spirit, tar-oil winter wash, etc., dabbed on to patches of American blight*

SECTION XXXII

EASY HOME PRESERVATION OF FRUITS

WITHOUT the use of sugar and with only the simplest apparatus, fruits can be home-preserved as satisfactorily as by any of the complicated rituals involving the use of expensive appliances. It can be done with the minimum fuss and the maximum gain. Methods are explained here.

Apples, Dried. Bruised or otherwise blemished apples which cannot go into store, and apples which cannot be stored whole because of lack of storage space, can be dried in the form of rings.

Cooking varieties are best for the purpose. The apples should be peeled (Fig. 437), bruised portions cut away, the cores scooped out and the fruit then sliced into ¼-in.-thick rings. These are then to be dried to a leathery—tough but not hard—condition, in a linen airing cupboard, or in an oven which has just been used for cooking, or on the plate rack above a lighted gas stove, or in front of an open fire.

The time taken to complete the drying will depend upon the periods when the mild heat is available. The process may need to be continued over several days, the apple rings being withdrawn and replaced as other cooking arrangements may require. The point is that drying must be completed slowly and no attempt made to shorten the period by using too great heat.

During the drying the rings may be threaded on short sticks, the ends of the latter to be supported in any way convenient so that the rings hang clear and can be turned occasionally. Or the rings can be placed in shallow boxes, these to be without tops and with bottoms formed of coarse canvas or muslin. The simplest form of drying box (or tray) consists of four slats of wood nailed together in the shape of a square or oblong, with canvas or muslin nailed over the bottom.

To prevent the apple rings discolouring before being dried they should be placed, directly they are cut, in salt water for five or six minutes. The solution is made by stirring two tablespoonfuls of salt in a gallon of water. When the rings are taken out of this they should be placed on a clean, dry cloth to get rid of the moisture. They are then ready to go into the drying boxes or on to the sticks.

Pears, Dried. Pears for drying are dealt with in exactly the same way as apples, except that they are cut into halves or quarters—according to their size—and not ringed. They should be almost ripe. Pears so ripe that they are soft are not suitable for drying.

Storing Dried Apples and Pears. When the leathery condition has been reached the dried fruit should be cooled off for about twelve hours in a cupboard or room free from flies, wasps and other pests. If these are present the fruit should be protected by covering it over with sheets of newspaper.

The apple rings or pear sections can then be stored, until wanted for use, in any dry place in tins, jars or paper bags. Exposure to damp or heat must be avoided. The time for which they will keep depends on observance of these points and the thoroughness of drying.

Using Dried Apples or Pears. When wanted for cooking a sufficient quantity of the rings or portions should be placed overnight in a bowl or basin and boiling water poured over them. This all-night soaking will plump them up to their original size.

Apples, Pears, Bottled in Water. Clean glass jars, boiling water and a moderate oven (temperature about 250 deg. Fahrenheit) are required for this method.

The apples should be peeled, cored and cut into slices ¼ in. thick. The pears (dessert varieties only and nearly ripe) should be peeled, cored and cut into halves or quarters according to size of fruit (Fig. 438).

After being soaked in salt water, as explained under Apples, Dried, to prevent discoloration, the prepared apples or pears are packed tightly (uncooked) into the jars so that these are completely filled. The packing can be done with fingers, the narrow end of a spoon, or with a piece of wood.

The packed bottles are then placed in the moderate oven for about thirty minutes, then taken out, filled with boiling water and sealed with airtight covers. If clip tops or screw tops are used these should be warmed first. Or covers can be made by dipping three layers of greaseproof or tissue paper in paste or gum and tying these, while still wet, over the mouths of the jars with string. It is essential that the jars be kept airtight.

To prevent jars being cracked by heat they should stand on a piece of wood or an asbestos mat while in the oven; and when brought out for tying down they should be placed on a similar base. The water in the jar must be boiling as it is sealed.

Store in a cool, dry place, not in warmth.

Plums, Damsons. For water-bottling, plums and damsons must be dry and firm, not over-ripe. Big plums, such as the Victoria variety, should be halved and the stones taken out. A half-dozen stones may be broken and the kernels put in with the plums; this gives them a nice nutty flavour.

They should then be dealt with as advised for bottled apples, but allowed to remain in the moderate oven until the fruit begins to split.

Apricots, Peaches, Nectarines. These are water-bottled in the same manner as plums, but the skins should first be removed. To expedite this job the fruit should be dropped into boiling water and allowed to remain there for a couple of minutes.

Cherries. Sweet cherries for bottling should be of the deep-red or near-black varieties. The lighter-coloured ones lose their taste in the process, which is the same as for plums.

Gooseberries, Blackberries, Loganberries, Raspberries. These can be water-bottled in the manner advised for plums. Gooseberries should be hard and green, not ripe and soft, and be topped and tailed and washed. They should

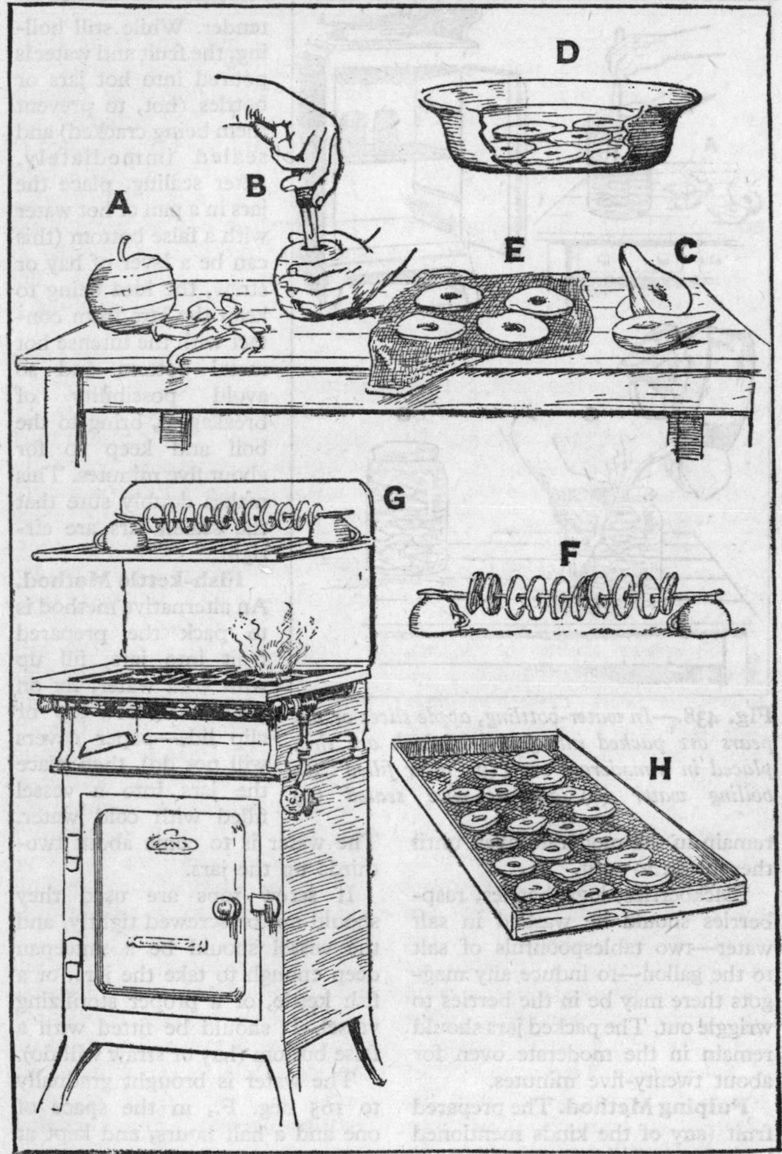

Fig. 437.—*Method of drying apple rings. Fruit is peeled* (A), *cored* (B), *sliced into rings which are soaked in salt water* (D), *taken out and dried* (E), *threaded on a stick* (F), *then placed over a gas-stove* (G) *or the rings are placed in a tray* (H) *for drying. Pears for drying are halved* (C) *or quartered*

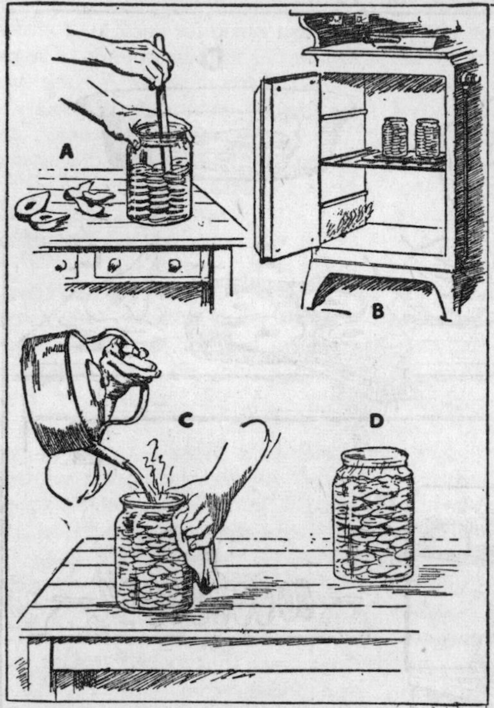

Fig. 438.—*In water-bottling, apple slices or cut pears are packed into jars* (A) *which are then placed in a moderate oven* (B), *later filled with boiling water* (C) *and at once sealed* (D)

tender. While still boiling, the fruit and water is poured into hot jars or bottles (hot, to prevent them being cracked) and sealed immediately. After sealing, place the jars in a pan of hot water with a false bottom (this can be a layer of hay or straw, the idea being to keep the jars from contact with the intense hot metal bottom and so avoid possibility of breakages), bring to the boil and keep so for about five minutes. This makes doubly sure that the sealed jars are airtight.

Fish-kettle Method. An alternative method is to pack the prepared fruit into jars, fill up with cold water, fix on the lids (screw-top or clip lids—paper covers will not do), then place the jars into a vessel filled with cold water. The water is to come about two-thirds up the jars.

If screw tops are used they should not be screwed tightly, and the vessel should be a saucepan deep enough to take the jars, or a fish kettle, or a proper sterilizing vessel. It should be fitted with a false bottom (hay or straw will do).

The water is brought gradually to 165 deg. F., in the space of one and a half hours, and kept at that temperature for ten minutes, in the case of apples, apricots, peaches, nectarines, plums (ripe and whole), damsons, gooseberries, blackberries, loganberries and

remain in the moderate oven until they begin to split.

Blackberries, loganberries, raspberries should be washed in salt water—two tablespoonfuls of salt to the gallon—to induce any maggots there may be in the berries to wriggle out. The packed jars should remain in the moderate oven for about twenty-five minutes.

Pulping Method. The prepared fruit (any of the kinds mentioned in this section) is placed in a saucepan and just covered with cold water, which is brought gradually to the boil. Gentle boiling continues until the fruit is quite raspberries. For halved or unripe plums the same temperature should be maintained for twenty minutes. Cherries should be raised, in one and a half hours, to 190 deg. and kept at that for ten minutes. Pears should be raised to 190 deg. in one and a half hours, and kept at that for 20 minutes.

If a bottling thermometer is not available, the water should be raised, in one and a half hours, to simmering point (when small bubbles are seen coming up from the bottom) and maintained at simmering point for the periods given in the preceding paragraph.

When the jars are removed from the vessel (and placed on wood or an asbestos mat), clip lids will have automatically tightened themselves; screw tops will need to be screwed up, finally, as tightly as possible.

Bottling in Syrup. If preferred fruit may be bottled in syrup instead of plain water. Use a thin syrup for sweet, ripe fruits and a thickish syrup for hard, sour fruits. Quantities are: six pounds of sugar to two quarts of water. For the thin syrup cook until sugar is dissolved. Thicker syrup is obtained by longer boiling—until the syrup becomes thick and sticky.

A little lemon juice added to the syrup will improve the flavour of pears or strawberries.

A Preserving Solution. Chemists sell tablets (with directions for use) for preparing Campden solution, no heat being required in this method of fruit preservation. Cleaned and dried, the fruit is packed in jars or any non-metal vessel that can be made airtight, and enough solution made up from the Campden tablets to cover the fruit is poured in.

The airtight cover, non-metal cap or lid, in place, the fruit will keep as long as required. The fruit must be cooked before use, the preservative being got rid of during the heating.

INDEX

Figures in italics denote illustrations

Index

Made and printed in Great Britain by Odhams (Watford) Ltd., Watford
S.256.4R.S.